Beatles Undercover

Kristofer K. Engelhardt

1998

We acknowledge the financial support of the Government of Canada through the Book Publishing Industry Development Program for our publishing activities.
Published by Collector's Guide Publishing Inc., Box 62034, Burlington, Ontario, Canada, L7R 4K2
Printed and bound in Canada by Webcom Ltd of Toronto
Beatles Undercover / Kristofer K. Engelhardt
ISBN 1-896522-43-2

The Beatles arriving in Boston, MA, for 1966 North American tour, photo courtesy of Guy Greve

Beatles Undercover

Kristofer K. Engelhardt

1998

Cover photos are by Tom Bert.
Tom Bert is a celebrity and commercial photographer, artist and poet. Bert has photographed more than 500 celebrities. Bert's work has appeared on album covers, billboards, television, book jackets, and in books and every major magazine. He is also a well-known automotive photographer who has worked for all the major car companies. Bert's photography has earned him a Grammy and several Gold and Platinum records. He has also received awards in advertising, poetry and painting. Tom Bert, whose photos appear throughout the book, can be contacted at: 775 Oakbrook Ridge, Rochester Hills, MI 48307 Tel. (248) 651-8998 or 650-0298.

FOREWORD

by Walter J. Podrazik

"Let me tell you about the time I worked with The Beatles."

A storyteller with that lead-in is guaranteed to catch the ear of any audience, crossing generations, continents, and musical tastes. Whether it is the tale of a cop handling security at their Shea Stadium concerts, a photographer setting up an album cover shot, or a radio disc jockey recalling a promotional interview, listeners inevitably find themselves drawn in.

Part of the attraction is that, however briefly, these people connected with The Beatles on a professional level. For one moment in time, they were a legitimate part of The Beatles story. They helped The Beatles be The Beatles.

Of all these people, the ones who made music with members of the group had the best experiences of them all. **Beatles Undercover** shares their stories. There are hundreds of tales. Some are brief connections – a surprise moment in the studio or a guest appearance at a concert. Others are far more involved, reflecting magical moments that turned a particular recording into a never-to-be-forgotten experience. In many cases, even The Beatles themselves never knew all the details, especially what happened before and after they left. The others involved never forgot. And now that they've shared their stories with Kristofer Engelhardt, their memories are in good hands.

Kris began this project seven years ago. Early on, he and I spoke by phone, sharing our mutual interest in these generally untold musical encounters with one or more of The Beatles. We've continued the conversations by phone and letter as his book developed and the stories unfolded.

I first developed an affection for these tales during the 1970s when preparing **All Together Now**, the first of three volumes co-authored with Harry Castleman. In these books, we chronicled all the recorded works associated with The Beatles, including these lesser known offerings, which we dubbed the "Beatles For Others." We were fascinated by the musical associations chosen by John Lennon, Paul McCartney, George Harrison, and Ringo Starr because we knew that – as the premier performing group of the world – they could work with anyone they wished. These are the people they chose. Something about these performers caught the attention of The Beatles. Sometimes the connection lasted only for that single encounter. Other times, the sessions led to long-lasting, on-going professional and personal relationships.

What adds an extra aura to these associations is that in many cases they quietly slipped by, almost out of sight. There might have been attendant publicity at the time of release, though not always. So, discovering these recordings is like unexpectedly finding The Beatles "hanging out" at a party. Suddenly, you want to take another look around, listening for just what the attraction was for the Fab Four. Most of the time, it's worth the effort. That's what Harry Castleman and I did in assembling the "Beatles For Others" sections for our three books. We listened to the music, scanned liner notes, read squibs in the rock press (especially in Britain), and conducted a handful of personal interviews. We always knew that there were some stories still left undiscovered and untold. During one chat with Harry Nilsson about our goal of chronicling every guest appearance, he smiled and said, "You'll never do it – there are too many no one knows about."

With this book, Kris Engelhardt comes closest to successfully answering that challenge. A man with a mission for over a decade, he has attempted to fill in the gaps once and for all. The results are amazing. Kris has dug up previously unknown behind-the-scenes associations. This is great news for any Beatles aficionado determined to have a truly complete Beatles collection. Now there are new discs to hunt down at second hand shops, or to bug labels to reissue on compact disc. Beyond that, Kris has also gone back to some of the already familiar connections and fleshed out the details of their stories. As often as possible, this involved one-on-one discussions by phone, fax, letter, or in person. Lucky thing. As time moves inexorably forward, some of the participants have passed on, sometimes far too soon. That's bad news for history because ultimately these are very personal stories, which can only be told by those who were there. When they are gone, so are their memories.

That is probably the most important aspect of this book. Kris Engelhardt has managed to convey a sense of wonder for not only rock music, but also for creative collaboration. These were special moments that should be celebrated and appreciated. As you read through the details of each Beatles encounter, you will inevitably find yourself struck by the wide range of talent at work. Rock. Pop. Jazz. Avant garde. Indian. Country. Rhythm and blues. Broadway. Comedy. The Beatles were not just about topping the rock charts. They were working with artists from all walks of life. Now, with a little help from Kris Engelhardt, you can see this collaborative handiwork up close and share in yet another magical, musical legacy of The Beatles.

Wally Podrazik, Chicago 1997

Walter J. Podrazik is co-author with Harry Castleman of three volumes on the recorded work of The Beatles: **All Together Now**, **The Beatles Again**, and **The End Of The Beatles?**

PREFACE

The Beatles have always been a popular subject of research, but somehow their contributions to other artists' recordings have been largely ignored. I find this surprising because these contributions represent some of The Beatles' best music! The need to share my love and knowledge on this subject motivated me to dedicate seven years of my life to writing **Beatles Undercover**.

This book was written while raising a family, running another business and getting on with life. I never gave up hope nor lost sight of my goal during the hard drive crashes; mounting phone, record and book bills and the endless hours of work in small offices, libraries, dressing rooms, tour buses and recording studios. That I was able to complete it while watching my parents and several other loved ones pass away makes it that much more of a personal journey and a victory.

My work was inspired by Harry Castleman and Walter Podrazik's book, **All Together Now**, published in 1975. I was challenged by their ability to discover and document The Beatles' contributions to other artists' recordings. Time eventually diminished the comprehensiveness of their book as it will mine. Before it does, I hope it's able to bring knowledge and enjoyment to those who read it. A research book of this nature can never be definitive, complete or wholly accurate – it is an ongoing process, an unknown puzzle made of thousands of pieces, with new pieces being created each day. I do not apologize for any of its mistakes or misinformation. I worked to the best of my abilities to prevent them. I will feel a tremendous sense of regret that I was unaware or unable to correct its shortcomings, but even George Harrison only recently learned that he was born a day earlier than he had always thought. I encourage those with any clarifications or additional information to contact me.

TABLE OF CONTENTS

INTRODUCTION

Beatles Undercover is a reference book which explores the origins and evolution of The Beatles' contributions to other artists' music, along with a brief biographical sketch of each of these artists. In short, this book is about The Beatles' admiration for and generous support of their friends and fellow musicians. It's neither a price guide nor a discography per se. It does not seek to expose the artists' personal lives or critique their work. For those of you who thought the music of John Lennon, Paul McCartney, George Harrison and Ringo Starr was confined to The Beatles and their solo recordings, you are in for a very big and pleasant surprise.

You Give Me Joy Joy

Veteran British rocker Tony Ashton accurately recounts life on the road as a rock star: "After several weeks of backbreaking bus rides, cheap motels and an increasing reliance on the falling-down juice, I'd noticed most of our number were on full automatic pilot, rapidly approaching 'zombiedom.' The daily routine had settled like dust into something like this – Drag yourself out of bed...toy with breakfast...straighten out with a beer...car to the airport...a few Scotches on the plane...car to the Holiday Inn (if we were lucky)...car to the gig for a sound check (if we were even luckier)...back to the hotel to eat...a few beers in the bar...back to the gig...play...survey the surroundings for potential female companionship...back to the hotel...hit the bar (if it was open)...wreck someone's room...hit the sack, with or without playmates. Repeat process ad infinitum."

You will be disappointed by this book if you are looking for these tales of sex, drugs and destruction, but you will find many references to rock 'n' roll. With the help of some influential friends and diligent efforts of my own, I was able to contact many of the musicians, or those closely involved (wives, friends, producers, engineers etc.), to whose recordings The Beatles contributed. I wanted to write a book with the full help and approval of as many musicians as I could contact. All the quotes in the text are taken from people (listed in the acknowledgments) that I personally interviewed or corresponded with (unless the quote is attributed to another source).

I have made a conscious effort to avoid including events that would embarrass or upset anyone. I felt it was more important to keep my focus on the subject of cataloguing The Beatles' contributions to other artists' recordings, and to the relevant musical events of their career. There were a few instances when it was relevant to the subject to mention artists' personal difficulties. I attempted to do this in the most sympathetic manner possible. I suspect that because I did not focus on their personal lives, I was taken into the confidence of most of the people I interviewed. Many of the people I talked to did recount the darker side of rock 'n' roll, but we never dwelled on it.

We've all heard and read the tabloid tales of the egocentric, sex crazed, drug addicted or burned out recluses we sometimes call rock stars. Obviously some of the people I talked to are, at least to some degree, a survivor of some of that. The vast majority of the "stars" I contacted were gracious, cooperative and coherent. A few were embittered by their years in the music business and totally disinterested in the subject of my book. For whatever reason (probably time restraints), a number of musicians chose not to respond to my repeated requests for assistance. There were surprisingly few unpleasant encounters and a number of solid friendships that were established as a result of my contacts. It was refreshing to learn that, for the most part, the people I talked to were just that – people – regular folks, who just happened to have a talent for making great music. Everyone still loved the music of The Beatles, and no one had a truly disparaging word to say about them as individuals. This, along with being able to reunite musicians who had lost touch with each other, was the most rewarding aspect of writing this book.

Some Harry Moments Not In The Nick Of Time

One of my earliest, and ultimately most embarrassing, experiences was with Harry Nilsson at Beatlefest '92 in Chicago. I was a little green at the time about the fine art of how to properly approach and interview people. I had given Nilsson a printout of my data on him and a list of questions that, unfortunately, I was only able to ask him before a large public forum. It was neither the proper time nor setting, and Harry seemed agitated, confrontational and unwilling to answer my detailed questions. He ridiculed my subject claiming there was no interest, dismissed my data as "all wrong" and asked me to leave him alone! I was publicly humiliated. My ego was badly bruised, but I was not discouraged. I tried to convince myself that it was just a hard day's night for Harry and myself and continued to pursue the principals of my book. Some months later I got a call from Nilsson. He had recently suffered a heart attack, and it was quite obvious from our conversation that he was in failing health. He explained that he had run across my printout while moving some things, had found my subject fascinating, and wanted to help in any way he could. I told him I would call back in a few weeks when he was feeling better. And then the news, Harry had died, and with him the chance to set the record straight.

In August of 1994 I contacted Nicky Hopkins at his home in Nashville. Nicky was one of the few musicians to contribute to a Beatles' recording session and worked with all four members after the breakup. He was a talent I greatly admired. My conversation with Nicky evolved into a deep two-hour discussion of the significance of my project. We also talked about our record collections, Phil Spector and Motown music. It was the most heartwarming conversation of my research. I think we both felt we had rediscovered a long lost friend who understood the value of documenting the history of Rock 'n' Roll. He warned me that no one was getting any younger, memories were fading and too many who could have provided firsthand accounts had died. He was eager to help and told me to send him some questions and call him in a few weeks. Before I was able to reestablish contact, the grim reaper sealed the mine of information that Nicky Hopkins was about to share. It would not be the last time the reaper would strike, professionally or personally.

Good News

The information in this book was gathered from the following sources – interviews that I conducted with musicians, recording engineers, producers, composers, noted authors, researchers and collectors knowledgeable of The Beatles' musical contributions to other artists' recordings. These interviews were conducted by phone, fax, postal correspondence, at fan conventions and backstage at performances. Additional research was conducted at reference libraries and recording studios. Most of the foundational information was taken from my own extensive library of records, tapes, books, fan club publications, record company press kits, music trade magazines and press clippings that I've accumulated over the last 30 years. I've used only those reference sources that have proven reliable, avoided those that were not, and verified my information from as many sources as possible.

Give Me Some Truth

The information in this book is only as good as my methods of research and the sources that I used. Unfortunately in many cases, the deeper I dug and the closer I got to the source, the fuzzier the picture became. Take young, impressionable musicians sometimes under the influence of mind altering substances and put them in the presence of their idols, The Beatles. Let some thirty years pass with myth and misinformation feeding their faded memories, and you are often left with little reliable information. It was unrealistic of me to expect that with the great passage of time and the countless sessions many of these musicians have attended, they would be able to remember the kind of minute details I required. Thankfully, most of them gave it their best effort. Not surprisingly, the more recent the recordings, the more clear and vivid the memories of people were.

One of the greatest challenges was sorting out the conflicting recollections of several people present at a particular event. When dealing with one artist, as opposed to several members of a group, there was naturally less conflicting information. I've tried to present all sides of the story and refrained from drawing conclusions, or quoting only one source, in the interest of objectivity. Imagine my frustration when artists would completely contradict what they told me in previous interviews. I'm sure that in some instances people told me what they thought I wanted to hear. Familiar stories were often retold in a degraded or self-serving form. On more than one occasion I had to take with a large barrel of salt what could be described kindly as fabrication.

With today's information highway, one would think it would be easy to track down data through record companies, unions and recording studios. On the few occasions when record companies did furnish me with information, it was usually superficial and often filled with inaccuracies. The promises of record companies to forward my inquiries to their artists rarely resulted in a response. Those familiar with unions, work permits and contractual restrictions know that musicians are sometimes credited for sessions they did not work on, while not being credited for sessions on which they did work. Today's multi-track recorders allow the final mix of a record to be made from any combination of tracks, including some that may have been previously recorded at another studio. An artist may

have contributed to sessions for a song only to be omitted from the final mix or have the song omitted from the record, but still receive credit. The confusion is usually created because the records' credits are general, and not specific to each song. More often a musician contributes to a recording and either deliberately (usually at their request) or inadvertently is not listed in the credits. In some cases, record companies have deliberately implied or claimed that a famous artist or musician had contributed to a record despite a lack of evidence. Add to all of this the often informal structure of recording studios with revolving door sessions that often last well into the night. Just imagine, especially in the drug hazed days of the 60s and 70s, how easily a name could be omitted from the credits or a tape could be mislabeled or put in the wrong box. Trusting studio tape boxes, diaries and union payroll sheets is useful but risky.

I've taken the liberty of correcting obvious mistakes in record information (misspellings, incorrect titles, composers, times, etc.). I've also exposed many of the long-held myths concerning The Beatles' contributions to other artists' recordings.

Grey Cloudy Lies

For over twenty years it has been accepted as fact, and reported in the most reliable reference books, that Paul McCartney contributed to Donovan's song, ***Atlantis***. That claim has never been challenged by anyone, except recently, by Donovan! He categorically denies that Paul McCartney had anything to do with the song. Why has it taken so long for the truth to be revealed? No one questioned; everyone accepted or assumed, myself included for a time! Unfortunately, I too will be held accountable for perpetrating a few myths.

In an interview with Allan Kozinn in October 1995, Paul McCartney explained one of the processes by which the three surviving Beatles came to a conclusion about events in their lives. During the interviews conducted for **The Beatles Anthology** film, Ringo recalled that while The Beatles were in Paris, George had a sore throat. George recalled it was Paul who had the sore throat. Paul recalled that it was John who had the sore throat. McCartney reasoned through a process of elimination that if Ringo and George knew they were not the ones with the sore throat and Paul knew he did not have a sore throat that it must have been John. If Lennon were alive, he no doubt would have remembered it being Ringo with the sore throat, thus completing the circle of confusion. In that interview McCartney was asked if **The Beatles Anthology** was the definitive statement. McCartney felt that The Beatles had tried as best as they could to make it the definitive story. But McCartney reminded us that there is no such thing as definitive, that life is not definitive!

Not surprisingly, there is even confusion concerning who first approached Yoko Ono with the idea of taking some of John's unfinished recordings and turning them into new Beatles' songs. Yoko says it was George and Beatles' assistant Neil Aspinall. McCartney alleges he first initiated the request but he is not sure. The research for this book presented many of the same problems and frequently states them throughout the text. When it was necessary, I used processes of elimination, similar to those McCartney used, to draw some conclusions.

You Say It's Your Birthday

There is nothing more frustrating than turning to three so-called reliable reference books and finding three different places and dates of birth for an artist, or no place or date at all! It seems inconceivable, but at the same time it also points out the danger in taking any one source as fact. I used the place and date of birth that was cited most often from reliable sources. This is by no means a guarantee of accuracy. Some artists like to shave a few years off their true date of birth. When in doubt, I tended to favor the earliest year of birth listed. Whenever possible, I went to the second most reliable source for a date of birth – the person in question (the first being the birth certificate.) I feel quite confident that the place and date of birth for those artists that I interviewed are accurate. I granted the request of all artists who preferred their birth names or dates not be revealed. As former Record Plant owner and John Lennon's recording engineer, Roy Cicala, once told me, "This is an industry obsessed with youth."

The Toppermost Of The Poppermost

During the early years, when The Beatles were feeling low and losing hope of ever becoming successful recording artists, John Lennon would often ask "Where are we going, fellas?" The group would always reply "To the top, Johnny!" Lennon would question, "What top?" "To the toppermost of the poppermost, Johnny!" To any struggling musician nothing seems more important, or elusive, than a number one record on the charts. The chart position of a record is still the primary measuring stick of success in the music business.

Charts are generally listed in major music trade publications on a weekly basis. Over the years, the methods and criteria for compiling charts have changed. They have generally been determined from information gathered by a variety of music industry and independent sources who poll or monitor retail sales and advance orders, along with juke boxes, radio and TV play lists. Regardless of what any publication might claim, it is not an exact science, and in some cases the results have been subjective or downright self-serving. It does not take a great deal of imagination to realize the number of ways that the charts can be unfairly influenced. Witness the payola scandals and fraudulent accounting practices that have plagued the music industry over the years. Brian Epstein was suspected by some of ordering large numbers of The Beatles' first single for his record store to influence its chart position. Sometimes retailers complain of having to be required to place large minimum orders for a particular record. However, new technology continues to improve the accuracy and accountability of the charts.

The chart positions and dates in this book are taken from a variety of sources, primarily music reference books, which no doubt gathered their information from major trade publications. These publications included Billboard, Cashbox, Melody Maker, New Musical Express and other national, regional or local organizations that ascertain a record's popularity and sales. Billboard has long been the primary source for chart information in the U.S., and today for much of the world. Charting systems in other countries are not always dominated by one publication or standardized polling system. The primary charts are the top 100 pop/rock singles and the top 200 albums. Over the years there have been a number of sub charts for everything from R&B (Rhythm & Blues or Black) to Classical, Jazz, C&W (Country), Dance, Alternative, Video and Regional releases. Some reference books rely on chart information from a variety of publications, and use those that post the highest position, or form a consensus. Dates listed regarding chart position can be misleading or unclear as to whether they represent the record's earliest date of release, when it first appeared on the charts or when it achieved its highest position. Sometimes the overall sales of a record represents a more realistic view of its popularity than its highest chart position. It is not always clear in some reference sources if sales represents number of copies or dollar amounts, the significance of which can vary over time.

For the sake of historical perspective, the reader would be well served not to place too much importance on sales and chart positions. I felt it was important to include this information only to establish the artists' degree of success relative to the charts. Unless noted otherwise, information listed is for the U.S. pop/rock charts. Because of the overall subjectivity of chart information, I have refrained from citing the highest chart position, opting instead to use the familiar categories of top 40, top 20, top 10, and when there is little doubt, number one. It should also be noted that some of an artist's most popular songs, which I often mention, have never appeared on the charts.

What You Got

The vast majority of the entries in this book pertain to the contributions (musical, backing vocal, production, arrangement, engineering assistance and compositions) of The Beatles' (John Lennon, Paul McCartney, George Harrison and Ringo Starr) to the recordings of other artists. Also included are liner notes written by, photographs taken by, or drawings or designs made by any of The Beatles specifically for another artist's record. Photographs of any of The Beatles included in the package of another artist's record are noted. However, photographs of a Beatle on one of their own releases that contain a contribution to another artist's recording, such as Ringo Starr's All-Starr Band records, are assumed present and therefore not noted.

There were few instances during The Beatles' early years together of them contributing in whole or in part to other artists' recordings. For the most part, The Beatles' contributions to other artists were initially limited to Lennon and McCartney donating their compositions to artists managed by Brian Epstein. When The Beatles created Apple Records, it increased the opportunity, and the necessity, for them to contribute to artists signed to the label. Each Beatle had an even greater opportunity and need to work with other artists following the breakup of the group.

When information was unavailable or credits were not specific, I often had to rely on my ears and my experience. This is where years of listening to The Beatles as musicians, a good sound system and a good set of ears pay off. It is usually easy to identify a Beatle singing in the background. Except for McCartney's infectious hooks and melodic writing style, most Beatles compositions are not immediately obvious. John Lennon's piano playing and acoustic guitar picking are fairly distinctive. George Harrison's slide guitar solos are easily recognizable. Ringo's steady back beat and unique fills usually make his drumming easily, though not conclusively, identifiable. Identifying technical contributions like arranging, mixing or producing just by listening alone is nearly impossible. Some recordings contain an easily recognizable contribution by a Beatle. Recordings do not lie, but they do not always reveal their secrets effortlessly. The challenge is to take the time to correctly identify the contents of the recording. Fortunately, this was usually a rewarding experience. However, there is always the danger of wanting to believe The Beatles made a contribution to a recording despite any evidence to support it. Admittedly, I have made some assumptions and judgment calls when listening to music to determine who might be playing what.

George Harrison produced a considerable volume of recordings for Apple Records and for his Dark Horse Records. He has also contributed a number of his compositions to other artists. Harrison seems confident and willing to work with a wide range of musicians on a frequent basis. Harrison, who was an owner of Handmade Films, made musical contributions to several of its films as well.

Paul McCartney was the most active contributor to other artists while The Beatles were together. Following the breakup, he devoted most of his energies to his group, Wings, and MPL (McCartney Productions Limited) projects. He did contribute to solo recordings by members of his group, Wings, including his wife Linda. Following McCartney's dissolution of Wings in the early 1980s, he began to work with a variety of his well-known peers in music. His contributions to other artists tended to be comprehensive, including composing, producing and playing a variety of instruments. His bass, keyboard and guitar work though unique, are often difficult to positively identify. He has also contributed to a number of film soundtracks.

Ringo Starr, like George Harrison, has contributed to a wide range of artists' recordings, though primarily as a session drummer. Ringo's good-natured personality will continue to make him the preferred choice among his musical peers. Ringo, having spent much of his life pursuing an acting career, has made contributions to film soundtracks.

Even if he was still alive, John Lennon would have contributed the least to other artists due in large part to his insecurity as an accomplished session musician. Though Lennon was adequate on keyboards and one of the steadiest rhythm guitarists in the business, he was not comfortable being a session musician or spending much time in the studio. He quickly grew impatient with numerous takes and countless over-dubs and remixing. Lennon's strength always lay in his personalized songwriting and powerful rock vocals. When he did contribute to other artists' recordings, it was usually limited to the role of songwriter or producer for his wife, Yoko Ono, or playing on recordings for friends like Elton John and Harry Nilsson. John Lennon was far too busy filming nearly every event in his life, and rarely had time to contribute to anyone else's films.

Act Naturally

The terms "film" and "video" are used synonymously throughout this book. Contributions to another artist's musical performance in a film or soundtrack (including contributions to other artists' work on scores) are included in this book. Films that any of The Beatles had any other type of role in, including technical assistance such as director, producer, screenwriter or appearance, are not included. Musical contributions exclusive to a film starring a number of people, are generally filed under "Various Artists", alphabetically by title. The exceptions are films with musical contributions that are billed as being by a particular artist – these are filed under the artist's name. Laser Videodiscs (LVDs) are listed in preference to video tape formats because of their superior audio and video quality.

Not A Discography Nor Collectors' Price Guide

One of the greatest difficulties in compiling a book of this nature is setting guidelines and determining the limits of what should and should not be included. This book was never intended to be a complete discography of every record (as opposed to recording) released in the world that contains a contribution by The Beatles; that would be an enormous task and serve little purpose. I have attempted only to include the generally best sounding and most readily available record that includes the particular recording to which a Beatle contributed. My research indicates that the majority of people who collect The Beatles' musical contributions to other artists' recordings prefer to have them in the best fidelity available, or in a (greatest hits) compilation package, as opposed to having the original first (often vinyl single) issue. Most of the first issue records that The Beatles contributed to do not fall into the highly priced collectibles category. Those which do are usually noted. Unfortunately, many of The Beatles' earliest contributions to other artists are still available only on their original 7" or 12" vinyl release and are nearly impossible to obtain, especially in acceptable condition.

Consequently, a great number of the records listed are Compact Disc (CD) reissues even if they are costly imports or less available than vinyl. If the CD was not issued in the United States (U.S.A.), I list the most comprehensive or readily available foreign CD, usually those from the United Kingdom (U.K.). If a record was available in the U.S., but a foreign release is more readily available, I usually list the foreign release. Unless noted otherwise, all record catalog numbers listed in the text are assumed to be U.S. numbers. CD and vinyl albums are both identified if there are differences in song mixes or lengths, or if the album package (jacket and contents) contain additional contributions (liner notes, photos etc.) Recordings are often remixed and edited for issue as singles. These records are not included unless they are noticeably different (or identified as such), or contain an additional contribution.

Though I realize most people do not own Laser Videodiscs (LVDs), for obvious reasons I list them as well as their corresponding CD releases. In some cases a contribution is available only on LVD. Unless noted otherwise, it should be assumed that all music LVDs listed usually include an introduction or dialogue and appearance by a Beatle as well.

Bogey Music

Unauthorized records, or bootlegs as they are more commonly known, are records that are not legally authorized for release by the artist and / or his record company. These so-called bootlegs began appearing as 12" vinyl pressings in the late 1960s, usually as low fidelity out-takes, demos and audience recordings of live performances. They were usually poorly made and distributed in limited quantities in plain white jackets with an insert briefly detailing the contents. Over the years, the quality of the recordings and jackets improved and began to (necessarily) resemble legitimate releases.

Naturally, once The Beatles broke up there was increased demand for their unreleased recordings. By the late 1970s, that demand was being met with hundreds of bootleg records featuring previously unreleased Beatles' (and solo) recordings, including those of artists to which they contributed. The arrival of the CD in the mid-1980s brought many improvements in the sound quality and packaging of bootlegs. Their smaller size also facilitated worldwide distribution. The release of unauthorized records became even more difficult for legitimate record companies and artists to prevent with changes in, or the expiration of, copyright protection laws in certain countries. In some cases, recordings that were more than a few decades old could be legally released by anyone. Recent embargoes, trade agreements and changes in international law and its enforcement have reduced (no doubt temporarily) the proliferation of unauthorized records.

I have included a number of The Beatles' contributions to other artists' recordings that, unfortunately, are currently only available on unauthorized records. Generally, I have listed only those recordings that are significantly different or unique from legitimate releases, and then usually only those available on CD with the highest fidelity. Their inclusion is in no way meant as an advertisement or endorsement of these illegal products. I do not condone theft or the violation of the rights of artists and record companies. Because of their clandestine nature, it is difficult to compile a complete list of all unauthorized records that contain contributions by The Beatles to other artists' recordings. Much of the information given on these records is quite often deliberately erroneous, so what is listed may not be accurate. I have endeavored to correct erroneous information when known.

To Beatle Or Not To Beatle?

Some may feel it's improper, but the terms "ex-Beatles" and "former Beatles" are not used in this book. Though The Beatles broke up in 1970, they have reformed in whole or part since that time. They are still more often referred to individually as a Beatle rather than a former or ex-Beatle. No matter what the circumstances or situation, no matter what their relationship with each other might be at any given time, they have been and will forever remain "The Beatles." The term "post-Beatle", as used ni this book, refers to activities after the break-up of The Bealtes in 1970.

I have always seen The Beatles and their solo recordings as one "body" of work, from the same source. It's just as accurate to say that The Beatles were contributing to each other's songs before the breakup as afterward. For this reason, I decided it was rather pointless to include The Beatles' contributions to each other's solo recordings. These contributions have been well documented, and I felt that they were really "within the family", and did not qualify as contributions to "other artists."

You Know My Name

All of the Beatles, particularly in the 1960s and 70s, resorted to using pseudonyms, or went uncredited, for their contributions. This was due to the contractual restrictions with their record companies, or to avoid drawing undue attention to themselves and away from the artist to whom they were contributing. George Harrison has often been the most ingenious at creating clever diversionary pseudonyms or avoiding credit altogether. This made the job of uncovering these contributions more difficult. Assumed names were also used to test the commercial viability of a recording without the notoriety of a Beatles' name added to it. McCartney was the first Beatle to deliberately go under an assumed name as the composer of Peter & Gordon's hit ***Woman***. Pseudonyms, or assumed names, have been replaced with their proper names, but are usually noted in the text. Recordings by Post-Beatles groups or assumed names (McCartney's Wings, Thrillington, The Country Hams or The Fireman and Harrison's Traveling Wilburys etc.), that do not feature a Beatle on a lead vocal, are not included. I felt these more properly came under the classification of solo Beatles' group recordings. However, I admit that it could be fairly argued that some of these recordings do technically qualify as contributions to other artists. Wings' recordings released under an individual member's name are included. I have included songs released from Ringo Starr's All-Starr Band tours that include a contribution from Ringo to songs performed (sung) by other artists. I have also included Plastic Ono Band recordings that feature vocals by anyone (usually Yoko Ono) other than John Lennon. Recordings released under the names of family members that The Beatles contributed to are also included. Any record that acknowledges, dedicates or thanks a Beatle only is not considered a contribution unless, of course, a specific contribution was made to the record or its recording.

Nowhere Man

Throughout my research I have discovered countless rumors and claims that one or more members of The Beatles contributed to other artists' recordings. I spent much time investigating these unconfirmed reports. I can say almost categorically that to date, despite rumors you may have heard, none of The Beatles have contributed to the following artists' recordings – Herb Alpert, Tasmin Archer, The Babys, Graham Bonnet, Brand X, The Byrds, Campbelltown Pipe Band, David Cassidy, Michael Chapman, Cerrone, Phil Collins, Cook & Moore, Suzy Cope, Culture Club, King Curtis, Kiki Dee, Bo Diddley, Fanny, Fresh, The Futz, Garland Jeffreys, Georgia Satellites, Johnny Hallyday, Jimi Hendrix Experience, Jools Holland, Kanda Bongo Man, Klaatu, Viktor Lazlo, Little Village, Lord Sitar, Nick Lowe, The Mamas And The Papas, Melissa Manchester, The Masked Marauders, Christine McVie, Joni Mitchell, Mortimer, Rab Noakes, NRBQ, Michael Parks, Don Preston, The Raspberries, Rudy Romero, Tim Rose, The Rutles, Shakespear's Sister, Gene Simmons, Nina Simone, Dave Stewart And The Spiritual Cowboys, Thee Image, Twiggy, Les Variations, Gene Vincent, Andy Williams or Karen Young.

Photographs or drawings of one or more of The Beatles appear on records by the following artists (though The Beatles did not contribute to these records in any way) – Carl Aubut, The Aztecs, Pete Best, David Essex, Rabbi Abraham Feinberg, The Firesign Theatre, Fresh, Fuzzbox, Louise Harrison, Jimmy Haskell (Sing A Song with The Beatles), The Merseyboys, The Mexicali Banditos,

EPILOGUE

THIS IS IT?

At this point you are probably wondering if this is it! In spite of my exhaustive efforts to discover every contribution any of The Beatles made to other artists' recordings, I undoubtedly missed a few. Time will tell. Who knows, maybe recordings exist of George Harrison's two performances with a group called The Four Bests that he gave during a visit to see his sister in Illinois in September 1963. One thing is certain, the surviving Beatles will continue to work with other artists and contribute to their recordings, which will entertain their fans and make a second volume of **Beatles Undercover** a necessity.

ABOUT THE EGO

Kristofer Karl Engelhardt's first public appearance was at Mercy Hospital (6 years before Madonna) on January 20, 1952 in Bay City, Michigan, where he still lives. He vividly remembers saving his allowance money to buy The Everly Brothers' 1958 single (which he still has) with ***Claudette*** on the B-side. He briefly entered show business in the 4th grade playing Jim in The Adventures of Huckleberry Finn, and became even more dramatic in high school. Kris began playing the guitar to the sounds of the Terry Knapp (aka Terry Knight) show on WTAC "The Big 600" in Flint, MI in the mid-1960s. Kris attended both of The Beatles' performances at Olympia Stadium in Detroit in 1966 which inspired him to begin seriously collecting their records. Today he has one of the most comprehensive collections of The Beatles' contributions to other artists' recordings in the world. Over the years he has appeared on a number of local TV and radio shows to talk about The Beatles and was the "Magical Mr. E" that hosted WMJT FM's "Breakfast With The Beatles" in the early 1990s. He graduated from the Culinary Institute of America in 1976 and has helped run a family-owned business for nearly 20 years. He enjoys fine food and wine, and spends his free time in the mountains of Puerto Rico or exploring coral reefs. He is currently working on another book on popular music.

Kristofer Engelhardt

ACKNOWLEDGEMENTS

There is no section in this book of which I am more proud than the acknowledgements.
After all, acknowledgements are what this book is all about!

Thanks to the following people for helping me during this project

Rodney Bingenheimer (for recollections)
Shirley Burns (for George Martin)
Dennis Duso (for knowing his rock and roll)
Chris Fonvielle (Top Of The Pops)
Guy Greve (for the photos)
Jo Jo Laine & Heidi Jo Hines
(for Denny Laine)
Chris Kenel (a great fan, friend and father)
Mark Lapidos (Beatlefest)
Phil Lopez (how was Woodstock?)
Peter Nash (for Bullshot)
May Pang (for detail)
Andy Rogers (for fine printing)
Aaron Salter (for the Donovan info.)
Roger Saunders (for Monty Python)
John Sinclair (for keeping the faith)
Pat Smith (for Spencer)
Joe Sunseri (on Tony Sheridan)
Joe Viglione (for the numbers)
Eddie Veltman
(for magazine and record loans)
Sir Ronald Watson C.B.E.
(for lasting friendship and support)
Steve Szablewski (for promotional designs)

Thanks to my fellow writers, authors & researchers

Andy Babiuk (The Chesterfield Kings)
Richard Barnes (for the Moon)
Alan Clayson (for reference)
Ray Coleman (for reference — R.I.P.)
Bill DeYoung (for numbers)
Glen Dundas (on Dylan)
Hans Gottfridsson (on Tony Sheridan)
Steve Granados (good luck)
Arno Guzek (for the Danish)
Bill Harry (for the Mersey Beat)
Harvey Kubernik (for numbers)
David Leaf (for the love of Brian)
Jeff Levy (for his "Apple Logs")
Mark Lewisohn
(for reference, forwards and plugs)
Chip Madinger (for reference and tapes)
Marc Roberty (for reference)
Garath Powlowski (R.I.P.)
Ron Scarlett (on Stills)
Tom Schultheiss of Popular Culture Ink.
(for integrity)
Ken Sharp (for reference)
Neville Stannard (for reference)
Joel Whitburn (for reference)
Allen Wiener (for reference and advice)
David "never Dave" Young
(the Phil-in-Spector)

Thanks to the following publications and organizations (past and present)

Angel Records (Randy Haecker)
AFM (for numbers)
ASCAP (for forwards)
Beatlefan (Bill King)
The Beatles Book (Andy Davis)
Beatles Unlimited
(Haarlem, Ditzhuyzen & Leeheer)
The Beatletter (Jim McNally)
Belmo's Beatleg News (Scott Belmer)
Billboard (for reference)
Blue Suede News (Dennis M. Dewitt)
BMI (for forwards)
British Equity (for numbers)
British Musician's Union (for numbers)
British Writers Guild (for numbers)
Bug Music-Hollywood & Nashville
(Angel Hurst)
Hal Carter Organization (for numbers)
Cashbox (for reference)
CEMA (Charles Levan)
Cilla's Circle Of Fans (Alan Hardy)
Club Sandwich
(Paul McCartney's Fun Club Magazine)
Country Music Foundation
(Ron Pugh & Alan Stoker)
Disc and Music Echo (for reference)
Discoveries (for reference)
East End Lights Magazine (Tom Stanton)
East West Records
EMI Records
(Heatley, Hughes & Pannetier)
Guinness (for reference and stout)
Goldmine (for reference)
Good Day Sunshine
(Charles Rosenay & Matt Hurwitz)
The Harrison Alliance (Patti Murawski)

Ice (The Monthly CD Newsletter)
In Dreams (Bert Kaufman for Roy Orbison)
The Paul McCartney Fan Club
(Club Sandwich)
Melody Maker (for reference)
New Musical Express (for reference)
The New Times (David A. Young)
New Zealand Wellington Rock 'n' Roll
Revival Club (for Devlin)
Playboy (for reference and lust)
PRS (for forwards)
Record Collector (for reference)
Rolling Stone Magazine (for reference)
Del Shannon Appreciation Society
(Brian Young)
Stony Plain Records (Holger Petersen)
Strawberry Fields Forever (Joe Pope)
True Brit (Mike Stax)
Westbury Music Consultants Ltd.
(Dan Cornish)
The Write Thing (Barb Fenick)

Very Special Thanks

I would like to thank the following groups, musicians, producers, engineers, managers and agents who willingly and unselfishly gave of their time to personally help me achieve this level of accuracy.

Dino Airali (for Larry Hosford)
Ashton, Gardner & Dyke (Tony Ashton
& Kim Gardner)
John Askew (aka: Johnny Gentle
& Darren Young)
Brian Auger (for photos and "Catcalls")
Randy Bachman
(for taking care of business)
Badfinger (Joey Molland & Mike Gibbins)
Long John Baldry (for numbers)
The Band (Levon Helm & Rick Danko)
Adrian Barber
(for preserving history and the environment)
Chris Barber (slow down)
Mike Batt (happy sails)
The Beach Boys (Brian Wilson
& Bruce Johnston — for fine tuning)
The Beat Brothers (Roy Young)
Barry Beckett (for numbers)
Cliff Bennett (had to get you into my book)
Lenny Berman (for the Moon and Clover)
Cilla Black (Robert Willis Jr.)
Graham Bonnet (for long letters)
Dan Bourgoise
(for remembering Del Shannon)
Pattie Boyd (for forwards)
David Bromberg (for The Holdup)
Gary Brooker (for following up)
Jack Bruce (for the 2% solution)
Brute Force (aka: Stephen Friedland
— your inner sun shines!)
T. Bone Burnett (good morning)
Lori Burton (for taking forever)
Johnny "Guitar" Byrne (for The Hurricanes)
Howie Casey (have sax will travel)
The Cate Brothers (Ernie Cate)
Felix Cavaliere (you rascal)
Cheech And Chong (Tommy Chong)
Clarence Clemons (Darlene Delano)
Joe Cocker (Ray Neapolitan)
Kip Cohen (for Herb Alpert)
Phil Collins (Annie Callingham)
Billy Connolly (that wacky singing rebel)
Lol Creme (for approval)
The Crickets (Jerry Allison)
Crowbar (Kelly Jay — for "doing time"
in Bay City)
The Charlie Daniels Band (Charlie Daniels)
Steve Cropper (for playing on everything)
Spencer Davis
(for knowledge on telephones)
Kiki Dee (thanks for the fax)
Delaney & Bonnie (Delaney Bramlett
& Bonnie (Bramlett) Sheridan)
Lynsey de Paul (for the Starkey stories)
Johnny Devlin (for the Kiwi rock)
Dr. John (aka: Mac Rebennack)
(thanks for the gumbo)
Lonnie Donegan (& Dave Radcliff)
Terry Doran (for the Grapefruit)
Jack Douglas (a Roy boy)
Gus Dudgeon (for Elton John)
Deed & Duane Eddy
(for the fine tuning and the twang)
Elephant's Memory
(Wayne "Tex" Gabriel & Gary Van Scyoc)
Geoff Emerick
(for Campbelltown Pipe Band)
Adam Faith (Alan Field)
Marianne Faithfull (for coming through)
Fanny (Patti Quatro, Jean & June Millington)
Mark Farner (for musical summers bro.)
Horst Fascher (a true survivor)
Dennis Ferrante (a Roy boy)
David Fishof (for trying)
Flo & Eddie and The Turtles (Mark Volman)
John & Robert Fogerty (for the grapevine)
Jeff Foskett (for the beach men)
The Fourmost (Brian O'Hara)
Peter Frampton (nice guy club member)
Kinky Friedman
(from one great American to another)
Georgia Satellites (Dan Baird)
Allen Ginsberg (R.I.P — & Bob Rosenthal)
Bob Glaub (for Jesse Ed Davis)
Andrew Gold (for knowing the numbers)

Graffiti Band
(Jim Ehinger & Bobby Tsukamoto)
Grapefruit (John Perry,
Geoff Swettenham & Pete Swettenham)
Sylvia Griffin (for detail)
Daryl Hall And John Oates
(& Paul Meissner)
John Hanti (for his generous hospitality)
Roy Harper (for being perfectly normal)
Tim Hauser (The Manhattan Transfer)
Ronnie Hawkins (keep rockin')
Jeff Healey (you're the best!)
Richard Hewson (for arranging his memory)
David Hood (for Aretha Franklin)
The Everly Brothers (Don Everly & Hooter)
Nicky Hopkins (for instant friendship
— R.I.P.)
Jim Horn (you're ageless)
Larry Hosford (the "Salinas Beatle")
House Of Cash (for Johnny Cash)
Jimmy Ienner (Roy boy)
Neil Innes (for the fax and charming chat)
Yusuf Islam (aka Cat Stevens)
Andy & Glyn Johns (any relation?)
Jimmy Johnson (for the Muscle in Shoals)
Kenney Jones (for the correct spelling)
Paul Jones (the sun will shine)
Michael Kamen (Zoe Lovell)
Jim Keltner (for being a true gentleman)
Bobby Keys (for knowing the numbers)
Aashish & Pranesh Khan
Lee Kiefer (for being a true gentleman)
The Knack (Bruce Gary)
Al Kooper (for knowing his rock and roll)
Larry Knechtel
Billy J. Kramer And The Dakotas
(Billy J. Kramer & Mike Maxfield)
Ulf Kruger (for Hamburg history)
Jon Landau Mgt. (for Bruce Springsteen)
Trevor Lawrence (for Perry and Harry)
Viktor Lazlo (for dispelling rumors)
Donovan Leitch (for answering
every question & to Carol Lawrence)
Mark Linett (for knowing the numbers)
Nils Lofgren (& to Eric Amble)
Jackie Lomax (for good memory)
Nick Lowe (for the compliments)
Vera Lynn (for the fax)
Jeff Lynne (for being a perfect gentleman)
Taj Mahal (for calling back)
Melissa Manchester (for trying)
Gered Mankowitz
Jimmy Markham (for knowing the numbers)
John Martin (for Gary Moore)
Dave Mason (thanks for calling)
Mike McCartney (our kid)
Ruth McCartney (for hanging in there)
Hugh McCracken (for taking forever)
Ian McLagan (for identification)
Terry Melcher
(for putting Doris on the phone music)
Adrian Mitchell
Zoot Money
(for the Gerry Marsden look alike)
Daniel Moore
Mortimer (Guy Masson)
Alan Moulder
(Karen Ciccone @ Fundamental Music)
Nervous (Justin Travis & Dean Watkyn)
Harry Nilsson (for the apologies — R.I.P.)
Don Nix
(for generosity and lasting friendship)
Rick Nowels (for Belinda Carlisle)
Barbara Orbison Productions
(for Roy Orbison)
Buck Owens Productions (Jim Shaw)
Hugh Padgham (for dispelling rumors)
Andy Paley (for the love of Brian)
Michael Parks (Calmella Gallien)
Van Dyke Parks (for the love of Brian)
"Papa" John Phillips (Robert Tucker)
David Peel & The Lower East Side
(Lenny Mars & Tom Doyle)
Richard Perry
(for producing a great memory)
Stan & Carl Perkins (country gentlemen)
Peter & Gordon (Peter Asher)
Tom Petty (for the approval)
Vini Poncia
Don Preston (hope you enjoy the single)
Jim Price (for being a true gentleman)
P.J. Proby (for keeping his Texas drawl)
The Radha Krsna Temple
(Mukunda Goswami — ISKCON)
The Raspberries (Eric Carmen)
Leon Redbone
(Sarah Forbes for August Records)
Noel Redding (for Jimi Hendrix)
Martha Reeves (for stories)
The Remo Four (Colin Manley)
The Righteous Brothers (Bobby Hatfield)
Mark Rivera (for all de dog soldiers)
Bruce Robb (at Cherokee)
Elizabeth Robbins (for Kate)
Kate Robbins (for "Tomorrow")
Todd Rundgren (Eric Gardner)
Michael Schenker
Tom Scott (nice guy club member)
Frank Serafine (for "Tana Mana")
Ravi Shankar (an honor)
Danny Sheridan (for Bonnie Sheridan)
Tony Sheridan
(for redemption and Becks Beer)
Carly Simon (for great advice)
Nina Simone (Rusty Michael/Fat City)
Sounds Incorporated
(John "St. John" Gillard & Griff West)
Dave Spinozza
Splinter (Bob Purvis)

Freddie Starr (Trudy Coleman)
Dave Stewart
(Hannah Eichler @ The Church Studios)
Bill Szymczyk (for Rudy Romero)
Bernie Taupin (Gilles Robigailles)
John Tavener (a whale of a guy)
John Taylor (for Joe Brown & Jim Capaldi)
10cc (Graham Gouldman & Eric Stewart)
Ron Terry (no bo)
Guthrie Thomas (for great conversation)
Russ Titelman (for great productions)
Doris Troy (you give me joy joy)
Twiggy (for dispelling rumors)
Lon & Derrek Van Eaton
(for generosity and friendship)
Tony Visconti (for bursting balloons)
Joe Walsh (David Spero)
Don Was (& Jane for the New Maroons)
Pete Waterman (for the "Ferry" info.)
Cynthia Webb (for coming through)
Jimmy Webb (for good memory)
Jerry Wexler (for Aretha Franklin)
Alan White
(for filling in some blanks and Yes)
Bobby Whitlock (Where There's A Will There's A Way)
Allan Williams (for Hamburg stories)
Andy Williams (for writing back)
Wings (Denny Laine,
Laurence Juber & Denny Seiwell)
Ron Wood (for answers)
Gary Wright (for detail)
Shelly Yakus
(for Johnny Winter & another Roy boy)

SUPER SPECIAL THANKS TO

my wife and friend, Deanna, for all of her help with editing and proofreading; my sons, Charles and Christopher, for waiting so long for dad to come out and play; Kim Adams Heritier for her keen eye and political correctness; Curtis Wozniak, the 100 proof reader; Michael Tiefenbacher, Ernie Clark and especially Thomas Jones for their endless amount of information and help; Wally Podrazik for the excellent foreword; Richard Long for the wonderful paint job; Steve Szablewski for covering my book; Tom Bert for the fantastic photos; Yoko Ono for permission; Levon Helm for opening doors; Roy Cicala for trust and hospitality; Brian Wilson for endless harmonies and inspiration and lastly, but not "leastly", the boys, the men, The Beatles.

Apologies To

anyone whose name I've forgotten to mention in the acknowledgments,
your help was greatly appreciated.

HOW TO USE THIS BOOK

Each entry in this book contains record "entry data" followed by text of bibliographical and / or historical nature. The text portions sometimes also expand on the record entry data. I have tried, wherever available, to include the following information in the entry data for each record or recording contribution:

Artist Name.
The book is arranged alphabetically by the artist or groups' official name, or as it is listed on the record package, or by what is known to be correct. In the case of a record with no specific artist listed, or a recording that is truly the product of a variety of artists, the record is filed under Various Artists.

RECORD DATA
Record ## title:
This is the title of the record (vinyl, CD, LVD), sometimes including alternate titles or subtitles. The *##* in record title is the record identifier used for reference by this book. Identifiers are simply assigned sequentially from the first to the last entry in the book. The record identifier plus the song identifier (see below) uniquely identifies each song listed in the book. All media (CD, LVD, VHS and vinyl) are refered to as records. If a song is known to have been recorded, but no record was made or planned, the record title is [None].

Label / Catalog number:
The label designation is the name of the record label, or subsidiary, as stated on the label or jacket, or what is known to be the correct label (subsidiaries are always used in preference to the parent or corporate label. The vast majority of the subsidiary labels belong to one of MCA, EMI, BMG, WEA, Polygram or Columbia/Sony.) In cases where a record is clearly intended to be cataloged or identified under more than one label, these are listed. Some labels have had more than one parent company, such as George Harrison's Dark Horse label which has been assigned to A&M, Warner Brothers and EMI over the years.

The catalog number (separated from the label by a slash) is the one listed on the record label. Where no catalog number is given on the record, the matrix number (the manufacturing number stamped into the plastic) is used. If the record has been issued under more than one catalog number by the label, the second number (if known) is appended to the first sepated by an ampersand (&).

Media:
Record items are designated as being album or single. Items designated as CD are CD's; items designated as LVD are laser videodisk; items designated as VHS are VHS videotape; and all other (non-designated) items are vinyl. The record size, in inches, is given. Multiple record sets are indicated in square brackets. An example media description is "Album 5" CD [5 CD set]." All records are stereo unless (mono) has been appended to the media description.

Producer:
This identifies the producer of the (contribution) songs as listed on the record package (which may not be the same as the producer for the rest of the record.) If there are discrepancies they are noted, and what is known to be correct is listed. If there are additional known, but uncredited producers, they are listed in square brackets. If the listed songs for the record don't all have the same producer, the producer information is moved down to the song data for each song.

The term producer is broadly defined. Many well-known producers exercise complete control over the artist by imposing their arrangements, distinctive style and sound. Other producers play a very passive role and allow the artists a good deal of control and decision making. It's also probably safe to say that not all recordings listing a Beatle as producer received their full, if any, attention (In these cases the term executive producer, usually referring to a managerial or financial role, is more appropriate.) The role of executive producer is not considered, in and of itself, a production contribution.

Jacket / Inserts:
Jacket describes the physical package in which the record is purchased. The term "Unique" is sometimes used to designate any jacket or package design that is considerably different from the standard international design used throughout the world (the U.K. and U.S. generally represent the primary standard design.)

Inserts (separted from Jacket by a slash) describes any items, other than the record(s), included within or with the jacket such as record sleeves, CD inserts, posters, etc.

Recording Location / Date:
Recording Location identifies the recording studio and its location (city, state [where applicable] and country) or live venue where the record was recorded. Studios or venues located in suburban communities are generally identified by the name of the major metropolitan area in which they lie. When a number of studios are listed in the record package, and do not specifically identify at which studio the contribution song(s) was recorded, all studios are listed (unless the details are otherwise known.)

Date identfies the date on which (or period over which) the contribution song was recorded.

If the listed songs for the record don't all have the same recording location and date, the location and date information is moved down to the song data for each song.

Song ##n title:
This is the title of the (contribution) song as given (and spelled) on or in the record package. The *##n* in song title label is the record identifier (as used for reference by this book, see above) plus a lower case letter to uniquely identify the song. The letters are sequentially assigned and restart at "a" for each record.

If a song is known to have been recorded during a performance or session with a Beatle contribution, but the actual song is not known, the song title is given as "Unknown". If the contribution is to a record package, such as liner notes, photographs by one of The Beatles, or an appearance in a film, as opposed to a song, no song title is given. Song listings are given only for songs to which a Beatle made a contribution (not all of the songs on a listed record.)

Song details:
The song details listed are the record side and track, and the running time for the song. For multiple record sets the record number is also included preceeding the side. If the details are not known (as when the song title is not known), or there are no applicable details (such as contributed liner notes) then no details are given and the "Song Details" label is omitted. Song times listed are usually as stated on the record label or package. If the time was not listed, or if there was a discrepancy in the times listed, I timed the songs . If the age of CDs and digital music has brought us anything, it's accurate times on records.

Composer:
This is the contribution song composer's name (first initial and last name) as listed on the record label or package. If there is a discrepancy, it is noted in the text, and what is known to be correct is given. Known, but uncredited, additional composers are appended in square brackets. When the specific song(s) that have a contribution by a Beatle is not known for a record, all of the record's composers may be listed. When a song's composer is unknown, no data is given and the "Composer" label is omitted.

In the case of the Lennon & McCartney songwriting partnership, when both writers are credited even though they did not write every song together, I still list the official writing credit (J. Lennon - P. McCartney) but underlined the specific composer.

Members of The Beatles have frequently contributed a composition of theirs to another artist or group to record and release prior to their release of the song. In a few rare instances the artist or record company would delay a release by months or even years, or not release the recording at all, sometimes at the request of the composers. Conversely, a Beatle occasionally will record one of his songs, and he, or his record company, holds it from release for months or even years, and gives another artist a chance to record and release the song. Some may feel that when a Beatle releases a recording of his own composition which another artist had previously released, the other artist's recording should, at that point, be reconsidered as a cover version and not a composition contribution from a Beatle. The general rules adopted in this book are as follows: if an artist recorded or legally released his version of a song before the composer did, it's considered a composition contribution. This circumstance could only be possible if the composer had initially intended to contribute the song to another artist with the likelihood that that artist would release it first. If there is evidence that a record company released a recording by an artist before its composer, without the consent of the composer, it is not considered a composition contribution. A compositions recorded by an artist subsequent to its composer, and not released before its composer's version, is considered a cover version. Cover versions of Beatles' compositions by artists featured in the book are mentioned only in the text. There are exceptions to all of these rules, but only in cases where there is substantial evidence indicating that the composition was indeed intended by its composer to be released by another artist first. Without these conditions, one could speculate as to the intent of any composers (or publishers) whose songs are recorded by someone other than themselves.

Release date / Country:
The release date denotes when the listed record was issued. If the song was additionally known to have been released at an earlier date, on any media, anywhere in the world, then the "first issued" date is appended (in round brackets.) Songs that were recorded, but, to date, not released, are listed as "Unreleased."

Every effort has been made to use the official record company release dates or to be consistent with release dates listed in reliable publications, unless it is known for a fact that the contribution recording was first available on a different date.

The country designation is the country where the record was manufactured, regardless of where it was primarily available (released.) If a portion of the record package was manufactured in a different country than where the record was manufactured, it is noted.

Musicians:
The musicians and the instruments they play are identified for each (contribution) song. This information was taken from the record package, or from a variety of reference sources, studio logs and/or interviews conducted with the musicians. The term musicians includes vocalists.

In cases where the record package lists the musicians for the entire record (but not for each specific song), exhaustive research and extensive listening were used to separate out, where possible, the individual musicians and the instruments that they play. Unfortunately, it is quite often the case that more than one musician will be listed for each instrument, complicating the process of making a positive identification. When it is unknown which specific musicians are involved, each musician is listed with an "&/or" notation. In some cases, the entire general musical credits of an album have, of necessity, been listed stating that "probably one or more of the following" musicians are involved. When all methods and available sources have failed to identify any of the musicians involved, the musicians list has been omitted. However, the list of musicians is usually complete.

References Symbols:
Throught the book, the note *(see ...)* has been abreviated by the use of an asterisk (*) suffix on names that are part of the text. For example; Eric Clapton* means *(see Eric Clapton)*.

The use of a cross (†) suffixing item data and / or text throughout the book is to indicated that suffixed items within a song or record are uniquely related to one another. For example; if George Harrison's name is suffixed in the musicians list (George Harrison: Guitar†;), and two recording dates are listed, one of which is suffixed with a cross (Jul 70 & Aug 70†), this indicates that Harrison played on tracks recorded in August, but not on tracks recorded in July.

Probable, Possible and Supposed:

These words are used as prefixes throughout the book to indicate the likelihood of involvement of a Beatle where there is no certainty.

The term "probable" indicates that the contribution is not definite, but that there is a strong likelihood of the contribution. Determining the degree of probability depends on whether one is refer ring to a record or specific song.

The term "possible" refers to anything ranging from a good to a remote chance of involvement. The range in degree of possible involvement can vary greatly from entry to entry.

The term "supposed" generally refers to those records that for too long have been considered or suggested by some as having Beatle involvement, but most likely do not. It was important that these so-called contributions be explored and either explained and dispelled, or left to future investigations to better determine the extent, if any, of a contribution.

Additional Considerations

The following information provides elaboration on some of the entry topics above.

Media:

Album 12" refers to an LP - long playing 12" vinyl album - that was the industry standard from the mid-1950s through the mid-1980s. Album 5" CD (Compact disc) refers to the (approximately) 5" (audio) laser-read digital discs which ahve been the industry standard since the mid-1980s. Album 12" LVD refers to Laser Videodisc, also known as Laser Discs or Video Laserdiscs. This format preceded the 5" (audio) CD by several years, though it has failed to achieve the same level of consumer acceptance of the VHS tape format. This is due in large part to the cost of Laser Videodiscs and players, even though the audio and video quality is far superior to that of any other commercially available pre-recorded video technology. The current high quality 12" Laser Videodisc is being replaced by the new 5" DVD (Digitial Versatile or Video Disc) format. Lasere Videodiscs have also been marketed in 8" and 5" formats.

Producer:

The Beatles, except for Ringo, have had much experience producing their own and other artists' recordings since the advent of their Apple Records label in the late 1960s. Personal managers, arrangers, engineers, A&R men, assistants, friends, group members and musicians may contribute as much to the recording as the designated producer, and may or may not receive co-production credits. People in these professions often go on to become full-time producers. Quite often a Beatle has assisted producers or engineers in mixing or arranging recordings for other artists but is not credited.

Jacket / Inserts:

Picture sleeves, title sleeves and record (company) label sleeves generally apply to 7", and occasionally 12", singles. The word sleeve generally indicates a lighter construction, usually paper as opposed to the cardboard that is used for 12" records. Jewel box refers to the hard plastic case that is currently the industry standard for compact discs. Double jewel box refers to a hinged, multi-CD jewel box (sometimes called a clam box.) Gatefold jacket refers to a record jacket that folds open like a book.

Occasionally a Beatle will have contributed to a record package, usually in the form of liner notes, jacket design or as a photographer. Beatles photos that occasionally appear within the insert material are noted.

Recording Location / Date:

Many of The Beatles' contributions to other artists' recordings were made at one or more of their private or home studios. John Lennon had a small studio in his Weybridge home in the 1960s. When Lennon moved to Tittenhurst Park in Ascot in the late 1960s, he called his home studio Ascot Sound Studios. When Ringo moved into Lennon's Ascot house, he renamed it Startling Studios. George Harrison built a state-of-the-art studio at his mammoth gothic home Friar Park, Henley on Thames. The studio's name has been abbreviated to FPSHOT. Early on in his solo career, Paul McCartney used two makeshift studios at his farm retreat in northern Scotland called Rude Studios and Spirit of Ranachan Studios. McCartney has since built a state-of-the-art studio near his home in Sussex called Hog Hill Studios or The Mill. McCartney also built a replica (Replica Studios) of EMI's Abbey Road Studio 2 (where The Beatles did most of their recording) at his MPL offices in London. (Please note that during the years covered in this book, many live venues and studios have changed ownership and names, or relocated under the same name.)

The date(s) listed for a song do not necessarily indicate all the dates on which the recording was made. The date given usually indicates the beginning date of the recording, the date on which the majority of the song was recorded, or the date on which The Beatles' contribution was made to the recording.

Anya Alexeyev

Record 1 title:
A Leaf
Label / Catalog number:
EMI Classics: CD LEAF 1
Jacket / Inserts:
Standard international design in jewel box / 2 page CD insert
Recording Location / Date:
On location at St. James' Palace, London, U.K. / 23 Mar 95

Media:
Single 5" CD
Producer:
John Fraser

Song 1a title:
A Leaf [live]
Release date / Country:
24 Apr 95 / U.K.

Song details:
Side 1, track 1 / 9 min. 56 sec.
Composer:
P. McCartney

Anya Alexeyev: Piano

Anya Alexeyev is a 22-year-old award-winning pianist from Russia. She is the daughter of the well-known pianist Dmitri Alexeyev, and a graduate of Britain's Royal College of Music. Anya caught the attention of Paul McCartney when she received the Queen Elizabeth Rose Bowl award in 1994, presented at the Royal College of Music by the school's titular president, Prince Charles. McCartney was asked to help organize and contribute to a benefit concert for the college. He composed a classical piece titled ***A Leaf*** which Anya Alexeyev performed at the benefit held at St. James' Palace in London on March 23, 1995. The event was billed as **An Evening With Paul McCartney And Friends** and was attended by 300 invited guests. ***A Leaf*** is a seven part piano composition including - I Andante Semplice, II Poco piu mosso, III Allegro ritmico, IV Andante, V Allegro ma non tanto, VI Moderato, and VII Andante semplice [II].

McCartney performed newly arranged versions of his Beatles songs ***For No One***, ***Eleanor Rigby***, ***Yesterday*** and ***Lady Madonna***, accompanied by horn player Michael Thompson and the Brodsky Quartet, who also backed Elvis Costello* on several numbers. McCartney and Costello also performed together. The benefit also featured Sally Burgess and Willard White performing portions of McCartney's ***Liverpool Oratorio*** *(see The Royal Liverpool Philharmonic Orchestra & Choir and Choristers of Liverpool Cathedral).* John Fraser, who has worked with McCartney on most of his classical music projects, produced a recording of the performance. Alexeyev's performance of ***A Leaf*** was issued as a CD single and other portions of the event were made available for promotional purposes. For his efforts, McCartney was offered honorary Fellowship Of The Royal College Of Music, Britain's highest honorary award to a musician, by Prince Charles.

All Occasion Brass Band

Record 2 title:
In The Presence Of The Lord
Label / Catalog number:
MCA / MCA 362
Jacket / Inserts:
Standard international design / Record label inner sleeve
Recording Location / Date:
Olympic Studios, London, U.K. / 71
Media:
Album 12"
Producer:
Jim Price for J.J. Productions (OM)

Song 2a title:
Oh Happy Day
Release date / Country:
1974 / U.S.A.
Track details:
Side 1, track 5 / 3 min. 33 sec.
Composer:
E. Hawkins

Ringo Starr: Drums, Klaus Voormann: Bass; Chris Spedding: Guitar; Jim Price: Horns; probably one or more of the following: Stu Blumberg, Jock Ellis, Jake The Rake, Dave McDaniels, C.B., Rev. D.S. Poncher; Steve Delaney, Carol Farhat, Ken Klinger, Chris Kimsey, Nat Seligman, Barbara Wood, Joe Zagarino, Dave Farrell, Greg Matheson

The All Occasion Brass Band is really a Jim Price project. Jim Price was born in Fort Worth, Texas on July 25, 1945, and is primarily a session horn player who came to The Beatles by way of the group Delaney & Bonnie & Friends*. He was a part of the Delaney & Bonnie & Friends tour in 1969 that included George Harrison. He was also part of the group when they backed up John Lennon at the UNICEF benefit at the Lyceum in London following the tour *(see Yoko Ono)*.

The All Occasion Brass Band's album, **In The Presence of The Lord**, has musical credits that contain a number of obvious pseudonyms like Pietro Frampini, surely better known as Peter Frampton*, and Christo Spedingo for Chris Spedding.

(Spedding would later become a member of Paul McCartney's makeshift band in his **Give My Regards To Broadstreet** film.) Part of the production credits of this album use the Sanskrit symbol for OM. Because George Harrison often uses this symbol, he has mistakenly been thought to be involved in the album's production.

Additionally, special appreciation is given to George Greif. George Harrison mentions a Mr. Greif in his song, ***Crackerbox Palace***. Harrison also talked about Mr. Greif on the promotional album, **A Personal Music Dialogue with George Harrison at 33 & 1/3**, explaining that Greif was a well-known manager who inspired the title for ***Crackerbox Palace***. Some have suggested that Greif (in this case and others relating to the subject of this book) is a borrowed pseudonym for Harrison, but there is absolutely no evidence to suggest this. According to Price, at least in this case, it's the real Greif.

The **In The Presence Of The Lord** album includes covers of George Harrison's songs ***My Sweet Lord*** and ***Isn't It A Pity***. Both songs appeared on Harrison's **All Things Must Pass** album on which Price played. The credits also thank Richard Starkey for his contribution to the instrumental album, who, according to Price, played drums on the song ***Oh Happy Day***. An article in the December 11, 1971 issue of **Melody Maker** claimed Ringo Starr was involved in the recording of Jim Price's 1972 solo album, **Kids Nowadays Ain't Got No Shame**. That year Price appeared in a musical scene in Nilsson and Ringo's film, **Son Of Dracula**. But, according to Price, ***Oh Happy Day*** was the only recording of his to which any of The Beatles contributed.

The Alpha Band

Record 3 title:
Spark In The Dark
Label / Catalog number:
Arista / AB 4145
Jacket / Inserts:
Standard international design / Custom inner-sleeve
Recording Location / Date:
Paramount Recording Studio, U.S.A. / (probably) Aug 77

Media:
Album 12"
Producer:
Steven Soles

Song 3a title:
Born in Captivity
Release date / Country:
26 Sep 77 / U.S.A.

Track details:
Side 1, track 2 / 3 min. 44 sec.
Composer:
A. Stahr

Steven Soles: Lead Vocals, Guitar & Percussion; T-Bone Burnett: Lead Vocals, Guitar & Percussion; David Mansfield: Mandolin, Dobro Guitar, Percussion, & Steel Guitar; K.O.Thomas: Piano; David Miner: Bass; Ringo Starr: Drums; Matt Betton: Drums

Song 3b title:
You Angel You
Release date / Country:
26 Sep 77 / U.S.A.

Track details:
Side 2, track 2 / 2 min. 44 sec.
Composer:
B. Dylan

Steven Soles: Lead Vocals & Acoustic Guitar; T-Bone Burnett: Lead Vocals & Acoustic Guitar; David Mansfield: Electric Guitar; David Miner: Bass; Ringo Starr: Drums; Matt Betton: Drums; Cindy Bullens: Harmony

T-Bone Burnette, 1980s, photo courtesy of Tom Bert

The Alpha Band was a trio fronted by T-Bone Burnett, born John Henry Burnett on January 14, 1948, in St. Louis, Missouri. Burnett is a well-known singer, songwriter and producer who has worked with Elvis Costello*, Bob Dylan*, Delaney Bramlett* and Roy Orbison* among many others. The other members of The Alpha Band were Steven Soles and David Mansfield. All three were members of Bob Dylan's **Rolling Thunder Revue** tour in 1975 *(see The Band, Kinky Friedman)*. Contrary to some reports, The Alpha Band had absolutely nothing to do with Bob Dylan's conversion to Christianity.

Ringo Starr's introduction to The Alpha Band's members began on January 25, 1976 when he performed with the **Rolling Thunder Revue** at

The Houston Astrodome. Starr contributed to the songs ***Born in Captivity*** and ***You Angel You*** on The Alpha Band's 1977 album, **Spark In The Dark**.

The Applejacks

Record 4 title:
Lennon & McCartney Song Book Vol. 2
Media:
Album 5" CD (mono)
Label / Catalog number:
Connoisseur Collection / VSOP CD 162
Producer:
Mike Smith
Jacket / Inserts:
Standard international design in jewel box with photo of John Lennon & Paul McCartney / 8 page CD booklet with photo of John Lennon & Paul McCartney
Recording Location / Date:
(probably) Decca Studios, London, U.K. / (probably) May 64

Song 4a title:
Like Dreamers Do
Track details:
Side 1, track 18 / 2 min. 30 sec.
Release date / Country:
31 May 91 (first issued 05 Jun 64) / U.K./E.E.C.
Composer:
J. Lennon - <u>P. McCartney</u>

Al Jackson: Lead Vocals; Martin Baggott: Lead Guitar; Phil Cash: Rhythm Guitar; Don Gould: Keyboards; Megan Davies: Bass; Gerry Freeman: Drums

The Applejacks hailed from Birmingham, England. They were previously known as The Crestas and The Jaguars. Their bass player was a woman, unusual for pop groups of that era. Their first single, ***Tell Me When***, was a top 10 in the U.K.

The AppleJacks' follow-up, ***Like Dreamers Do***, reached the U.K. top 20. It was an early Paul McCartney composition once included by The Beatles in their live repertoire, which is probably why this up-tempo pop song was chosen as one of three Lennon and McCartney originals for The Beatles' Decca Records audition on New Year's Day 1962. (The other two Lennon and McCartney compositions were ***Hello Little Girl*** *(see The Fourmost, Gerry And The Pacemakers)* and ***Love Of The Loved*** *(see Cilla Black)*.) Ironically, this song was produced by Mike Smith who oversaw The Beatles' Decca Records auditions and was probably responsible for their being turned down by the label. The song was likely recorded in the same studios as The Beatles' audition. The Applejacks did a cover of The Beatles' song ***Baby's In Black*** in 1965. The Decca audition version of ***Like Dreamers Do*** was officially released by The Beatles on their album, **Anthology 1**, in 1995.

Artists United Against Apartheid

Record 5 title:
Sun City [Various Artists]
Media:
Single 7"
Label / Catalog number:
Manhattan / B50017
Producer:
Little Stven Van Zandt & Arthur Baker
Jacket / Inserts:
Standard international design Picture sleeve
Recording Location / Date:
One or more of the following studios: Shakedown Sound, Hit Factory, Electric Lady, M&I Recording, Unique, Right Track, Soundworks & Power Station, New York, NY, Cherokee & The Outpost, Los Angeles, CA, Syncro Sound, Boston, MA, U.S.A.; Eel Pie & Fallout Shelter, London, Startling, Ascot, U.K.; Windmill Lane, Dublin, Ireland

Song 5a title:
Sun City [single version]
Release date / Country:
11 Nov 85 / U.S.A.
Track details:
Side 1, track 1 / 4 min. 58 sec.
Composer:
S. Van Zandt

One or more of the following: Run DMC: Vocals; Grandmaster Melle Mel & Duke Bootee: Vocals; Afrika Bambaataa & Kurtis Blow: Vocals; Big Youth & All Rappers: Vocals; David Ruffin: Vocals; Pat Benatar: Vocals; Eddie Kendrick: Vocals; Bruce Springsteen: Vocals; George Clinton: Vocals; Joey Ramone: Vocals; Jimmy Cliff & Daryl Hall: Vocals; Darlene Love: Vocals; Linton Kwesi Johnson & All Rappers: Vocals; Bonnie Raitt: Vocals; Ruben Blades & John Oates: Vocals; Lou Reed: Vocals; Bobby Womack: Vocals; Jackson Browne & Bob Dylan: Vocals; Peter Garrett: Vocals; Nona Hendryx & Kashif: Vocals; Bono: Vocals; Ringo Starr: Drums; Zak Starkey: Drums; Keith Le Blanc:Drums & Drum Programming; Tony Williams: Drums; Pete Townshend: Guitar; Stanley Jordan: Guitar; Little Steven Van Zandt: Guitar & Drum Programming; Doug Wimbish: Bass; Ron Carter: Acoustic Bass; Herbie Hancock: Keyboards; Richard Scher: Keyboards; Robbie Kilgore: Keyboards; Zoe Yanakis: Keyboards; Miles Davis: Trumpet; Clarence Clemons: Saxophone; Shankar: Double Violin; Ray Barretto: Conga; Sonny Okosuns: Talking Drum; Jam Master Jay: Scratcher; D.J. Cheese: Scratcher; Benjamin Newberry: Drum Programming; BLT: B. Vocals; B.J. Nelson: B. Vocals; Lottie Golden: B. Vocals; Tina B: B. Vocals; Daryl Hannah: B. Vocals; Kevin McCormick: B. Vocals; The Dunnes Stores Strikers: B. Vocals; Annie Brody Dutka: B. Vocals; Gil Scott-Heron: B. Vocals; Robert Gordon: B. Vocals; Steve Walker: B. Vocals

Record 6 title:
Sun City [Various Artists]
Media:
Album 5" CD
Label / Catalog number:
Razor & Tie/Capitol / RE 2007
Producer:
Little Steven Van Zandt & Arthur Baker
Jacket / Inserts:
Standard international design in jewel box / 10 page CD booklet
Recording Location / Date:
One or more of the following studios: Shakedown Sound, Hit Factory, Electric Lady, M&I Recording, Unique, Right Track, Soundworks & Power Station, New York, NY, Cherokee & The Outpost, Los Angeles, CA, Syncro Sound, Boston, MA, U.S.A.; Eel Pie & Fallout Shelter, London, Startling, Ascot, U.K.; Windmill Lane, Dublin, Ireland

Song 6a title:
Sun City [LP version]
Release date / Country:
1993 (first issued 18 Nov 85) / U.S.A.
Track details:
Side 1, track 1 / 7 min. 10 sec.
Composer:
S. Van Zandt
Performers as above.

Song 6b title:
Sun City [version II]
Release date / Country:
1993 (first issued 18 Nov 85) / U.S.A.
Track details:
Side 1, track 4 / 5 min. 43 sec.
Composer:
S. Van Zandt
Performers as above.

Song 6c title:
Sun City (The Last Remix) [aka Dub version]
Release date / Country:
1993 (first issued 18 Nov 85) / U.S.A.
Track details:
Side 1, track 8 / 9 min. 37 sec.
Composer:
S. Van Zandt
Performers as above; also includes - Desmond Tutu: Vocals.

Artists United Against Apartheid was organized by "Little Steven" Steven Van Zandt, who is best known for his long association with Bruce Springsteen*. In 1985, Van Zandt decided to organize a campaign to discourage performers from working in Sun City. Sun City is a major international tourist resort in Bophuthatswana, within South Africa. Bophuthatswana was one of several native

tribal homelands set up by the white government of South Africa in an attempt to diffuse criticism of Apartheid (racial segregation) by allowing blacks autonomous self-rule. The world community, for the most part, generally denounced the creation of these homelands as divisive and deceptive, and refused to recognize them as independent nations. Sun City, unlike South Africa as a whole at the time, had the appearance of being racially tolerant and integrated. It attracted many performers who normally refused to appear in segregated South Africa because they felt it was a step in the right direction. Van Zandt and the Artists United Against Apartheid felt that Sun City was a facade, not a showcase.

Van Zandt hastily and masterfully organized some of music's top jazz, rhythm & blues, rap and rock performers to contribute to this project on behalf of "The Africa Fund." Among them were Ringo and his son Zak, who drummed on the backing tracks used on the four versions of the song ***Sun City***. Ringo and Zak's contribution were recorded at Startling Studios, Ascot, U.K.

In September 1973, Ringo bought John Lennon's home in Tittenhurst Park, Ascot. Lennon had lived there barely two years before moving to New York in 1971. Lennon, unable to return to England because of the threat of not being allowed back in the U.S., decided to sell the house to Ringo. The home contained a recording studio Lennon called Ascot Sound. Ringo renamed the studio Startling Studios (like one of his publishing companies) after his last name and opened it up to commercial use. The studio was used by a number of well-known musical acts as well as by Ringo himself. The home was eventually sold, and the new owner eliminated the studio, reportedly along with a very large number of master tapes, during renovations. Ringo and Zak also appear in the video release for the **Sun City** project. The LP custom inner sleeve contains a photo of Zak and Ringo taken by his wife Barbara Bach. The **Sun City** CD contains three versions (all but the single version) of ***Sun City***, totaling over twenty-two and a half minutes of ***Sun City***. The Sun City project was also released on laser video disk (IMG / 1985 ID5150).

Ashton, Gardner & Dyke

Record 7 title:
The Worst Of Ashton, Gardner & Dyke

Label / Catalog number:
Repertoire / REP 4458-WY

Media:
Album 5" CD

Producer:
Tony Ashton, Kim Gardner, Roy Dyke & "Kneaded and leavened by George Harrison"

Jacket / Inserts:
Standard international design in jewel box / 6 page CD booklet & 28 page Repertoire Records catalogue

Recording Location / Date:
De Lane Lea Sound Centre, London, England / (probably) Jul 70 &/or (possibly) Mar 70

Song 7a title:
I'm Your Spiritual Breadman

Release date / Country:
May 94 (first issued 28 Sep 70) / Germany

Track details:
Side 1, track 2 / 3 min. 16 sec.

Composer:
T. Ashton & [G. Harrison]

Tony Ashton: Lead Vocals; Keyboards; Kim Gardner: Bass; Roy Dyke: Drums; Eric Clapton: Lead Guitar; George Harrison: Electric Swivel Guitar; Bobby Keys: Saxophone; Jim Price: Trumpet; Phil & His Boogie Brass provide brass & reeds

Ashton, Gardner & Dyke formed in 1968. Tony Ashton and Roy Dyke had previously been members of the Liverpool band The Remo Four*. Bass player Kim Gardner was born on January 27, 1946 in Dulwich, England. He had previously been a member of The Birds and then The Creation.

Ashton, Gardner & Dyke were a supporting act for the Delaney & Bonnie & Friends* tour in December 1969 which included George Harrison and Eric Clapton. Ashton denies reports that he took part with the tour's members in John Lennon and Yoko Ono's* performance on December 15, 1969 at London's Lyceum Ballroom, though he was present.

Several months later Harrison and Clapton contributed to Ashton, Gardner & Dyke's recording ***I'm Your Spiritual Breadman***. George is listed in the credits as "George O'Hara Smith" (a pseudonym he used on his **All Things Must Pass** album) and Eric Clapton as "Sir Cedric Clayton." According to Ashton, "I played the song for George and he liked it, and I asked him if he'd like to play on it and produce it. He said sure, and he was so good about it. He just did the general production and helped out with some of the lyrics on the middle eight. The song was originally going to be the A-side of the single, but that ended up being ***Resurrection Shuffle*** (a top five in the U.K. and a top 40 in the U.S.) which our record company thought was more commercial." **The Worst of Ashton, Gardner & Dyke** album also contains a song titled ***Sweet Pattie O'Hara Smith*** in tribute to George Harrison's wife, Pattie (Boyd) Harrison, later to become Mrs. Eric Clapton. Ashton laments, "Isn't it a pity my keyboard work on Harrison's recording ***Isn't It A Pity*** went uncredited." Over the years there has been speculation about possible Beatles involvement in other Ashton, Gardner & Dyke recordings, but according to Ashton and Gardner, ***I'm Your Spiritual Breadman*** was the only song of theirs that contained any involvement by a Beatle

Ashton, Gardner & Dyke broke up in early 1973 after several moderately successful albums. Roy Dyke and Kim Gardner went on to join Badger *(see Jackie Lomax)* and worked with Chris Barber* as well as other artists. Roy Dyke currently lives and works in Germany but still dabbles in music. Kim Gardner now owns and operates a bar in the Los Angeles, California area.

Tony Ashton worked with a number of artists, including Jon Lord and Ian Paice of the group Deep Purple. (Lord is a neighbor and good friend of George Harrison and contributed to his album **Gone Troppo**. On December 14, 1984, Harrison made a guest appearance onstage with Deep Purple in Sydney, Australia, performing ***Lucille***. This has fueled speculation, in spite of any evidence, that Harrison may have contributed to some of Lord's recordings.) Portions of the album **First Of The Big Bands**, by Ashton and Lord, were recorded at Apple Studios, but Ashton said none of The Beatles contributed to it. Tony Ashton was also a member of Paul McCartney's **Rockestra** ensemble on October 3, l978 for ***So Glad To See You Here*** and ***Rockestra Theme***. Ashton continues to play in pubs and clubs in England and Europe and is currently working on his autobiography. His tribute song to John Lennon, ***The Big Freedom Dance***, was released in 1996.

Chet Atkins

Record 8 title:
Chet Atkins Picks On The Beatles
Media:
Album 5" CD
Label / Catalog number:
RCA / 07863-53531-2
Producer:
Chet Atkins & Bob Ferguson
(re-produced for CD by Steve Lindsey)
Jacket / Inserts:
Standard international design in jewel box / 4 page CD booklet with Liner notes by George Harrison
Release date / Country:
1996 (first issued Mar 66) / U.S.A.
Composer:
J. Lennon - P. McCartney
Recording Location / Date:
RCA "Nashville Sound" Studio, Nashville, Tennessee U.S.A.

Chet Atkins was born on June 20, 1924 in Luttrell, Tennessee. Both of his parents played the piano and his father often gave lessons on the instrument. Young Chet grew to become one of the most accomplished guitarists in the history of country & western music. He has won nine CMA Awards as Musician of the Year and thirteen Grammies. He has contributed to dozens of recordings by some of the biggest names in country and rock music, including Hank Williams, Elvis Presley and The Everly Brothers*. Atkins, who served an executive role with RCA Records for several decades, was instrumental in developing and promoting some of the biggest names in country music.

Chet Atkins, Photo courtesy of Tom Bert

George Harrison obviously wrote five paragraphs of liner notes for the album of Beatles' covers titled **Chet Atkins Picks On The Beatles** because of his respect and admiration for Atkins. The album jacket's front photo features a clever display of models of The Beatles with their faces "picked" off along with Atkins' Gretsch guitar – the same make Harrison used. On the jacket's back there's a photo of Atkins wearing a Beatles' wig.

Atkins also played guitar on the song, ***Walking In The Park With Eloise***, by The Country Hams. The song was composed by Paul McCartney's father James. It included McCartney on washboard and bass, Wings' brief drummer, Geoff Britton, and equally famous country & western pianist, Floyd Cramer, during Wings' recording sessions in Nashville in the summer of 1974.

In 1973, Atkins was inducted into the Country Music Hall of Fame. He released a cover of John Lennon's song ***Imagine*** in 1989. Atkins teamed up with singer Suzy Bogguss performing ***All My Loving*** for the 1995 country music Beatles tribute album titled **Come Together: America Salutes The Beatles**. Chet Atkins was featured on Paul McCartney's 1995 radio series, **Oobu Joobu**.

I have appreciated Chet Atkins as a musician since long before the tracks on this album were written; in fact, since I was the ripe young age of seventeen. Since then I have lost count of the number of Chet's albums I have acquired, but I have not been disappointed with any of them.

For me, the great thing about Mr. Atkins is not the fact that he is capable of playing almost every type of music but the conviction in the way he does it. Whilst listening to CHET ATKINS PICKS ON THE BEATLES I got the feeling that these songs had been written specifically with Chet in mind. The fact that they were not proves his eminence as an artist—the perfect example being *Yesterday*. Chet, by himself, gets far more out of this than some of the people known as "class" singers do with a full orchestral arrangement to boot!

I'll Cry Instead, She's a Woman and *Can't Buy Me Love,* having a country feeling about them, lend themselves perfectly to Chet's own style of picking, which has inspired so many guitarists throughout the world (myself included, but I didn't have enough fingers at the time).

All the other tracks have Chet adding harmonies and harmonics in the least expected places, bringing out that crystal-clear sound of the guitar to his audience's benefit.

One thing remains very clear to me at the end of this LP, and that is why this sleeve note must end here. Chet Atkins did not get to be a great guitarist by writing sleeve notes, but by years of devoted practice on the instrument he so obviously loves.

GEORGE HARRISON

Attitudes

Record 9 title:
Ain't Love Enough / The Whole World's Crazy
Label / Catalog number:
Dark Horse / DH 10004
Release date / Country:
09 Dec 75 / U.S.A.
Media:
Single 7"
Producer:
Lee Kiefer & Attitudes
Composer:
D. Foster - B. G. Russell - B. Russell - P. Stallworth
Jacket / Inserts:
Unique Picture sleeve with photo by George Harrison
Recording Location / Date:
Sunswept Recorders, Los Angeles, CA, U.S.A. / 1975

Paul Stallworth: Vocals & Bass; David Foster: Piano & B. Vocals; Danny Kortchmar: Guitars & Vocals; Jim Keltner: Drums, Percussion & B. Vocals

Record 10 title:
Good News
Label / Catalog number:
Dark Horse / DH 3021
Jacket / Inserts:
Standard international design / Custom inner-sleeve
Recording Location / Date:
(probably) Producer's Workshop, A&M &/or Sunswept Recording Studios, Los Angeles, CA, U.S.A. / (probably) late 76 or early 77

Media:
Album 12"
Producer:
Jay Lewis & Attitudes

Song 10 title:
Good News
Release date / Country:
05 May 77 / U.S.A.

Track details:
Side 2, track 5 / 3 min. 45 sec.
Composer:
P. Stallworth

Paul Stallworth: Lead Vocals & Bass; David Foster: Piano & B. Vocals; Danny Kortchmar: Guitars & B. Vocals; Jim Keltner: Drums, Percussion & B. Vocals; Ringo Starr: Drums; Booker T. Jones: Organ; Tower Of Power Horn Section (Horn Arrangement by Greg Adams); Jorge Calderon: B. Vocals; Y. Rankin: B. Vocals

Attitudes was conceived by Lee Kiefer and comprised of well-known studio musicians Dave Foster, Danny "Kootch" Kortchmar *(see James Taylor)*, Paul Stallworth and Jim Keltner. Keyboard player and producer David Foster was a founding member of the group Skylark. He has contributed to Paul McCartney, George Harrison and Ringo Starr's recordings over the years. Guitarist Kortchmar has contributed to Starr and Harrison's recordings. Bass player Paul Stallworth has also worked with Harrison. Jim Keltner has been a backup drummer for Harrison, Starr and John Lennon on recordings too numerous to mention.

Keltner and several other musicians *(see All Occasion Brass Band, Bobby Whitlock, Bobby Keys, Leon Russell)* came to The Beatles' attention via Delaney & Bonnie & Friends*. John Lennon added Keltner to his backing band Elephant's Memory* during his **One-To-One** benefit concert.

George Harrison recruited him on his 1974 U.S. tour. Ringo Starr formed his first of many All-Starr Band tours in 1989 and included Jim Keltner in the line-up. Keltner is also the drummer for Harrison's "supergroup" Traveling Wilburys *(see Bob Dylan, Jeff Lynne, Roy Orbison, Tom Petty)*, adding to his long list of credits playing with virtually every major name in rock 'n' roll. He joined another band in the 1990s called Little Village with John Hiatt, Ry Cooder and Nick Lowe.

Album credits for **Attitudes** (Dark Horse / SP 22008) give "special thanks to Ohnothimagen," a self-deprecating pseudonym Harrison used at the time. Attitudes' first single, ***Ain't Love Enough***, was issued with a picture sleeve photo taken by Harrison.

Credits for Attitudes' second and final album, **Good News**, the title track of which features Ringo, also give "special thanks" to George Harrison. According to Jim Keltner, Harrison did not contribute to any of Attitudes' recordings, and the thanks to him was merely for his support of the group.

Randy Bachman

Record 11 title:
Ringo Starr And His Third All-Starr Band Volume 1
Label / Catalog number:
Blockbuster Exclusive / 0ERE4<5297>
RINGOSTARR ADFL
Jacket / Inserts:
Standard international design / 4 page CD insert
Recording Location / Date:
Nippon Budakon Hall, Tokyo, Japan / 27 Jun 95
Media:
Album 5" CD
Producer:
Greg Delancy (Mixer)
Ringo Starr and David Fishof(Executive Producers)

Song 11a title:
No Sugar Tonight [live]
Release date / Country:
12 Aug 97 / U.S.A.
Track details:
Side 1, track 6 / 4 min. 15 sec.
Composer:
R. Bachman

Randy Bachman: Lead Vocals & Lead Guitar; Mark Farner: Guitar & B. Vocals; Ringo Starr: Drums; Zak Starkey: Drums; John Entwistle: Bass; Felix Cavaliere: Keyboards, Percussion & B. Vocals; Billy Preston: Keyboards & B. Vocals; Mark Rivera: Percussion & B. Vocals

Song 11b title:
You Ain't Seen Nothin' Yet [live]
Release date / Country:
08 Dec 97 / U.S.A.
Track details:
Side 1, track 10 / 3 min. 39 sec.
Composer:
R. Bachman

Randy Bachman: Lead Vocals & Lead Guitar; Mark Farner: Guitar; Ringo Starr: Drums; Zak Starkey: Drums; John Entwistle: Bass; Felix Cavaliere: Keyboards; Billy Preston: Keyboards; Mark Rivera: Acoustic Guitar

Randy Bachman was born on September 27, 1943 in Winnipeg, Manitoba, Canada. Bachman was a founding member of the group The Guess Who *(see Burton Cummings)* for whom he composed, sang and played guitar. Bachman recalls, "The Guess Who always had a fascination with England and when the new Liverpool sound began its influence in Winnipeg, we radically changed our stage show to cover every track on every Beatles' album. We tried to write original material like The Beatles. The Beatles were everything to us."

Bachman left The Guess Who in 1970 and released a solo album titled **Axe**. Soon after, he and his younger brother Robbie along with Chad Allan (another founding member of The Guess Who) formed the band Brave Belt. Their albums **Brave Belt I** in 1971 and **Brave Belt II** released the following year, failed to yield any major hits in the U.S.

In 1972, Randy's brother Tim and Fred Turner replaced Allan, and the group was renamed Bachman-Turner Overdrive. Their first release was a self-titled album in 1973. Tim later left the group and was replaced by Blair Thornton. 1974 was the group's banner year. Their single, ***Let It Ride***, became their first top 30. The album **Bachman-Turner Overdrive II** was a top five and contained the single ***Takin' Care of Business***, which hovered just outside the top 10. Later in the year the album **Not Fragile** was released. Both the album and its single ***You Ain't Seen Nothin' Yet*** climbed to the top of the charts and were also huge international hits. Their 1975 album **Four-Wheel** was a top five, and their song ***Roll On Down The Highway*** made the top 20 while another song, ***Hey You***, just missed it.

Randy Bachman, late 1980s, photo courtesy of Tom Bert

Randy Bachman left Bachman-Turner Overdrive in 1977 and released a solo album titled **Survivor** with help from Burton Cummings. Meanwhile, Bachman-Turner Overdrive officially became known as BTO and continued on and off for several more years with various members departing and reforming under both group names. (The confusion would eventually cause Randy to take legal action over the rights to the group names.) Randy formed a new group called Ironhorse that had a top 40 with the song ***Sweet Lui-Louise*** in 1979. During this period he also formed another short-lived group called Union. In 1983 the original members of The Guess Who (including Bachman) briefly reunited for a tour and album. In 1984, Randy and Tim Bachman along with Turner regrouped to release another self-titled Bachman-Turner Overdrive album.

Ringo Starr twice utilized The Guess Who's pool of talent for his All-Starr Band. In 1992, Burton Cummings was a member and in 1995, Randy Bachman joined the growing list of All-Starrs. Bachman remembers, "When my phone rang and the voice said, 'Hello, this is Ringo calling from Monaco. Welcome to the band.' I was speechless. It was a dream come true. It was the ultimate rock 'n' roll bar band led by the world's greatest rock drummer."

During the tour Bachman performed the BTO hits ***Takin' Care Of Business*** and ***You Ain't Seen Nothin' Yet*** and The Guess Who's hit ***No Sugar Tonight***, all featuring Ringo on drums. Bachman said, "Playing guitar on Ringo's songs every night and looking back over my shoulders and hearing and seeing him playing drums on my songs was the highlight of my musical career. Every show was memorable; I don't see anything that will eclipse it. I would have done it for nothing. It was a privilege. For his birthday my wife and I had a newly discovered star named after him called 'The Ringo Starr.'" Randy Bachman is still takin' care of business writing songs, recording and touring.

Badfinger

Record 12 title:
Magic Christian Music

Media:
Album 5" CD

Label / Catalog number:
Apple/Capitol / CDP 7 97579 2

Jacket / Inserts:
Standard international design in jewel box / 8 page CD booklet

Song 12a title:
Carry On Till Tomorrow

Track details:
Side 1, track 8 / 4 min. 47 sec.

Producer:
Mal Evans & [Paul McCartney]

Composer:
T. Evans - P. Ham

Release date / Country:
19 Nov 91 (first issued 09 Sep 70) / U.S.A.
Recording Location / Date:
EMI-Abbey Road Studios, London, U.K. / 22 & 26 Aug 69

Tom Evans: Guitar & Lead Vocals; Pete Ham: Guitar & B. Vocals; Ron Griffiths: Bass; Mike Gibbins: Drums; George Martin: String Arrangement & Conductor

Song 12b title:
Come And Get It
Track details:
Side 1, track 1 / 2 min. 21 sec.
Producer:
Paul McCartney
Composer:
P. McCartney
Release date / Country:
19 Nov 91 (first issued 9 Jan 70) / U.S.A.
Recording Location / Date:
EMI-Abbey Road Studios, London, U.K. / 22 & 26 Aug 69

Tom Evans: Lead Vocals & Guitar; Pete Ham: Guitar; Ron Griffiths: Bass; Mike Gibbins: Drums; Paul McCartney: Piano & Maracas

Song 12c title:
Crimson Ship
Track details:
Side 1, track 2 / 3 min. 42 sec.
Producer:
Tony Visconti & [Paul McCartney]
Composer:
T. Evans - P. Ham
Release date / Country:
19 Nov 91 (first issued 09 Jan 70) / U.S.A.
Recording Location / Date:
Trident Studios, London, U.K. / (probably) Aug or Sep 69

Pete Ham: Lead Vocals, Guitar & Keyboards; Ron Griffiths: Bass; Tom Evans: Lead Vocals & Guitar; Mike Gibbins: Drums

Song 12 dtitle:
Rock Of All Ages
Track details:
Side 1, track 7 / 3 min. 16 sec.
Producer:
Mal Evans & Paul McCartney
Composer:
T. Evans - P. Ham - M. Gibbins - [P. McCartney]
Release date / Country:
19 Nov 91 (first issued 09 Jan 70) / U.S.A.

Recording Location / Date:
IBC Studios, London, U.K. / 18 Sep 69

Tom Evans: Lead Vocals & Bass; Pete Ham: Guitar; Mike Gibbins: Drums; Paul McCartney: Piano & (probable) B. Vocals

Record 13 title:
Straight UP
Media:
Album 5" CD
Label / Catalog number:
Apple / CDP 0777 7 81403 20
Producer:
George Harrison & [Todd Rundgren]
Jacket / Inserts:
Standard international design in jewel box / 12 page CD booklet

Song 13a title:
Day After Day
Track details:
Side 1, track 9 / 3 min. 10 sec.
Release date / Country:
25 May 93 (first issued 13 Dec 71) / U.S.A.
Composer:
P. Ham

Recording Location / Date:
EMI-Abbey Road Studios, London, U.K. / 03 Jun 71

Pete Ham: Lead Vocals & Lead Guitar; Joey Molland: Guitar & B. Vocals; Tom Evans: Bass & B. Vocals; Mike Gibbins: Drums; George Harrison: Lead Guitar; Leon Russell: Piano

Song 13b title:
I'd Die Babe
Release date / Country:
25 May 93 (first issued 13 Dec 71) / U.S.A.
Recording Location / Date:
EMI-Abbey Road Studios, London, U.K. / (probably) Jun 71
Track details:
Side 1, track 5 / 2 min. 33 sec.
Composer:
J. Molland

Joey Molland: Lead Vocals & Guitar; Pete Ham: Guitar & Keyboards; Tom Evans: Bass & B. Vocals; Mike Gibbins: Drums; George Harrison: Electric & Acoustic Guitar

Song 13c title:
Name Of The Game
Release date / Country:
25 ay 93 (first issued 13 Dec 71) / U.S.A.
Recording Location / Date:
EMI-Abbey Road Studios, London, U.K. / Jun 71
Track details:
Side 1, track 6 / 5 min. 17 sec.
Composer:
P. Ham

Pete Ham: Lead Vocals & Guitar; Joey Molland: Guitar & B. Vocals; Tom Evans: Bass & B. Vocals; Mike Gibbins: Drums; Leon Russell: Keyboards

Song 13d title:
Suitcase
Release date / Country:
25 May 93 (first issued 13 Dec 71) / U.S.A.
Recording Location / Date:
EMI-Abbey Road Studios, London, U.K. / 31 May 71
Track details:
Side 1, track 7 / 2 min. 52 sec.
Composer:
J. Molland

Joey Molland: Lead Vocals & Guitar; Pete Ham: Slide Guitar; Tom Evans: Bass & B. Vocals; Mike Gibbins: Drums & Maracas; Klaus Voormann: Keyboards; Leon Russell: Guitar; Kathie Molland: Tambourine

Badfinger was unquestionably Apple Records' most successful group of recording artists, except for The Beatles. They were Joey Molland (born June 21, 1947), Tom Evans (born June 5, 1947), both from Liverpool, England; Pete Ham (born April 27, 1947) and Mike Gibbins (born March 12, 1949), both from Swansea, Wales. The band's members were naturally influenced by and in awe of their idols, The Beatles. Evans had been a fan since 1962 when he regularly saw The Beatles perform at the Cavern Club in Liverpool. Unfortunately, Badfinger were often unfairly accused of imitating The Beatles.

Badfinger originally called themselves The Iveys (patterned after The Hollies). They began backing

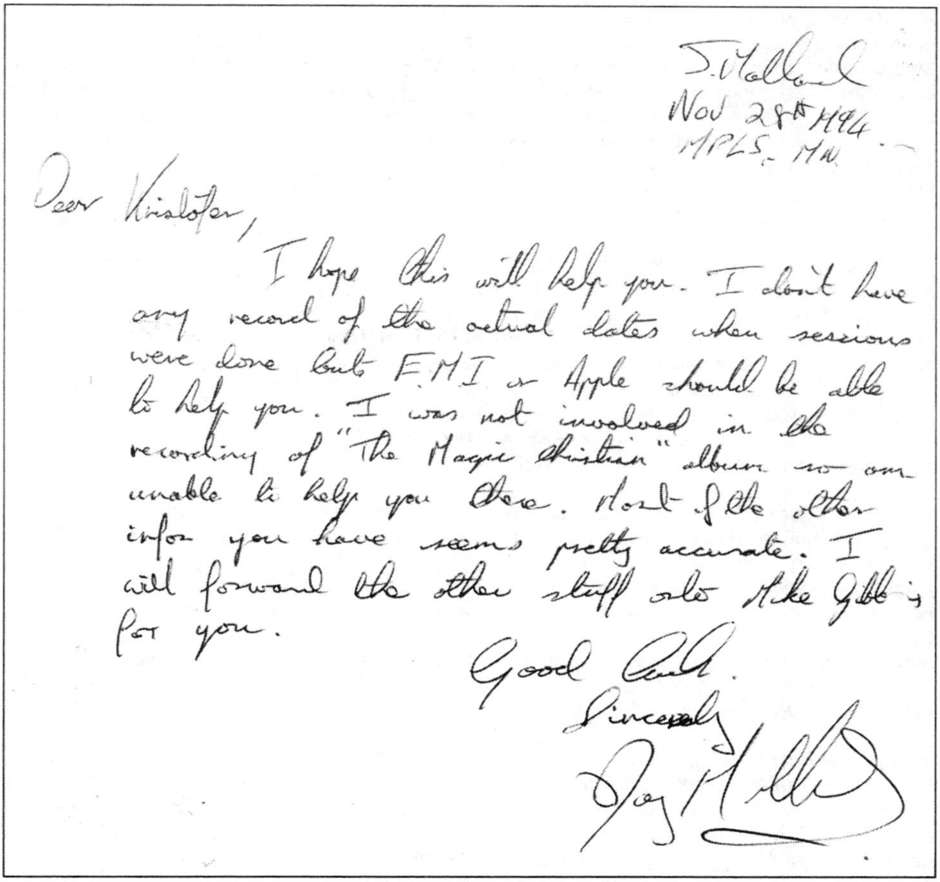
J. Molland
Nov 28th 1994
MPLS. MN.

Dear Kristofer,

I hope this will help you. I don't have any record of the actual dates when sessions were done but E.M.I or Apple should be able to help you. I was not involved in the recording of "The Magic Christian" album so am unable to help you there. Most of the other info you have seems pretty accurate. I will forward the other stuff also Mike Gibbs is for you.

Good Luck.

Sincerely

Joey Molland

Letter from Joey Molland to Kristofer Engelhardt

recording artist David Garrick in 1966. They came to Apple Records via their manager, former band-leader Bill Collins who knew Paul McCartney's father *(see Mike McGear)* and were signed to the label in July 1968. They released their first Apple album in 1969, titled after their first single, ***Maybe Tomorrow***, a minor hit earlier that year. But the album's extremely limited release delayed The Iveys' success. The Iveys were considering a new name for the group. John Lennon had originally suggested the name Prix, which wisely was rejected, and McCartney wanted to call the band Home or Mama's Boys. According to Tom Evans, The Beatles' assistant Neil Aspinall and The Iveys were listening to The Beatles' song ***Lady Madonna***, and Aspinall commented that it sounded a lot like the song ***Bad Penny Blues***. The words bad and penny jokingly developed into Badfinger, a bit of Liverpool slang that had also been used as a working title for The Beatles' song ***With A Little Help From My Friends***. Original member, Ron Griffiths, left the group and was replaced by Joey Molland. Hamish Stuart (a member of Paul McCartney's band in the late 1980s) was also considered as a replacement for Griffiths.

Paul McCartney initially took Badfinger under his wing and gave them his song, ***Come And Get It***. He took the band into the studio and auditioned each member to determine who would sing the lead vocals. It became Badfinger's first hit single and the soundtrack theme for the film **The Magic Christian** *(see Peter Sellers, Terry Southern & Ringo Starr)*. (***Come And Get It*** was also covered by the groups The Magic Christians in 1970 and The Saltbee in the mid-'90s.) (The Beatles' [McCartney's demo] recording of the song was officially released on their 1996 album, **Anthology 3**.)

McCartney arranged for Badfinger to provide two additional recordings, ***Carry On Till Tomorrow*** and

Rock Of All Ages, for the film The Magic Christian. There is some confusion surrounding the production credits on these and another Badfinger song, ***Crimson Ship***. Neither the **Magic Christian Music Soundtrack** nor the first issue of Badfinger's **Magic Christian Music** album lists production credits for these songs. However, when the CD of **Magic Christian Music** with extended credits was released, the producer was listed as Mal Evans (The Beatles' roadie and assistant) on ***Carry On Till Tomorrow*** and Tony Visconti *(see Mary Hopkin)* on ***Crimson Ship*** and ***Rock Of All Ages***. Visconti does not recall exactly what he produced for Badfinger. According to Mike Gibbins, McCartney was involved in the initial production on these three songs but did not want to be credited. Tom Evans has also stated that McCartney was involved in the production of these songs.

According to Gibbins, McCartney also helped write ***Rock Of All Ages*** and played piano on the recording. Evans has also gone on record as saying that McCartney played piano on the track and that he and McCartney did a take sharing the lead vocals but that McCartney decided against using it. Molland thinks McCartney contributed some backing vocals to the song though Gibbins does not agree. However, it does sound like McCartney doing his best Little Richard* vocal impersonation in the background. Gibbins and Evans have been the source for most of the information on McCartney's musical contributions to Badfinger's recordings as Molland was not a member at the time. The fade-out on the soundtrack and Apple single version of ***Rock Of All Ages*** is approximately six seconds longer than the version on Badfinger's first Apple album, **Magic Christian Music**.

Apple Records initially rejected ***No Matter What*** as Badfinger's follow-up single to ***Come And Get It***, suggesting they record and release the Ringo Starr composition, ***It Don't Come Easy***, instead. The group (for both their sake and Ringo's) wisely resisted, and ***No Matter What*** became one of their biggest hit singles. Evans and Ham did end up singing backing vocals on Ringo's first single success, ***It Don't Come Easy***. Badfinger's members served as backing musicians for a number of solo Beatles' projects in the early 1970s. The group played on Harrison's **All Things Must Pass** album and were part of the backing band at **The Concert For Bangla Desh**. Ham also took part in sessions for what would become Harrison's album **Living In The Material World**. Molland and Evans contributed to John Lennon's album, **Imagine**.

George Harrison began to produce tracks for Badfinger's third album, titled **Straight Up**, in 1971. He became sidetracked, after producing only four songs, to help organize **The Concert For Bangla Desh** and turned over the production reins to Todd Rundgren*. Along with producing the remainder of the album, Rundgren also worked on the four tracks begun by Harrison. The album's lead-off single and another of the group's biggest hits was ***Day After Day***, produced by Harrison and featuring his trademark slide guitar in unison with Pete Ham. Harrison also contributed rhythm and acoustic guitar to his production of ***I'd Die Babe***. Another song Harrison produced for the album was ***Name Of The Game***. Molland recalled Nicky Hopkins* playing piano on the track. Hopkins did not recall playing on any of Badfinger's recordings. Gibbins said it was Leon Russell* who played piano on ***Name Of The Game***. Russell seems the more likely candidate as he played on ***Day After Day*** and the fourth track Harrison produced for Badfinger called ***Suitcase***. Other sources have suggested it was Gary Wright* who played on the track.

Ironically, Badfinger's biggest success would come at the hands of Harry Nilsson's* cover of their song ***Without You***, that became a multimillion dollar seller for him. Though Badfinger was Apple Records' most successful band, they fell under the same neglect as all other Apple artists as a result of Allen Klein's budget-cutting management and left the label disgruntled and disillusioned. It was no accident that Badfinger titled their last three albums for Apple **No Dice, Straight Up** [your] and **Ass. Ass** contained a song called ***The Winner***, written by Molland about John Lennon, who he felt was constantly complaining and angry in public.

Badfinger moved to Warner Bros. in 1973 but failed to recapture the early success they had at Apple. On April 23, 1975, their leader and primary songwriter Pete Ham took his life. Molland went on to join the group Natural Gas, Gibbins joined Flying Aces, and Evans joined The Dodgers. Badfinger, with original members Molland and Evans, released two albums in the late 1970s. On November 19, l983, tragedy struck again when Tom Evans also took his life. Molland and Gibbins reunited in l984 to continue the highly augmented Badfinger legend, but the two have been unable to sustain a long-term partnership. Molland, who has released two solo albums, still tours under the Badfinger name. A collection of the late Pete Ham's early demos was issued in 1997 and Gibbins has an album in the can tentatively titled **A Place In Time**. A book and film documentary on

Badfinger were also recently released.

The Band

Record 14 title:
The Last Waltz [Various Artists]
Label / Catalog number:
MGM/UA / ML 100482
Jacket / Inserts:
Standard international design with photo of Ringo Starr on jacket front / Record label inner sleeve
Recording Location / Date:
On location at Winterland Arena, San Francisco, CA, U.S.A. / 25 Nov 76
Media:
Album 12" LVD
Producer:
Robbie Robertson

Bob Dylan: Lead Vocals & Guitar; Robbie Robertson: Guitar & B. Vocals; Rick Danko: Bass & B. Vocals; Levon Helm: Drums & B. Vocals; Garth Hudson: Keyboards; Richard Manuel: Keyboards & B. Vocals; Eric Clapton: Guitar & B. Vocals; Neil Diamond: B. Vocals; Joni Mitchell: B. Vocals; Neil Young: B. Vocals; Van Morrison: B. Vocals; Dr. John: B. Vocals; Ronnie Hawkins: B. Vocals; Ron Wood: Guitar & B. Vocals; Paul Butterfield: B. Vocals; Ringo Starr: Drums; Bobby Charles: B. Vocals

Song 14a title:
I Shall Be Released
Release date / Country:
1985 / U.S.A.
Track details:
Side 2, track 12 / 3 min. 53 sec.
Composer:
B. Dylan

Song 14b title:
I Shall Be Released/[Ending Jam] [live]
Release date / Country:
(probably) 1987
(first issued 10 Apr 78) / U.S.A.
Track details:
CD2, track 11 / 3 min. 53 sec. [1 min. 29 sec.]
Composer:
B. Dylan-/[R. Starkey-L. Helm]

These songs are also included on Warner Bros / 3146-2 / Album 5" [2 CD set] / Standard international design in jewel box / Two 20 page CD booklets.

The Band originally consisted of four Canadians from Ontario - Robbie Robertson (born July 5, 1944 in Toronto), Eric Garth Hudson (born August 2, 1937 in London), Richard Manuel (born April 3, 1945 in Stratford), Rick Danko* and one American, Arkansas native, Levon Helm*. Another Arkansas native, Ronnie Hawkins*, formed the group in the early 1960s as his backup band calling them The Hawks. The Band achieved notoriety as Bob Dylan's* backup band in the mid-1960s and went on to become successful on their own starting with the legendary album, **Music From Big Pink**.

The Band continued to work with Dylan throughout the second half of the 1960s and went to England to perform with Dylan at the Isle Of Wight rock festival on August 29, 1969. The Beatles (minus McCartney) attended the event and spent much time with The Band and Dylan during their visit to England.

The Band's (minus Richard Manuel) first contribution to a Beatles' recording was on ***Sunshine Life For Me (Sail Away Raymond)***, a George Harrison composition recorded by Ringo Starr for his album, **Ringo**. Robbie Robertson also

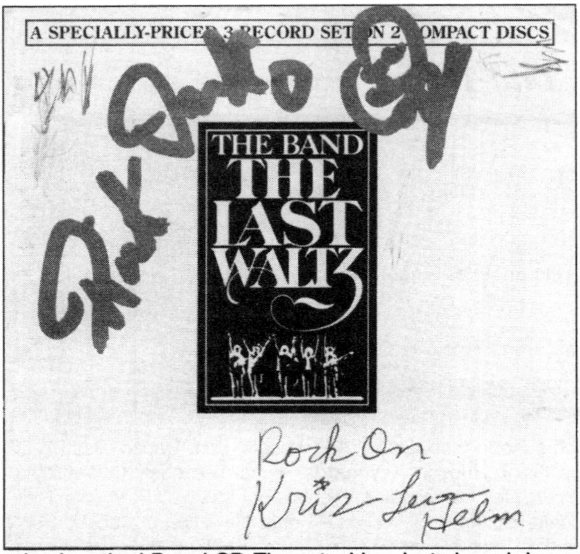

played on Ringo's follow-up album, **Goodnight Vienna**.

The Band gave a farewell concert on Thanksgiving Day 1976 at Winterland Arena, the site of their very first performance, which was made into a documentary film on the group by Martin Scorsese. The concert included guest performances by Eric Clapton*, Dr. John*, Ron Wood*, Bob Dylan, Ronnie Hawkins and Ringo Starr, among others. **The Last Waltz**, as both the film and the live album were aptly titled, was the last time all the original members of The Band would ever perform together. Unfortunately, the laser videodisk for **The Last Waltz** does not include the ***Ending Jam***, which Ringo also contributed to, though it is contained on the LP and CD. The actual jam lasted much longer than what was officially released on record (about half an hour) with many of the musicians returning to the stage. The entire ***Ending Jam*** is available on the bootleg CD **The Complete Last Waltz**.

Richard Manuel took his life on March 4, 1986, during one of The Band's (minus Robertson) reunion tours. Rick Danko and Levon Helm were members of Ringo Starr's All-Starr Band tour in 1989 and were joined by Garth Hudson on one occasion during the tour. The Band reformed in 1992 around original members Helm, Danko and Hudson, along with new members Jim Weider on guitar, Randy Ciarlante helping out on drums and Richard Bell *(see Crowbar)* helping out on keyboards. In 1993, The Band released **Jericho**, their first album of new studio recordings in eighteen years. Ringo Starr and the All-Starrs are listed in the album's credits under "project support," though according to Helm, Ringo did not contribute to the album. In 1994, The Band was inducted into the Rock and Roll Hall of Fame. All the original surviving members, except for Levon Helm, were in attendance. **The Authorized Video Biography** of The Band released in 1995, included cameo appearances by George Harrison and Ringo Starr. In 1996, The Band released **High On The Hog**, their follow up to **Jericho**, again with thanks to Ringo Starr but again without his participation. To date, Robbie Robertson has not rejoined the group but continues to maintain a solo career performing, recording and acting. Meanwhile, The Band maintains a popular following on tour performing classics such as ***The Weight***, ***The Night They Drove Old Dixie Down***, ***Up On Cripple Creek***, ***Rag Mama Rag*** and ***Life Is A Carnival***.

Band Aid

Record 15 title: Do They Know It's Christmas? [Various Artists]
Media: Single 12"
Label / Catalog number: Columbia / 44-05157
Jacket / Inserts: Standard international design / Record label inner sleeve
Recording Location / Date: Sarm West Studios, London, U.K. / 25 Nov 84

Song 15a title: Do They Know It's Christmas? (Remix)
Track details: Side 1, track 1 / 6 min. 16 sec.

Release date / Country:
14 Dec 84 / U.S.A.
Producer:
Midge Ure & Trevor Horn (Remixed by Trevor Horn)

Composer:
B. Geldof - M. Ure

Song 15b title:
Feed The World
Release date / Country:
14 Dec 84 / U.S.A.
Producer:
Midge Ure & Trevor Horn

Track details:
Side 2, track 2 / 4 min. 15 sec.
Composer:
B. Geldof - M. Ure

Band Aid (Adam Clayton, Phil Collins, Bob Geldof, Steve Norman, Chris Cross, John Taylor, Paul Young, Tony Hadley, Glenn Gregory, Simon Le Bon, Simon Crowe, Marilyn, Keren Woodward, Martin Kemp, Jody Watley, Bono, Paul Weller, James Taylor, Peter Blake, George Michael, Midge Ure, Martin Ware, John Keeble, Gary Kemp, Roger Taylor, Sarah Dallin, Siobhan Fahey, Peter Briquette, Francis Rossi, Robert "Kool" Bell, Dennis Thomas, Andy Taylor, Jon Moss, Sting, Rick Parfitt, Nick Rhodes, Johnny Fingers, David Bowie, Boy George, Holly & Paul McCartney): Vocals &/or Messages

By the fall of 1984, Ethiopia, which had seen several years of severe drought and war, was in the throes of a massive famine. Boomtown Rats' band leader, Bob Geldof (born on October 5, 1954, in Dublin, Ireland), suddenly became the respectable advocate for Ethiopian famine relief, eventually leading to a Nobel Prize. Geldof was a politically outspoken rebel of the post-punk, new-wave British rock scene. He was so appalled by the sight of starving Ethiopians on TV newscasts that he recruited a small army of British rock stars to record two songs and use the proceeds to assist in the famine relief. Some artists (including Paul McCartney) who were unable to attend the recording sessions, contributed a prerecorded message. The response to Geldof's plea far exceeded anyone's expectations and led to a worldwide outpouring of support and contributions.

Geldof took the "Band Aid" idea one step farther. On July 13, 1985, he organized what was the biggest rock benefit to date, staging a live, dual venue that was internationally telecast from Wembley Stadium in London and John F. Kennedy Stadium in Philadelphia. The bill included most of the biggest names in rock 'n' roll, including Paul McCartney, who performed ***Let It Be*** only to have his microphone fail!

Chris Barber & His Band

Record 16 title:
The Songs Lennon and McCartney Gave Away (Various Artists)

Media:
Album 12"

Label / Catalog number:
EMI / NUT 18 [0C 054-07 003]

Producer:
Chris Barber, Giorgio Gomelsky, Reggie King & [Paul McCartney]

Jacket / Inserts:
Standard international design with sketches of John Lennon, Paul McCartney, & Ringo Starr / Record label inner sleeve

Recording Location / Date:
Chappell Studios, London, U.K. / 20 Jul 67

Song 16a title:
Cat Call [aka Catswalk]

Track details:
Side 2, track 10 / 3 min. 03 sec.

Release date / Country:
13 Apr 79 (first issued 20 Oct 67) / U.K.

Composer:
P. McCartney

Chris Barber: Trombone; Pat Halcox: Trumpet; Ian Wheeler: Alto Saxophone; John Slaughter: Guitar; "Stu" Morrison: Banjo; Jackie Flavelle: Bass; Graham Burbidge: Drums; Brian Auger: "Catcalls" & Organ; Barry Jenkins: "Catcalls;" Vic Briggs: "Catcalls;" Viv Prince: Cymbal dropping & "Catcalls;" Paul McCartney: Keyboard, Yell, "Catcalls" & B. Vocals; Jane Asher: "Catcalls;" Madeleine Hirsiger: "Catcalls;" Ottilie Patterson: "Catcalls;" John Ryan: "Catcalls;" Gustav Karl Lovenz Schneeweiss-Moody "Catcalls" & B. Vocals; Giorgio Gomelsky: Voice

Brian Auger, John Slaughter, Paul McCartney, Jackie Flavelle & Chris Barber, Chappell Studios, London, 1967, photo courtesy of Brian Auger

Chris Barber was born on April 17, 1930, in Welwyn, England. His Chris Barber Jazz Band has been a British institution since 1954. He teamed up with Lonnie Donegan* and played on his ground-breaking international skiffle hit, ***Rock Island Line***. Barber's biggest hit was ***Petite Fleur*** in 1959 which was a top 10. Barber and his band have continued to play over two hundred dates a year since their formation.

Chris Barber had known The Beatles since their days at the Cavern when it was still a jazz club. Shortly after Paul McCartney bought his St. John's Wood home in the mid-1960s from a friend of Barber's, the two stopped by for a visit. Barber asked McCartney if he had any songs he'd written that he never used. McCartney said he had one song The Beatles never used because it was an instrumental and offered ***Catswalk*** to Barber. ***Catswalk*** dates back to The Beatles' early days at the

Cavern Club in Liverpool. A Beatles' recording of ***Catswalk***, probably made at a Cavern Club rehearsal, has turned up on numerous bootleg records.

According to Barber, initial sessions for the recording of ***Catswalk*** took place in a studio at his Marquee Club in London. Barber said the version of ***Catswalk*** done at The Marquee, and attended by McCartney, was a straightforward jazz number. However, McCartney decided the song should be done as a more lighthearted "big production number with catcalls as a sort of joke song or put-on," as Barber described it. So the second (released) version was recorded at Chappell Studios according to McCartney's specifications. Brian Auger, who remembers playing organ on ***Cat Call***, and Barber confirmed that McCartney was heavily involved in the production of the recording. Barber also recalls McCartney playing one-handed organ on the song, but Auger remembers McCartney playing piano. According to Barber, ***Cat Call*** was the only recording of his to which any of The Beatles contributed.

Viv Prince, Paul McCartney & Brian Auger, Chappell Studios, London, 1967
photo courtesy of Brian Auger

Count Basie

Record 17 title:	***Media:***
Basie On The Beatles	Album 12"
Label / Catalog number:	***Producer:***
Happy Tiger / HT 1007	Dick Peirce
Release date / Country:	***Composer:***
(probably) 1970 / U.S.A.	J. Lennon - P. McCartney / G. Harrison
Jacket / Inserts:	
Standard international design with Liner Notes by Ringo Starr / Record label inner sleeve	

Count Basie, Ann Arbor, MI, early 1970s, photo courtesy of Tom Bert

The legendary jazz band leader and pianist Count Basie was born on August 21, 1904 in Red Bank, New Jersey. Both of his parents were amateur musicians who encouraged their son's interest in music. Basie first took up the drums but later switched to the piano, studying under Fats Waller. He first made a name for himself during the Harlem renaissance in the 1920s. By the mid-1930s he had formed the Count Basie Orchestra and played with, among other jazz legends, Benny Goodman and Duke Ellington. His hits included ***One O'clock Jump***, ***L'il Darlin'*** and ***April In Paris***.

Basie On The Beatles is a Count Basie album of Beatles covers with liner notes written by Ringo Starr. According to the liner notes, on October 1, 1969, Ringo asked Basie if he would do an arrangement of ***Night And Day*** for his **Sentimental Journey** album (the album actually credits Chico O'Farrill as the arranger of ***Night And Day***). Five days later a complete score arrived, so Ringo gave thanks by writing the liner notes. Count Basie died on April 26, 1984.

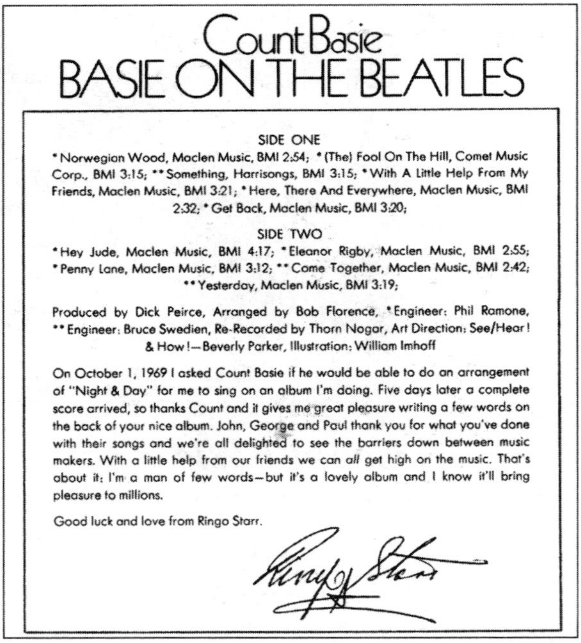

Count Basie
BASIE ON THE BEATLES

SIDE ONE

*Norwegian Wood, Maclen Music, BMI 2:54; *(The) Fool On The Hill, Comet Music Corp., BMI 3:15; **Something, Harrisongs, BMI 3:15; *With A Little Help From My Friends, Maclen Music, BMI 3:21; *Here, There And Everywhere, Maclen Music, BMI 2:32; *Get Back, Maclen Music, BMI 3:20;

SIDE TWO

*Hey Jude, Maclen Music, BMI 4:17; *Eleanor Rigby, Maclen Music, BMI 2:55; *Penny Lane, Maclen Music, BMI 3:12; **Come Together, Maclen Music, BMI 2:42; **Yesterday, Maclen Music, BMI 3:19;

Produced by Dick Peirce, Arranged by Bob Florence, *Engineer: Phil Ramone, **Engineer: Bruce Swedien, Re-Recorded by Thorn Nogar, Art Direction: See/Hear! & How!—Beverly Parker, Illustration: William Imhoff

On October 1, 1969 I asked Count Basie if he would be able to do an arrangement of "Night & Day" for me to sing on an album I'm doing. Five days later a complete score arrived, so thanks Count and it gives me great pleasure writing a few words on the back of your nice album. John, George and Paul thank you for what you've done with their songs and we're all delighted to see the barriers down between music makers. With a little help from our friends we can *all* get high on the music. That's about it: I'm a man of few words—but it's a lovely album and I know it'll bring pleasure to millions.

Good luck and love from Ringo Starr.

Mike Batt

Record 18 title:
Mike Batt's The Hunting Of The Snark (Various Artists)
Media:
Album 5" CD
Label / Catalog number:
Epic/Adventure / CD SNARK 1 (CDEPC 57023)
Producer:
Mike Batt
Jacket / Inserts:
Standard international design in jewel box / 12 page CD booklet
Recording Location / Date:
CTS, London & FPSHOT (Friar Park Studio, Henley-on-Thames)†, U.K. / 26 Jan 85†

Song 18a title:
Children Of The Sky
Track details:
Side 1, track 2 / 5 min. 30 sec.
Release date / Country:
24 Nov 86 / U.K.
Composer:
M. Batt
(Spoken Verse by Lewis Carroll)

Mike Batt: Lead Vocals, Piano, Arrangement & Conductor; Tom Nicholl: Drums; Frank McDonald: Bass; Chris Spedding: Guitar; Alan Parker: Guitar; Ray Cooper: Percussion; Sir John Gielgud: Narration; John Hurt: Narration; The London Symphony Orchestra: Orchestrations; George Harrison: Guitar*

Mike Batt was born on February 6, 1949 in Southampton, England. He began his career in music at the age of eighteen as a producer for Liberty / United Artists Records but left two years later to form his own publishing company. In 1969, towards the end of his stay with Liberty, he released a cover of The Beatles' song ***Your Mother Should Know***. Today he works in the classical and popular music fields as a producer, arranger, composer and conductor. He has conducted The London Symphony Orchestra*, The London Philharmonic Orchestra and The Royal Philharmonic Orchestra, among others. He has served in the positions of directorship of The Performing Rights Society Ltd. and vice president of the British Academy Of Songwriters, Composers and Authors.

Mike Batt, photo courtesy of Mike Batt

Batt began working in the popular music field producing the groups Hapshash And The Coloured Coat and Groundhogs. He first saw success in 1974 with the TV show **The Wombles** and the group of the same name with whom he had eight hit singles and four gold albums. He has since worked with or written for a wide range of artists, including Steeleye Span (**All Around My Hat**), Andrew Lloyd Webber (**Phantom Of The Opera**), Cliff Richard (***Please Don't Fall In Love*** and the album **Cover Shot**), Art Garfunkel (**Bright Eyes**) *(see Paul Simon)* and David Essex (**A Winter's Tale**), among others. He is the first composer to ever win the Ivor Novello Award for "Best Film Music" two years in a row, first for **Watership Down** and then **Caravans**. Besides his work with other artists, he has managed a successful solo career. He had a hit with the song ***Summertime City*** in 1975. His albums **Schizophonia** and **Tarot Suite**, recorded with The London Symphony Orchestra, produced the European hit songs ***Railway Hotel***, ***Lady Of The Dawn***, ***The Winds Of Change*** and ***The Ride To Agadir***. Batt made some recordings around 1971 at The Beatles' Apple Studios in London but none of The Beatles participated. Batt made a three-year sail around the world that included a visit to the Caribbean island of Montserrat in February 1981. While there he met Paul McCartney, who was an admirer of his work, and the two began to socialize. McCartney invited Batt to his recording sessions at George Martin's* AIR Studios on the island.

Batt composed and scored the musical, **The Hunting of The Snark** that was based on Lewis Carroll's 1874 poem "Snark." The recordings contained musical contributions from a number of artists, including Julian Lennon*. Batt told his friend and percussionist, Ray Cooper, that he wanted to have George Harrison overdub some guitar on his song ***Children Of The Sky***. Cooper offered to take the tapes to Harrison, who in turn invited Batt to his Friar Park (FPSHOT) home studios for the overdub session. Batt recalled "As he was doing the overdub I'd be sort of pointing to the next fret as if to say move your finger up to there. I thought to myself, I don't even play guitar and here I am pointing to George Harrison's frets during a live overdub! That was crazy, and yet he was very tolerant of my presence; we had a good time doing it. George suggested I come over to do some jamming and writing together, which we later did, but nothing ever came of it. Later I said, 'When are we going to get together and write this masterpiece?' He said, 'Well actually something crap would do to start with.' It's a great quote; he has such a dry sense of humor. It was a lovely experience working with him." Batt said Harrison did not sing backing vocals on ***Children Of The Sky*** as had been reported.

The Beach Boys

Record 19 title:
Fourth Of July. A Rockin' Celebration Of America (Various Artists)
Media:
Album 12"
Label / Catalog number:
Love Foundation For American Music Entertainment And Art / [matrix #] PLAT 86 (mail order only)
Producer:
Ted Mather
Jacket / Inserts:
Unique / Artist Courtesy slip & Love Foundation flyer
Recording Location / Date:
On location at The Mall, Washington DC, U.S.A. / 04 Jul 84

Song 19a title:
Back In The U.S.S.R. [live]
Track details:
Side 1, track 1 / 3 min. 00 sec.
Release date / Country:
Dec 86 / U.S.A.
Composer:
J. Lennon - P. McCartney

Jeff Foskett: Lead Vocals & Guitar; Mike Love: Lead Vocals; Ringo Starr: Drums; Alan Jardine: Guitar & B. Vocals; Carl Wilson: Guitar & B. Vocals; Ed Carter: Bass & B. Vocals; Bruce Johnston: Hand Claps & B. Vocals; Mike Kowalski: Percussion & B. Vocals; John Lodge: Acoustic Guitar & B. Vocals; Justin Hayward: Acoustic Guitar & B. Vocals; Mike Meros: Synthesizer & Keyboards; Billy Hinsche: Electric Piano; Brian Wilson: Piano & B. Vocals

Record 20 title:
Good Vibrations (Thirty Years Of The Beach Boys)
Media:
Album 5" CD [5 CD set]
Label / Catalog number:
Capitol / C2 0777 7 81294 2 4 (CDP 0777 7 81296 2 2)
Producer:
Brian Wilson
Jacket / Inserts:
Standard international design in jewel box in box set / 60 page booklet, decal & 4 page CD inserts on 4 CDs
Recording Location / Date:
One or more of the following studios: United Western, Goldstar, Columbia &/or Brian Wilson's Home Studio / 12 Apr 67

Song 20a title:
Vegetables
Release date / Country:
29 Jun 93 / U.S.A.
Track details:
Side 1, track 26 / 3 min. 28 sec.
Composer:
B. Wilson - V.D. Parks

Brian Wilson: Lead Vocals; Al Jardine: B. Vocals; Mike Love: B. Vocals; Carl Wilson: B. Vocals; Dennis Wilson: B. Vocals; Bruce Johnston: B. Vocals; Paul McCartney: (possible) Munching Sounds

Record 21 title:
Smiley Smile & Wild Honey
Media:
Album 5" CD
Label / Catalog number:
Capitol / CDP 7 93696 2
Producer:
The Beach Boys
Jacket / Inserts:
Standard international design in jewel box / 24 page CD booklet
Recording Location / Date:
One or more of the following studios: United Western, Goldstar, Columbia &/or Brian Wilson's Home Studio / (probably) 10-11 Apr 67

Song 21a title:
Vegetables
Release date / Country:
04 Sep 90 (first issued 18 Sep 67) / U.S.A.
Track details:
Side 1, track 2 / 2 min. 05 sec.
Composer:
B. Wilson - V.D. Parks

Al Jardine: Vocals; Mike Love: Vocals; Carl Wilson: Vocals; Dennis Wilson: Vocals; Bruce Johnston: Vocals; Brian Wilson: Vocals; Paul McCartney: (possible) Munching Sounds

Record 22 title:
The Beach Boys
Media:
Album 5" CD
Label / Catalog number:
Caribou/Brother / ZK 39946
Producer:
Steve Levine
Jacket / Inserts:
Standard international design in jewel box / 12 page CD booklet
Recording Location / Date:
Red Bus Studios, London, U.K. / (probably) Aug 84

Song 22a title:
California Calling
Release date / Country:
27 Sep 85 (first issued 10 Jun 85) / U.S.A.
Track details:
Side 1, track 6 / 2 min. 46 sec.
Composer:
A. Jardine - B. Wilson

Alan Jardine: Lead Vocals & Electric Guitars; Mike Love: Lead Vocals; Ringo Starr: Drums & Timpani; Brian Wilson: Piano, DX1 & Vocal Arrangement; Simon Humphrey: Bass; Julian Lindsay: Organ; John Alder: Electric Guitars; Steve Levine: Fairlight Programming; The Beach Boys: Vocal Arrangement

Record 23 title:
The Pet Sounds Sessions

Label / Catalog number:
Capitol / C2 7243 8 37662 2 2

Release date / Country:
04 Nov 97 (first issued 16 May 66) / U.S.A.

Jacket / Inserts:
Standard international design in jewel box in box set / 40 page booklet, 128 page booklet with interview with Paul McCartney & advert. insert

Recording Location / Date:
Western, Gold Star, Sunset & (probably), Columbia & Capitol Studios, Los Angeles, CA, U.S.A. / Jul 65 & Nov 65 - Apr 66

Media:
Album 5" CD [4 CD set]

Producer:
Brian Wilson

Composer:
B. Wilson - T. Asher - M. Love - T. Sachen

Brian Wilson: Lead Vocals & Organ; Mike Love: Lead Vocals; Carl Wilson: Lead Vocals & Guitar; Al Jardine: B. Vocals; Dennis Wilson: B. Vocals; Bruce Johnston: B. Vocals; Hal Blaine: Drums & Temple Blocks; Jerry Williams: Percussion; Richie Frost: Drums; Carol Kaye: Bass; Chuck Berghofer: String Bass; Lyle Ritz: Ukulele & String Bass; Jerry Cole: Guitar; Barney Kessel: Guitar; Bill Pitman: Guitar; Ray Pohlman: Guitar & Bass; Al de Lory: Piano, Organ & Harpsichord; Mike Melvoin: Harpsichord; Paul Tanner: Theremin; Don Randi: Piano; Larry Knechtel: Keyboards; Carl Fortina: Accordion; Frank Marocco: Accordion; Frank Capp: Timpani & Bells; Roy Caton: Trumpet; Jack Nimitz: Saxophone; Steve Douglas: Flute & Tenor Saxophone; Plas Johnson: Tenor Saxophone; Jay Migliori: Flute & Baritone Saxophone; Julius Wechter: Finger Cymbals, Tambourine, Timpini, Latin Percussion & Vibes; Glen Campbell: Guitar & (probable) Banjo; Mike Deasy: Guitar; Tommy Tedesco: Guitar; Barney Kessel: Guitar; Jerry Cole: Guitar; Jim Horn: Flute & Alto Saxophone; Lee Hartman: Saxophone; Bill Green: Flute & Alto Saxophone; Billy Strange: Guitar; Arnold Belnick: Violin; Ralph Schaeffer: Violin; Sid Sharp: Violin; Tibor Zelig: Violin; Bill Kurasch: Violin; Lenny Malarsky: Violin; Justin DiTullio: Cello; Joe Saxon: Cello; Jesse Ehrlich: Cello; Harry Hyams: Viola; Derrel Terwilliger: Viola; Norm Botnick: Viola; Joe DiFiore: Viola; Al Casey: Guitar; Jim Gordon: Drums; Gary Coleman: Timpani & Bongos; Jules Jacob: Flute; Alan Robinson: French Horn; Jim Getzoff: Violin; Jerry Reisler: Violin; Tommy Morgan: Harmonica; Nick Martinis: Drums; Gail Martin: Trombone; Ernie Tack: Trombone; James Henderson: Trombone; Lew McCreary: Trombone

The Beach Boys formed in 1961 in Southern California. They originally consisted of brothers Brian Wilson (born June 20, 1942) who played bass, Dennis Wilson (born December 4, 1944) who played drums, Carl Wilson (born December 21, 1946) who played lead guitar and their cousin Mike Love (born March 15, 1941), the group's front man. All were born in the Los Angeles, California area. The group also included a schoolmate of Brian's named Alan Jardine (born, September 3, 1942, in Lima, Ohio) on rhythm guitar. Jardine left the group between early 1962 and mid-1963 to attend college. He was replaced by David Marks, a neighbor of the Wilsons, during his studies.

Carl Wilson, Irvine, CA, late 1980s, photo courtey of Tom Bert

For the most part the group's leader, gifted songwriter, and producer is Brian, who modeled their sound on the four-part harmonies of The Four Freshmen. Lyrically, their early songs were based almost entirely around four themes - summer (***All Summer Long***), surfing (***Surfin' U.S.A.***, ***Surfer Girl*** and ***Surfin' Safari***), cars (***Fun, Fun, Fun***, ***Shut Down*** and ***Little Deuce Coupe***) and girls (***California Girls***, ***Help Me, Rhonda*** and ***Don't Worry Baby***). The Beach Boys were one of the most popular U.S. rock 'n' roll groups in the early 1960s. Their only regular competition in the charts was The Four Seasons.

Like nearly all other domestic acts, The Beach Boys' popularity was tested by the onslaught of the British music invasion spearheaded by The Beatles in 1964. They were keenly aware of The Beatles' impact on the American music landscape not only because they coincidentally happened to be on the same record label, but because they alphabetically preceded The Beatles in record bins. Naturally, they envied and admired each others' work. The Beach Boys showed their appreciation

of The Beatles' music by recording cover versions of ***I Should Have Known Better***, ***Tell Me Why*** and ***You've Got To Hide Your Love Away*** for their 1965 **Party** album. By this time, Brian, who had apparently suffered a nervous breakdown, had retired from the pressures of touring with The Beach Boys to devote more time to writing and producing. Glen Campbell, then a well-known session guitarist, briefly filled in for Brian. Campbell was replaced by Bruce Johnston (born June 27, 1942, in Peoria, Illinois) who joined the group on April 9, 1965. Johnston and Terry Melcher had previously produced and sung on recordings for The Beach Boys-styled group, The Rip Chords, during their days as staff producers at Columbia Records. Johnston had also worked with Phil Spector*, whose productions Brian greatly admired.

The Beatles' album **Rubber Soul**, released in December 1965, impressed and inspired Brian Wilson into producing the album, **Pet Sounds**, that is regarded as his best work. **Pet Sounds** was an introspective album that ignored The Beach Boys' familiar themes. In turn, Paul McCartney was so impressed with **Pet Sounds** that he has since dubbed it his all-time favorite album and claims it motivated and inspired The Beatles during their recording of the album **Sgt. Pepper's Lonely Hearts Club Band**. When **Pet Sounds** was released on CD in 1990, it was supposed to include a printed interview with Paul McCartney. Due to production problems, it could not be included but was made available separately on request. The interview was included in the 1997 CD box set release **The Pet Sounds Sessions**. In Paul's closing remarks in the interview he affectionately states "I'm still a big fan. I figure, with what you're gonna write here, he'll know that. Just let Brian know that I love him, and that I still think he's gonna do great things. Tell him good luck, stay healthy for me and think good, positive thoughts." The box set also included a printed interview with George Martin*.

It was during **Pet Sounds** period that The Beach Boys hired former (and future) Beatles' press officer Derek Taylor, who was instrumental in helping The Beach Boys break into the British market. Bruce Johnston vividly remembers the excitement that was generated when he played **Pet Sounds**, which had not yet been released in the U.K., for Lennon, McCartney and Keith Moon* during a visit to England in May 1966. By the end of the year, The Beach Boys had topped the U.S. and U.K. charts with their classic rock mini-symphony **Good Vibrations** and unseated The Beatles in New Musical Express magazine's annual poll as the World's Best Group.

In the continuing musical one-upmanship between The Beatles and The Beach Boys, Brian Wilson began work on the follow-up to **Pet Sounds** several months before The Beatles began recording their epic album, **Sgt. Pepper's Lonely Hearts Club Band**. Brian was producing a concept album based on humor and the elements (fire, water, air and earth) to be called **Smile**. The Beach Boys were attempting to form their own record company called Brother Records, and numerous legal battles with Capitol Records threatened the album's release. Though **Pet Sounds** had received the highest critical acclaim, it was up to then a relative commercial failure. Members of the band feared losing their surf and hot rod music followers. They expressed concern over the musical direction Brian was charting and the time it was taking to complete the album. After nearly a year of on and off recordings, a frustrated and disillusioned Brian Wilson abandoned **Smile**. While the world delighted in the sounds of **Sgt. Pepper** and the "Summer of Love", The Beach Boys had temporarily become a forgotten surf band from another era. Their follow-up single, ***Heroes And Villains***, did well in the charts, but it was perceived as somewhat of a letdown after ***Good Vibrations*** and all the hype surrounding **Smile**. In September 1967, they released the album **Smiley Smile** on their Brother Records label. For the most part, it contained tracks hurriedly recorded at Brian's house, including some of the tracks intended for **Smile**. Its minimal production by Brian (credited to The Beach Boys) marked a shift in focus towards other members of the group (especially Carl) who would have to assume more responsibilities in the future. In many respects, The Beatles' **Get Back / Let It Be** project two years later and their difficulties with their Apple Records label bore a striking similarity to the **Smile / Smiley Smile** episode. Sadly, the **Smile** experience marked the end of Brian Wilson's creative marathon.

One song from the **Smile** sessions, ***Vegetables***, has been a source of debate concerning Paul McCartney's involvement. In the liner notes of the **Smiley Smile** CD, Al Jardine states "The night before a big tour, I was out in the studio recording the vocal for ***Vegetables*** when, to my surprise, Paul McCartney walked in and joined Brian at the console. And, briefly, the two most influential musical Gemini's in the world had a chance to work together. I remember waiting for long periods of time between takes to get to the next section or verse. Brian seemed to have lost track of the session. Paul would come on the talk-back and say something like 'good take, Al'." Concluding that McCartney helped with the production of ***Vegetables*** depends on one's definition of production and the degree of his actual involvement. McCartney has never been officially credited as producer on any of the releases of ***Vegetables***. Most authorities on The Beach Boys dismiss the notion that McCartney should be acknowledged as having helped produce ***Vegetables***. Bruce Johnston said, "Paul was just in the booth, more as support of Brian because he thought so highly of **Pet Sounds**. According to Brian, "Paul attended the sessions with Derek Taylor and gave suggestions but he didn't actually produce anything. His being there was an inspiration."

The Beach Boys' tour referenced by Al began on April 13 on the East Coast, making a session the night before in Los Angeles unlikely. Most reliable sources place the session with McCartney on the 10th, and his departure for London on the 11th, making it likely that the sessions were held on the evening of the 10th and early morning of the 11th of April 1967. Brad Elliott, author of the 1982 book **Surf's Up! The Beach Boys On Record, 1961 - 1981**, states that on the 11th McCartney attended a Beach Boys' session and, along with DJ Rodney Bingenheimer and Roger McGuinn, sang background vocals on an unreleased version of ***Vegetables***. Brian said, "We were just warming up, they're not on the final track." Bingenheimer recalls the sessions taking place late at night at Columbia Studios, "There were a lot of different people there, studio people; I think Dean Torrence (of the surf and hot rod duo Jan & Dean) was there; Brian had everyone there name off a vegetable; McCartney named off a vegetable but I don't remember what one." Bingenheimer did not recall McCartney having anything to do with the production of ***Vegetables***. However, no Beach Boys' versions have surfaced featuring different people naming off vegetables. Elliott's book further states that McCartney also added bass to a Beach Boys' recording of ***On Top Of Old Smokey*** that evening. The Beatles' road manager Mal Evans, who reported on McCartney's trip to Los Angeles in the July 1967 issue of The Beatles Book monthly magazine, stated McCartney played guitar on ***On Top Of Old Smokey***. Brian does not recall The Beach Boys recording that song. If the song was performed it probably was nothing more than a warm-up jam that either was not recorded or not saved.

Mike Love, photo courtesy of Tom Bert

The **Smiley Smile** CD liner notes also claim that McCartney joined The Beach Boys munching on raw vegetables for percussion. In the winter 1994 issue No. 72 of McCartney's fan magazine Club Sandwich, Paul answered questions sent in by club members. One fan asked the following question - Is it true that you can be heard munching vegetables on The Beach Boys track ***Vegetables***? The CD liner notes say so. McCartney replied, "Do they? Well, I was certainly at a few Beach Boys sessions, and if someone gave me, say, an apple, I would have munched it, and if there'd been a microphone nearby I suppose it might have gone down on tape. But I don't remember doing it knowingly." Brian said, "I had brought some vegetables down there for the atmosphere. Paul was chewing on a stick of celery."

In 1993, portions of the original **Smile** sessions were officially released as a part of the CD box set **Good Vibrations (Thirty Years Of The Beach Boys)**. It includes a version of ***Vegetables*** that is considerably longer and more complex than the version on **Smiley Smile** reportedly recorded the night McCartney was in attendance. This version also features munching sounds, and although it's listed as being recorded on April 12, 1967, it sounds as though it was begun much earlier. The reported sequence of recordings suggests that the more complex recordings produced by Brian are from the earlier **Smile** sessions, and the more sparsely produced versions are from the **Smiley Smile** sessions that came much later. Perhaps this is the version to which Brad Elliott is referring. Both of the versions of ***Vegetables*** released by The Beach Boys obviously contain fragments of recordings from different sessions. With all the confusion surrounding these sessions and the large volume of bits and pieces of tape that were intended to be used in the **Smile** project, Brian is not certain if McCartney's munching sounds were used on any of the released versions.

In the fall of 1967 The Beach Boys began recording sessions for what would become their album **Wild Honey**. The album yielded two hit singles, ***Darlin'*** and the title track. Another track recorded during the fall sessions was a cover of The Beatles' song, ***With A Little Help From My Friends***, that did not see release until 1983 on The Beach Boys' album, **Rarities**. (The **Rarities** concept was an idea Capitol Records had borrowed from their Beatles' album of the same title that they had released several years earlier.)

Bruce and Mike were among a select group of invited guests at a costume party The Beatles threw on December 21, 1967, at the Royal Lancaster Hotel in London for the cast and crew of the **Magical Mystery Tour** film. According to Bruce, The Beatles danced around the two Beach Boys and joined them onstage in a performance of ***Sloop John B.***

In February 1968, Mike Love, along with The Beatles, was a student of Transcendental Meditation at Maharishi Mahesh Yogi's (aka Mahesh Prasad Verma) ashram in Rishikesh, India. While there, The Beatles wrote most of the songs that would comprise their **The Beatles** (white) album. Paul came up with the song ***Back In The U.S.S.R.***, which The Beatles recorded very much in the style of The Beach Boys. McCartney had reportedly auditioned the song in India for Love who suggested he include references to Soviet girls just as The Beach Boys had done in their song ***California Girls***.

Another song included on **The Beatles** was ***Helter Skelter***. Prosecutors trying Charles Manson for ordering his followers to murder actress Sharon Tate and others claimed that Manson was motivated by the lyrics of ***Helter Skelter***. Dennis Wilson had befriended Manson and his followers prior to the murders and had recorded Manson's composition ***Cease To Exist***, retitled ***Never Learn Not To Love***, included on The Beach Boys' album **20 / 20**. This album included the hits ***I Can Hear Music*** and ***Do It Again***. According to Bruce, McCartney had agreed to do a cameo as a clerk in the video for ***Do It Again*** when he was in Los Angeles in June 1968 but was unable to attend the shoot due to a scheduling conflict.

By 1970, The Beach Boys had left the Capitol label for Reprise Records and spent the first half of the decade touring and turning out albums with decreasing contributions from Brian. It was reported in the July 10 & 17, 1971 issues of Melody Maker magazine that Harrison turned up in the studios while The Beach Boys were filming a TV special with Ike and Tina Turner* in New York. The articles also stated that Harrison was reported to have recorded with The Beach Boys — possibly on the final tracks for the album [**Surf's Up**]. Harrison was also reported to have showed up backstage with The Beach Boys and Ike and Tina at the Shaeffer Music Festival in New York. Bruce Johnston has no recollection of Harrison turning up for any of these events and discounts the report. However, according to Brian, "George was there [during a session for the **Surf's Up** album] but he didn't play."

In 1971 Dennis Wilson co-starred with James Taylor* in the film **Two-Lane Blacktop**. That year, Dennis severely injured his hand, and drumming duties were filled by Ricky (aka Rikki) Fataar. (Fataar would later play the part of George Harrison [Stig O'Hara] in The Beatles parody band, The Rutles *[see The Bonzo Dog Band, Monty Python].*) Fataar had been a member of The Beach Boy's Brother Records recording group, Flame, along with Blondie Chaplin, who several months later officially replaced Bruce Johnston. The two brief members left the group in 1974. During this period, Brian's mental and physical health had been declining and only one Beach Boys' song, ***Sail On Sailor***, achieved any amount of airplay.

Kristofer Engelhardt and Brian Wilson, Detroit, MI, 1991, photo by Dennis Duso

In 1976, The Beach Boys garnered the media's attention with their attempts to rehabilitate Brian and return him to his former role within group. McCartney's attendance of Brian's thirty-fourth birthday party, included in the 1976 NBC-TV Special **The Beach Boys: It's OK**, was certainly an acknowledgment of McCartney's long-felt admiration and respect for the talents of Brian Wilson.

Backstage pass, courtesy of Bruce Johnston

After lengthy mental and physical therapy, Brian seemed to be on the road to recovery and his creative powers briefly resurfaced on the 1977 album, **Love You**. That year saw the release of Dennis' album, **Pacific Ocean Blue**. Since that time, all the Beach Boys (excluding Al) have issued solo albums. The group scored a top 40 with the song *Good Timin'* in 1979. But by the early 1980s, Brian's mental and physical health had dramatically deteriorated as had that of his brother Dennis, who was effectively dismissed from touring.

In 1978, Bruce Johnston officially rejoined The Beach Boys, though he had continued to record, uncredited, with the group during his so-called departure. Ironically, during his absence from the group, he received a Grammy Award for Song Of The Year for composing Barry Manilow's 1976 mega-hit, *I Write The Songs*, making him the only Grammy winning Beach Boy. He also made a brief cameo appearance in Robert Stigwood's 1978 film **Sgt. Pepper's Lonely Hearts Club Band**.

On December 28, 1983, a legally intoxicated Dennis Wilson drowned while free-diving in the frigid waters of Marina Del Rey Harbor to recover items that lay beneath where his repossessed boat had once been docked. Special permission was granted by President Reagan so that the Beach Boy, who most epitomized the image of the surfer, could be buried at sea.

The Beach Boys have attempted to make the Fourth of July an annual concert celebration. Ringo made a guest appearance with The Beach Boys at the July 4, 1984 celebration in both Washington DC & Miami playing drums on *Back In The U.S.S.R.* Ringo and The Beach Boys also performed *You Can't Do That* and *Day Tripper* in Washington, DC and *Dizzy Miss Lizzie* and *Slow Down* in Miami. Portions of this concert were televised in the U.S. The Beach Boys' live version of *Back In The U.S.S.R.* with Ringo was released in 1986 on the mail order only album, **Fourth Of July - A Rockin' Celebration Of America**, though it incorrectly lists the song as being recorded in 1985. Ringo was scheduled for the '85 show but canceled at the last minute.

Ringo played on the song *California Calling* from the 1985 album simply titled **The Beach Boys** that yielded the hit *Getcha Back*. Also released that year was the retrospective film, **An American Band**, that included footage of McCartney's attendance at Brian's birthday party from the 1976 NBC-TV special. The Beach Boys, along with The Beatles, were inducted into the Rock and Roll Hall of Fame in 1988. That year, The Beach Boys topped the charts with the song *Kokomo*. Mike, Al and Bruce attended the Natural Law Political Party fund-raiser at the Royal Albert Hall in London on April 6, 1992, at the request of George Harrison. The Party promotes Transcendental Meditation as a means of solving political problems.

Brian contributed backing vocals to Ringo's 1992 album **Time Takes Time**. He also appeared in the 25th Anniversary TV documentary of **The Making Of Sgt. Pepper**. Brian made a guest appearance on Paul McCartney's 1995 radio series, **Oobu Joobu**, that also featured some of his music.

McCartney was thanked in the credits of the Brian Wilson retrospective, **I Just Wasn't Made For These Times**, though he did not contribute to the film. Brian said, "I thanked him for the inspiration and his energy and enthusiasm about music — it's very contagious; it rubbed off on me." Brian and Ringo sang *Barbara Ann* to a musical who's who of guests at a birthday party Ringo threw for his wife Barbara on August 26, 1996. Brian contributed to Ringo's 1998 album **Vertical Man**. A promotional sampler of Brian's critically acclaimed 1998 album **Imagination** included an interview of Wilson conducted by John Lennon's son Sean. Wilson continues to regain his mental health and footing in the music world as a solo artist and on The Beach Boys' recordings.

In 1997, David Marks was asked to fill in for Carl Wilson who lost a battle with cancer on February 6, 1998. Remarkably, The Beach Boys have managed to stay together for over 35 years and continue to be one of the most popular group of recording and performing artists in the world.

Cliff Bennett And The Rebel Rousers

Record 24 title:
Lennon & McCartney Songbook
Media:
Album 5" CD
Label / Catalog number:
Connoisseur Collection / VSOP CD 150
Producer:
Paul McCartney & David Paramor
Jacket / Inserts:
Standard international design in jewel box with photo of John Lennon & Paul McCartney / 4 page CD booklet with photos of John Lennon & Paul McCartney
Recording Location / Date:
EMI-Abbey Road Studios, London, U.K. / late Jul 66

Song 24a title:
Got To Get You Into My Life
Track details:
Side 1, track 10 / 2 min. 29 sec.
Release date / Country:
02 Jul 90 (first issued 05 Aug 66) / U.K./E.E.C.
Composer:
J. Lennon - P. McCartney

Cliff Bennett: Lead Vocals; Chas Hodges: Bass & Lead Guitar; Maurice Groves: Saxophone; Sid Phillips: Saxophone; Roy Young: Keyboards, Mike Burt: Drums; Paul McCartney: Piano & Arrangement

Cliff Bennett was born on June 4, 1940 in Slough, England. The Beatles and Cliff Bennett probably first met during their engagements at the Star Club in Hamburg, Germany in December of 1962. (Roy Young, a future member of The Rebel Rousers [named after the Duane Eddy* song] took part in one of The Beatles' recordings with Tony Sheridan*.) The London-based Cliff Bennett And The Rebel Rousers recorded for Parlophone Records a full year before The Beatles did. They had numerous personnel changes over the years, and the band briefly included Nicky Hopkins*. Their first big hit was the song ***One Way Love*** in 1964 that reached the U.K. top 10. The Beatles' manager, Brian Epstein, represented the group for a period of time.

Cliff Bennett And The Rebel Rousers appeared on the same bill with The Beatles during their 1966 tour of Germany. Prior to the tour, The Beatles had recorded the song, ***Got To Get You Into My Life***, for their album, **Revolver**. Bennett recalled, "we were on tour in Germany when Paul came into the dressing room and said, 'We've written a great song, John and I, and we think it would be ideal for you.' They actually demonstrated the song right there for us on acoustic guitar. Following a break in the tour, Paul came into the studio to help produce the song. Dave Paramor, our producer, just took a back seat. He let Paul come in and help with the arrangement and this and that. He was great because he was encouraging everybody; he was a great believer in our band. Paul played a little piano, the glissando, on the backing track and we finished at about midnight. We put the vocals on the following day. Paul came back with his jacket over his pajamas and wearing slippers (because he only lived around the corner) to finish the song off, which I thought was hilarious." Bennett also said that additional horn players were brought in to play on the song. Contrary to reports, he said McCartney did not contribute to any other of his recordings. Bennett's version of ***Got To Get You Into My Life*** reached the top 10 in the U.K. Any chance of American success for his version was doomed when The Beatles simultaneously released their version on the **Revolver** album. Though it was not released before The Beatles' version, because of McCartney's direct involvement, it is obvious he intended it as a composition contribution to Bennett. (***Got To Get You Into My Life*** has since been covered by Blood, Sweat & Tears and Earth, and Wind & Fire, among aothers.)

Bennett had some success in Europe but was virtually unknown in America. Roy Young replaced Cliff Bennett in The Rebel Rousers in 1968 but disbanded the group to form the Roy Young Band the following year. (The Roy Young Band released a cover of The Beatles' song ***Revolution*** in 1970.) Bennett's new band, The Cliff Bennett Band, as they were known when they released a cover of The Beatles' ***Back In The U.S.S.R.*** in late 1968, broke up in June 1969. Bennett was involved in several other bands, including Toe Fat, Cliff Bennett's Rebellion, and Shanghai. He has reformed The Rebel Rousers, with several original members, and they have had a fair amount of success touring Britain and Europe.

Chuck Berry

Record 25 title:
The Mike Douglas Show with John Lennon & Yoko Ono

Media:
VHS [5 VHS set]

Release date / Country:
26 May 98 / U.S.A.

Producer:
WBS in association with Mike Douglas Entertainments Inc. & Michael Krauss

Jacket / Inserts:
Unique in box set / 48 page hard bound book with photos of John Lennon

Recording Location / Date:
Philadelphia, PA, U.S.A. / 16 Feb 72

Song 25a title:
Johnny B. Goode [live]

Track details:
Tape 3 / 2 min. 56 sec.

Label / Catalog number:
Rhino / R3 2438 (R3 2430)

Composer:
C. Berry

Chuck Berry: Lead Vocals & Guitar; John Lennon: Lead Vocals & Guitar; Gary Van Scyoc: Bass; Adam Ippolito: Keyboards; Richard Frank Jr.: Drums; Stan Bronstein: Saxophone & Tambourine; Wayne Gabriel: Guitar; Jerry Rubin: Percussion; Yoko Ono: Percussion

Song 25b title:
Memphis, Tennessee [live]

Track details:
Tape 3 / 3 min. 09 sec.

Label / Catalog number:
Rhino R3 2438 (R3 2430)

Composer:
C. Berry

Chuck Berry: Lead Vocals & Guitar; John Lennon: Lead Vocals & Guitar; Gary Van Scyoc: Bass; Adam Ippolito: Keyboards; Richard Frank Jr.: Drums; Stan Bronstein: Saxophone & Tambourine; Wayne Gabriel: Guitar; Jerry Rubin: Percussion; Yoko Ono: Percussion & B. Vocals

Chuck Berry was born on October 18, 1926, in San Jose, California but has lived most of his life in the St. Louis area. His musical career, which has spanned five decades, has been plagued by run-ins with numerous law enforcement agencies whose actions some say have bordered on racism and harassment. Aside from being a musician most of his life, Berry has also worked as a hair-dresser, a nightclub owner, an auto worker and has appeared in a number of films. When he's not touring, he's usually at his amusement complex, Berry Park, near St. Louis. His songwriting, guitar style and stage "duckwalk" rightfully earned him the title of one of rock 'n' roll's founding fathers.

Berry's rise to stardom began in 1955 with the top 10 song ***Maybellene***. The following year, he released ***You Can't Catch Me*** and his classic ***Roll Over Beethoven***. In 1957 he had two more top 10 songs, ***School Day*** and ***Rock And Roll Music***. He added ***Sweet Little Sixteen***, ***Johnny B Goode*** and ***Carol*** to his growing list of rock 'n' roll classics in 1958.

Berry's string of hits ended in 1959 with ***Little Queenie*** and ***Memphis, Tennessee*** after he was arrested for violation of the Mann Act. Berry was accused of transporting a fourteen-year-old girl over state lines for immoral purposes. The girl reported Berry to the authorities after he allegedly fired her as a hat-check girl at his St. Louis nightclub when he suspected she was a prostitute. Berry was finally convicted of the crime in early 1962 and spent the next two years in prison.

While Berry was behind bars the landscape of American music was changing. A southern California surf band named The Beach Boys* rewrote the lyrics to Berry's ***Sweet Little Sixteen*** and retitled it ***Surfin' U.S.A.*** which became their first top 10 song. When Berry was released from prison in 1964, he was greeted with the sounds of The Beatles and The Rolling Stones echoing his music back from England. That same year he had hits with ***Nadine (Is It You?)*** and a rewrite of ***School Day*** titled ***No Particular Place To Go***. He began touring the U.K., where he was always popular, and released the albums **St. Louis To Liverpool** and **Chuck Berry In London**.

Berry remained active during the second half of the 1960s recording sporadically and touring, but he failed to recapture the success he had in the 1950s. John Lennon and Ringo Starr attended Chuck Berry and Del Shannon's* performances at Brian Epstein's Saville Theatre in London on February 19, 1967. Berry appeared on the same bill as Lennon and the Plastic Ono Band at the Toronto Rock 'n' Roll Revival on September 13, 1969, though the two did not meet then.

Nearly every rock 'n' roll band has cut its teeth on Chuck Berry's music and The Beatles were no exception. Their early repertoire was filled with his songs including such Berry classics as ***Too Much Monkey Business***, ***Carol***, ***Johnny B Goode***, ***Memphis, Tennessee***, ***Roll Over Beethoven***, ***Sweet Little Sixteen***, ***Rock And Roll Music***, ***I Got To Find My Baby***, ***I'm Talking About You***, and ***Little Queenie***. All of these songs would show up on The Beatles' or their solo records. All but ***Little Queenie*** were sung by John Lennon. Other Berry songs The Beatles frequently jammed on or performed included ***Thirty Days***, ***Maybellene***, ***Reelin' And Rockin'***, ***Vacation Time***, ***Almost Grown***, ***Around And Around***, ***Brown-Eyed Handsome Man*** and ***School Day***. ***Memphis, Tennessee*** was one of the songs John sang at The Beatles' audition for Decca Records in 1962. (George Harrison still considers ***Roll Over Beethoven*** one of his top 10 favorite songs.) Paul McCartney has admitted that he copied the bass riff of his composition ***I Saw Her Standing There*** from ***I'm Talking About You***.

Chuck Berry, Detroit, MI, mid-1970s, photo courtesy of Tom Bert

When John Lennon wrote The Beatles' hit single, ***Come Together***, he borrowed a line and some of the melody from Chuck Berry's song ***You Can't Catch Me***. Record industry mogul Morris Levy, who owned the publishing rights to ***You Can't Catch Me***, sued Lennon for copyright infringement. As part of an out-of-court settlement, Lennon agreed to record three songs, including ***You Can't Catch Me***, that Levy owned the publishing rights to for his oldies album **Rock 'N' Roll**.

John and Yoko* were the guest co-hosts on The Mike Douglas TV Show for a week in mid-February 1972. One of the guests John wanted to have on the show was his idol, Chuck Berry, whom he had never met. Lennon introduced Berry as "my hero," and said "if you were to try and give rock 'n' roll another name you might call it Chuck Berry." John sang duet vocals with Berry on ***Memphis, Tennessee*** and backing vocals on ***Johnny B Goode***. John played guitar on both tracks and was backed by his newly acquired band, Elephant's Memory*, Yoko and political activist Jerry Rubin. In spite of Lennon's duet vocals on ***Memphis, Tennessee***, these two performances are more properly classified as John Lennon contributions to Chuck Berry. Berry was backed by Elephant's Memory the following year on his album, **Bio**.

Ironically, Berry's first and only bona fide number one on the pop charts was his sexually suggestive, live audience participation recording ***My Ding-A-Ling*** in 1972. He was backed on the live recording by future Paul McCartney guitarist Robbie McIntosh. Chuck Berry was given a lifetime achievement award by NARAS at the 1985 Grammy Awards. The following year, Berry became a charter inductee into the Rock and Roll Hall of Fame. In 1987 John Lennon's son, Julian Lennon*, appeared in the Chuck Berry film **Hail! Hail! Rock 'n' Roll**. A recording of Berry's ***Johnny B. Goode*** was included on the interstellar record enclosed on the space probe Voyager 2 sent out beyond our solar system. Berry continues to tour and often uses pickup or house bands because they usually know all of his songs.

Cilla Black

Record 26 title:
Cilla 1963 - 1973 The Abbey Road Decade
Media:
Album 5" CD [3 CD set]
Label / Catalog number:
Zonophone / 7243 8 57053 2 8
Producer:
George Martin
Jacket / Inserts:
Unique / 32 page CD booklet with photos of Paul McCartney & John Lennon

Song 26a title:
It's For You
Track details:
CD1, track 7 / 2 min. 20 sec.
Release date / Country:
04 Jul 97 (first issued 31 Jul 64) / U.K.
Composer:
J. Lennon - P. McCartney
Recording Location / Date:
EMI-Abbey Road Studios, London, U.K. / 02 Jul 64

Cilla Black: Lead Vocals; John Lennon: Arrangement; Paul McCartney: Piano & Arrangement; Johnny Person: Piano; Kenny Clarke: Drums; Judd Proctor: Guitar; George Martin: Orchestra Conductor

Song 26b title:
Love Of The Loved
Track details:
CD1, track 1 / 2 min. 01 sec.
Release date / Country:
04 Jul 97 (first issued 27 Sep 63) / U.K.
Composer:
J. Lennon - P. McCartney
Recording Location / Date:
EMI-Abbey Road Studios, London, U.K. / 28 Aug 63

Cilla Black: Lead Vocals; George Martin: Orchestra Conductor

Song 26c title:
M'Innamoro (Step Inside Love) (Italian Version)
Track details:
CD2, track 23 / 2 min. 21 sec.
Release date / Country:
04 Jul 97 (probably first issued Mar 68) / U.K.
Composer:
J. Lennon - P. McCartney - (Mogol: Translation)
Recording Location / Date:
EMI-Abbey Road Studios, London, U.K. / 28 Feb 68 & (probably) Mar 68

Cilla Black: Lead Vocals; Mike Vickers: Musical Direction & Arrangement; Vicki Brown: B. Vocals; Judd Proctor: Guitar

Song 26d title:
Step Inside Love
Track details:
CD2, track 1 / 2 min. 21 sec.
Release date / Country:
04 Jul 97 (first issued 08 Mar 68) / U.K.
Composer:
J. Lennon - P. McCartney
Recording Location / Date:
EMI-Abbey Road Studios, London, U.K. / 28 Feb 68

Cilla Black: Lead Vocals; Mike Vickers: Musical Direction & Arrangement; Vicki Brown: B. Vocals; Judd Proctor: Guitar

Song 26e title:
Step Inside Love (Original Demo)
Release date / Country:
04 Jul 97 / U.K.
Recording Location / Date:
EMI-Abbey Road Studios, London, U.K. / 21 Nov 67
Track details:
CD3, track 12 / 2 min. 51 sec.
Composer:
J. Lennon - P. McCartney

Cilla Black: Lead Vocals; Paul McCartney: B. Vocals & Acoustic Guitar

Song 26f title:
Step Inside Love (First Take)
Release date / Country:
04 Jul 97 / U.K.
Recording Location / Date:
EMI-Abbey Road Studios, London, U.K. / 21 Nov 67
Track details:
CD3, track 14 / 2 min. 23 sec.
Composer:
J. Lennon - P. McCartney

Cilla Black: Lead Vocals

Cilla Black was born Priscilla White on May 27, 1943, and nicknamed "Cil" by fellow Liverpudlians. She got her start in show business by casually getting up on Liverpool club stages and singing with bands like The Big Three, Faron's Flamingoes, King Size Taylor and the Dominoes and Rory Storm & The Hurricanes. She often sang the song ***Boys*** with The Hurricanes' drummer, Ringo Starr. She decided to change her last name as a result of an article in Liverpool's Mersey Beat music magazine in which editor Billy Harry mistakenly referred to her as Cilla Black. Brian Epstein did not need much persuading from The Beatles to sign Cilla to a contract with his management company, NEMS Enterprises, once he had heard her perform. Cilla's first major appearances were during The Beatles' 1963 Christmas Shows in London. She also appeared on the U.K. TV specials **Around The Beatles** in 1964 and **The Music Of Lennon And McCartney** in 1965.

Cilla had long been a favorite of The Beatles, particularly Paul McCartney. She exclusively recorded three of his compositions. The first, ***Love Of The Loved*** (an early Lennon and McCartney standard that Lennon originally wanted Liverpool singer Beryl Marsden to record), barely broke the U.K. top 40. Both Lennon and McCartney attended the recording session, but it is doubtful they contributed to the recording. An acetate of McCartney's acoustic guitar demo of the song for Cilla still exists. The Beatles' recording of the song is available on a number of the Decca audition releases. (***Love Of The Loved*** has since been covered by The E-Types, Michelle Torr, and The Saltbee.) Lennon and McCartney reportedly also attended the sessions for Cilla's first number one song in the U.K., ***Anyone Who Had A Heart***, written by Bacharach and David. However there is no indication they contributed to this recording either.

Cilla's next attempt at a McCartney song was ***It's For You***. Both John and Paul were again present in the studio this time to help arrange the song on which McCartney also played piano. Apparently, McCartney had recorded two demos for Cilla of ***It's For You*** that were each quite different. Cilla recorded three versions in all, but it was the final version with McCartney on piano that was released and became a U.K. top 10. McCartney recalls plugging the song to DJs during The Beatles visit to the U.S. in 1964

The American band, Three Dog Night, did an unusual arrangement of ***It's For You*** in 1968, but with more critical than commercial success. (***It's For You*** has since been covered by The Bowery Boys, Springwell, Tony Merrick, Mother Folkers, and The Saltbee.)

Step Inside Love, another top 10, was the third and final McCartney composition for Cilla. He wrote it specifically for her to sing as the theme song to her first TV series titled **Cilla**, that had its debut January 30, 1968 on BBC. Ringo appeared on the show on February 6, singing a duet with Cilla of ***Act Naturally*** and covers of two standards - ***Do You Like Me?*** and ***Nellie Dean***. On November 21, 1967, the BBC produced a two-minute promotional film of McCartney rehearsing ***Step Inside Love*** with Cilla at Chappell Studios in London. The rehearsal, featuring McCartney on acoustic guitar singing along with Cilla, has turned up on bootleg records. The two also recorded a demo of the song that featured McCartney on backing vocals and acoustic guitar. Later in the day Cilla recorded a finished version of the song, though it's unlikely McCartney contributed to it. However, the version of the song that was first released was a re-recording made on February 28, 1968, at Abbey Road Studios.

McCartney, who was at the Maharishi Mahesh Yogi's ashram in India at the time, was not present. Cilla later overdubbed her vocals, sung in Italian, to the February 28 backing that was released in Italy. Alan Hardy of Cilla's Circle Of Fans fan-club thinks it's quite likely that Cilla also dubbed the vocals to ***Step Inside Love*** in French and Spanish, though there is no indication that these versions exist. McCartney recorded a brief version of the song during sessions for **The Beatles** (the white album) in 1968 that was included on their 1996 album, **Anthology 3**.

Cilla's last major hit was ***Something Tells Me (Something's Gonna Happen Tonight)*** that reached number three on the U.K. charts in 1971. George Harrison attempted to bolster Cilla's recording career by producing two songs for her he had written, ***You've Got To Stay With Me*** and ***I'll Still Love You*** (originally titled ***When Every Song Is Sung***.) The songs were recorded at Apple Studios in 1972 with an all-star line-up including George on guitar, Ringo Starr on drums, Klaus Voormann *(see Paul Jones)* on bass and Eric Clapton* on guitar. (Harrison had earlier offered ***I'll Still Love You*** to Apple artists Mary Hopkin* and Ronnie Spector* and later to Leon Russell*. ***I'll Still Love You*** was eventually recorded by Ringo and included on his album **Rotogravure**.) Apparently, Cilla was unhappy with the results due in part to painful dental work done before the session. Harrison had also written the song ***The Light That Has Lighted The World*** for Cilla to record but ended up recording it for his **Living In The Material World** album instead. She re-recorded ***I'll Still Love You*** again in 1974 with a different producer. To date, none of these recordings have been released by Cilla. Ringo once offered Cilla ***Back Off Boogaloo***, but she preferred ***Photograph***. Ringo rightly felt ***Photograph*** would be a hit for him and was unwilling to turn it over to Cilla.

Success has always eluded Black outside the U.K. Her only top 40 in the U.S. was an adaptation of the Italian ballad, ***You're My World***, which was a number one for her in the U.K. She's had a good deal of chart success covering songs written by Bacharach and David and her husband Bobby Willis. Over the years Cilla has recorded covers of The Beatle tracks ***Yesterday***, ***For No One***, ***The Long And Winding Road***, ***Across The Universe*** and ***In My Life***. She also covered McCartney's song ***Junk*** and Lennon's ***Oh My Love***.

On September 7, 1993, it was reported that Cilla and Ringo were at EMI's Abbey Road Studios for a recording session, though as yet nothing has been released. That month, Ringo and McCartney contributed video material for a Cilla Black U.K. TV special.

In 1996, London's Daily Mirror made the unlikely claim that EMI had discovered 20 tracks of Black singing with The Beatles. According to Cilla's son Robert Willis, about 30 tracks were discovered including covers of The Beatles' songs but only one (***Step Inside Love***) featured any contributions from a Beatle.

In 1997 EMI Records released **Cilla 1963 - 1973 The Abbey Road Decade**, a three-CD retrospective of Cilla's recordings for the label. The set contained ***Love Of The Loved***, ***It's For You*** and the four recordings of ***Step Inside Love***, as well as Cilla's covers of ***Yesterday*** and ***For No One***. The set's booklet included photos of Cilla with McCartney and John Lennon. According to Cilla's son, a film documentary tentatively titled **A Girl In The Beat Boys World** is in the making. Cilla Black continues to be one of Britain's most popular television entertainers.

John Foster And Sons Ltd. Black Dyke Mills Band

Record 27 title:
Thingumybob / Yellow Submarine
Label / Catalog number:
Apple / 1800
Jacket / Inserts:
Record label sleeve

Media:
Singles 7" (mono)
Producer:
Paul McCartney

Song 27a title:
Thingumybob
Release date / Country:
26 Aug 68 / U.S.A.
Track details:
Side 1, track 1 / 1 min. 51 sec.
Composer:
J. Lennon - P. McCartney
Recording Location / Date:
On location at Victoria Hall, Bradford, Saltaire, Yorkshire, U.K. / 30 Jun 68

The Black Dyke Mills Band: all instruments; Paul McCartney: Conductor & Arrangement; Geoffrey Brand: Conductor

Song 27b title:
Yellow Submarine
Release date / Country:
26 Aug 68 / U.S.A.
Track details:
Side 2, track 1 / 2 min. 56 sec.
Composer:
J. Lennon - P. McCartney
Recording Location / Date:
On location at the Square Of The Victoria Hall, Bradford, Saltaire, Yorkshire, U.K. / 30 Jun 68

The Black Dyke Mills Band: all instruments; Paul McCartney: Conductor & Arrangement; Geoffrey Brand: Conductor

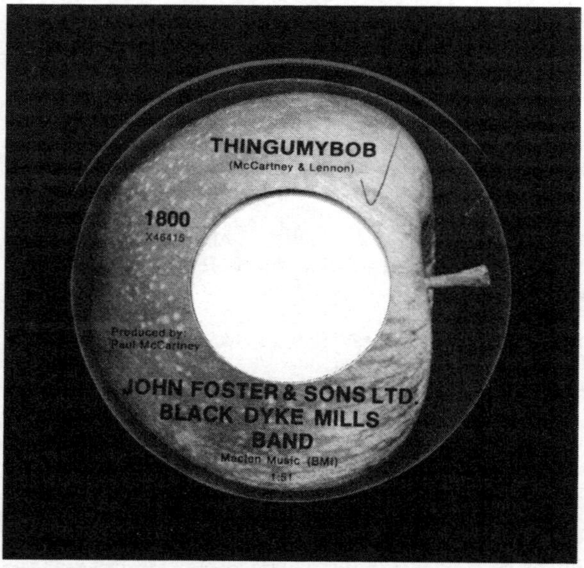

Paul McCartney was commissioned to write the title theme of ITV's London Weekend Television comedy series called **Thingumybob**. The Black Dyke Mills Band, a well-known British brass band of thirty-nine members founded in the 1940s by the Yorkshire firm of John Foster and Sons Ltd., was recruited. ***Thingumybob*** was recorded at Victoria Hall in Bradford, Yorkshire, and ***Yellow Submarine*** was recorded outside in the square. The main conductor was Geoffrey Brand, but McCartney also helped in the conducting and arranging of his composition that also credits him as producer.

Thingumybob was issued as one of the first four Apple Records' releases along with The Beatles' ***Hey Jude***. It is one of the rarer Apple Records' singles, particularly those copies that have ***Yellow Submarine*** on the green (un-split) apple A-side. ***Yellow Submarine***, also a McCartney composition, may have been chosen as a tie-in to help promote The Beatles' animated film ***Yellow Submarine***. Though the recordings are catchy, up-tempo instrumental numbers, they were hardly promoted or successful in the wake of ***Hey Jude***, that captured all the attention received by The Beatles' newly launched record label. Paul McCartney would later employ the Black Dyke Mills Band on the song, ***Love Awake***, on his album **Back To The Egg**. The Black Dyke Mills Band continues to perform in the U.K.

Blind Faith

Record 28 title:
Blind Faith
Label / Catalog number:
RSO / 825 094-2
Jacket / Inserts:
Standard international design in jewel box / 4 page CD booklet
Recording Location / Date:
Morgan Studio, London, U.K. / 07 Oct 69
Media:
Album 5" CD
Producer:
Blind Faith

Song 28a title:
Exchange And Mart
Release date / Country:
1986 / Germany
Track details:
Side 1, track 7 / 4 min. 15 sec.
Composer:
S. Winwood - E. Clapton - G. Baker - R. Grech

Eric Clapton: Guitar; Alan White: Drums; Rick Grech: Violin & Bass; Steve Winwood: Mandolin; George Harrison: (probable) Guitar

Song 28b title:
Spending All My Days
Release date / Country:
1986 / Germany
Track details:
Side 1, track 8 / 3 min. 00 sec.
Composer:
S. Winwood - E. Clapton - G. Baker - R. Grech

Rick Grech: Lead Vocals & Bass; Eric Clapton: Guitar; Alan White: Drums; (probably) Steve Winwood: Keyboards; George Harrison: (probable) Guitar

Blind Faith was the second "supergroup" formed in the late 1960s, the first being Crosby, Stills & Nash. The group named itself Blind Faith because of all the pre-publicity and hype they received before ever having released a record or performed in public. Members were Eric Clapton*, Steve Winwood, Ginger Baker and Rick Grech.

Eric Clapton, Saginaw, MI, 1979, photo by Kristofer Engelhardt

Steve Winwood was born May 12, 1948, in Birmingham, England. He gained notoriety in The Spencer Davis Group before he formed the band Traffic along with Dave Mason*, Jim Capaldi* and Chris Wood. Traffic appeared in The Beatles' film, **Magical Mystery Tour**, but their performance was edited out of the released version. During one of Traffic's many respites, Winwood became the lead vocalist, mandolin and keyboard player for Blind Faith. Years later Winwood would contribute to George Harrison's self titled-album in 1979 and to his song ***Flying Hour***, available only with the limited edition book, **Songs By George**

Harrison, published by Genesis in 1988. Winwood's 1986 solo album, **Back In The High Life**, was certified triple-platinum and included the number one song, ***Higher Love***.

Drummer, Ginger Baker (born Peter Baker on August 19, 1939 or 1940, depending on your source, in London, England) was a holdover from the band Cream that also included Clapton and Jack Bruce*. Baker would later move to Akeja, Nigeria (outside Lagos) and build ARC Studios. Paul McCartney recorded portions of his album **Band On The Run** at ARC. Baker has claimed he helped out on drums and production assistance on the album, though he is not credited.

Eric Clapton began spending much time with Delaney & Bonnie & Friends* who were the opening act during Blind Faith's only U.S. tour. Blind Faith, unable to forge their identity with a public that wanted to hear Cream and Traffic songs, decided to break up after about year. Clapton, Winwood and Grech all decided they would record solo albums. Clapton toured and recorded with Delaney & Bonnie & Friends throughout the fall of 1969 and winter of 1970. With the help of Delaney Bramlett, he released the album **Eric Clapton**. Baker formed the short-lived group Ginger Baker's Air Force that included, among others, Denny Laine*, Grech and Winwood. Winwood's solo recordings turned into Traffic's album **John Barleycorn Must Die**. Grech soon joined Steve Winwood in a reformed Traffic with Dave Mason and well-known session drummer, Jim Gordon, both of whom also had a stint with Delaney & Bonnie & Friends. Gordon also contributed to several Beatles solo recordings. Grech left Traffic in late 1971 and joined the band KGB.

Rick Grech was born on November 1, 1946, in Bordeaux, France. He was a violin and bass player who first gained notice in the group Family. It has long been rumored that George Harrison was asked to join Blind Faith. It's unlikely that Harrison, still a member of the quickly disintegrating Beatles, would have taken the offer to be a full-time member of another band seriously. He was eager to expand his solo efforts after being with The Beatles for so long. Harrison did, however, join Clapton on tour with Delaney & Bonnie & Friends while The Beatles were still officially together. Harrison was reported to have taken part in sessions with members of Blind Faith for a Rick Grech album in October 1969.

When the **Blind Faith** album was reissued on a German CD, it contained two previously unreleased jams, ***Exchange And Mart***, and ***Spending All My Days*** credited as being recorded on October 7, 1969. Are these the last known recordings by Blind Faith as indicated in the CD booklet notes, or are they songs from the never completed Rick Grech solo album? According to Marc Roberty, a noted Eric Clapton musical biographer, they are from the Rick Grech sessions and include Harrison on guitar. However, other experts on the group question Roberty's claim that Harrison appears on these two recordings. Roberty mentions that other musicians, including Baker, Clapton, Winwood, Trevor Burton, Jim Capaldi, Chris Wood and Graham Bond also participated in the sessions though it's not clear if he is referring to these two tracks. Denny Laine was also reported to be involved in these sessions. It is surprising that Roberty lists Alan White on drums and does not list who plays mandolin or keyboards. This seems unusual because the CD lists Winwood, Clapton, Baker and Grech as the composers. One would have to assume that the composers of these two loose "jams" played their respective instruments. Alan White confirmed that he drummed on ***Exchange And Mart*** and ***Spending All My Days*** and that the sessions were for Rick Grech, but he does not recall whether Harrison was present.

Grech reportedly recorded at Olympic Studios in London in 1970, and Harrison supposedly produced several tracks for Grech in 1971. A collection of Grech odds and ends, including his work with other groups titled **The Last Five Years** (RSO / 9 SO 876 in the U.S.) was also released. It's anybody's guess at this stage what, if any, contributions Harrison may have made to the album. The song, ***Hey Mr. Policeman***, does include Harrison-styled guitar work, and ***Face in The Clouds*** features a lead sitar!

On September 14, 1979, Grech, along with a host of other rock dignitaries, took part in the grand finale of Paul McCartney's annual "Buddy Holly Week" celebration at London's Hammersmith Odeon. Rick Grech died on March 17, 1990.

Colonel Doug Bogie

Record 29 title:
Cokey Cokey / Away In A Manger
Label / Catalog number:
Ring O' / 2017 104
Jacket / Inserts:
Record label sleeve
Media:
Singles 7"
Producer:
Doug Bogie
Recording Location / Date:
1975

Song 29a title:
Away In A Manger
Release date / Country:
21 Nov 75 / U.K.
Track details:
Side 2, track 1 / 3 min. 54 sec.
Composer:
Trad Arr. D. Bogie

Colonel Doug Bogie: Lead Vocals; Ringo Starr: (possible) Drums; Eric Clapton: (possible) Guitar

There is no official credit of Ringo playing drums on the single ***Cokey Cokey / Away In A Manger***, credited to one mysterious Colonel Doug Bogie. Bogie was reported to be one of Ringo's favorite performers. A variety of sources have long claimed that Ringo plays drums on ***Away In A Manger***. Ringo signed Bogie to his short-lived Ring O'Records label. The single also supposedly features Eric Clapton* on guitar, further bolstering the possibility that Ringo is involved somewhere on this single. Listening to this single could easily lead one to believe that both Clapton and Ringo contributed to at least ***Away In A Manger***. The single was also available on ABC Records in the U.S. Some at ABC erroneously claimed that the Colonel was Ringo under a pseudonym.

The Bonzo Dog Band

Record 30 title:
The Bonzo Dog Band Cornology Vol. 2 - The Outro
Label / Catalog number:
EMI / 0777 7 99597 2 2 (CZ 500)
Jacket / Inserts:
Unique in Jewel box / 16 page CD booklet
Recording Location / Date:
Chappell Studios, London, U.K. / Jul 68
Media:
Album 5" CD
Producer:
Paul McCartney & Gus Dudgeon

Song 30a title:
I'm The Urban Spaceman
Release date / Country:
22 Jun 92 (first issued 11 Oct 68) / U.K.

Track details:
Side 1, track 6 / 2 min. 22 sec.
Composer:
N.Innes

Neil Innes: Lead Vocals; Paul McCartney: Ukulele; probably the following: Roger Ruskin Spear: Saxophone, Kazoos, Jew's Harp & Models; Rodney Desborough Slater: Reeds & Trumpet; Vivian Stanshall: Tuba & Tube Percussion; "Leg's" Larry Smith: Drums; Vernon Dudley Bohay-Nowell: Banjo; Martin "Sam Spoons" Stafford: Tambourine; Dennis Cowan: Bass

The core members of The Bonzo Dog Band were the Englishmen Vivian Stanshall (born March 21, 1943, in Shillingford), Neil Innes (born December 9, 1944, in Essex), Rodney Slater (born November 8, 1944 in Lincolnshire), Roger Ruskin Spear (born June 29, 1943, in Wormwood Scrubbs) and "Legs" Larry Smith*. Other members included Large Sydney Nicholls, James Chambers aka Jim Stobes, Bob Kerr, John Parry, Raymond Lewitt, Martin "Sam Spoons" Stafford, Leon Williams and Vernon Dudley Bohay-Nowell. The group first called themselves The Bonzo Dog Dada Band in keeping with their reverence for the anti-art Dada Movement. The name was soon modified to The Bonzo Dog Doo Dah Band before finally being shortened to The Bonzo Dog Band. The band was a loose consortium of poets, musicians and comedians.

The Beatles and The Bonzos crossed paths many times — first during the filming of The Bonzo Dog Band's cameo appearance in The Beatles' TV special, **Magical Mystery Tour**, performing a song called ***Death Cab For Cutie***. The Bonzo's were invited to a post-production party for **Magical Mystery Tour** that The Beatles gave at the Royal Lancaster Hotel on December 21, 1967 just prior to its premiere. The Beatles and The Bonzo Dog Band jammed together during the party on rock oldies that included ***Lawdy Miss Clawdy*** and ***Long Tall Sally***. The following year, Paul McCartney lent his production hand (under the pseudonym Apollo C. Vermouth) and played ukulele for The Bonzos' only top 10 song in the U.K., ***I'm The Urban Spaceman***. Though the group had a large cult following, particularly in the U.K., they never had an impact on the U.S. charts.

According to Neil Innes, none of The Beatles contributed to The Bonzos' song ***Fresh Wound*** as had been rumored. He also dispelled several long-held rumors about possible Beatles' contributions to a number of Bonzo-related projects. To the best of Neil's knowledge, none of The Beatles contributed to ***Witchi Tai To / Jam***, a 1969 single by Topo D. Bil produced by "Legs" Larry Smith. He also has no knowledge of them contributing to ***Labio Dental Fricative / Paper Round***, a February 1970 single by "Vivian Stanshall & The Sean Head Showband" or Stanshall's album **Men Opening Umbrellas Ahead**.

The Bonzos did a wonderful Lennon parody titled ***Give Booze A Chance***. The Bonzos broke up in 1970 after five years of their inspired madness — but then regrouped briefly in 1972, again shuffling the membership. The cultural climate of experimentation in the 1960s did not survive the disco '70s, and various Bonzo members drifted into other projects. Innes became part of the group Grimms in 1973 that included Stanshall and Paul McCartney's brother Mike *(see Mike McGear, Roger McGough & Mike McGear, Scaffold).*

During the 1970s, George Harrison's association with Bonzo members "Legs" Larry Smith and Innes increased as did his association with Eric Idle of Monty Python*. Innes appeared in the Harrison music video for ***Crackerbox Palace*** directed by Idle. Innes and Idle were the creators and hosts of the BBC-TV comedy series **Rutland Weekend Television** at the time. Harrison appeared on the show on December 26, 1975, performing ***The Pirate Song***, a parody written by Harrison and Idle about George's plagiarism suit over ***My Sweet Lord*** *(see Delaney & Bonnie & Friends).* An album titled **The Rutland Weekend Television Song Book** was issued. The final liner note on the album is "**Warning.** There is to be no mention of George Harrison on this record." This is in response to part of ***The Pirate Song*** skit with Harrison in which he wishes not to be George Harrison. According to Neil Innes, George Harrison did not contribute to **The Rutland Weekend Television Song Book** album in any way.

The Rutles made their U.S. debut on producer Lorne Michaels' NBC-TV show, **Saturday Night Live**, that had featured both Harrison and members of Monty Python in the past. Michaels agreed to produce The Rutles in a full-length TV-parody documentary on the history of The Beatles titled **All You Need Is Cash**. The documentary was based in part on rough cuts, compliments of Harrison, of **The Long And Winding Road**, the tentative title of a mid-1970s version of The Beatles' **Anthology** film. Harrison had long seen The Beatles' experience as a surreal absurdity and was greatly amused by the parody. The documentary featured Innes as "Ron Nasty" (John Lennon), Idle as "Dirk McQuickly" (Paul McCartney), John Halsey as "Barry Wom" (Ringo Starr), and Rikki (aka Ricky) Fataar as "Stig O'Hara" (George Harrison) *(see The Beach Boys)*. The documentary featured a cameo role by George Harrison who interviews Michael Palin (pictured in the soundtrack album) who plays The Rutles' press officer "Eric Manchester" (Derek Taylor). It also featured cameo roles by Mick Jagger* as himself *(see The Rolling Stones)* and Ron Wood* as a Hell's Angel. Other characters included "Leggy Mountbatten" (Brian Epstein), "Dick Jaws" (Dick James), "Ron Decline" (Allen Klein) "Bill Murray The K" (DJ Murray The K) and Roger McGough* as himself. The documentary included such Rutles' classics as ***Hold My Hand*** and ***Ouch***, and featured the albums **Meet The Rutles**, **Tragical History Tour**, **Sgt. Rutters**, and **Let It Rot**. Most of the general public missed the point, but for those knowledgeable about the history of The Beatles and willing to laugh at themselves and Beatlemania, it was a brilliantly accurate parody. Naturally, George Harrison was delighted with the results. Apparently, John Lennon was also amused, though Ringo and especially Paul were initially reported to be a little sensitive about the parody. **The Rutles - All You Need Is Cash** was first aired on March 22, 1978 and was issued on laser videodisk in 1991.

In 1990, Rhino Records released **The Rutles** on CD that included six bonus tracks not released on the vinyl version of The Rutles' **All You Need Is Cash**. In the December 1992 volume 5 number 4 issue of Belmo's Beatleg news, a reader wrote in saying he worked with Eric Idle on the film **Too Much Sun**. He claimed that Idle told him George Harrison sang backing vocals on the Rutles' track ***Blue Suede Schubert***. According to Neil Innes, "George didn't contribute to any of The Rutles recordings in any way, but he was very supportive throughout the project."

Vivian Stanshall died in a house fire on March 5, 1995. McCartney gave tribute to Viv in the press and in his Club Sandwich fan club magazine. Paul McCartney featured the music of The Bonzo Dog Band on his 1995 radio series **Oobu Joobu**. "Legs" Larry Smith plans to release a Bonzo Dog tribute album titled **It Was A Great Party...Till Somebody Found A Hammer**. It reportedly may include contributions from Paul McCartney and Ringo Starr, as well as a George Harrison song written with Jim Capaldi*, titled ***Doin' The Bonzo Dog***. Neil Innes continues to be a popular guest at Beatles Conventions.

David Bowie

Record 31 title:
Young Americans
Media:
Album 5" [2 CD set]
Label / Catalog number:
Rykodisc / RCD 10140
Jacket / Inserts:
Standard international design in jewel box / 8 page CD booklet
Recording Location / Date:
Electric Ladyland Studios, New York, NY, U.S.A. / Jan 75

These songs are also included Fame '90 / Rykodisc / RCD5 1018 / Album 5" [2 CD set] / 26 Mar 90 (first issued 10 Mar 75) / U.S.A.

Song 31a title:
Across The Universe
Track details:
CD1, track 6 / 4 min. 30 sec.
Producer:
David Bowie & Harry Maslin
Composer:
J. Lennon - P. McCartney
Release date / Country:
14 May 91 / U.S.A.

David Bowie: Lead Vocals & Guitar; John Lennon: Guitar; Earl Slick: Guitar; Carlos Alomar: Guitar; Emir Kassam: Bass; Willie Weeks: Bass; Dennis Davis: Drums; Andy Newmark: Drums

Song 31b title:
Fame
Producer:
David Bowie & Harry Maslin
Release date / Country:
14 May 91 / U.S.A.
Track details:
CD1, track 8 / 4 min. 12 sec.
Composer:
D. Bowie - J. Lennon - C. Alomar

David Bowie: Lead Vocals & Guitar; John Lennon: Guitar & B. Vocals; Earl Slick: Guitar; Carlos Alomar: Guitar; Emir Kassam: Bass; Willie Weeks: Bass; Dennis Davis: Drums; Andy Newmark: Drums; Ralph McDonald: Percussion; Pablo Rosario: Percussion; Larry Washington: Percussion; Jean Fineberg: B. Vocals; Jean Millington: B. Vocals

Song 31c title:
Fame '90 (Absolutely Nothing Premeditated / Epic Mix)
Producer:
David Bowie & Harry Maslin / 1990 Dave Barratt
Release date / Country:
14 May 91 / U.S.A.
Track details:
CD2, track 5 / 14 min. 22 sec.
Composer:
D. Bowie - J. Lennon - C. Alomar

David Bowie: Lead Vocals & Guitar; John Lennon: Guitar & B. Vocals; Earl Slick: Guitar; Carlos Alomar: Guitar; Emir Kassam: Bass; Willie Weeks: Bass; Dennis Davis: Drums; Andy Newmark: Drums; Ralph McDonald: Percussion; Pablo Rosario: Percussion; Larry Washington: Percussion; Jean Fineberg: B. Vocals; Jean Millington: B. Vocals

Song 31d title:
Fame '90 (Gass Mix)
Producer:
David Bowie & Harry Maslin / 1990, Jon Gass
Release date / Country:
14 May 91 / U.S.A.
Track details:
CD2, track 3 / 3 min. 34 sec.
Composer:
D. Bowie - J. Lennon - C. Alomar

David Bowie: Lead Vocals & Guitar; John Lennon: Guitar & B. Vocals; Earl Slick: Guitar; Carlos Alomar: Guitar; Emir Kassam: Bass; Willie Weeks: Bass; Dennis Davis: Drums; Andy Newmark: Drums; Ralph McDonald: Percussion; Pablo Rosario: Percussion; Larry Washington: Percussion; Jean Fineberg: B. Vocals; Jean Millington: B. Vocals

Song 31e title:
Fame '90 (Hip Hop Mix)
Producer:
David Bowie & Harry Maslin / 1990, Arthur Baker
Release date / Country:
14 May 91 / U.S.A.
Track details:
CD2, track 4 / 5 min. 55 sec.
Composer:
D. Bowie - J. Lennon - C. Alomar

David Bowie: Lead Vocals & Guitar; John Lennon: Guitar & B. Vocals; Earl Slick: Guitar; Carlos Alomar: Guitar; Emir Kassam: Bass; Willie Weeks: Bass; Dennis Davis: Drums; Andy Newmark: Drums; Ralph McDonald: Percussion; Pablo Rosario: Percussion; Larry Washington: Percussion; Jean Fineberg: B. Vocals; Jean Millington: B. Vocals

Song 31f title:
Fame '90 (House Mix)
Producer:
David Bowie & Harry Maslin / 1990, Arthur Baker
Track details:
CD2, track 2 / 5 min. 56 sec.
Composer:
D. Bowie - J. Lennon - C. Alomar

Release date / Country:
14 May 91 / U.S.A.

David Bowie: Lead Vocals & Guitar; John Lennon: Guitar & B. Vocals; Earl Slick: Guitar; Carlos Alomar: Guitar; Emir Kassam: Bass; Willie Weeks: Bass; Dennis Davis: Drums; Andy Newmark: Drums; Ralph McDonald: Percussion; Pablo Rosario: Percussion; Larry Washington: Percussion; Jean Fineberg: B. Vocals; Jean Millington: B. Vocals

Song 31g title:
Fame '90 (with Queen Latifah)
Producer:
David Bowie & Harry Maslin/1990, D.J. Mark
Release date / Country:
14 May 91 / U.S.A.
Track details:
CD2, track 1 / 4 min. 04 sec.
Composer:
D. Bowie - J. Lennon - C. Alomar

David Bowie: Lead Vocals & Guitar; Queen Latifah: Lead Vocals; John Lennon: Guitar & B. Vocals; Earl Slick: Guitar; Carlos Alomar: Guitar; Emir Kassam: Bass; Willie Weeks: Bass; Dennis Davis: Drums; Andy Newmark: Drums; Ralph McDonald: Percussion; Pablo Rosario: Percussion; Larry Washington: Percussion; Jean Fineberg: B. Vocals; Jean Millington: B. Vocals

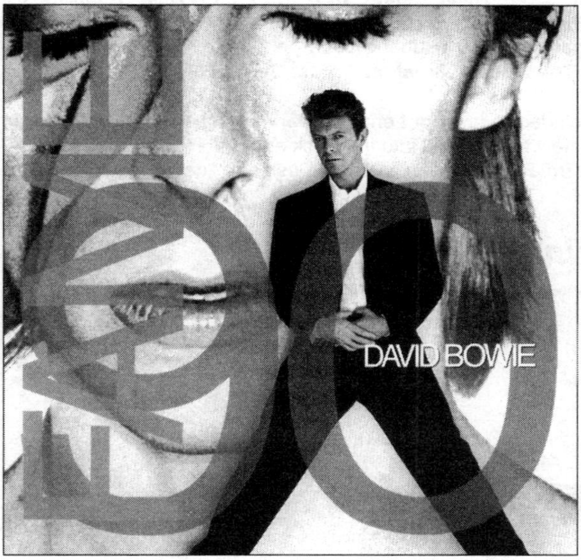

David Bowie was born David Jones on January 8, 1947 in London, England. He later adopted the name Bowie (after the knife) so as not to be confused with actor Davy Jones (Jones would go on to gain fame in the group The Monkees). Bowie is best known for his androgynous appearance and musical transformations throughout his long career. David took up the guitar and saxophone as a young teen. He first worked as a commercial artist before fronting a number of unsuccessful pop groups in the mid-1960s. Uncertain of a career in music, he also pursued acting. This no doubt helped him create such stage characters as Ziggy Stardust and the Thin White Duke, establishing him as a glitter rock star and pioneer of rock androgyne. Bowie had a great deal of difficulty getting his musical career started and reportedly was rejected as a possible candidate for The Beatles' record label, Apple, by Paul McCartney.

In spite of (or because of) Bowie's ever-changing personae and musical styles, his audience grew steadily throughout the 1970s and '80s. Some of Bowie's more memorable hit songs are ***Space Oddity***, ***Changes***, ***The Jean Genie***, ***Rebel Rebel***, ***Young Americans***, ***Fame***, ***Golden Years***, ***Boys Keep Swinging***, ***Ashes To Ashes***, ***Let's Dance***, ***Modern Love***, and ***Blue Jean***. Bowie also found time to produce and write songs for other artists while cultivating his acting career. He appeared on Broadway in the leading role of **The Elephant Man** and starred in the films **The Man Who Fell To Earth**, **The Hunger** and **Labyrinth**.

David Bowie first met John Lennon at a birthday party for Elizabeth Taylor in February 1974 in Los Angeles. By January of 1975, Bowie and Lennon were residents of New York City who occasionally ran into one another. Bowie visited Lennon one night and the two began sketching each other. John expressed an interest in visiting Bowie in the studio. According to May Pang, Lennon and guitarist Carlos Alomar composed the music to the song ***Fame*** on the spot in the studio while Bowie went off and composed the lyrics. Pang said Lennon's portion of the composition was inspired by the song ***Shame, Shame, Shame***, a hit at the time by the group Shirley & Company. According to Bowie, Alomar borrowed a riff from The Flares' song ***Footstompin***. John ended up singing background vocals on the song as well as playing guitar on it and Bowie's cover of John's Beatles song, ***Across The Universe***. Bowie omitted two songs scheduled for inclusion on his just completed **Young Americans** album to include the two songs to which Lennon contributed. ***Fame*** became Bowie's first number one single in the U.S. Claims of a recording of ***Let's Twist Again*** by Lennon and Bowie together on bootleg records is, apparently, false.

It is also worth noting that ***Young Americans*** guitarist Earl Slick, and drummer Andy Newmark, also worked on Lennon's last studio albums **Double Fantasy** and **Milk And Honey**. Newmark and ***Young Americans*** bass player Willie Weeks have also worked extensively with George Harrison.

When ***Fame*** was first issued in 1975, it mistakenly listed L. Andross (it's Luther Vandross) along with Bowie and Lennon as the song's composers. All subsequent issues since 1978 correctly list C. Alomar in place of L. Andross. ***Fame*** was also included in the soundtrack to the successful film, **Pretty Woman**. As a result of its re-exposure, a CD titled **Fame '90** containing no less than five newly remixed and extended versions of ***Fame*** was released in March 1990. In May 1991, this CD was reissued along with the newly issued CD **Young Americans**. Additional mixes of ***Fame*** also exist on obscure or promotional records. They include ***Fame (Acapulco Rap Mix)***, ***Fame (Dave Barratt Mix)***, ***Fame (Humberto Gatics Sonic Mix)***, ***Fame (Bonus Beat Mix)*** aka ***Fame (Bonus-Beats International)***, ***Fame (Queen Latifah's Rap Version)*** and ***Fame (DJ Mark Mix)***. All the remixed versions contained some portion of the original recording featuring John Lennon. A video for ***Fame*** was included on the 1991 laser videodisk **The World's Greatest Artists Sing LENNON A Tribute**.

Bowie's 1989 album **Tin Machine** included a cover of Lennon's ***Working Class Hero***. David Bowie continues to record, perform and act. He was inducted into the Rock and Roll Hall of Fame in 1996. Bowie edged past Paul McCartney as Britain's richest musician in Business Age magazine rankings in 1997.

Delaney Bramlett

Record 32 title:
Delaney & Friends - Class Reunion
Label / Catalog number:
Prodigal / P6-10017S1
Jacket / Inserts:
Standard international design / Record label inner sleeve
Media:
Album 12"
Producer:
Ray Ruff & Jimmy Bowen

Song 32a title:
For Old Time's Sake
Release date / Country:
1977 / U.S.A.
Recording Location / Date:
Heritage Recording Studio, Los Angeles, CA, U.S.A. / 1977
Track details:
Side 2, track 3 / 3 min. 02 sec.
Composer:
R. Sharp

Delaney Bramlett: Lead Vocals; Ringo Starr: Drums; Jim Keltner: Drums; additionally, one or more of the following: Spider Taylor: Lead Guitar; Randy Sharp: Guitar; Chuck Rainey: Bass; Chris Etheridge: Bass; Rick Sutherland: Keyboards; Jim Hobson: Keyboards; Stu Perry: Drums; Sidney Sharp: Strings; Samuel Boghossian: Strings; Harry Hyams: Strings; Ronald Folsom: Strings; Murray Adler: Strings; James Getzoff: Strings; David D. Turner: Strings; Jesse Ehrlich: Strings; Raymond Kelley: Strings; William Kurasch: Strings; Chuck Findley: Horns; Ollie Mitchell: Horns; Jackie Kelso: Horns; Slyde Hyde: Horns; Quitman Dennis: Horns; Clydie King: B. Vocals; Sherlie Matthews: B. Vocals; Monalisa Young: B. Vocals; Susie Allanson: B. Vocals; Pat Erickson: B. Vocals; Patti Quatro: B. Vocals

Song 32b title:
I Think I Got It
Track details:
Side 2, track 1 / 3 min. 12 sec.

Release date / Country:
1977 / U.S.A.
Composer:
D. Bramlett
Recording Location / Date:
Gold Star Recording Studio, Los Angeles, CA, U.S.A. / 1977

Delaney Bramlett: Lead Vocals; Ringo Starr: Drums; Jim Keltner: Drums; additionally, one or more of the following: Spider Taylor: Lead Guitar; Randy Sharp: Guitar; Chuck Rainey: Bass; Chris Etheridge: Bass; Rick Sutherland: Keyboards; Jim Hobson: Keyboards; Stu Perry: Drums; Sidney Sharp: Strings; Samuel Boghossian: Strings; Harry Hyams: Strings; Ronald Folsom: Strings; Murray Adler: Strings; James Getzoff: Strings; David D. Turner: Strings; Jesse Ehrlich: Strings; Raymond Kelley: Strings; William Kurasch: Strings; Chuck Findley: Horns; Ollie Mitchell: Horns; Jackie Kelso: Horns; Slyde Hyde: Horns; Quitman Dennis: Horns; Clydie King: B. Vocals; Sherlie Matthews: B. Vocals; Monalisa Young: B. Vocals; Susie Allanson: B. Vocals; Pat Erickson: B. Vocals; Patti Quatro: B. Vocals

Song 32c title:
I Wish It Would Rain
Track details:
Side 1, track 3 / 2 min. 58 sec.
Release date / Country:
1977 / U.S.A.
Composer:
N. Whitfield - B. Strong - R. Penzabene
Recording Location / Date:
Gold Star Recording Studio, Los Angeles, CA, U.S.A. / 1977

Delaney Bramlett: Lead Vocals; Ringo Starr: Drums; additionally, one or more of the following: Spider Taylor: Lead Guitar; Randy Sharp: Guitar; Chuck Rainey: Bass; Chris Etheridge: Bass; Rick Sutherland: Keyboards; Jim Hobson: Keyboards; Stu Perry: Drums; Jim Keltner: Drums; Sidney Sharp: Strings; Samuel Boghossian: Strings; Harry Hyams: Strings; Ronald Folsom: Strings; Murray Adler: Strings; James Getzoff: Strings; David D. Turner: Strings; Jesse Ehrlich: Strings; Raymond Kelley: Strings; William Kurasch: Strings; Chuck Findley: Horns; Ollie Mitchell: Horns; Jackie Kelso: Horns; Slyde Hyde: Horns; Quitman Dennis: Horns; Clydie King: B. Vocals; Sherlie Matthews: B. Vocals; Monalisa Young: B. Vocals; Susie Allanson: B. Vocals; Pat Erickson: B. Vocals; Patti Quatro: B. Vocals

Song 32d title:
Locked Up In Alabama
Track details:
Side 1, track 1 / 4 min. 30 sec.
Release date / Country:
1977 / U.S.A.
Composer:
D. Bramlett
Recording Location / Date:
Gold Star Recording Studio, Los Angeles, CA, U.S.A. / 1977

Delaney Bramlett: Lead Vocals; Ringo Starr: Drums; Jim Keltner: Drums; additionally, one or more of the following: Spider Taylor: Lead Guitar; Randy Sharp: Guitar; Chuck Rainey: Bass; Chris Etheridge: Bass; Rick Sutherland: Keyboards; Jim Hobson: Keyboards; Stu Perry: Drums; Sidney Sharp: Strings; Samuel Boghossian: Strings; Harry Hyams: Strings; Ronald Folsom: Strings; Murray Adler: Strings; James Getzoff: Strings; David D. Turner: Strings; Jesse Ehrlich: Strings; Raymond Kelley: Strings; William Kurasch: Strings; Chuck Findley: Horns; Ollie Mitchell: Horns; Jackie Kelso: Horns; Slyde Hyde: Horns; Quitman Dennis: Horns; Clydie King: B. Vocals; Sherlie Matthews: B. Vocals; Monalisa Young: B. Vocals; Susie Allanson: B. Vocals; Pat Erickson: B. Vocals; Patti Quatro: B. Vocals

Song 32e title:
You Were The Light
Track details:
Side 2, track 5 / 3 min. 17 sec.
Release date / Country:
1977 / U.S.A.
Composer:
R. Sharp
Recording Location / Date:
Heritage Recording Studio, Los Angeles, CA, U.S.A. / 1977

Delaney Bramlett: Lead Vocals; Ringo Starr: Drums; additionally, one or more of the following: Spider Taylor: Lead Guitar; Randy Sharp: Guitar; Chuck Rainey: Bass; Chris Etheridge: Bass; Rick Sutherland: Keyboards; Jim Hobson: Keyboards; Stu Perry: Drums; Jim Keltner: Drums; Sidney Sharp: Strings; Samuel Boghossian: Strings; Harry Hyams: Strings; Ronald Folsom: Strings; Murray

Adler: Strings; James Getzoff: Strings; David D. Turner: Strings; Jesse Ehrlich: Strings; Raymond Kelley: Strings; William Kurasch: Strings; Chuck Findley: Horns; Ollie Mitchell: Horns; Jackie Kelso: Horns; Slyde Hyde: Horns; Quitman Dennis: Horns; Clydie King: B. Vocals; Sherlie Matthews: B. Vocals; Monalisa Young: B. Vocals; Susie Allanson: B. Vocals; Pat Erickson: B. Vocals; Patti Quatro: B. Vocals

Record 33 title:
We Can't Be Seen Together
Label / Catalog number:
Columbia / 4-45781
(probably promotional only)
Jacket / Inserts:
Record label sleeve
Recording Location / Date:
United Western Studios, Los Angeles, CA, U.S.A. / (probably) 1973

Media:
Single 7"
Producer:
Delaney Bramlett & Doug Gilmore

Song 33a title:
We Can't Be Seen Together
Release date / Country:
1973 / U.S.A.

Track details:
Side 1, track 1 / 2 min. 27 sec.
Composer:
D. Bramlett - D. Gilmore - [G. Harrison]

Delaney Bramlett: Lead Vocals & Guitar; Tim Hedding: Keyboards; Larry Savola: Trombone; Jerry Jumonville: Saxophone; Darrell Leonard: Trumpet; Ron Grayson: Drums; Robert Wilson: Bass

Delaney Bramlett released several albums on Columbia Records following the breakup of his marriage and musical act with Bonnie in 1972. Delaney's recording of ***We Can't Be Seen Together*** was issued by Columbia, probably only as a promotional single, in 1973. According to Delaney and Bonnie*, George Harrison helped write the song around the time of the Delaney & Bonnie & Friends tour with Eric Clapton. Delaney said he did not credit George on ***We Can't Be Seen Together*** because he felt Harrison should have credited him for helping write ***My Sweet Lord***.

Album liner notes of **Delaney & Friends-Class Reunion** state in part: "there comes a time in every artist's life when he wants to say 'thank you' to those who have helped on this album, past albums, jam sessions, concerts, and who have 'just been my friends.' THANK YOU. Ringo Starr, George Harrison, Paul McCartney, John Lennon." Also included in the thank you list of almost 300 people are many of the artists that have worked with The Beatles.

However, none of The Beatles are listed among the musicians credited as playing on **Delaney & Friends-Class Reunion**. According to Delaney Bramlett, Ringo did drum on five songs included on **Class Reunion** and four unreleased songs from the album's sessions, one of which is titled ***When This Day Ends***.

David Bromberg

Record 34 title:
David Bromberg
Label / Catalog number:
Columbia / C 31104
Jacket / Inserts:
Standard international design / Record label inner sleeve & Lyric insert
Recording Location / Date:
On location at World Control Headquarters, Philadelphia, PA
& Columbia Studios, New York, NY, U.S.A. / 1970 or 1971
Media:
Album 12"
Producer:
David Bromberg

Song 34a title:
The Holdup [live-version one]
Release date / Country:
16 Feb 72 / U.S.A.
Track details:
Side 2, track 4 / 3 min. 00 sec.
Composer:
G. Harrison - D. Bromberg

David Bromberg: Lead Vocals & Acoustic Guitar; George Harrison: Slide Guitar; David Nichterne: Piano; Jody Stecher: Mandolin; David Amram: French Horn; Willow Scarlett: Harmonica; Steve Burgh: Bass; Steve Mosley: Drums

David Bromberg was born September 19, 1945, in Philadelphia, Pennsylvania. He has virtually dedicated his life to stringed instruments, collecting, making, repairing and playing violins, mandolins, banjos and guitars. He spent a great deal of his youth in the New York City area and became a part of the Greenwich Village folk scene. His recording career has been more critically than commercially successful, though his albums have sold relatively well. Bromberg has worked as both producer and session player with a great number of famous musicians. He contributed to Ringo Starr's star-studded album **Ringo** in 1973 and to his 1977 album **Ringo The 4th**. David has since retreated to a more subtle and domestic life-style in Chicago, though he still occasionally records and makes the scene at folk festivals.

David Bromberg and George Harrison appeared together on the David Frost TV show on December 3, 1971, performing the song ***The Holdup***. George and David mentioned during the show that they had composed the song over Thanksgiving dinner (at Al Aronowitz's house) the year before. According to Bromberg, ***The Holdup*** was written in Englewood, NJ, with George Harrison in about a half an hour; "it just came out of us. It was recorded live in Philadelphia, and George overdubbed the slide guitar part at a church in New York City that is still Columbia's largest studio. George isn't credited, but everyone else is on the insert; that's all folks!" Bromberg recorded two versions of ***The Holdup***, though the second, a studio version, does not include Harrison's slide guitar. It's available on the U.S. CD **Out Of The Blues - Best of David Bromberg** (Columbia / CK 34467).

Gary Brooker

Record 35 title:
Lead Me To The Water
Label / Catalog number:
Line / LICD 9.00015 0
Jacket / Inserts:
Standard international design in jewel box / 4 page CD booklet
Recording Location / Date:
The Farm Studios, Surrey, U.K. / 1982
Media:
Album 5" CD
Producer:
Gary Brooker

Song 35a title:
The Cycle
Release date / Country:
1987 (first issued 01 Mar 82) / Germany
Track details:
Side 1, track 5 / 3 min. 20 sec.
Composer:
G. Brooker

Gary Brooker: Lead Vocals & Keyboards; George Harrison: B. Vocals; Phil Collins: Drums & B. Vocals; Tim Renwick: Guitar; Dave Markee: Bass; Phil Aaberg: Keyboards

Song 35b title:
Mineral Man
Release date / Country:
1987 (first issued 01 Mar 82) / Germany
Track details:
Side 1, track 1 / 3 min. 19 sec.
Composer:
G. Brooker

Gary Brooker: Lead Vocals & Keyboards; George Harrison: Guitar; Phil Collins: Drums; Eric Clapton: Guitar; Albert Lee: Guitar; Peter Maunu: Guitar; Tim Renwick: Guitar; Dave Markee: Bass; Mel Collins: Saxophones; Kent Middleton: Percussion

Gary Brooker, Detroit, MI, photo courtesy of Pat Henry

Keyboard player Gary Brooker was born on May 29, 1945 in Essex, England. He was a founding member and lead vocalist of the mid-'60s to mid-'70s group Procol Harum. Their mega hit, ***A Whiter Shade Of Pale***, in the psychedelic "Summer of Love" in 1967, was not only in competition with the album **Sgt. Pepper**, but a favorite of The Beatles as well. Their only other major hit was in 1972 with an orchestrated re-recording of the song ***Conquistador*** from their 1967 debut album. Procol Harum began as an R&B band in the early '60s called The Paramounts, which included Brooker on keyboards and guitarist Robin Trower, who years later took the spotlight as a solo guitarist. The group recorded a cover of The Beatles' song ***It Won't Be Long*** in 1964. They were signed with Brian Epstein's management company, NEMS Enterprises, and as a result were one of the acts billed on The Beatles' British tour in December 1965. The group also covered The Beatles' song ***Eight***

Days A Week in 1975.

Brooker has had a close personal and working relationship with Eric Clapton* and George Harrison. He contributed to Harrison's albums **All Things Must Pass** in 1970, **Somewhere In England** released in 1981 and **Gone Troppo** released the following year. Harrison is listed as playing guitar in the general credits of Brooker's 1982 album **Lead Me To The Water**. According to Brooker, Harrison plays on the song ***Mineral Man***, and sings backing vocals on ***The Cycle***. (The **Lead Me To The Water** album also includes contributions from drummer Steve Holly. Holly was a member of Paul McCartney's band Wings, when Brooker contributed to McCartney's songs ***Rockestra Theme*** and ***So Glad To See You***.)

Gary Brooker contributed keyboards to Ringo's 1983 album **Old Wave**. He joined Ringo Starr's All-Starr Band tour in 1997 performing ***The Devil Came From Kansas*** and ***Whiter Shade Of Pale***, with backing from Ringo on drums. Brooker continues to write, record and tour, sometimes under the Procol Harum name. He has also been involved in several projects with the London Symphony Orchestra*.

Record 36 title:
About Love And Life

Media:
Album 5" CD

Label / Catalog number:
Polydor / 847 266-2

Producer:
Sam Brown

Jacket / Inserts:
Standard international design in jewel box / 24 page CD booklet

Recording Location / Date:
FPSHOT (Friar Park Studios, Henley-on-Thames)†, EMI-Abbey Road Studios, London, U.K. & Wisseloord, Holland / (probably) 1990

Song 36a title:
Lu Le La

Track details:
Side 1, track 10 / 4 min. 07 sec.

Release date / Country:
Sep 90 / Holland

Composer:
N. Lancaster - C. Corbett

Vicki Brown: Lead Vocals; Phil Palmer: Guitar; Ian Maidman: Bass; Tim Goldsmith: Drums; Jesse Bailey: Piano & Keyboards; Andre Hoekstra: Percussion; George Harrison: Slide Guitar†; Joe Brown: Ukulele: Tony Palmer: Steel Drums; Chris Ballin: B. Vocals; Mario Frendo: B. Vocals; Derek Green: B. Vocals; Paul A. Lee: B. Vocals; Zetia Massiah: B. Vocals; Juliet Roberts: B. Vocals; Iris Sutherland: B. Vocals

Vicki (Haseman) Brown was born on August 23, 1940 in Liverpool, England. She was a member of the singing groups The Vernons Girls and The Breakways. The Vernons Girls toured with The Beatles during the autumn of 1963. The group recorded the novelty song ***We Love The Beatles***. Other members of the group also recorded the novelty number ***We Love You Beatles*** under the name Carefrees. Neither song included Vicki.

Vicki married early '60s rock guitarist Joe Brown of Joe Brown And His Bruvvers fame. Vicki enjoyed much success, particularly in Holland where she, along with the New London Choral, had a top five in 1986 with the song ***Stay With Me Till The Morning***. The following year she had a top 20 there with the song ***Can't Let Go***.

Joe Brown is also no stranger to The Beatles, who opened numerous shows for him during the early 1960s. The Beatles included Joe's hit ***A Picture Of You***, sung by George, in their repertoire in 1962 and performed the song during their second BBC radio appearance. Joe released a cover of ***With A Little Help From My Friends*** in June 1967 that made the U.K. top 30.

Vicki and Joe were neighbors of George Harrison and contributed to his 1982 album **Gone Troppo**.

Vicki sang the duet vocals with George on the title track of the film **Shanghai Surprise** *(see Various Artists - Shanghai Surprise)*. Harrison, who has been greatly influenced by Joe's ukulele playing, wrote the foreword for his autobiography, **Brown Sauce: The Life And Times Of Joe Brown**, in 1986. In late 1986, Vicki Brown appeared as one of the backing vocalists in the Paul McCartney video for ***Only Love Remains***. Joe joined Harrison and Carl Perkins* for a musical jam at HandMade Films' 10th anniversary celebration in 1988. Harrison contributed slide guitar to the song ***Lu Le La*** from Vicki's 1990 album, **About Love And Life**. Vicki Brown died on June 16, 1991, after a long battle with cancer. The couple's daughter, Sam Brown, who produced ***Lu Le La***, has also had a successful recording career.

In 1992, George Harrison appeared in one of the musical sequences in the documentary **Mister Roadrunner** performing on ukulele the song, ***Between The Devil And The Deep Blue Sea***, with a backup band that included Joe Brown, Jools Holland, Ray Cooper and Herbie Flowers. That year Harrison announced that he would soon be working with Joe on some recordings, but nothing has emerged beyond the jams the two neighbors frequently have together.

Jack Bruce

Record 37 title:
Songs For A Tailor

Media:
Album 5" CD

Label / Catalog number:
Polydor / 835 242-2

Producer:
Felix Pappalardi

Jacket / Inserts:
Standard international design in jewel box / 4 page CD booklet

Recording Location / Date:
Morgan Studios, London, U.K. / 11 May 69

Song 37a title:
Never Tell Your Mother She's Out Of Tune

Track details:
Side 1, track 1 / 3 min. 39 sec.

Release date / Country:
Jun 88 first issued 29 Aug 69) / U.S.A.

Composer:
J. Bruce - P. Brown

Jack Bruce: Lead Vocals, Piano & Bass; George Harrison: Guitar; Harry Beckett: Trumpet; Henry Lather: Trumpet; Dick Heckstall-Smith: Tenor & Soprano Saxophones; Art Theman: Tenor & Soprano Saxophones; Jon Hiseman: Drums

John "Jack" Bruce, was born on May 14, 1943, in Glasgow, Scotland into a very worldly and musical family. He won a scholarship as a teenager to the Royal Scottish Academy of Music for cello and composition. Since that time Bruce has been a member of Alexis Korner's Blues Inc., The Graham Bond Organization (including Ginger Baker), Manfred Mann *(see Paul Jones)* and John Mayall's Bluesbreakers *(see Eric Clapton)*. The Graham Bond Quartet, including Bruce and Baker, backed Duffy Power on his 1963 cover of The Beatles' song ***I Saw Her Standing There***. Bruce will be remembered most as the writer and front man for the legendary psychedelic blues band Cream, that included Clapton and Baker.

Backstage pass for Ringo Starr All-Starr Band "Happy birthday Jack!"

When Cream broke up in 1968, Clapton and Baker joined forces with Steve Winwood and Rick Grech to form Blind Faith*. Jack Bruce recorded the solo album **Songs For A Tailor**, asking Harrison to play on ***Never Tell Your Mother She's Out Of Tune***, "because I was impressed with Harrison's guitar work on Cream's song ***Badge***. George showed up an hour early and was quite nervous and careful to be in tune. It was done as a live track in the studio. The session was very good and very easy and a lot of fun." Bruce said the Harrison pseudonym, L'Angelo Misterioso, (used for ***Badge***) *(see Jesse Ed Davis)* was used to avoid royalty payments.

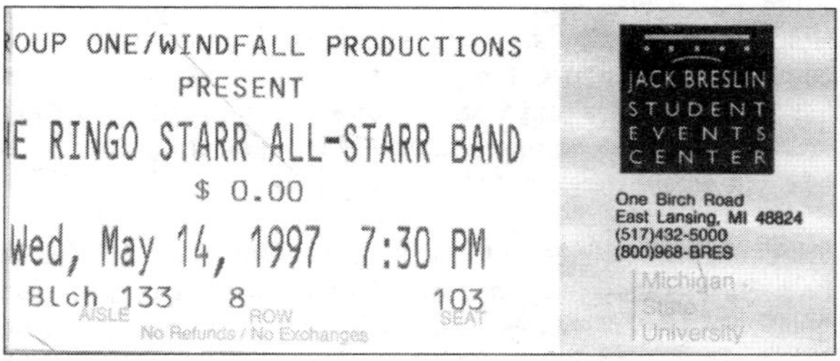

Ticket stubfor Ringo Starr All-Starr Band "Happy birthday Jack!"

Bruce revived the power trio concept in the 1970s with (Leslie) West, Bruce and (Corky) Laing; in the 1980s with Robin Trower and Bill Lordan in BLT; and finally in the 1990s with Gary Moore* and Bruce's old partner Ginger Baker in BBM. Bruce made a brief cameo appearance in Robert Stigwood's 1978 film **Sgt. Pepper's Lonely Hearts Club Band**. He continues to collaborate with the well-known names of rock. Cream reunited for a performance at their induction into the Rock and Roll Hall of Fame in 1993.

Bruce was a member of Ringo Starr's All-Starr Band tour in 1997 performing ***Sunshine Of Your Love***, ***I Feel Free*** and ***White Room*** with Ringo backing him on drums. Ginger Baker made a guest appearance playing drums during Bruce and the All-Starrs' performance of ***White Room*** in Denver, Colorado. Bruce is also scheduled to be part of the All-Starr's 1998 tour.

Brute Force

Record 38 title:
King Of Fuh

Media:
Single 7" (mono)

Label / Catalog number:
Apple / 8

Producer:
The Tokens (Phil Margo, Mitch Margo, Hank Medress & Jay Siegel) & [Stephen Friedland] [Remixed by George Harrison]

Jacket / Inserts:
Record label sleeve

Recording Location / Date:
Olmsted Studios, New York, NY, U.S.A.† & (probably) Trident Studios, London, U.K. / (probably) spring 1968† & (probably) Dec 68 & or Jan 69

Song 38a title:
King Of Fuh

Track details:
Side 1, track 1 / 3 min. 01 sec.

Release date / Country:
16 May 69 / U.K.

Composer:
Brute Force (S. Friedland)

Stephen Friedland: Lead Vocals, Keyboards & Mellotron; Phil Margo: Drums; Mitch Margo: Bass; George Harrison: (possible) Orchestral Arrangement; Royal Philharmonic Orchestra

Brute Force was born Stephen Friedland on September 29, 1940, in Jersey City, New Jersey. Stephen is primarily a variety entertainer with an act incorporating his talents as comedian, musician and songwriter. Offstage he has been a bit part actor on TV and in a number of films, including **Ghostbusters** and **Sea Of Love**. Stephen is also a Yoga teacher, paralegal and long-distance swimmer. In 1968 he attempted to swim the Bering Strait, making it as far as the international dateline. The event was chronicled in the September 20, 1968 issue of **Life** magazine.

Friedland was initiated into the music business by Billy Gussak (a session drummer for Bill Haley). In 1964 he joined the group The Tokens, of the ***The Lion Sleeps Tonight*** fame, playing keyboard and guitar. He became professionally known as Brute Force, and in the later 1960s, along with The Tokens, recorded a song he had written about a land called Fuh and its king. Stephen recalls, "The song was inspired by a poem I had written back in '67 about a furry king who went where he wanted to go, and did what he wanted to do. 'Furry king' led to 'fuh king.' So I saw the syllables of the common expletive and turned them around to 'King Of Fuh,' and weaved those words into a song that's really about individuality and beauty...a song that explores language taboo."

Steve Friedland aka Brute Force, photo courtesy Steve Friedland

Friedland was a friend Tom Dawes, of the Brian Epstein-managed group The Cyrkle. (The Cyrkle adopted the unusual spelling of their name at the suggestion of John Lennon and toured America with The Beatles in 1966.) Friedland gave Dawes a tape of ***King Of Fuh***. Dawes gave the tape to Nat Weiss a business associate and close friend of Brian Epstein's and The Beatles. George Harrison heard the

3 Savile Row
London W.1.
10/2/69.

Dear Brute Force,

first let me introduce myself, I am Road Manager for the Beatles, and was with George at Nat Weiss's flat when we first heard your record King of Fuh.

I was at the session when he added the strings and reduced the track and on this side we use the Royal Philharmonic Orchestra. We only played the backing track, and when we finished we played the vocal track as well. It was terribly funny for the whole orchestra fell about laughing and really enjoyed the whole thing, and were delighted when George said they would get a promotion copy.

We have a slight problem in that at the moment E.M.I. refuse to distribute the record, saying that there is a rude word on the record, no good telling them it's all in the mind. We will overcome this problem shortly I am sure so don't worry about it at the moment.

Hope you enjoy these first pressings I have enclosed and please give my regards to Nat.

One more thing I would like to add is that I have spoken with Peter Asher who has just returned to America, and was delighted to hear that the contracts have been signed.

So

Welcome to the Apple Family
Love and Peace
Mal.

Letter from Beatles' road manager Mal Evens, 1969, courtesy of Steve Friedland song at Weiss's apartment in New York in November 1968. Sometime between December 1968 and early February 1969, Harrison decided to work on the recording and release it on Apple Records. Friedland received a letter from The Beatles' road manager, Mal Evans, explaining that George Harrison had remixed ***King Of Fuh*** and added a string section provided by the Royal Philharmonic Orchestra. Evans also recounted how amused the orchestra members were by the song. Friedland thinks Harrison may have "kicked up the percussion a bit; really a super mix."

When management at EMI Records, who were responsible for pressing and distributing Apple Records, heard the lyrics to ***King Of Fuh*** (the story of a Fuh King), they refused to have anything to do with it. Consequently, Apple had the record pressed elsewhere and distributed it themselves primarily as a mail order item. Friedland guesses about 2,000 copies were pressed. Though promotional copies were distributed by Apple in England, the clever but profane song never had a chance of receiving any airplay. It is one of the rarest and most valuable Apple Records' releases. ***King Of Fuh*** was released as a single (Brute Force Records / BFR 100) backed with ***The Tapeworm Of Love*** in the U.S. on July 20, 1971.

Ironically, Friedland was also a staff writer for Bright Tunes Music Corp *(see Delaney & Bonnie & Friends)* which was owned by The Tokens. Stephen wrote The Chiffons' top 40 song ***Nobody Knows What's Goin' On (In My Mind But Me)***. His version was used for the B-side of Apple's ***King Of Fuh*** single. Friedland doubts George Harrison did anything to ***Nobody Knows***.

Stephen still performs ***King Of Fuh*** in his variety comedy act. The original Apple release is available on his cassette tape **SFFS, Stephen Friedland Funny Songs**. The cassette contains a photo of Stephen taken by Linda Eastman (McCartney) *(see Linda McCartney)* at Columbia Studios in New York in 1967. He has also written a musical based upon ***King Of Fuh*** called ***The Fuh King Thing*** and is working with his daughter Lilah on a music video of ***King Of Fuh***.

Lori Burton

Composer:
C. Sigman - G. Winkler - F. Rauch
Producer:
Roy Cicala & John Lennon
Recording Location / Date:
Record Plant (East) Studios, New York, NY, USA / 13 Jan 75
Song 39a title:
Answer Me, My Love
Release date / Country:
[Unreleased]

Lori Burton: Lead Vocals; John Lennon: Arrangement; probably one or more of the following: Patrick Jude: Percussion; Mark Rivera: Saxophone; John Corbert: Keyboards; Vinnie Appice: Drums; Daniel Elfassy: Drums; Joe Bassin: Trombone; Bob Livingood: Trumpet; Rick: Bass; Kenny Papa; Kenny Sambolin

Composer:
R. Cicala - J. Lennon
Producer:
Roy Cicala & John Lennon
Recording Location / Date:
Record Plant (East) Studios, New York, NY, USA / (probably) Jan 75
or (possibly) mid-to late 1974
Song 30b title:
Incantation
Release date / Country:
[Unreleased]

Lori Burton: Lead Vocals; probably one or more of the following: Patrick Jude: Percussion; Mark Rivera: Saxophone; John Corbert: Keyboards; Vinnie Appice: Drums; Daniel Elfassy: Drums; Joe Bassin: Trombone; Bob Livingood: Trumpet; Rick: Bass; Kenny Papa; Kenny Sambolin

Composer: Shanklin	***Song 39c title:*** The Big Hurt
Producer: Roy Cicala & John Lennon	***Release date / Country:*** [Unreleased]
Recording Location / Date: Record Plant (East) Studios, New York, NY, USA / (probably) Jan 75	

Lori Burton: Lead Vocals; probably one or more of the following: Patrick Jude: Percussion; Mark Rivera: Saxophone; John Corbert: Keyboards; Vinnie Appice: Drums; Daniel Elfassy: Drums; Joe Bassin: Trombone; Bob Livingood: Trumpet; Rick: Bass; Kenny Papa; Kenny Sambolin

Lori Burton was born Dolores Diana Squeglia on September 30, 1940 in New Haven, Connecticut into a highly musical family. Her brother, James Anthony, was a fill-in drummer for Karen Carpenter onstage. Her father, who sang and played saxophone, had a fifteen-piece band called the Jimmy Nichols Orchestra. By the age of five, Lori began to sing with her father's orchestra, usually at weddings and talent shows. By the age of twelve she had adopted several stage names, including Dolly Renay, and sang with her father in nightclubs. She began writing songs in high school.

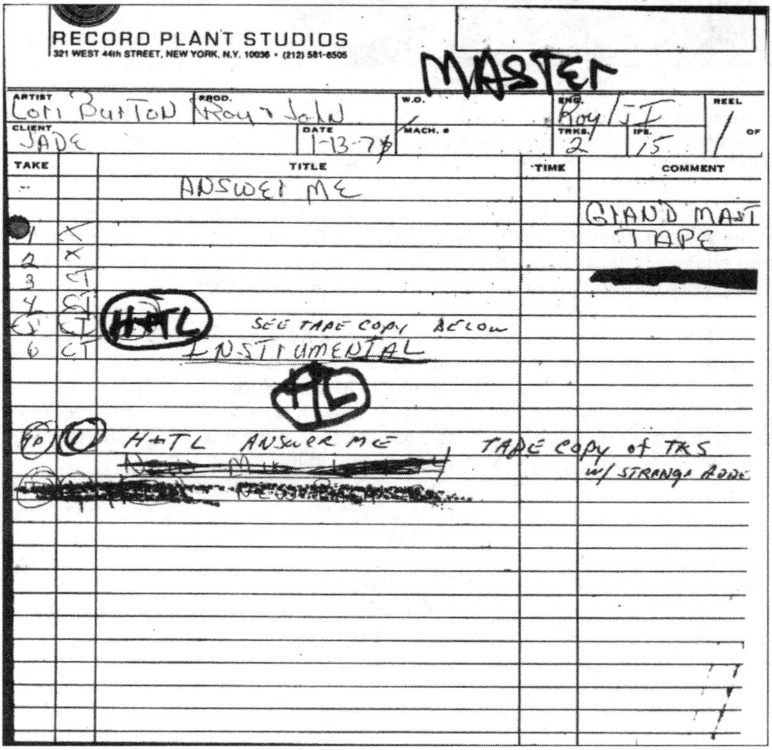

Tape box cover for "Answer Me" from Record Plant Studios, courtesy of Roy Cicala

Lori Burton married her childhood sweetheart, Roy Cicala, of West Haven, Connecticut. Lori continued to sing and write songs, while Roy pursued his career as a recording engineer. Lori was signed to Morris Levy's Roulette Records in 1964. Roulette felt the name Dolores Squeglia was too ethnic, so Dolores was shortened to Lori and Burton was adopted from Richard Burton. (Burton was a popular figure at the time due to his affair with Elizabeth Taylor.) Her first record was a song called ***That Boy Is Mine***. Shortly after signing with Roulette, she met Pam Sawyer. By 1965, Lori and Pam had two of their compositions on the charts - The (Young) Rascals' *(see Felix Cavaliere)* debut single ***Ain't Gonna Eat Out My Heart Anymore*** (later covered by Michael Jackson*) and Patti Labelle

Acetate for "Lets's Spend TheNight Together", courtesy of Roy Cicala

& The Blue Bells' debut single for Atlantic titled ***All Or Nothing***. Lori and Pam also wrote the song, ***Forget About Me*** by Prince Harold that reached the top of the rhythm & blues charts in 1966. The two were also briefly signed as writers for Motown Records in the mid-1960s.

Lori released her first solo album titled **Breakout** for Mercury Records in 1967. She began performing again, but soon grew tired of the demands of touring. In 1968 Lori and her husband Roy began writing and producing together. One of their more successful productions was a remake of The Box Tops' 1967 hit ***The Letter*** by the group The Arbors in 1969.

Most of Lori's time in the early 1970s was divided between raising the couple's two children and helping to manage The Record Plant (East) Studios. Lori has been less active in the music business the last two decades, but in 1995 she reunited with Pam Sawyer. They wrote the song ***House Of Secrets*** about incest. Lori feels it is one of the best songs the two have written.

By the early 1970s, Roy Cicala had become one of the music industry's top engineers and was the owner of The Record Plant (East) Studios in New York. During this period, some of today's top producers and engineers, including Jack Douglas, Jimmy Iovine, Jimmy Ienner, Dennis Ferrante and Shelly Yakus, were learning their craft under the tutelage of Roy Cicala.

Roy first met John Lennon in the summer of 1971 when he helped engineer overdubs for Lennon's album **Imagine**. It was the beginning of a long professional (and personal) relationship that included Roy's work on the Lennon albums **Sometime In New York City**, **Mind Games**, **Walls And Bridges**, **Rock 'N' Roll**, **Menlove Ave** and John & Yoko's final recordings at the Record Plant shortly before Lennon's death in 1980. Roy once told Lennon that the only song of John's he never liked was the one with the yeah, yeah, yeah (***She Loves You***) in it!

Sometime near the dawn of 1975, Lennon agreed to help Roy produce some recordings for Lori. Lori had previously sung backing vocals on Lennon's ***#9 Dream*** (listed as one of the 44th Street Fairies that included May Pang, Joey Dambra and Lennon) and (uncredited) on ***Luck Of The Irish***. Lennon wanted to do some of the recordings for Lori in the disco style popular at the time. Information concerning Lennon's contributions to Lori Burton's recordings is sketchy at best and taken from existing Record Plant tape boxes and extensive interviews with those present. However, there is some disagreement as to the events and the extent of Lennon's involvement. There seems to be general agreement that Lennon contributed to at least four Lori Burton recordings – ***The Big Hurt***, ***Answer Me, My Love***, ***Let's Spend The Night Together*** and ***Incantation***.

According to May, ***Answer Me, My Love*** was an old Nat King Cole number that Lennon had liked and had rearranged for Lori. Record Plant tape boxes list John Lennon as producing ***Answer Me, My Love*** on January 13, 1975, which falls into the period Pang thinks most of Lennon's work on Burton's recordings took place. ***The Big Hurt*** was a cover of the Toni Fisher hit from 1960.

Lori and May Pang are both certain that Lennon produced the songs ***Answer Me, My Love***, ***The Big Hurt*** and, to a lesser degree, Lori's duet with Patrick Jude of ***Let's Spend The Night Together***. According to Jude, Lennon also arranged The Rolling Stones cover.

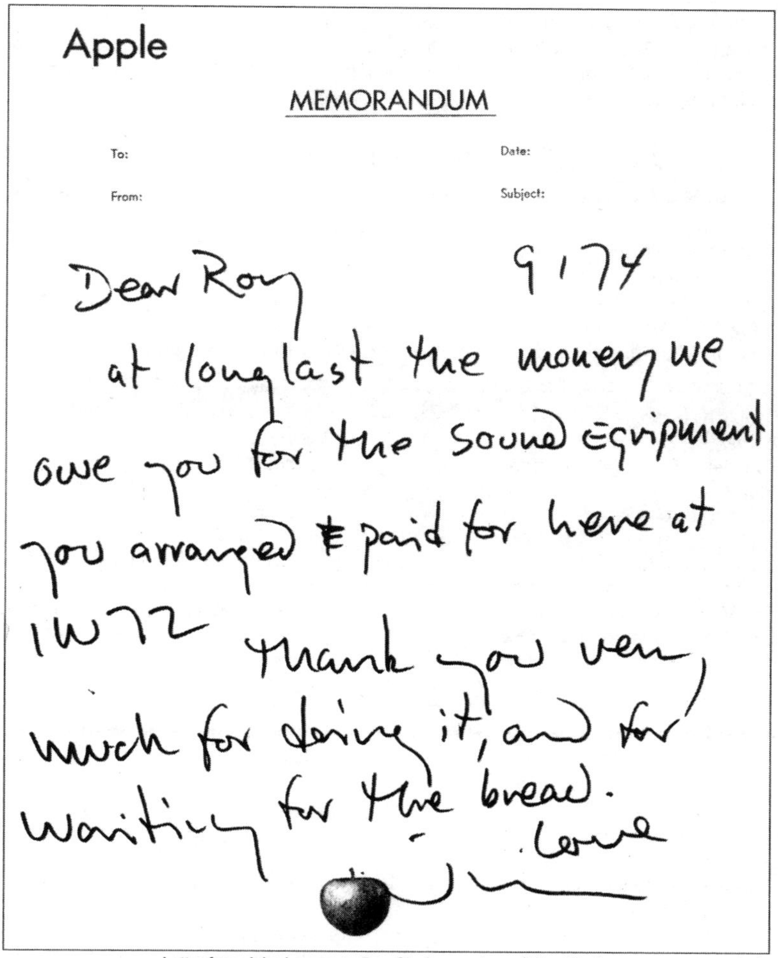

Apple

MEMORANDUM

To: Date:

From: Subject:

Dear Roy 9 1 74

at long last the money we owe you for the sound equipment you arranged & paid for here at 1W72 thank you very much for doing it, and for waiting for the bread.

Love

Letter from John Lennon to Roy Cicala, courtesy of Roy Cicala

Lori was backed by a group of musicians Roy discovered called Bomf, fronted by singer and actor Patrick Jude. The group had originally been called Community Apple when they were fronted by singer Joey Dambra. The group eventually became known as Dog Soldier*.

According to Lori, ***Incantation*** was a song Roy had originally written the music and lyrics for called ***Jubilation*** recorded by Community Apple. Lennon rewrote the lyrics and retitled it ***Incantation***. Lennon's lyrics were inspired by an Indian he had met named Rolling Thunder. Roy then recorded Lennon's version of the song with a group called Visitor, but he was not happy with their version either so he had Lori sing the song. Patrick Jude also sang a version of the song recorded with Dog Soldier. May Pang was not aware of Lennon producing any versions of ***Incantation***. However, Lori and Patrick are certain that Lennon helped produce each of their respective versions.

By the accounts of all present, Lennon did not play on any of these tracks, including those for Lori Burton. Some of these recordings were exclusively released accompanying the book Beatles Undercover.

Roy and Lori were divorced in 1979. The Record Plant (east) closed in 1989, and Roy moved to Brazil where he recorded some of that country's musicians. He recently returned to the New York area and has opened a new studio with John Hanti called IIWII (it is what it is), a favorite saying between him and his long-lost fishing buddy, John Lennon. Roy still commands a great deal of respect and admiration as one of the music industry's top engineers and producers. He has recently worked with Patti Smith. Well-known studio guitarist Hugh McCracken said, "he's probably the best mixer on the whole darn planet!" Others refer to him as elephant ears because of his keen sense of hearing.

Lori Burton and Patrick Jude

Record 40 title:
Let's Spend The Night Together
Label / Catalog number:
Cutting Room
Recording Location / Date:
Record Plant (East) Studios, New York, NY, USA / (probably) Jan 75
Media:
Single 10" [Acetate]
Producer:
Roy Cicala & John Lennon

Song 40a title:
Let's Spend The Night Together
Release date / Country:
Unreleased / U.S.A.
Track details:
3 min. 14 sec.
Composer:
M. Jagger - K. Richard

Lori Burton: Lead Vocals; Patrick Jude: Lead Vocals & (probable) Percussion; John Lennon: Arrangement; probably one or more of the following: Mark Rivera: Saxophone; John Corbert: Keyboards; Vinnie Appice: Drums; Daniel Elfassy: Drums; Joe Bassin: Trombone; Bob Livingood: Trumpet; Rick: Bass; Kenny Papa; Kenny Sambolin

Jim Capaldi

Record 41 title:
Some Come Running
Label / Catalog number:
Island / 7 91024-2
Jacket / Inserts:
Standard international design in jewel box / 8 page CD booklet
Recording Location / Date:
FPSHOT (Friar Park Studios, Henley-on-Thames)† & Backyard Studios, Surrey, U.K. / Jul 88
Media:
Album 5" CD
Producer:
Jim Capaldi

Song 41a title:
Oh Lord Why Lord?
Release date / Country:
01 Nov 88 / U.S.A.
Track details:
Side 1, track 8 / 4 min. 24 sec.
Composer:
P. Trim - M. Bouchar

Jim Capaldi: Lead Vocals & Drums; Chris Parren: Keyboards; George Harrison: Guitar†; Eric Clapton: Guitar; Rosko Gee: Bass; Andy Mac Pherson: Mix

Jim Capaldi was born on August 2, 1944 in Evesham, England. It's hardly surprising that both George Harrison's and Eric Clapton's names would show up on a Jim Capaldi album. The two have worked with Jim and his associates in Traffic *(see Blind Faith, Dave Mason)* for decades. The song ***Oh Lord Why Lord?*** is dedicated to South African activist Steve Biko. George also makes a cameo appearance in the music video for the song.

Belinda Carlisle

Record 42 title:
Runaway Horses
Media:
Album 5" CD
Label / Catalog number:
MCA / MCAD 6339
Producer:
Rick Nowels
Jacket / Inserts:
Standard international design in jewel box / 12 page CD booklet
Recording Location / Date:
One on One, Los Angeles, CA, U.S.A., & FPSHOT (Friar Park Studios, Henley-on-Thames)†, U.K. / 1988 or 1989

Song 42a title:
Deep Deep Ocean
Release date / Country:
03 Oct 89 / U.S.A.
Track details:
Side 1, track 7 / 4 min. 05 sec.
Composer:
B. Steinberg - T. Kelly - A. Sky

Belinda Carlisle: Lead Vocals; George Harrison: Six String Guitar & Twelve String Bass†; Charles Judge: Keyboards & Acoustic Piano; Ben Schultz: Guitar; John Pierce: Bass; Kenny Aronoff: Drums; X.Y. Jones: Guitar; Ellen Shipley: B. Vocals; Maria Vidal: B. Vocals; Donna Delory: B. Vocals; Bekka Bramlett: B. Vocals

Song 42b title:
Leave A Light On
Release date / Country:
03 Oct 89 / U.S.A.
Track details:
Side 1, track 1 / 4 min. 33 sec.
Composer:
R. Nowels - E. Shipley

Belinda Carlisle: Lead Vocals; George Harrison: Slide Guitar†; Rick Nowels: Guitar; Charles Judge: Keyboards; Ben Schultz: 12 String Guitar; John Pierce: Bass; Rudy Richman: Drums; X.Y. Jones: Guitar; Ellen Shipley: B. Vocals; Maria Vidal: B. Vocals; Donna Delory: B. Vocals; Bekka Bramlett: B. Vocals

Belinda Carlisle was born on August 17, 1958 in Hollywood (Los Angeles), California. She has become the most successful member of the Los Angeles band The Go-Go's. The group, formed in 1978, had two top 10s, ***We Got The Beat*** and ***Vacation*** in 1982. They also had two top 20s, ***Our Lips Are Sealed*** in 1981 and ***Head Over Heels*** in 1984, before disbanding in 1985. The Go-Go's, including Carlisle, have reunited on several occasions since their initial formation in 1978.

Carlisle's solo career got off to a successful start with the single ***Mad About You***, which reached the top five in 1986. The following year, her recording ***Heaven Is A Place On Earth*** reached the top of the charts in the U.S. and U.K. She just missed the number one spot in 1988 with the song ***I Get Weak***. That year she had another top 10 with ***Circle In The Sand***. Carlisle is currently married to Morgan Mason, son of actor James Mason, and is living in the south of France.

Rick Nowels, who produced Carlisle's 1989 album **Runaway Horses** and wrote many of its songs recounts, "I met George Harrison at a party in Los Angeles in 1987 and he complimented me on ***Heaven Is A Place On Earth*** which I had produced and co-written for Belinda. A year later when I was working on **Runaway Horses**, we decided to contact George to see if he was interested in playing on a couple of tracks for the album. George said he would be happy to play, and to send him the tapes, and tell him what we wanted and what songs to play on. I wrote him very specific notes and asked him to play on ***Leave A Light On*** and ***Deep Deep Ocean***. I arranged ***Leave A Light On*** with a sixteen bar solo instead of an eight bar solo to give George some room to stretch. After I got the tapes back, to my delight, George called me at A&M Studios and asked if it was all right and said I owed him a beer. He even wrote specific notes on how to mix it. He was very friendly. I can't wait to buy George that beer and thank him again." ***Leave A Light On*** was a major international hit due in no small part to Harrison's searing slide guitar solo. Virgin Records' U.K. CD single / VSCD 1210 contains an 8 minute, 7 second extended mix of ***Leave A Light On***.

Johnny Cash

Record 43 title:
Water From The Wells Of Home
Label / Catalog number:
Mercury / 834 778-2
Jacket / Inserts:
Standard international design in jewel box / 4 page CD booklet
Recording Location / Date:
The Mill Studios, Sussex, U.K. & Nashville, TN, U.S.A. / 09 May 88
Media:
Album 5" CD
Producer:
Paul McCartney

Song 43a title:
New Moon Over Jamaica
Release date / Country:
08 Nov 88 / U.S.A.
Track details:
Side 1, track 9 / 3 min. 12 sec.
Composer:
T. Hall - J. Cash - P. McCartney

Johnny Cash: Lead Vocals & (probable) Rhythm Guitar; Paul McCartney: Bass, Vocals & Guitar; Hamish Stuart: Guitar & B. Vocals; Chris Whitten: Drums & B. Vocals; Marty Stuart &/or Mark Howard: Mandolin; Ralph Mooney &/or Lloyd Green: Pedal Steel Guitar; Jack Clemont, &/or Mark Howard, &/or Emmylou Harris: Rhythm Guitar; Joey Miskulin: Accordion; Jack Clement, &/or Lloyd Green: Dobro Guitar; Jack Clement: (probable) Ukulele; June Carter Cash: Autoharp & B. Vocals; Linda McCartney: B. Vocals; Tom T. Hall: B. Vocals; Cindy Cash: B. Vocals

Johnny Cash, Detroit, MI, early 1970s, photo courtesy og Tom Bert

Johnny Cash was born in Kingsland, Arkansas on February 26, 1932. He took up guitar as a youth and worked briefly in radio. In the mid-1950s he found his way to Sam Phillips' Sun Records along-side Elvis, Jerry Lee Lewis and Carl Perkins*. He had several country and western hits, including ***Cry, Cry, Cry***; ***Folsom Prison Blues***; and ***I Walk The Line***. Cash was one of the first and most frequent country artists to have crossover success on the pop charts. He was also one of the first to work with a wide range of well-known country and rock artists over the years, including among others, Kris Kristofferson, Waylon Jennings, Willie Nelson, Jerry Lee Lewis, Carl Perkins, Roy Orbison* and U2.

In 1963, Cash scored his first number one on the pop charts with the song ***Ring Of Fire*** written by his friends and country stars, Merle Haggard and June Carter. Cash and Carter become a duet act and were married in 1968, shortly after Cash's divorce from his first wife. That year he recorded an album live at Folsom Prison that was a million-seller, and he teamed up with Bob Dylan* on Dylan's country album **Nashville Skyline**. He had his own musical variety TV show for several years, and hit the top of the charts again with ***A Boy Named Sue*** in 1969.

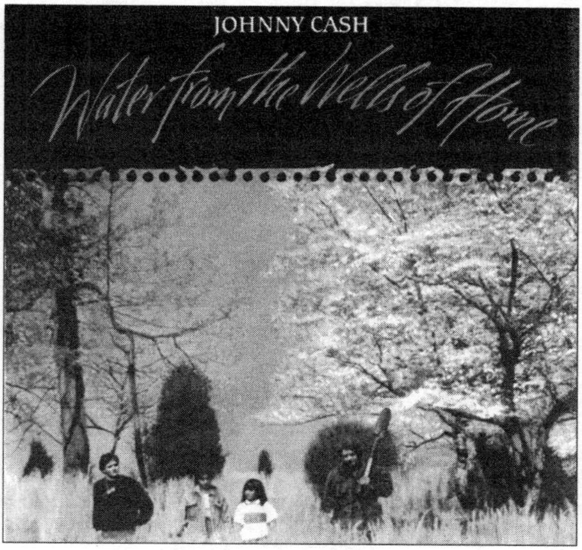

Cash has won numerous Grammy Awards and is a member of the Nashville Songwriter's Hall of Fame. He is also a member of the Country Music Hall of Fame, and in 1992 he was inducted into the Rock and Roll Hall of Fame. He has long performed at benefits — particularly for prisoners, Native Americans and religious organizations. His daughter, Rosanne Cash, from his first marriage, is a country music star. His son, John Carter Cash, also has a career in music.

Both Johnny Cash and Paul McCartney have had a long love affair with the island nation of Jamaica. While on vacation there, the two met (Cash has a home on the island) and composed the song ***New Moon Over Jamaica***. McCartney featured the original reggae demo of the song on his 1995 radio series **Oobu Joobu**. A country version was arranged and recorded with Cash at McCartney's studio near his home in Sussex, England. The song appeared on **Water From The Wells Of Home**, a superstar-studded album from the "man in black." Cash also recorded a cover of McCartney's ***Man We Was Lonely*** during the sessions at McCartney's studio. Cash's version of the song, which has yet to be released, almost certainly contains some contribution from McCartney.

Record 44 title:
Ringo Starr And His Third All-Star Band Volume 1

Media:
Album 5" CD

Label / Catalog number:
7 Blockbuster Exclusive / [matrix #] 0ERE4<5297>RINGOSTARR ADFL

Producer:
Greg Delancy (Mixer) Ringo Starr and David Fishof (Executive Producers)

Jacket / Inserts:
Standard international design / 4 page CD insert

Recording Location / Date:
Nippon Budakon Hall, Tokyo, Japan / 27 Jun 95

Song 44a title:
People Got To Be Free [live]

Release date / Country:
12 Aug 97 / U.S.A.

Track details:
Side 1, track 7 / 4 min. 33 sec.

Composer:
F. Cavaliere - E. Brigati

Felix Cavaliere: Lead Vocals & Keyboards; Mark Farner: Guitar & B. Vocals; Ringo Starr: Drums; Zak Starkey: Drums; John Entwistle: Bass; Randy Bachman: Guitar; Billy Preston: Keyboards & B. Vocals; Mark Rivera: Saxophone, Percussion & B. Vocals

Felix Cavaliere was born on November 29, 1944 in Pelham, New York. Cavaliere studied classical piano as a youngster. He was part of a "doo-wop" group in high school consisting of two black and two white members that he called The Stereos because, he said, "stereo was new at the time." He formed a band called Felix & The Escorts while a student at Syracuse University. Felix recalled, "My

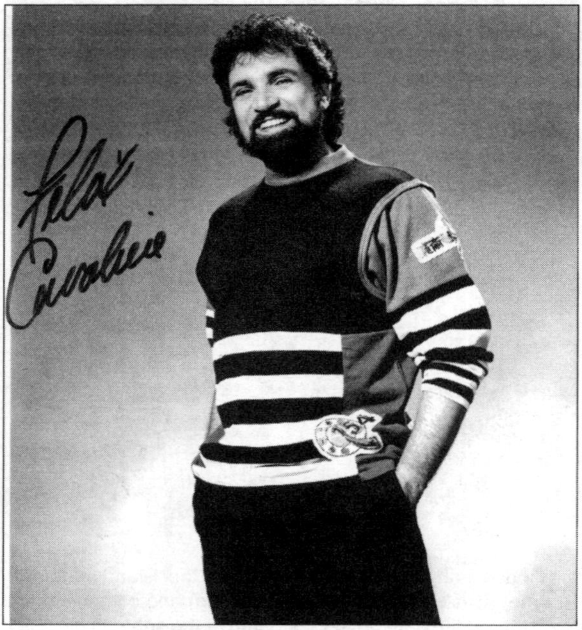

Photo courtesy of Felix Cavaliere

father wanted me to be a doctor but after a few years in school he realized I had a band but no grades." Cavaliere joined the group Joey Dee and the Starliters that also included New Yorker David Brigati. Cavaliere hired a jazz drummer from New York named Dino Danelli to play in a band in Las Vegas.

When The Beatles' song ***I Want To Hold Your Hand*** broke in the U.S., Danelli and Cavaliere were so inspired that they vowed to strike out on their own and put together a band like The Beatles. Felix returned to New York and rejoined the Starliters that now included a guitarist from Canada named Gene Cornish. Cornish had recently recorded a novelty song called ***I Wanna Be A Beatle*** released as a single by Gene Cornish & The Unbeetables.

In late 1964, Cavaliere decided to form a band with Cornish, Brigati's brother Eddie, and Danelli who was also a friend of Eddie's. The group briefly backed comedian Soupy Sales who provided them with the name The Rascals. They were a resident act at a trendy floating nightclub called The Barge in the upscale Hamptons area of Long Island, New York. Promoter Sid Bernstein became their manager after seeing them at the club. Their powerful covers and self-penned rhythm & blues also caught the attention of another club patron, Ahmet Ertegun, head of Atlantic Records who signed them up as the label's first white act.

Bernstein, who was the promoter for The Beatles' appearance at Shea Stadium on August 15, 1965, had The Rascals sit in the stadium's dugout for a special surprise. He used the occasion to flash "The Rascals Are Coming" across the stadium's scoreboard, so enraging The Beatles' manager Brian Epstein that he made Bernstein remove it!

According to Cavaliere, Bernstein feared the group could be sued because there was another group known as The Harmonica Rascals. Cavaliere said Bernstein, unbeknownst to the group and much to their dismay, legally modified their name to The Young Rascals toward the end of 1965.

Cavaliere recalled "we went absolutely bananas because the obvious inference was to The Little Rascals (a child comedy team). It stuck with us our whole career and was a big problem because it was so uncool, but the damage was done."

The Young Rascals' first single ***I Ain't Gonna Eat Out My Heart Anymore***, written by Pam Sawyer and Lori Burton*, made it into the top 60 in early 1966. Their follow-up single, ***Good Lovin'***, went to the top of the charts. Their third single, ***You Better Run***, reached the top 20 in the summer of 1966 and marked the beginning of their string of hits written by Cavaliere and Brigati. In 1967 ***Lonely Too Long***, ***A Girl Like You*** and ***How Can I Be Sure*** reached the top 10, and ***Groovin'*** (their only U.K. top 10) became their second number one. In 1968 the group managed to change their name back to The Rascals and scored a top 20 with ***It's Wonderful***, a top 10 with ***A Beautiful Morning*** and their last number one with ***People Got To Be Free***.

The Rascals were one of the acts who performed at the **Peace For Christmas** concert for UNICEF on December 15, 1969 at London's Lyceum Ballroom, which also featured a performance by John Lennon, Yoko Ono* and George Harrison. The Rascals left Atlantic for Columbia Records in 1970, but by 1971 Brigati and Cornish had left the group. Several new members were brought in, but the group broke up in 1972. Felix lamented, "unfortunately our history is not too good — it's pretty sad as a matter of fact. We had a good band. We had a record deal six months after we started the group! I did not realize that along with the talent of the group were four dominant males, but that's the way it goes."

Felix Cavaliere released a self-titled solo album produced by Todd Rundgren* in 1974 and an album titled **Destiny** the following year. In 1980, he had a top 40 with the song ***Only A Lonely Heart Sees*** from his album **Castles In The Air**. The Rascals (minus Brigati) got together for a U.S. tour in 1988. The following year Cornish and Danelli filed suit against Cavaliere over the use of The Rascals' name. In 1991 Cavaliere was part of The Peace Choir, organized by Yoko Ono and John Lennon's son Sean, who made a recording of Lennon's ***Give Peace A Chance***. Cavaliere's latest release was his 1994 album **Dreams In Motion**, produced by Don Was.

Cavaliere was a member of Ringo Starr's All-Starr Band in 1995. He wove a number of other artists' hits into his All-Starr's performances, including ***Love Train*** and ***Respect Yourself*** during ***People Got To Be Free***; ***My Girl***, ***Apples, Peaches, Punkin Pie*** and ***Just My Imagination*** during ***Groovin'***; and ***La Bamba*** during ***Good Lovin'***. Ringo played drums on all of Cavaliere's performances with the All-Starrs. According to Felix, (along with the filmed and recorded performances in Tokyo), there were plans to film and record the All-Starrs in Reno, Nevada. That show and the remainder of the tour were canceled when Ringo learned that his daughter was quite ill. Felix declares "I'm very fortunate that I'm still able to be involved in music. I've been very lucky over the years and I had a dream come true working with Ringo."

Cheech And Chong

Record 45 title:
Cheech And Chong's Greatest Hits
Media:
Album 5" CD
Label / Catalog number:
Warner Bros / 3614-2
Producer:
Lou Adler
Jacket / Inserts:
Standard international design in jewel box / 4 page CD booklet
Recording Location / Date:
A&M Studios, Los Angeles, CA, U.S.A. / 1973

Song 45a title:
Basketball Jones
Track details:
Side 1, track 4 / 4 min. 00 sec.
Release date / Country:
(first issued 20 Aug 73) / U.S.A.
Composer:
T. Chong - C. Marin

Cheech Marin: Lead Vocals; Tommy Chong: B. Vocals; George Harrison: Guitar; Carole King: Electric Piano; Nicky Hopkins: Piano; Tom Scott: Saxophone; Billy Preston: Organ; Klaus Voormann: Bass; Jim Keltner: Percussion; George Bohanon: Horns; Dick Hyde: Horns; Paul Hubinon: Horns; Jimmy Karstein: Drums; Michelle Phillips: B. Vocals; Darlene Love: B. Vocals; Fanita Jones: B. Vocals; Jean King: B. Vocals; Viva Marshall: B. Vocals & Hi

Tommy Chong was born on May 23, 1938 in Edmonton, Alberta, Canada. He is partly of Asian descent and appropriately does not remember the birth date of his Mexican / American partner, Richard "Cheech" Marin, born on July 13, 1946 in Los Angeles, California. The two met after Cheech reportedly fled to Canada to avoid being drafted during the war in Vietnam. Chong had been a guitarist with Bobby Taylor & The Vancouvers. Initially he and Cheech started out as a rock band, but they soon realized their talents lay more with comedy than music. By the early 1970s they were the kings of drug culture humor based around marijuana. Ironically, Marin's father was a cop with the LAPD for 30 years.

Tommy Chong, Detroit, MI, mid-1970s
photo courtesy of Tom Bert

While hanging around A&M Studios during the early development of his Dark Horse Record acts, Harrison was asked by Cheech and Chong to contribute guitar to their song, ***Basketball Jones***. The song was a parody of ***Love Jones*** by the group Brighter Side Of Darkness. The comic duo's spoof on the Black American male's passion for basketball probably was not fully appreciated by the English-born Harrison according to Chong. Judging from the list of musicians, it is likely that the song was recorded sometime during the recording sessions for Ringo Starr's album **Ringo**, or perhaps in the fall of 1973. ***Basketball Jones*** was originally featured on the highly successful comedy album **Los Cochinos**.

Cheech Marin, Detroit, MI, mid-1970s
photo courtesy of Tom Bert

When drug humor began to burn out in the late 1970s, Cheech and Chong turned to films, including **Up In Smoke** and a lead role in the Monty Python* spin-off film **Yellowbeard**. Cheech continued to make films after the duos' breakup in 1985. He has also been a regular on such well-known TV series' as **Golden Palace** and **Nash Bridges**. Chong continues to do stand-up comedy and is searching for a new "Cheech" partner. His daughters Rae Dawn and Robbie are successful actresses.

The Christians

Record 46 title:
Ferry Cross The Mersey
Label / Catalog number:
PWL / PWL PWCD 41
Jacket / Inserts:
Jewel box / CD insert
Recording Location / Date:
PWL Studios, London, U.K. / 20 Apr 89
Media:
Single 5" CD
Producer:
Michael Stock, Matt Aitken & Pete Waterman

Song 46a title:
Ferry Cross The Mersey
Release date / Country:
02 May 89 / U.K.
Track details:
Side 1, track 1 / 3 min. 55 sec.
Composer:
G. Marsden

Russell Christian: Vocals; Garry Christian: Vocals; Henry Priestman: Vocals; Holly Johnson: Vocals; Paul McCartney: Vocals & Guitar; Gerry Marsden: Vocals; Michael Stock: Vocals & instruments; Matt Aitken: Vocals & instruments; Pete Waterman: Vocals & instruments

On April 15, 1989, a semi-final cup football (soccer) match between Liverpool and Nottingham Forest took place in Hillsborough (Sheffield), England. Ninety-six people were killed and over 400 others had to be hospitalized after being trapped within the confines of an over crowded section of the stadium. Gerry Marsden *(see Gerry And The Pacemakers)* along with Paul McCartney, The Christians, Holly Johnson, and Stock, Aitken and Waterman recorded a remake of Marsden's ***Ferry Cross The Mersey*** and donated the proceeds to aid in the relief of the families.

The Christians are Henry Priestman and brothers Russell Christian and Garry Christian. They are a popular soul and pop vocal group from Liverpool who had a string of U.K. top 40 songs between 1987 and 1989 including ***Forgotten Town***, ***Hooverville (They Promised Us The World)***, ***Born Again***, ***Ideal World***, ***Harvest For The World*** and ***Words***. The Christians performed The Beatles' song, ***Revolution***, at **The John Lennon Scholarship Concert** in Liverpool on May 5, 1990.

Holly Johnson was a member of the Liverpool band Frankie Goes To Hollywood. Their 1983/84 hit ***Relax*** was a top 10 in the U.S. and though banned by the BBC was a number one in the U.K. Their follow-up, ***Two Tribes***, was also a number one in the U.K., as was the single and album titled **Welcome To The Pleasure Dome**. The group was never able to duplicate the success it had in 1984 and disbanded in 1987.

Michael Stock, Matt Aitken and Pete Waterman became one of the U.K.'s most successful songwriting and production teams during the 1980s. Their handiwork created such U.K. hits as ***You Spin Me Round*** by Dead Or Alive in 1984, ***Respectable*** by Mel And Kim and ***Never Gonna Give You Up*** by Rick Astley in 1987. They formed a production company and record label, PWL. (PWL is an abbreviation for Pete Waterman Limited which Waterman opted for after Paul McCartney warned that using his full name was too egotistical.) More hits followed including ***I Should Be***

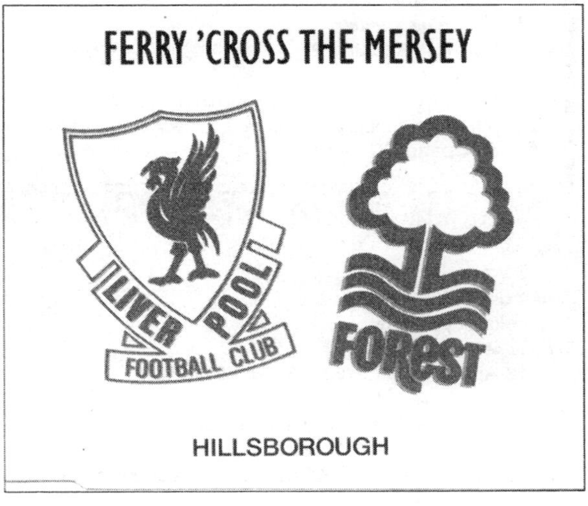

So Lucky by Kylie Minogue. By the end of the decade the team had racked up over a dozen chart topping singles in the U.K. Stock and Aitken have since parted company with Pete Waterman.

Mike Stock has said working with McCartney on the charity was one of his biggest thrills. According to Pete Waterman, McCartney not only sang on *Ferry Cross The Mersey* but played guitar on it as well and that Stock, Aitken and Waterman furnished the balance of the instrumental backing. Waterman considers the events surrounding the charity to be one of the greatest times of his life. He says he first met The Beatles right after they dropped the "Silver" from their name. He later worked at Apple for a brief period. Waterman advises anyone who wants a hit record to analyze The Beatles, then he says, "we might start hearing music again!"

John Christie

Record 47 title:
4th Of July
Label / Catalog number:
Capitol / 3928
Jacket / Inserts:
Unique Picture sleeve
Media:
Single 7"
Producer:
Dave Clark & [Mike Smith]

Song 47a title:
4th Of July
Release date / Country:
01 Jul 74 / U.S.A.
Track details:
Side 1, track 1 / 2 min. 27 sec.
Composer:
P. McCartney - L. McCartney

John Christie: Lead Vocals

The *4th Of July* was produced by Dave Clark, leader of the popular mid-1960s band The Dave Clark Five. Clark turned to music and television production following the demise of the DC5. Apparently, Clark, during sessions he produced for John Christie, requested a song from McCartney who sent him a home demo of *4th Of July*. Christie contributed to **Dave Clark's Time — The Musical**, in 1986, which also included contributions from, among others, Jimmy Helms* and Julian Lennon*.

Eric Clapton

Record 48 title:
Crossroads
Label / Catalog number:
Polydor / 835 261-2
Jacket / Inserts:
Standard international design in jewel box in box set / 32 page booklet with photos of George Harrison & Ringo Starr; songwriting & publishing insert & 4 page CD insert
Media:
Album 5" CD [4 CD set]

Song 48a title:
Badge
Producer:
Felix Pappalardi
Release date / Country:
18 Apr 88 (first issued 05 Feb 69) / U.S.A
Recording Location / Date:
IBC Studios, London, U.K. / Dec 68
Track details:
CD2, track 4 / 2 min. 45 sec.
Composer:
G. Harrison - E. Clapton - [R. Starkey]

Eric Clapton: Lead Vocals & Lead Guitar; Jack Bruce: Bass; Ginger Baker: Drums; George Harrison:

Rhythm Guitar; Felix Pappalardi: Piano & Mellotron

Song 48b title:
Roll It Over
Track details:
CD2, track 13 / 4 min. 29 sec.
Producer:
Phil Spector
Composer:
E. Clapton - B. Whitlock
Release date / Country:
18 Apr 88 (first issued 14 Sep 70) / U.S.A.
Recording Location / Date:
(probably) Apple Studios, London or (possibly) FPSHOT (Friar Park Studios, Henley-on-Thames), U.K. / (probably) 18 Jun 70

Eric Clapton: Lead Vocals & Guitar; George Harrison: Guitar & B. Vocals; Dave Mason: Guitar & B. Vocals; Bobby Whitlock: Lead Vocals & Piano; Carl Radle: Bass; Jim Gordon: Drums

Song 48c title:
Tell The Truth
Track details:
CD2, track 12 / 3 min. 23 sec.
Producer:
Phil Spector
Composer:
E. Clapton - B. Whitlock
Release date / Country:
18 Apr 88 (first issued 14 Sep 70) / U.S.A.
Recording Location / Date:
(probably) Apple or (possibly) Trident Studios, London, U.K.
/ (probably) 18 Jun 70 (possibly) 05 Aug 70

Eric Clapton: Lead Vocals & Guitar; Bobby Whitlock: Guitar; Carl Radle: Bass; Jim Gordon: Drums; George Harrison (possible) Guitar

Record 49 title:
Journeyman
Media:
Album 5" CD
Label / Catalog number:
Reprise/Duck / 9 26074-2
Producer:
Russ Titelman
Jacket / Inserts:
Standard international design in jewel box / 8 page CD booklet
Recording Location / Date:
Power Station Studios, NYC, U.S.A. / Apr 89

Song 49a title:
Run So Far
Track details:
Side 1, track 8 / 4 min. 06 sec.
Release date / Country:
07 Nov 89 / U.S.A.
Composer:
G. Harrison

Eric Clapton: Lead Vocals & Guitar; George Harrison: Guitar & Harmony Vocals; Rob Mounsey: Synthesizer; Robbie Kondor: Synthesizer Programming; Greg Phillinganes: Synthesizer; Alan Clark: Synthesizer; Darryl Jones: Bass; Jim Keltner: Drums & Drum Programming; Jimmy Bralower: Drum Programming; Carol Steele: Percussion

Record 50 title:
Nobody's Child - Romanian Angel Appeal (Various Artists)
Media:
Album 5" CD
Label / Catalog number:
Warner Bros / 9 26280-2
Producer:
Russ Titelman
Jacket / Inserts:
Standard international design in jewel box / 16 page CD booklet
Recording Location / Date:
Power Station Studios, New York, NY, U.S.A. / Apr-May 89

Song 50a title:
That Kind Of Woman
Track details:
Side 1, track 10 / 3 min. 56 sec.
Release date / Country:
24 Jul 90 / U.S.A.
Composer:
G. Harrison

Eric Clapton: Lead Vocals & Guitar; George Harrison: Guitar & B. Vocals; Nathan East: Bass; Rob Mounsey: Keyboards; Robbie Kondor: Keyboards; Jim Keltner: Drums

Record 51 title:
Songs I Forgot
Media:
Album 5" CD (mono)
Label / Catalog number:
Planet Records / U.S. Audio 1005 [Unauthorized record]
Producer:
Danish Television
Jacket / Inserts:
Unique / 1 page CD insert
Recording Location / Date:
On location at Falkoner Theatre, Copenhagen, Denmark / 12 Dec 69

Song 51a title:
Don't Know Why [live]
Track details:
Side 1, track 10 / 5 min. 14 sec.
Release date / Country:
1995 / Japan
Composer:
D. Bramlett - E. Clapton

Eric Clapton: Lead Vocals & Lead Guitar; Delaney Bramlett: Rhythm Guitar; Bonnie Bramlett: Vocals & Tambourine; Billy Preston: Keyboards; Carl Radle: Bass; Jim Gordon: Drums; Bobby Whitlock: Organ & B. Vocals; Jim Price: Trumpet & Trombone; Bobby Keys: Saxophone; Tex Johnson: Congas & Bongo Drums; Rita Coolidge: B. Vocals; George Harrison: Guitar

Eric Patrick Clapton was born on March 30, 1945 in Ripley, Surrey, England. His mother Patricia Clapton was in her mid-teens when she gave birth to him. His father, Edward Fryer, was a Canadian soldier stationed in England during the war. Eric was raised by his grandparents, Rose and Jack Clapp. Rose's first husband, and Patricia's father, was named Reginald Clapton.

Eric Clapton's career in rock and blues began in 1963 with a band called The Roosters, which included Brian Jones, later of The Rolling Stones*, Paul Jones* and Tom McGuinness of Manfred Mann. Clapton went on to briefly join Casey Jones and The Engineers before settling on the blues oriented Yardbirds. He left The Yardbirds a year later when the band took a successful turn towards what would become the foundations of hard rock and heavy metal pioneered by future Yardbird and Led Zeppelin member, Jimmy Page. Seeking a band to serve his blues apprenticeship, he joined John Mayall's Bluesbreakers in 1965. Among the many sit-in members of the Bluesbreakers were drummer Ginger Baker and bass player Jack Bruce* (also briefly with Manfred Mann).

In 1967 Clapton, Baker and Bruce formed the highly successful psychedelic blues band Cream which, ironically, also laid the foundations for the heavy metal sound. Cream broke up amid constant tension between Bruce and Baker. (The band performed for the first and only time since their breakup during their induction into the Rock and Roll Hall of Fame in 1993.)

Clapton and Baker joined forces with Rick Grech on bass and Steve Winwood on keyboards to form yet another "supergroup," Blind Faith*, in 1969. But it was to be even shorter-lived than Cream. Clapton, tired of being the front man in the limelight, looked for a band with which to play sideman. He found it in the southern U.S. gospel-rock Delaney & Bonnie & Friends*. In 1970, Clapton formed what would prove to be his last group, Derek And The Dominos. Thereafter he billed himself as a solo act.

Eric Clapton's relationship with The Beatles is a very long and winding one. A popular graffiti in London during the mid-1960s was the slogan "Clapton is God." George Harrison, a deeply religious man, must have believed it for the two have been the closest of friends ever since, despite Harrison's first wife, Pattie Boyd, leaving him to marry Clapton. Their musical association officially began in December 1964 when the Yardbirds opened for **Another Beatles Christmas Show**, a three-week engagement at London's Hammersmith Odeon Theatre. Clapton was one of the many rock-star elite present during The Beatles' live telecast, via satellite, performance of ***All You Need Is Love*** for the BBC's program **Our World**, on June 25, 1967. In December 1967, Harrison recruited Clapton to play on his first solo album, the soundtrack to the film **Wonderwall**. Between 1968 and 1970, Eric was helping Harrison on the recordings for Apple Records artists Jackie Lomax, Doris Troy and Billy Preston.

On September 6, 1968, Clapton contributed his famous guitar work on Harrison's ***While My Guitar Gently Weeps*** from **The Beatles** (the white album). He supposedly also played on ***Not Guilty*** also from **The Beatles** album sessions — though none of the versions that have surfaced seem to feature Clapton. Harrison recorded a version for his 1979 album **George Harrison**. The Beatles' version of ***Not Guilty*** was officially released on their album **Anthology 3** in 1996. George also wrote the song ***Savoy Truffle*** about Eric Clapton's love for chocolate and the dental problems it caused him, based on Mackintosh's Good News Chocolates. On December 11, 1968, Clapton, along with Mitch Mitchell of Jimi Hendrix Experience, Keith Richards of The Rolling Stones and John Lennon, performed ***Yer Blues*** for The Rolling Stones' film **Rock And Roll Circus**.

It was soon after the recordings for **The Beatles** that Harrison and Clapton began their first real collaboration with the song ***Badge***. Harrison had written a set of lyrics with a little help from Ringo and had presented the idea to Clapton for inclusion on what was planned to be Cream's last album, **Goodbye**. At the time of presentation to Clapton, the song was untitled; and above some of the lyrics Harrison had handwritten the musical term "Bridge." Clapton thought it said "Badge." Both found the misinterpretation amusing, so the song was duly titled. As often happened at the time, due to contractual restraints, Harrison's rhythm guitar contribution was credited to L'Angelo Misterioso. Harrison used this alias on several occasions during this period *(see Jack Bruce, Jesse Ed Davis)*. Harrison lists ***Badge*** as one of his top 10 favorite songs. In the spring of 1969, Harrison was inspired by a break in the often gray British weather to write ***Here Comes The Sun*** in Clapton's backyard.

On September 13, 1969, Clapton was recruited by John Lennon at the last minute as a member of Lennon's makeshift Plastic Ono Band for a performance at a **Toronto's Rock 'n' Roll Revival**. The result was **The Plastic Ono**

Band - Live Peace In Toronto 1969 album. Clapton also played on the studio recording for Lennon's *Cold Turkey* single. (Lennon had offered the song to The Beatles as the follow-up single to *Something / Come Together*, but was turned down due to the timing and controversial lyrics.)

In the fall of 1969, George joined the Delaney & Bonnie & Friends tour of England and Scandinavia featuring Eric Clapton. Delaney & Bonnie had been the opening act for Blind Faith on their U.S. tour. An album, **Delaney & Bonnie & Friends - On Tour With Eric Clapton**, was released. There have also been several bootlegs of the performances at the Falkoner Theatre in Copenhagen, Denmark that include the Clapton and Delaney Bramlett composition *Don't Know Why*, featuring Clapton on lead vocals. When Delaney & Bonnie & Friends returned to England after the tour, they backed up John Lennon and Yoko Ono* at The Lyceum in London for a UNICEF **Peace For Christmas** benefit concert, later featured on the John and Yoko album **Sometime in New York City**.

Following the breakup of The Beatles in the spring of 1970, Clapton assisted George Harrison on his first bona fide post-Beatles solo album **All Things Must Pass**. At the time Clapton was forming his first real band, Derek And The Dominos, as front man out of the remnants of the Delaney & Bonnie & Friends touring band. The Dominos included Carl Radle, Jim Gordon, Bobby Whitlock* and later Duane Allman of the Allman Brothers Band. Though highly acclaimed, the band would be short-lived and released only one studio album titled *Layla And Other Assorted Love Songs*. The title song *Layla* was a thinly veiled reference to the portrait of the woman on the album's front jacket and the object of Clapton's affections, George's wife, Pattie Boyd Harrison.

Derek And The Dominos' first single *Tell The Truth / Roll It Over* was produced by Phil Spector*. The recordings were really an outgrowth of sessions held between June and August 1970 for the **All Things Must Pass** album. The single was quickly withdrawn at the band's request because they preferred their newly recorded version produced by Tom Dowd. (Had anyone at Atlantic Records listened closely to the sexually suggestive lyrics of *Roll It Over* they probably would never have released it.) Several reliable publications, including Marc Roberty's book **Eric Clapton: The Complete Recording Sessions 1963 - 1992**, credit Harrison as playing guitar on the single version of *Tell The Truth* and *Roll It Over*. The 1988 retrospective box set **Crossroads** does not credit Harrison on *Tell The Truth*, but it does credit him on *Roll It Over*. There was no attempt to hide any of Harrison's contributions on **Crossroads**. His full permission was given, and his previous aliases were replaced with his real name in the credits. It seems unlikely, given the overall completeness of the credits of **Crossroads**, that there would be any reason to omit Harrison's contribution if there was one.

There is even more confusion concerning the studios used and dates the songs were recorded. Credits in **Crossroads** list *Roll It Over* as being recorded at Harrison's home studio and gives the date only as summer 1970 during sessions for the **All Things Must Pass**. **Crossroads'** credits list *Tell The Truth* as being recorded at Trident Studios on August 5, 1970. Roberty's book lists both songs being recorded on June 18, 1970, at Apple Studios, London. Previous reliable accounts list both songs as being recorded in June. It is unlikely that Harrison had a fully operational studio in his recently acquired home. No other known recordings were made at Harrison's studio at such an early date. **Crossroads** lists *Roll It Over* as being mixed at Trident Studios on August 5, 1970, the same day *Tell The Truth* was recorded, so perhaps this is where the confusion over their origin began.

Bobby Whitlock is quite sure that *Tell The Truth* and *Roll It Over* were recorded at EMI's Abbey Road Studios and that George did not contribute to either song. However, he does remember going up to Harrison's home to do some recording during this period. **Crossroads** also lists Dave Mason* as playing guitar and singing on *Roll It Over*. Whitlock is also certain that Dave Mason was not around when *Tell The Truth* and *Roll It Over* were recorded. (Mason is credited as playing guitar on **All Things Must Pass**.) Whitlock correctly points out that only he and Clapton played guitar and sang lead vocals on both songs. If Whitlock is mistaken, then it would seem more likely that the two songs were recorded at different times, and possibly at different studios. Whitlock also revealed that the George O'Hara-Smith Singers credited on the album **All Things Must Pass** was actually him, Clapton and Harrison. Some sources have stated that it was just Harrison multi-tracked, while others include Phil Spector as one of the O'Hara-Smith Singers. Given the circumstances, Harrison almost certainly contributed to *Roll It Over* and he cannot be totally ruled out as contributing to *Tell The Truth*.

Bonnie Bramlett, Delaney Bramlett & Eric Clapton, Scandinavia, 1969, photo courtesy of Delaney Bramlett

Eric's next musical project with George Harrison was **The Concert For Bangla Desh** on August 1, 1971 at New York's Madison Square Garden. Unfortunately, Clapton's personal problems began to seriously interfere with his career and relationship with Harrison over the next few years. The credits for the song ***Bye Bye Love*** on Harrison's 1974 album **Dark Horse** list "Rhythm Ace and Pattie + Eric Clapton." The credits also contain a religious message to Clapton and a hello to George's future wife, Olivia "Ohliv'ere" Arias. The album notes that Eric Clapton appears through the courtesy of RSO Records. Marc Roberty states emphatically in the preface of his book **Eric Clapton The Complete Recording Sessions 1963 - 1992** that Clapton did not contribute to any songs on George Harrison's **Dark Horse** album. Given the bitterness and reference to Eric and Pattie's romantic involvement in the amended lyrics of this Everly Brothers* hit, it is unlikely that the musical credit to Clapton was anything more than symbolic. There are a number of other unsubstantiated claims of Harrison and Clapton collaborations. Clapton's 1976 album **No Reason To Cry** thanks "Geoffrey Harrison," leading some to speculate that this is actually George Harrison and that he may have contributed to the album — though there is absolutely no evidence to indicate that he did.

Clapton contributed ***This Be Called A Song***, on which he plays guitar, to Ringo's 1976 album **Rotogravure**. Clapton made another composing and guitar contribution to Ringo's 1983 album **Old Wave** that saw only limited release at the time. (Clapton was also reported to have been involved in Ringo's aborted Chips Moman album sessions recorded in Memphis in 1987.)

Harrison, along with Elton John*, joined Clapton during his performance of ***Further On Up The Road*** at the Civic Hall, Guildford, U.K. on December 7, 1978. The appearance was featured in the film **Eric Clapton And His Rolling Hotel** released in 1980. The song is also available on a number of bootleg records. Clapton's next officially credited work with Harrison was on ***Love Comes To Everyone*** from the 1979 album **George Harrison**. Harrison referred to "slowhand" (Clapton's nick-name) in his 1982 song ***Mystical One***.

In May 1979, Eric Clapton almost pulled off the impossible when he was able to bring together Ringo, George and Paul McCartney at his post-wedding reception (to Pattie, Harrison's ex-wife), which included a musical jam.

Clapton's association with The Beatles went into high gear beginning with the 1985 Carl Perkins'* TV Special **Blue Suede Shoes (A Rockabilly Session with Carl Perkins and Friends Starring George Harrison, Ringo Starr, Eric Clapton, Rosanne Cash & Dave Edmunds)**. The event inspired the semi-retired musician and film executive Harrison to actively return to recording and performing.

In 1986, Paul McCartney joined Clapton, Tina Turner *(see Ike & Tina Turner)* and Elton John, among others, in **The Prince's Trust All-Star Rock Concert**. In 1987, Harrison performed at the **Prince's Trust Rock Concert** accompanied by both Clapton and Starr. This re-emergence by Harrison led to one of his most successful albums, **Cloud Nine**, in 1987, again featuring the talents of Clapton and Starr.

In 1989 Harrison donated his composing and musical talent to Clapton's superstar album **Journeyman**, produced by Russ Titleman who also helped produce the album **George Harrison**. Two Harrison compositions were recorded, ***Run So Far*** and ***That Kind Of Woman***, although the latter was rejected by Clapton for **Journeyman**. Harrison then offered the song to Gary Moore* by whom it was first released. Like the Clapton version, it featured Harrison on guitar. Clapton's version was finally released on the Romanian children's charity album **Nobody's Child**. Harrison initially offered ***Cheer Down*** to Clapton for **Journeyman**, but it too was bypassed. Harrison's version was featured in the soundtrack of the movie **Lethal Weapon 2**, which also featured the music of Eric Clapton.

Harrison has appeared backstage at Clapton performances on numerous occasions, and on May 1, 1990, he joined Eric onstage at the Los Angeles Forum playing guitar on ***Crossroads*** and ***Sunshine Of Your Love***. Clapton's marriage to Pattie unofficially ended in 1986 when Eric fathered Conor Clapton by Lory Del Santo. Conor died tragically, falling from his mother's apartment window in New York City in 1991. Clapton and Harrison also toured Japan together in December 1991. Harrison was backed by Clapton and his band resulting in the George Harrison album **Live In Japan**. Harrison did not appear on stage during Clapton's set. Clapton backed McCartney on several songs during their performance at the **Music For Montserrat** benefit concert organized by George Martin*, held on September 15, 1997 at London's Royal Albert Hall. Eric Clapton, who has been no stranger to the excesses of rock's life-style, has lived the blues, paid his dues and survived to become one of music's living legends.

John Cleese / Bill Oddie / Ringo Starr

Record 52 title:
The Anti-Heroin Project
It's A Live-In World (Various Artists)

Media:
Albums 12" [2 LP set]

Label / Catalog number:
EMI / AHP LP 1 11/12

Producer:
Charlie Foskett & [Bill Oddie]

Jacket / Inserts:
Unique with gatefold / Record label inner sleeve

Recording Location / Date:
Startling Studios, Ascot, U.K. / Aug 86

Song 52a title:
Naughty Atom Bomb

Track details:
LP2, Side 1, track 2 / 3 min. 00 sec.

Release date / Country:
24 Nov 86 / U.K.

Composer:
K. Craddock - C. Gibson

Bill Oddie: Lead Vocals; Ringo Starr: Drums & B. Vocals; Michael Palin: B. Vocals; John Cleese: Voice

Though Ringo Starr is credited for performing on the song ***Naughty Atom Bomb*** along with John Cleese *(see Monty Python)* and Bill Oddie of The Goodies, the lead vocals are predominately by Oddie. The song was recorded as a contribution to the Anti-Heroin Phoenix House charity album **It's A Live-In World**. The album does not list any detailed credits for the song, but it was reported to have been recorded in August 1986 at Startling Studios located in Ringo's home at the time. The song also includes Michael Palin of Python fame. In a 1990 interview, Cleese seemed to have no recollection of Ringo's involvement in the recording and thought that Bill Oddie had written and produced the track. Others involved recall that there were two sessions and that Ringo's contributions ended up on the final mix. Cleese is probably right about Oddie being involved in the production, as Charlie Foskett is credited primarily as executive producer on the album. The album also includes an anti-heroin message by Starr called ***You Know It Makes Sense***, a contribution by Ringo's son Zak and McCartney's cousin Kate Robbins* to the title track, and the song ***Simple As That*** by Paul McCartney.

Clarence Clemons

Record 53 title:
Ringo Starr And His All-Starr Band
Label / Catalog number:
Pioneer Artists / PA-090-007
Media:
Album 12" LVD
Producer:
Tim Snow (film);
Joe Walsh & Jim Nipar (music)
Jacket / Inserts:
Standard international design / Record label inner sleeve
Recording Location / Date:
On location at Greek Theatre, Los Angeles, CA, U.S.A. / 03 Sep 89

Song 53a title:
Quarter To Three [live]
Release date / Country:
Jul 90 / U.S.A.
Track details:
Side 2, track (17) 5/ 3 min. 50 sec.
Composer:
F. Guida - J. Royster - G. Anderson - E. Barge

Clarence Clemons: Lead Vocals & Saxophone; Billy Preston: Keyboards & B. Vocals; Jim Keltner: Drums; Ringo Starr: Drums; Levon Helm: Drums; Nils Lofgren: Guitar & B. Vocals; Joe Walsh: Guitar & B. Vocals; Rick Danko: Bass & B. Vocals; Dr. John: Keyboards & B. Vocals This song is also included on Rykodisc / RCD 10190 & RCD5-1019 / Albums 5" [2 CD set] / released 12 Oct 90 / Side 1, track 8 / Unique Jewel box in box set / 6 page CD booklet, sticker postcard & Rykodisc info. post-card & CD insert.

Song 53b title:
You're A Friend Of Mine [live]
Release date / Country:
Jul 90 / U.S.A.
Track details:
Side 1, track 9 / 5 min. 43 sec.
Composer:
N. Walden - J. Cohen - C. Clemons

Clarence Clemons: Lead Vocals & Saxophone; Billy Preston: Keyboards & B. Vocals; Jim Keltner: Drums; Ringo Starr: Drums; Levon Helm: Drums; Nils Lofgren: Guitar; Joe Walsh: Guitar; Rick Danko: Bass; Dr. John: Keyboards

Clarence Clemons is known affectionately as "The Big Man" because of his size and the sound he makes on his saxophone. He was born on January 11, 1942 in Norfolk, Virginia and attended Maryland State College on football and music scholarships. He played semi-pro football with the Newark Bears and the Jersey Generals before injuries sustained in a car accident forced him to fall back on music as a career.

In 1971, he began working with Bruce Springsteen* and has been a member of his E Street Band since its formation in the mid-1970s. He has also pursued a solo career with several successful albums and has worked as a back-up and session musician for countless contemporaries, including Aretha Franklin*, Alvin Lee*, Roy Orbison* and The Grateful Dead. His song ***You're A Friend Of Mine*** that he recorded with Jackson Browne, reached the top 20 in 1986. Clarence has had several bands of his own including Red Bank Rockers, Clarence Clemons and Aja, and Clarence Clemons & The Blues Crew.

In 1989, he went on tour as a member of Ringo Starr's All-Starr Band performing ***You're A Friend Of Mind*** and ***Quarter To Three*** with Ringo backing him on drums. Clemons now divides his time between music, acting and script writing. He has appeared in the films **Fatal Instinct** and **Bill And Ted's Excellent Adventure** and has a recurring role in the CBS-TV series **Nash Bridges**.

Clarence Clemons, photo courtesy of Pat Henry

Joe Cocker

Record 54 title:
Joe Cocker!
Label / Catalog number:
A&M / CD 4224
Jacket / Inserts:
Standard international design in jewel box / 4 page CD booklet
Recording Location / Date:
Sunset Sound &/or A&M Studios, Los Angeles, CA, U.S.A. / Spring 1969
Media:
Album 5" CD
Producer:
Denny Cordell & Leon Russell

Song 54a title:
Something
Release date / Country:
1986 (first issued Nov 69) / U.S.A.
Track details:
Side 1, track 7 / 3 min. 32 sec.
Composer:
G. Harrison

Joe Cocker: Lead Vocals; one or more of the following: Chris Stainton: Piano, Organ & Guitar; Alan Spenner: Bass; Bruce Rowlands: Drums; Henry McCullough: Guitar; Leon Russell: Piano, Organ & Guitar; Milt Holland: Percussion; Sneeky Pete: Guitar; Clarence White: Guitar; Paul Humphries: Drums; Merry Clayton: B. Vocals; Bonnie Bramlett: B. Vocals; Rita Coolidge: B. Vocals; Patrice Holloway: B. Vocals; Shirley Mathews: B. Vocals; George Harrison (supposed) Guitar

Joe Cocker was born John Cocker on May 20, 1944 in Sheffield, England. Cocker, a former gas fitter, has long been an admirer of The Beatles. As a struggling young musician, he did a cover version of The Beatles' ***I'll Cry Instead***, issued under the name Vance Arnold & The Avengers in 1964.

In 1968, Cocker teamed up with Chris Stainton and Henry McCullough forming what would become The Grease Band. He released yet another Beatles cover, ***With A Little Help From My Friends***, with guests Steve Winwood *(see Blind Faith)*, Albert Lee and Jimmy Page. The song topped the charts in the U.K. Lennon and McCartney were so impressed that they took out a congratulatory ad in Britain's New Musical Express. His performance of the song at the **Woodstock Music And Art Fair** in 1969 made him an international star. His popularity at the time was due, in part, to his near-spastic contortions and flailing arms during his performances.

According to Joe Cocker, Harrison and McCartney invited him to pick a recording from what would eventually become The Beatles' album **Abbey Road**. His first choice was reportedly ***Oh Darling***, (Cocker claims that it was ***Golden Slumbers***) a song certainly suited to Cocker's vocal style, but McCartney apparently vetoed his choice and urged Cocker to record ***She Came In Through The Bathroom Window***. Cocker said Harrison and McCartney helped him record rough reference demos of ***Something*** and ***She Came In Through The Bathroom Window*** at Apple Studios. Numerous photos of Harrison in Apple Studios playing guitar and piano and singing to Cocker have appeared in The Beatles Book monthly magazine over the years. Judging from Harrison's appearance and the first date of publication of the photos, the sessions probably took place in April of 1969. It is uncertain whether Cocker sang to Harrison's backing demo or if it still exists on tape. Mark Lewisohn, a noted authority on The Beatles, stated in his book **The Beatles Recording Sessions** that Harrison played guitar on Cocker's version of ***Something***. However, Cocker says he took the tapes back to Los Angeles and completely re-recorded both songs for his album **Joe Cocker!**. Glyn Johns, who was one of the recording engineers for **Joe Cocker!**, also recalls the songs being re-recorded in Los Angeles. This rules out any musical involvement by Harrison, or McCartney for that matter, on any of Cocker's released recordings. ***She Came In Through The Bathroom Window*** became a top 30 for Cocker. The Beatles had second thoughts and wisely decided to release George Harrison's version of ***Something*** as his first A-side single with The Beatles before Cocker's release.

In early 1971 it was reported in Britain's Disc magazine that George Harrison and Leon Russell sat in on a Joe Cocker session, but this is discounted by Cocker. In June 1971, Melody Maker magazine reported that Ringo contributed to some sessions with Cocker, Steve Winwood and Chris Stainton at Island Studios. According to Cocker, Ringo merely stopped in to visit and jammed with the band during the sessions. Cocker doubts if any tapes, if they were made, still exist and that nothing with Ringo was ever released.

Cocker's career has been filled with many highs and lows along with numerous personnel changes. Grease Band member Henry McCullough joined Paul McCartney's first incarnation of Wings in 1972. Cocker has had the uncanny ability to make unusual song choices, adapt them to his unique vocal style, and turn them into hits like ***The Letter*** and ***Cry Me A River***. His biggest hit came in 1974 with a cover of Billy Preston's ***You Are So Beautiful***. Most of his recent success has been with songs featured in popular films. ***Up Where We Belong***, a duet with Jennifer Warnes from the film **An Officer And A Gentlemen**, was a major international hit in 1982. ***When The Night Comes*** from the film **An Innocent Man** was a chart success in 1990.

Cocker performed ***Come Together*** and ***Isolation*** at **The John Lennon**

Joe Cocker, Detroit, MI, early 1970s, photo courtesy of Tom Bert

Scholarship Concert held on May 5, 1990 in Liverpool. ***Isolation*** was included on the 1991 laser video disk **The World's Greatest Artists Sing LENNON A Tribute**. Following the performance, he embarked on a tour with a backing band that included former Wings' drummer Steve Holly, and released an album that included a cover of The Beatles' song ***You've Got To Hide Your Love Away***. Cocker was the opening act for some of Ringo Starr's All-Starr Band performances in Europe in 1992.

Alma Cogan

Record 55 title:
A Celebration
Media:
Album 12" [2 LP set]
Label / Catalog number:
EMI / EM 1280
Producer:
(possibly) John Lennon & Paul McCartney
Jacket / Inserts:
Unique with gatefold with photo of The Beatles
Recording Location / Date:
(probably) EMI-Abbey Road Studios, London, U.K. / 04 Oct 65

Song 55a title:
Eight Days A Week
Track details:
3 min. 50 sec.
Release date / Country:
02 Nov 87 (first issued 26 Nov 65) / U.K.
Composer:
J. Lennon - P. McCartney

Alma Cogan: Lead Vocals; Stan Foster: Conductor & Arrangement; Paul McCartney: (possible) Arrangement assistance; John Lennon: (possible) Arrangement assistance

Record 56 title:
It's You / I Knew Right Away
Media:
Single 7" (mono)
Label / Catalog number:
Columbia (EMI) / DB 7390
Producer:
(probably) Norman Newell
Jacket / Inserts:
Record label sleeve
Recording Location / Date:
EMI-Abbey Road Studios, London, U.K. / 1964

Song 56a title:
I Knew Right Away
Track details:
Side 1, track 1 / 2 min. 00 sec.
Release date / Country:
30 Oct 64 / U.K.
Composer:
A. Cogan - S. Foster

Alma Cogan: Lead Vocals; Paul McCartney: (possible) Tambourine

Alma Cogan was born on May 19, 1932 in London, England. She was one of Britain's most popular and flamboyant female singers from the early 1950s through the mid-1960s. She was known as "the girl with the laugh in her voice." The Beatles grew up listening to Cogan's hits like ***Bell Bottom Blues***, ***Sugartime*** and ***Dreamboat***. The Beatles first met Alma Cogan on January 12, 1964, during rehearsals for the TV show **Sunday Night At The London Palladium**. They hit it off immediately and became frequent guests at her family home. She became very close friends of Brian Epstein and John Lennon who nicknamed her Sara Sequin. She also crossed paths with The Beatles at EMI's Abbey Road Studios.

It was not surprising that Paul McCartney would be rumored to be involved in Cogan's recordings. Numerous reliable publications have listed McCartney as playing tambourine on the B-side of the October 1964 Cogan single ***I Knew Right Away***. Noted Beatles researchers Harry Castleman and

Walter Podrazik first cataloged McCartney's involvement in their book **All Together Now**. Castleman and Podrazik later located a copy of the single. When they detected no tambourine they did some further investigation and concluded in their book **The End Of The Beatles?** that McCartney "had nothing to do with that single." Another Beatles researcher, Arno Guzek, did some further checking with EMI, who confirmed that McCartney had no involvement in the recording. However, Brian Southall (a publicity executive for EMI Records, U.K.) clearly states in his book **Abbey Road** that McCartney played tambourine on *I Knew Right Away*. In Mark Lewisohn's 1987 book **25 Years In The Life** McCartney is listed as playing tambourine on the A-side of the single, *It's You*. McCartney's Club Sandwich fan magazine denies his involvement in its spring 1988 issue, apparently based on previous dismissals. Perhaps all of these sources are quoting each other's misinformation. However, it certainly sounds as if there is a tambourine buried in the mix at the beginning of *I Knew Right Away*, though it does not sound like there is any tambourine on *It's You*.

Lennon and McCartney most certainly did attend Cogan's recording session for her cover of *Eight Day's A Week* in October 1965. It is doubtful that John or Paul contributed musically to the number that starts off as a tender love song with full orchestration and ends as a big band jazz number. However, it is possible that they gave their advice on how the song should be arranged and produced. The single's B-side was a cover of The Beatles' current hit single *Help!*. When the single was released it had the sub-title *The Beatles Help Alma For Christmas*, fueling speculation that they may have lent a hand with the recording. Alma also recorded covers of *Yesterday*, *Ticket To Ride* and *I Feel Fine*. Cogan died in October 26, 1966, after a battle with cancer. McCartney contributed brief liner notes to the 1987 Cogan retrospective album **A Celebration** that also featured a photo of Alma with The Beatles.

Billy Connolly / Chris Tummings & The Singing Rebels Band

Record 57 title:
Filmtracks - The Best Of British Film Music

Media:
Album 5" CD [2 CD set]

Label / Catalog number:
London Filmtrax / MCPS 820 252-2 (820254-2)

Producer:
Mike Moran

Jacket / Inserts:
Unique / 8 page CD booklet

Recording Location / Date:
FPSHOT (Friar Park Studios, Henley-on-Thames) / 1984

Song 57a title:
Freedom

Track details:
CD2, track 10 / 4 min. 37 sec.

Release date / Country:
Jul 85 (first issued 31 May 85) / Germany

Composer:
E. Clapton - I. La Frenais

Billy Connolly: Lead Vocals & Guitar; George Harrison: Guitar & B. Vocals; Eric Clapton: Guitar; Ringo Starr: Drums; Christopher Tummings: Keyboards & B. Vocals; Chris Stainton: Bass; Ray Cooper: Drums; Mike Moran: Keyboards; Jon Lord: Keyboards; Jenny Bogle: B. Vocals; Anastasia Rodriquez: B. Vocals

Billy Connolly was born on November 24, 1942 in Glasgow, Scotland. He was a member of the late '60s group Humblebums early on in his career. He later had a number one in the U.K. with a parody cover of Tammy Wynette's song *D.I.V.O.R.C.E.* He introduced Paul McCartney's Rockestra at the **Concerts For The People Of Kampuchea** at London's Hammersmith Odeon in December 1979. Connolly has since become a successful character actor and comedian in the U.K. and U.S. Connolly recorded a cover of *Being For The Benefit Of Mr. Kite* produced by George Martin* that was released in 1998.

Connolly was given a co-starring role in HandMade Films' **Water**. The film also starred Michael

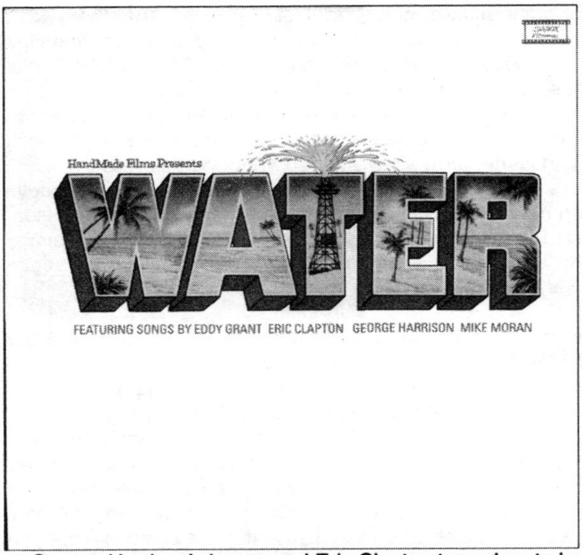

Caine, Valerie Perrine, Brenda Vaccaro and Leonard Rossiter. Billy suspects he got the part because "They couldn't imagine anyone else crazy enough to do it and because I had a musical background." The film is a comedy about colonialism, revolution and exploitation and is set in the fictitious Caribbean island of Cascara (actually St. Lucia).

George Harrison was the executive producer of **Water**. He also contributed to the film's music and made a cameo appearance in the performance of the song ***Freedom*** with Ringo, Eric Clapton and co-star Billy Connolly, as members of The Singing Rebels Band *(see Chris Tummings & The Singing Rebels Band, Jimmy Helms)*. Connolly recounts, "The song was recorded at George Harrison's house and Eric Clapton turned up to hear us record and ended up playing on the recording." The U.K. vinyl album soundtrack of **Water** (London Filmtrax / YEAR 2 820 263-1) and the single released from it (Audiotrax / ATX 10) contain slightly different photos of George and Ringo from their cameo performance of ***Freedom***. The film premiered on January 18, 1985, and was issued on VHS in 1987.

Elvis Costello

Record 58 title:
All This Useless Beauty
Media:
Album 5" CD
Label / Catalog number:
Warner Bros / 9 46198-2
Producer:
Geoff Emerick & Elvis Costello
Jacket / Inserts:
Standard international design in jewel box / 10 page CD booklet
Recording Location / Date:
Windmill Lane Recording, Dublin, Ireland &/or Westside Studio, London, U.K. / (probably) 1995 or 1996

Song 58a title:
Shallow Grave
Track details:
Side 1, track 7 / 2 min. 01 sec.
Release date / Country:
14 May 96 / U.S.A.
Composer:
P. McCartney - D. Mac Manus

Elvis Costello: Lead Vocals, Guitars & Bass; Bruce Thomas: Bass; Steve Nieve: Keyboards; Pete Thomas: Drums

Record 59 title: Mighty Like A Rose
Media: Album 5" CD
Label / Catalog number: Warner Bros / 9 26575-2
Producer: Mitchell Froom, Kevin Killen & D.P.A. Mac Manus
Jacket / Inserts: Standard international design in jewel box / 12 page CD booklet
Recording Location / Date: Ocean Way Studio, Los Angeles, CA, U.S.A. & (possibly) Westside Studio, London, U.K. / (probably) Sep - Oct 90

Song 59a title: Playboy To A Man
Track details: Side 1, track 11 / 3 min. 17 sec.
Release date / Country: 14 May 91 / U.S.A.
Composer: P. McCartney - D. Mac Manus

Elvis Costello: Lead Vocals, Guitar & Organ; Marc Ribot: Guitar; Jerry Scheff: Bass; Jim Keltner: Drums; Larry Knechtel: Piano; Mitchell Froom: Piano & Organ; Benmont Tench: Piano

Song 59b title: So Like Candy
Track details: Side 1, track 9 / 4 min. 36 sec.
Release date / Country: 14 May 91 / U.S.A.
Composer: P. McCartney - D. Mac Manus

Elvis Costello: Lead Vocals & Guitars; Marc Ribot: Guitars; Jerry Scheff: Bass; Jim Keltner: Drums; Larry Knechtel: Piano; Mitchell Froom: Mellotron, Chamberlain & Celeste; T. Bone Wolk: Bass

Record 60 title: Spike
Media: Album 5" CD
Label / Catalog number: Warner Bros / 9 25848-2
Producer: Elvis Costello, Kevin Killen & T-Bone Burnett
Jacket / Inserts: Standard international design in jewel box / 16 page CD booklet
Recording Location / Date: One or more of the following studios: Ocean Way, Los Angeles, CA, Southlake, New Orleans, Los Angeles, U.S.A; Windmill Land, Dublin, Ireland &/or Air, London, U.K. / 1987 or 1988

Song 60a title: Pads, Paws and Claws
Track details: Side 1, track 10 / 2 min. 54 sec.
Release date / Country: 07 Feb 89 / U.S.A.
Composer: P. McCartney - D. Mac Manus

Elvis Costello: Lead Vocals, Guitars, Piano & Bass; Marc Ribot: Guitars; Jerry Marotta: Drums; Michael Blair: Marimba and Martian-Dog Bark; Jerry Scheff: Bass; T-Bone Burnett: Bass

Song 60b title: This Town
Track details: Side 1, track 1 / 4 min. 26 sec.
Release date / Country: 07 Feb 89 / U.S.A.
Composer: D. Mac Manus

Elvis Costello: Lead Vocals, Guitars, Piano, Organ, Tambourine & Melodica; Paul McCartney: Bass & B. Vocals; T-Bone Burnett: Guitars; Ralph Forbes: Electric Drums; Jim Keltner: Snare Drums; Michael Blair: Glockenspiel & Bells; Cait O' Riordan: Maracas; Roger McGuinn: 12 String Electric Guitar

Song 60c title:
Veronica
Release date / Country:
07 Feb 89 / U.S.A

Track details:
Side 1, track 4 / 3 min. 10 sec.
Composer:
P. McCartney - D. Mac Manus

Elvis Costello: Lead Vocals & Guitar; Paul McCartney: Bass; T-Bone Burnett: Guitar; Jerry Marotta:

Drums; Michael Blair: Glockenspiel & Tympani; Benmont Tench: Piano & Spinet; Mitchell Froom: Electric Piano & Chamberlain

Record 61 title:
The Elvis Costello Hour
Label / Catalog number:
Warner Bros / WBWM 165
PRO-C-3488 (promotional only)
Jacket / Inserts:
Unique in cassette case / 1 page insert
Recording Location / Date:
One or more of the following studios: Ocean Way, Los Angeles, CA, Southlake, New Orleans, LA, U.S.A; Windmill Land, Dublin, Ireland &/or Air, London, U.K. / 1987 or 1988

Media:
Cassette Tape
Producer:
Elvis Costello, Kevin Killen & T-Bone Burnett

Song 61a title:
This Town (The Bastard Mix)
Release date / Country:
07 Feb 89 / U.S.A.

Track details:
Side 1, track 4 / 4 min. 26 sec.
Composer:
D. Mac Manus

Elvis Costello: Guitars, Piano, Organ, Tambourine & Melodica; Paul McCartney: Bass & B. Vocals; T-Bone Burnett: Guitars; Ralph Forbes: Electric Drums; Jim Keltner: Snare Drums; Michael Blair: Glockenspiel & Bells; Cait O' Riordan: Maracas; Roger McGuinn: 12 String Electric Guitar

Elvis Costello, born Declan Mac Manus, is the son of Joe Loss & His Orchestra leader, Ross Mac Manus (who once performed on the same bill as The Beatles). Costello was his grandmother's maiden name. Costello was born in London, England on August 25, 1954. When his parents divorced, he moved to Liverpool with his mother. By the age of fifteen he was playing the guitar and writing songs. He moved back to London in the early 1970s and began performing when he was not working as a computer operator for cosmetics giant Elizabeth Arden. He quit his job in 1975 and went to work as a roadie for Brinsley Schwarz (Brinsley Schwarz had opened for Paul McCartney and Wings' U.K. tour in 1973). Costello became good friends with the band's bass player, Nick Lowe. Several years later, Costello was signed to Stiff Records on the advice of Lowe, now staff producer for the label and Costello.

Costello and his backing group, The Attractions, quickly gained fame as a brash and abrasive, post-punk, new-wave group in the late 1970s. Costello has long maintained a cult

following — primarily for his excellent songwriting. He had chart success in the U.K., particularly in the late 1970s and early 1980s, but has not fared as well in the U.S. singles charts in spite of respectable album sales. Nonetheless, his songs ***(What's So Funny 'Bout) Peace, Love And Understanding***, ***Pump It Up***, ***Oliver's Army***, ***Accidents Will Happen***, ***Radio, Radio***, ***Man Out Of Time***, ***Clubland*** and ***Everyday I Write The Book*** are destined to become rock classics.

In 1983, Costello contributed his recording of Yoko Ono's ***Walking On Thin Ice*** for a tribute album to her titled **Every Man Has A Woman**. In the summer of 1987, Paul McCartney approached Costello with the idea of writing and recording together. McCartney accurately sensed that Costello would provide a competitive, counterpoint working relationship reminiscent of the one Paul had with John Lennon. To date twelve co-compositions have been released, seven by McCartney (***My Brave Face***, ***You Want Her Too***, ***Don't Be Careless Love***, ***Back On My Feet***, ***That Day Is Done***, ***Mistress And Maid*** and ***The Lovers That Never Were***). Costello issued two co-compositions on his album **Spike**, two on **Mighty Like A Rose**, and one on **All This Useless Beauty** that also thanks McCartney. A promotional cassette tape **The Elvis Costello Hour** contains an alternate mix of ***This Town*** called ***The Bastard Mix*** (actually the ***Sweetheart*** mix!). When Costello released ***So Like Candy*** as a single on October 14, 1991, he included a demo version of ***Veronica*** on the B-side, but it does not contain any musical contribution by McCartney. ***Veronica*** proved to be one of Costello's highest charting singles. There are at least two McCartney-Mac Manus songs yet to be released by either artist, ***I Don't Want To Confess*** and ***Tommy's Coming Home***.

Costello and McCartney performed their first public duet together on March 23, 1995 at St. James Palace in London at a benefit for the Royal College Of Music *(see Anya Alexeyev)*. They performed their co-composition ***Mistress And Maid*** and The Beatles' ***One After 909***. The entire performance is available on the bootleg CD **Paul McCartney, Elvis Costello & Friends - A Royal Performance** (Strawberry Records / STR 005). A portion of ***One After 909*** was also featured on McCartney's 1995 radio series **Oobu Joobu**. **Oobu Joobu** featured several of Costello's songs including his demo with McCartney of ***The Lovers That Never Were***.

Costello recently covered Lennon's composition ***You've Got To Hide Your Love Away***, and McCartney's ***Step Inside Love*** *(see Cilla Black)*. He has also performed a number of The Beatles' songs in public over the years including ***All You Need Is Love*** and ***Baby's In Black***. The 1990s continue to see Elvis Costello tour, write, record and explore new musical styles.

The Crickets

Record 62 title:
T-Shirt
Label / Catalog number:
Epic / EK 44446
Jacket / Inserts:
Standard international design in jewel box / 2 page CD insert
Recording Location / Date:
Hog Hill Studios, Sussex, U.K. / Spring 1988
Media:
Album 5" CD
Producer:
Paul McCartney

Gordon Payne: Guitar & Vocals; Jerry Allison: Guitar & Drums; Joe B. Mauldin: Bass; Paul McCartney: Piano & B. Vocals

The Crickets were Buddy Holly's back-up band originally consisting of Sonny Curtis on guitar, Don Guess on bass and Jerry Allison on drums. Niki Sullivan replaced Curtis and Joe Mauldin replaced Guess just as the group was becoming successful. Over the years, The Crickets have also included Larry Welborn, Tommy Allsup, Glen Hardin, Gordon Payne, Jerry Naylor and country star Waylon Jennings.

In the fall of 1958, Buddy Holly (born Charles Hardin Holley on September 7, 1936 in Lubbock, Texas) left The Crickets and his producer Norman Petty and moved to New York. There he proposed marriage to Puerto Rican, Maria Santiago, on the first date. Following their marriage, Holly went on

Song 62a title:
T-Shirt
Release date / Country:
04 Nov 88 (first issued 29 Aug 88) / U.S.A.
Track details:
Side 1, track 5 / 3 min. 05 sec.
Composer:
J. Imray

a northern Midwest tour. On February 3, 1959, a small private plane carrying Ritchie Valens, The Big Bopper (J. P. Richardson), and Holly crashed shortly after take-off from Clear Lake, Iowa during a snow storm, killing all on board.

The Crickets continued to record and perform throughout the 1960s as a group (built around the core of Curtis and Allison), as solo artists, and as back-up for other artists. Sonny Curtis got on the British music invasion bandwagon in February 1964 with the release of his novelty song ***A Beatle I Want To Be***, and his cover album of Beatles' songs **Beatle Hits Flamenco Style**. The Crickets also did covers of ***I Want To Hold Your Hand***, ***From Me To You***, ***Please Please Me***, ***She Loves You*** and ***I Saw Her Standing There*** in 1964. Most of The Crickets' post-Buddy Holly success has been enjoyed in England.

Hardin, Curtis and Allison recorded The Crickets' album **Rockin' 50's Rock 'n' Roll** (Barnaby / 9 Z 30268) in 1970 with help from Eric Clapton* and Delaney Bramlett*. Rumors have persisted that George Harrison or Ringo Starr may have contributed to the album tracks produced by Bramlett. The album's liner notes contain a reprinted, signed message from all four Beatles dated January 24, 1963. It reads, "Dear Crickets: When we were rehearsing for a TV show the other day, we met someone who had known you during your recent trip to England, and they told us how you had complimented us. We also heard from E.M.I. in London that you had a copy of our record. Well, we'd just like to say that we take this as a great compliment and appreciate it very much. Yours sincerely, The Beatles." Because The Beatles did not intentionally contribute this message to the album, it is not considered a contribution. However, the message also helped fuel speculation that The Beatles were in some way involved in the album. According to Jerry Allison and Delaney Bramlett, none of The Beatles contributed musically to the album.

There are many artists who greatly influenced The Beatles. The primary ones were Chuck Berry*, Little Richard*, Carl Perkins* and Elvis Presley, but it was Buddy Holly that gave Lennon and McCartney the greatest encouragement to attempt songwriting. If a kid about their age with horn-rimmed glasses from Lubbock, Texas, could write a dozen or so three-chord hits in as many months, then John and Paul could too. The earliest known recording The Beatles, then known as the Quarry Men, ever made was of Buddy Holly & The Crickets' ***That'll Be The Day*** in 1958. The recording was included on The Beatles' 1995 album **Anthology 1**. It was probably no accident that the name The Beatles bore a striking similarity to The Crickets. Other Buddy Holly and The Crickets' songs that have been released both by The Beatles and as solo artists include ***Peggy Sue***, ***Mailman, Bring Me No More Blues***, ***Words Of Love*** and ***Crying, Waiting, Hoping***. The Beatles often included these, and other Buddy Holly and The Crickets' songs such as ***It's So Easy***, ***Maybe Baby***, ***Think It Over*** and ***Don't Ever Change***, during their live performances prior to 1963.

Paul McCartney purchased most of the Buddy Holly music publishing catalogue in 1976. Not surprisingly, Holly admirer, George Harrison, also bid to obtain the Holly catalogue. In September 1976, McCartney launched "Buddy Holly Week" in London as an annual event to celebrate Holly's birthday. McCartney is usually in attendance and occasionally performs onstage with The Crickets. McCartney produced Denny Laine's* 1977 album of Holly covers titled **Holly Days**.

McCartney, in association with the BBC, produced the 1985 documentary **The Real Buddy Holly Story**. McCartney narrated and performed covers of Holly's material in the documentary that is available on video cassette and laser videodisk. Buddy Holly was inducted as a charter member into the Rock and Roll Hall of Fame in 1986.

In 1988, McCartney got together with a newly formed Crickets at his studio in Sussex to produce and perform on the song ***T-Shirt***. ***T-Shirt*** was the winning song from the previous year's Buddy Holly Week song competition. McCartney was pictured on the back of the U.K. 12" single and was also featured briefly in the video for the song. The song was released in time for the twelfth anniversary of Buddy Holly Week celebrations with a T-Shirt design competition. McCartney also made an appearance in the 1990 film documentary of The Crickets, **My Love Is Bigger Than A Cadillac**.

Crowbar

Record 63 title:
KE32746
Label / Catalog number:
Epic / KE 32746
Jacket / Inserts:
Standard international design / Record label inner sleeve
Recording Location / Date:
Record Plant (East) Studio A, New York, NY, U.S.A. / (probably) Jul or Aug 73
Media:
Album 12"
Producer:
Jack Douglas

Song 63a title:
Rocky Mountain Tragedy
Release date / Country:
(probably) Jan 74 / U.S.A.
Track details:
Side 2, track 2 / 5 min. 30 sec.
Composer:
K. Jay - R. Greenway

Kelly Jay: Lead Vocals & (probable) Keyboards; one or more of the following: Sonnie Bernardi: Drums, Percussion & Vocals; Jozef Chirowski: Keyboards, Percussion, Flute & Vocals; John Gibbard: Acoustic, Electric & Slide Guitars & Vocals; Roland Greenway: Bass & Vocals; Rheal Lanthier: Acoustic & Electric Guitars & Vocals. Additionally thanked are: Michael Brecker, Randy Brecker, The Rock, Paul Prestopino, Steve Hunter, Sneaky Pete, Hugh McCracken, Wade Marcus, Jay Messina, Ed Sprigg, John Pearson, New York's Record Plant-Studios B and C with John Lennon: (possible) B. Vocals; Yoko Ono (possible) B. Vocals; May Pang, Lou Reed and Smiler's Delight

Crowbar was a Canadian band, of mostly Toronto area musicians, led by Kelly Jay. Jay was born Henry Blake Fordham in Toronto, Canada on December 1, 1941. The core of what was to become Crowbar formed in 1965 with Jay and Ascot Revue members Roly Greenway and Rheal Lanthier. Several years later, Ronnie Hawkins* asked Kelly to help put together a new backing band for him. The group included Jay, Greenway, Lanthier, and new members Richard "King Biscuit Boy" Newell, John "Ghetto" Gibbard, Larry Atamanuik, Johnny "Rhythm" Rutter and Richard Bell *(see The Band)*. They dubbed themselves the Full Tilt Boogie Band. Over time there were personnel changes. Atamanuik left for the band Seatrain, and Bell joined Janis Joplin taking with him the Full Tilt Boogie Band name. Ronnie Hawkins remarked "those boys are dumber than a crowbar" and the name stuck. With the addition of Sonnie Bernardi and Ray Harrison (who replaced Jozef Chirowski), Crowbar was born.

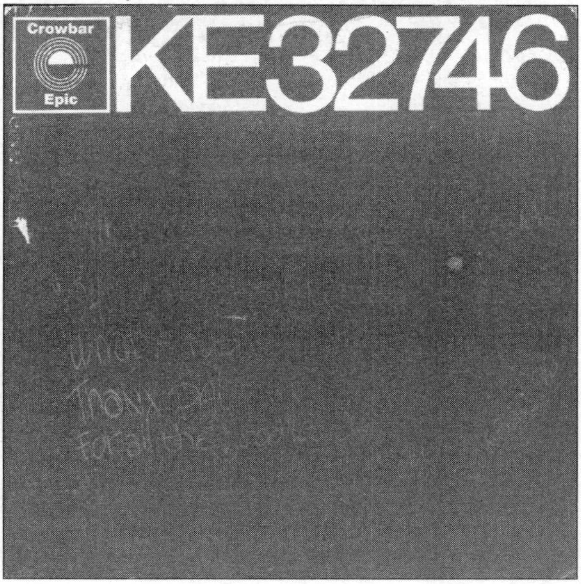

Crowbar first met John Lennon and Yoko Ono* at the **Toronto Rock 'n' Roll Revival** on September 13, 1969. They met John and Yoko again a few months later when the couple were staying at Ronnie Hawkins' house outside Toronto. Shortly thereafter, Crowbar parted with Hawkins to go out on their own. They had two hits in Canada, ***Million Dollar Weekend*** and ***Oh What A Feeling*** that also received airplay in the U.S.

Crowbar journeyed to the Record Plant (East) Studios in New York City, probably around July or August, to record an album for Epic

Records. Yoko Ono was also at the Record Plant recording her album **Feeling The Space** and befriended Crowbar, paying a few bar tabs along the way. A short time later, John Lennon showed up to record his album **Mind Games.** Kelly said Lennon recruited members of Crowbar to sing background vocals and do hand claps for the **Mind Games** album (probably on the song *Only People*).

Crowbar's producer, Jack Douglas, did not feel that Kelly Jay's storytelling at the beginning of their song *Rocky Mountain Tragedy* was very convincing. Douglas asked Kelly, "What do you drink?" Kelly replied "C.C., Canadian Club would be nice." "Fine," said Douglas, "all we've got is Southern Comfort." Kelly, who had eaten a large amount of Waldorf salad earlier in the day, proceeded to down a good portion of the bottle. The re-take of the track went down very well, but the Southern Comfort did not. Kelly ended up on his knees in the heavily mirrored bathroom of the Record Plant relieving himself of the whiskey and the Waldorf. He felt a pair of hands on the back of his neck and a voice with a heavy Liverpool accent saying "Go ahead Kelly, puke it up man, I know how you feel. That feels better doesn't it Kelly?" Kelly says, "I remember turning my head slightly and seeing these boots and slurping a little on them and saying, Oh God, sorry Mr. Lennon!"

Kelly also said, "I remember Jack Douglas clearly saying that, after we left for the night, he grabbed John and Yoko as they were leaving. He put everybody in this hallway and got them both to sing on the chorus of *Rocky Mountain Tragedy*." Jack Douglas admitted, "It's been more than twenty years and I really can't remember whether I used John and Yoko on any of the Crowbar sessions, but it's possible." Dennis Ferrante, a recording engineer at Record Plant, did say that when they needed echo on a song they recorded in the hallway. Yoko recorded a promotional radio spot for Crowbar's Epic album **KE32746** (the record catalogue number was used for title). John, Yoko and May Pang are all thanked in the album's credits. The last song on the album, *Nothing Lasts Forever*, ironically ended up being Crowbar's last recording. Five of the original members reformed Crowbar in 1996, though they are not to be confused with another current band by the same name.

The Crowd

Record 64 title: You'll Never Walk Alone / Messages	***Media:*** Single 7"
Label / Catalog number: Spartan / BRAD 1	***Producer:*** Graham Gouldman & Ray Levy
Jacket / Inserts: 20 May 85	***Recording Location / Date:*** Unique Picture sleeve

Song 64a title: Messages

Release date / Country: 07 Jun 85 / U.K.

Track details: Side 2, track 1 / 3 min. 17 sec.

Composer: G. Gouldman - P. McCartney - T. Healy - G. Holton - P. Lynott - R. Harris - R. Marie - C. Norman - A. Nolans - I. Kilmister - K. Dee - K. Chegwin - J. Conteh

The Crowd: (Paul McCartney, Tim Healy, Gary Holton, Phil Lynott, Rolf Harris, Rose Marie, Chris Norman, Ann Nolans, Ian "Lemmy" Kilmister, Kiki Dee, Keith Chegwin, & John Conteh) Messages; Graham Gouldman: Keyboards

On May 11, 1985, fifty-five people were killed and several hundred more injured in a fire at a soccer stadium in Bradford, England. Gerry Marsden *(see Gerry And The Pacemakers)* gathered a large group of musicians to record a new version of The Pacemakers' hit *You'll Never Walk Alone* as a charity record to benefit the families and survivors of the disaster. Though McCartney was unable to attend the sessions for *You'll Never Walk Alone*, he, like others, telephoned in a "Message" of sympathy and support that was included on the record's B-side. Denny Laine*, a member of Paul's band Wings throughout the 1970s and Ringo Starr's son, Zak, sing in the chorus of the A-side of *You'll Never Walk Alone* with backing and production by Graham Gouldman *(see 10cc)*. The McCartney "Message" is also contained on a 12" single release.

Burton Cummings

Record 65 title:
Live From Montreaux (Various Artists)
Label / Catalog number:
Videoarts Music / VALJ-3369
Jacket / Inserts:
Unique / Lyric & translation insert
Recording Location / Date:
On location at Montreaux Jazz Festival, Montreaux, Switzerland / 13 Jul 92
Media:
Album 12" LVD
Producer:
Jim Beach & Louise Velazquez (film); Ringo Starr (music)

Song 65a title:
American Woman [live]
Release date / Country:
(probably) Nov 93 / Japan
Track details:
Side 2, track 8 / 5 min. 50 sec.
Composer:
R. Bachman - B. Cummings - G. Peterson - M. Cale

Burton Cummings: Lead Vocals & Harmonica; Ringo Starr: Drums; Joe Walsh: Acoustic & Electric Guitar; Todd Rundgren: Guitar; Nils Lofgren: Acoustic & Electric Guitar; Dave Edmunds: Guitar; Timothy B. Schmit: Bass; Tim Cappello: Percussion; Zak Starkey: Drums This song is also included on Rykodisc / RCD 20264 / Album 5" CD / Standard international design in jewel box / 12 page CD booklet.

Song 65b title:
No Time [live]
Release date / Country:
(probably) Nov 93 / Japan
Track details:
Side 1, track 3 / 4 min. 31 sec.
Composer:
R. Bachman - B. Cummings

Burton Cummings: Lead Vocals & Guitar; Ringo Starr: Drums; Joe Walsh: Guitar; Todd Rundgren: Guitar; Nils Lofgren: Guitar; Dave Edmunds: Guitar; Timothy B. Schmit: Bass; Tim Cappello: Percussion; Zak Starkey: Drums

For anyone in Canada, the names Burton Cummings and The Guess Who are those of musical legends. The band evolved from humble beginnings in their native Winnipeg, Manitoba, Canada, originally consisting of Randy Bachman*, Chad Allan, Bob Ashley and Garry Peterson; but the band would undergo a number of personnel changes throughout their career.

In 1965, Burton Cummings, born on December 31, 1947 in Winnipeg, Canada joined The Guess Who. Cummings' lead vocals and songwriting had a major impact on the band's sound. The group had million sellers with the songs ***These Eyes*** and ***Laughing*** in 1969, and ***No Time***, ***American Woman*** and ***No Sugar Tonight*** in 1970. Bachman, at odds with Cummings and unable to reconcile his religious beliefs with the rock 'n' roll life-style of the band, left at the height of their success. Cummings continued to turn out hits like ***Hand Me Down World***, ***Share The Land***, and ***Albert Flasher***, but personnel changes continued to erode the band into little more than a back-up for Cummings. Cummings finally disbanded the group following their final hit, ***Clap For The Wolfman***, a tribute to the legendary DJ Wolfman Jack who did a cameo on the record. The Guess Who, minus the forces of Bachman and Cummings, regrouped in 1978. They have recorded sporadically, including a cover of The Beatles' song ***Taxman***, and continue to make appearances along with personnel changes.

Cummings had one major hit on his own, ***Stand Tall***, shortly after he went solo. His 1979 album **Dream Of A Child**, became the first Canadian album to ever go triple platinum. His 1991 album **Plus Signs** also went platinum in Canada.

In 1992, Cummings joined Ringo Starr's All-Starr Band tour performing ***American Woman*** and ***No Time*** with Ringo backing him on drums. He received the band's greatest crowd response (excluding Ringo of course) at the Canadian and U.S. dates near the Canadian border. Randy Bachman joined Ringo's All-Starr Band tour in 1995.

Roger Daltrey

Record 66 title:
One Of The Boys
Label / Catalog number:
MCA / 2271
Jacket / Inserts:
Standard international design / Custom inner-sleeve
Recording Location / Date:
Ramport Studios, London, U.K. &/or Pathe Marconi Studios, Paris, France / 1976 &/or 1977
Media:
Album 12"
Producer:
David Courtney & Tony Meehan

Song 66a title:
Giddy
Release date / Country:
13 May 77 / U.S.A.
Track details:
Side 2, track 2 / 4 min. 46 sec.
Composer:
P. McCartney

Roger Daltrey: Lead Vocals; one or more of the following: Brian Odgers: Bass; John Entwistle: Bass; Stuart Tosh: Drums; Jimmy McCulloch: Guitar; Paul Keogh: Guitar; Rod Argent: Keyboards; Phil Kenzie: Saxophone; Jimmy Jewell: Saxophone; Tony Rivers: B. Vocals; John Perry: B. Vocals; Stuart Calver: B. Vocals; Tony Meehan: Arrangements; Hank B. Marvin: Special Thanks; Alvin Lee: Special Thanks; Eric Clapton: Special Thanks; Andy Fairweather Low: Special Thanks; Mick Ronson: Special Thanks

Roger Daltrey was born on March 1, 1944 in London, England. He is best known as the lead singer of the group The Who. Daltrey's vocals grace such classics by The Who as ***My Generation***, ***I Can See For Miles***, ***Magic Bus***, ***See Me, Feel Me***, ***Won't Get Fooled Again***, ***Behind Blue Eyes***, ***Join Together***, ***Squeeze Box*** and ***Who Are You***. The Who often covered The Beatles' songs during their performances early in their career. During the mid-60s The Who were managed by Allen Klein.

In 1973 Daltrey released his first album, self-titled **Daltrey**, that included the U.K. top five hit ***Giving It All Away***. Daltrey released his second solo album, **Ride A Rock Horse**, in 1975. He had a top 20 in the U.S. with the song ***Without Your Love*** in 1980. He has released several more solo albums and appeared in a number of films during the last two decades.

Daltrey starred in two films in 1975, **Tommy**, and Ken Russell's **Lisztomania**, in which Ringo Starr played The Pope. The soundtrack album, as well as the 1992 laser videodisk, features a photo of Pope Ringo from the film on the back of their jackets.

Roger Daltrey's 1977 album **One Of The Boys** included the song ***Giddy*** written by Paul McCartney. The "Rode All Night" portion of ***Giddy*** was recorded by McCartney during sessions for his album **Ram** and though never released, is available on bootleg CDs. Jimmy McCulloch is listed in the general musical credits of **One Of The Boys**. McCulloch was probably a member of McCartney's band Wings at the time Daltrey's version of ***Giddy*** was recorded, though it is not known if he plays guitar on the track. McCartney has yet to release his version of ***Giddy***.

Rick Danko

Record 67 title:
Ringo Starr And His All-Starr Band
Label / Catalog number:
Rykodisc / RCD 10190 & RCD5-1019
Media:
Album 5" [2 CD set]
Producer:
Tim Snow (film);
Joe Walsh & Jim Nipar (music)
Jacket / Inserts:
Unique in box set in Jewel box / 6 page CD booklet, sticker postcard, Rykodisc info. postcard & CD insert
Recording Location / Date:
On location at Greek Theatre, Los Angeles, CA, U.S.A. / 03 Sep 89

Song 67a title:
Raining In My Heart [live]
Release date / Country:
12 Oct 90 / U.S.A.
Track details:
Side 1, track 9 / 5 min. 14 sec.
Composer:
B. Holly

Rick Danko: Lead Vocals & Bass; Billy Preston: Keyboards; Jim Keltner: Drums; Ringo Starr: Drums; Levon Helm: Mandolin; Nils Lofgren: Guitar; Garth Hudson: Accordion; Joe Walsh: Guitar; Clarence Clemons: Saxophone; Dr. John: (probable) Keyboards

Record 68 title:
Ringo Starr And His All-Starr Band
Label / Catalog number:
Pioneer Artists / PA-090-007
Media:
Album 12" LVD
Producer:
Tim Snow (film);
Joe Walsh & Jim Nipar (music)
Jacket / Inserts:
Standard international design / Record label inner sleeve
Recording Location / Date:
On location at Greek Theatre, Los Angeles, CA, U.S.A. / 03 Sep 89

Song 68a title:
Shape I'm In [live]
Release date / Country:
Jul 90 / U.S.A.
Track details:
Side 1, track 10 / 4 min. 19 sec.
Composer:
R. Robertson

Rick Danko: Lead Vocals & Bass; Billy Preston: Keyboards; Jim Keltner: Drums; Ringo Starr: Drums; Levon Helm: Drums; Nils Lofgren: Accordion; Garth Hudson: Accordion; Joe Walsh: Guitar; Clarence Clemons: Saxophone; Dr. John: Keyboards

Rick Danko was born December 9, 1943 in Simcoe, Ontario, Canada. Danko is best known as one of the core members of the group The Band*. Rick, along with fellow member of The Band, Levon Helm* , was part of Ringo Starr's All-Starr Band tour in 1989 and performed ***Raining In My Heart*** and ***Shape I'm In*** with Ringo backing him on drums. He also contributed to Ringo Starr's 1973 album **Ringo**.

Apart from The Band, Rick has released several solo albums and has contributed to a large number of other artists' recordings over the years, including Robbie Robertson. He is also the member of a trio with Eric Andersen and Jonas Fjeld. Their 1992 album, **Danko / Fjeld / Anderson**, received critical praise and was awarded album of the year in the sparsely populated Norway where it sold over 100,000 copies.

Rick Danko, Woodstock, NY, 1994,
photo by Kristofer Engelhardt

Jesse Ed Davis

Record 69 title:
Keep Me Comin'
Label / Catalog number:
Epic/Sony / ESCA 7523
Media:
Album 5" CD
Producer:
Jesse Ed Davis
Jacket / Inserts:
Standard international design in jewel box / 4 page CD booklet & 24 page lyric translation insert
Recording Location / Date:
Paramount Recorders, Los Angeles, CA, U.S.A. / 05 Dec 72 - Feb 73

Song 69a title:
Unknown
Release date / Country:
21 Jan 94 (first issued 1973) / Japan
Composer:
J. Davis - J. Angelos - A. Williams - J. Gordon

Jesse Ed Davis: Lead Vocals & Guitar; one or more of the following: James Gordon: Keyboards; Bob Glaub: Bass; Jim Keltner: Drums; Bobby Torres: Congas; Felix Falcon: Percussion; John Angelos: Harmonica; Bobby Bruce: Violin; Bill Plummer: Bass; Gary Barone: Trumpet & Flugelhorn; Jerry Jumonville: Alto Saxophone; Clifford Scott: Tenor Saxophone; John Smith: Tenor Saxophone; George Bohannon: Trombone; Jacques Ellis: Trombone; Howard Johnson: Baritone Saxophone; Oma Drake: B. Vocals; Julie Tillman: B. Vocals; Carolyn Willis: B. Vocals; Patti Daley: B. Vocals; Chris O'Dell: B. Vocals; Russell Saunkeah: B. Vocals; Billy Davis: B. Vocals; Johnny Angel: B. Vocals; Leon, Bonnie, Merry, Mick, Nino, Billy, Rod, Bette Y El Mysterioso (probably George Harrison: possible Involvement): Cameo Appearances; Peter Waddington, Steve Delaney, Rusty Pelican & Marshall Brevitz: Honorable Mention

Record 70 title:
Live! The Silver Wilburys
Label / Catalog number:
[none] / SWP 87-2 [Unauthorized Record]
Jacket / Inserts:
Unique in Jewel box / 2 page CD insert
Recording Location / Date:
On location at Palomino Club, Los Angeles, CA, U.S.A. / 19 Feb 87
Media:
Album 5" CD (mono)
Producer:
(probably) Palomino Club

Song 70a title:
Farther On Down The Road
(You Will Accompany Me) [live]
Release date / Country:
1988 / Korea
Track details:
Side 1, track 1 / 3 min. 53 sec.
Composer:
T. Mahal - J. Davis

Jesse Ed Davis: Lead Vocal & Guitar; George Harrison: Guitar; Taj Mahal: Harmonica & B. Vocals; Jim Ehinger: Keyboards; Bobby Tsukamoto: Bass; Mark Shark: Guitar; Gary Ray: Drums

Record 71 title:
Ululu
Label / Catalog number:
ATCO / SD 33-382
Media:
Album 12"
Producer:
Jesse Ed Davis, Albhy Galuten
& (possibly) George Harrison
Jacket / Inserts:
Standard international design with Gatefold / Record label inner sleeve
Recording Location / Date:
One or more of the following studios: Criteria Sound, Miami, FL; Record Plant (West), or The Village Recorder, Los Angeles, CA, U.S.A. / 1971 &/or 1972

Song 71a title:
Sue Me, Sue You Blues
Release date / Country:
06 Mar 72 (first issued 25 Jan 72) / U.S.A.
Track details:
Side 1, track 4 / 2 min. 45 sec.
Composer:
G. Harrison

Jesse Ed Davis: Lead Vocals & Guitar; Dr. John: Keyboards; Billy Rich: Bass; Jim Keltner: Drums; Merry Clayton: B. Vocals; Vanetta Fields: B. Vocals; Clydie King: B. Vocals; The Charles Chalmers Singers: B. Vocals; George Harrison: (possible) Guitar

Jesse Ed Davis, or "Indian Ed" as he was known to friends, was a full-blooded native American Indian from Oklahoma. He gained recognition as a member of the band Taj Mahal*, during which time he met John Lennon on the set of The Rolling Stones'* **Rock And Roll Circus** TV special. He came to George Harrison's attention via the Delaney & Bonnie & Friends* connection *(see also Eric Clapton, Leon Russell).* Davis was known primarily as a session guitarist. Over the years he worked for a wide range of artists including: B.B. King*, Steve Miller* and Rod Stewart*.

Davis' first album, **Jesse Davis**, released in 1970 (available on Japanese CD ATCO / 9 18P2-2921), includes contributions from Eric Clapton, Leon Russell and Jackie Lomax whom George Harrison frequently worked with at the time. Portions of the album were recorded at Olympic Studios in London. Harrison or possibly other members of The Beatles have long been suspected of contributing to **Jesse Davis** in spite of any solid evidence. However, Jackie Lomax thinks Harrison may have contributed to the sessions for the **Jesse Davis** album.

Davis' 1972 album **Ululu** contains Harrison's ***Sue Me, Sue You Blues***, released a full year and a half before Harrison's version. Harrison probably felt the song about The Beatles suing each other was too controversial for him to release at the time. It has again been suggested that Harrison also contributes to the Davis version, but the difficulty lies in the fact that Davis' slide guitar style is somewhat similar to Harrison's. Davis was given the song by Harrison in Los Angeles in the summer of 1971 shortly before his appearance at Harrison's **The Concert For Bangla Desh**. An article in the January 1993 issue of Beatles Book monthly magazine mentions that in late 1971 George took part in sessions for a Jesse Ed Davis album. This would almost certainly have to be the album **Ululu**. It is possible that along with writing ***Sue Me, Sue You Blues***, Harrison may also have helped arrange, produce and/or play guitar on Davis' recording. However, Jim Keltner, who drummed on **Ululu**, said that he did not recall Harrison being present at any of the sessions, including ***Sue Me, Sue You Blues***.

The liner notes for Davis' 1973 album **Keep Me Comin'** list a cameo appearance by Bette Y El Mysterioso. In all likelihood this is a pseudonym for George Harrison who had used the pseudonym L'Angelo Misterioso on several occasions. The same group of musicians who have worked extensively with Harrison are also present on this record. The cameo appearances also mention a Leon, Bonnie, and Billy, no doubt referring to Russell, Bramlett and Preston*. It is not yet known to which songs, if any, on **Keep Me Comin'** Harrison might have contributed. The tracks on the album are ***Big Dipper***; ***She's A Pain***; ***Where Am I Now (When I Need Me)***; ***Natural Anthem***; ***Who Pulled The Plug?***; ***Ching, Ching, China Boy***; ***Bacon Fat***; ***No Diga Mas***; ***6:00 Bugalu*** and ***Keep Me Comin'***.

Keep Me Comin' included a 7" EP interview with KMET-FM Los Angeles' Mitch Reed in some early copies. During the interview, Davis talked about the making of **Keep Me Comin'** and his association with George Harrison. He revealed how he came to record Harrison's ***Sue Me, Sue You Blues*** and that he had a recording of himself and Harrison jamming Beatles' songs. He also talked about how he came to perform at **The Concert For Bangla Desh**. Bass player Bob Glaub and Jim Keltner, who were at most of the sessions for **Keep Me Comin'**, do not recall Harrison being present. Keltner said some of the album was recorded at Criteria Sound Studios in Miami. Keltner and Glaub confessed it was possible that Harrison might have overdubbed some guitar when they were not present. No direct involvement by any of The Beatles on Jesse Ed Davis' studio recordings has ever been confirmed. However, the possibility exists considering the amount of work Davis did on solo Beatles recordings.

Davis was a constant companion of Lennon and Ringo during their stays in Los Angeles between 1973 and 1974. He made major contributions to Lennon's 1974 album **Walls And Bridges**, his 1975 album **Rock 'N' Roll**, and his posthumous album **Menlove Avenue** released in 1986. Davis performed the Lennon composition ***Mucho Mungo*** on the Westwood One radio series **The Lost Lennon Tapes**, and claimed he was Lennon's inspiration for the song. However, May Pang, Lennon's companion at the time the song was written, disputes Davis' claim. He contributed to Ringo's 1974 album **Goodnight Vienna** and his 1976 album **Rotogravure**. George Harrison also used the talents of Davis on his 1975 album **Extra Texture**.

On February 19, 1987, Harrison, John Fogerty* and Bob Dylan* left their seats at the Palomino Club in Hollywood to join Jesse Ed Davis' Graffiti Band and Taj Mahal onstage for a jam session. The performance is available on the bootleg CD **Live! The Silver Wilburys** that features Jesse Ed singing lead vocals on ***Farther On Down The Road (You Will Accompany Me)***. Jesse Ed Davis died on June 22, 1988.

Delaney & Bonnie & Friends

Record 72 title:
Artifacts III (Not Fade Away: 1969-1971)
Media:
Album 5" CD [4 CD set]
Label / Catalog number:
Big Music / BIGBX 009.4 (BIG 4033)
[Unauthorized Record]
Producer:
Unknown-audience recording
Jacket / Inserts:
Unique in Jewel box in box set / 24 page box set CD booklet
& (4) 2 page CD inserts
Recording Location / Date:
On location at Falkoner Theatre, Copenhagen, Denmark / 10 Dec 69

Song 72a title:
Only You Know And I Know [live]
Release date / Country:
(probably) Feb 95 / Italy
Track details:
CD1, track 3 / 4 min. 34 sec.
Composer:
D. Mason

Delaney Bramlett: Lead Vocals & Rhythm Guitar; Bonnie Bramlett: Lead Vocals & Tambourine; Eric Clapton: Lead Guitar; Billy Preston: Keyboards; Guitar; George Harrison: Guitar; Carl Radle: Bass; Jim Gordon: Drums; Bobby Whitlock: Organ & B. Vocals; Jim Price: Trumpet & Trombone; Bobby Keys: Saxophone; Tex Johnson: Congas & Bongo Drums; Rita Coolidge: B. Vocals.

Record 73 title:
Delaney & Bonnie & Friends - On Tour
With Eric Clapton
Media:
Album 5" CD
Label / Catalog number:
Atco / 33326-2
Producer:
Jimmy Miller & Delaney Bramlett
Jacket / Inserts:
Standard international design in jewel box / 6 page CD booklet

Song 73a title:
Coming Home [live]
Release date / Country:
Jun 89 (first issued 07 Apr 70) / U.S.A.
Track details:
Side 1, track 7 / 5 min. 30 sec.
Composer:
B. Bramlett - E. Clapton
Recording Location / Date:
On location at Fairfield Hall, Croydon, U.K. / 07 Dec 69

Delaney Bramlett: Lead Vocals & Rhythm Guitar; Bonnie Bramlett: Vocals & Tambourine; Eric Clapton: Lead Guitar; Dave Mason: Guitar; Carl Radle: Bass; Jim Gordon: Drums; Bobby Whitlock: Organ & B. Vocals; Jim Price: Trumpet & Trombone; Bobby Keys: Saxophone; Tex Johnson: Congas & Bongo Drums; Rita Coolidge: B. Vocals; George Harrison: Guitar

Song 73b title:
I Don't Want To Discuss It [live]
Release date / Country:
Jun 89 (first issued 07 May 70) / U.S.A.
Track details:
Side 1, track 4 / 4 min. 55 sec.
Composer:
Beatty - Cooper - Shelby

Recording Location / Date:
Probably on location at Fairfield Hall, Croydon, or possibly at Colston Hall, Bristol
or Empire Theatre, Liverpool, U.K. / (probably) 02, 05, or 07 Dec 69

Delaney Bramlett: Lead Vocals & Rhythm Guitar; Bonnie Bramlett: Lead Vocals & Tambourine; Eric Clapton: Lead Guitar; Dave Mason: Guitar; Carl Radle: Bass; Jim Gordon: Drums; Bobby Whitlock: Organ & B. Vocals; Jim Price: Trumpet & Trombone; Bobby Keys: Saxophone; Tex Johnson: Congas

& Bongo Drums; Rita Coolidge: B. Vocals; George Harrison: Guitar

Song 73c title:
Little Richard Medley: Tutti-Frutti / The Girl Can't Help It / Long Tall Sally / Jenny Jenny [live]
Track details:
Side 1, track 8 / 5 min. 45 sec.
Release date / Country:
Jun 89 (first issued 07 Apr 70) / U.S.A.
Composer:
R. Penniman - R. W. Trout - R. A. Blackwell
Recording Location / Date:
Probably on location at Fairfield Hall, Croydon, or possibly at Colston Hall, Bristol or Empire Theatre, Liverpool, U.K. / (probably) 02, 05, or 07 Dec 69

Delaney Bramlett: Lead Vocals & Rhythm Guitar; Bonnie Bramlett: Vocals & Tambourine; Eric Clapton: Lead Guitar; Dave Mason: Guitar; Carl Radle: Bass; Jim Gordon: Drums; Bobby Whitlock: Organ & B. Vocals; Jim Price: Trumpet & Trombone; Bobby Keys: Saxophone; Tex Johnson: Congas & Bongo Drums; Rita Coolidge: B. Vocals; George Harrison: Guitar

Song 73d title:
Only You Know And I Know [live]
Track details:
Side 1, track 3 / 4 min. 10 sec.
Release date / Country:
Jun 89 (first issued 07 Apr 70) / U.S.A.
Composer:
D. Mason
Recording Location / Date:
On location at Fairfield Hall, Croydon, U.K. / 07 Dec 69

Delaney Bramlett: Lead Vocals & Rhythm Guitar; Bonnie Bramlett: Lead Vocals & Tambourine; Eric Clapton: Lead Guitar; Dave Mason: Guitar; Carl Radle: Bass; Jim Gordon: Drums; Bobby Whitlock: Organ & B. Vocals; Jim Price: Trumpet & Trombone; Bobby Keys: Saxophone; Tex Johnson: Congas & Bongo Drums; Rita Coolidge: B. Vocals; George Harrison: Guitar

Song 73e title:
Poor Elijah - Tribute To Johnson (Medley) [live]
Track details:
Side 1, track 2 / 5 min. 00 sec.
Release date / Country:
Jun 89 (first issued 07 May 70) / U.S.A.
Composer:
D. Bramlett - J. Ford - L. Russell
Recording Location / Date:
Probably on location at Fairfield Hall, Croydon, or possibly at Colston Hall, Bristol or Empire Theatre, Liverpool, U.K. / (probably) 02, 05, or 07 Dec 69

Delaney Bramlett: Lead Vocals & Rhythm Guitar; Bonnie Bramlett: Lead Vocals & Tambourine; Eric Clapton: Lead Guitar; Dave Mason: Guitar; Carl Radle: Bass; Jim Gordon: Drums; Bobby Whitlock: Organ & B. Vocals; Jim Price: Trumpet & Trombone; Bobby Keys: Saxophone; Tex Johnson: Congas & Bongo Drums; Rita Coolidge: B. Vocals; George Harrison: Guitar

Song 73f title:
That's What My Man Is For [live]
Track details:
Side 1, track 5 / 4 min. 30 sec.
Release date / Country:
Jun 89 (first issued 07 Apr 70) / U.S.A.
Composer:
B. Griffin
Recording Location / Date:
Probably on location at Fairfield Hall, Croydon, or possibly at Colston Hall, Bristol or Empire Theatre, Liverpool, U.K. / (probably) 02, 05, or 07 Dec 69

Bonnie Bramlett: Lead Vocals & Tambourine; Delaney Bramlett: Rhythm Guitar & Vocals; Eric Clapton: Lead Guitar; Dave Mason: Guitar; Carl Radle: Bass; Jim Gordon: Drums; Bobby Whitlock: Organ & B. Vocals; Jim Price: Trumpet & Trombone; Bobby Keys: Saxophone; Tex Johnson: Congas & Bongo Drums; Rita Coolidge: B. Vocals; George Harrison: Guitar

Song 73g title:
Things Get Better [live]
Track details:
Side 1, track 1 / 4 min. 20 sec.
Release date / Country:
Jun 89 (first issued 07 Apr 70) / U.S.A.
Composer:
Floyd - Cropper - Wayne

Recording Location / Date:
Probably on location at Fairfield Hall, Croydon, or possibly at Colston Hall, Bristol or Empire Theatre, Liverpool, U.K. / (probably) 02, 05, or 07 Dec 69

Delaney Bramlett: Lead Vocals & Rhythm Guitar; Bonnie Bramlett: Lead Vocals & Tambourine; Eric Clapton: Lead Guitar; Dave Mason: Guitar; Carl Radle: Bass; Jim Gordon: Drums; Bobby Whitlock: Organ & B. Vocals; Jim Price: Trumpet & Trombone; Bobby Keys: Saxophone; Tex Johnson: Congas & Bongo Drums; Rita Coolidge: B. Vocals; George Harrison: Guitar

Song 73h title:
Where There's A Will, There's A Way [live]
Release date / Country:
Jun 89 (first issued 07 Apr 70) / U.S.A.
Track details:
Side 1, track 6 / 4 min. 57 sec.
Composer:
B. Bramlett - B. Whitlock
Recording Location / Date:
Probably on location at Fairfield Hall, Croydon, or possibly at Colston Hall, Bristol or Empire Theatre, Liverpool, U.K. / (probably) 02, 05, or 07 Dec 69

Delaney Bramlett: Vocals & Rhythm Guitar; Bonnie Bramlett: Vocals & Tambourine; Eric Clapton: Lead Guitar; Dave Mason: Guitar; Carl Radle: Bass; Jim Gordon: Drums; Bobby Whitlock: Vocals & Organ; Jim Price: Trumpet & Trombone; Bobby Keys: Saxophone; Tex Johnson: Congas & Bongo Drums; Rita Coolidge: B. Vocals; George Harrison: Guitar

Record 74 title:
Falkoner
Label / Catalog number:
Shalom / 8420 [Unauthorized Record]
Jacket / Inserts:
Unique / Record label inner sleeve
Media:
Album 12" (mono)
Producer:
Unknown-audience recording
Recording Location / Date:
On location at Falkoner Theatre, Copenhagen, Denmark / 10 Dec 69

Song 74a title:
Coming Home [live]
Release date / Country:
mid 1970s / U.S.A.
Track details:
Side 2, track 3 / 6 min. 45 sec.
Composer:
B. Bramlett - E. Clapton

Delaney Bramlett: Lead Vocals & Rhythm Guitar; Bonnie Bramlett: Vocals & Tambourine; Eric Clapton: Lead Guitar; Billy Preston: Keyboards; Carl Radle: Bass; Jim Gordon: Drums; Bobby Whitlock: Organ & B. Vocals; Jim Price: Trumpet & Trombone; Bobby Keys: Saxophone; Tex Johnson: Congas & Bongo Drums; Rita Coolidge: B. Vocals. George Harrison: Guitar

Song 74b title:
12 Little Richard Medley: Tutti-Frutti / The Girl Can't Help It / Long Tall Sally / Jenny Jenny [live]
Release date / Country:
mid 1970s / U.S.A.
Track details:
Side 2, track 4 / 6 min. 22 sec.
Composer:
R. Penniman - R. W. Trout - R. A. Blackwell

Delaney Bramlett: Lead Vocals & Rhythm Guitar; Bonnie Bramlett: Vocals & Tambourine; Eric Clapton: Lead Guitar; Billy Preston: Keyboards; Guitar; George Harrison: Guitar; Carl Radle: Bass; Jim Gordon: Drums; Bobby Whitlock: Organ & B. Vocals; Jim Price: Trumpet & Trombone; Bobby Keys: Saxophone; Tex Johnson: Congas & Bongo Drums; Rita Coolidge: B. Vocals

Record 75 title:
Songs I Forgot
Label / Catalog number:
Planet Records / U.S. Audio 1005
[Unauthorized Record]
Jacket / Inserts:
Unique / 1 page CD insert
Recording Location / Date:
On location at Falkoner Theatre, Copenhagen, Denmark / 12 Dec 69
Media:
Album 5" CD (mono)
Producer:
Danish Television

Song 75a title:
I Don't Want To Discuss It [live]
Release date / Country:
1995 / Japan
Track details:
Side 1, track 13 / 5 min. 38 sec.
Composer:
Beatty - Cooper - Shelby

Delaney Bramlett: Lead Vocals & Rhythm Guitar; Bonnie Bramlett: Lead Vocals & Tambourine; Eric Clapton: Lead Guitar; Billy Preston: Keyboards; George Harrison: Guitar; Carl Radle: Bass; Jim Gordon: Drums; Bobby Whitlock: Organ & B. Vocals; Jim Price: Trumpet & Trombone; Bobby Keys: Saxophone; Tex Johnson: Congas & Bongo Drums; Rita Coolidge: B. Vocals

Song 75b title:
My Baby Specializes [live]
Release date / Country:
1995 / Japan
Track details:
Side 1, track 12 / 4 min. 34 sec.
Composer:
D. Porter - I. Hayes

Delaney Bramlett: Lead Vocals & Rhythm Guitar; Bonnie Bramlett: Vocals & Tambourine; Eric Clapton: Lead Guitar; Billy Preston: Keyboards; George Harrison: Guitar; Carl Radle: Bass; Jim Gordon: Drums; Bobby Whitlock: Organ & B. Vocals; Jim Price: Trumpet & Trombone; Bobby Keys: Saxophone; Tex Johnson: Congas & Bongo Drums; Rita Coolidge: B. Vocals.

Song 75c title:
Poor Elijah - Tribute To Johnson
(Medley) [live]
Release date / Country:
1995 / Japan
Track details:
Side 1, track 9 / 5 min. 00 sec.
Composer:
D. Bramlett - J. Ford - L. Russell

Delaney Bramlett: Lead Vocals & Rhythm Guitar; Bonnie Bramlett: Lead Vocals & Tambourine; Eric Clapton: Lead Guitar; Billy Preston: Keyboards; George Harrison: Guitar; Carl Radle: Bass; Jim Gordon: Drums; Bobby Whitlock: Organ & B. Vocals; Jim Price: Trumpet & Trombone; Bobby Keys:

Saxophone; Tex Johnson: Congas & Bongo Drums; Rita Coolidge: B. Vocals

Song 75d title:
That's What My Man Is For [live]
Release date / Country:
1995 / Japan
Track details:
Side 1, track 14 / 4 min. 59 sec.
Composer:
B. Griffin

Bonnie Bramlett: Lead Vocals & Tambourine; Delaney Bramlett: Rhythm Guitar & Vocals; Eric Clapton: Lead Guitar; Billy Preston: Keyboards; George Harrison: Guitar; Carl Radle: Bass; Jim Gordon: Drums; Bobby Whitlock: Organ & B. Vocals; Jim Price: Trumpet & Trombone; Bobby Keys: Saxophone; Tex Johnson: Congas & Bongo Drums; Rita Coolidge: B. Vocals

Song 75e title:
Where There's A Will, There's A Way [live]
Release date / Country:
1995 / Japan
Track details:
Side 1, track 11 / 5 min. 01 sec.
Composer:
B. Bramlett - B. Whitlock

Delaney Bramlett: Vocals & Rhythm Guitar; Bonnie Bramlett: Vocals & Tambourine; Eric Clapton: Lead Guitar; Billy Preston: Keyboards; George Harrison: Guitar; Carl Radle: Bass; Jim Gordon: Drums; Bobby Whitlock: Vocals & Organ; Jim Price: Trumpet & Trombone; Bobby Keys: Saxophone; Tex Johnson: Congas & Bongo Drums; Rita Coolidge: B. Vocals

Delaney Bramlett* was born on July 1, 1939 in Pontotoc, Mississippi. Bonnie Lynn O'Farrell was born November 8, 1944 in Acton, Illinois, the daughter of a steel mill worker in East St. Louis. Delaney had his first taste of success as a member of the Shindogs on ABC-TV's rock-music program **Shindig** (which had featured The Beatles). Bonnie knew singing would be her lifelong occupation when she joined her church choir at the age of five.

Bonnie got her first big break as one of Ike and Tina Turner's* Ikettes. Bonnie does not remember it so much as a break, as a risk: "I could have been killed! There was an attempt made on our lives because of the integration thing. I was fifteen years old at the time. I was a white chick with black dudes, and I was as virgin as the day I was born. Ike and all the guys were nothing but gentlemen. I wore a black wig that must have weighed fifty pounds and Man Tan, and it turned me bright orange and streaked; it was so funny; I was having a great time though; it was my dream; all I ever wanted to be was an Ikette!" Bonnie said she sang St. Louis dry and headed for California. There she met Delaney Bramlett in 1967 and a week later they were married.

Delaney & Bonnie Bramlett proved to be a great catalyst bringing together some of the best studio musicians and spawning some of the greatest talents in rock 'n' roll. The band would introduce British rock (including John Lennon, George Harrison and Ringo Starr) to some of the best of America's studio musicians. Eric Clapton* reportedly first saw Delaney & Bonnie during a U.S. tour with Cream. His interest in their brand of gospel and rhythm & blues was apparently rekindled with the help of George Harrison. They were soon hired as the opening act of Blind Faith's* only tour, in the summer of 1969, in America. Following the tour, Clapton, dissatisfied with the musical direction of Blind Faith, departed, leaving it one of rock's shortest-lived "supergroups." He immediately began working with Delaney & Bonnie.

George Harrison first saw Delaney & Bonnie perform at a private party in Los Angeles in the fall of 1968. According to Bonnie, Harrison took tapes of the group back to England. Alan Pariser, an associate of The Beatles, attempted to have them signed to The Beatles' Apple Records label. Their album **The Original Delaney & Bonnie - Accept No Substitute** was tentatively scheduled for release on Apple Records as SAPCOR 7 on May 23, 1969, but was withdrawn and issued in the U.S. on Elektra EKS 74039. The album featured the original group of "Friends" including Leon Russell*, Jim Price *(see All Occasion Brass Band)*, Bobby Whitlock*, Bobby Keys*, Jerry McGee, Jim Keltner *(see Attitudes)*, Carl Radle and Rita Coolidge. None of The Beatles contributed to the album. Copies of the withdrawn album on the Apple label do exist and command a very high price among record collectors.

In late fall of 1969, Delaney & Bonnie followed Eric Clapton back to England and began recording and rehearsing for a tour that included Dave Mason* and their backup band of Friends. Many of these Friends would later work on numerous solo Beatles' recordings. George Harrison and Ringo Starr were in attendance at Delaney & Bonnie & Friends' English tour opener at the Royal Albert Hall on December 1, 1969. Following the concert, Harrison decided to join the tour as one of the Friends.

A live album was released titled **Delaney & Bonnie & Friends - On Tour With Eric Clapton** that included George Harrison. Harrison's involvement went uncredited except for the "Special Thanks to: Mysterioso." The album cover featured a picture of Bob Dylan's* two feet hanging out the window of a Rolls Royce. According to Delaney, the entire tour was recorded. Delaney and Bonnie think the live album was compiled primarily from their performances at Fairfield Hall, Croydon on December 7 and Colston Hall, Bristol on December 2. They also thought it was possible that some of their performance at the Empire Theatre in Liverpool on December 5 was also included on the album. Bonnie said, "These were our best shows." Delaney also said that some of the material on the album might have been from the Albert Hall shows but he is not sure. Bonnie doubts that much, if anything, from the Albert Hall show was used for the album because "it was opening night and we were still getting all the bugs out of the sound equipment." Marc Roberty claims in his book **Eric Clapton - The Complete Recording Sessions, 1963 - 1992** that only the Albert Hall and Fairfield Hall shows were recorded and that the Fairfield Hall shows were used for the album. If there are any songs on the album that were recorded at Albert Hall, then obviously they cannot include Harrison! ***Coming Home*** and ***Only You Know And I Know*** were, based on the introductions, recorded at Croydon.

The album represented only a portion of the entire performances given at each show during the tour. The group also performed a number of other songs like ***My Baby Specializes***, ***Tell Me***, ***Mississippi's Burning***, ***Come On In My Kitchen***, ***Howling For My Baby***, and a few other Howlin' Wolf* and Robert Johnson songs. Clapton was featured singing ***Don't Know Why***, that he had written with Delaney. Delaney and Bonnie also revealed that the shy Harrison was finally goaded into singing some oldies during the tour, mostly Carl Perkins* numbers like ***Everybody's Trying To Be My Baby***, ***Blue Suede Shoes*** and the Rosie And The Originals ballad ***Angel Baby***. Delaney suspects that Atlantic probably still has the out-takes, including Harrison's brief set.

Following the English tour, Harrison accompanied the group to Denmark for several shows at the Falkoner Theatre in Copenhagen. The December 12 show was filmed for Danish Television. Some of the Falkoner Theatre performances are available on bootlegs titled **Falkoner**, **Songs I Forgot** and **Artifacts III.** By this stage of the tour, Harrison had taken over the guitar work of the departed Dave Mason, and Billy Preston* had joined in on keyboards. According to Delaney, he asked Harrison to attempt the slide guitar parts played by Mason, setting in motion Harrison's now familiar trademark guitar style. Delaney also revealed that George's behavior on the tour was more reminiscent of his Hamburg days than one might expect from the spiritual Beatle in 1969.

Delaney said, "During the tour George asked me how to write a gospel song. I used the chord pattern of the Chiffons' 1963 hit ***He's So Fine*** as a demonstration. (The Chiffons were part of the billing for The Beatles' first American concert in early 1964.) George and the tour group worked on a gospel anthem based around my demonstration that developed into his song ***My Sweet Lord***." When Harrison released the song about a year later, Delaney asked George why he had not been given credit for helping to develop the smash hit. (Delaney recalled writing another song with Harrison titled ***We Can't Be Seen Together***.) Bonnie contests Delaney's recollections on the origins of ***My Sweet Lord*** and said that the song was probably born out of an ad-lib medley of gospel songs including ***Oh Happy Day*** that the band jammed on one night in a hotel room during the tour. According to Delaney, when Harrison was sued for plagiarism by Bright Tunes, the owners of ***He's So Fine***, he asked Delaney to testify. Delaney said he was advised by his attorneys not to involve himself.

Harrison maintained in court that ***My Sweet Lord*** was primarily inspired by the Edwin Hawkins Singers' arrangement of the traditional gospel song ***Oh Happy Day***, that was a hit at the time. Harrison employed the services of the Edwin Hawkins Singers to back Billy Preston on his version of ***My Sweet Lord***. Apparently, Preston's version was recorded and scheduled for release as a single before Harrison's release but ended up being released as a single shortly after Harrison's release. The court found Harrison guilty of plagiarism. Harrison was also double-dealed by his manager Allen Klein, who bought the rights to ***He's So Fine*** and sued for damages. The two eventually settled with Harrison being able to own the rights to ***My Sweet Lord***.

On December 15, following the completion of the tour, the entourage (including Harrison) backed up John Lennon and Yoko Ono* at London's Lyceum Gallery for a UNICEF benefit performance that would end up on the album **Sometime In New York City**. Around this time, Delaney & Bonnie issued a single of a studio version of the song ***Coming Home*** backed with ***Groupie (Superstar)*** that was a moderate hit. (***Groupie***, retitled ***Superstar***, became a million selling song for the brother and sister duo The Carpenters in 1971.)

Eric Clapton, Bonnie Bramlett, Delany Bramlett & George Harrison, Scandinavia, 1969
photo courtesy of Delany Bramlett

Most of the Friends split from Delaney & Bonnie to join Joe Cocker's* Mad Dogs And Englishmen tour, which also included Leon Russell. In the summer of 1970, after the Mad Dogs and Englishmen tour had ended, Carl Radle, Jim Gordon and Bobby Whitlock teamed up with Eric Clapton to form the short-lived group Derek And The Dominos.

Delaney & Bonnie, and a new set of Friends, went on to record several more albums. However, 1971 proved to be the couple's most successful year in terms of chart success with the top 20 singles ***Never Ending Song Of Love*** and ***Only You Know And I Know***. Not all the Friends were specifically listed in their album credits leading to speculation that Harrison, or some of the other Beatles, might have contributed. In 1972, Atco records released ***Where There's A Will, There's A Way*** as a single. According to Delaney, the single, as the record label states, was nothing more than an edited version of what appears on the **Delaney & Bonnie & Friends - On Tour With Eric Clapton** album. Bonnie seems quite sure that none of Beatles, including Harrison, contributed to any of their recordings, other than those from the tour with Eric Clapton in 1969. Delaney thinks it's possible that Harrison contributed to some of their studio recordings, but he's not sure. Delaney & Bonnie recorded one more album, ironically titled **D&B Together**, before their marriage, and musical act, ended in 1972. Delaney and Bonnie each released several solo albums following their breakup.

In the mid-1970s, Bonnie was rehearsing for a tour with drummer Joe English when Joe got the call from Paul McCartney to join his band Wings. Her cover version of The Beatles' song ***I've Just Seen A Face*** was issued as a single in 1978. During this period, Bonnie was briefly a member of The Allman Brothers Band. On August 8, 1988, Bonnie Bramlett became Bonnie Sheridan in a marriage ceremony to producer / manager and Eli Radish Band founder, Danny Sheridan. Danny encouraged Bonnie to take up acting. She appeared in the music oriented films **Fame** and **The Doors**, and was a member of the cast of TV's highly rated sitcom, **Roseanne**. In 1990, Rhino Records released the CD **The Best Of Delaney & Bonnie**.

In May 1992, Bandaloo Doctors, consisting of Bonnie on vocals, Danny on bass, Jimmy Crespo on guitar and Dallas Taylor on drums, began rehearsing in a Hollywood studio. Down the hall, Ringo Starr and his All-Starr Band were rehearsing for their tour. After only three days of rehearsing, Ringo dropped in and asked the band to be the opening act for his tour. Danny Sheridan said that Ringo was very generous, helpful, and enthusiastic about Bandaloo Doctors.

Delaney continues to write, record and do session work, most recently for Huey Lewis and Phil Driscoll, and he recently recorded a cover of The Beatles' song ***With A Little Help From My Friends***. The Bramlett's daughter, Bekka, has recently enjoyed some success as a singer and became a member of Fleetwood Mac *(see Mick Fleetwood)* in 1994, but is no longer with the group.

Johnny Devlin & The Devils

Record 76 title:
25 Rare Recycled RCA Rock Relics
[Various Artists]

Media:
Album 12" (mono)

Label / Catalog number:
RCA / VPL 1 0240

Producer:
Johnny Devlin

Jacket / Inserts:
Unique with Gatefold / Record label inner sleeve

Recording Location / Date:
AWA Studios, Sydney, Australia / (probably) Jan 65

Song 76a title:
Won't You Be My Baby?

Release date / Country:
1979 (first issued 1965) / Australia

Track details:
Side 1, track 7 / 2 min. 38 sec.

Composer:
J. Devlin - [P. McCartney]

Johnny Devlin: Lead Vocals

Johnny Devlin was born on May 11, 1938 in Raetihi, New Zealand. Devlin's late 1950s cover of ***Lawdy Miss Clawdy*** became New Zealand's first gold record. It made the Elvis-styled Devlin a teen idol at home, and in Australia, which he has called home for most of his life. Later he wrote a song called ***Surfside*** recorded by The Denvermen that became the first instrumental to reach the top of the charts in Australia.

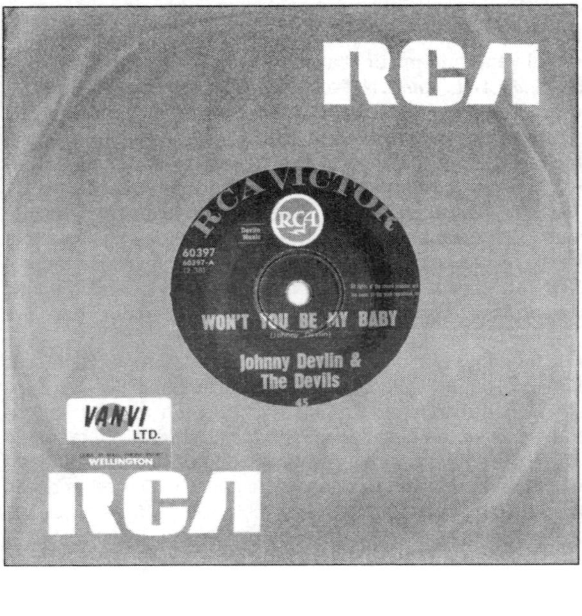

Devlin's career was given a brief boost by the exposure he and his group The Devils received from being one of the supporting acts on The Beatles' tour of Australia and New Zealand in June 1964. Devlin said, "Touring with The Beatles was probably the highlight of my career. They were fabulous. They invited me to all of their parties. I had written a song called ***Won't You Be My Baby?*** and I played it to Paul McCartney backstage at Sydney Stadium, but he didn't like it. He just sort of took the guitar and fiddled around with it a bit and he said, 'Why don't you do this?' He put a couple of chords in here, there and everywhere and it sounded better. I recorded it in early 1965 and it was a minor hit single in Australia. I was A&R (Artist and Repertoire) manager for RCA in Australia at the time, and it was my last released for them." Devlin cannot recall if he used studio musicians or The Devils (probably Bob Taylor, Kevin McKeefry, Colin Luck and Barry Coupland) to back him on ***Won't You Be My Baby***. The recording was included on the 1979 various artists album **25 Rare Recycled RCA Rock Relics** and is also available on Devlin's LP **Stag-O-Lee** (Canetoad Records / CTLP-006) in Australia. None of these records lists McCartney as co-composer but Devlin said, "I thought in all fairness that I should mention Paul as contributing to it; I'm quite sure the song is registered in both of our names."

Devlin relocated to England and signed with CBS Records soon after the release of ***Won't You Be My Baby***. He had a couple of singles issued there, one of which, ***My Strength, Heart And Soul***, was a top 10 on Radio London's charts. After two years he had to return to Australia due to work permit difficulties. Over the years Devlin has sporadically recorded, performed on the club circuit, made TV appearances and rock documentaries and managed other artists. He has received several composer's awards in Australia. Devlin is currently working on a TV special in celebration of his 40 years in show business.

Dog Soldier

Record 77 title:
April Rainbow
Label / Catalog number:
Cutting Room
Recording Location / Date:
Record Plant (East) Studios, New York, NY, USA / 22 Jan 75
Media:
Single 10" [Acetate]
Producer:
Roy Cicala & John Lennon

Song 77a title:
April Rainbow
Release date / Country:
[Unreleased] / U.S.A.
Track details:
3 min. 05 sec.
Composer:
J. Corbert

Patrick Jude: Lead Vocals; probably one or more of the following: Mark Rivera: Saxophone; John Corbert: Keyboards; Vinnie Appice: Drums; Joe Bassin: Trombone; Bob Livingood: Trumpet; Rick: Bass; Kenny Papa; Kenny Sambolin; Joe Crupi: Guitar

Record 78 title:
[None]
Recording Location / Date:
Record Plant (East) Studios, New York, NY, USA / 22 Jan 75
Producer:
Roy Cicala & John Lennon

Song 78a title:
Everyday Living
Release date / Country:
[Unreleased]
Track details:
3 min. 01 sec.
Composer:
P. Jude - M. Rivera - J. Corbert - V. Appice

Patrick Jude: Lead Vocals; probably one or more of the following: Mark Rivera: Saxophone; John Corbert: Keyboards; Vinnie Appice: Drums; Joe Bassin: Trombone; Bob Livingood: Trumpet; Rick: Bass; Kenny Papa; Kenny Sambolin; Joe Crupi: Guitar

Record 79 title:
[None]
Producer:
Roy Cicala & John Lennon
Recording Location / Date:
Record Plant (East) Studios, New York, NY, USA / 1974 or 1975

Song 79a title:
Incantation
Track details:
3 min. 55 sec.
Release date / Country:
Released exclusively with the book Beatles Undercover
Composer:
R. Cicala - J. Lennon

Patrick Jude: Lead Vocals & (possible) Percussion; probably one or more of the following: Mark Rivera: Saxophone; John Corbert: Keyboards; Vinnie Appice: Drums; Joe Bassin: Trombone; Bob Livingood: Trumpet; Rick: Bass; Kenny Papa; Kenny Sambolin; Joe Crupi: Guitar

Record 80 title:
[None]
Producer:
Roy Cicala & John Lennon
Recording Location / Date:
Record Plant (East) Studios, New York, NY, USA / (probably) Jan 75

Song 80a title:
You Can't Do That
Release date / Country:
[Unreleased]
Composer:
J. Lennon - P. McCartney

Patrick Jude: Lead Vocals & (possible) Percussion; probably one or more of the following: Mark Rivera: Saxophone; John Corbert: Keyboards; Vinnie Appice: Drums; Joe Bassin: Trombone; Bob Livingood: Trumpet; Rick: Bass; Kenny Papa; Kenny Sambolin; Joe Crupi: Guitar

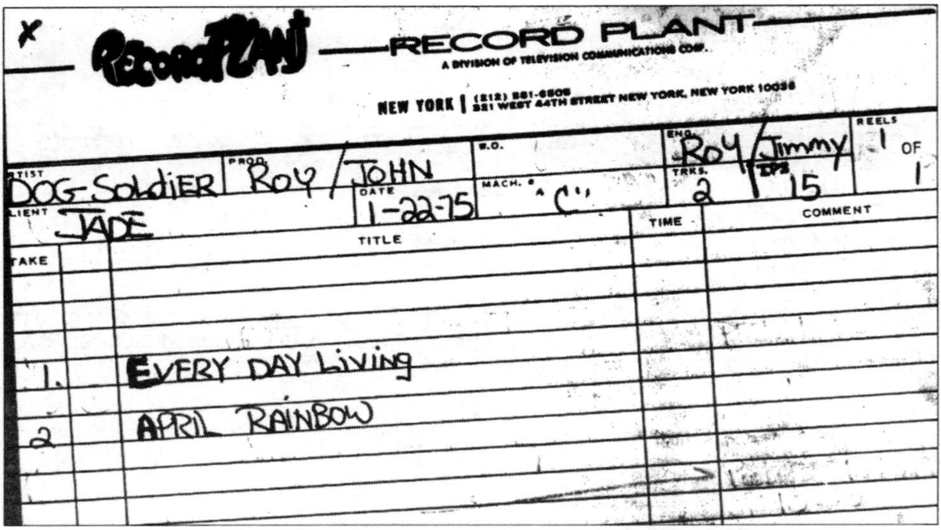

Tape box cover for "April Rainbow" from Record Plant Studio, courtesy of Roy Cicala

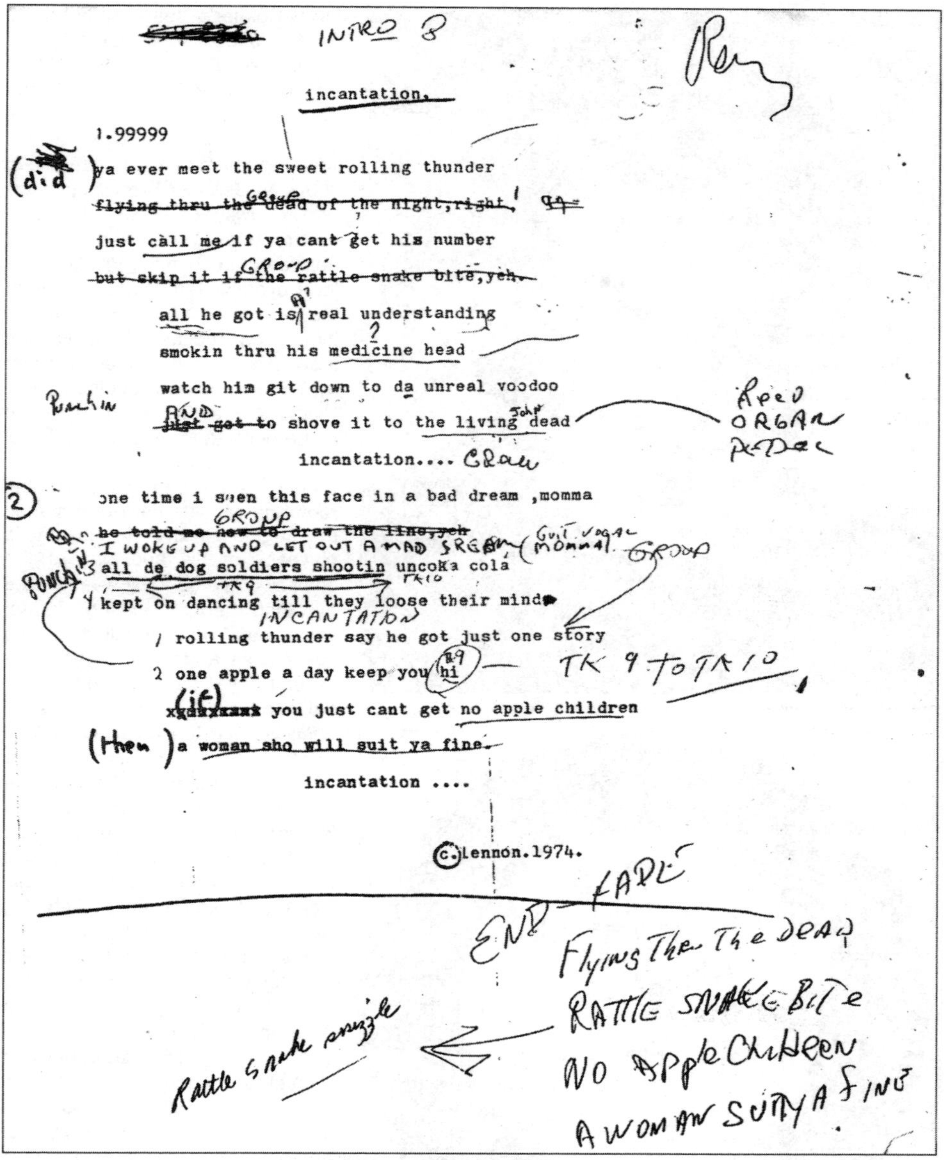

INTRO 8

incantation.

1.99999

(did) ya ever meet the sweet rolling thunder

flying thru the dead of the night,right.

just call me if ya cant get his number

but skip it if the rattle snake bite,yeh.

all he got is real understanding

smokin thru his medicine head

watch him git down to da unreal voodoo

just got to shove it to the living dead

incantation....

one time i seen this face in a bad dream ,momma

he told me how to draw the line,yeh

I WOKE UP AND LET OUT A MAD SCREAM (MOMMA)

all de dog soldiers shootin uncoka cola

kept on dancing till they loose their mind.

INCANTATION

rolling thunder say he got just one story

one apple a day keep you hi

(if) you just cant get no apple children

(then) a woman sho will suit ya fine.

incantation ....

(c) Lennon.1974.

END FADE

Flying Thru The dead

RATTLE SNAKE BITE

NO Apple Children

A WOMAN SUIT YA FINE

Rattle snake sizzle

Lyric sheet for "Incantation", courtesy of Patrick jude

The band Dog Soldier (not to be confused with the mid-'70s U.K band of the same name) was originally called Community Apple. Community Apple was fronted by singer Joey Dambra, who sang backing vocals on John Lennon's song ***#9 Dream***. Following the departure of Dambra and other members of the group, they became known as Bomf, which stood for Band Of Mother Fuckers *(see Lori Burton)*, and finally, Dog Soldier. According to May Pang, Lennon had nothing to do with the name Bomf, but he did come up with the name Dog Soldier that was taken from John's lyrics to the song ***Incantation***. The band was dubbed John Lennon etc. when they backed Lennon at his last live performance on April 18, 1975, at the Waldorf Astoria Hotel for **A Salute to Sir Lew Grade**.

Patrick Jude, photo courtesy of Patrick Jude

Dog Soldier's lead singer was Patrick Jude, born Patrick Jude Petrullo on February 25, 1951 in Hoboken, New Jersey. Patrick has been a singer, dancer and stage and screen actor most of his life. After two years of playing the role of Judas in **Jesus Christ Superstar** on Broadway, he decided to return to fronting a rock band. He answered an ad in the Village Voice for a dynamic lead singer and front man for a recording band that led him to an audition at the Record Plant (East) Studios. Record Plant owner and sound engineer Roy Cicala took Jude to another studio in the building to meet the writer of the lyrics they wanted him to sing. As Jude entered the studio control room, he saw the back of a man in the engineer's chair listening to a playback of his audition. As the chair swung around he was greeted by John Lennon saying, "Great voice man!" Jude recalled, "I was speechless and couldn't sleep for several days." Patrick said he later did hand claps on Lennon's song ***Whatever Gets You Thru The Night***.

Acetate for "April Rainbow", courtesy of Roy Cicala

Another member of Dog Soldier was Mark Rivera. Rivera has been blowing his saxophone on the road and in studios since 1967. He has worked for a wide range of musicians including Hall & Oates* , Simon & Garfunkel *(see Paul Simon)* and Joe Walsh*, but he is best known for his work with Billy Joel. Mark filled a variety of roles (saxophone, percussion acoustic guitar, keyboards and backing vocals) on Ringo Starr's All-Starr Band tours in 1995 and 1997. The drummer in Dog Soldier was Vinnie Appice, who went on to drum in Rick Derringer's band in the mid-'70s. His brother Carmine Appice is the drummer for the group Vanilla Fudge.

According to Jude, Lennon was involved in four of Dog Soldier's recordings done at the Record Plant in late 1974 or early 1975. Two of the songs, ***Everyday Living*** and ***April Rainbow***, were Dog Soldier compositions that John produced. Another song was ***Incantation***, a number originally written by Roy Cicala with new lyrics written by Lennon. John also produced Dog Soldier's version of The Beatles' ***You Can't Do That*** written by Lennon. Jude said almost an album's worth of Dog Soldier material was recorded and was probably going to come out on Apple. He thinks the album was going to be titled **Incantation**. According to Cicala, "because

Dog Soldier had mostly original songs, John and Capitol Records wanted them to record a cover version of ***You Can't Do That***. When we were ready to mix the whole album, John got back together with Yoko and disappeared."

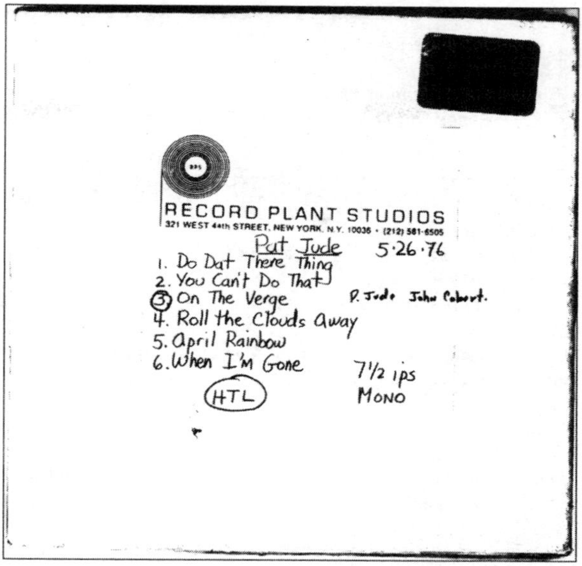

RECORD PLANT STUDIOS
321 WEST 44th STREET, NEW YORK, N.Y. 10036 • (212) 581-6505
Pat Jude 5·26·76
1. Do Dat There Thing
2. You Can't Do That
3. On The Verge
P. Jude John Calvert.
4. Roll the Clouds away
5. April Rainbow
6. When I'm Gone
7½ ips
MONO
HTL

Tape box cover for
"You Can't Do That"
from Record Plant Studio,
courtesy of Roy Cicala

Lonnie Donegan

Record 81 title:
Puttin' On The Style
Label / Catalog number:
United Artists / UA-LA 827-H
Jacket / Inserts:
Standard international design with Gatefold with photo of Ringo Starr / Record label inner sleeve
Recording Location / Date:
Larrabee Studios, Los Angeles, CA, U.S.A. / Jul &/or Aug 77

Media:
Album 12"
Producer:
Adam Faith

Song 81a title:
Ham 'n' Eggs
Release date / Country:
09 an 78 / U.S.A.

Track details:
Side 1, track 3 / 3 min. 10 sec.
Composer:
Trad Arr. by: L. Donegan

Lonnie Donegan: Lead Vocals & 12-String Guitar; Ringo Starr: Drums; Dave Wyntor: Bass; Peter Jameson: Acoustic & Slide Guitar; Peter Banks: Guitar; Peter Wingfield: Piano; Leo Sayer: Harp

Song 81b title:
Have A Drink On Me (Take A Whiff On Me)
Release date / Country:
09 Jan 78 / U.S.A.

Track details:
Side 1, track 2 / 3 min. 00 sec.
Composer:
H. Ledbetter - J. Lomax - A. Lomax - L. Donegan - P. Buchanan

Lonnie Donegan: Lead Vocals & Banjo; Ringo Starr: Drums; Dave Wyntor: Bass; Peter Jameson: Acoustic & Slide Guitar; Peter Wingfield: Piano; Albert Lee: Lead Guitar; Southern California Community Choir-Arr. Rev. James Cleveland: B. Vocals

Record 82 title:
[None]
Producer:
Lonnie Donegan
Recording Location / Date:
Essex Studios, London & FPSHOT (Friar Park Studios, Henley-on-Thames)†, U.K. / 1979

Song 82a title:
Everybody's Making It Big But Me
Release date / Country:
[Unreleased]
Composer:
C. Hodges - D. Peacock

Lonnie Donegan: Lead Vocals & Banjo; George Harrison: Guitar†; Dave Peacock: Bass; Chas Hodges: Guitar; Mick Burt: Drums

Song 82b title:
Massage Parlour
Release date / Country:
[Unreleased]
Composer:
C. Hodges - D. Peacock

Lonnie Donegan: Lead Vocals & Guitar; George Harrison: Guitar†; Dave Peacock: Bass; Chas Hodges: Guitar; Mick Burt: Drums

Song 82c title:
Punchy And The Willer Warbler
Release date / Country:
[Unreleased]
Composer:
C. Hodges - D. Peacock

Lonnie Donegan: Lead Vocals & Guitar; George Harrison: Guitar†; Dave Peacock: Bass; Chas Hodges: Guitar; Mick Burt: Drums

Lonnie Donegan was born Anthony Donegan on April 29, 1931 in Glasgow, Scotland, but was raised in London, England. His father was a violinist in the National Scottish Orchestra and his mother was an English teacher. Lonnie began playing drums at age thirteen but switched to guitar and banjo several years later. The name Lonnie was borrowed from the blues artist Lonnie Johnson. His early career included membership in a variety of jazz bands including a stint with Chris Barber's Jazz Band *(see Chris Barber & His Band).*

During his membership in Barber's band, Donegan recorded a skiffle version of ***Rock Island Line*** that became an international smash hit in 1956. Donegan was dubbed the "king of skiffle." He inspired many an English youth, including John Lennon, Paul McCartney and George Harrison, to take up guitar, washboard and tea chest bass, laying the foundation for a generation of British rock stars. Harrison and McCartney attended Donegan's performances at Liverpool's Empire Theatre as teenagers. One of the songs that survive on tape from a John Lennon and The Quarry Men performance for the Woolton Parish Fete at St. Peter's Church (the day John met Paul McCartney) was Donegan's current hit ***Puttin' On The Style***. The Westwood One radio series **The Lost Lennon Tapes** featured home demos of Lennon during the '70s singing several Donegan classics. It's also not surprising that the first bands Ringo was in were called The Eddie Clayton Skiffle Group and Darktown Skiffle Group.

Donegan's music consisted mostly of adaptations of American folk, country and western, and rhythm & blues classics, or comedy numbers. His U.K. hits included, among many others, ***Cumberland Gap***, ***Lost John***, ***Don't You Rock Me Daddy-O***, ***Putting On The Style***, ***Have A Drink On Me (Take A Wiff On Me)*** ***My Old Man's A Dustman*** and ***Does Your Chewing Gum Lose Its Flavor (On The Bedpost Overnight)*** which was also a hit in the U.S. Donegan established a folk music society that also acted as his fan-club; one member was George Harrison. Donegan thinks The Beatles played at one of the fan-club's meetings at the Cavern Club in Liverpool.

Donegan's success waned following the British music invasion in the mid-1960s that he had helped inspire. He continued to perform in cabarets around the world until heart problems slowed his pace in the mid-1970s. Donegan was featured in the 1982 film documentary **The Complete Beatles**. He became active in music publishing and acting and played the leading role in the British musical comedy **Mr. Cincers** in 1984. Donegan is now semi-retired and living in the south of Spain.

At a party Paul McCartney threw in Los Angeles following Wings' final U.S. concert in 1976, Ringo, Leo Sayer, Adam Faith*, and Elton John* started singing Donegan songs together. At McCartney's suggestion, Faith got the assembled to commit to helping him record a new album for Donegan featuring some of his greatest hits. Unfortunately, when it came time to record, McCartney was unavailable. Ringo Starr, however, contributed to the album along with a number of other Donegan admirers including Klaus Voormann *(see Paul Jones)*, Ron Wood*, Zoot Money*, Jim Keltner *(see Attitudes)* and Nicky Hopkins*. Donegan recalls the session that Ringo contributed to as being recorded at Larrabee Studios in Los Angeles. Donegan said he made some recordings with Chas & Dave and George Harrison in 1979 that may be released in the future.

Donovan

Record 83 title:
Donovan Rising
Media:
Album 5" CD
Label / Catalog number:
Permanent / PERM CD 2
Producer:
Patrick Hehir
Jacket / Inserts:
Unique in Jewel box / 4 page CD booklet with lyrics & photos of George Harrison, John Lennon & Paul McCartney; John Lennon: Quotation
Recording Location / Date:
On location at Carnegie Hall, New York, NY, U.S.A. / (sometime between) 1968 - 1971

Song 83a title:
Hurdy Gurdy Man [live]
Track details:
Side 1, track 3 / 6 min. 04 sec.
Release date / Country:
Nov 90 (first issued 1973) / U.K.
Composer:
D. Leitch - [G. Harrison]

Donovan Leitch: Lead Vocals & Guitar

Record 84 title:
No. 3 Abbey Road N.W.8
Media:
Album 5" CD
Label / Catalog number:
Vigotone / VT-116 [Unauthorized Record]
Producer:
Paul McCartney
Jacket / Inserts:
Unique in Jewel box / 4 page CD booklet
Recording Location / Date:
Paul McCartney's home studio, 7 Cavendish Ave, St. John's Wood, London, U.K. / (probably) Nov 68 - Jan 69

Song 84a title:
Good Morning Mr. Wind
Track details:
Side 1, track 6 / 1 min. 31 sec.
Release date / Country:
1993 / U.S.A.
Composer:
D. Leitch

Donovan Leitch: Lead Vocals & Guitar; Paul McCartney: Guitar & Voice

Song 84b title:
Lalena
Release date / Country:
1993 / U.S.A.
Track details:
Side 1, track 4 / 3 min. 26 sec.
Composer:
D. Leitch

Donovan Leitch: Lead Vocals & Guitar; Paul McCartney: Guitar & B. Vocals

Song 84c title:
Land Of Gisch
Release date / Country:
1993 / U.S.A.
Track details:
Side 1, track 8 / 0 min. 48 sec.
Composer:
D. Leitch

Donovan Leitch: Lead Vocals & Guitar; Paul McCartney: Voice

Song 84d title:
The Walrus And The Carpenter
Release date / Country:
1993 / U.S.A.
Track details:
Side 1, track 7 / 1 min. 07 sec.
Composer:
D. Leitch - L. Carroll

Donovan Leitch: Lead Vocals & Guitar; Paul McCartney: Voice

Song 84e title:
Unicorn
Release date / Country:
1993 / U.S.A.
Track details:
Side 1, track 3 / 1 min. 04 sec.
Composer:
D. Leitch

Donovan Leitch: Lead Vocals & Guitar

Record 85 title:
Troubadour The Definitive Collection / 1964-1976
Media:
Album 5" CD [2 CD set]
Label / Catalog number:
Epic/Legacy / E2K 46986 (EK 48691)
Producer:
Mickie Most
Jacket / Inserts:
Unique in box set in Jewel box / 12 page box set booklet with photos of The Beatles & 40 page CD booklet with photos of The Beatles
Recording Location / Date:
Trident Studios, London, England / Oct 66

Song 85a title:
Mellow Yellow
Release date / Country:
Aug 92 (first issued 24 Oct 66) / U.S.A.
Track details:
CD1, track 13 / 3 min. 40 sec.
Composer:
D. Leitch

Donovan Leitch: Lead Vocals & Acoustic Guitar; John Paul Jones: Bass; Bobby Orr: Drums; Danny Moss: Horns; Ronnie Ross: Horns; Paul McCartney: Voice

Donovan Leitch was born in Glasgow, Scotland on May 10, 1946. He has spent most of his musical career as a folk singer, though much of his commercial success in the U.S. was achieved with his more rock-oriented material in the mid- to late-1960s. His self-penned ***Catch The Wind*** hit the U.K. top 10 in March 1965 and was followed by ***Colours*** in July. He was billed as the English Bob Dylan*, a comparison that he accurately rejects to this day. Ironically, it was Dylan who introduced Donovan to The Beatles during his British tour in 1965. Donovan's only number one hit was ***Sunshine Superman***, originally subtitled ***For John and Paul*** as a tribute to Lennon and McCartney. Donovan also contributed the lyrics "Sky of blue, sea of green" to The Beatles' song ***Yellow Submarine***, though he was not one of the guests making noise in the background, and he did not help write ***Eleanor Rigby*** as was rumored.

In the fall of 1966, Donovan's song ***Mellow Yellow*** had reached the top 10 about the time that the psychedelic drug culture was first blooming. There were rumors that the song was a message about the euphoric effects of smoking banana peels. In reality, it was about an electric dildo. After failing to get high on banana peels, rumor mongers claimed that some of the whispered phrases in the song were sung by none other than Paul McCartney, but close listening reveals them to be by Donovan. Apparently, very few people paid much attention to interviews Donovan later gave identifying McCartney as one of the revelers in the party portion of the song. In McCartney's World Tour Program from 1989, Paul lists under session work, "Donovan (bass on a few tracks around ***Mellow Yellow***)." However, Donovan does not recall McCartney making bass contributions to any of his recordings. Donovan dropped by The Beatles' recording sessions for ***A Day In The Life*** and appeared in a documentary film that was made of the sessions, a portion of which appeared in **The Beatles Anthology** film.

Donovan's friendship with The Beatles grew during their stay together at the Maharishi Mahesh Yogi's ashram in Rishikesh, India in early 1968. While there, Donovan and The Beatles began swapping musical ideas. Donovan taught John Lennon a style of guitar playing he used on his songs ***Julia*** and ***Dear Prudence*** from **The Beatles** (white) album. Lennon also incorporated the style on a number of his solo recordings as well. Donovan denied reports that he helped write The Beatles' song ***Rocky Raccoon***. He did say that, while in India, he helped George Harrison write the unreleased song ***Dhera Dun***, which Harrison briefly performed in **The Beatles Anthology** film. One of Donovan's hits written at the ashram, ***Jennifer Juniper***, was about Harrison's sister-in-law Jenny Boyd.

Donovan's musical style began reflecting his turn towards Eastern mysticism. His hit ***Hurdy Gurdy Man***, was about the Maharishi, and was also written at the ashram in India. George Harrison contributed a verse to the song which Donovan said was omitted from the studio version because of Jimmy Page's long guitar solo. When Donovan performed ***Hurdy Gurdy Man*** live at Carnegie Hall in New York, he described the situation and included the Harrison lyrics. This live version of ***Hurdy Gurdy Man*** was first issued in the U.K. on the CD **Donovan Rising** on Permanent Records (PERM CD 2.) The CD booklet, in black and white, featured a group photo with Donovan, Mike Love *(see The Beach Boys)*, Mia Farrow, Maharishi, Lennon, McCartney, Harrison and The Beatles' wives and girlfriends. The booklet also featured a photo, circa 1969/70, of George with Donovan, and a quotation from Lennon in 1968 that reads "Donovan is as important and influential as Bob Dylan and we are...listen the man's a poet." The first U.S. issue of ***Hurdy Gurdy Man*** with the Harrison lyrics was on the promotional CD single featuring the same photo of The Beatles at the Maharishi's camp in India, only this time as the front cover and in color. The live version is also available on the U.S. CD **Donovan The Classics Live** (Great Northern Arts / GNA 61007-2.) Only the U.K. CD is listed, as it is the most complete in terms of Beatles involvement. The first release of ***Hurdy Gurdy Man*** with the Harrison lyrics was issued in 1973 on Donovan's album **Live In Japan**.

Donovan and McCartney did some rehearsing together in the basement of Paul's Cavendish home in St. John's Wood in 1968 that first appeared in 1980 on side two of the bootleg album, **No. 3 Abbey Road N.W.8**. Donovan also worked with McCartney on Mary Hopkin's* debut album **Postcard** for Apple Records.

Ever the story teller, Donovan recorded a song about the mythical lost continent "Atlantis" that became one of his biggest hits. Since the release of ***Atlantis*** in late 1968, it has been widely reported, even in the most reliable publications, and taken as gospel, that Paul McCartney contributed backing vocals and tambourine to the song. However, the gospel according to Donovan states McCartney did not contribute to ***Atlantis*** in any way.

Donovan has released a number of albums since the height of his popularity in the late 1960s. The songs from his 1973 album **Cosmic Wheels** were published by Apple Music when Donovan was being managed by Allen Klein. Several Apple Custom label acetates of Donovan's demos exist, though, according to Donovan, they contain no contributions by any of The Beatles. He made a brief cameo appearance in Robert Stigwood's 1978 film **Sgt. Pepper's Lonely Hearts Club Band**. Donovan did not contribute to Harrison's 1987 album **Cloud Nine**, as was rumored. He did write a song for Harrison called ***Dear Heart***, though he is not sure if Harrison has recorded it.

In 1992, Epic/Legacy Records released a double CD retrospective box set titled **Troubadour** that contains ***Mellow Yellow*** and two photos of Donovan with The Beatles in India in 1968. Some of the

CD liner notes are written by The Beatles' press officer and Apple publicist Derek Taylor. In the set, Donovan thanks the following for their influence on his career: Bob Dylan*, George Harrison, John Lennon, Paul McCartney, Allen Ginsberg*, Maharishi Mahesh Yogi, Dave Mason*, Jim Keltner *(see Attitudes)*, and Allen Klein.

Paul McCartney featured Donovan's music on his 1995 radio series **Oobu Joobu**. Donovan continues to maintain his loyal following, and his career and music are currently enjoying a revival. His 1996 album **Sutras** has received critical praise, as have his children, Donovan Jr. and Ione Skye, for their acting roles.

Dr. John

Record 86 title:
Ringo Starr And His All-Starr Band
Label / Catalog number:
Pioneer Artists / PA-090-007
Jacket / Inserts:
Standard international design / Record label inner sleeve
Recording Location / Date:
On location at Greek Theatre, Los Angeles, CA, U.S.A. / 03 Sep 89
Media:
Album 12" LVD
Producer:
Tim Snow (film);
Joe Walsh & Jim Nipar (music)

Song 86a title:
Iko Iko [live]
Release date / Country:
Jul 90 / U.S.A.
Track details:
Side 1, track 4 / 6 min. 05 sec.
Composer:
R.L. Hawkins - B. Hawkins - J. Johnson - J. Crawford

Dr. John: Lead Vocals & Keyboards; Billy Preston: Keyboards; Jim Keltner: Drums; Ringo Starr: Drums; Levon Helm: Drums; Nils Lofgren: Guitar; Joe Walsh: Guitar; Rick Danko: Bass; Clarence Clemons: Saxophone

This song is also included on Rykodisc / RCD 10190 & RCD5-1019 / Albums 5" [2 CD set] / released 12 Oct 90 / Unique in box set in Jewel box's / 6 page CD booklet, sticker postcard & Rykodisc info. postcard & CD insert

Song 86b title:
Right Place Wrong Time [live]
Release date / Country:
Jul 90 / U.S.A.
Track details:
Side 2, track 4 (16) / 3 min. 52 sec.
Composer:
M. Rubennack

Dr. John: Lead Vocals & Keyboards; Billy Preston: Keyboards; Jim Keltner: Drums; Ringo Starr: Drums; Levon Helm: Drums; Nils Lofgren: Guitar; Joe Walsh: Guitar; Rick Danko: Bass; Clarence Clemons: Saxophone

Dr. John was born Malcolm John Rebennack on November 21, 1940 in New Orleans, Louisiana. His father owned a record store and his mother was a model who first introduced young "Mac" to the world by helping get his picture on the cover of Ivory Soap boxes. Dr. John, who also goes under the name Mac Rebennack, is regarded as one of the finest purveyors of the New Orleans sound, mixing jazz, funk, gospel, and rhythm & blues, along with his own brand of Cajun Voodoo, into a style that's been called swamp rock. He has had some success as a solo artist with such well-known hits as ***Right Place, Wrong Time*** and ***Such A Night***, but he's also been recognized over the last thirty years as a top songwriter and session player for such artists as Eric Clapton*, Taj Mahal*, Chris Barber *(see Chris Barber & His Band)* and Phil Spector*, among many others. John started out as a guitar player but switched to the keyboards in the 1960s. He often bills himself as **Dr. John The Night Tripper** and dresses up in wild Mardi Gras and witch doctor style costumes, complete with feathered headdress.

In early December 1973, John Lennon, along with Cher, Bobby Womack, Elton John* and Bonnie

Dr. John, New York City, NY, late 1980s, photo courtesy of Tom Bert

Bramlett *(see Delaney & Bonnie & Friends)*, joined Dr. John on stage while he performed ***Cold, Cold*** and ***Mama Don't Know*** at Hollywood's Troubadour Club. Lennon's contributions were limited to repetitive discordant sounds on keyboards. The get-together probably took place following one of the recording sessions for Lennon's album **Rock 'N' Roll**, to which Dr. John had contributed. Dr. John contributed to Ringo Starr's 1974 album **Goodnight Vienna**, his 1976 album **Rotogravure**, and his 1978 album **Bad Boy**. He also worked with Ringo on The Manhattan Transfer's* album **Coming Out**.

Dr. John's 1975 album **Hollywood Be Thy Name** initially contained a custom inner sleeve with two photos of Ringo Starr, and credits Ringo as "Master Of Ceremonies." According to Dr. John, Ringo played the part of "Master Of Ceremonies" in a film to promote **Hollywood Be Thy Name**, but did not contribute musically to the album. It's possible that Ringo is buried in some of the crowd noise included on the album. The footage was shot at Cherokee Studios in Los Angeles which was decorated and renamed Willie Purple's Nightclub for the occasion. Unfortunately, the promotional film was never used. Dr. John recorded a cover of The Beatles' song **Yesterday**, and made a brief cameo appearance in Robert

Stigwood's 1978 film **Sgt. Pepper's Lonely Hearts Club Band.**

Dr. John was a member of Ringo's All-Starr Band tour in 1989. During the tour, John performed ***Iko Iko*** and ***Right Place, Wrong Time*** with Ringo backing him on drums. John also performed ***Candy*** and ***Such A Night*** on the tour, but to date they have not been released. Dr. John is still in high demand as a session player and continues to play the club circuit.

Bob Dylan

Record 87 title:
Bobfest Rehearsals October 1992

Media:
Album 5" CD [2 CD set]

Label / Catalog number:
Yellow Cat / YC 036/37 [Unauthorized Record]

Jacket / Inserts:
Unique in Jewel box with photo of George Harrison / 4 page CD booklet with photos of George Harrison

Recording Location / Date:
On location at Madison Square Garden, New York, NY, U.S.A. / (probably) 16 Oct 92

Song 87a title:
My Back Pages [rehearsal - 4 takes]

Track details:
CD1, track 11-15 / 26 min. 49 sec. [combined time]

Release date / Country:
Feb 97 / U.S.A.

Composer:
B. Dylan

Bob Dylan: Guitar & Vocals; George Harrison: Guitar & Vocals; Eric Clapton Guitar & Vocals; Neil Young: Guitar & B. Vocals; G. E. Smith: Guitar; Anton Fig: Drums; Tom Petty: Guitar & B. Vocals; Roger McGuinn: Guitar & Vocals; Jim Keltner: Drums; Donald Dunn: Bass; Steve Cropper: Guitar; Al Kooper: Organ; Stan Lynch: Percussion

Record 88 title:
New Morning

Media:
Album 5" CD

Label / Catalog number:
Columbia / CK 30290

Producer:
Bob Johnson

Jacket / Inserts:
Standard international design with slight variation in Jewel box / 4 page CD insert

Recording Location / Date:
Columbia Studios, New York, NY, U.S.A. / (probably) 01 May 70 &/or 05 Jun 70

Song 88a title:
Went To See The Gypsy

Track details:
Side 1, track 4 / 2 min. 48 sec.

Release date / Country:
25 Jul 89 (first issued 21 Oct 70) / U.S.A.

Composer:
B. Dylan

Bob Dylan: Lead Vocals & (possible) Piano; probably the following: Bob Johnson: (probable) Piano; Charlie Daniels: Bass; George Harrison: (probable) Electric Guitar; Al Kooper: Keyboards; Russ Kunkel: Drums

Record 89 title:
Odds & Ends (Unsurpassed Maestro Vol 1)
Media:
Album 5" CD
Label / Catalog number:
Sick Cat / 006 [Unauthorized Record]
Producer:
Bob Johnson
Jacket / Inserts:
Unique in Jewel box / 4 page CD insert
Recording Location / Date:
Columbia Studio B, New York, NY, U.S.A. / 01 May 70

Song 89a title:
Working On A Guru
Track details:
Side 1, track 8 / 3 min. 38 sec.
Release date / Country:
1993
Composer:
B. Dylan

Bob Dylan: Lead Vocals & Acoustic Guitar; George Harrison: Electric Guitar; Russ Kunkel: Drums; Charlie Daniels: Bass

Record 90 title:
Shot Of Love
Media:
Album 5" CD
Label / Catalog number:
Columbia / CK 37496
Producer:
Chuck Plotkin & Bob Dylan
Jacket / Inserts:
Standard international design in jewel box / 4 page insert
Recording Location / Date:
Clover Recorders, Los Angeles, CA, U.S.A. / May 80

Song 90a title:
Heart Of Mine
Track details:
Side 1, track 2 / 4 min. 32 sec.
Release date / Country:
18 Jun 90 (first issued 10 Aug 81) / U.S.A.
Composer:
B. Dylan

Bob Dylan: Lead Vocals & Piano; Jim Keltner: Drums; Chuck Plotkin: Drums; Donald "Duck" Dunn: Bass; Wm "Smitty" Smith: Organ; Ron Wood: Guitar; Ringo Starr: Drums (Tom Tom); Clydie King: B. Vocals

Record 91 title:
The 30th Anniversary Concert Celebration
Media:
Album 5" CD [2 CD set]
Label / Catalog number:
Columbia / C2K 53230
Producer:
Jeff Rosen & Don DeVito
Jacket / Inserts:
Standard international design in double jewel box with photo of George Harrison / 14 page CD booklet with photos of George Harrison
Recording Location / Date:
On location at Madison Square Garden, New York, NY, U.S.A. / 16 Oct 92

Song 91a title:
Knockin' On Heaven's Door [live]
Track details:
CD2, track 13 / 5 min. 38 sec.
Release date / Country:
24 Aug 93 / U.S.A.
Composer:
B. Dylan

Bob Dylan: Lead Vocals & Guitar; George Harrison: Guitar & B. Vocals; Neil Young: Guitar & B. Vocals; Eric Clapton Guitar & B. Vocals; Ron Wood: Guitar & B. Vocals; G. E. Smith: Guitar; Tom Petty

Guitar & B. Vocals; Roger McGuinn: Guitar & B. Vocals; George Thorogood: Guitar & B. Vocals; Jim Keltner: Drums; Booker T. Jones: Keyboards; Anton Fig: Drums; Al Kooper: Keyboards; Donald Dunn: Bass; Steve Cropper: Guitar; Tracy Chapman: B. Vocals; June Carter: B. Vocals; Johnny Cash: B. Vocals; Kris Kristofferson: B. Vocals; Paddy Clancy: B. Vocals & Guitar; Bobby Clancy: B. Vocals; Liam Clancy: B. Vocals; Robbie O'Connell: B. Vocals; Tommy Makem: B. Vocals; Rosanne Cash: B. Vocals; Mary-Chapin Carpenter: B. Vocals; Shawn Colvin: B. Vocals; Chrissie Hynde: B. Vocals; Richie Havens: B. Vocals; Lou Reed: B. Vocals; Stan Lynch: Percussion & B. Vocals; Sinead O'Connor: B. Vocals; Sylvia Hawkins: B. Vocals; Willie Nelson: B. Vocals

This song is also included on Columbia Music Video / ML2 49165 / Albums 12" LVD [2 disc set] / Disk 2, Side 4, track 3 / Standard international design with Gatefold.

Song 91b title:
My Back Pages [live]
Release date / Country:
24 Aug 93 / U.S.A.
Track details:
CD2, track 12 / 4 min. 39 sec.
Composer:
B. Dylan

Bob Dylan: Guitar & Vocals; George Harrison: Guitar & Vocals; Eric Clapton Guitar & Vocals; Neil Young: Guitar & Vocals; G. E. Smith: Guitar; Anton Fig: Drums; Tom Petty: Guitar & Vocals; Roger McGuinn: Guitar & Vocals; Jim Keltner: Drums; Donald Dunn: Bass; Steve Cropper: Guitar; Al Kooper: Organ; Stan Lynch: Percussion This song are also included on Columbia Music Video / ML2 49165 / Albums 12" LVD [2 disc set] / Disk 2, Side 4, track 2 / Standard international design with Gatefold.

Record 92 title:
The Bootleg Series Volumes 1-3
[rare & unreleased] 1961-1991
Media:
Albums 5" CD [3 CD set]
Label / Catalog number:
Columbia / C3K 47382 (CK 47400)
Producer:
Bob Johnson
Jacket / Inserts:
Standard international design in jewel box in box set / (3) CD inserts
& 72 page box set booklet
Recording Location / Date:
Columbia Studio B, New York, NY, U.S.A. / 01 May 70

Song 92a title:
If Not For You
Release date / Country:
25 Mar 91 / U.S.A.
Track details:
CD2, track 15 / 3 min. 32 sec.
Composer:
B. Dylan

Bob Dylan: Lead Vocals, Guitar & Harmonica; George Harrison: Electric Guitar; Charlie Daniels: Bass; Russ Kunkel: Drums

Record 93 title:
The Concert For Bangla Desh
Media:
Album 5" CD [2 CD set]
Label / Catalog number:
Capitol/Apple / CDP 7 93265 2
Producer:
George Harrison & Phil Spector
Jacket / Inserts:
Standard international design in double Jewel box / 34 page CD booklet with
photo of George Harrison & Ringo Starr
Recording Location / Date:
On location at Madison Square Garden, New York, NY, U.S.A.
/ 01 Dec 71 [evening]

Song 93a title:
Mr. Tambourine Man [live]
Release date / Country:
01 Aug 91 (first issued 20 Dec 71) / U.S.A.
Track details:
CD2, track 6 / 4 min. 06 sec.
Composer:
B. Dylan

Bob Dylan: Lead Vocals, Acoustic Guitar & Harmonica; George Harrison: Electric Guitar; Leon Russell: Bass; Ringo Starr: Tambourine

Song 93b title:
A Hard Rain's Gonna Fall [live]
Release date / Country:
01 Aug 91 (first issued 20 Dec 71) / U.S.A.
Track details:
CD2, track 3 / 5 min. 04 sec.
Composer:
B. Dylan

Bob Dylan: Lead Vocals, Acoustic Guitar & Harmonica; George Harrison: Electric Guitar; Leon Russell: Bass; Ringo Starr: Tambourine

This song is also included on The Concert For Bangla Desh / Warner Bros / NJL-38583 / Album 12" LVD / Side 2, track 4 / released 1990 in Japan / Standard international design with variations with photo of George Harrison on back / Record label inner sleeve & 4 page translation insert (see below.)

Song 93c title:
Blowin' In The Wind [live]
Release date / Country:
01 Aug 91 (first issued 20 Dec 71) / U.S.A.
Track details:
CD2, track 5 / 3 min. 34 sec.
Composer:
B. Dylan

Bob Dylan: Lead Vocals, Acoustic Guitar & Harmonica; George Harrison: Electric Guitar; Leon Russell: Bass; Ringo Starr: Tambourine

This song is also included on The Concert For Bangla Desh / Warner Bros / NJL-38583 / Album 12" LVD / Side 2, track 6 / released 1990 in Japan / Standard international design with variations with photo of George Harrison on back / Record label inner sleeve & 4 page translation insert (see below.)

Song 93d title:
It Takes A Lot To Laugh,
It Takes A Train To Cry [live]
Release date / Country:
01 Aug 91 (first issued 20 Dec 71) / U.S.A.
Track details:
CD2, track 4 / 2 min. 54 sec.
Composer:
B. Dylan

Bob Dylan: Lead Vocals, Acoustic Guitar & Harmonica; George Harrison: Electric Guitar; Leon Russell: Bass; Ringo Starr: Tambourine

This song is also included on The Concert For Bangla Desh / Warner Bros / NJL-38583 / Album 12" LVD / Side 2, track 5 / released 1990 in Japan / Standard international design with variations with photo of George Harrison on back / Record label inner sleeve & 4 page translation insert (see below.)

Song 93e title:
Just Like A Woman [live]
Release date / Country:
01 Aug 91 (first issued 20 Dec 71) / U.S.A.
Track details:
CD2, track 7 / 4 min. 14 sec.
Composer:
B. Dylan

Bob Dylan: Lead Vocals, Acoustic Guitar & Harmonica; George Harrison: Electric Guitar & B. Vocals; Leon Russell: Bass; Ringo Starr: Tambourine

This song is also included on The Concert For Bangla Desh / Warner Bros / NJL-38583 / Album 12" LVD / Side 2, track 7 / released 1990 in Japan / Standard international design with variations with photo of George Harrison on back / Record label inner sleeve & 4 page translation insert (see below.)

Record 94 title:
The Concert For Bangla Desh
Media:
Album 12" LVD
Label / Catalog number:
Warner Bros / NJL-38583
Producer:
Allen Klein (film);
George Harrison & Phil Spector (music)
Jacket / Inserts:
Standard international design with variations with photo of George Harrison on back / Record label inner sleeve & 4 page translation insert
Recording Location / Date:
On location at Madison Square Garden, New York, NY, U.S.A. / 31 Jul 71 [Rehearsal]

Song 94a title:
If Not For You [rehearsal]
Track details:
Side 1, track 1 / 0 min. 32 sec.
Release date / Country:
1990 (first issued Oct 83) / Japan
Composer:
B. Dylan

Bob Dylan: Lead Vocals & Acoustic Guitar; George Harrison: Acoustic Guitar & B. Vocals

Record 95 title:
Under The Red Sky
Media:
Album 5" CD
Label / Catalog number:
Columbia / CK 46794
Producer:
Don & Dave Was
Jacket / Inserts:
Standard international design in jewel box / 12 page CD booklet
Recording Location / Date:
(probably) Ocean Way, (possibly) The Complex & The Record Plant (West) Studios, Los Angeles, CA, U.S.A. / Mar - Apr 90

Song 95a title:
Under The Red Sky
Track details:
Side 1, track 2 / 4 min. 03 sec.
Release date / Country:
11 Sep 90 / U.S.A.
Composer:
B. Dylan

Bob Dylan: Lead Vocals & Acoustic Guitar; George Harrison: Slide Guitar; Waddy Wachtel: Guitar; Al Kooper: Keyboards; Don Was: Bass; Kenny Aronoff: Drums

Record 96 title:
Volume Four And A Half [Various Artists]
Media:
Album 5" CD (mono)
Label / Catalog number:
Adam VIII LTD / CD 49-021
[Unauthorized Record]
Producer:
Unknown-audience, Allen Klein (film);
George Harrison & Phil Spector (music)
Jacket / Inserts:
Unique in Jewel box / 1 page CD insert
Recording Location / Date:
On location at Madison Square Garden, New York, NY, U.S.A. / 01 Aug 71 [afternoon]

Song 96a title:
A Hard Rain's Gonna Fall [live]
Track details:
Side 1, track 23 / 5 min. 30 sec.
Release date / Country:
1991 / Germany
Composer:
B. Dylan

Bob Dylan: Lead Vocals, Acoustic Guitar & Harmonica; George Harrison: Electric Guitar; Leon Russell: Bass; Ringo Starr: Tambourine

Song 96b title:
Love Minus Zero / No Limit [live]
Release date / Country:
1991 / Germany
Track details:
Side 1, track 21 / 4 min. 20 sec.
Composer:
B. Dylan

Bob Dylan: Lead Vocals, Acoustic Guitar & Harmonica; George Harrison: Electric Guitar; Leon Russell: Bass; Ringo Starr: Tambourine

Record 97 title:
Yesterday
Label / Catalog number:
Winged Wheel / WW 9420
[Unauthorized Record]
Jacket / Inserts:
Unique in cardboard gatefold / CD insert
Recording Location / Date:
Columbia Studio B, New York, NY, U.S.A. / 01 May 70
Media:
Album 5" CD
Producer:
Bob Johnston

Song 97a title:
All I Have To Do Is Dream
Release date / Country:
(probably) Feb 95 / Italy
Track details:
Side 1, track 3 / 2 min. 44 sec.
Composer:
B. Bryant

Bob Dylan: Lead Vocals & Acoustic Guitar; George Harrison: Electric Guitar & B. Vocals; Charlie Daniels: Bass; Russ Kunkel: Drums

Song 97b title:
Cupid
Release date / Country:
(probably) Feb 95 / Italy
Track details:
Side 1, track 2 / 3 min. 45 sec.
Composer:
S. Cooke

Bob Dylan: Lead Vocals & Acoustic Guitar; George Harrison: Electric Guitar & B. Vocals; Charlie Daniels: Bass; Russ Kunkel: Drums

Song 97c title:
Da Doo Ron Ron
Release date / Country:
(probably) Feb 95 / Italy
Track details:
Side 1, track 17 / 2 min. 06 sec.
Composer:
P. Spector - J. Barry - E. Greenwich

Bob Dylan: Lead Vocals, Acoustic Guitar & Harmonica; George Harrison: Electric Guitar & B. Vocals; Charlie Daniels: Bass; Russ Kunkel: Drums

Song 97d title:
Medley: Don't Think Twice, It's All Right / Corrnia Corrina
Release date / Country:
(probably) Feb 95 / Italy
Track details:
Side 1, track 14 / 1 min. 46 sec.
Composer:
B. Dylan / Trad

Bob Dylan: Lead Vocals & Acoustic Guitar; George Harrison: Electric Guitar & B. Vocals; Russ Kunkel: Drums; Charlie Daniels: Bass; Bob Johnston: Piano

Song 97e title:
Fishin Blues [or: I'm a-Goin' Fishin' or: Telephone Line]
Track details:
Side 1, track 9 / 1 min. 50 sec.
Release date / Country:
(probably) Feb 95 / Italy

Bob Dylan: Lead Vocals & Acoustic Guitar; George Harrison: Electric Guitar; Charlie Daniels: Bass; Russ Kunkel: Drums

Song 97f title:
Gates Of Eden
Track details:
Side 1, track 4 / 4 min. 19 sec.
Release date / Country:
(probably) Feb 95 / Italy
Composer:
B. Dylan

Bob Dylan: Lead Vocals & Acoustic Guitar; George Harrison: Electric Guitar & B. Vocals; Charlie Daniels: Bass; Russ Kunkel: Drums

Song 97g title:
Ghost Riders In The Sky
Track details:
Side 1, track 1 / 3 min. 41 sec.
Release date / Country:
(probably) Feb 95 / Italy
Composer:
S. Jones

Bob Dylan: Lead Vocals & Acoustic Guitar; George Harrison: Electric Guitar & B. Vocals; Charlie Daniels: Bass; Russ Kunkel: Drums

Song 97h title:
Honey, Just Allow Me One More Chance
Track details:
Side 1, track 10 / 2 min. 36 sec.
Release date / Country:
(probably) Feb 95 / Italy
Composer:
H. Thomas - B. Dylan

Bob Dylan: Lead Vocals & Acoustic Guitar; George Harrison: Electric Guitar; Charlie Daniels: Bass; Russ Kunkel: Drums

Song 97i title:
I Don't Believe You (She Acts Like We Never Have Met)
Track details:
Side 1, track 6 / 3 min. 14 sec.
Release date / Country:
(probably) Feb 95 / Italy
Composer:
B. Dylan

Bob Dylan: Lead Vocals & Acoustic Guitar; George Harrison: Electric Guitar; Charlie Daniels: Bass; Russ Kunkel: Drums

Song 97j title:
I Threw It All Away
Track details:
Side 1, track 5 / 2 min. 30 sec.
Release date / Country:
(probably) Feb 95 / Italy
Composer:
B. Dylan

Bob Dylan: Lead Vocals & Acoustic Guitar; George Harrison: Electric Guitar & B. Vocals; Charlie Daniels: Bass; Russ Kunkel: Drums

Song 97k title:
Just Like Tom Thumb's Blues
Track details:
Side 1, track 16 / 3 min. 56 sec.
Release date / Country:
(probably) Feb 95 / Italy
Composer:
B. Dylan

Bob Dylan: Lead Vocals, Harmonica & Guitar; George Harrison: Guitar & B. Vocals; Charlie Daniels: Bass; Bob Johnston: Piano; Russ Kunkel: Drums

Song 97l title:
Mama You've Been On My Mind
Release date / Country:
(probably) Feb 95 / Italy
Track details:
Side 1, track 13 / 3 min. 09 sec.
Composer:
B. Dylan

Bob Dylan: Lead Vocals & Acoustic Guitar; George Harrison: Guitar & B. Vocals; Bob Johnston: Piano; Charlie Daniels: Bass; Russ Kunkel: Drums

Song 97m title:
Matchbox
Release date / Country:
(probably) Feb 95 / Italy
Track details:
Side 1, track 7 / 3 min. 35 sec.
Composer:
C. Perkins - [Trad]

Bob Dylan: Lead Vocals & Acoustic Guitar; George Harrison: Electric Guitar & B. Vocals; Charlie Daniels: Bass; Russ Kunkel: Drums

Song 97n title:
One Too Many Mornings [take one]
Release date / Country:
(probably) Feb 95 / Italy
Track details:
Side 1, track 18 / 2 min. 16 sec.
Composer:
B. Dylan

Bob Dylan: Lead Vocals & Acoustic Guitar; George Harrison: Electric Guitar & B. Vocals; Charlie Daniels: Bass; Bob Johnston: Piano; Russ Kunkel: Drums

Song 97o title:
One Too Many Mornings [take two]
Release date / Country:
(probably) Feb 95 / Italy
Track details:
Side 1, track 19 / 3 min. 46 sec.
Composer:
B. Dylan

Bob Dylan: Lead Vocals & Acoustic Guitar; George Harrison: Electric Guitar & B. Vocals; Charlie Daniels: Bass; Bob Johnston: Piano; Russ Kunkel: Drums

Song 97p title:
Rainy Day Women Nos. 12 & 35
Release date / Country:
(probably) Feb 95 / Italy
Track details:
Side 1, track 11 / 1 min. 07 sec.
Composer:
B. Dylan

Bob Dylan: Lead Vocals & Acoustic Guitar; George Harrison: Electric Guitar; Charlie Daniels: Bass; Russ Kunkel: Drums

Song 97q title:
Song To Woody
Release date / Country:
(probably) Feb 95 / Italy
Track details:
Side 1, track 12 / 4 min. 26 sec.
Composer:
B. Dylan

Bob Dylan: Lead Vocals, Acoustic Guitar & Harmonica; George Harrison: Electric Guitar; Charlie Daniels: Bass; Russ Kunkel: Drums

Song 97r title:
Yesterday
Release date / Country:
(probably) Feb 95 / Italy
Track details:
Side 1, track 15 / 3 min. 15 sec.
Composer:
J. Lennon - P. McCartney

Bob Dylan: Lead Vocals & Acoustic Guitar; George Harrison: Guitar & B. Vocals; Bob Johnston: Piano; Charlie Daniels: Bass; Russ Kunkel: Drums

Song 97s title:
Your True Love
Release date / Country:
(probably) Feb 95 / Italy
Track details:
Side 1, track 8 / 1 min. 36 sec.
Composer:
C. Perkins

Bob Dylan: Lead Vocals & Acoustic Guitar; George Harrison: Electric Guitar & B. Vocals; Charlie Daniels: Bass; Russ Kunkel: Drums

Bob Dylan, Los Angeles, CA, late 1980s, photo courtesy of Tom Bert

Bob Dylan, born Robert Zimmerman in Duluth, Minnesota on May 24, 1941, was raised in the small town of Hibbing in northern Minnesota. It was an unlikely setting for this Jewish child who would grow up to become a protest singer in New York City's Greenwich Village. Dylan began his musical career emulating traditional American blues and folk singers like Woody Guthrie. He moved to Greenwich Village in January 1961 and quickly established himself as a rising folk singer, securing a contract with Columbia Records in October 1961. True to form throughout much of his career, Dylan abandoned one style in favor of another, becoming a protest singer crafting social and political lyrics that helped to inspire the social revolution of the 1960s. Due to his quirky vocals, he quickly became known primarily as a songwriter to more commercial folk acts like girlfriend Joan Baez, and Peter, Paul & Mary who reached the top 10 with his songs ***Blowin' In The Wind*** and ***Don't Think Twice, It's Alright*** in 1963.

Bob Dylan has loomed large in The Beatles story. The Beatles, ever eager to discover new American music, gave their first serious listen to Dylan while visiting a radio station in Paris in January 1964. They took some of Dylan's records back to their hotel room and, as John Lennon later remarked, "fell in love." The Beatles first met Dylan in their hotel room in New York City in August 1964 during their North American tour. Dylan, who had apparently misinterpreted the lyrics ("I can't hide" as "I get high") to The Beatles' first U.S. hit ***I Want To Hold Your Hand***, brought along some marijuana. Though the accounts of the event vary, Lennon is said to have initially passed on the marijuana cigarette to Ringo, claiming in typical Lennon humor that Ringo was his "official taster." Before long, however, all the Beatles had been turned on by Bob Dylan.

Never musically content, Dylan shifted gears on July 25, 1965, when he picked up an electric guitar at the prestigious Newport Folk Festival. He was booed and condemned as a traitor to what was termed folk-rock, which he helped launch by befriending Jim (Roger) McGuinn and The Byrds *(see Stephen Stills)* who had a number one hit with his song ***Mr. Tambourine Man***. It would hardly be the last time Dylan would be ridiculed for his tendencies to change and vacillate. That year, a group called The Turtles reached the top 10 with ***It Ain't Me Babe***, and a young singer named Cher reached the top 20 with ***All I Really Want To Do***, both written by Dylan. Dylan also scored in the charts for the first time in 1965 with ***Subterranean Homesick Blues***, that reached the top 40, and ***Like A Rolling Stone***, that became his first million-selling single. Dylan began backing himself with members of a group called The Hawks who eventually renamed themselves The Band* *(see also Levon Helm, Rick Danko, Ronnie Hawkins)*.

The Beatles also joined the folk-rock voyage recording "Dylanesque" songs, written by John Lennon, like ***I Don't Want To Spoil The Party***, ***I'm A Loser***, ***You've Got To Hide Your Love Away***, ***It's Only***

Love and ***Norwegian Wood***. Dylan reportedly wrote the song ***Fourth Time Around*** based on ***Norwegian Wood***.

In the booklet from the Dylan box set **Biograph** it mentions: "It's an interesting footnote to music history that along an early English tour [probably 1965 or 1966], Dylan would visit the home of John Lennon and the two would pen a song together. 'I don't remember what it was, though,' said Dylan. 'We played some stuff into a tape recorder but I don't know what happened to it. I can remember playing it and the recorder was on. I don't remember anything about the song.' Lennon would later comment on their relationship. 'I've grown up enough to communicate with him...Both of us were always uptight, you know, and of course I wouldn't know whether he was uptight because I was so uptight, and then when he wasn't uptight, I was — all that bit. But we just sat it out because we just liked being together.'" The 1966 documentary film of Dylan's British tour titled **Eat The Document** included a segment with Lennon that was later edited out.

Dylan was involved in a serious motorcycle accident near his home in Woodstock, New York in the summer of 1966. He was at his commercial peak at the time of the accident. His double album **Blonde On Blonde** had just spawned the hits ***Rainy Day Women Nos. 12 & 35*** and ***I Want You***.

The Beatles' turn towards acid rock and Dylan's low profile, due in large part to the injuries he suffered, provided little opportunity for interaction between himself and The Beatles. The Beatles included a photo of Dylan on the cover of their album **Sgt. Pepper's Lonely Hearts Club Band**.

Dylan spent much of 1967 recording with The Band at their Big Pink Studios. Though widely bootlegged, the first of these recordings were not officially released until 1975 on the album **The Basement Tapes**. The June 28 edition of the British music weekly Melody Maker did a feature on the album, but incorrectly identified Richard Manuel as Ringo Starr in the album photos. Admittedly, Manual, wearing a hat, did look a lot like Ringo at the time. Unfortunately, this case of mistaken identity would lead to speculation that Ringo contributed to the album in some way, which of course is untrue. Dylan's song ***The Mighty Quinn (Quinn The Eskimo)*** from these sessions was covered by the group Manfred Mann *(see Paul Jones)* reaching top 10 in the U.S. and the number one spot on the U.K. charts in 1968.

If you are in a receptive state of mind, Dylan's first post-accident album, **John Wesley Harding**, released in 1968, appears to contain The Beatles' **Rubber Soul** photographs hidden in the tree on the jacket cover. The album included the song ***All Along The Watchtower*** which Jimi Hendrix turned into a top 10. What emerged from Dylan by 1968 again looked and sounded very different. The direction now was country rock and the persona was isolated and elusive at best, shunning public appearances. Suddenly, the musical spokesman of the counter-culture was a hit on country, as well as the pop charts, with his 1969 single ***Lay Lady Lay***.

George Harrison spent some time at Dylan's home in Woodstock, NY in November 1968. While there the two wrote ***I'd Have You Anytime*** (Dylan contributed the bridge). Apparently, Harrison also wrote ***All Things Must Pass*** during his stay with Dylan. On August 31, 1969, George, Ringo and John Lennon attended a then-rare Dylan performance on Isle Of Wight, and met with him and The Band prior to the show. After the show, Dylan flew to Lennon's home where Lennon tried unsuccessfully to get Dylan to contribute to his recording of ***Cold Turkey***.

Harrison took part in Dylan's day-long recording sessions on May 1, 1970 at Columbia Studio B in New York at least 25 songs were recorded. Only one for certain has been officially released – An alternate version of ***If Not For You***, not used on the **New Morning** album, was included some twenty years later on Columbia's Dylan album **The Bootleg Series**. (Harrison also included a cover version of the song on his **All Things Must Pass** album.)

Long-time Dylan sideman Al Kooper, who played on and produced some of the **New Morning** sessions, is certain that George plays guitar on the version of ***Went To See The Gypsy*** that was used for **New Morning**. It's the one song on **New Morning** that does sound as if it was taken from the May 1 sessions with Harrison. Clinton Heylin's book **Bob Dylan: The Recording Sessions 1960 - 1994** does not list any of the tracks from the session with Harrison as being used on **New Morning**.

Twenty of the remaining 23 songs known to have been recorded at the May 1 sessions have turned

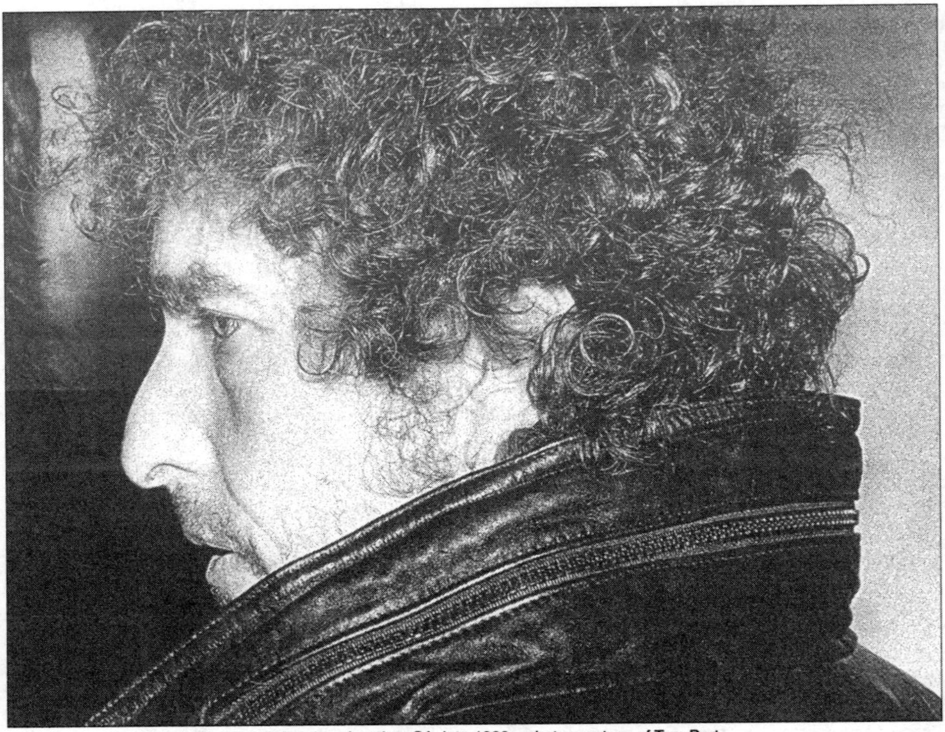

Bob Dylan, Los Angeles, CA, late 1980s, photo courtesy of Tom Bert

up on at least two bootleg CDs, ***Possum Belly Overalls*** and ***Yesterday***. The remaining three tracks that have yet to see the light of day are alternate versions of ***Sign On The Window***, ***Time Passes Slowly*** and ***It Ain't Me Babe***. The first part of the session was little more than a warm-up consisting of Dylan numbers and oldies, including a swipe at McCartney's Beatles song ***Yesterday***. As the session progressed, it became more focused. Clinton Heylan lists two separate and distinct sessions taking place – afternoon and evening. Heylin's book lists Dylan (guitar, piano, harmonica and vocals), Harrison (guitar), Ron Cornelius (guitar), Alvin Rogers (drums - afternoon only), Russ Kunkel (drums - evening only), Charlie Daniels (bass) and Al Kooper (guitar, piano and vocals). Al Kooper has stated that he did not attend any of the sessions with Harrison, and that he never sang on any recordings for **New Morning**. Charlie Daniels said the drummer throughout the session was Russ Kunkel, and that Ron Cornelius was not present. It is apparent from listening to the recordings that most, if not all, of the piano was played by producer Bob Johnston. Charlie Daniels also thinks he played acoustic guitar on a couple of tracks. Daniels said that Harrison played electric guitar throughout the session, and that his involvement was supposed to be kept secret for legal reasons. Daniels does not think that any of the takes from the session ended up on **New Morning**.

Two George Harrison songs – ***Every Time Somebody Comes To Town*** and ***I'd Have You Anytime*** – featuring Dylan, also appear on bootlegs. These two songs were probably recorded during the same visit to New York, or possibly during Harrison's visit to see Dylan in late 1968. Harrison's song ***Behind That Locked Door*** was written about Dylan during his reclusive period in the early 1970s. George Harrison is rumored to have helped Leon Russell* produce ***Watching The River Flow*** and ***When I Paint My Masterpiece*** from a Dylan session in March 1971. But Jim Keltner *(see Attitudes)*, who drummed on the sessions, denies that.

It came as no surprise when Bob Dylan accepted Harrison's invitation to appear at **The Concert For Bangla Desh**, on August 1, 1971, to help raise relief money for the starving people of that country. ***Love Minus Zero / No Limit***, performed only during the afternoon show, was omitted during the evening show in favor of ***Mr. Tambourine Man***, which was included on the album, but omitted from the film. ***Love Minus Zero / No Limit*** has since appeared on several bootlegs.

John Lennon's 1970 album **John Lennon / Plastic Ono Band** contained the Dylanesque song ***Working Class Hero***, and the song ***God***, in which Lennon sings "I don't believe in Zimmerman." In 1972, Lennon, eager to go on a "political" tour that was to culminate in San Diego at the Republican National Convention's nomination of Richard Nixon, sought Dylan's support. Dylan and activist beat poet Allen Ginsberg* co-wrote and recorded the song ***Going To San Diego***, along with an album's worth of material that Lennon almost had released on Apple Records.

Melody Maker magazine stated in its March 10, 1973 issue that Lennon was "in Los Angeles with Dylan to help remix their tapes he had cut down in Mexico City in January." This would have to be in reference to the songs Dylan cut at CBS Studios in Mexico City for the soundtrack to the film **Pat Garrett And Billy The Kid**. John Lennon would never have left the U.S. at this time because he was fighting a deportation order and knew he would almost certainly have been refused reentry. There is no evidence to indicate that Lennon left New York for Los Angeles in February 1973, as he was beginning his across-town move into the Dakota apartments in New York. None of the available data on Dylan's February sessions in Los Angeles suggest any Lennon involvement.

Throughout the early 1970s, Dylan dabbled in films and made brief public appearances. But the early 1970s were a period of low profile and low output for Dylan, forcing Columbia Records to issue a series of previously unreleased studio and live recordings and greatest hits albums. By the mid-1970s, Dylan left Columbia for David Geffen's Asylum Records. He reunited with his old backup group The Band (now successful in their own right). Together they recorded a new studio album and went on an extensive tour, which also yielded a highly successful live album.

In 1975, Dylan embarked on his long vagabond **Rolling Thunder Revue** tour featuring numerous guest appearances, including Ringo Starr for one night, on January 25, 1976 at the Houston Astrodome *(see The Alpha Band, Kinky Friedman)*. On November 24, 1976, Dylan, again along with Ringo Starr, appeared at The Band's **Last Waltz** farewell concert to pay tribute. Dylan's song ***Abandoned Love*** recorded during this period but not released until 1985, was also recorded by George Harrison, whose version remains unreleased. By the mid-1970s, Dylan was back with Columbia Records, where he has remained to this day. The late 1970s and early 1980s saw a Bob Dylan who had returned to the stage with a vengeance, and had renewed his popularity with the sort of music he was most identified with – folk-rock and the occasional protest song.

In 1979, Bob Dylan created the greatest controversy of his career when he converted to Christianity, and was baptized in Pat Boone's swimming pool. The born-again Bob was now a gospel artist urging audiences and fellow musicians alike to, as the lyrics of his current single proclaimed, "serve somebody." By the mid-1980s, Dylan had toned down his proselytizing, adopting a broader and more tolerant view of religion. In the late 1970s, John Lennon, living in self-imposed musical exile in the Dakota apartment building in New York, reacted cynically to Dylan's religious convictions composing several brilliant Dylan parodies with posthumous titles like ***Serve Yourself*** (***Gotta Serve Somebody***), ***Lord Take This Makeup Off Of Me*** (***Knockin' On Heaven's Door***) and ***Ballad Of Reuter's News Of The World***.

Dylan's single ***Heart Of Mine***, from his 1981 album **Shot Of Love**, features Ringo on drums. The B-side was ***Groom's Still Waiting At The Alter*** which was included on some versions of **Shot Of Love**, but omitted from others. There is a good bit of confusion surrounding just who plays on this track. Dylan says, in his **Biograph** release, that "maybe" Ringo plays on this track, but that he "can't remember." In the April 1993 record collectors magazine DISCoveries cover issue on Ringo Starr, they quote Ringo as saying: "We had a discussion — Bob and I. I said to him thanks a lot. I come all the way down for the session and you wipe me off." Bob replied, "You're not listening!" Perhaps Ringo is referring to the A-side of the single. Jim Keltner, the credited drummer on the track, is certain that Ringo was not present at the sessions for ***Groom's Still Waiting At The Alter***. Keltner correctly recalls that it was an entirely different session and group of musicians to those on ***Heart Of Mine***.

In 1985, George Harrison recorded and released the Dylan song ***I Don't Want To Do It*** for the soundtrack of the film **Porky's Revenge**. Harrison had considered releasing his version of the song on his 1970 album **All Things Must Pass**. Harrison reportedly talked Ringo into recording ***I Don't Want To Do It*** during sessions for his **Rotogravure** album in 1976, but his version remains unreleased. Dylan has yet to release his version of the song.

In 1986, Dylan released the album **Knocked Out Loaded** that thanks a "George" in the credits, though it is not known if this is George Harrison. Further investigation of the recording dates, musicians and studios used for the tracks that appear on the album do not reveal any Harrison involvement. It is always possible that Harrison may have contributed to recordings left off the album.

On February 19, 1987, Harrison, Dylan and John Fogerty* joined Taj Mahal* and the Graffiti Band, featuring Jesse Ed Davis*, onstage at Hollywood's Palomino Club for an hour plus jam. On October 17, 1987, Harrison joined Dylan onstage at Wembley Arena in London playing his distinctive slide guitar on ***Rainy Day Women Nos. 12 & 35***. The performance will, no doubt, eventually show up on bootlegs. On June 13, 1989, Ringo joined Dylan onstage at Les Arenes in Frejus, France, drumming on ***Highway 61 Revisited*** and ***Like A Rolling Stone***.

On January 20, 1988, Bob Dylan, along with The Beatles, was inducted into the Rock and Roll Hall of Fame at ceremonies held in the Grand Ballroom of the Waldorf-Astoria Hotel in New York City. The now traditional jam of the assembled at the end of the evening's events included Harrison joining Dylan on a rendition of ***All Along The Watchtower***.

The year 1988 also saw the greatest collaboration yet between Harrison and Dylan. Harrison, attempting to record a B-side for a single off his highly successful album **Cloud Nine**, recruited Tom Petty* to help. Petty, who had been working with Dylan at the time, suggested they rehearse the number over at Dylan's home studio. It just so happened that Roy Orbison* was performing in the area and was also asked to drop by and help. Harrison's and Petty's producer, Jeff Lynne*, and everyone's session drummer, Jim Keltner, rounded out the group. The group hit it off so well that they decided to record an entire album together and called the new "supergroup" Traveling Wilburys. The album was such a critical and commercial success that a second album was recorded and released two years later.

George Harrison contributed slide guitar to the title track of Dylan's **Under The Red Sky** album in 1990. The credits list the album as being recorded at Ocean Way, The Complex Studios and The Record Plant (West) Studios, in Los Angeles. Several reference books on Dylan list **Under The Red Sky** as being recorded at The Complex and Record Plant, but according to Al Kooper, the basic tracks were done at Ocean Way. Pat Schneider, a recording engineer working at Ocean Way at the

George Harrison, Duane Eddy and Bob Dylan, Los Angeles, CA, late 1980s, photo courtesy of Tom Bert

time, also recalls the session being done there. Dylan performed The Beatles' song ***Nowhere Man*** during a tour in 1990.

On October 16, 1992, some of the biggest names in music including The Band, Johnny Cash*, Eric Clapton*, Roger McGuinn, Tom Petty, Ron Wood* and George Harrison gathered at Madison Square Garden to celebrate the 30th anniversary of Bob Dylan as a recording artist. Harrison performed two songs: ***If Not For You*** (not included on **The 30th Anniversary Concert Celebration** album or video release) and ***Absolutely Sweet Marie***, and he joined in on the finale of ***My Back Pages*** and ***Knockin' On Heaven's Door***. Portions of the George Harrison rehearsal for the performance are available on the bootleg CD **Bobfest Rehearsals October 1992**.

To date, the only Beatle who has never worked with Bob Dylan is Paul McCartney, and with his recent willingness to collaborate with artists like Elvis Costello*, the chances are improving – though a Dylan / McCartney collaboration still seems difficult to imagine. One thing almost certain is that both George Harrison and Ringo Starr, who still like to turn up at Dylan concerts and recording sessions, will continue to work with him. Today Bob Dylan continues to tour and record, remaining as musically unpredictable, and popular, as ever, and maintaining, but denying, his status as a living legend.

Duane Eddy

Record 98 title:
Duane Eddy
Media:
Album 5" CD
Label / Catalog number:
Capitol / CDP 7 46897 2
Jacket / Inserts:
Standard international design in jewel box with photo of Paul McCartney and George Harrison (vinyl only) / 8 page CD booklet

Song 98a title:
Rockestra Theme
Track details:
Side 1, track 2 / 4 min. 00 sec.
Release date / Country:
19 Jun 87 / U.S.A.
Composer:
P. McCartney
Producer:
Paul McCartney
Recording Location / Date:
The Mill Studios, Sussex, U.K. / 04 Feb 87

Duane Eddy: Guitar; Phil Pickett: Piano & B. Vocals; Nick Glennie-Smith: Keyboards, Fairlight & B. Vocals; Jim Horn: Tenor Saxophone; Charlie Morgan: Drums & B. Vocals; Paul McCartney: Bass & B. Vocals

Song 98b title:
The Trembler
Track details:
Side 1, track 6 / 3 min. 30 sec.
Release date / Country:
19 Jun 87 / U.S.A.
Composer:
R. Shankar - D. Eddy

Producer:
Jeff Lynne & [George Harrison]
Recording Location / Date:
FPSHOT (Friar Park Studios, Henley-on-Thames), U.K. / late Jan, early Feb 87

Duane Eddy: Guitar; George Harrison: Slide Guitar; Jeff Lynne: Keyboards & Synthesizers; Jim Horn: Tenor Saxophone; Jim Keltner: Drums; Jeff Lynne: Bass

Song 98c title:
Theme For Something Really Important
Release date / Country:
19 Jun 87 / U.S.A.
Producer:
Jeff Lynne & [George Harrison]
Recording Location / Date:
FPSHOT (Friar Park Studios, Henley-on-Thames), U.K. / late Jan, early Feb 87
Track details:
Side 1, track 3 / 4 min. 09 sec.
Composer:
J. Lynne

Duane Eddy: Guitar; George Harrison: Slide Guitar; Jeff Lynne: Keyboards & Synthesizers; Jim Horn: Baritone Saxophone; Jim Keltner: Drums; Jeff Lynne: Bass

Record 99 title:
Duane Eddy
Label / Catalog number:
Capitol / 12CL 463
Jacket / Inserts:
Unique PS with photo of Paul McCartney
Recording Location / Date:
The Mill Studios, Sussex, U.K. / 04 Feb 87
Media:
Single 12"
Producer:
Paul McCartney & remixed by Bert Bevan†

Song 99a title:
Rockestra Theme [extended version†]
Release date / Country:
21 Sep 87 / U.K.
Track details:
Side 1, track 1 / 6 min. 26 sec.
Composer:
P. McCartney

Duane Eddy: Guitar; Phil Pickett: Piano & B. Vocals; Nick Glennie-Smith: Keyboards, Fairlight & B. Vocals; Jim Horn: Tenor Saxophone; Charlie Morgan: Drums & B. Vocals; Paul McCartney: Bass & B. Vocals

Duane Eddy was born in Corning, New York on April 26, 1938. He began playing guitar at the age of five, emulating his hero, the "singing cowboy" and actor Gene Autry. At the age of 13, Eddy's family moved to Arizona where, in 1955, he began playing professionally. Eddy teamed up with producer Lee Hazlewood and created a sound that went on to earn him the title of best selling rock 'n' roll instrumentalist of all time because of his signature twangy guitar style.

Eddy's trademark Gretsch guitar, and his hit songs ***Rebel Rouser*** and ***Ramrod***, featuring his backup band The Rebels, caught the attention of a teenager named George Harrison in 1958. George and his brother Peter also formed a group named The Rebels. (The Beatles often performed ***Ramrod*** and other songs made popular by Eddy in their live set in the early '60s.) Eddy has turned out more than 30 hits during his career including ***Cannonball***, ***The Lonely One***, ***Forty Miles Of Bad Road***, ***Yep***, ***Pepe***, ***Theme From Dixie***, ***(Dance With The) Guitar Man***, ***Boss Guitar***, and his cover of the theme song from the TV series ***Peter Gunn***. In 1960, he had a big hit with ***Because They're Young*** from the movie of the same title. Eddy also appeared in the film performing another one of his hits, ***Shazam***. Duane appeared in several films in the early 1960s including **A Thunder Of Drums** co-starring Richard Boone. A friendship between the two led to Eddy's appearance in two episodes of Boone's long-running CBS-TV series **Have Gun Will Travel**. Duane's recording of the series' theme song, ***The Ballad Of Paladin***, (a tribute to Boone) was a hit on both sides of the Atlantic in 1962.

When the British magazine New Musical Express asked George Harrison in 1963 who his favorite band was, he replied "the Duane Eddy Group." (Rebels' members Jim Horn*, Steve Douglas and Larry Knechtel went on to become members of Phil Spector's* famous "wrecking crew," and earned a reputation as some of the world's best session players. Knechtel also found success in the 1970's group Bread.) Eddy all but vanished from the charts following the British music invasion of 1964. He released a cover of George Harrison's Beatles song ***Something*** in 1970. He made a few appearances in films and contributed to other artists' recordings including Phil Everly's *(see The Everly Brothers)* first solo album in 1973, which Eddy also produced. In 1975, Eddy's ***Play Me Like You Play Your***

Guitar was a top 10 on every major chart in the world except the U.S. He teamed up with the group The Art Of Noise to make a new recording of *Peter Gunn* which became another worldwide hit. The recording earned Eddy the Grammy Award for Best Rock Instrumental of 1986, returning him to the spotlight.

Duane Eddy, Los Angeles, CA, late 1980s, photo courtesy of Tom Bert

In 1987, Eddy enlisted the help of Paul McCartney and George Harrison for his Capitol album **Duane Eddy**. McCartney produced Eddy on a cover of the Wings' song *Rochestra Theme* that was recorded at Paul's studio near his home in Sussex. An extended version of the song, remixed by Bert Bevans, was released on a U.K. 12" single. **Rockestra** was even suggested as a possible title for the **Duane Eddy** album. (McCartney featured Eddy's cover of *Rockestra Theme* on an episode of his 1995 radio series **Oobu Joobu**. The series was produced by Duane's longtime friend Eddy Pumer, who had initially put Duane in touch with McCartney. The episode, which commemorated the 30th anniversary of the release of *Yesterday*, also included a brief rendition of *Yesterday* which Eddy recorded for the occasion along with a message of congratulations.)

The recordings with Harrison for **Duane Eddy** began in late January 1987 at Harrison's home studio in Henley. A week later Eddy began recording sessions with McCartney at his studio. By early to mid-February, Eddy was back recording at Harrison's studio. According to Eddy and Jeff Lynne, Harrison (though not credited) helped Lynne produce *Theme For Something Really Important* and *The Trembler*. *The Trembler* had the unusual co-authorship of Shankar / Eddy. In an interview in the November 1987 issue of Guitar Player magazine, Harrison recounted that Ravi Shankar had made a tape of the basic melody some years earlier. Harrison played the tape for Lynne and the two decided to simplify the song before Eddy added his part. Eddy remembers Harrison humming the melody to him and then writing the bridge creating the Shankar / Eddy collaboration that he says pleased Harrison immensely. Eddy said Harrison also came up with the title for the track

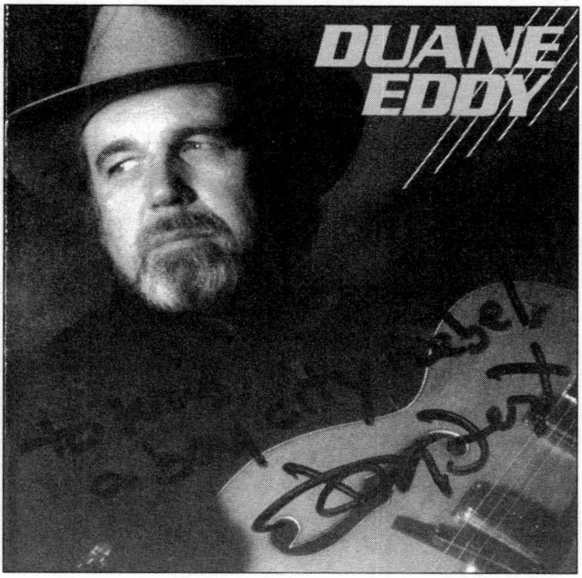

Rockabilly Holiday on the album. (The title was a word play on rockabilly and singer Billie Holiday, though Harrison did not actually contribute to the song.) At the same time, Eddy also played guitar on some sessions for Harrison's **Cloud Nine** album, but Eddy said, "it just didn't sound right for the songs and wasn't used." Lynne and Eddy also recall having some great jams together with George, Jim Horn and James Burton during the recordings at Harrison's home studio.

Duane Eddy was inducted into the Rock and Roll Hall in 1994 along with John Lennon. His unique sound has made him one of rock's most influential and successful instrumentalists. He continues to work with some of the world's finest musicians and released an album titled **Ghostrider** in 1996. His many recordings, – which continue to grace soundtracks such as **Forrest Gump**, **Broken Arrow** and **Scream 2** – and advertisements alike, have easily exceeded 100 million in worldwide sales.

Dave Edmunds

Record 100 title:
Live From Montreaux
Label / Catalog number:
Videoarts / VALJ-3369
Jacket / Inserts:
Unique / Lyric & translation insert
Recording Location / Date:
On location at Montreaux Jazz Festival, Montreaux, Switzerland / 13 Jul 92

Media:
Album 12" LVD
Producer:
Jim Beach & Louise Velazquez (film); Ringo Starr (music)

Song 100a title:
Girls Talk [live]
Release date / Country:
(probably) Nov 93 / Japan

Track details:
Side 1, track 5 / 3 min. 25 sec.
Composer:
E. Costello

Dave Edmunds: Lead Vocals & Guitar; Ringo Starr: Drums; Joe Walsh: Acoustic Guitar; Todd Rundgren: Tambourine; Burton Cummings: Keyboards; Nils Lofgren: Acoustic Guitar; Timothy B. Schmit: Bass; Tim Cappello: Percussion; Zak Starkey: Drums This song is also included on Rykodisc / RCD 20264 / Album 5" CD / released 14 Sep 93 in the U.S. / Side 1, track 7 / Standard international design in jewel box / 12 page CD booklet.

Song 100b title:
I Hear You Knocking [live]
Release date / Country:
(probably) Nov 93 / Japan

Track details:
Side 2, track 7 (20) / 3 min. 48 sec.
Composer:
Bartholomew - King

Dave Edmunds: Lead Vocals & Guitar; Ringo Starr: Drums; Joe Walsh: Guitar; Todd Rundgren: Guitar & B. Vocals; Burton Cummings: Keyboards; Nils Lofgren: Guitar & B. Vocals; Timothy B. Schmit: Bass & B. Vocals; Tim Cappello: Percussion; Zak Starkey: Drums

Dave Edmunds was born April 15, 1944 in Cardiff, Wales and is most often identified with the revival of rockabilly music in England. His first chart hit was a remake of Smiley Lewis' ***I Hear You Knocking*** in 1970. Dave has been rocking since the mid-1960s in such recording groups as Image, Human Beings and Love Sculpture. He was also a member of Rockpile, along with Nick Lowe, in the '70s. In 1979 he hit the charts again with a cover of Elvis Costello's* ***Girls Talk***. As a part of Rockpile, Edmunds took part in the Rockestra that backed McCartney and Wings when they performed the ***Rockestra Theme*** on December 29, 1979 at the Hammersmith Odeon Theatre in London, U.K. The benefit performance was released on the album **Concerts For The People Of Kampuchea**.

Dave Edmunds is a widely respected guitarist, but he has also become a successful record producer. He has produced, among others, Brinsley Schwarz, Flamin' Groovies, The Everly Brothers*, Dion, K. D. Lang, The Fabulous Thunderbirds, Status Quo, Del Shannon* and The Stray Cats. Edmunds has also done a bit of acting, co-starring with David Essex in the film **Stardust**.

In 1983, Edmunds briefly joined Paul McCartney's make-shift band for his **Give My Regards To Broadstreet** film and soundtrack released in 1984. That year, Edmunds, a neighbor and friend of George Harrison, helped drag Harrison out of semi-retirement to produce his recording of Bob Dylan's* *I Don't Want To Do It*. The recording was for the soundtrack of the film **Porky's Revenge**, which Edmunds was producing. Harrison had originally considered the song for his album **All Things Must Pass** in 1970. Edmunds also persuaded Harrison to perform before a live audience for **Blue Suede Shoes - A Rockabilly Session With Carl Perkins* And Friends** TV special on October 21, 1985. Edmunds was the person Harrison put in charge of contacting Jeff Lynne* when George sought his services as producer. Edmunds was reported to have been involved in Ringo's aborted Chips Moman album sessions recorded in Memphis in 1987. He was the musical director for **The John Lennon Scholarship Concert** held on May 5, 1990 in Liverpool and performed *A Day In The Life*, *Strawberry Fields Forever* and *The Ballad Of John And Yoko*. Only *The Ballad Of John And Yoko* was included on the 1991 laser videodisk **The World's Greatest Artists Sing LENNON A Tribute**. Edmunds joined Ringo Starr's All-Starr Band tour in 1992 performing *Girls Talk* and *I Hear You Knocking* with Ringo backing him on drums.

Elephant's Memory

Record 101 title:
Elephant's Memory
Media:
Album 12"
Label / Catalog number:
Apple / SMAS 3389
Producer:
John Lennon & Yoko Ono
Jacket / Inserts:
Standard international design with Gatefold / Custom inner-sleeve with photo of John Lennon
Recording Location / Date:
Record Plant (East) Studios, New York, NY, U.S.A. / Apr - May 72

Song 101a title:
Baddest Of The Mean
Track details:
Side 1, track 2 / 8 min. 46 sec.
Release date / Country:
18 Sep 72 / U.S.A.
Composer:
S. Bronstein - R. Frank - G. Van Scyoc - A. Ippolito - W. Gabriel

Stan Bronstein: Lead Vocals & Saxophone; Wayne "Tex" Gabriel: Guitar & B. Vocals; Rick Frank: Drums, & Percussion; Adam Ippolito: Keyboards, B. Vocals & Trumpet; Gary Van Scyoc: Bass & B. Vocals

Song 101b title:
Chuck 'N Bo
Track details:
Side 1, track 4 / 4 min. 33 sec.
Release date / Country:
18 Sep 72 / U.S.A.
Composer:
S. Bronstein - R. Frank - W. Gabriel

Stan Bronstein: Lead Vocals & Saxophone; Wayne "Tex" Gabriel: Guitar & B. Vocals; Rick Frank: Drums & B. Vocals; Adam Ippolito: Keyboards & B. Vocals; Gary Van Scyoc: Bass & B. Vocals; John Lennon: Percussion & B. Vocals; Yoko Ono: B. Vocals

Song 101c title:
Cryin' Blacksheep Blues
Track details:
Side 1, track 3 / 4 min. 27 sec.
Release date / Country:
18 Sep 72 / U.S.A.
Composer:
R. Frank - S. Bronstein - D. Price

Stan Bronstein: Lead Vocals & Saxophone; Wayne "Tex" Gabriel: Guitar; Rick Frank: Drums & Percussion; Adam Ippolito: Keyboards & Trumpet; Gary Van Scyoc: Bass & B. Vocals; John Lennon: Guitar & B. Vocals

Song 101d title:
Gypsy Wolf
Release date / Country:
18 Sep 72 / U.S.A.
Track details:
Side 2, track 1 / 3 min. 58 sec.
Composer:
S. Bronstein - R. Frank

Stan Bronstein: Lead Vocals & Saxophone; Wayne "Tex" Gabriel: Guitar & B. Vocals; Rick Frank: Drums, Cherokee Indian Drum, B. Vocals & Percussion; Adam Ippolito: Keyboards & B. Vocals; Gary Van Scyoc: Bass & B. Vocals; John Lennon: B. Vocals; Yoko Ono: B. Vocals

Song 101e title:
Liberation Special
Release date / Country:
18 Sep 72 / U.S.A.
Track details:
Side 1, track 1 / 5 min. 28 sec.
Composer:
R. Frank - S. Bronstein

Stan Bronstein: Lead Vocals & Percussion; Wayne "Tex" Gabriel: Guitar & B. Vocals; Rick Frank: Drums & B. Vocals; Adam Ippolito: Keyboards; Gary Van Scyoc: Bass & B. Vocals; Martha Velez: B. Vocals; Toni Wine: B. Vocals; Hilda Harris: B. Vocals; Linda November: B. Vocals

Song 101f title:
Life
Release date / Country:
18 Sep 72 / U.S.A.
Track details:
Side 2, track 3 / 3 min. 42 sec.
Composer:
W. Gabriel

Wayne "Tex" Gabriel: Lead Vocals & Guitar; Rick Frank: Drums & Percussion; Adam Ippolito: Keyboards; Gary Van Scyoc: Bass & B. Vocals; Stan Bronstein: Saxophone; Keith Johnson: Trumpet; Martha Velez: B. Vocals; Toni Wine: B. Vocals; Hilda Harris: B. Vocals; Linda November: B. Vocals

Song 101g title:
Local Plastic Ono Band
Release date / Country:
18 Sep 72 / U.S.A.
Track details:
Side 2, track 6 / 2 min. 00 sec.
Composer:
R. Frank

Rick Frank: Lead Vocals, Drums & Percussion; Wayne "Tex" Gabriel: B. Vocals; Adam Ippolito: B. Vocals; Gary Van Scyoc: Bass & B. Vocals; Stan Bronstein: Saxophone, Sea Green Alto Saxophone, B. Vocals & Percussion; Yoko Ono: Breath Rhythms & B. Vocals: John Lennon: B. Vocals

Song 101h title:
Madness
Release date / Country:
18 Sep 72 / U.S.A.
Track details:
Side 2, track 2 / 3 min. 10 sec.
Composer:
A. Ippolito - R. Frank - S. Bronstein

Stan Bronstein: Lead Vocals & Saxophone; Wayne "Tex" Gabriel: Guitar & B. Vocals; Rick Frank: Drums & Percussion; Adam Ippolito: Keyboards; Gary Van Scyoc: B. Vocals & Bass; Martha Velez: B. Vocals; Toni Wine: B. Vocals; Hilda Harris: B. Vocals; Linda November: B. Vocals

Song 101i title:
Power Boogie
Release date / Country:
18 Sep 72 / U.S.A.
Track details:
Side 2, track 5 / 3 min. 50 sec.
Composer:
S. Bronstein - R. Frank - C. Robison
[additionally sleeve lists: C. Robison
and label lists: Myer]

Stan Bronstein: Lead Vocals; Wayne "Tex" Gabriel: Guitar & B. Vocals; Rick Frank: Drums, B. Vocals & Percussion; Adam Ippolito: Keyboards & B. Vocals; Gary Van Scyoc: Bass & B. Vocals; John Lennon: Guitar & B. Vocals; Yoko Ono: B. Vocals; David Peel: B. Vocals; Myron Yules: B. Vocals

Song 101j title:
Wind Ridge
Release date / Country:
18 Sep 72 / U.S.A.
Track details:
Side 2, track 4 / 3 min. 20 sec.
Composer:
G. Van Scyoc - [J. Lennon]

Gary Van Scyoc: Lead Vocals, Bass & Acoustic Guitar; Wayne "Tex" Gabriel: Guitar; Rick Frank: Drums; John Lennon: Electric Piano

In early 1972, John Lennon, fueled by recent appearances for political causes, entertained the idea of touring. So, at the suggestion of political activist Jerry Rubin, he went to see New York City's East Village based band Elephant's Memory. Lennon was impressed by their raw brand of rock 'n' roll and hired the group. At the time, the band included drummer Rick Frank (born February 12, 1942 in New York City, New York), saxophonist Stan Bronstein (born July 17, 1938 in Brooklyn, New York), bass guitarist Gary Van Scyoc (born November 21, 1946 in Waynesburg, Pennsylvania), keyboard player Adam Ippolito, and Wayne "Tex" Gabriel (born December 24, 1955).

Elephant's Memory formed in 1969 and first gained notice for their contributions to the soundtrack of the film **Midnight Cowboy**. Between 1969 and 1974, the band went through numerous personnel changes including, briefly, Carly Simon*. Other members included Chris Robinson and Myron Yules, both of whom made brief contributions to the **Elephant's Memory** album, along with Martha Velez. They had only one minor hit, the song ***Mongoose*** in 1969.

The band's first assignment was to back up John and Yoko* and Chuck Berry* during the Lennons' week long appearance on **The Mike Douglas TV Show** in February 1972. In March, they backed up the Lennons on their **Sometime In New York City** album. Their next backing assignment was for the May 11, 1972 appearance by John and Yoko on **The Dick Cavett TV Show**.

During the spring of 1972, the Lennons assisted on and produced **Elephant's Memory** for the group that was released on The Beatles' Apple Records label. According to Gary Van Scyoc, John wrote a major piano line for the song ***Wind Ridge***, but refused to take credit for it. John also wanted the song to be the single. In the November 6, 1971 issue of Melody Maker magazine, John Lennon mentioned a song he had written about Chuck Berry and Bo Diddley. This led to speculation that the song ***Chuck 'N Bo*** by Elephant's Memory might have been co-written or inspired by John, but Wayne Gabriel and Gary Van Scyoc deny this. Elephant's Memory also toured with Diddley before their involvement with Lennon, which probably helped inspire their song. According to Van Scyoc, Lennon hated his song ***Forty-Two Down The Line*** which was the only number from the sessions that was not released.

Elephant's Memory backed the Lennons for the **One-To-One** benefit concert on the afternoon and evening of August 30, 1972, at New York's Madison Square Garden. Unlike other brief appearances with the Lennons, this was a full-length, large-arena concert. A week later on September 6, Elephant's Memory backed the Lennons on **Jerry Lewis' Muscular Dystrophy Telethon**. According to Van Scyoc, Lennon bought Elephant's Memory $100,000 worth of musical equipment and rehearsed with the band in preparation for a tour that would also serve as a forum for the Lennons' political message. By the beginning of 1973 however, the Lennons were urged by their legal advisers to keep a low political profile until John's deportation case was resolved. As a result, the Lennons were forced to abandon any plans for a tour, leaving little use for a backup band.

The group's last official assignment with the Lennons was to back up Yoko on her album **Approximately Infinite Universe**. Elephant's Memory recorded a song, without assistance from the Lennons, called ***Everglade Woman***, probably scheduled for release as Apple single # 1856. But Elephant's Memory had to look for another record label, as Apple Records manager Allen Klein was attempting to eliminate all but The Beatles from the Apple Records artist roster. Elephant's Memory split amicably with the Lennons after less than a year as their backup band.

The band went on to back Chuck Berry on his 1973 album **Bio**, but fell apart several years later as core members began to depart. Elephant's Memory guitarist Wayne "Tex" Gabriel went on to form the early 1980's band Limozine. He was asked to be a member of Ringo's 1995 All-Starr Band, but the proper arrangements were not able to be made in time for him to join the tour.

Bill Elliott And Elastic Oz Band

Record 102 title:
God Save Us
Label / Catalog number:
Apple / 1835
Jacket / Inserts:
Standard international design PS
Recording Location / Date:
Ascot Sound Studios, Ascot† & (probably) Apple
or (possibly) EMI-Abbey Road Studio, London, U.K. / 01 Jun 71†
Media:
Single 7"
Producer:
John Lennon, Yoko Ono, Mal Evans & Phil Spector

Song 102a title:
God Save Us
Release date / Country:
07 Jul 71 / U.S.A.
Track details:
Side 1, track 1 / 3 min. 10 sec.
Composer:
J. Lennon - Y. Ono

Bill Elliott: Lead Vocals; John Lennon: Guitar & B. Vocals; Ringo Starr: Drums; Bobby Keys: (probable) Saxophone; Klaus Voormann: Bass; Diane: Keyboards

The Elastic Oz Band was formed by John Lennon in an attempt to lend support to the leftist underground British magazine OZ. Several of its editors were sentenced to fifteen months in prison for violating England's Obscene Publications Act as a result of the 1970 issue No. 28 of OZ dubbed "the school kids' issue." Most of the violations had to do with the publication of sexually oriented drawings sent in by some students. John Lennon, among other prominent people, was a subscriber to the magazine – a fact that was used in the editors' defense. Lennon was outraged by the harsh sentence and by the apparent censorship of the press.

John, along with Yoko*, Phil Spector* and The Beatles' assistant Mal Evans, produced a benefit single to help pay the legal expenses of the defendants' appeal of the court's ruling. Lennon was at the height of his political activity in England. He had recently recorded ***Power To The People*** and publicly supported several leftist causes.

Musician and writer Charles Shaar Murray recounted some of the events surrounding the recording of ***God Save Us*** in the May 1997 issue of Mojo music magazine. Murray said the session he attended took place at Lennon's home studio in Ascot and included himself and Lennon on acoustic guitar; Ringo on drums; Klaus Voormann on bass; Oz editors Felix Dennis, Richard Neville and Jim Anderson on percussion; a woman named Diane on piano and acoustic guitar; a fellow called Magic Michael handling the lead vocals and assorted backing vocalists. Murray recalls Phil Spector producing the session and that Yoko Ono and Mal Evans were also in attendance. Apparently, someone named Michelle also played acoustic guitar. However, as Murray noted, when the song was released the acoustic guitars had been replaced by electric guitars and the lead vocals were now sung by Bill Elliott *(see Splinter)*.

A version of ***God Save Us***, featuring Lennon on lead vocals, was aired for the first time in 1988 on the Westwood One radio series **The Lost Lennon Tapes**. Apparently, John did not want to give the impression that the benefit record was to be his latest single, so he decided not to use his vocal track. That the released version contains a horn section, but does not contain any noticeable number of backing vocalists or percussion, leads one to suspect that possibly only a portion of the backing from the session Murray attended survived, or that the backing was completely re-recorded later.

Though he was not present, Bob Purvis, Elliott's partner in Splinter, said Elliott recorded his vocal overdubs at Apple Studios. Other reports claim the song was recorded, at least in part, at EMI's Abbey Road Studios. The A-side was credited to Bill Elliott And The Elastic Oz Band (a la Plastic Ono Band), while the B-side, ***Do The Oz*** (sung by Lennon), was simply credited to Elastic Oz Band. Because Lennon sings the lead vocals on ***Do The Oz***, it is not considered a contribution to another artist's recording.

John and Yoko were among more than one thousand who demonstrated on August 11, 1971 supporting the OZ defendants and protesting the British government's policy in Northern Ireland. An Interview with John and Yoko, along with their rendition of ***Keep Right On To The End Of The Road***, was featured on a flexi-disc included in an issue of OZ later that summer.

John Entwistle

Record 103 title:
Ringo Starr And His Third All-Starr Band Volume 1

Media:
Album 5" CD

Label / Catalog number:
Blockbuster Exclusive / [matrix #] 0ERE4<5297>RINGOSTARR ADFL

Producer:
Greg Delancy (Mixer) Ringo Starr and David Fishof (Executive Producers)

Jacket / Inserts:
Standard international design / 4 page CD insert

Recording Location / Date:
Nippon Budakon Hall, Tokyo, Japan / 27 Jun 95

Song 103a title:
Boris The Spider [live]

Track details:
Side 1, track 8 / 2 min. 34 sec.

Release date / Country:
12 Aug 97 / U.S.A.

Composer:
J. Entwistle

John Entwistle: Lead Vocals & Bass; Mark Farner: Guitar & B. Vocals; Ringo Starr: Drums; Zak Starkey: Drums; Randy Bachman: Guitar; Felix Cavaliere: Keyboards; Billy Preston: Keyboards & B. Vocals; Mark Rivera: Percussion

John Entwistle was born on October 9, 1944 in London, England. He and a school mate named Pete Townshend shared membership in several bands in the late 1950s. Entwistle went on to play bass in a band call The Detours that included Roger Daltrey*. Before long, Townshend was asked to join the group. With the addition of Keith Moon* the band evolved into what eventually became known as The Who.

Entwistle wrote a number of songs for The Who, most notably ***Boris The Spider***, ***Fiddle About*** and ***My Wife***. (The 1972 album **Tommy**, performed by The London Symphony Orchestra and Chambre Choir with Guest Soloists, featured Ringo Starr singing ***Fiddle About***.) He also acted as the musical director on The Who's soundtracks **Quadrophenia** and **The Kids Are Alright** and was responsible for compiling The Who's album of out-takes titled **Odds And Sods** in 1974.

Entwistle was the first member of The Who to pursue a solo career, releasing an album titled **Smash Your Head Against The Wall** in 1971. His next album, **Whistle Rhymes**, was released the following year. He formed a studio band called Rigor Mortis and released the album **Rigor Mortis Sets In** in 1973. In 1975 he formed the group John Entwistle's Ox (his nickname) and had an album release titled **Mad Dog**. Entwistle's last solo album **Too Late The Hero** was released in 1981. Entwistle contributed to Ringo Starr's 1983 album **Old Wave** helping Ringo compose the song ***Everybody's In A Hurry But Me*** on which he played bass. He produced recordings for the band Nightfly which included Ringo's son Zak. Entwistle was a member of Ringo Starr's All-Starr band during their 1995 tour and performed ***Boris The Spider***, with Ringo backing him on drums, and ***My Wife***.

The Escorts

Record 104 title:
From The Blue Angel
Label / Catalog number:
Edsel / EDCD 422
Recording Location / Date:
Maximum Sound Studios, London, U.K. / Nov 66
Media:
Album 5" CD (mono)
Jacket / Inserts:
Unique / 16 page CD booklet

Song 104a title:
From Head To Toe
Release date / Country:
Jun 95 (first issued 18 Nov 66) / U.K.
Producer:
(probably) Paul McCartney
Track details:
Side 1, track 11 / 2 min. 28 sec.
Composer:
W. Robinson

John Kinrade: Guitar & Vocals; Mike Gregory: Bass & Vocals; Paddy Chambers: Guitar & Vocals; Paul Comerford: Drums; Paul McCartney: Tambourine

Song 104b title:
Night Time
Release date / Country:
Jun 95 (first issued 18 Nov 66) / U.K.
Producer:
(possibly) Paul McCartney
Track details:
Side 1, track 12 / 2 min. 50 sec.
Composer:
P. Chambers - (probably) P. McCartney

John Kinrade: Guitar & Vocals; Mike Gregory: Bass & Vocals; Paddy Chambers: Guitar & Vocals; Paul Comerford: Drums

The Escorts were a popular Liverpool band in the mid-1960s originally consisting of Terry Sylvester on rhythm guitar, John Kinrade on lead guitar, Mike Gregory on bass and John Foster on drums. Ringo Starr, who was Foster's cousin, helped The Escorts get bookings early in their career. The Escorts also have the distinction of being on the same bill as The Beatles the last time they played at the Cavern on August 3, 1963. Foster left the group and was followed on drums by Pete Clarke, Kenny Goodlass and finally Paul Comerford. Terry Sylvester left The Escorts for the Swinging Blue Jeans and later joined The Hollies. He was replaced by Frank Townshend who was then replaced by Paddy Chambers of the trio Paddy, Klaus and Gibson. The Klaus in the trio was Klaus Voormann *(see Paul Jones)*. The other member was Gibson Kemp, who replaced Ringo Starr in Rory Storm & The Hurricanes* when he left to join The Beatles. Gibson later married Beatle Stu Sutcliffe's fiancee, Astrid Kirchherr. Paddy, Klaus and Gibson were managed by Brian Epstein's NEMS Enterprises for a time. Mike Gregory and Kenny Goodlass went on to join the Swinging Blue Jeans after The Escorts broke up in 1967.

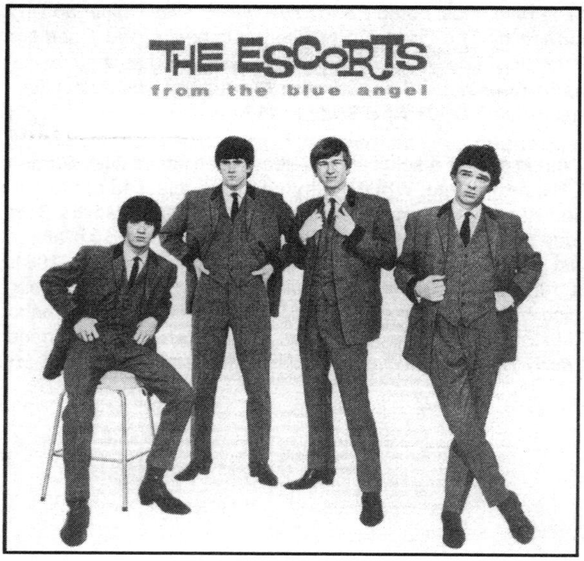

For years it was reported that Paul McCartney had produced the

A-side of The Escorts' final single ***From Head To Toe / Night Time*** (Columbia / DB 8061), released in the U.K. on November 18, 1966. Later reports claimed that McCartney's only involvement was as tambourine player. The book **The Beatles London**, co-written by noted Beatles researcher Mark Lewisohn, states that McCartney played tambourine and co-produced ***From Head To Toe***, reopening the debate about McCartney's role as producer. More recent reports claim McCartney also helped compose the single's B-side ***Night Time***. Additionally, there are rumors that he may also play on the cut. The full extent of McCartney's involvement may never be known, but it's likely he is involved with more than just the tambourine on the A-side of this record.

The Everly Brothers

Record 105 title:
EB 84
Label / Catalog number:
Mercury / 822 431-2
Media:
Album 5" CD
Producer:
Dave Edmunds
Jacket / Inserts:
Standard international design in jewel box / 12 page CD booklet (printed in U.S.A.)
Recording Location / Date:
Maison Rouge Studios, London, U.K. / (probably) 1984

Song 105a title:
On The Wings Of A Nightingale
Release date / Country:
16 Nov 88 (first issued 05 Oct 84) / Germany/U.S.A.
Track details:
Side 1, track 1 / 2 min. 34 sec.
Composer:
P. McCartney

Don Everly: Vocals; Phil Everly: Vocals; Dave Edmunds: Guitar; Pete Wingfield: Keyboards; Albert Lee: Guitar; John Giblin: Bass; Terry Williams: Drums; Gerry Conway: Drums; Phil Donnelly: Guitar; Paul McCartney: Guitar & (possible) Keyboards

Record 106 title:
Heartaches & Harmonies
Label / Catalog number:
Rhino / R2 71779
Media:
Albums 5" [4 CD set]
Producer:
Dave Edmunds (remixed by Paul McCartney)
Jacket / Inserts:
Jewel box in Standard international design box set / (4) CD insert, 64 page box set booklet with introduction by Paul McCartney & Gibson guitar postcard
Recording Location / Date:
Maison Rouge Studios, London, U.K. / 1984

Song 106a title:
On The Wings Of A Nightingale [single version]
Release date / Country:
18 Oct 94 (first issued Aug 84) / U.S.A.
Track details:
CD4, track 19 / 2 min. 34 sec.
Composer:
P. McCartney

Don Everly: Vocals; Phil Everly: Vocals; Dave Edmunds: Guitar; Pete Wingfield: Keyboards; Albert Lee: Guitar; John Giblin: Bass; Terry Williams: Drums; Gerry Conway: Drums; Phil Donnelly: Guitar; Paul McCartney: Guitar & (possible) Keyboards

Don Everly was born on February 1, 1937 in Brownie, Kentucky. Shortly after his birth, the family moved to Chicago, Illinois, where his brother Phil was born on January 19, 1939. The two boys performed with their country music star parents, Ike and Margaret Everly, until they were old enough to head out on their own. The Everly Brothers were undeniably two of the founding fathers of country

Phil Everly, Los Angeles, CA, early 1980s, photo courtesy of Tom Bert

rock, dominating the charts from 1957 to 1961. Among their songs that hit the top 20 are such classics as ***Bye Bye Love***, ***Wake Up Little Susie***, ***All I Have To Do Is Dream***, ***Bird Dog***, ***Devoted To You***, ***('Til) I Kissed You***, ***Let It Be Me***, ***When Will I Be Loved***, ***Cathy's Clown***, ***Walk Right Back*** and ***Crying In The Rain***. Their career was given a boost by the songwriting talents of Felice and Boudleaux Bryant. Their popularity seemed to fade with the onset of the British music invasion of 1964.

The influence that The Everly Brothers had on The Beatles, particularly the songwriting of Lennon and McCartney, has for the most part been underestimated. Those in doubt need to listen to The Beatles' 1963 version of ***One After 909***. (McCartney apparently paid a little tribute by mentioning Phil and Don in the lyrics of his 1976 Wings' hit ***Let 'Em In***.)

The Everly Brothers continued to record and tour throughout the 1960s and landed a summer replacement TV show for CBS in 1970. In 1973, a myriad of personal problems came to a head during a performance in California, and the duo went their separate ways. Each brother continued to record separately. It took nearly ten years for the brothers to straighten out their own personal lives and patch up their differences for an attempt at a reunion.

On September 23, 1983, The Everly Brothers staged a reunion concert at The Royal Albert Hall in London, which caught Paul McCartney on film in the audience and was later released on video. The studio album that followed, titled **EB 84**, was a critical, though unfortunately not a major commercial, success. It was no surprise that Paul McCartney gladly contributed his composition ***On The Wings Of A Nightingale*** to **EB 84**. He attended the sessions, adding guitar, and remixed the single version of the song that was a moderate chart success. The single version was included on The Everly Brothers' CD box set **Heartaches & Harmonies** which contains a booklet with an introduction by McCartney. Don Everly is not certain, but he thinks McCartney may have contributed keyboards to the song as well. McCartney's version of the song has yet to be released, though his demo version appears on a number of bootlegs. To date, the duo have covered two Beatles songs, McCartney's ***Hey Jude*** and ***Let It Be***. The Everly Brothers were inducted into the Rock and Roll Hall of Fame in 1986.

Adam Faith

Record 107 title: Free As A Bird
Label / Catalog number: FAB / FAB 1 [Unauthorized Record]
Jacket / Inserts: Unique / 8 page CD booklet
Recording Location / Date: Wembley Studios, Studio One, London, U.K. / 16 Apr 65
Media: Album 5" CD
Producer: (probably) Francis Hitching

Song 107a title: I Need Your Lovin' [live]
Release date / Country: (probably) Jan 96
Track details: Side 1, track 11 / 2 min. 13 sec.
Composer: Robinson - Gardner

Adam Faith: Lead Vocals; Doris Troy: B. Vocals; John Lennon: B. Vocals; George Harrison: B. Vocals; probably one or more of the following: Ray Davies: Guitar & B. Vocals; Dave Davies: Guitar & B. Vocals; Pete Quaife: Bass; Mike Avory: Drums; Jeff Beck: Guitar; Chris Dreja: Guitar; Jim McCarty: Drums; Keith Relf: B. Vocals & Harmonica; Paul Samwell-Smith: Bass; Peter Noone: B. Vocals; Derek Leckenby: Guitar; Keith Hopwood: Guitar; Karl Green: Bass; Barry Whitwam: Drums

Record 108 title: I Survive
Label / Catalog number: Warner Bros / BS 2791
Jacket / Inserts: Standard international design / Record label inner sleeve
Recording Location / Date: Kingsway Recorders, London, U.K. / 1974
Media: Album 12"
Producer: Adam Faith & David Courtney

Song 108a title: Change
Release date / Country: 02 Sep 74 / U.S.A.
Track details: Side 1, track 5 / 4 min. 00 sec.
Composer: A. Faith - D. Courtney

Adam Faith: Lead Vocals; Bob Henritt: Drums; Russ Ballard: Guitar; Dave Wintour: Bass; Dave Courtney: Piano; Del Newman: String Arrangement; Paul McCartney: Synthesizer

Song 108b title: Goodbye
Release date / Country: 02 Sep 74 / U.S.A.
Track details: Side 2, track 3 / 4 min. 01 sec.
Composer: A. Faith - D. Courtney

Adam Faith: Lead Vocals; Bob Henritt: Drums; Russ Ballard: Guitar & Piano Solo; Dave Wintour: Bass; Dave Courtney: Piano; Paul McCartney: Synthesizer

Song 108c title: Never Say Goodbye
Release date / Country: 02 Sep 74 / U.S.A.
Track details: Side 2, track 2 / 4 min. 04 sec.
Composer: A. Faith - D. Courtney

Adam Faith: Lead Vocals; Bob Henritt: Drums; Russ Ballard: Guitar; Dave Wintour: Bass; Dave Courtney: Piano; Paul McCartney: Synthesizer

Song 108d title:
Star Song
Release date / Country:
02 Sep 74 / U.S.A.
Track details:
Side 2, track 5 / 5 min. 58 sec.
Composer:
A. Faith - D. Courtney

Adam Faith: Lead Vocals; Bob Henritt: Drums; Russ Ballard: Guitar; Dave Wintour: Bass; Dave Courtney: Piano; Andrew Powell: String Arrangement; Linda McCartney: B. Vocals; Paul McCartney: B. Vocals

Adam Faith was born Terry Nelhams on June 23, 1940 in London, England. He, like many other British youngsters, was greatly influenced by Lonnie Donegan* and the Skiffle craze. Faith and Cliff Richards reigned supreme among male teen idols in Britain in the late 1950s and early '60s. He topped the U.K. charts with the songs ***What Do You Want*** and ***Poor Me***. He turned more and more towards acting like many of his teen idol contemporaries on both sides of the Atlantic at the time.

On April 16, 1965, Faith appeared on the popular mid-1960s British TV show **Ready Steady Goes Live!**. Musical guests included Doris Troy* and the groups The Kinks, The Yardbirds and Herman's Hermits. Also appearing on the show were John Lennon and George Harrison, who had stopped by to promote The Beatles' new single ***Ticket To Ride***. At the end of the show almost everyone assembled to back Adam Faith on a sing-along of Don Gardner & Dee Dee Ford's 1962 song ***I Need Your Lovin'*** that included prominent backing vocals by Lennon, Harrison and Doris Troy. However, Faith does not recall singing the song. Faith recorded a cover of The Beatles' song ***I Wanna Be Your Man*** released later that year.

Faith was best known to Americans as a regular on Jack Good's mid-1960s TV rock show **Shindig**, though he never had much chart success in the U.S. other than with the song ***It's Alright*** which made the top 40. Later he starred in the two U.K. TV series **Budgie** and **Love Hurts**. Faith also found success as a manager and has produced a number of artists including Leo Sayer, Roger Daltrey* and Lonnie Donegan.

Faith took over the role of Mike in the 1975 film **Stardust**. **Stardust** was the sequel to the 1973 film **That'll Be The Day** in which Ringo played the role of Mike. Ringo turned down his role in the sequel. The British soundtrack album jackets of **That'll Be The Day** and **Stardust** contain photos of Ringo Starr. Both films starred David Essex. (Paul McCartney and Wings backed Essex during his performance of ***Gonna Make You A Star*** on **Top Of The Pops** on November 21, 1974 [taped the 20th].)

Faith attempted a musical comeback (after a serious auto accident) in 1974 with the album **I Survive** which received fair reviews, but failed to reestablish him as a force in music. He called upon his old friends Paul and Linda McCartney* who contributed to the album as a personal favor. In 1977, he took part in the **Scouse The Mouse** project along with Ringo Starr. Faith, who has also found success in the financial world, is currently hosting a financial advice show called **Dosh** on British TV.

Marianne Faithfull

Record 109 title:
Lennon & McCartney Song Book
Label / Catalog number:
Connoisseur Collection / VSOP CD 150
Media:
Album 5" CD
Producer:
Tony Calder [Mike Leander & Paul McCartney]
Jacket / Inserts:
Standard international design in jewel box with photo of John Lennon & Paul McCartney / 4 page CD booklet with photos of John Lennon & Paul McCartney
Recording Location / Date:
Decca Studios, London, U.K. / 09 Oct 65 or 11 Oct 65

Song 109a title:
Yesterday
Release date / Country:
02 Jul 90 (first issued 22 Oct 65) / U.K./E.E.C.

Track details:
Side 1, track 23 / 2 min. 15 sec.
Composer:
J. Lennon - P. McCartney

Marianne Faithfull: Lead Vocals; Singers from the Royal College of Music

Marianne Faithfull was born on December 29, 1946 in London, England the daughter of Baroness Erisso Sacher-Masoch and Major Glynn Faithfull, a psychologist and university lecturer. Sadly, Marianne Faithfull is often remembered more for her scandalous relationship with The Rolling Stones*, and Mick Jagger* in particular, than for her tremendous talent. Americans remember her most for her trance-like rendition of the Jagger and Richards' composition ***As Tears Go By***. The song was top 30 in the U.S., and a top 10 in the U.K., in 1964 while Faithfull was still attending St. Joseph's Convent School. In 1965, her songs ***Come And Stay With Me***, ***This Little Bird*** and ***Summer Nights*** reached the top 30 in the U.S. and the top 10 in the U.K. She also recorded a cover of John Lennon's Beatles song ***I'm A Loser***.

On October 9, 1965, (some sources list the October 11) Paul McCartney visited Faithfull in the studios during her recording of ***Yesterday***. Marianne said "Paul and I had a very close and unique friendship. He helped me on a lot of my work, he always had a special kind of vision. I was very young and he's quite a patriarchal kind of guy. I looked up to him! He was very obsessed with his craft. He helped me a lot with ***Yesterday***. He sat down and started to explain, to teach me and this went on for a long time. It was a serious lesson and I knew that one day it would be useful to me. What he was suggesting was everything that was done on ***Yesterday***. I wouldn't call him a co-producer really, it's more than that. I guess co-producer is as good a word as any, but it doesn't quite cover it." In Barry Miles' 1997 authorized biography **McCartney Many Years From Now**, McCartney recalls attending Faithfull's session for ***Yesterday*** at Decca Studios, but does not remember if he contributed anything to it. Faithfull admits, and McCartney confirms, that she was not the sort of person who easily welcomed suggestions. During the session McCartney got to know the musical director, Mike Leander. (In 1967, McCartney had Leander arrange the score of his Beatles' song ***She's Leaving Home*** because George Martin* was unavailable. Several months later, Leander arranged a Lennon and McCartney instrumental called ***Shirley's Wild Accordion*** for The Beatles' **Magical Mystery Tour** soundtrack that was never used.)

McCartney stressed to Marianne the importance of releasing her version of ***Yesterday*** before Matt Monro's* cover version. Faithfull's version was released on October 22, 1965, and was a U.K. top 40. Monroe's version was released two weeks earlier and reached the top 10 on the U.K. charts. A 22 second film clip of McCartney performing ***Yesterday*** was used as an introduction to Faithfull's rendition of the song on **The Music Of Lennon & McCartney**, which first aired on British TV on December 17, 1965.

Faithfull married art dealer John Dunbar in 1965. The following year, Dunbar invited John Lennon to a private preview of an avant-garde art exhibition at his Indica Gallery titled **Unfinished Paintings and Objects**. The date – November 9, the artist – Yoko Ono, the rest, as they say, is history. Dunbar was also involved in making avant-garde films with Paul McCartney. Faithfull sang in the chorus of The Beatles' song ***Yellow Submarine***. By the end of 1966, she had separated from Dunbar and become Mick Jagger's steady girlfriend.

Faithfull was certainly one of "the beautiful people" of the swinging 1960s. She was also the infamous naked woman rolled up in a rug that police referred to when they made a drug raid at the house of Keith Richards on February 12, 1967. Luckily, George Harrison had left the party just before the raid. Marianne appeared along with Jagger and Richards in a film documentary of The Beatles' recording ***A Day In The Life***.

A picture of Paul McCartney, Glyn Johns and Mick Jagger together at a Faithfull recording session appears in McCartney's Club Sandwich summer 1996 No. 78. In the issue, readers are asked to help identify when the picture was taken and what song was being recorded. The photo shows McCartney wearing the identical outfit he wore at the press party to launch the album **Sgt. Pepper's Lonely Hearts Club Band** held on May 19, 1967 at Brian Epstein's home in London. Documents indicated that Faithfull recorded The Beatles' song ***With A Little Help From My Friends*** at Decca Studios on May 20, 1967. McCartney therefore must have attended a late night / early morning session on the 19th / 20th. He almost certainly had a hand in making it possible for Faithfull to record the then as-yet-unreleased Beatles' song that he composed. Mike Leander is listed as the producer for the sessions. It is not known if McCartney directly contributed to the recording. Faithfull has little recollection of her recording of ***With A Little Help From My Friends***, which remains unreleased.

Marianne appeared along with Jagger and Richards in the live telecast, via satellite, of The Beatles' performance of ***All You Need Is Love*** for the BBC's program **Our World** on June 25, 1967. Faithfull, along with Jagger and The Beatles, attended a seminar in August that year in Bangor, Wales on Transcendental Meditation given by Maharishi Mahesh Yogi.

Paul McCartney stated in his "interview" issue of Club Sandwich, winter 1994 No. 72, that he offered Faithfull a song he had written called ***Etcetera***. "I offered it to Marianne Faithfull and Mick Jagger, who were looking for a song for Marianne to record, but it wasn't what she wanted. I think she was looking for an ***Eleanor Rigby*** and instead I offered her an ***Etcetera***." (McCartney recalled in Miles' biography that ***Etcetera*** was a poor attempt to come up with a song for Faithfull and that maybe she was looking for something more baroque like ***Yesterday***.) McCartney recorded a demo of ***Etcetera*** during the sessions for **The Beatles** (white album.) Marianne does not recall McCartney offering her a song called ***Etcetera***, but said "When disco came along, I said to myself this isn't what Paul meant! What did he mean? Then I figured it out and made **Broken English**. I didn't want an ***Eleanor Rigby***, I wanted "Lucy Jorden!" He'll know exactly what I mean, the two songs are definitely stepsisters."

During the second half of the 1960s Faithfull had all but given up her singing career and turned to acting, but she had become increasingly dependent on drugs. By 1970 her relationship with Mick Jagger was at an end. Faithfull reappeared on the charts with the song ***The Ballad Of Lucy Jordan*** from her critically acclaimed album **Broken English** in 1979. The album also included her cover of John Lennon's song ***Working Class Hero***. Her voice was now void of its youthful innocence, which served as a reminder of the personal difficulties she had overcome. She denies reports that she recorded any songs with George Harrison, but she did record a cover of his song ***Beware Of Darkness*** in 1970, which was first released in 1984. She continues to release albums on a regular basis and make appearances in films and on TV. Her autobiography, **Faithfull**, was published in 1994.

Mark Farner

Record 110 title:
Ringo Starr And His Third All-Starr Band Volume 1

Media:
Album 5" CD

Label / Catalog number:
Blockbuster Exclusive / [matrix #] 0ERE4<5297>RINGOSTARR ADFL

Producer:
Greg Delancy (Mixer) Ringo Starr and David Fishof (Executive Producers)

Jacket / Inserts:
Standard international design / 4 page CD insert

Recording Location / Date:
Nippon Budakon Hall, Tokyo, Japan / 27 Jun 95

Song 110a title:
The Loco-Motion [live]

Track details:
Side 1, track 4 / 3 min. 07 sec.

Release date / Country:
12 Aug 97 / U.S.A.

Composer:
G. Goffin - C. King

Mark Farner: Lead Vocals & Lead Guitar; Ringo Starr: Drums; Zak Starkey: Drums; John Entwistle: Bass; Randy Bachman: Guitar & B. Vocals; Felix Cavaliere: Keyboards & B. Vocals; Billy Preston: Keyboards & B. Vocals; Mark Rivera: Percussion & B. Vocals

Singer and guitarist Mark Farner was born on September 29, 1948 in Flint, Michigan. Farner, like Ted Nugent, Bob Seger and Dick Wagner, is a living legend of the Michigan rock scene from the mid-'60s to mid-'70s. Farner played in a couple of well-known bands in the state including The Bossmen, fronted by Wagner, and also Terry Knight & The Pack. Knight, a former top 40 AM radio DJ in the southeastern Michigan area who went by his real name, Terry Knapp, gave up the spotlight several months after the group's top 50 song ***I (Who Have Nothing)***. The group was renamed the Fabulous Pack that also included Donald Brewer.

In 1968, Farner and Brewer recruited bassist Mel Schacher, a latter-day member of ? [Question Mark] and the Mysterians (of ***96 Tears*** fame), another Michigan based band. The group appointed Knight to be their manager and producer. Knight then dubbed the band Grand Funk Railroad after the Grand Trunk Railroad line. They signed with Capitol Records in 1969, and over the next six years, would become America's first and most successful heavy-metal rock group. To date, they've sold more than 25 million records. Within their first three years alone they racked up one gold and five platinum albums in spite of constant bashing from the critics. In 1970, their song ***I'm Your Captain***, from the **Closer To Home** album, was a top 30. They were a major concert draw and in 1971 sold out New York's Shea Stadium, breaking the attendance record previously held by The Beatles. In 1972, the group fired Knight. They replaced him with Andy Cavaliere and retained attorney John Eastman *(see Linda McCartney)*, setting into motion long and bitter legal disputes with Knight that would ultimately take its toll on the group. That year the trio became a quartet with the addition of the fourth Flint area native Craig Frost who, according to Farner, was hired as a sideman to play keyboards. Initially, Grand Funk's albums (the "Railroad" was dropped from their name between '73 and '75) fared better on the charts than their singles. However, in 1973 Todd Rundgren* produced an anthem to the excesses of touring titled ***We're An American Band*** which became Grand Funk's first number one song. In 1974 they accomplished one of music's rarest feats by taking their cover of Little Eva's number one song ***The Loco-Motion*** to the top of the charts. Their 1975 singles ***Some Kind Of Wonderful*** and ***Bad Time*** reached the top 10, but the group planned to break up following the release of their prophetically titled album **Born To Die**. They decided to record one more album, **Good Singin' Good Playin'**, released in 1976 and produced by Frank Zappa*. Grand Funk Railroad only reached the top 40 in the U.K. once with the song ***Inside—Looking Out*** in 1971.

In 1977, Brewer, Schacher and Billy Elworthy formed the group Flint that released only one album. Farner's self-titled solo album, produced by Dick Wagner, was released that year. Grand Funk reformed around Farner, Brewer and bassist Dennis Bellinger in 1981. They disbanded again in 1983 after releasing two albums that failed to reignite their careers. Brewer and Frost went on to become members of Bob Seger's backing band. Farner released several Christian-rock oriented albums in the late '80s and early '90s. His song ***Isn't It Amazing*** was a number two on the Inspirational chart.

Farner regained the spotlight as a member of Ringo Starr's All-Starr band during their 1995 tour, and performed ***The Loco-Motion*** and ***Some Kind Of Wonderful*** with Ringo backing him on drums. (Ringo reportedly recorded a version of ***Some Kind Of Wonderful*** produced by Chips Moman in Memphis in 1987.) Farner made a guest appearance during Ringo's All-Starr Band performance of ***With A Little Help From My Friends*** at the Universal Amphitheatre in Los Angeles on May 3, 1997. Grand Funk reformed with all three original members in 1997 for a world tour and a live album titled **Bosnia**.

Fred Fascher

Record 111 title:
The Beatles Live / At The Star Club in Hamburg, Germany; 1962

Media:
Album 5" CD

Label / Catalog number:
Overseas / 38 CP-44

Producer:
Adrian Barber & Ted Taylor; (re-produced by: Larry Grossberg)

Jacket / Inserts:
Unique in Jewel box / 24 page CD booklet with photo of John Lennon

Recording Location / Date:
Star-Club, Hamburg, Germany / 25 Dec 62

Song 111 title:
Be-Bop-A-Lula

Track details:
Side 1, track 23 / 2 min. 29 sec.

Release date / Country:
Sep 85 (first issued 08 Apr 77) / Japan

Composer:
G. Vincent - T. Davis

Fred Fascher: Lead Vocals; George Harrison: Lead Guitar; John Lennon: Rhythm Guitar; Paul McCartney: Bass; Ringo Starr: Drums

See Horst Fascher.

Roy Young, Paul McCartney and George Harrisonat the Star-Club, Hamburg, Germany, spring 1962, photo courtesy of Roy Young

Horst Fascher

Record 112 title:
The Beatles Live / At The Star Club in Hamburg, Germany; 1962

Media:
Album 5" CD

Label / Catalog number:
Overseas / 38 CP-44

Producer:
Adrian Barber & Ted Taylor; (re-produced by: Larry Grossberg)

Jacket / Inserts:
Unique in Jewel box / 24 page CD booklet with photo of John Lennon

Recording Location / Date:
Star-Club, Hamburg, Germany / 25 Dec 62

Song 112a title:
Hallelujah, I Love Her So

Track details:
Side 1, track 24 / 2 min. 10 sec.

Release date / Country:
Sep 85 (first issued 08 Apr 77) / Japan

Composer:
R. Charles

Horst Fascher: Lead Vocals; George Harrison: Lead Guitar; John Lennon: Rhythm Guitar; Paul McCartney: Bass; Ringo Starr: Drums

Horst Fascher was born on February 5, 1936, in Hamburg, Germany. In 1960, Fascher, a former German boxing champion, was a bouncer at Bruno Koschmider's Kaiserkeller Club in the St. Pauli district of the port city of Hamburg, Germany. St. Pauli has long been known as one of Europe's vice capitals. It was a magnet for off duty seamen and the large number of foreign troops stationed in Germany after the war. St. Pauli was a breeding ground for crime, and home to a sizable number of gangsters. The area was filled with every variety of entertainment including legalized prostitution, strip clubs and pick-up bars headlining American rock 'n' roll acts.

Supplementing these acts were a number of lesser-known and affordable English acts covering the latest American hits. Among them were Roy Young, Derry And The Seniors *(see Freddie Starr)*, The Undertakers *(see Jackie Lomax)*, Billy J. Kramer & The Dakotas*, The Strangers, Gerry And The Pacemakers*, Cliff Bennett And The Rebel Rousers* and The Beatles.

Allan Williams, a Liverpool club owner and booking agent, arranged The Beatles' first visit to St. Pauli in August 1960. They took up residency at Koschmider's Indra Club on Grosse Freiheitstrasse, just off the main avenue, in the area known as Reeperbahn. In October, Koschmider moved them to his more up-scale Kaiserkeller Club on the same street. It was there that Horst Fascher met and befriended The Beatles, acting as bodyguard, and looking out for their interests and safety in the notorious St. Pauli. For The Beatles, St. Pauli was the epitome of sex, drugs and rock 'n' roll, and served as a proving ground and playground.

Kristofer Engelhardt and Horst Fascher at press party for Canadian Abuse Prevention Foundation - "Imageine Sweepstakes," 1996, CN Tower, Toronto, Canada, photo courtesy of Brad Forder

Fascher soon went to work at Peter Eckhorn's newly opened Top Ten Club on Reeperbahn, featuring Tony Sheridan and The Beat Brothers *(see Tony Sheridan)*. (Fascher also served as Roy Young and Sheridan's manager for a number of years.) The Beatles were regular visitors in their off hours and began performing with Sheridan, a violation of their contract with Koschmider. This ultimately led to their expulsion from Germany for a time. Eckhorn quickly arranged with The Beatles for them to play at his Top Ten Club from late March to July 1961. As a result of The Beatles' direct negotiations with Eckhorn, they informed Williams that they did not feel he was entitled to his management percentage, and that led to his parting with the group. Eckhorn, along with Sheridan, journeyed to Liverpool in late December to negotiate with The Beatles' new manager, Brian Epstein, for another engagement the following year, but was unwilling to meet Epstein's fee. During this visit, Sheridan persuaded Ringo Starr to join his band and return with him to Hamburg.

Three weeks later, Manfred Weissleder sent Roy Young and Fascher to Liverpool where they signed a contact with Epstein to have The Beatles help open Weissleder's plush new Star-Club on Grosse Freiheit in April 1962. Fascher had been hired to help manage the Star-Club, which would soon feature Sheridan as well. Horst's brother Fred (born April 23, 1945) worked at the club as a headwaiter. The Beatles made a return engagement at the Star-Club during the first half of November, before their final engagement during the second half of December 1962. It was at the Star-Club that The Beatles first met and shared the bill with Little Richard*, and his band member Billy Preston*, among others like Gene Vincent whom they considered musical heroes.

The Beatles' final engagement at the Star-Club ran from December 18 through the 31, 1962. Well-known producer Adrian Barber, who had also been a member of the popular Liverpool group Cass And The Cassanovas, later renamed The Big Three, was the sound and stage manager of the Star-Club in 1962. According to Barber, he and Ted Taylor put Taylor's tape recorder on a table with a single microphone pointed towards the Star-Club stage to record performances as an ambiance test. Taylor, known as "Kingsize" because of his robust stature, fronted the group Kingsize Taylor and the Dominoes. Taylor ended up with the tapes that had captured his group, Cliff Bennett And The Rebel Rousers, and The Beatles in performance. Hans Gottfridsson, in his book **The Beatles From Cavern To Star-Club**, has concluded that released recordings of The Beatles at the Star-Club were compiled from recordings of four sets made on three separate occasions in December, most likely on December 21, 25, 28, 30 or 31. Gottfridsson has determined that the recordings of The Beatles with lead vocals by Horst Fascher and his brother Fred *(see Fred Fascher)* were made on Christmas Day.

The tapes lay forgotten for nearly a decade until Taylor and Allan Williams "rediscovered" them. They tried to interest, among other companies, Polydor and The Beatles' Apple Records in an agreement to buy the recordings with the condition that they be given a percentage of the sales of any release. Any release by Apple had to be approved by The Beatles, who reportedly were as opposed to releasing the recordings as they were to working with each other at the time. When Harrison and Ringo met with Williams in 1975, they refused to deal with him for the tapes.

In 1976, Williams and Taylor sold the tapes to Paul Murphy of Lingasong Records in England. Murphy (aka Paul Rogers) had been an A&R man and producer for Polydor Records as well as a part-time member of one of Rory Storm's early bands *(see Rory Storm & The Hurricanes)*. After unsuccessfully trying to market the tapes to other record companies, including Apple and EMI, Lingasong sold the worldwide distribution rights to Double H Licensing Co. Double H proceeded to invest a considerable amount of money and expertise into trying to improve the tapes' sound quality. At the time, EMI was preparing to release the live **The Beatles At The Hollywood Bowl** album. Once release of the Star-Club recording was imminent, legal wrangling with EMI over who owned the rights to the recordings ensued. EMI rightfully claimed ownership, as The Beatles were under contract to them at the time the recordings were made, though Double H implied they were recorded prior to The Beatles being under contract. The British High Court ruled that because The Beatles had passed over purchase of the crudely made tapes, and because EMI had done little to claim ownership in the past, they did not have a case. Though they appealed, EMI probably felt the inferior sounding Star-Club recording was not worth a serious fight and would not be a major threat to sales of **The Beatles At The Hollywood Bowl** album. (The Beatles and Apple Records returned to the courts in 1996 and were able to halt Lingasong's release of the Star-Club recordings on CD as they had successfully done against Sony Music several years earlier.)

The recording of **The Beatles Live! At The Star-Club In Hamburg, Germany; 1962** was first issued in Germany by Bellaphon Records in April 1977. A few weeks later, EMI released **The Beatles At The Hollywood Bowl**, the first previously unreleased recordings of The Beatles issued by EMI since the group's breakup in 1970. Its release was, no doubt, in part expedited by the impending release of The Star-Club recordings. The Star-Club recordings were released shortly thereafter by Lingasong Records in the U.S. and U.K. The Star-Club recordings were subsequently released in a variety of formats on a number of labels throughout the world, and were often incorrectly identified, or included numbers not performed by The Beatles.

At first, there was some confusion as to the lead vocalist on the two songs ***Be-Bop-A-Lula*** and ***Hallelujah, I Love Her So***. The initial releases of the Star-Club recordings identified the lead vocalist on these songs as a Star-Club waiter named Horst Obber. The word "ober" is a term often used in Germany for waiter. Fights were a frequent occurrence in the St. Pauli clubs and waiters often acted as bouncers. In Fascher's position as bouncer and manager, he, no doubt, was referred to as "ober," which probably led to the confusion concerning his actual name. According to Fascher, this was not the first time he had performed with The Beatles. Fascher said "when I had two or three beers, I was a little more confident and I would get up and sing sometimes! I would only sing the songs I knew the words to because my English was not so good at the time."

On December 15, 1978, Sheridan was the headline act for the opening night at a new Star-Club in Hamburg in which Fascher was involved. Ringo Starr and George Harrison were in attendance. Fascher said that Paul McCartney has remained a close friend over the years, especially during troubled times. Fascher is an occasional guest at Beatles conventions in Europe and works as a rock music promoter.

Ferry Aid

Record 113 title:
Let It Be - The Zeebrugge Ferry Disaster
March 6th, 1987

Media:
Single 12"

Label / Catalog number:
Profile / PRO 7147

Producer:
Stock, Aitken & Waterman

Jacket / Inserts:
Standard international design PS (version 2) with alternate photo of Paul McCartney / Record label inner sleeve

Recording Location / Date:
PWL Studios, London, U.K. / 14-16 Mar 87

Song 113a title:
Let It Be

Track details:
Side 1, track 1 / 6 min. 30 sec.

Release date / Country:
May 87 (first issued 23 Mar 87) / U.S.A.

Composer:
J. Lennon - P. McCartney

Paul McCartney: Vocal Contribution; Mike Stock: Keyboards; Matt Aitken: Keyboards; Luke Goss: Drums; Mark Knopfler; Bass Gary Moore: Guitar

On March 6, 1987, the passenger ferry boat Herald of Free Enterprise, bound for England, capsized shortly after its departure from Zeebrugge, Belgium. One hundred and eighty-eight people, mostly British citizens, were killed. As frequently happens in such tragedies, some of Britain's top pop stars (often including Paul McCartney) quickly assembled to make a benefit recording. McCartney, unable to attend the sessions, gave the producers permission to lift his vocal introduction to The Beatles' song ***Let It Be*** that was mixed into the intro of the all-star recording. Though technically the recording contains nothing more than a sample of a Beatles' recording, it is nonetheless a specific contribution by McCartney. The song was issued the following week in 7" (edited) and 12" (extended) formats. It went straight to No. 1 on the U.K. charts, prompting the U.S. record company Profile to issue it two months later. Americans had little connection to the ferry boat disaster in the English Channel, and barely responded to the cause. The U.S. picture sleeve, though nearly identical to the U.K.

sleeve, substituted, apparently at McCartney's request, a more flattering photo of him than the one used on the U.K. sleeve. McCartney was also featured in the video for the song.

First Mistake

Record 114 title:
Gotta Sing, Gotta Dance
Label / Catalog number:
Monopol / L4949 [(probably) Unauthorized Record]
Jacket / Inserts:
Unique PS
Recording Location / Date:
(probably) Sweden / (probably) 1986
Media:
Single 7"

Song 114a title:
Gotta Sing, Gotta Dance
Release date / Country:
1986 / Sweden
Track details:
Side 1, track 1
Composer:
P. McCartney

In 1973 it was reported that Paul McCartney would write songs for a musical film titled **Gotta Sing, Gotta Dance**. The film was to star Twiggy (Lawson), a well-known model and friend of the McCartney's, but the film was never made. McCartney performed the choreographed title theme on his **James Paul McCartney** TV special that year.

Over a decade later an obscure band called First Mistake issued their version of ***Gotta Sing, Gotta Dance***. The B-side of the single is ***Gotta Sing, Gotta Dance (Party Mix)***. The label does not carry an MPL copyright and the catalogue number is identical to The Beatles' first single ***Love Me Do*** for EMI. If this is not coincidental, it may indicate that it is not an authorized release.

Mick Fleetwood

Record 115 title:
The Visitor
Label / Catalog number:
Great Expectations / PIPCD 020
Jacket / Inserts:
Standard international design in jewel box / 6 page CD booklet
Recording Location / Date:
Ghana Film Industries Studios, Accra, Ghana & Jimmy Page's Sol Studios (The Mill), Cookham, Berkshire, U.K. / Jan - Feb 81
Media:
Album 5" CD
Producer:
Richard Dashut & Mick Fleetwood

Song 115a title:
Walk A Thin Line
Release date / Country:
09 Nov 90 (first issued 30 Jun 81) / France
Track details:
Side 1, track 6 / 3 min. 19 sec.
Composer:
L. Buckingham

George Hawkins: Lead Vocals, Bass, Piano & Guitar; George Harrison: 12 String Guitar, Slide Guitar & B. Vocals; Mick Fleetwood: Drums & Percussion; Adjo Group: B. Vocals; Sara Recor: B. Vocals

Mick Fleetwood was born on June 24, 1947 in Redruth, England. Fleetwood, a drummer, along with bass player John McVie, is one of the founders and namesakes of the band Fleetwood Mac. Numerous personnel and musical changes seem to have become the band's trademark. Fleetwood, McVie and Peter Green had been early members of John Mayall's band, The Bluesbreakers *(see*

Mick Fleetwood, Irvine, CA, late 1980s, photo courtesy of Tom Bert

Eric Clapton). The three, along with blues freak Jeremy Spencer formed the initially blues-oriented band, Fleetwood Mac. Fleetwood Mac almost signed to Apple Records in 1969, but got a better offer from Immediate Records. In 1970, Green left the band and Danny Kirwan joined. Also joining the band was Christine Perfect, who soon became known as Christine McVie after marrying John. In 1971, Spencer left and was replaced by Bob Welch, then Kirwan left and was replaced by Bob Weston and Dave Walker. All but Fleetwood and the McVies departed before the most famous and longest lasting line-up was formed in 1975 with the addition of Lindsey Buckingham and Stevie Nicks.

During the next five years, with this lineup, Fleetwood Mac would release their three most successful albums: **Fleetwood Mac**, **Rumors** (one of music's all-time best selling albums), and **Tusk**. Their songs ***Rhiannon (Will You Ever Win)***, ***Say You Love Me***, ***Go Your Own Way***, ***Dreams***, ***Don't Stop***, ***You Make Loving Fun***, ***Sara***, ***Hold Me*** and ***Gypsy*** have become rock classics. As in the past, the band continued to be plagued by personal problems; still, they managed to stay together while pursuing solo projects.

Mick Fleetwood traveled to Ghana, West Africa in 1981 to record a decidedly African-flavored album titled **The Visitor**. The album included the song ***Walk A Thin Line*** which featured a guest appearance by George Harrison that was recorded in England. Fleetwood had been married to Harrison's sister-in-law, Jenny Boyd.

Christine McVie released her solo album **Christine McVie** in 1984. In the February 1983 issue of Creem magazine's rock 'n' roll news page, it mentions that Paul McCartney, Ringo Starr and George Harrison would all be making guest appearances on the forthcoming solo album by Christine McVie of Fleetwood Mac. That month Beatles Book monthly magazine also reported that McCartney was rumored to be producing McVie's album at AIR Studios in Montserrat, but dispelled the rumor in its May 1983 issue. When the album was issued in 1984, its detailed credits fail to mention involvement by any of The Beatles. None of The Beatles contributed to the album according to its producer Russ Titelman. A spokesman for McVie also stated that none of The Beatles contributed to any other recordings of hers.

Lindsey Buckingham left Fleetwood Mac shortly after their 1987 album **Tango In The Night**. Rick Vito and Billy Burnette were brought in to supplement the band on tours. Burnette, who recorded a cover of The Beatles' ***I've Just Seen A Face*** in 1986, is the son of the rockabilly star Johnny Burnette. Vito left the group in 1991 and Stevie Nicks departed in 1993.

In 1992, Nicks joined Ringo Starr And His All-Starr Band during their encore performance of ***With A Little Help From My Friends*** at the Greek Theatre in Los Angeles. In 1995, she sang a duet with Ringo on the song ***Lay Down Your Arms*** from the CD **For The Love Of Harry: Everybody Sings Nilsson** *(see Harry Nilsson)*. Nicks has been the only member of Fleetwood Mac who has enjoyed a great amount of chart success on her own.

In 1995, Fleetwood Mac released the album **Time** that included new members Dave Mason* and Bekka Bramlett, the daughter of Delaney & Bonnie *(see Delaney & Bonnie & Friends).* Shortly after its release, Fleetwood disbanded the group. In 1997, Fleetwood, Buckingham, Nicks and the McVie's reunited and released a live album titled **The Dance**. Fleetwood Mac was inducted into the Rock and Roll Hall of Fame in 1998.

John Fogerty

Record 116 title:
Live! The Silver Wilburys
Label / Catalog number:
[none] / SWP 87-2 [Unauthorized Record]
Jacket / Inserts:
Unique in Jewel box / 2 page CD insert
Recording Location / Date:
On location at Palomino Club, Los Angeles, CA, U.S.A. / 19 Feb 87
Media:
Album 5" CD (mono)
Producer:
(probably) Palomino Club

Song 116a title:
Blue Suede Shoes [live]
Release date / Country:
1988 / Korea
Track details:
Side 1, track 7 / 2 min. 50 sec.
Composer:
C. Perkins

John Fogerty: Vocals & Guitar; George Harrison: Guitar & Vocals; Jesse Ed Davis: Guitar; Taj Mahal: Harmonica; Bob Dylan: Guitar; Jim Ehinger: Keyboards; Bobby Tsukamoto: Bass; Mark Shark: Guitar; Gary Ray: Drums

Song 116b title:
Knock On Wood [live]
Release date / Country:
1988 / Korea
Track details:
Side 1, track 4 / 3 min. 55 sec.
Composer:
S. Cropper - E. Floyd

John Fogerty; Lead Vocals & Guitar; Jesse Ed Davis: Guitar; George Harrison: Guitar; Taj Mahal: Harmonica & B. Vocals; Bob Dylan: Guitar; Jim Ehinger: Keyboards; Bobby Tsukamoto: Bass; Mark Shark: Guitar; Gary Ray: Drums

Song 116c title:
In The Midnight Hour [live]
Release date / Country:
1988 / Korea
Track details:
Side 1, track 5 / 3 min. 20 sec.
Composer:
S. Cropper - W. Pickett

John Fogerty: Lead Vocals & Guitar; Jesse Ed Davis: Guitar; George Harrison: Guitar; Taj Mahal: B. Vocals; Bob Dylan: Guitar; Jim Ehinger: Keyboards; Bobby Tsukamoto: Bass; Mark Shark: Guitar; Gary Ray: Drums

Song 116d title:
Proud Mary [live]
Release date / Country:
1988 / Korea
Track details:
Side 1, track 9 / 4 min. 23 sec.
Composer:
J. Fogerty

John Fogerty: Lead Vocals & Guitar; Jesse Ed Davis: Guitar; George Harrison: Guitar; Taj Mahal: B. Vocals; Bob Dylan: Guitar; Jim Ehinger: Keyboards; Bobby Tsukamoto: Bass; Mark Shark: Guitar; Gary Ray: Drums

Multi-instrumentalist John Fogerty, born on May 28, 1945 in Berkeley, California, was the primary creative force in the band Creedence Clearwater Revival that included Stu Cook, Doug Clifford, and John's older brother Tom. John Fogerty's songwriting, production and distinctive vocals, and the groups' unique sound, best described as a cross between rockabilly and swamp rock, were the keys to their lasting popularity. The band's members had been together since 1959 under various names but without much success.

Things began to improve shortly after they changed their name to Creedence Clearwater in 1967. In 1968, they reached the top 20 for the first time with a remake of Dale Hawkins' *(see Ronnie Hawkins)* ***Suzie Q***, but in 1969 they ignited the U.S. charts. C.C.R., or Creedence as they were often referred to, were America's most popular rock band between 1969 and 1971. During that period they recorded nine million-selling singles and five million-selling albums. In 1969 alone they had top 10s with ***Proud Mary***, ***Bad Moon Rising***, ***Green River***, ***Fortunate Son*** and ***Down On The Corner***. The following year they reached the top 10 with ***Travelin' Band***, ***Who'll Stop The Rain***, ***Up Around The Bend***, ***Run Through The Jungle*** and ***Lookin' Out My Back Door***. In 1971 they had the million-selling singles ***Have You Ever Seen The Rain*** and ***Sweet Hitch-Hiker***. But John Fogerty's prominence, and the departure of brother Tom, led to the group's rapid disintegration and they broke up in 1972.

John Fogerty, Los Angeles, CA, late 1980s, photo courtesy of Tom Bert

Tom and John Fogerty embarked on solo careers, but chart success eluded them. By the late 1970s, the brothers had all but dropped out of the music business. Fogerty restarted his career with the 1985 hit single ***The Old Man Down The Road*** and album **Centerfield**. Tom Fogerty died of complications from tuberculosis in 1990. Stu Cook and Doug Clifford became the rhythm sections of various groups, including The Don Harrison Band, and are currently touring as Cosmo's Factory, the title of one of C.C.R's albums. Creedence Clearwater Revival was inducted into the Rock and Roll Hall of Fame in 1993. Fogerty's latest album, **Blue Moon Swamp**, was released in 1997.

On February 19, 1987, Fogerty joined Taj Mahal* and the Graffiti Band, featuring Jesse Ed Davis*, and George Harrison and Bob Dylan* for a late night hour-long jam at Hollywood's Palomino Club. The jam is available on the bootleg CD titled **Live! The Silver Wilburys** and on copies of the club's house video of the performance circulating among collectors.

The Fourmost

Record 117 title:
Lennon & McCartney Song Book Volume 2

Media:
Album 5" CD (mono)

Label / Catalog number:
Connoisseur Collection / VSOP CD 162

Producer:
George Martin

Jacket / Inserts:
Standard international design in jewel box with photo of John Lennon & Paul McCartney / 8 page CD booklet with photo of John Lennon & Paul McCartney

Recording Location / Date:
EMI-Abbey Road Studios, London, U.K. / 03 Jul 63

Song 117a title:
Hello Little Girl
Release date / Country:
31 May 91 (first issued 30 Aug 63) / U.K./E.E.C.
Track details:
Side 1, track 23 / 1 min. 50 sec.
Composer:
J. Lennon - P. McCartney

Billy Hatton: Vocals & Bass; & Brian O'Hara: Vocals & Lead Guitar; Mike Millward: Vocals & Rhythm Guitar; Dave Lovelady; Drums

Record 118 title:
Rosetta / Just Like Before
Label / Catalog number:
CBS / 4041
Jacket / Inserts:
Unique PS (printed in Holland)
Recording Location / Date:
Jan 69
Media:
Single 7" (mono)
Producer:
Paul McCartney

Song 118a title:
Just Like Before
Release date / Country:
21 Feb 69 / U.K.
Track details:
Side 1, track 2 / 2 min. 30 sec.
Composer:
A. Benny [aka B. O'Hara]

Brian O'Hara: Lead Vocals & Guitar; Dave Lovelady: Drums & B. Vocals; Billy Hatton: Bass & B. Vocals; Joey Bowers: Guitar & B. Vocals

Song 118b title:
Rosetta
Release date / Country:
21 Feb 69 / U.K.
Track details:
Side 1, track 1 / 2 min. 11 sec.
Composer:
E. Hines - H. Woode

Brian O'Hara: Lead Vocals & Guitar; Paul McCartney: Piano & Arrangement; Dave Lovelady: Drums & B. Vocals; Billy Hatton: Bass & B. Vocals; Joey Bowers: B. Vocals & Guitar

Record 119 title:
The Songs Lennon & McCartney Gave Away
Label / Catalog number:
EMI / NUT 18 (0C 054-07 003)
Jacket / Inserts:
Standard international design with sketch of John Lennon & Paul McCartney / Record label inner sleeve
Recording Location / Date:
EMI-Abbey Road Studios, London, U.K. / Oct or Nov 63
Media:
Album 12"
Producer:
George Martin

Song 119a title:
I'm In Love
Release date / Country:
13 Apr 79 (first issued 15 Nov 63) / U.K.
Track details:
Side 1, track 10 / 2 min. 07 sec.
Composer:
J. Lennon - P. McCartney

18 Billy Hatton: Vocals & Bass; Brian O'Hara: Vocals & Lead Guitar; Mike Millward: Rhythm Guitar; Dave Lovelady; Drums

The Fourmost, whose highly educated members were born and raised in the Liverpool area, originally called themselves The Four Jays and then The Four Mosts before revising their name. They were good friends of, and often shared the same bill with, The Beatles. Like The Beatles, they were

known as much for their unique brand of humor as their music.

The group originally consisted of Brian Redman on drums; Joey Bowers on rhythm guitar and vocals; Billy Hatton, born June 6, 1941 on bass and vocals; and Brian O'Hara, born March 12, 1942 on lead guitar and vocals. By 1962, Dave Lovelady, born October 16, 1942, had replaced Redman on drums and Mike Millward, born May 9, 1942, had replaced Bowers on rhythm guitar. Millward died in 1966 and Bowers reclaimed his old position with the band. George Peckham, another brief member of the group, went on to work for The Beatles' Apple Records.

The Beatles first recorded ***Hello Little Girl*** at their Decca Records audition along with a dozen or so standards and two other Lennon and McCartney compositions. After they failed the audition, they never again attempted to record ***Hello Little Girl***. It was instead given to Brian Epstein's NEMS Enterprises managed group Gerry And The Pacemakers* to record, but they decided not to release their version (it was finally released in 1991). The song was then turned over to another NEMS Enterprises managed group, The Fourmost, who had a U.K. top 10 with it in the fall of 1963. ***Hello Little Girl*** is apparently the first song John Lennon ever wrote. Brian O'Hara recalls "We were given a demo of Lennon and Harrison playing acoustic guitars and singing the song; we had about two days to learn it and we rehearsed it on the way down to the studio in the bus we had. Lennon was reading his poetry on the other side of the tape, but I think we sent it back to Brian Epstein after we were done with it." A low-fidelity, alternate version of The Fourmost's ***Hello Little Girl*** appears on the bootleg Beatles' CD **Maybe You Can Drive My Car** (Yellow Dog/Orange / 019). (The Decca audition version of ***Hello Little Girl*** was officially released by The Beatles on their album **Anthology 1** in 1995.)

In November 1963, The Fourmost issued their second single, another Lennon and McCartney song written by John titled ***I'm In Love*** that reached the U.K. top 20. John and Paul also gave Billy J. Kramer *(see Billy J. Kramer & The Dakotas)* a chance to record and release the song around the same time as The Fourmost. EMI decided to leave Kramer's version in their vaults (it was finally released in 1991). Both Kramer's and The Fourmost's versions of ***I'm In Love*** qualify as contributions, though the Kramer version is the preferred, as it does involve an uncredited production assistance by John Lennon. (***I'm In Love*** has since been covered by Maxine Brown, Solomon Burke, Sandy Nelson, Junior Parker, Wilson Pickett, and The Saltbee.) There are bootleg records that contain Lennon's performance of the song.

The Fourmost were also given the Lennon and McCartney composition ***One And One Is Two*** *(see The Strangers with Mike Shannon)*. According to O'Hara, "McCartney came into the studio and played bass on ***One And One Is Two***, but there just wasn't any meat in the song and we couldn't get anywhere with it."

The Fourmost, being more of a cabaret / comedy act, were perfect to fill the bill on The Beatles' 1963 Christmas Shows. Their biggest hit was a song called ***A Little Loving*** in 1964. They had three other hits in the U.K., ***How Can I Tell Her?***, ***Baby I Need Your Lovin*** and ***Girls Girls Girls***, but The Fourmost were virtual unknowns in the U.S. Their song ***I Love You Too*** from the soundtrack to Gerry And The Pacemakers' 1965 film **Ferry Cross The Mersey**, in which they appeared, was also included on the bootleg Beatles record **Indian Rope Trick**. It was labeled as Paul McCartney with The Fourmost, but O'Hara said McCartney had absolutely nothing to do with ***I Love You Too***. The Fourmost also recorded a cover of McCartney's Beatles song ***Here, There And Everywhere*** in 1966.

In 1969, McCartney suggested to Brian O'Hara that The Fourmost should record the old jazz standard ***Rosetta*** as a single, and even volunteered to arrange and produce it for them. McCartney also produced the single's B-side, ***Just Like Before***. O'Hara wrote the song under the pseudonym A. Benny and said it was assigned to Apple Publishing in thanks for McCartney's contributions to The Fourmost. According to O'Hara and Lovelady, McCartney liked the way the group could mimic ('a pinch off The Mills Brothers') instruments with their voices, which The Beatles had done on ***Lady Madonna***. So O'Hara made trumpet sounds and the rest of the group made trombone sounds on ***Rosetta***. Lovelady was playing piano at the session, but Brian O'Hara suggested he play it badly, correctly anticipating that McCartney would lay down the piano track. Later that year, the group released a cover of the McCartney's Beatles song ***Maxwell's Silver Hammer*** under the name Format, though the group never officially changed their name.

The core members of The Fourmost carried on for another decade, but they tired of the one night stands and packed it by the early 1980s. New members carried on with the group name for a while. Hatton, Lovelady and Bower and his wife formed a group called Clouds that performed in the U.K. until 1993.

Peter Frampton

Record 120 title:
Wind Of Change
Label / Catalog number:
A&M / PCCY-10231
Jacket / Inserts:
Standard international design in jewel box / 4 page CD booklet & translation sheet
Recording Location / Date:
Olympic Studios, London, U.K. / Nov 71 - Feb 72
Media:
Album 5" CD
Producer:
Peter Frampton

Song 120a title:
Alright
Release date / Country:
Oct 91 (first issued 10 Jul 72) / Japan
Track details:
Side 1, track 10 / 4 min. 21 sec.
Composer:
P. Frampton

Peter Frampton: Lead Vocals, Guitars & Percussion; Ringo Starr: Drums; Klaus Voormann: Bass; Billy Preston: Piano & Organ; Frank Carillo: Rhythm Guitar, Percussion & B. Vocals; Andrew Bown: Percussion & B. Vocals

Song 120b title:
The Lodger
Release date / Country:
Oct 91 (first issued 10 Jul 72) / Japan
Track details:
Side 1, track 8 / 5 min. 40 sec.
Composer:
P. Frampton

Peter Frampton: Lead Vocals, Guitars & Door Percussion; Ringo Starr: Drums; Frank Carillo: Guitars; Andrew Bown: Bass; Jim Price: Brass

Peter Frampton was born on April 22, 1950 in Beckenham, Kent, England. He quickly became known as a guitar whiz kid, making his professional debut at the age of ten, and appeared on the British pop musical TV show **Ready Steady Go!** when he was fourteen. He joined the band The Herd at the age of sixteen, and by nineteen established himself as a British pop hero in the band Humble Pie.

Frampton was soon in demand as a session player on a number of other artists' recordings, including Doris Troy's* 1970 star-studded album for Apple Records. It was during this time that he first met and worked with George Harrison and Ringo Starr. This led to his playing (uncredited) acoustic guitar on several songs on Harrison's 1970 album **All Things Must Pass**. He said "I use to live around the corner from Ringo and hang out at his house when neither of us were busy." Frampton played on Harry Nilsson's* 1972 album **Son Of Schmilsson** along with Harrison and Starr, and he made an appearance in a musical scene in Nilsson and Ringo's film **Son Of Dracula**. He now says nostalgically "I was just a whore then; I'd play for anybody!"

Photo courtesy of Peter Frampton

Nineteen seventy-two saw the release of Frampton's first solo album, **Wind Of Change**, that featured Ringo drumming on the songs ***Alright*** and ***The Lodger***. Frampton recalled that the only time he ever had to audition for anyone was when he asked Ringo to play on his recordings; "he liked everything!" According to Frampton, an early backing track of ***Lady Lieright***, featuring Ringo on drums, was recorded, but a more "unplugged" version without Ringo ended up on the album. Frampton returned the favor by playing guitar on Ringo's 1976 album **Rotogravure**.

Frampton's constant touring of the U.S. finally paid off in 1976 with the release of **Frampton Comes Alive**, that sold well over ten million copies. The album yielded the hit singles ***Show Me The Way***, ***Baby I Love Your Way*** and ***Do You Feel Like We Do***. He had another major hit with the title track of his follow-up album **I'm In You** in 1977. He was reportedly in the running as a replacement for Mick Taylor in The Rolling Stones*, and was voted one of the top 10 rock guitarists in a New York Times poll in the mid-1970s.

Frampton, along with the group The Bee Gees, starred and performed in Robert Stigwood's 1978 musical film **Sgt. Pepper's Lonely Hearts Club Band**, which fully elevated him to the status of teeny bopper heart throb. He now prefers to forget the film that detracted from his more serious musical side at the time.

Frampton was a member of David Bowie's touring band in 1987. He has released over a dozen albums since **Wind Of Change**. His latest studio album, **Relativity**, was issued in 1994 and **Frampton Comes Alive II** was released the following year. He continues to record and remains in demand as a session guitarist for a wide range of artists.

Frampton proved he has lost none of his guitar skills or ability to work an audience during his appearances as a member of Ringo Starr's All-Starr Band tour in 1997. During the tour, he performed ***Show Me The Way***, ***Baby I Love Your Way***, ***All I Want To Be (Is By Your Side)*** and ***Do You Feel Like We Do*** with Ringo backing him on drums. He also performed ***Norwegian Wood*** in tribute to John Lennon.

Aretha Franklin

Record 121 title:
Lennon & McCartney Songbook
Label / Catalog number:
Connoisseur Collection / VSOP CD 150
Media:
Album 5" CD
Producer:
Jerry Wexler, Tom Dowd & Arif Mardin
Jacket / Inserts:
Standard international design in jewel box with photo of John Lennon & Paul McCartney / 4 page CD booklet with photos of John Lennon & Paul McCartney
Recording Location / Date:
Atlantic Recording Studios, New York, NY, U.S.A. / (probably) 26-30 May 69; (possibly) Oct 69 or Dec 69

Song 121a title:
Let It Be
Release date / Country:
02 Jul 90 (first issued 21 Feb 70) / U.K./E.E.C.
Track details:
Side 1, track 2 / 3 min. 28 sec.
Composer:
J. Lennon - P. McCartney

Aretha Franklin: Lead Vocals & (possible) Keyboards; one or more of the following: Barry Beckett: Keyboards; David Hood: Bass; Roger Hawkins: Drums; King Curtis: (probable) Saxophone; Cissy Houston: (probable) B. Vocals; Sylvia Shemwell: (probable) B. Vocals; Estelle Brown: (probable) B. Vocals; Myrna Smith: (probable) B. Vocals; Jimmy Johnson: Guitar; Eddie Hinton: Guitar; Jerry Weaver: (possible) Guitar

Aretha Franklin, also affectionately referred to as the Lady or Queen of Soul, was born on March 25, 1942 in Memphis, Tennessee. She has spent most of her life in Detroit, Michigan where she was raised by her father, the Reverend C. L. Franklin, a well-known gospel preacher and singer. Her mother, who left the family when Aretha was six and died four years later, was also a gospel singer. Aretha's path to musical stardom was fostered at an early age by gospel singers Mahalia Jackson, James Cleveland and the Ward Sisters, who were friends of her family.

Aretha became one of the world's most successful female singers by covering other artists' minor hits and rearranging them to suit her dynamic soul and gospel voice. She began making recordings in her father's church in Detroit for Checker Records when she was fourteen years old. In 1960, she branched out from gospel to light jazz and rhythm & blues, and signed on with John Hammond of Columbia Records.

Franklin remained with Columbia for six years, but with only limited success. By 1967 she had switched to Atlantic Records and producer Jerry Wexler, and had her first major hit with the song ***I Never Loved A Man (The Way I Love You)***. She quickly followed up with three more hits that year, ***Respect***, ***Baby I Love You*** and ***(You Make Me Feel Like A) Natural Woman***.

In 1968, she racked up six more hits: ***Chain Of Fools***, ***Since You've Been Gone***, ***Think***, ***I Say A Little Prayer***, ***The House That Jack Built*** and ***See Saw***. Between the decades of the 1970s and 1990s, she recorded dozens of hit albums and singles including such songs as ***Son Of A Preacher Man***, ***Don't Play That Song***, ***Spanish Harlem***, ***Rock Steady***, ***Bridge Over Troubled Water*** and ***Freeway of Love***. Her career has been littered with numerous civic and honorary awards, Billboard Magazine Awards, Grammy Awards and American Music Awards. She has performed at national political conventions, presidential inaugurations and at baseball's World Series. Aretha Franklin was inducted into the Rock and Roll Hall of Fame in 1987.

Aretha Franklin and The Beatles have long admired each other's music. In 1969, Franklin recorded a cover of The Beatles' song ***Eleanor Rigby*** with moderate chart success. The Beatles were unsure of what to do with recordings they had made early in 1969 during rehearsals for a possible live concert and accompanying documentary film that would later become the album and the motion picture **Let It Be**. They were virtually breaking up during the recordings, and consequently none of them were very pleased with the results. Many of the songs rehearsed and recorded for the **Let It Be** sessions were rejected out of hand by the group and ended up being re-recorded for inclusion on solo Beatles albums. Meanwhile, The Beatles began recordings for what would become their final recorded album **Abbey Road**.

Apparently, Paul McCartney felt the song ***Let It Be*** from the sessions was suited for Aretha Franklin's gospel voice. The song was familiar to Beatles fans who had found it available on bootleg records taken from acetates of the **Let It Be** album that had been circulating since the summer of 1969. According to Aretha's producer, Jerry Wexler, "They sent me an acetate, I don't remember if it was Paul or The Beatles organization, with the suggestion that I do the song with Aretha. I loved it very much. I played it for Aretha and she didn't like it! As time went on, she decided that she did like it, so we cut it and had it in the can. I got a legal stop order from them [The Beatles] mandating that I could not put out the record. Once their record was out, I could legally put it out. I could have legally put it out before The Beatles' version if I would have acted in time." The Beatles' version of ***Let It Be*** was officially presented to the world on the Ed Sullivan Show on March 1, 1970, and its earliest record release was on March 6. Billboard magazine reported the album **This Girl's In Love With You** by Aretha Franklin, which contained her version of ***Let It Be***, was released on February 21, 1970. However, release dates are routinely delayed and rescheduled without notice. If Billboard's date is correct, then Aretha's version preceded The Beatles' first official release anywhere in the world by about two weeks. If the release was indeed delayed, as Wexler maintains it legally had to be, the information in Billboard may be misleading. A 7" EP promotional single was released by Atlantic Records with sleeve notes about ***Let It Be*** written by Wexler. Because the song was originally intended for Franklin to release first, and because it may have been released first, it is considered a contribution. The song was probably recorded in May 1969 according to David Hood and Jimmy Johnson, who played on the session. Some sources list it as being recorded in October or December 1969.

Franklin also covered McCartney's Beatles song ***The Long And Winding Road*** on her 1972 album **Young, Gifted And Black**. Wexler also revealed that Franklin began recording a cover of McCartney's Beatles song ***The Fool On The Hill***, but it was never completed.

Kinky Friedman

Record 122 title:
Lasso From El Paso
Label / Catalog number:
Epic / PE 34304
Jacket / Inserts:
Standard international design / Record label inner sleeve
Recording Location / Date:
Cherokee Studios, Los Angeles, and probably one or more of the following: Shangri-La, Haji Sound, Los Angeles, CA & Sugar Hill, Houston, TX, U.S.A. / (probably) Apr 76
Media:
Album 12"
Producer:
Huey P. Meaux

Song 122a title:
Men's Room, L.A.
Release date / Country:
05 Nov 76 / U.S.A.
Track details:
Side 2, track 2 / 2 min. 10 sec.
Composer:
B. Fowler

Kinky Friedman: Lead Vocals; Ringo Starr "The Voice Of Jesus;" one or more of the following: Jim Atkinson: Guitar & B. Vocals; T-Bone Burnett: Guitar & Keyboards; Tom Culpepper: Guitar; Kinky Friedman: Guitar; Bill Ham: Guitar; Mick Ronson: Guitar; Steve Soles: Guitar; Ron Wood: Guitar; Brian Clarke: Bass; Rick Danko: Bass & B. Vocals; Terry Danko: Bass & B. Vocals; Rob Stoner: Bass; Ira Wilkes: Bass; Major Boles: Drums & Percussion; Gary Burke: Drums & Percussion; Teddy Jack Eddy: B. Vocals, Drums & Percussion; Levon Helm: Guitar, B. Vocals, Drums & Percussion; Richard Manuel: Keyboards, Drums & Percussion; Dahrell Norris: Drums & Percussion; Howie Wyeth: Drums

& Percussion; Ken Lauber: Keyboards; Jewford Shelby: Keyboards; Red Young: Keyboards; Snakebite Jacobs: Horns; Tracey Balin: B. Vocals; Roscoe West: B. Vocals; The Rolling Thunder Revue: B. Vocals; Van Dyke Parks: Keyboards; Lowell George: Guitar

Richard "Kinky" Friedman was born on November 1, 1944 in Chicago, Illinois. His family relocated to Texas where Kinky has lived most of his life. Friedman first recorded with the surf music band King Arthur And The Carrots in 1966. Since that time he has been known primarily as a country singer, songwriter and leader of The Texas Jewboys. His political, humorous, and vulgar lyrics, combined with outrageous stage outfits, have not always endeared him to the mainstream country music crowd, especially with songs like ***They Ain't Makin' Jews Like Jesus Anymore***, ***Get Your Biscuits In The Oven And Your Buns In Bed*** and ***Ride 'em Jewboy***. However, he is a favorite in more diverse, liberal environs like Austin, Texas, New York and Los Angeles. He has written for Rolling Stone magazine and has nine successful mystery novels to his credit. He has all but given up his music career stating "when the horse dies, get off," though he does perform on occasion – usually at a book store signing.

Ringo Starr's contribution to the album **Lasso From El Paso** was the result of his involvement in Bob Dylan's **Rolling Thunder Revue** tour that included Friedman *(see Alpha Band, The Band, Bob Dylan)*. The title of the album was taken from Friedman's song ***Asshole From El Paso***. Kinky recalls Ringo's "Voice Of Jesus" portion of the song ***Men's Room, L.A.*** as being recorded at Cherokee Studios in Los Angeles. According to Kinky, Ringo was "flying by Jewish radar and improvised it on the spot." **Lasso From El Paso** was issued on CD (Epic / EPC 474609-2) in France in 1993.

Gerry & The Pacemakers

Record 123 title:
The Best of Gerry & The Pacemakers, The Definitive Collection

Media:
Album 5" CD

Label / Catalog number:
United Artists / CDP-7-96093-2

Producer:
George Martin

Jacket / Inserts:
Unique in Jewel box / 12 page CD booklet

Song 123a title:
Hello Little Girl

Track details:
Side 1, track 6 / 1 min. 51 sec.

Release date / Country:
08 Oct 91 / U.S.A.

Composer:
J. Lennon - P. McCartney

Recording Location / Date:
EMI-Abbey Road Studios, London, U.K. / 17 Jul 63

Gerry Marsden: Lead Vocals & Lead Guitar; Les Chadwick: Bass & B. Vocals; Les Maguire: B. Vocals; Freddie Marsden: Drums

Song 123b title:
How Do You Do It?
Release date / Country:
08 Oct 91 (first issued Mar 63) / U.S.A.
Recording Location / Date:
EMI-Abbey Road Studios, London, U.K. / 22 Jan 63

Track details:
Side 1, track 1 / 1 min. 53 sec.
Composer:
M. Murray

Gerry Marsden: Lead Vocals & Lead Guitar; Les Chadwick: Bass; Les Maguire: Piano; Freddie Marsden: Drums; John Lennon: Arrangement; Paul McCartney: Arrangement

Guitarist Gerard "Gerry" Marsden was born on September 24, 1942 in Liverpool, England. Gerry, along with his older brother Freddie, the band's drummer, formed the core of what would eventually be called Gerry And The Pacemakers, one of Liverpool's most popular groups. They were joined by John Leslie Chadwick on bass and Les Maguire, formerly of The Undertakers *(see Jackie Lomax)*, on keyboards. The group's early members included Brian O'Hara *(see The Fourmost)*. They spent much of their formative years playing the same venues as The Beatles in Liverpool, England and in Hamburg, Germany, developing a close and competitive relationship with the group under Brian Epstein's management. Like The Beatles, and other Epstein-managed NEMS Enterprises artists, Gerry And The Pacemakers were signed to EMI and produced by George Martin*.

During the summer of 1962, George Martin mailed a demo to The Beatles of the Mitch Murray song ***How Do You Do It*** performed with backing by The Dave Clark Five. Martin intended this song to be The Beatles' first single for EMI. The Beatles, who wanted one of their compositions to be their first single, disliked the song and re-arranged it considerably before halfheartedly recording it in early September at their second session for EMI. Murray reportedly had written the song with the idea of having it recorded by Adam Faith*. The Beatles persuaded Martin to instead release the Lennon and McCartney composition ***Love Me Do*** as their first single. The song failed to reach the U.K. top 10, and Martin again urged them to reconsider ***How Do You Do It***. Martin felt sure the song could be a number one and challenged the group to write a number one. They met Martin's challenge with a rearranged version of ***Please Please Me*** that became The Beatles' first number one song in the U.K. George Martin was still convinced ***How Do You Do It*** was a potential number one. He was vindicated in early 1963 when his production of The Beatles' arrangement of ***How Do You Do It*** became Gerry And The Pacemakers' first number one in the U.K. Several months later, Gerry And The Pacemakers' second single ***I Like It***, another Mitch Murray composition, also reached the number one spot in the U.K.

Manager Brian Epstein took advantage of the Lennon and McCartney songwriting team's name recognition, assigning their leftovers to his stable of NEMS Enterprises' artists. In 1963, Gerry And The Pacemakers recorded ***Hello Little Girl***, an early Lennon composition that was a popular Beatles favorite at the Cavern and a song familiar to them. However, Gerry, like The Beatles, passed on the song as a single release (it was finally released on the CD **The Best of Gerry & The Pacemakers, The Definitive Collection** in 1991). The song was then given to The Fourmost*, who made it a U.K. top 10. The Pacemakers' version of ***Hello Little Girl*** is considered a contribution because it was given to them first and recorded before The Fourmost's version. The Beatles also recorded the song during their January 1, 1962, Decca audition, but after being turned down by Decca they never again recorded the song.

Gerry And The Pacemakers made it three-in-a-row at the top of the U.K. charts in 1963, with the ballad ***You'll Never Walk Alone***. In 1964, the group had three more U.K. top 10 hits with ***I'm The One***, ***Don't Let The Sun Catch You Crying***, and ***Ferry Cross The Mersey***, the title song to their first and only film released near the end of the year. By 1965, Gerry And The Pacemakers, like many of the British music invasion bands, had all but faded from the charts. Their only U.K. top 20 that year was ***I'll Be There***, though the group stayed together until 1967. All of their U.K. hits were successful on the U.S. charts, though to a lesser degree.

Gerry Marsden has since played a variety of roles onstage and television and has occasionally performed with a new group of Pacemakers on nostalgia tours. Gerry And The Pacemakers recorded a cover of John Lennon's song ***Imagine*** released in 1981 shortly after Lennon's death. In 1985 Marsden re-recorded ***You'll Never Walk Alone***, along with an all-star cast that included Paul

McCartney, as a benefit single to aid the families of the Bradford City Football Club Disaster Fund *(see The Crowd)*. That year Gerry issued an album titled **Lennon / McCartney Songbook**, containing covers of their classics, for which McCartney provided the liner notes *(see Gerry Marsden)*. Four years later, Marsden and McCartney again came to the aid of families hit by disaster by donating proceeds of a re-recording of ***Ferry Cross The Mersey*** to The Hillsborough Football Disaster Fund *(see The Christians, Holly Johnson, Paul McCartney, Gerry Marsden & Stock Aitken Waterman)*. The Beatles' recordings of ***How Do You Do It*** and ***Hello Little Girl*** were officially released on their album **Anthology 1** in 1995.

Allen Ginsberg

Record 124 title:
The Ballad Of The Skeletons
Media:
Single 5" CD
Label / Catalog number:
Mouth Almighty/Mercury / 697 120 101-2
Producer:
Lenny Kaye
Jacket / Inserts:
Unique in Jewel box / 4 page CD booklet with photo of Paul McCartney
Recording Location / Date:
Kampo Culture Center, New York, NY, U.S.A. & The Mill, Sussex, U.K. / (probably) Oct 95 & May - Jun 96

Song 124a title:
The Ballad Of The Skeletons
Release date / Country:
15 Oct 96 / U.S.A.
Track details:
Side 1, track 1 / 7 min. 46 sec.
Composer:
A. Ginsberg - P. Glass - P. McCartney

Allen Ginsberg: Lead Vocals; Paul McCartney: Guitar, Maracas, Hammond Organ & Drums; Mark Ribot: Guitar; Lenny Kaye: Bass; David Mansfield: Guitar; Philip Glass: Keyboards

Song 124b title:
The Ballad Of The Skeletons [Clean]
Release date / Country:
15 Oct 96 / U.S.A.
Track details:
Side 1, track 4 / 7 min. 46 sec.
Composer:
A. Ginsberg - P. Glass - P. McCartney

Allen Ginsberg: Lead Vocals; Paul McCartney: Guitar, Maracas, Hammond Organ & Drums; Mark Ribot: Guitar; Lenny Kaye: Bass; David Mansfield: Guitar; Philip Glass: Keyboards

Song 124c title:
The Ballad Of The Skeletons [Edit]
Release date / Country:
15 Oct 96 / U.S.A.
Track details:
Side 1, track 2 / 4 min. 07 sec.
Composer:
A. Ginsberg - P. Glass - P. McCartney

Allen Ginsberg: Lead Vocals; Paul McCartney: Guitar, Maracas, Hammond Organ & Drums; Mark Ribot: Guitar; Lenny Kaye: Bass; David Mansfield: Guitar; Philip Glass: Keyboards

Legendary Beat Poet and political activist Irwin Allen Ginsberg was born on June 3, 1926 in Newark, New Jersey. This son of a poet was surrounded by controversy throughout most of his career, starting with the publication of his book **Howl and Other Poems** in 1956. The book set the tone for his politically and sexually abrasive stream-of-consciousness literary style. He defined the beatnik generation of the 1950s and became the spokesman of pacifism credited with coining the phrase "flower power" in the turbulent 1960s. Though Allen Ginsberg's prose ceased on April 5, 1997, his chants will echo through the ages.

On May 9, 1965, Bob Dylan* invited Ginsberg to his room at the Savoy Hotel in London, England to meet The Beatles following his performance at Albert Hall. Ginsberg, and his friend and biographer Barry Miles (also a friend and biographer of Paul McCartney's) made occasional visits to McCartney's home in London in the mid-1960s. Ginsberg was also in the studio during The Rolling

Allen Ginsberg, Mt. Pleasant, MI, circa 1990

Stones'* recording of ***We Love You*** the night Lennon and McCartney sang background vocals on the song. Zapple Records, a spoken-word and avant-garde division of Apple Records, apparently considered releasing an album in 1969 of Ginsberg performing material written by poet William Blake.

Contrary to widely published accounts, Ginsberg was not present during Lennon's Montreal "bed-in" recording of ***Give Peace A Chance***, though Lennon did phone Ginsberg, who was in New York at the time. Ginsberg made a cameo appearance in Yoko Ono's* **Film No. 12 (Up Your Legs Forever)**. He did spend some time with the Lennons shortly after their move to New York's Greenwich Village in 1971. He was one of the invited guests at Yoko's one woman art show **This Is Not Here** that opened on John's 31st birthday in Syracuse, New York on October 9, 1971. Following the opening, Ginsberg joined Lennon, Ringo, Elliot Mintz, Phil Spector*, Nicky Hopkins*, Klaus Voormann *(see Paul Jones)*, Jim Keltner *(see Attitudes)*, the wives and girlfriends of most of the musicians and others for a jam session that has since been released on the bootleg CD **John Lennon - Let's Have A Party** (Quality Compact Productions / QCP 72003). Ginsberg began the jam with a series of mantras and did Blake's ***Nurse's Song*** before the jam turned to rock and blues standards.

On November 17 and 20, 1971, Allen Ginsberg, with help from Bob Dylan, recorded an album's worth of material at the Record Plant (East) Studios in New York City after Lennon and his manager Allen Klein indicated a release on Apple Records was possible. Ginsberg described the recordings as "a mixture of political reference, gay vaudeville, mantras, musical interpretations of William Blake's poetry and blues songs." The album was tentatively titled **Holy Soul & Jelly Roll** and was to include, among other songs, ***Going To San Diego***, ***Nurse's Song*** and ***September On Jessore Road***. According to Ginsberg, Lennon told him the album would not be released on Apple because he was secretly trying to break off his business ties with Klein (which he later did). Lennon was also forced to retreat from his political activism at the time because of his U.S. deportation order. These factors, the political and sexual nature of the album's lyrics, and its limited commercial appeal, effectively ruled out any chance of it ever being released on Apple. For years there was speculation that Lennon might have contributed to these recordings in some way, which certainly seemed possible considering the circumstances. The inclusion of the song ***Going To San Diego*** on the Westwood One radio series **The Lost Lennon Tapes** also seemed to suggest Lennon's involvement. According to Ginsberg, however, Lennon never directly contributed any of his recordings – though he and John did do much improvisational jamming at Lennon's Greenwich Village apartment. Ginsberg said Lennon did suggest that he use a string quartet arrangement similar to what The Beatles had used on ***Eleanor Rigby*** for ***September On Jessore Road*** after hearing Ginsberg's performance of the song at the **John Sinclair Freedom Rally**. Rhino Records released a four-CD retrospective Ginsberg box set titled **Holy Soul Jelly Roll: Poems and Songs 1949 - 1993** that included the recordings originally intended to be released by Apple. Ginsberg also appeared onstage at the **One-To-One** benefit concert on August 30, 1972 at Madison Square Garden for the ***Give Peace A Chance*** encore.

Ginsberg gave a poetry reading billed as **Return Of The Reforgotten** at the Royal Albert Hall in London on October 16, 1995. He was accompanied by Paul McCartney on electric guitar during the reading of ***The Ballad Of The Skeletons***. The performance was videotaped, and portions were broadcast on U.S. television. The collaboration was the result of a visit Ginsberg had made to the McCartney's home during which he asked Paul to recommend some guitarists. ***The Ballad Of The Skeletons*** is a political song that Ginsberg later recorded, with help from McCartney, and released a CD single in time for the 1996 U.S. elections. The CD single also contains a "clean" version of the song, which omits profanities, and an edited version. McCartney took Ginsberg's advice and collaborated with poet Tom Pichard on his ***Standing Stone*** poem *(see The London Symphony Orchestra & Chorus)*. Just before Ginsberg's death, Billboard magazine reported plans were underway for McCartney, Dylan, Beck and Ginsberg to team up for a music and spoken word performance on MTV's **Unplugged**.

Godley & Creme

Record 125 title:
Freeze Frame
Label / Catalog number:
Polydor / 831 555-2
Jacket / Inserts:
Standard international design in jewel box / 4 page CD insert
Recording Location / Date:
Surrey Sound Studios, Surrey, U.K. / 1979
Media:
Album 5" CD
Producer:
Kevin Godley & Lol Creme

Song 125a title:
Get Well Soon
Release date / Country:
1988 (recording first issued: 30 Nov 79) / U.S.A.
Track details:
Side 1, track 8 / 4 min. 35 sec.
Composer:
K. Godley - L. Creme

Kevin Godley: Lead Vocals, Cowbell & Percussion; Lol Creme: Lead Guitar, Bass, Keyboards, Harmonica & B. Vocals

Godley and Creme were members of the group 10cc* along with Eric Stewart and Graham Gouldman. McCartney's involvement with Godley and Creme began during his work on his brother Mike (McCartney) McGear's album **McGear**. The album was recorded at Strawberry Studios, which was partly owned by Stewart. Godley and Creme left 10cc to concentrate on inventing new musical devices, and were pioneers in the production of musical videos, including several over the years for McCartney. One of their more famous videos was George Harrison's Beatles tribute **When We Was Fab** that includes a cameo by Ringo Starr, though it did not include an appearance by Paul McCartney as has been rumored.

Godley and Creme had a major hit, titled ***Cry***, in 1985. They briefly reunited with Stewart and Gouldman for a 10cc album released in 1992. In 1995, Kevin Godley directed the music video for The Beatles' single ***Real Love***.

Grapefruit

Record 126 title:
Around Grapefruit
Label / Catalog number:
Repertoire / REP 4363-WP
Jacket / Inserts:
Standard international design in jewel box / 6 page CD booklet
Media:
Album 5" CD

Song 126a title:
C'mon Marianne
Release date / Country:
Aug 93 (recording first issued: Jul 68) / Germany
Producer:
Grapefruit & Terry Melcher
Track details:
Side 1, track 5 / 2 min. 36 sec.
Composer:
Brown - Bloodworth

Recording Location / Date:
(probably) Trident or Advision Studios, London, U.K. / 1968

John Perry: Lead Vocals & Electric Guitar; Pete Swettenham: Acoustic Guitar & B. Vocals; Geoff Swettenham: Drums & B. Vocals; George Alexander: Bass & B. Vocals; John Lennon: Horn Arrangement

Song 126b title:
Lullaby
Release date / Country:
Aug 93 probably first issued: Jan 69) / Germany
Producer:
Paul McCartney & (probably) John Lennon
Recording Location / Date:
Advision Studios, London, U.K. / (probably) Mar - Apr 68 or (possibly) Jan 68
Track details:
Side 1, track 6 / 3 min. 29 sec.
Composer:
G. Alexander

George Alexander: Lead Vocals & Bass; John Perry: Acoustic Guitar; Pete Swettenham: Acoustic Guitar & B. Vocals; Geoff Swettenham: Drums & B. Vocals

Song 126c title:
Yes
Release date / Country:
Aug 93 first issued: Apr 68) / Germany
Producer:
Grapefruit [Paul McCartney]
Recording Location / Date:
Advision Studios, London, U.K. / (probably) Mar - Apr 68 or (possibly) Jan 68
Track details:
Side 1, track 4 / 2 min. 20 sec.
Composer:
J. Perry

John Perry: Lead Vocals & Acoustic Guitar; Pete Swettenham: Acoustic Guitar, Keyboards & B. Vocals; Geoff Swettenham: Drums & B. Vocals; George Alexander: Bass & B. Vocals

The group Grapefruit consisted of George Alexander (born Alexander Young on December 28, 1946 in Glasgow, Scotland), Geoff Swettenhan (born March 8, 1948), his brother Pete Swettenham (born April 24, 1949), and John Perry (born July 16, 1949) all born in London, England. All but Alexander were in a band called the Sugarbeats before becoming members of the group Tony Rivers And The Castaways, managed by Brian Epstein's NEMS Enterprises. Tony Rivers And The Castaways recorded a cover version of The Beatles' song ***Nowhere Man***, released in 1966. Paul McCartney attended a Tony Rivers And The Castaways performance at Epstein's Saville Theatre on November 19, 1967.

Terry Doran, a friend of Brian Epstein and The Beatles from Liverpool who worked for Apple Music Publishing, signed Alexander as a songwriter for Apple. (Alexander came from a very musical family. His brother George, whose first name Alexander borrowed, was in the mid-'60s group The Easybeats and his brothers Angus and Malcolm are members of the group AC/DC.) John Perry said, "I met Doran who told me he worked for a company called Apple. Later I found out it was The Beatles' company. Had I known that I would have been down there in five minutes! We had this idea of forming a four-piece group that would replace The Beatles' pop image because they were sort of psychedelic at the time. Apple liked the idea, and it was there that I met George Alexander, whose songs we liked."

The group was signed to Apple Publishing and managed by Doran. On December 11, 1967, they were christened Grapefruit at the suggestion of John Lennon (after Yoko Ono's book of the same title). On January 17, 1968, The Beatles (minus Harrison) attended a press reception at the London headquarters of RCA records (Apple did not yet have a record label) to launch Grapefruit. (Some time later, Lennon, McCartney and Starr attended a press reception for Grapefruit held at The Hanover Grand's Banqueting Rooms.) The group's first single, ***Dear Delilah***, was released two days later.

According to several reliable publications, Lennon and McCartney visited Grapefruit at IBC Studios in London and probably participated for their debut recording session that produced the recording ***Dear Delilah***. The Swettenhams and Perry agree none of The Beatles contributed to, or were present for, the recording of ***Dear Delilah***. However, they recall Lennon and McCartney attending one of their first recording sessions. Pete remembers McCartney hanging around playing tambourine but does not think anything resulted from those first sessions.

Terry Melcher, who is listed as the producer of ***Dear Delilah***, does not recall any of The Beatles being present for the recording, and said he handled all the production by himself. (Melcher, the son of actress Doris Day, was a songwriter and producer known for his work with The Byrds and Bruce Johnston of The Beach Boys*. Melcher, no doubt, came at the suggestion of The Beatles' press officer and Apple publicist Derek Taylor, who had been a publicist for The Byrds and The Beach Boys.)

Grapefruit said they, not Melcher, produced their second single ***Yes / Elevator***. The group recalls McCartney being present to give advice and help (padding drums etc.) with the recording of ***Yes***. On May 26, 1968, McCartney directed a promotional video for ***Elevator*** at the Albert Memorial Statue in London.

In July of 1968, Grapefruit's third single, ***C'mon Marianne***, was released. Perry said, "Lennon basically arranged the brass part of ***C'mon Marianne***. I think Terry Melcher produced it though." Pete also remembers Lennon suggesting an arrangement for horns on ***C'mon Marianne***. However, Mike Vickers, formerly of the group Manfred Mann, scored Lennon's ideas for the arrangement. (Vickers conducted the orchestra on the live telecast, via satellite, of The Beatles' performance of ***All You Need Is Love*** for the BBC's program **Our World** on June 25, 1967.)

Grapefruit's fourth single ***Someday***, released in December of 1968, was followed by their first album **Around Grapefruit**. The album primarily consisted of the group's first four singles and a few other tracks recorded along the way. Grapefruit members said most of the album's tracks were probably recorded at Advision Studios, but they also used Regent Sound, IBC, De Lane Lea Sound Centre, Trident Studios and EMI's Abbey Road Studios for some of their recordings. The album's liner notes were written by Derek Taylor. The only producer mentioned on the album is Terry Melcher. Melcher admitted he produced some of Grapefruit's first recordings in England, but had to return to the U.S. Grapefruit said they took over the production role on many of their songs, but Melcher did the final mixing. According to Mark Lewisohn, a noted authority on The Beatles, both Lennon and McCartney acted as uncredited executive producers of **Around Grapefruit**. Perry recalls, "McCartney, Harrison and Lennon stopped by during a couple of other sessions. I remember Lennon trying to get me to play something on the guitar to sound like an airplane landing. We were tied up with them quite deeply."

According to Perry and the Swettenhams, the backing track of the song ***Lullaby*** from **Around Grapefruit** was produced and engineered by McCartney and Lennon at Advision. (This explains why a demo acetate of ***Lullaby*** was discovered many years later among John Lennon's personal belongings that some mistook to be an unreleased Beatles' demo.) Spencer Davis, who also attended the session, said McCartney handled most of the duties, and thinks Paul sang in the background as well. Perry and the Swettenhams do not recall McCartney or Lennon performing on ***Lullaby***, or playing on any other recordings of theirs. Geoff said, "I think I would remember if Paul had played something on one of our tracks." Grapefruit later decided to add an orchestra to the recording. Perry recalls, "Lennon and McCartney wanted to put ***Lullaby*** out as a single. We didn't like their version. Can you believe it? How bloody stupid can you get?"

Though Grapefruit was the first group signed to Apple Publishing, they never appeared on Apple Records. Perry did, however, end up appearing on one of Apple Records' releases, ***Hey Jude***. He recalls, "I was in Trident Studios and Paul ushered me over to the microphone to sing on the chorus; when I put on the headphones they were very loud, and I shouted an obscenity." (Perry's remark can be faintly heard at about 2:58 into the recording.)

Grapefruit's association with Apple Publishing ended in November 1968. During The Beatles' recording sessions for the album **Let It Be** in January 1969, John Lennon suggested the as-then-yet-unreleased Beatles' song ***Two Of Us*** might be suitable for Grapefruit to record. Grapefruit never recorded the song. (Several months later the Apple group Mortimer recorded ***Two Of Us***, but they too never ended up having a release on the label and their version remains unreleased.)

Grapefruit released a second album through RCA in 1969 titled **Deep Water** and a single, ***Sha-Sha / Universal Party***, in 1971 on the Deram label before disbanding. Geoff worked with Badfinger* briefly, almost joining the group. He is now an accountant. Pete remained involved in music for a time and assisted Geoff Emerick with the sound engineering of Paul McCartney's 1974 album **Band On The Run**. He is currently a project manager for a communications company. John Perry has maintained his musical career concentrating on Christian and gospel recordings. He has also worked with Cliff Richard (singing on ***Devil Woman*** among other songs.) All three members reside in England. George Alexander was last known to be living in Germany.

Terry Doran and Derek Taylor went on to become assistants for George Harrison for a time. Taylor returned to work for the revived Apple Records label in the 1990s, but died of cancer in 1997. Doran, who has worked much of his life in auto sales, currently lives in London. Terry Melcher owns and operates a restaurant in California, but is still involved in the music business, and recently wrote a number of songs for The Beach Boys.

Sylvia Griffin

Record 127 title:
Love's A State Of Mind
Label / Catalog number:
Rocket/Phonogram / 870 377-2/BLACD 7
Jacket / Inserts:
Unique PS (printed in U.K.)
Recording Location / Date:
Air Studio, London & FPSHOT (Friar Park Studios, Henley-on-Thames)†, U.K. / 16 Jan 88 & 05 Mar 88†

Media:
Single 5" CD
Producer:
Chris Thomas

Song 127a title:
Love's A State Of Mind
Release date / Country:
27 May 88 / Germany/U.K.

Track details:
Side 1, track 1 / 3 min. 14 sec.
Composer:
S. Griffin - R. Bowkett

Sylvia Griffin: Lead Vocals; David Paton: Bass; Charlie Morgan: Drums; Robbie McIntosh: Guitar; Rod Bowkett: Keyboards; George Harrison: Slide Guitar†

Sylvia Griffin was originally trained as an opera singer. She has branched out into stage musicals, performing on the cabaret circuit, doing session work, and writing songs. She recently toured with the Natural Theatre Company in **Henry VIII - Diary Of A Serial Killer**, a comedy about Henry VIII returning from the dead to advise Prince Charles on how to handle women.

Griffin met George Harrison at a party given by Elton John. Harrison liked her song and agreed to play on it. Robbie McIntosh, the other guitarist on ***Love's A State Of Mind***, became a member of Paul McCartney's band in 1988.

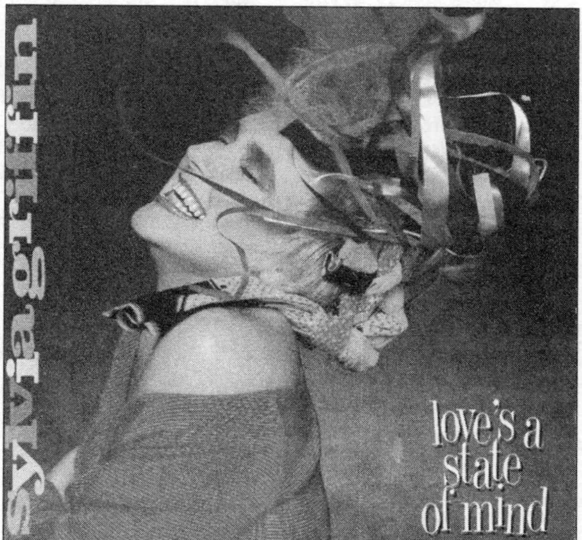

Daryl Hall And John Oates

Record 128 title:
Along The Red Ledge
Media:
Album 5" CD
Label / Catalog number:
RCA / B20D-41022
Producer:
David Foster
Jacket / Inserts:
Standard international design in jewel box / 20 page CD booklet with translation
Recording Location / Date:
Davlen, &/or Sunset Studios, Los Angeles, CA &/or Hit Factory, New York, NY, U.S.A. / (probably) 1978

Song 128a title:
The Last Time
Track details:
Side 1, track 3 / 2 min. 47 sec.
Release date / Country:
1989 (first issued: 21 Aug 78) / Japan
Composer:
D. Hall

Daryl Hall: Lead Vocals; George Harrison: Guitar; John Oates: B. Vocals; probably one or more of the following: Kenny Passarelli: Bass; Caleb Quaye: Guitar; Roger Pope: Drums; David Kent: Synthesizer

Daryl Hall and John Oates are one of the most commercially successful duo's in the history of popular music. Hall was born Daryl Hohl on October 11, 1949 in Pottstown, Pennsylvania, and John Oates was born on April 7 1949, in New York City, New York. Both took an avid interest in music at an early age and met in 1967 during a battle of the bands competition in Philadelphia. They soon teamed up to play in various "doo-wop" and rhythm & blues bands.

By 1972 Hall and Oates' brand of blue-eyed soul attracted Atlantic Records, but in 1975, after three ineffectual albums with the label, they signed with RCA. The following year they had their first of many million sellers with the song ***Sara Smile***. Meanwhile, Atlantic wisely decided to reissue their 1974 single ***She's Gone*** that quickly became a top 10. Their first number one single for RCA was ***Rich Girl*** in 1977. In 1978, George Harrison was one of a growing list of admirers who contributed to their album **Along The Red Ledge**. From 1981 through 1985, Hall and Oates topped the charts with the songs ***Kiss On My List***, ***Private Eyes***, ***I Can't Go For That***, ***Maneater*** and ***Out Of Touch***, and made the top 10 with ***You Make My Dreams***, ***Did It In A Minute***, ***One On One***, ***Family Man***, ***Adult Education***, ***Say It Ain't So*** and ***Method of Modern Love***.

In 1986, the dynamic duo took a break to pursue solo projects. Hall released the album **Three Hearts In The Happy Ending Machine** to which he reportedly asked Paul McCartney to contribute. McCartney apparently declined due to his schedule. In 1988, the duo signed to Arista Records and had a top 10 with the song ***Everything Your Heart Desires***. Their last top 20 song was ***So Close*** in 1990. Hall and Oates appeared at **The John Lennon Scholarship Concert** held on May 5, 1990 in Liverpool and performed ***Don't Let Me Down*** and ***Julia***. ***Don't Let Me Down*** was included on the 1991 laser videodisk **The World's Greatest Artists Sing LENNON A Tribute**. Although Hall and Oates have been less active on the charts in recent years, they continue to delight large audiences wherever they perform their seemingly endless list of hits.

Roy Harper

Record 129 title:
An Introduction To Roy Harper [Various Artists]
Label / Catalog number:
Chrysalis / PRO 620 (promotional only)
Jacket / Inserts:
Unique / Record label inner sleeve
Recording Location / Date:
EMI-Abbey Road Studios, London, U.K. / 1976
Media:
Album 12"
Producer:
Bob Harris

Song 129a title:
Conversation with Paul McCartney
Release date / Country:
Feb 76 / U.S.A.
Track details:
Side 2 / 1 min. 34 sec. (in total)
Composer:
Paul McCartney (Promotional Interview)

Record 130 title:
One Of Those Days In England (Bullinamingvase)
Label / Catalog number:
Science Friction / HUCD021
Jacket / Inserts:
Standard international design in jewel box
/ 16 page CD booklet with photo of Paul McCartney
Media:
Album 5" CD

Song 130a title:
One Of Those Days In England (Part 1)
Release date / Country:
Nov 96 (recording first issued: 11 Feb 77) / Austria
Track details:
Side 1, track 1 / 3 min. 25 sec.
Composer:
R. Harper

Producer:
Roy Harper & Peter Jenner
Recording Location / Date:
EMI-Abbey Road Studios, London, U.K. / (probably) winter 1976

Roy Harper: Lead Vocals & Guitar; Andy Roberts: Guitar & B. Vocals; Henry McCullough: Guitar; David Lawson: Keyboards; B.J. Cole: Steel Guitar; Dave C. Drill: Bass; John Halsey: Drums; Paul McCartney: B. Vocals; Linda McCartney: B. Vocals

Song 130b title:
One Of Those Days In England
(Parts 2-10) [Part 10 reprise†]
Release date / Country:
Nov 96 (first issued: 11 Feb 77) / Austria
Track details:
Side 1, track 6-(10†) / 1 min. 58 sec.†
Composer:
R. Harper
Producer:
Roy Harper & John Leckie
Recording Location / Date:
EMI-Abbey Road Studios, London, U.K. / (probably) fall 1976 & (probably) winter 76†

Roy Harper: Lead Vocals & Guitars; Andy Roberts: Guitars & B. Vocals; Henry McCullough: Guitars; David Lawson: Keyboards; Dave C. Drill: Bass; John Halsey: Drums; Paul McCartney: B. Vocals; Linda McCartney: B. Vocals; Alvin Lee: Guitar

Roy Harper was born on June 12, 1941, in Manchester, England. He is alternately referred to as poet, actor, musician and sheep farmer. Harper is also well-known for his eccentric behavior.

Though virtually unknown as a solo artist in the U.S., Harper is highly respected by his musical peers in the U.K., and has worked with Led Zeppelin and Pink Floyd, among many others. Harper has released nearly twenty albums in the four decades he has been recording.

Paul McCartney was also impressed with Harper and agreed to do a brief interview contained on the album **An Introduction To Roy Harper**, used to promote Harper's 1976 album **When An Old Cricketer Leaves The Crease**. The 1994 best of Roy Harper CD titled **An Introduction To.....Roy Harper** incorrectly claims it includes an interview (probably from 1976) with McCartney. The CD does include ***One Of Those Days In England (Part 1)*** from Harper's 1977 album **One Of Those Days In England (Bullinamingvase)**. According to Harper, Paul and Linda McCartney* sang backing vocals on ***One Of Those Days In England (Part 1)***, which is the single version of the song that opens the album. The final track on the vinyl album is a continuous suite titled ***One Of Those Days In England (Parts 2-10)***. Harper said that Paul and Linda also sang backing vocals on the reprise ***One Of Those Days In England (Part 10)***. ***Part 1*** was recorded after ***Parts 2-10*** at the suggestion of producer Peter Jenner, who thought the song would have hit potential if a shorter, single version was recorded. According to Harper, Henry McCullough (a former member of Paul McCartney's band Wings at the time) plays guitar on ***One Of Those Days In England (Part 1)***. Jimmy McCulloch, who was Henry's replacement in Wings at the time, contributed to other portions of the album. Harper is currently working with the Canadian group, The Tea Party.

Rolf Harris

Record 131 title:
The Fab Four — Radio-Active Vol. 8
Label / Catalog number:
Pyramid / RFT CD 016 [Unauthorized Record]
Jacket / Inserts:
Unique in Jewel box / 2 CD inserts
Recording Location / Date:
BBC Paris Studios, London, U.K. / 18 Dec 63
Media:
Album 5" CD (mono)
Producer:
Bryant Marriott

Song 131a title:
Tie Me Kangaroo Down, Sport
Release date / Country:
1988
Track details:
Side 1, track 17 / 2 min. 42 sec.
Composer:
R. Harris

Rolf Harris: Lead Vocals; John Lennon: B. Vocals; George Harrison: B. Vocals & Electric Guitar; Paul McCartney: Bass & B. Vocals; Rolf Harris: Wobbleboard

Rolf Harris, the son of Welsh parents, was born on March 30, 1930 in Perth, Australia. Harris learned to play the piano as a youngster, and became an accomplished painter and cartoonist. With horn-rims and a goatee, Harris looked the part of the teaching job he gave up before moving from Australia to England to seek a career in show business. Over the years he has become best known as a variety entertainer on British TV, incorporating his talents in comedy, music and drawing for adult and children's audiences.

He first gained notoriety in 1960 with his novelty song ***Tie Me Kangaroo Down, Sport*** that went on to become a million selling international hit. The song featured Harris playing an unusual instrument he had developed called the Wobbleboard made out of a sheet of Masonite. His second hit ***Sun Arise*** in 1962, was based on an Australian aboriginal chant.

Harris first met The Beatles when he interviewed them for the BBC. Later he appeared on the bill with them at their first Royal Albert Hall performance on April 18, 1963. The show was called **Swinging Sound '63**, and was broadcast live by the BBC. Harris was The Beatles' guest host on the first in a series of BBC radio shows titled **From Us To You** taped on December 18, 1963 and broadcast on the 26th. During the show, The Beatles backed Harris on a version of ***Tie Me Kangaroo***

Down, Sport that featured revised lyrics referring to the group.

Harris was also a part of The Beatles' 1963 Christmas Shows that began in London several days later. A cartoon of the show, drawn by Harris, was sent to members of The Beatles Fan Club as a souvenir. Rolf Harris recorded a song called ***Ringo For President*** which was released in the summer of 1964. He was awarded the MBE in 1968 and the OBE in 1977. Harris still records, performs and makes regular appearances on British TV and radio.

Bobby Hatfield

Record 132 title:
Oo Wee Baby, I Love You
Label / Catalog number:
Warner Bros / WB 7566
Jacket / Inserts:
Record label sleeve
Recording Location / Date:
Apple Studios, London, U.K. / Jan 72
Media:
Single 7"
Producer:
Richard Perry

Song 132a title:
Oo Wee Baby, I Love You So
Release date / Country:
01 Mar 72 / U.S.A.
Track details:
Side 1, track 1 / 3 min. 35 sec.
Composer:
R. Parker

Bobby Hatfield: Lead Vocals; Ringo Starr: Drums; Chris Stainton: Keyboards; Klaus Voormann: Bass; Bobby Keys: (probable) Saxophone

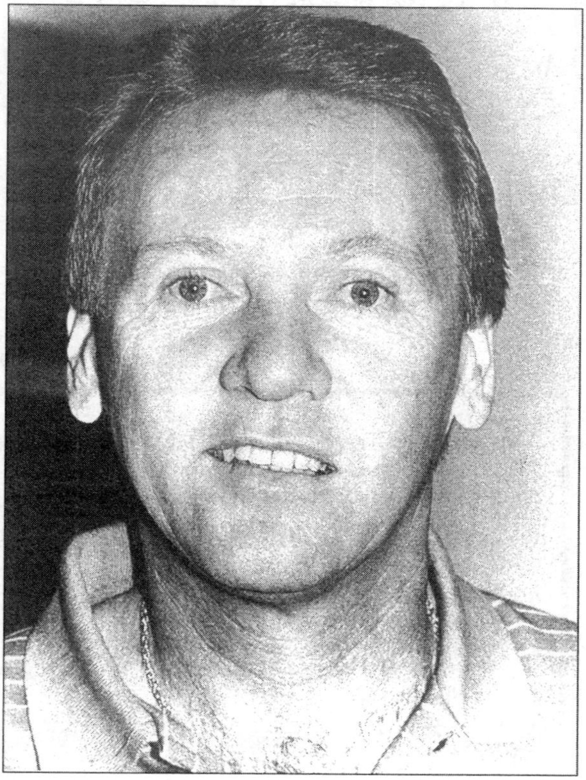

Bobby Hatfield,
Los Angeles, CA, early 1980s,
photo courtesy of Tom Bert

Bobby Hatfield was born August 10, 1940 in Beaver Dam, Wisconsin, but his family relocated to Anaheim, California when he was a youngster. Bobby began singing professionally while in college and soon teamed up with another blue-eyed soul singer named Bill Medley. They named themselves The Righteous Brothers. They were one of the supporting acts on The Beatles' tour of the U.S. in 1964. Their greatest success came at the hands of Phil Spector* who produced their top 10 songs ***You've Lost That Lovin' Feelin'***, ***Unchained Melody***, ***Ebb Tide*** and ***Just Once In My Life*** between late 1964 and late 1965. Their contract with Spector's Philles Records was bought out by Verve (MGM) Records with whom they had one top 10 song ***(You're My) Soul And Inspiration*** in 1966. Bill Medley had left The Righteous Brothers by 1968. He and Hatfield continued to work as solo artists, but Hatfield also worked under The Righteous

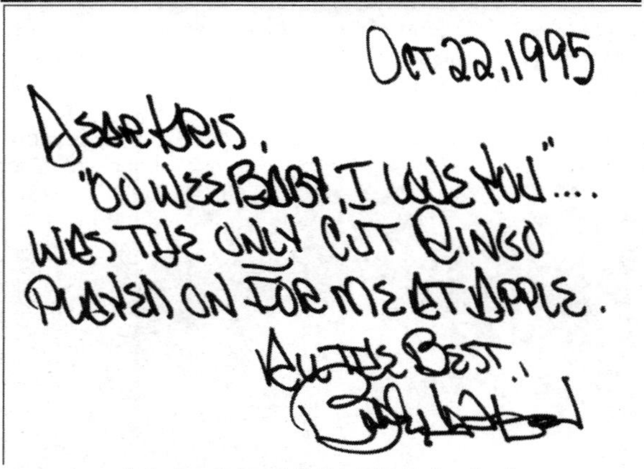
Oct 22, 1995

Dear Kris,
"Oo Wee Baby, I Love You"....
was the only cut Ringo
played on for me at Apple.
All the Best,

Letter from Bobby Hatfield to Kristofer Engelhardt

Brothers name with stand-in Jimmy Walker.

In December 1971, Hatfield was working with producer Richard Perry. Perry was called to London to work with the all-girl group Fanny at Apple Studios. He decided to fly Hatfield over to London to continue work on his recordings at Apple. The Beatles had been impressed by Perry's production of Tiny Tim, and, in late 1969, Ringo asked Perry to arrange the title track for his first solo album **Sentimental Journey**. According to Perry, "Ringo was great, he never turned me down, and he sat in on the Hatfield session as a favor."

The Righteous Brothers have reformed on numerous occasions. In 1974 they recorded a tribute to some of rock's late great stars titled ***Rock And Roll Heaven*** that was a top five song. In 1981, they performed a reworked version of the song on an **American Bandstand** anniversary TV special as a tribute to John Lennon. Medley received a Grammy Award for ***(I've Had) The Time Of My Life***, a duet with Jennifer Warnes featured in the popular 1987 film **Dirty Dancing**. Three years later ***Unchained Melody*** re-entered the charts as a result of its inclusion in the film **Ghost**. The Righteous Brothers still perform together occasionally.

Ronnie Hawkins

Record 133 title:
John Lennon On Ronnie Hawkins The Short Rap / John Lennon On Ronnie Hawkins The Long Rap

Media:
Single 7"

Label / Catalog number:
Cotillion / PR-104-PL & PR-105-PL (promotional only)

Producer:
(probably) Ritchie Yorke

Jacket / Inserts:
Record label sleeve

Recording Location / Date:
On location at Ronnie Hawkins' home, Mississauga (Toronto), Ont. Canada / 18-20 Dec 69

Song 133a title:
John Lennon on Ronnie Hawkins
The Short Rap
Release date / Country:
1970 / U.S.A.

Track details:
Side 1, track 1 / 0 min. 06 sec.

Composer:
J. Lennon

John Lennon (Promotional Interview)

Song 133b title:
John Lennon on Ronnie Hawkins
The Long Rap
Release date / Country:
1970 / U.S.A.

Track details:
Side 1, track 2 / 1 min. 24 sec.

Composer:
J. Lennon

John Lennon (Promotional Interview)

Ronnie Hawkins, also affectionately known as The Hawk, was born on January 10, 1935 in Huntsville, Arkansas – "two days after Elvis," he says proudly. Ronnie is well-known for his story-telling, and rubbed shoulders with most of the founding fathers of rock at its dawn. But he never hit the big time, and frequently refers to himself as "a legend in my spare time."

From the age of five, Ronnie knew that he wanted to be a music star like his uncle Delmar "Skipper" Hawkins and cousin Dale Hawkins (of ***Suzie Q*** fame). By high school, Hawkins was forming bands and playing local clubs. He entered college, but dropped out and joined the army, though he never stopped performing. He went on to back Carl Perkins* and Conway Twitty, who told Ronnie that Canada was the land of endless gigs. In 1958, Hawkins headed north of the border along with his band, which included Levon Helm*.

Hawkins signed to Roulette Records in 1959 and recorded a string of records with a couple of minor hits, including ***Forty Days***, ***Mary Lou*** and ***Odessa***. His band, The Hawks, would eventually be made up of Helm and four Canadian musicians - Robbie Robertson, Rick Danko, Richard Manuel and Garth Hudson. The band would go on to fame and fortune, first as Bob Dylan's* folk-rock backing band, and later on their own, known simply as The Band*. Hawkins adopted Canada as his homeland, which permitted him to be, as he says, "a big fish in a small pond."

Photo courtesy of Ronnie Hawkins

In mid-December 1969, John Lennon returned to Toronto to promote his new album release **Live Peace In Toronto 1969**, recorded there in September, and to make plans for a rock 'n' roll peace festival to be held there the following summer (it never happened). While in Toronto, Lennon needed a little peace and quiet in order to sign his limited-edition erotic lithographs, and Ronnie Hawkins' farm house on the outskirts of Toronto was chosen. While at the house, Lennon heard Ronnie's latest recording, ***Down In The Alley***, featuring Duane Allman on guitar, and was so impressed that he offered to record a radio spot specifically to promote Hawkins' single. It was issued as part of a two-single promotional set to radio stations. Several variations of the promotional single exist and are highly sought-after collectors' items. Unfortunately, Lennon's promotion came at a price – during the couples' stay, they left Hawkins with a very large amount of unpaid trans-Atlantic telephone bills.

It was reported that Ringo Starr performed at a benefit concert organized by Hawkins to aid sufferers of schizophrenia in Peterborough, Ontario, Canada, on June 30, 1996. Later reports confirmed that the person identified as Ringo was a well-known impersonator.

Though The Hawk has never been a major draw in the States, he maintains legendary status in Canada, where he performs straight-ahead rhythm & blues and rockabilly to enthusiastic crowds. Hawkins has recorded over two dozen albums during his five decades in the music business. He has done some bit part acting over the years, and hosted the TV series **Honky Tonk**. Ronnie's a little "bigger" than he used to be, but his storytelling, sense of humor and voice are still in excellent condition.

Screamin' Jay Hawkins

Record 134 title:
Screamin' The Blues
Label / Catalog number:
Red Lightnin' / RLCD0075
Jacket / Inserts:
Standard international design in jewel box / 4 page CD booklet
Recording Location / Date:
(possibly) Houston, TX or A&R Studios, New York, NY, U.S.A. / (possibly) 1970 or Jan 71
Media:
Album 5"
Producer:
(possibly) Paul McCartney

Song 134a title:
Monkberry Moon Delight
Release date / Country:
(probably) 1993 (first issued: 1979) / U.K.
Track details:
Side 1, track 15 / 3 min. 18 sec.
Composer:
P. McCartney - L. McCartney

Screamin' Jay Hawkins: Lead Vocals & Piano; Paul McCartney: (possible) Drums & (possible) B. Vocals; Linda McCartney: (possible) B. Vocals

Screamin' Jay Hawkins was born Jalacy Hawkins in Cleveland, Ohio on July 18, 1919 or 1929, depending on your source. Hawkins started out on piano and saxophone as a youngster, but turned to boxing, eventually becoming a Golden Gloves champion in 1943. By the early 1950s, Hawkins had begun a musical career that would span several decades. He toured with The Fats Domino Revue, and as part of Alan Freed's package tours in the mid-1950s.

Hawkins is best remembered as the flamboyant "drunken screamer" of the 1956 hit ***I Put A Spell On You***, as well as for being carried offstage in a flaming coffin as part of his act. He suffered second degree burns and temporary blindness during one of his pyrotechnic performances in 1976. His style no doubt influenced such 1960's artists as Screaming Lord Sutch and Arthur Brown. Hawkins has also appeared in several rock oriented films. He entered the charts in 1993 with a cover of Tom Waits' song ***Heartattack And Vine***.

One of the pre-concert songs played over the public-address system on McCartney's 1993 tour was ***Monkberry Moon Delight*** by Screamin' Jay Hawkins. Hawkins' version of the song can be found on his compilation CD titled **Screamin' The Blues**. The liner notes credited the song as "probably being recorded in Houston in 1970." There is no record of McCartney being in Houston during this period. If the liner notes are correct, and the song was recorded in Houston in 1970, then McCartney probably allowed Hawkins to record the song with the idea of having him release it before McCartney's version released in 1971. That would qualify the song as a composition contribution by McCartney.

The Hawkins arrangement is virtually identical to the McCartney version, but with slightly different (original or misinterpreted?) lyrics. The drumming intro sounds identical to that of ***My Dark Hour*** (played by McCartney) by The Steve Miller Band*, and the background vocals sound like they might possibly be sung by Paul and Linda McCartney*. Hawkins may have recorded the song after McCartney's screaming version was released, feeling that the song and arrangement were perfect for his vocal style and faithfully reproduced the background vocals to sound like the McCartney version.

Perhaps McCartney gave Hawkins the song in or before 1970 and adopted Hawkins' arrangement for his album **Ram**. If indeed McCartney plays drums and / or sings backing vocals on the track, it was probably recorded during the early phases of **Ram** at A&R Studios in New York City in January 1971. When McCartney arrived in New York to record, he was without a band and began auditioning musicians and looking for a permanent drummer. Hawkins, who lived and performed in New York during much of the 1970s, may have attended the early sessions for **Ram** – or McCartney might have attended one of Hawkins' sessions in New York – and they had a go at ***Monkberry Moon Delight***. The track following ***Monkberry Moon Delight*** on the CD gives the credits as "same as above", but does not sound at all like it was recorded at the same sessions as ***Monkberry Moon Delight***. Hawkins' version of ***Monkberry Moon Delight*** was probably released for the first time on the album **Screamin' The Blues** in 1979.

The Jeff Healey Band

Record 135 title:
Hell To Pay
Label / Catalog number:
Arista / ARCD 8632
Jacket / Inserts:
Standard international design in jewel box / 8 page CD booklet & ad insert
Recording Location / Date:
Le Studio, Morin Heights, Quebec, Canada & Rumbo Recorders, Los Angeles, CA, U.S.A. / Feb 90
Media:
Album 5" CD
Producer:
Ed Stasium

Song 135a title:
While My Guitar Gently Weeps
Release date / Country:
25 May 90 / U.S.A.
Track details:
Side 1, track 7 / 5 min. 13 sec.
Composer:
G. Harrison

Jeff Healey: Lead Vocals & Guitar; Joe Rockman: Bass; Tom Stephen: Drums; George Harrison: Acoustic Guitar & B. Vocals; Jeff Lynne: B. Vocals & Acoustic Guitar; Paul Shaffer: Keyboards

Norman Jeffery Healey was born on March 25, 1966, with cancer in both eyes and was soon adopted by Bud and Yvonne Healey in Toronto, Canada. By his first birthday Jeff was totally blind. He received his first guitar at age three, and his father, who played steel guitar, taught him to play on his lap where it has remained ever since. By fourteen he was playing bars and clubs in Toronto, and in 1985 he formed the Jeff Healey band with Joe Rockman and Tom Stephen. Most Americans got their first glimpse of Healey in the 1989 film **Road House**. Their first album had two hit singles and was a million seller.

For years Healey's band had successfully included The Beatles' song ***While My Guitar Gently Weeps***, written by George Harrison, in their live set. They recorded the song in 1990, despite objections from their record company who did not feel it was appropriate for inclusion on their albums. Once the song was recorded, they attempted to contact George Harrison to see if he was interested in possibly contributing to the song. To their surprise, they received a call from Harrison who instructed them to send the tape to Rumbo Recorders where he was working on Jeff Lynne's* **Armchair Theatre** album. According to Healey, the tape was returned within a matter of days. Healey's brilliant and unique style of playing had obviously caught the attention and respect of Harrison who,

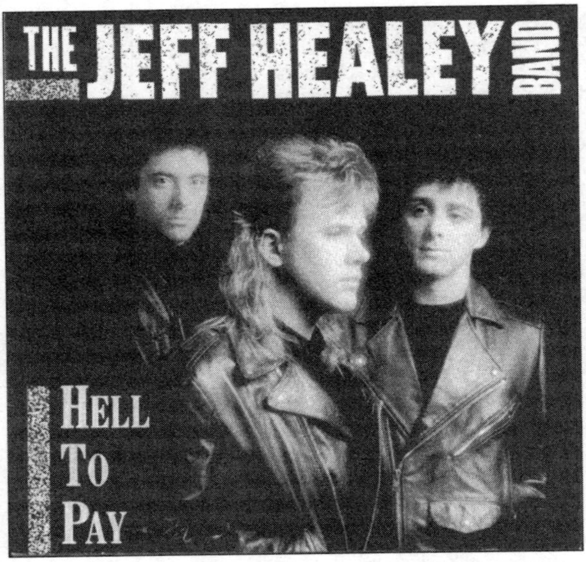

along with Lynne, overdubbed guitar and backing vocals to Healey's version of ***While My Guitar Gently Weeps***.

The Jeff Healey Band was the opening act for Ringo Starr And His All-Starr Band's performance in Toronto in 1992. Healey joined the All-Starrs during Ringo's performance of ***Yellow Submarine***, ***Act Naturally*** and ***With A Little Help From My Friends***. The Jeff Healey Band has also recorded a cover version of The Beatles' song ***Yer Blues*** to be included on their album **Cover To Cover**. Jeff Healey has over twelve thousand records in his personal collection that he draws upon for the radio shows he often hosts.

Levon Helm

Record 136 title:
Ringo Starr And His All-Starr Band
Label / Catalog number:
Pioneer Artists / PA-090-007
Media:
Album 12" LVD
Producer:
Tim Snow (film);
Joe Walsh & Jim Nipar (music)
Jacket / Inserts:
Standard international design / Record label inner sleeve
Recording Location / Date:
On location at Greek Theatre, Los Angeles, CA, U.S.A. / 03 Sep 89

Song 136a title:
The Weight [live]
Release date / Country:
Jul 90 / U.S.A.
Track details:
Side 1, track 5 / 5 min. 48 sec.
Composer:
R. Robertson

Levon Helm: Vocals & Drums; Billy Preston: Keyboards & B. Vocals; Jim Keltner: Drums; Ringo Starr: Drums; Vocals; Nils Lofgren: Guitar; Joe Walsh: Guitar & B. Vocals; Rick Danko: Bass & Vocals; Clarence Clemons: Saxophone, B. Vocals & Tambourine; Dr. John: Keyboards & Vocals; Garth Hudson: Accordion

This song is also included on Rykodisc / RCD 10190 & RCD5-1019 / Albums 5" [2 CD set] / Side 1, track 4 / released 12 Oct 90 / Unique in box set in Jewel box / 6 page CD booklet, sticker postcard & Rykodisc info. postcard / CD insert.

Song 136b title:
Up On Cripple Creek [live]
Release date / Country:
Jul 90 / U.S.A.
Track details:
Side 2, track 1 (13) / 5 min. 43 sec.
Composer:
R. Robertson

Levon Helm: Lead Vocals & Drums; Billy Preston: Keyboards & B. Vocals; Jim Keltner: Drums; Ringo Starr: Drums; Nils Lofgren: Guitar; Joe Walsh: Guitar & B. Vocals; Rick Danko: Bass & B. Vocals; Clarence Clemons: Saxophone; Dr. John: Keyboards

Mark Levon (it's actually Lavon) Helm was born on May 26, 1942 in Marvell, Arkansas and began his musical career with Ronnie Hawkins*. In 1958, Helm and Hawkins headed for Toronto, Canada and eventually hooked up with four Canadian musicians that would later become known simply as The Band*. Levon drifted in and out of The Band until 1967, when he joined the group permanently. Helm has had a fairly successful career as an actor co-starring in a number of films including **Coal Miner's Daughter**, **The Right Stuff**, **End Of The Line** and **The Doll Maker**. He has also been the narrator for a number TV documentaries on music over the years.

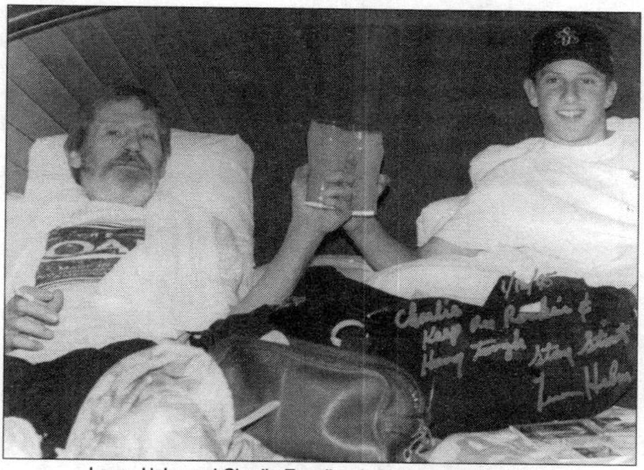

Levon Helm and Charlie Engelhardt, Kalamazoo, MI, 1995, photo by Kristofer Engelhardt

Levon, like other members of The Band, had previously worked with Ringo Starr on his solo album **Ringo**. Starr invited Levon and Jim Keltner *(see Attitudes)*, whom he felt were two of the best drummers in the business, to back him up on his All-Starr Band tour in 1989. During the tour, Helm performed ***Up On Cripple Creek*** and ***The Weight*** with Ringo backing him on drums.

Jimmy Helms

Record 137 title:
Water [Various Artists]
Label / Catalog number:
London Filmtrax / YEAR 2 820 263-1
Jacket / Inserts:
Unique with photo of George Harrison & Ringo Starr on back of jacket / Record label inner sleeve
Recording Location / Date:
1984

Media:
Album 12"
Producer:
Mike Moran

Song 137a title:
Celebration
Release date / Country:
28 Jun 85 (first issued: 31 May 85) / U.K.

Track details:
Side 2, track 4 / 3 min. 45 sec.
Composer:
G. Harrison - M. Moran

Jimmy Helms: Lead Vocals; George Harrison: Guitar

Song 137b title:
Focus Of Attention
Release date / Country:
28 Jun 85 / U.K.

Track details:
Side 1, track 6 / 2 min. 06 sec.
Composer:
M. Moran - D. Clement - G. Harrison

Jimmy Helms: Lead Vocals

Helms' recording career in England dates back to the 1960s. He had a top 10 there with the song ***Gonna Make You An Offer You Can't Refuse*** in 1973. Helms has contributed to a number of other artists' projects and recordings, including those of The Scaffold*. The songs ***Focus Of Attention***, with George Harrison as co-composer, and ***Celebration***, with Harrison as co-composer and guitarist, were performed by Jimmy Helms and featured in the soundtrack of HandMade Films' **Water**. The soundtrack also features the song ***Freedom***, by Billy Connolly / Chris Tummings and The Singing Rebels Band*.

David Hentschel

Record 138 title:
Sta*rtling Music
Label / Catalog number:
Ring O'Records / ST 11372
Jacket / Inserts:
Standard international design / Record label inner sleeve
Recording Location / Date:
Startling Studio, Ascot, U.K. / Sep 74
Media:
Album 12"
Producer:
David Hentschel & John Gilbert

Song 138a title:
Step Lightly
Release date / Country:
17 Feb 75 / U.S.A.
Track details:
Side 1, track 3 / 3 min. 39 sec.
Composer:
R. Starkey

David Hentschel: Synthesizer; Ringo Starr: Finger Clicks; John Gilbert: Finger Clicks

David Hentschel began his musical career as a recording engineer at Trident Studios in London. When Trident bought a synthesizer in 1973, Hentschel took to the instrument with a passion. He has worked with a number of artists including Harry Nilsson*, Carly Simon*, Jim Webb* and on Paul McCartney's album **Red Rose Speedway**. He is probably recognized most for his synthesizer work on Elton John's* song ***Funeral For A Friend***.

Hentschel's manager John Gilbert introduced him to Ringo Starr, who was scouting for talented artists in the mid-1970s for his newly formed record label, Ring O'Records. Hentschel was given the task of doing a synthesizer version of Ringo's most successful album **Ringo** (a project not unlike McCartney's orchestration of his album **Ram** under the pseudonym **Thrillington**). Ring O'Records, much like George Harrison's Dark Horse label and McCartney's MPL, was Ringo's attempt at trying to reorganize his financial affairs, outside Apple, within the context of helping struggling musicians who managed to attract his attention. Hentschel has gone on to become a successful producer.

Mary Hopkin

Record 139 title:
Post Card
Label / Catalog number:
Apple / CDP 7975782
Jacket / Inserts:
Standard international design in jewel box with modified U.K.-style jacket back with design and notes by: Paul McCartney / 8 page CD booklet
Media:
Album 5" CD
Producer:
Paul McCartney

Song 139a title:
En Aquellos Dias ("Those Were The Days" - sung in Spanish)
Release date / Country:
19 Nov 91 (first issued: 25 Oct 68) / Germany
Recording Location / Date:
Trident & EMI-Abbey Road Studios, London, U.K. / Jul 68
Track details:
Side 1, track 18 / 5 min. 09 sec.
Composer:
G. Raskin

Mary Hopkin: Lead Vocals & Acoustic Guitar; Paul McCartney: Acoustic Guitar & (possible) Percussion; Gilbert Webster: Cembalon

Song 139b title:
Happiness Runs (Pebble And The Man)
Release date / Country:
19 Nov 91 (first issued: 21 Feb 69) / Germany
Recording Location / Date:
EMI-Abbey Road Studios, London, U.K. / Nov 68 - Jan 69

Track details:
Side 1, track 3 / 2 min. 03 sec.
Composer:
D. Leitch

Mary Hopkin: Lead Vocals & Guitar; Paul McCartney: Bass; Donovan Leitch: Guitar

Song 139c title:
Inch Worm
Release date / Country:
19 Nov 91 (first issued: 21 Feb 69) / Germany
Recording Location / Date:
(probably) EMI-Abbey Road, or Trident or (possibly) Apple Studios, London, U.K. / Nov 68 - Jan 69

Track details:
Side 1, track 8 / 2 min. 33 sec.
Composer:
F. Loesser

Mary Hopkin: Lead Vocals

Song 139d title:
Lord Of The Reedy River
Release date / Country:
19 Nov 91 (first issued: 21 Feb 69) / Germany
Recording Location / Date:
EMI-Abbey Road Studios, London, U.K. / Nov 68 - Jan 69

Track details:
Side 1, track 2 / 2 min. 37 sec.
Composer:
D. Leitch

Mary Hopkin: Lead Vocals; Paul McCartney: Guitar; Donovan Leitch: Guitar & B. Vocals

Song 139e title:
Love Is The Sweetest Thing
Release date / Country:
19 Nov 91 (first issued: 21 Feb 69) / Germany
Recording Location / Date:
(probably) EMI-Abbey Road, or Trident or (possibly) Apple Studios, London, U.K. / Nov 68 - Jan 69

Track details:
Side 1, track 4 / 3 min. 43 sec.
Composer:
R. Noble

Mary Hopkin: Lead Vocals; Paul McCartney: (probable) Guitar & (probable) Bass

Song 139f title:
Lullaby Of The Leaves
Release date / Country:
19 Nov 91 (first issued: 21 Feb 69) / Germany
Recording Location / Date:
(probably) EMI-Abbey Road, or Trident or (possibly) Apple Studios, London, U.K. / Nov 68 - Jan 69

Track details:
Side 1, track 10 / 2 min. 33 sec.
Composer:
J. Young - B. Petkere

Mary Hopkin: Lead Vocals; Paul McCartney: (probable) Guitar

Song 139g title:
Prince En Avignon
Release date / Country:
19 Nov 91 (first issued: 21 Feb 69) / Germany
Recording Location / Date:
(probably) EMI-Abbey Road, or Trident or (possibly) Apple Studios, London, U.K. / Nov 68 - Jan 69

Track details:
Side 1, track 13 / 3 min. 20 sec.
Composer:
J. Bourtayre

Mary Hopkin: Lead Vocals; Paul McCartney: (probable) Guitar, (probable) Drums & (probable) Bass

Song 139h title:
Quelli Erano Giorni ("Those Were The Days" - sung in Italian)
Track details:
Side 1, track 17 / 5 min. 08 sec.
Release date / Country:
19 Nov 91 (first issued: 25 Oct 68) / Germany
Composer:
G. Raskin
Recording Location / Date:
Trident & EMI-Abbey Road Studios, London, U.K. / Jul 68

Mary Hopkin: Lead Vocals & Acoustic Guitar; Paul McCartney: Acoustic Guitar & (possibly) Percussion; Gilbert Webster: Cembalon

Song 139i title:
Someone To Watch Over Me
Track details:
Side 1, track 12 / 2 min. 02 sec.
Release date / Country:
19 Nov 91 (first issued: 21 Feb 69) / Germany
Composer:
I. Gershwin - G. Gershwin
Recording Location / Date:
EMI-Abbey Road Studios, London, U.K. / Nov 68 - Jan 69

Mary Hopkin: Lead Vocals; The Mike Cotton Sound (Jim Garforth: Drums; Bernie: Bass; Mike Cotton: Horns; Nick: Horns; Derek Tearle: Guitar); Paul McCartney: Arrangement; George Martin (probable) Piano

Song 139j title:
The Game
Track details:
Side 1, track 14 / 2 min. 40 sec.
Release date / Country:
19 Nov 91 (first issued: 21 Feb 69) / Germany
Composer:
G. Martin
Recording Location / Date:
EMI-Abbey Road Studios, London, U.K. / Nov 68 - Jan 69

Mary Hopkin: Lead Vocals; George Martin: Piano; Jeanne Dolmetsch: Recorder; Marguerite Dolmetsch; Recorder; Paul Blood: Recorder; Brian Blood: Recorder; Peter Blood: Recorder; Christine Blood: Recorder

Song 139k title:
The Honeymoon Song
Track details:
Side 1, track 6 / 2 min. 07 sec.
Release date / Country:
19 Nov 91 (first issued: 21 Feb 69) / Germany
Composer:
M. Theodorakis
Recording Location / Date:
Trident Studio, London, U.K. / Nov 68 - Jan 69

Mary Hopkin: Lead Vocals; Paul McCartney: Tambourine & (possible) Guitar; The Mike Cotton Sound (Jim Garforth: Drums; Bernie: Bass; John Beecham: Horns; Mike Cotton: Horns; Nick: Horns; Derek Tearle: Guitar)

Song 139l title:
The Puppy Song
Track details:
Side 1, track 7 / 2 min. 42 sec.
Release date / Country:
19 Nov 91 (first issued: 21 Feb 69) / Germany
Composer:
H. Nilsson
Recording Location / Date:
(probably) EMI-Abbey Road, or Trident or (possibly) Apple Studios, London, U.K. / Nov 68 - Jan 69

Mary Hopkin: Lead Vocals; Paul McCartney: (probable) Piano & (probable) Bass

Song 139m title:
There's No Business Like Show Business
Track details:
Side 1, track 15 / 4 min. 03 sec.

Release date / Country:
19 Nov 91 (first issued 21 Feb 69) / Germany
Composer:
I. Berlin
Recording Location / Date:
EMI-Abbey Road Studios, London, U.K. / Nov 68 - Jan 69

Mary Hopkin: Lead Vocals; The Mike Cotton Sound (Jim Garforth: Drums; Bernie: Drums); George Martin: Piano; Paul McCartney: Conductor

Song 139n title:
Those Were The Days
Track details:
Side 1, track 1 / 5 min. 08 sec.
Release date / Country:
19 Nov 91 (first issued 26 Aug 68) / Germany
Composer:
G. Raskin
Recording Location / Date:
Trident & EMI-Abbey Road Studios, London, U.K. / Jul 68

Mary Hopkin: Lead Vocals & Acoustic Guitar; Paul McCartney: Acoustic Guitar & (possible) Percussion; Gilbert Webster: Cembalon

Song 139o title:
Turn! Turn! Turn! (To Everything There Is A Season)
Track details:
Side 1, track 16 / 2 min. 50 sec.
Release date / Country:
19 Nov 91 (first issued 26 Aug 68) / Germany
Composer:
P. Seeger
Recording Location / Date:
(probably) Trident or (possibly) EMI Abbey Road Studios, London, U.K. / Jul 68

Mary Hopkin: Lead Vocals & Acoustic Guitar

Song 139p title:
Voyage Of The Moon
Track details:
Side 1, track 9 / 5 min. 52 sec.
Release date / Country:
19 Nov 91 (first issued: 21 Feb 69) / Germany
Composer:
D. Leitch
Recording Location / Date:
EMI-Abbey Road Studios, London, U.K. / Nov 68 - Jan 69

Mary Hopkin: Lead Vocals; Paul McCartney: Guitar; Donovan Leitch: Guitar

Song 139q title:
Y Blodyn Gwyn
Track details:
Side 1, track 5 / 3 min. 08 sec.
Release date / Country:
19 Nov 91 (first issued 21 Feb 69) / Germany
Composer:
E. J. Hughes - R. H. Jones
Recording Location / Date:
(probably) EMI-Abbey Road, Trident or (possibly) Apple Studios, London, U.K. / Nov 68 - Jan 69

Mary Hopkin: Lead Vocals

Song 139r title:
Young Love
Track details:
Side 1, track 11 / 2 min. 11 sec.
Release date / Country:
19 Nov 91 (first issued: 21 Feb 69) / Germany
Composer:
C. Joyner - R. Carty
Recording Location / Date:
EMI-Abbey Road Studios, London, U.K. / Nov 68 - Jan 69

Mary Hopkin: Lead Vocals; The Mike Cotton Sound (Jim Garforth: Drums; Bernie: Bass; John Beecham: Horns; Mike Cotton: Horns; Nick: Horns; Derek Tearle: Guitar); The London Welsh Choir: B. Vocals; Paul McCartney: Arrangement

Record 140 title:
Those Were The Days
Label / Catalog number:
Apple / 7243 8 30197 2 4
Jacket / Inserts:
Standard international design in jewel box / 12 page CD booklet
Media:
Album 5" CD
Producer:
Paul McCartney

Song 140a title:
Lontano Dagli Occhi
Release date / Country:
27 Mar 95 (first issued 07 Mar 69) / U.K.
Recording Location / Date:
Morgan Studios, London, U.K. / 1-2 Mar 69
Track details:
Side 1, track 7 / 3 min. 22 sec.
Composer:
S. Endrigo - S. Bardotti

Mary Hopkin: Lead Vocals; Paul McCartney: Arrangement, (probable) Bass & (probable) Piano

Song 140b title:
Goodbye
Release date / Country:
27 Mar 95 (first issued 28 Mar 69) / U.K.
Recording Location / Date:
(probably) EMI-Abbey Road, Trident or Apple Studios, London, U.K. / 1968 or 1969
Track details:
Side 1, track 2 / 2 min. 23 sec.
Composer:
J. Lennon - P. McCartney

Mary Hopkin: Lead Vocals & Guitar; Paul McCartney: Acoustic Guitars, Bass & Thigh-slap Percussion

Song 140c title:
Que Sera, Sera (What Will Be, Will Be)
Release date / Country:
27 Mar 95 (first issued: 19 Sep 69) / U.K.
Recording Location / Date:
EMI-Abbey Road Studios, London, U.K. / Jul or Aug 69
Track details:
Side 1, track 6 / 3 min. 05 sec.
Composer:
J. Livingston - R. Evans

Mary Hopkin: Lead Vocals; Paul McCartney: Electric Guitar, Acoustic Guitar, Bass & Arrangement; Ringo Starr: Drums

Song 140d title:
Sparrow
Release date / Country:
27 Mar 95 (first issued 28 Mar 69) / U.K.
Recording Location / Date:
Morgan Studios, London, U.K. / 1-2 Mar 69
Track details:
Side 1, track 8 / 3 min. 09 sec.
Composer:
B. Gallagher - G. Lyle

Mary Hopkin: Lead Vocals; Paul McCartney: (probable) Bass

Song 140e title:
The Fields Of St. Etienne
Release date / Country:
27 Mar 95 (first issued 19 Sep 69) / U.K.
Recording Location / Date:
(probably) EMI-Abbey Road, or (possibly) Apple or Trident Studio, London, U.K. / Aug 69
Track details:
Side 1, track 10 / 3 min. 08 sec.
Composer:
B. Gallagher - G. Lyle

Mary Hopkin: Lead Vocals & (probable) Acoustic Guitar; Paul McCartney: Acoustic Guitar & (probable) Bass; Ringo Starr: Drums

Record 141 title:
An Jenem Tag / Turn! Turn! Turn!
(To Every Thing There is A Season)
Label / Catalog number:
Apple / 0-23 910
Jacket / Inserts:
Record label sleeve
Recording Location / Date:
Trident Studios & EMI-Abbey Road Studios, London, U.K. / Jul 68
Media:
Single 7" (mono)
Producer:
Paul McCartney

Song 141a title:
An Jenem Tag ["Those Were The Days" - sung in German]
Release date / Country:
25 Oct 68 / Germany
Track details:
Side 1, track 1 / 5 min. 06 sec.
Composer:
G. Raskin

Mary Hopkin: Lead Vocals & Acoustic Guitar; Paul McCartney: Acoustic Guitar & (possible) Percussion; Gilbert Webster: Cembalon

Record 142 title:
Le Temps des Fleurs ("Those Were The Days"-sung in French) / Turn! Turn! Turn
Label / Catalog number:
Apple / APF 503
Jacket / Inserts:
Picture sleeve
Recording Location / Date:
Trident & EMI-Abbey Road Studios, London, U.K. / Jul 68
Media:
Single 7" (mono)
Producer:
Paul McCartney

Song 142a title:
Le Temps des Fleurs ("Those Were The Days" - sung in French)
Release date / Country:
25 Oct 68 / France
Track details:
Side 1, track 1 / 5 min. 06 sec.
Composer:
G. Raskin

Mary Hopkin: Lead Vocals & Acoustic Guitar; Paul McCartney: Acoustic Guitar & (possible) Percussion; Gilbert Webster: Cembalon

Mary Hopkin was born May 3, 1950 in Pontardawe, Glamorgan, Wales. She started singing in her church choir when she was four years old. As a teenager she performed in local clubs and on television in Wales. She sang primarily Welsh folk songs but was also influenced by American and British folksingers like Donovan*.

Hopkin was brought to the attention of Paul McCartney by the swinging '60s model, actress and singer known as Twiggy, who had seen Hopkin on the U.K. TV talent show **Opportunity Knocks**. McCartney was duly impressed and signed Hopkin to The Beatles' newly formed Apple Records label in May 1968. McCartney quickly took Mary under his tutelage and, though not her personal manager, guided and directed her career her first year at Apple. He made a number of promotional appearances for her, including a spot on ITV. Mary claims she sang in the chorus of The Beatles' songs ***Hey Jude*** and ***Let It Be***, though she is not certain if she is featured on the versions of ***Let It Be*** that were released. Linda McCartney stated in the 1989 Paul McCartney World Tour book, "The first thing I ever did was with The Beatles. I sang harmonies on ***Let It Be***. It was supposed to be me and Mary Hopkin, but she had to go home."

Hopkin's debut on Apple Records was the single ***Those Were The Days***, a Lithuanian folk song adapted by American folksingers Gene (Raskin) and Francesca. For years, McCartney had been urging artists like future Wings' member Denny Laine* and his band The Moody Blues to record the song. McCartney was so sure of the song's potential as an international hit that he had Hopkin record vocal overdubs in French, German, Italian, and Spanish. McCartney's long held convictions proved correct when the song became an international million selling hit. It was held from the number one position in many countries only by The Beatles' Apple debut single ***Hey Jude***. Many years later, John Lennon's first wife, Cynthia, also recorded a version of the song.

McCartney was convinced that Hopkin would become an international star and help launch Apple Records globally. Over a period of months he produced her debut album **Post Card**, on which he also played. The track listing (on a post card) on the back of the album's jacket was handwritten by McCartney along with some doodles that differed on the U.S. and U.K. vinyl album versions. Paul's wife, Linda, took the jacket's front photo. To further bolster her international appeal, three more non-English recordings were produced by McCartney: ***Y Blodyn Gwyn*** in Welsh, ***Prince en Avignon*** in French, and ***Lontano Dagli Occhi*** in Italian. (***Lontano Dagli Occhi*** was first issued in Italy as a single and included on Mary's final album for Apple). Unfortunately for Mary, **Post Card** was more of a showcase for McCartney's love affair with show tunes than for her Welsh folk music.

Though there are no specific musical credits on **Post Card**, it is well-known that McCartney contributed a significant amount of the instrumental backing, including guitars. It's also quite likely that he played some piano and possibly drums. Ringo Starr, who contributed to some of Mary's later recordings produced by McCartney, may have contributed some drums and / or percussion. Other contributors to **Post Card** included Donovan Leitch, The Mike Cotton Sound, who had been a part of The Beatles Christmas Show in 1964, and George Martin* who conducted the orchestra and played piano.

The follow-up single to ***Those Were The Days*** was McCartney's catchy melody ***Goodbye***. Hopkin's great vocal, along with the Lennon-McCartney composing credit, was enough to make it a U.S. top 20 and a U.K. top 10 in 1969. A promotional video was shot (though never broadcast) of McCartney and Hopkin recording the song. A McCartney demo of ***Goodbye*** has appeared on a number of bootleg records. (***Goodbye*** has since been covered by I Ribelli, Gunter Kallman Chorus and Little Big Horns.)

McCartney's last work with Hopkin was on her third U.S. single ***Que Sera, Sera (What Will Be, Will Be) / The Fields Of St. Etienne*** (Apple / 1823), released in the U.S. nearly a year after the two songs were recorded. The single was apparently first issued with the catalogue number Apple 16 in France on September 19, 1969, shortly after it was recorded. (The Apple 16 catalogue number was also apparently assigned to the never released song ***On Our Way Home [Two Of Us]*** by Mortimer.) Apparently, both sides of the single feature only Paul and Ringo on the musical backing. Hopkin reportedly was not thrilled with the results of either song, and did not want the single released. The songs were later included on Mary's "best of" album **Those Were The Days**, with the production on ***Que Sera, Sera*** erroneously credited to Mickie Most. When the CD of the album was released, it still listed Most as producer (an error carried over from the original vinyl album credits). George Harrison reportedly offered his composition ***I'll Still Love You*** (originally titled ***When Every Song Is Sung***) to

Several more singles produced by Mickie Most and Mary's future husband, Tony Visconti, along with a final Apple album produced by Visconti, rounded out Hopkin's final days with the label. Like most of Apple's artists, Mary became disillusioned with the company and let her contract expire. **Those Were The Days**, featuring the remainder of McCartney's contributions, was Hopkin's last Apple album. The album was issued in Germany with a different jacket design, slightly different song contents and titled **The Best Of Mary Hopkin**.

During the 1970s, Hopkin settled into a semi-domestic life-style with her husband Tony Visconti. Visconti gained notoriety producing Badfinger*, David Bowie*, T. Rex* and others. He also worked with Paul and Linda McCartney on several projects. Mary served as back-up vocalist (under the name Mary Visconti) for several artists, including Bowie. She released a couple of singles on her husband's Good Earth record label, and an album sung entirely in Welsh. Her marriage to Visconti ended in the early 1980s. Tony Visconti continues to produce and is now married to May Pang *(see Yoko Ono)*, the former secretary and girlfriend of John Lennon.

Mary became a member of the trio Sundance in 1980. In 1984, she joined a group called Oasis that also included Peter Skellern*. Mary contributed, along with other artists, to a 1988 album project of Dylan Thomas' **Under Milk Wood**, produced by George Martin. She continues to write songs and occasionally release new recordings.

Nicky Hopkins

Record 143 title:
The Tin Man Was A Dreamer
Label / Catalog number:
Sony / SRCS 6450
Media:
Album 5" CD
Producer:
Nicky Hopkins & David Briggs
Jacket / Inserts:
Standard international design in jewel box / 4 page CD booklet & 24 page lyric translation
Recording Location / Date:
Apple Studios, London, U.K. / Jan - Apr 73 &/or Jul 73

Song 143a title:
Banana Anna
Release date / Country:
01 Feb 95 (first issued 23 Apr 73) / Japan
Track details:
Side 1, track 7 / 3 min. 40 sec.
Composer:
N. Hopkins - J. Williams

Nicky Hopkins: Vocals & Piano; Jerry Williams: Vocals; George Harrison: Guitar; Klaus Voormann: Bass; Bobby Keys: Saxophone; Prairie Prince: Drums; Ray Cooper: Percussion & Congas

Song 143b title:
Edward
Release date / Country:
01 Feb 95 (first issued: 23 Apr 73) / Japan
Track details:
Side 1, track 3 / 5 min. 20 sec.
Composer:
N. Hopkins

Nicky Hopkins: Piano & Organ; George Harrison: Guitar; Klaus Voormann: Bass; Bobby Keys: Saxophone; Prairie Prince: Drums; Ray Cooper: Percussion & Congas

Song 143c title:
Speed On
Release date / Country:
01 Feb 95 (first issued: 23 Apr 73) / Japan
Track details:
Side 1, track 5 / 4 min. 01 sec.
Composer:
N. Hopkins - J. Williams

Nicky Hopkins: Vocals & Piano; Jerry Williams: Vocals; George Harrison: Lead Guitar; Klaus Voormann: Bass; Bobby Keys: Saxophone; Prairie Prince: Drums; Ray Cooper: Percussion & Congas; Mick Taylor: Rhythm Guitar; Jim Horn: Saxophone; Jim Price: Trumpet

Song 143d title:
Waiting For The Band
Release date / Country:
01 Feb 95 (first issued: 23 Apr 73) / Japan
Track details:
Side 1, track 2 / 2 min. 16 sec.
Composer:
N. Hopkins

Nicky Hopkins: Vocals & Piano; Jerry Williams: Vocals; George Harrison: Slide Guitar; Klaus Voormann: Bass; Bobby Keys: Saxophone; Prairie Prince: Drums; Ray Cooper: Percussion

Nicky Hopkins was born on February 24, 1944 in London, England. Hopkins was a classically trained musician who attended Britain's Royal Academy of Music. He is best remembered for his keyboard session work with The Rolling Stones*, The Who, The Small Faces *(see Rod Stewart, Kenney Jones, Ian McLagan)*, The Steve Miller Band*, Ravi Shankar*, Carly Simon* and Marc Bolan *(see T. Rex)*, among others. Hopkins has also enjoyed membership in Screaming Lord Sutch's Savages, The Cyril Davies All Stars, The Jeff Beck Group, Quicksilver Messenger Service, Sky *(see John Williams)*, Sweet Tuesday and Night.

Hopkins first met The Beatles in Hamburg, Germany as a member of Cliff Bennett And The Rebel Rousers* during one of their performances at the Star-Club. Hopkins was one of the few rock musicians to contribute to a Beatles' recording playing keyboards on the single version of ***Revolution***. He also contributed to the following solo Beatles albums - Lennon's **Imagine**, **Walls And Bridges** and **Some Time In New York City**; Harrison's **Living In The Material World**, **Dark Horse** and **Extra Texture**; Starr's **Ringo** and **Goodnight Vienna**; and McCartney's **Flowers In The Dirt**. Additionally, he played on John and Yoko's ***Happy Xmas*** single in 1971. He also played keyboards on ***Jet*** and ***Listen To What The Man Said*** for McCartney's appearance on the BBC-TV show **Wogan**, taped on November 19, 1987 and broadcast the following day. McCartney teamed up with Hopkins and others for the 1988 charity single ***Children In Need*** *(see Spirit Of Play)*. Nicky recorded a cover of The Beatles' song ***Yesterday***.

The Tin Man Was A Dreamer was one of Hopkins' several attempts at a solo career. The album was recorded at Apple Studios, probably during the sessions for George Harrison's album **Living In The Material World** using most of the same musicians. On September 6, 1994, Nicky Hopkins died of complications from intestinal problems he had suffered from for many years. If there's a rock 'n' roll heaven, Nicky's in the band!

Jim Horn

Record 144 title:
Work It Out
Label / Catalog number:
Warner Bros / 9 25911-2
Media:
Album 5" CD
Producer:
Larry Knechtel & Jim Horn
Jacket / Inserts:
Standard international design in jewel box / 8 page CD insert with photo of George Harrison
Recording Location / Date:
FPSHOT (Friar Park Studios, Henley-on-Thames) U.K. & Nightingale Studios, Nashville, TN, U.S.A. / (probably) 1987 (possibly) 1989

Song 144a title:
Take Away The Sadness
Release date / Country:
Mar 90 / U.S.A.
Track details:
Side 1, track 2 / 4 min. 00 sec.
Composer:
R. Tandy - J. Horn

Larry Knechtel: Keyboards & Synthesizers; Michael Rhodes: Bass; Paul Leim: Drums; George Harrison; Slide Guitar; Larry Byrom: Electric Guitar; Jim Horn: Soprano Saxophone

Jim Horn was born in Los Angeles, California. With the encouragement of his mother, he began taking music lessons at the age of eight, and was playing trumpet and saxophone several years later.

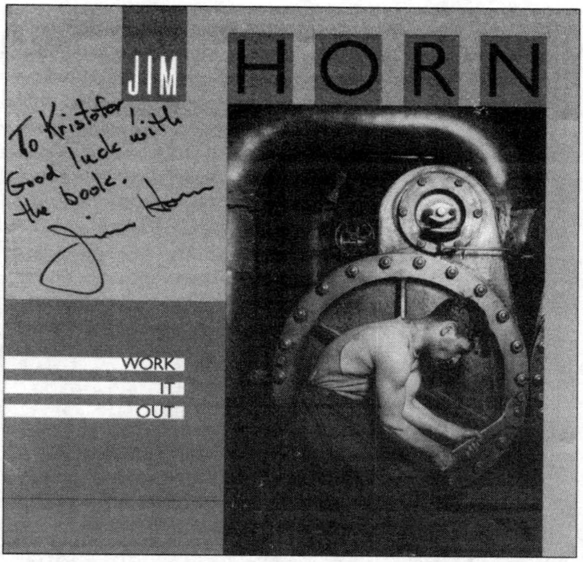

He has long been considered one of the top session horn players, and has been a steady working partner with Duane Eddy* for years.

Horn has contributed to many of George Harrison's solo recordings. He took part in **The Concert For Bangla Desh** in 1971, and was a member of Harrison's backing band during his 1974 U.S. tour. He has also worked with the "supergroup" Traveling Wilburys *(see Bob Dylan, Jeff Lynne, Roy Orbison, Tom Petty)*. Harrison, Petty and Lynne gladly returned the favor by contributing to Horn's 1990 instrumental album **Work It Out**.

He also contributed to Ringo's albums **Ringo** and **Time Takes Time**. George and Ringo made cameo appearances and spoke about Jim Horn in a video sampler for his 1988 album **Neon Nights**. Horn plans to include those comments on an album he is recording of some favorite songs he has played on, including George's ***Cloud Nine*** and Ringo's ***Don't Go Where The Road Don't Go***.

Larry Hosford

Record 145 title:
Crosswords

Media:
Album 12"

Label / Catalog number:
Shelter / SRL 52003

Producer:
Dino Airali & Larry Hosford

Jacket / Inserts:
Standard international design / 4 page lyric insert and bio.

Recording Location / Date:
Capitol Records Studio B, Los Angeles, CA, U.S.A. / (probably) Nov 75

Song 145a title:
Direct Me

Track details:
Side 1, track 3 / 3 min. 30 sec.

Release date / Country:
02 Aug 76 / U.S.A.

Composer:
L. Hosford

Larry Hosford: Lead Vocals & Acoustic Guitar; Pat Hubbard: B. Vocals; Ann Hughes: B. Vocals; Gary Roda: Pedal Steel Guitar & B. Vocals; Duane Sousa: Bass & B. Vocals; Jim Norris: Drums, Percussion & B. Vocals; Doug Haywood: B. Vocals; Dino Airali: B. Vocals; Frank Reckard: Acoustic Guitar; George Harrison: Slide Guitar; Leon Russell: Piano & Vibes

Song 145b title:
Wishing I Could

Track details:
Side 1, track 5 / 3 min. 14 sec.

Release date / Country:
02 Aug 76 (first issued 06 Jul /76) / U.S.A.

Composer:
L. Hosford

Larry Hosford: Lead Vocals & Acoustic Guitar; Harold Bradley: Acoustic Guitar; Billy Sanford: Acoustic Guitar; Bob Moore: Bass; Buddy Harman: Drums; Leon Russell: B. Vocals; George Harrison: B. Vocals; Jerry Miller: Acoustic Guitar; Tom Scribner: "The Lost Sound Of The Musical Saw;" Jeff Gylkinson: Harmonica

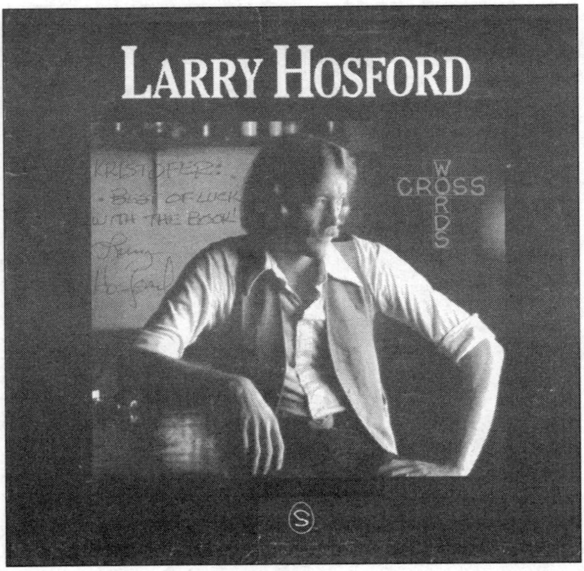

Larry Hosford was born on September 9, 1943 in Salinas, California. Hosford began playing guitar with his father, who was a barn dance fiddler. He began working with a group called the E-Types in the mid-1960s whom Larry describes as "a Beatles clone band – the Salinas Beatles." Their cover of The Beatles' song ***Love Of The Loved*** was released in 1964. Larry next worked with a rock band called Snail that had two albums for Cream Records. Hosford says his musical heroes are Bob Dylan, John Deere, Lefty Frizzell, Jimmy Rogers, and Willie Nelson (Hosford's vocals are reminiscent of Nelson's) which resulted in his shift towards country rock music. Producer Dino Airali liked Hosford's country rock style and got him signed to Shelter Records. He had two albums for the label – **A.K.A. Lorenzo** and **Crossword**. Hosford had moderate chart success in the mid-1970s with the songs ***Long Distance Kisses*** and ***King Takes The Queen***. He continues to record and perform with his Larry Hosford Band, mostly in his native California.

Dino Airali, the co-producer of Larry Hosford's 1976 album **Crossword**, said he met George Harrison through his good friend David Foster *(see Attitudes)* and helped him negotiate a deal to sign with Harrison's record label, Dark Horse. Airali said, "I went over and met George and we talked for awhile and got along real well. He eventually had me become the General Manager of Dark Horse Records. During that time, I had an obligation to finish Larry Hosford's album for Shelter Records. I told George about that, and he said he would love to be able to just be looked at as a guitar player hired to do a session. So I played Larry's music for him and he liked it. I asked him if he would like to play guitar on the session and he said 'sure.' Tom Scott* was also there, so I asked Tom if he wanted to play and he said, 'yeah.' Leon Russell*, who I had known for years, liked Larry's writing and he added his keyboard part, so it was that kind of thing." Harrison had recently worked with Scott, Foster and Russell on his 1975 album **Extra Texture**, that also thanked Airali.

According to Hosford, "Harrison had gone home with my tapes and was all prepared when he got to the studio. He was loose and very easy to work with, which made me want to be loose too. He played slide guitar on ***Direct Me***, and then he and Leon and I went to the piano and worked up the three-part harmony for ***Wishing I Could***. Three-part harmony 'like we use to do with the lads,' as George said."

Howlin' Wolf

Record 146 title:
The London Howlin' Wolf Sessions
Label / Catalog number:
Chess / DIDX 005222
Jacket / Inserts:
Standard international design / 8 page CD booklet
Recording Location / Date:
Olympic Studios, London, U.K. / 02 May 70

Media:
Album 5" CD
Producer:
Norman Dayron

Song 146a title:
I Ain't Superstitious
Release date / Country:
1989 (first issued 26 Jul 71) / U.S.A.
Track details:
Side 1, track 2 / 3 min. 29 sec.
Composer:
W. Dixon

Howlin' Wolf: Lead Vocals; Eric Clapton: Lead Guitar; Steve Winwood: Piano; Bill Wyman: Bass; Charlie Watts: Drums & Percussion; Hubert Sumlin: Rhythm Guitar; Ringo Starr: Drums; Klaus Voormann: Bass; Joe Miller: Horns; Jordan Sandke: Horns; Dennis Lansing: Horns

Howlin' Wolf was born Chester Arthur Burnett on June 10, 1910 in West Point, Mississippi and brought up on a cotton plantation. He began playing guitar at an early age, and practiced with such blues legends as Charley Patton and his brother-in-law, Sonny Boy Williamson (Rice Miller). He formed a band in Memphis in the late 1940s that included James Cotton, Little Junior Parker, Ike Turner *(see Ike & Tina Turner)*, and Willie Johnson. Wolf began his recording career with Sam Phillips of Sun Records. In the early 1950s, Wolf moved to Chicago and signed with Chess Records, where he recorded such Blues classics as ***Spoonful***, ***Smokestack Lightnin***, ***Little Red Rooster*** and ***I Ain't Superstitious***. Wolf's style of blues had a major influence on British artists like The Rolling Stones*, Eric Clapton*, and The Yardbirds.

It was not surprising then that such rock luminaries as Clapton, Ian Stewart, Charlie Watts, Bill Wyman, Steve Winwood *(see Blind Faith)* and Ringo Starr (using his then popular "Richie" pseudonym) would contribute to **The London Howlin' Wolf Sessions** released in 1971. Ringo drummed on the track ***I Ain't Superstitious***. The wolf ceased to howl on January 10, 1976.

Indian Mosk

Record 147 title:
None
Label / Catalog number:
Apple
Producer:
John Lennon & Peter Bendrey
Recording Location / Date:
Record Plant (East) Studios, New York, NY, USA / 16 Nov 71

Song 147a title:
Bodhnath (Gellupka) I
Release date / Country:
Unreleased
Composer:
Unknown

Indian Mosk: Vocals

Song 147b title:
Bodhnath Part II
Release date / Country:
Unreleased
Composer:
Unknown

Indian Mosk: Vocals

Indian Mosk is listed as the artist on a box of unreleased recordings found in the old Record Plant's (East) tape library with John Lennon listed as producer. The recording engineer on the sessions was Jack Douglas, who would later produce John and Yoko's 1980 sessions for **Double Fantasy** and **Milk And Honey**. When contacted about the Indian Mosk recording sessions, Douglas drew a complete blank and was at a loss for any idea who Indian Mosk was or for what use the recordings were intended. The tape box lists the client as Apple Records. Other tape boxes, dating from the same period, suggest that this may have been intended for use in a soundtrack to an ABKCO (Allen & Betty Klein Co.) film. ABKCO had released soundtrack albums on Apple Records for the films **Come Together** and **El Topo**. It's more likely that the recording was intended for use in some John and Yoko project that was later abandoned. May Pang theorizes that John put his name to the project

to identify him as the specific client, and that Peter Bendrey, the Lennons' personal assistant, probably did most, if not all, of the production *(see Tibetan Chants)*.

Front door of Record Plant (east) Studios, New York, photo by Kristofer Engelhardt

Michael Jackson with Paul McCartney

Record 148 title:
Thriller
Label / Catalog number:
Epic / EK 38112
Jacket / Inserts:
Standard international design in jewel box / 12 page CD booklet with sketch of Paul McCartney
Recording Location / Date:
Ocean Way &/or West Lake Audio, Studios, Los Angeles, CA, U.S.A. / Apr 82
Media:
Album 5" CD
Producer:
Quincy Jones

Song 148a title:
The Girl Is Mine
Release date / Country:
(first issued 25 Oct 82) / U.S.A.
Track details:
Side 1, track 3 / 3 min. 42 sec.
Composer:
M. Jackson

Michael Jackson: Vocals & Vocal Arrangement; Paul McCartney: Vocals; Greg Phillinganes: Rhodes; David Paich: Piano & Rhythm Arrangement; David Foster: Synthesizer & Synthesizer Arrangement; Steve Porcaro: Synthesizer Programming; Dean Parks: Guitar; Steve Lukather: Guitar; Louis Johnson: Bass; Jeff Porcaro: Drums; Quincy Jones: Vocal Arrangement & Rhythm Arrangement; Jerry Hey: String Arrangement and Conductor; Jerry Vinci: Concertmaster

Michael Jackson was born August 29, 1958 in the steel-mill town of Gary, Indiana. Michael and his brothers Tito, Jermaine, Jackie and Marlon first began performing in the Gary area in the mid-1960s and became known as The Jackson Five. The boys' father Joe, who played guitar in a local band called the Falcons, had also been his sons' manager throughout much of their careers. National success eluded them until they were signed to Motown Records in 1969. A string of number one hits followed including ***I Want You Back***, ***ABC***, ***The Love You Save*** and ***I'll Be There***, along with nearly a dozen top 20 songs. Most of the Jackson family's of nine children are musically gifted, including sisters Janet and La Toya. However, it was obvious that Michael (who was fronting the group from a very early age) was the most gifted. The band left Motown in 1975 and, for contractual reasons, simply became known as The Jacksons.

Michael had already been a solo artist since 1971 scoring hits with the songs ***Got To Be There***, ***Rockin' Robin***, and ***Ben***. In 1977, Michael played the part of the Scarecrow in the film version of **The Wiz**, a black cast musical adaptation of **The Wizard Of Oz**. Legendary producer Quincy Jones, in charge of the soundtrack, teamed up with Jackson two years later to produce Michael's comeback album **Off The Wall**. The album produced the number one hits ***Don't Stop 'Til You Get Enough*** and ***Rock With You***, and the top 10 hits ***She's Out Of My Life*** and ***Off The Wall***.

In 1982, Michael Jackson released what to date is the biggest-selling album of all time, **Thriller**, producing the top 10 songs ***Beat It***, ***The Girl Is Mine***, ***Billie Jean***, ***Human Nature***, ***Wanna Be Startin' Somethin'***, ***P.Y.T. (Pretty Young Thing)*** and ***Thriller***. Jackson's videos for the songs were also highly successful, particularly because of their special effects and Jackson's self-choreographed dance scenes.

The Michael Jackson / Paul McCartney association has been a long and winding, not to mention rough, road. Michael Jackson recounted in his autobiography **Moonwalk** that he first met McCartney at a party to celebrate the completion of Wings' album **Venus And Mars**, on March 24, 1975, on the ocean liner Queen Mary docked at Long Beach, California. The guests, among others, included George Harrison and the sixteen-year-old child superstar of The Jacksons who was invited by McCartney's daughter Heather.

According to **Moonwalk**, shortly after the **Venus And Mars** party, the two formally met at a party to which McCartney had invited Jackson. During the party, McCartney began to sing the song ***Girlfriend*** to Jackson, telling him he had written it for Jackson to record. McCartney and Jackson exchanged phone numbers, but apparently never found the time to get together to record the song. McCartney ended up recording the song for inclusion on his 1978 album **London Town**. During the recording of Jackson's album **Off The Wall**, producer Quincy Jones suggested that Michael record a cover of a McCartney song he had recently heard called ***Girlfriend***. Considering the unusual coincidence, Jackson decided to record the song for inclusion on his **Off The Wall** album. However, according to McCartney, as quoted in Ray Coleman's book **Yesterday & Today**, the song ***Girlfriend*** was not composed with Jackson in mind.

Jackson phoned McCartney at his home in England on Christmas Day 1980 telling Paul he wanted to work together. In May 1981, Jackson visited McCartney in England, and the two co-wrote ***The Man*** and the hit ***Say Say Say*** and recorded them in London. Horns were added to the songs in Los Angeles in April 1982. Essentially, McCartney wrote the music and Jackson the lyrics. In February 1983, Jackson returned to England to finish the recordings for both songs with McCartney. They were featured on the McCartney album **Pipes Of Peace** released later that year. Jackson was also included in McCartney's music video for ***Say Say Say***.

During McCartney's April 1982 visit to Los Angeles, he recorded a vocal duet for Jackson's song ***The Girl Is Mine***, the first single off Jackson's album **Thriller**. The **Thriller** album gives special thanks to McCartney in the credits. The single was issued in a picture sleeve with a photo of Jackson and McCartney, and it was also issued as a picture disc in the U.K.

Now friends, Jackson asked McCartney for some business recommendations. McCartney gave Jackson three bits of advice that he took to heart – get a manager you can trust; make and own music videos; and invest in music publishing (as McCartney had successfully done). Jackson jokingly suggested (or so McCartney thought) that he was going to buy his (the Lennon - McCartney catalogue) songs.

In March 1985, Jackson visited McCartney again at his home in England. Now a very wealthy man as a result of the sales of **Thriller**, Jackson again hinted to Paul that he might buy his songs. The Beatles had lost controlling interest in their Northern Songs Publishing Company in March 1969 and sold off their minority shares to the controlling interest ATV (Associated Television) in October 1969. This came about as a result of their financial difficulties at Apple, disputes over being managed by Allen Klein, and the legacy of Brian Epstein's mismanagement. After John Lennon's death, McCartney and Yoko Ono joined forces to try to buy back the catalogue priced at around $25 million, but apparently Ono convinced McCartney that she could get it for a lower price if he was willing to hold out a little longer. McCartney understandably had difficulty with the fact that he would have to pay $25 million to buy back songs he had written and originally owned.

On August 10, 1985, Michael Jackson bought the publishing rights to the vast majority of the Lennon - McCartney compositions for $47,500,000 (other sources claim $53 million). The catalogue he purchased also included a number of George Harrison and Ringo Starr (Starkey) compositions, and songs written separately by Lennon and McCartney following the breakup of The Beatles. Apparently a clause in the U.S. copyright laws allows for a renewal of copyrights by the heirs if the composer dies within the first 28-year phase of a copyright, regardless of any previous publishing agreements. In effect, Yoko Ono, or whoever is rightful heir, will probably end up owning Lennon's portion of the copyright for a time when it comes up for renewal. Negotiations by McCartney and Yoko to stop Jackson from allowing the songs to be used for commercials have been ongoing for some years. McCartney and Jackson's friendly relationship ended as a result of the purchase.

In November 1995, Jackson and Sony Music Publishing announced a joint publishing venture, Sony / ATV Music Publishing, that merged Jackson's ATV Music holdings, which include his Lennon - McCartney catalogue, with Sony. Jackson reportedly received close to $100 million for the merger.

Lennon's son Sean made a cameo appearance in Jackson's film **Moonwalker** and has been a guest at Jackson's home. Jackson performed John Lennon's Beatles song ***Come Together*** in **Moonwalker** that was included on the 1991 laser videodisk **The World's Greatest Artists Sing LENNON A Tribute**.

In 1994, Michael Jackson's career suffered a setback amid allegations of sexual misconduct. That year he married Elvis Presley's daughter, Lisa Marie, but the two parted in 1996. Jackson's 1995 **HIStory Past, Present & Future - Book I** album included ***The Girl Is Mine*** along with a photo of McCartney and his cover of ***Come Together***.

Mick Jagger

Record 149 title:
Leon Russell

Media:
Album 5" CD

Label / Catalog number:
DCC/Shelter / GZS-1049

Producer:
Denny Cordell & Leon Russell

Jacket / Inserts:
Standard international design in jewel box with die-cut cardboard slip cover / 8 page CD booklet

Recording Location / Date:
Olympic Sound Studios, London, U.K. / Sep - Oct 69

Song 149a title:
(Can't Seem To) Get A Line On You [Shine A Light]

Track details:
Side 1, track 17 / 4 min. 16 sec.

Release date / Country:
18 Nov 93 / Japan/Canada

Composer:
L. Russell [M. Jagger - K. Richards]

Mick Jagger: Lead Vocals; Chris Stainton: Guitar; Ringo Starr: Drums; Bill Wyman: Bass; Leon Russell: Piano

Record 150 title:
The Lost Lennon Tapes [Various Artists]
Label / Catalog number:
Westwood One Radio Network
/ [Matrix #] LT 91-03 (promotional only)
Jacket / Inserts:
Unique "Lost Lennon Tapes" / Cue Sheets
Recording Location / Date:
Record Plant (West) Studios, Los Angeles, CA
/ (probably) Dec 73 or Jan 74 or (possibly) Jun 74
Media:
Album 12" [2 LP set]
Producer:
John Lennon

Song 150a title:
Too Many Cooks
Release date / Country:
14 Jan 91 / U.S.A.
Track details:
3 min. 22 sec.
Composer:
Bond - Dumbar - Wayne

Mick Jagger: Lead Vocals; probably one or more of the following: Jim Keltner: Drums; Bruce Gary: Drums; Harry Nilsson: B. Vocals & Keyboards; Jesse Ed Davis: Guitar; Danny Kortchmar: Guitar; Jack Bruce: Bass; Bobby Keys: Horns; Trevor Lawrence: Horns; Al Kooper: Keyboards; Joe De Aguero: Percussion; Rocky Djubano: Percussion; Mike Finnegan: Keyboards; Wolfgang Metz: Bass; Paul Stallworth: Bass; Steve Madaio: Trumpet; Jim Price: Horns

Mick Jagger, like other members of The Rolling Stones*, has long maintained a solo career and contributed to a number of other artists' recordings. The song ***(Can't Seem To) Get A Line On You*** appears for the first time on the 1993 reissue of the Leon Russell* gold CD **Leon Russell**. The lead vocals are sung by Jagger, so it is more correctly classified as a Mick Jagger recording. However, it is actually an early working version of The Rolling Stones'* song ***Shine A Light*** that appears on their album **Exile On Main Street**.

Mick Jagger, Detroit, MI, 1970s, photo courtesy of Tom Bert

A recording of a song called ***Too Many Cooks***, sung by Mick Jagger, was apparently produced in part by John Lennon. ***Too Many Cooks*** was the result of a weekly jam session in Los Angeles, affectionately known as The Jim Keltner Fan-Club, that centered on Keltner *(see Attitudes)*. Its star-studded backing was confirmed by attendants Jack Bruce*, Bruce Gary, Bobby Keys*, Jim Keltner, Lee Kiefer, Al Kooper and May Pang, John's lover during his "lost weekend." By all accounts Jack Bruce played bass, Keys played saxophone, Harry Nilsson* sang backing vocals, and Jesse Ed Davis* and Danny Kortchmar played guitar.

There is not unanimous agreement concerning the following accounts of the session for ***Too Many Cooks***. According to Keltner and Kiefer, Ringo was at the session, but did not participate. Keltner thought producer Richard Perry helped Lennon with the editing during the session, but Kiefer, Pang and Kooper categorically deny Perry's presence. Keltner also thought the song was recorded sometime in May or June 1974. Rolling Stone magazine first reported on the recording in their July 18, 1974 issue, lending support to Keltner's date. However, Kiefer and Pang insist ***Too Many Cooks*** was recorded in late December 1973 during a break in Lennon's **Rock 'N' Roll** album sessions. Jack Bruce said the session had to take place sometime between January and March 1974, when he was at the Record Plant recording his album **Out Of The Storm**. According to Jack Bruce, "The session began with Lennon doing ***Stand By Me*** for hours before it evolved into the recordings for ***Too Many Cooks***." Drummer Bruce Gary (later a member of The Beatles-styled group The Knack) said Keltner walked out of the studio and that he ended up drumming on the track. Gary concurs with Jack Bruce's recollections of when the song was recorded, but is certain they only jammed on ***Bring It On Home To Me***, and that it was after the takes for ***Too Many Cooks***. (Lennon would end up recording both songs for his **Rock 'N' Roll** album.) Gary does not recall Ringo or Al Kooper being at the sessions, and said it was Billy Preston who played keyboards on ***Too Many Cooks***.

Lee Kiefer said he engineered ***Too Many Cooks*** and arranged for the session that he described as a group production involving himself, Kortchmar, Kooper, Jagger and Lennon. Kiefer remembers both Preston and Kooper playing keyboards on the recording. Additionally, he thinks Nilsson and Mike Finnegan played keyboards, Paul Stallworth and Wolfgang Metz played bass, Steve Madaio and Jim Price played horns, and Joe De Aguero and Rocky Djubano played percussion on the track. Kiefer recalls, "we had the doors open at Record Plant's (West) Studio A and a lot of people participated in the session; you could hear cars burning rubber in the parking lot! We even had Record Plant employees singing backing vocals, and there were some guys whose names I don't remember playing acoustic guitar." Kiefer said they recorded only one backing track, and that both Keltner and Gary drummed on it, but that there were three takes of the song.

May Pang recalls two versions of ***Too Many Cooks*** being recorded. She said the song was never considered for release on Apple Records, as had been reported. According to Pang, the song was not released because Jagger was unhappy with the results. **The Lost Lennon Tapes** promotional radio series is the closest this song has come to an official release. The song also appears on numerous bootleg records.

Elton John

Record 151 title:
To Be Continued...
Label / Catalog number:
MCA / MCAD4 10110
Media:
Album 5" CD [4 CD Box Set]
Producer:
Gus Dudgeon
Jacket / Inserts:
Standard international design in jewel box in box set / 40 page box set booklet with photos of John Lennon, Paul McCartney & Ringo Starr, credit insert, 4 page CD insert
Recording Location / Date:
Caribou Ranch Studios, Nederland, CO, U.S.A. / (probably) Aug 74

Song 151a title:
Lucy In The Sky With Diamonds
Release date / Country:
12 Nov 90 (first issued 15 Nov 74) / U.S.A.
Track details:
CD3, track 3 / 6 min. 15 sec.
Composer:
J. Lennon - P. McCartney

Elton John: Lead Vocals, Mellotron Harpsichord & Keyboards; Dee Murray: Bass & B. Vocals; Nigel Olsson: Drums & B. Vocals; Davey Johnstone: Guitar, Sitar, B. Vocals; Ray Cooper: Tambourine & Gong; John Lennon: Guitars, B. Vocals & Arrangement

Elton John Band Featuring John Lennon and The Muscle Shoals Horns

Record 152 title:
Artifacts III (Sue Me Sue You: 1972-1975) [Various Artists]
Media:
Album 5" CD [4 CD box set]
Label / Catalog number:
Big Music / BIGBX 009.4 (BIG 4034) [Unauthorized Record]
Producer:
Gus Dudgeon
Jacket / Inserts:
Unique in Jewel box in box set / 24 page box set booklet & (4) 2 page CD inserts
Recording Location / Date:
Record Plant (East) Studios, New York, NY, U.S.A. / 24 Nov 74

Song 152a title:
I Saw Her Standing There [rehearsal]
Track details:
CD2, track 19 / 2 min. 54 sec.
Release date / Country:
(probably) Feb 95 / Italy
Composer:
J. Lennon - P. McCartney

Elton John: Vocals & Piano; John Lennon: Vocals & Guitar; Ray Cooper: Percussion; Davey Johnstone: Guitar; Dee Murray: Bass; Nigel Olsson: Drums; Muscle Shoals Horns: Horns

Record 153 title:
Made In England
Media:
Extended Play 5" CD
Label / Catalog number:
Rocket / 422-852 173-2
Producer:
Gus Dudgeon (remixed by Gus Dudgeon†)
Jacket / Inserts:
Standard international design in jewel box / CD insert
Recording Location / Date:
On location at Madison Square Garden, New York, NY, U.S.A. & Metropolis Studios, London, U.K.† / 28 Nov 74 (remixed: Mar 95†)

Song 153a title:
I Saw Her Standing There [live]
Track details:
Side 1, track 4 / 3 min. 23 sec.
Release date / Country:
09 Aug 95 (first issued 24 Feb 75) / U.S.A.
Composer:
J. Lennon - P. McCartney

Elton John: Vocals & Piano; John Lennon: Vocals & Guitar; Ray Cooper: Percussion; Davey Johnstone: Guitar; Dee Murray: Bass; Nigel Olsson: Drums; Muscle Shoals Horns: Horns

Song 153b title:
Lucy In The Sky With Diamonds [live]
Track details:
Side 1, track 3 / 6 min. 07 sec.
Release date / Country:
09 Aug 95 (first issued 13 Mar 81) / U.S.A.
Composer:
J. Lennon - P. McCartney

Elton John: Vocals & Piano; John Lennon: Vocals, Guitar & Arrangement; Davey Johnstone: Guitar; Dee Murray: Bass; Nigel Olsson: Drums; Muscle Shoals Horns: Horns

Song 153c title:
Whatever Gets You Thru The Night [live]
Track details:
Side 1, track 2 / 4 min. 09 sec.
Release date / Country:
09 Aug 95 (first issued 13 Mar 81) / U.S.A.
Composer:
J. Lennon

Elton John: Vocals & Piano; John Lennon: Vocals & Guitar; Davey Johnstone: Guitar; Dee Murray: Bass; Nigel Olsson: Drums; Muscle Shoals Horns: Horns

Elton John was born Reginald Kenneth Dwight on March 25, 1947 in Pinner, England. He began playing the piano at the age of three, and when he was eleven, he received a scholarship to study at London's Royal Academy of Music. He joined the group Bluesology in the early 1960s. By the end of 1966, Bluesology included Elton Dean and Long John Baldry.

Reg, as he was still known, left Bluesology in 1967 to devote more time to songwriting and adopted the name Elton John from Dean and Baldry's names. Later that year, he was paired with lyricist Bernie Taupin* with the help of Liberty Records. In 1968, John and Taupin were signed on as staff writers for Dick James Music Publishing (DJM), who also handled The Beatles. John proved to be a prolific keyboard composer, whose melodies were often anonymously paired with Taupin's lyrics. By 1969, Elton was doing session work and releasing his recordings on the DJM label.

Elton's rise to stardom began in the U.S. with the rave reviews he received of his performance at Los Angeles' Troubadour club on August 25, 1970. Elton hopped from the club circuit to arena rock superstardom in a matter of months. He became the Liberace of glitter rock, wearing outrageous glasses and sporting outlandish costumes that included duck suits and sequined baseball uniforms.

Elton's admission of bisexuality in 1976 signaled a departure from the limelight, and several changes in his personal and professional direction. He briefly retired from performing in public in 1977, and began to experiment with other musical styles and lyricists, but without much success.

In 1979, Elton reunited with Taupin and returned to the stage. By 1982, the hits were pouring out of him again. In spite of his tremendous success, Elton, like so many of his peers and idols, fell victim to the excesses of the rock world. Ever the trouper, he continued throughout the 1980s performing tirelessly to the point of vocal cord damage. He managed to pull himself back from the edge of self-destruction in 1990.

Some of the many memorable hits of Elton John include ***Your Song***, ***Rocket Man***, ***Daniel***, ***Candle In The Wind***, ***Bennie And The Jets***, ***Funeral For A Friend / Love Lies Bleeding***, ***Don't Let The Sun Go Down On Me***, ***Philadelphia Freedom***, ***Crocodile Rock***, ***Empty Garden***, ***I Guess That's Why They Call It The Blues***, and ***I'm Still Standing***. John was inducted into the Rock and Roll Hall of Fame in 1994. That year he received a Grammy and an Oscar for ***Can You Feel The Love Tonight*** from the soundtrack to the film **The Lion King**. It would be an understatement to say that Elton John is one of the most prolific and gifted songwriters and entertainers of the twentieth century. He has also been active in his support of various social causes, particularly the fight against AIDS.

Elton performed his song ***Candle In The Wind***, (originally written in tribute to Marilyn Monroe) at Princess Diana's funeral in 1997. It included a new set of lyrics written by Taupin in tribute to the Princess. Following the funeral, George Martin* produced Elton's recording of the tribute to raise money for the Diana, Princess of Wales Memorial Fund. In a little over a month, nearly 32 million copies were shipped making it the biggest selling single recording in history.

Elton John is one of those special few who have worked with all four Beatles. The Beatles first became aware of him during their visits to Dick James' offices in the late 1960s. He first worked with Ringo Starr in the T. Rex* film **Born To Boogie**. During the summer of 1974, Elton played piano on his composition ***Snookeroo*** for Ringo's **Goodnight Vienna** album.

Elton first met John Lennon during the recordings for Lennon's album **Rock 'N' Roll** in Los Angeles in October 1973. The two quickly became good friends. The following summer, he performed on Lennon's **Walls And Bridges** album. According to Lennon, who had yet to have a number one solo single, Elton was certain ***Whatever Gets You Thru The Night*** was going to be a number one, and made a disbelieving Lennon promise that, if it was, he would have to perform it live at Madison Square Garden with Elton. In the retrospective box set **To Be Continued...**, Elton claims that his promise to Lennon was about whether **Walls And Bridges** would go number one. Lennon's version of the promise makes more sense because Elton's major contribution to **Walls And Bridges** was on the song ***Whatever Get You Thru The Night***. Furthermore, Lennon already had a number one album with **Imagine**. In either case, the album and the single both reached the number one spot the same week

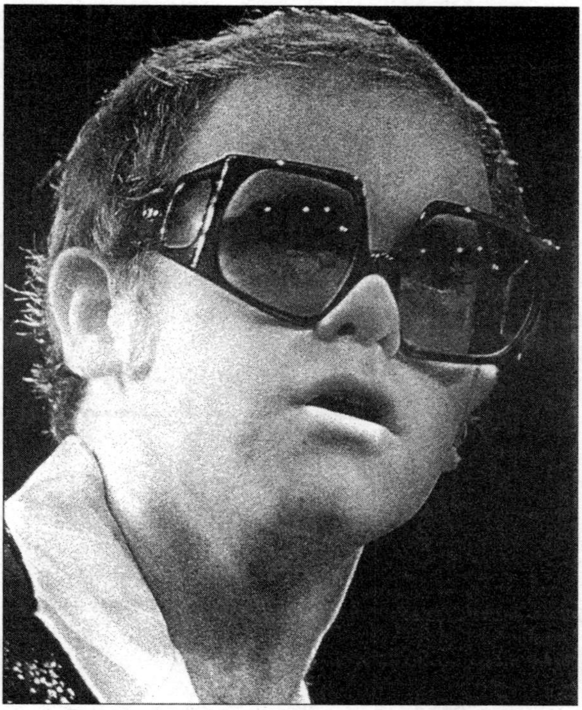
Elton John, Detroit, MI, mid-1970s, photo courtesy of Tom Bert

and, much to Lennon's horror, Elton persuaded him to keep his promise. The stage was literally set for Lennon's triumphant return to live performances. Lennon was physically sick from the terror of having to be Beatle John before his adopted hometown and his estranged wife, at the time, Yoko Ono*. Many doubted he would perform, but true to his word the nervous Lennon strolled onstage and confidently performed ***Whatever Gets You Through The Night***, ***Lucy In The Sky With Diamonds*** and ***I Saw Her Standing There*** with Elton. Elton has stated that the band was brought to tears by the nearly 10 minutes of applause Lennon received.

These three live recordings are difficult to categorize as they appear on both John Lennon and Elton John records, and all three numbers are Lennon or Beatles numbers, with lead vocals sung by both Lennon and Elton. These songs are generally categorized as John Lennon contributions to an Elton John performance. They are officially credited as the Elton John Band Featuring John Lennon And The Muscle Shoals Horns, and controlled by Dick James Music (Elton) and not EMI (Lennon). The songs have appeared on a variety of records, including singles with picture sleeves that feature photos of Lennon. The 1995 extended play **Made In England** contains the entire live performance in digitally remixed sound. Over the years Elton has performed several Beatles' songs in public, including ***Back In The U.S.S.R.***

During the summer of 1974, Lennon visited Elton at the Caribou Ranch Recording Studios in Colorado. While there, Elton recorded the Lennon compositions ***Lucy In The Sky With Diamonds*** and ***One Day At A Time***. Most reliable publications list Lennon as contributing guitar and background vocals to ***Lucy In The Sky With Diamonds***, but the detailed credit sheet in **To Be Continued...** only list Lennon on guitar. However, Lennon can clearly be heard singing in the background. Lennon also stated on numerous occasions that he came up with the new reggae bridge for the song. ***Lucy In The Sky With Diamonds*** was the first single issued by Elton that he did not write – that didn't matter, it was still a hit!

Most reliable publications also list Lennon playing guitar on ***One Day At A Time***, but the credit sheet on **To Be Continued...** only lists him on background vocals, which are not readily detectable. According to Gus Dudgeon, who produced both songs, "John only performed on ***Lucy***. However, he was so unimpressed with his playing, other than the reggae bit which was, in fact, his idea, that we wiped all of it, other than that section. Half the time he couldn't remember the chords and had to get Davey Johnstone to show them to him. He also sang on the backing vocals of ***Lucy***, but made no contribution to ***One Day At A Time***. Unfortunately, as no one bothered to ask me for information for the **To Be Continued...** booklet, it's inaccurate. This kind of thing happens all the time, and it really pisses me off." The **To Be Continued...** credit sheet also fails to mention that John Lennon plays guitar on the Madison Square Garden performance of ***I Saw Her Standing There***, calling into question its overall reliability.

Elton John remained one of Lennon's few close friends during Lennon's "house-husband" retirement, and was named godfather of his second son, Sean Ono Lennon. Elton was deeply affected by the murder of John Lennon. He and Taupin wrote the most moving of all Lennon tributes, ***Empty***

Garden, which Elton performed at Madison Square Garden in August 1982. He was joined onstage by Yoko Ono and his godson Sean. George Harrison joined Elton onstage for ***Empty Garden*** on March 19, 1982 in Sydney, Australia. He released another tribute song to Lennon titled ***The Man Who Never Died*** in 1985.

A film clip of Elton singing ***Imagine*** from his Central Park concert was included on the 1991 laser videodisk **The World's Greatest Artists Sing LENNON A Tribute**. Elton played with Paul McCartney in 1986, and with George and Ringo in 1987 at The Prince's Trust rock concerts. Elton also played on George Harrison's highly successful 1987 album **Cloud Nine**. Elton backed McCartney on several songs and sang a verse of ***Hey Jude*** during their performance at the **Music For Montserrat** benefit concert on September 15, 1997 at London's Royal Albert Hall. On May 21, 1998, Elton performed ***Great Balls Of Fire*** and ***Twist And Shout*** backed by Ringo on drums at the **Cinema Against AIDS** benefit at the **Cannes Film Festival**.

Kenney Jones

Record 154 title:
None

Producer:
Mentor Williams

Recording Location / Date:
(probably) Record Plant (West) or (possibly) Wally Heider Studios,
Los Angeles, CA, U.S.A. / Mar or Apr 75

Song 154a title:
Baby Blue Eyes

Release date / Country:
Unreleased

Composer:
M. Williams

Kenney Jones: Lead Vocals & Drums; Al Kooper: Keyboards; Mentor Williams: Guitar; Denny Laine: Guitar & B. Vocals; Danny "Kootch" Kortchmar; Paul McCartney: Bass & (possible) B. Vocals; Linda McCartney: Keyboards

Song 154b title:
So High (Rock Me Baby, Roll Me Away)

Release date / Country:
Unreleased

Composer:
M. Williams

Kenney Jones: Lead Vocals & Drums; Al Kooper: Keyboards; Mentor Williams: Guitar; Denny Laine: Guitar & B. Vocals; Danny "Kootch" Kortchmar; Paul McCartney: Bass & (possible) B. Vocals; Linda McCartney: Keyboards

Drummer Kenney Jones was born September 16, 1948 in London, England *(see Ian McLagan, Rod Stewart)*. It was reported in Melody Maker on May 10, 1975, that Kenney Jones had cut a single in Los Angeles, produced by Mentor Williams with contributions from Paul and Linda McCartney*. According to Kenney Jones, Paul played bass on the songs ***So High (Rock Me Baby, Roll Me Away)*** and ***Baby Blue Eyes***, and might have sung backing vocals. Jones could not remember the studio where the songs were recorded, but thinks it might have been The Record Plant (West), or possibly Wally Heider Studios in Los Angeles. Unfortunately, these recordings remain unreleased.

Jones contributed to McCartney's ***Rockestra Theme*** and ***So Glad To See You Here*** from McCartney and Wings' **Back To The Egg** album. Jones was also a part of the Rockestra that backed McCartney and Wings when they performed the ***Rockestra Theme*** on December 29, 1979 at the Hammersmith Odeon Theatre in London, U.K. The benefit performance was released on the album **Concerts For The People Of Kampuchea**.

Paul Jones

Record 155 title:
And The Sun Will Shine / The Dog Presides
Label / Catalog number:
Columbia (EMI) / DB 8379
Jacket / Inserts:
Record label sleeve
Recording Location / Date:
EMI-Abbey Road Studios, London, England, U.K. / Feb 68
Media:
Single 7" (mono)
Producer:
Peter Asher

Song 155a title:
And The Sun Will Shine
Release date / Country:
08 Mar 68 / U.K.
Track details:
Side 1, track 1 / 3 min. 00 sec.
Composer:
R. Gibb - B. Gibb - M. Gibb

Paul Jones: Lead Vocals; Jeff Beck: Guitar; Paul Samwell-Smith: Bass; Nicky Hopkins: Keyboards; Paul McCartney: Drums; Clair Asher: B. Vocals; Dr. Richard Asher: B. Vocals; Mike Vickers: Arrangement and Conductor

Song 15b title:
The Dog Presides
Release date / Country:
08 Mar 68 / U.K.
Track details:
Side 1, track 2 / 2 min. 45 sec.
Composer:
P. Jones

Paul Jones: Lead Vocals & Harmonica; Paul Samwell-Smith: Bass; Jeff Beck: Guitar; Paul McCartney: Drums

Paul Jones was born Paul Pond on February 24, 1942 in Portsmouth, England. He was an original member, and the lead vocalist, of the British band Manfred Mann. Later members of the band would include Jack Bruce* *(see also Cream)* on bass, who was replaced by Klaus Voormann.

Klaus Voormann was born in Berlin, Germany on April 29, 1942. He and his girlfriend, Astrid Kirchherr, met The Beatles during their engagement at the Kaiserkeller Club in Hamburg in 1960. Astrid soon fell in love with The Beatles' bass player Stuart Sutcliffe, who later left The Beatles and remained in Germany with his fiancee Astrid to study painting. Voormann moved to England shortly after The Beatles became a worldwide success. He, along with Liverpool musicians Patty Chambers *(see The Escorts)* and Gibson Kemp *(see Rory Storm & The Hurricanes)*, formed the short-lived trio Patty, Klaus & Gibson, who were briefly managed by Brian Epstein. Voormann, who was also a gifted artist, received a Grammy Award for his design of The Beatles' **Revolver** album cover. When Paul McCartney announced he was leaving The Beatles, rumors circulated that Voormann might be drafted as a replacement. Voormann played bass on dozens of solo

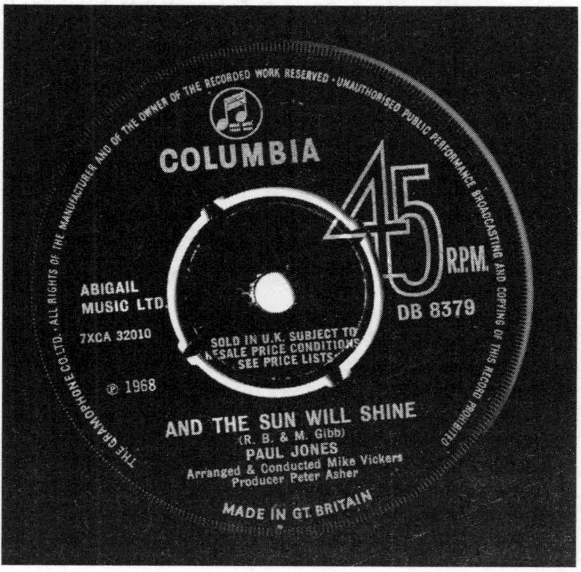

Klaus Voormann and Astrid Kirchherr at Beatlefest NY/NJ 1988, photo courtesy of Donna Doremus

Beatles recordings and designed the **Ringo** album lyric booklet. In 1984, Klaus and his group Trio covered the Yoko Ono song ***Wake Up***, included on her guest star Yoko Ono tribute album **Every Man Has A Woman** *(see Spirit Choir)*. Voormann designed the picture sleeve for George Harrison's 1988 single **When We Was Fab**, and was commissioned by The Beatles in 1995 to handle the art work for their **Anthology** project.

Paul Jones left Manfred Mann in 1966 to concentrate on solo music projects and an acting career. He had two hits ***High Time*** and ***Bad Boy***, and formed several more short-lived bands, including The Paul Jones Band. In 1968, he recorded The Bee Gees' song ***And The Sun Will Shine***, produced by Peter Asher *(see Peter & Gordon)* with an all-star line-up.

Asher mentioned to Jones that Paul McCartney, then dating his sister Jane, was looking to do some session work as a drummer and wondered if Jones was interested in having him play on his sessions. According to Jones, who accepted McCartney's offer, the sessions were completely arranged by Asher, who also brought along his sister Clair to play keyboards and their mother Margaret to sing backing vocals. Peter said, "Nicky Hopkins played keyboards, and Clair and my father sang backing vocals on ***And The Sun Will Shine***." Jones said, "McCartney also played drums on ***The Dog Presides***."

Jones has been quite active over the years working as a musician, disc jockey and actor. In 1979 he formed a band called The Blues Band, with which he still performs, and he recently reformed Manfred Mann with original members Tom McGuiness and Mike Hugg. Jones starred in the film **Privilege**, and has landed roles in stage productions of **Cats**, **Guys And Dolls**, **Hamlet**, **The Beggar's Opera**, **Conduct Unbecoming** and **Joseph and The Amazing Technicolor Dream Coat**.

Laurence Juber

Record 156 title:
Standard Time

Label / Catalog number:
Breaking Records / BREAK 1

Jacket / Inserts:
Unique / 1 page insert

Recording Location / Date:
Spirit of Ranachan, Scotland† & Air Studios London, England, U.K. / Jun 78† & 1979

Media:
Album 12"

Producer:
Laurence Juber & Richard Niles and Paul McCartney & Chris Thomas

Song 156a title:
Maisie

Release date / Country:
09 Jul 82 / U.S.A.

Track details:
Side 1, track 3 / 3 min. 10 sec.

Composer:
L. Juber

Laurence Juber: Guitars; Paul McCartney: Bass; Denny Laine: Harmonica; Steve Holly: Drums

Laurence Juber was born on November 12, 1952 in London, England. He was interested in music from an early age, and began playing guitar at eleven. He attended Goldsmith's College and the University of London and earned a bachelor's degree in music in 1975. Juber joined the National Youth Jazz Orchestra and moved on to session work backing Cleo Laine, Shirley Bassey, John Williams*, Jimmy Rafferty and others. He was cast as the backup guitarist for Denny Laine's appearance on the BBC's **David Essex Show**. Laine was sufficiently impressed to recommend him to McCartney.

Laurence Juber became the third and final lead guitarist for Paul McCartney's band Wings in the summer of 1978 as they began recordings for the album **Back To The Egg**. It proved to be Wings' last studio album. In November and December 1979, Juber and Wings toured the U.K., and in January 1980 they embarked on their fateful tour of Japan, doomed before it ever began. McCartney was found to be in possession of marijuana by customs officials at the airport in Tokyo and was briefly jailed then deported, forcing the tour's cancellation. McCartney began to pursue solo projects following his return to England. Wings was left hanging in midair before being set free by McCartney in 1981.

In early 1980, during the period Wings was in limbo, Juber went to work on an instrumental solo album of old standards titled **Standard Time**. All the songs were part of McCartney's publishing catalogue that he wanted Juber to record. The album was originally intended to be more of a demonstration record of Juber's talents than a commercial release. Following the breakup of Wings, Juber decided to independently release five of the standards on his Breaking Records label. The 1982 album, which kept its original title, was limited to 1,000 copies making it a difficult-to-obtain collectors' item.

One song on **Standard Time** is a Juber composition called ***Maisie***, recorded during the **Back To The Egg** album sessions, which featured McCartney on bass. According to Juber, McCartney was also involved in the production of ***Maisie***. Juber often guests at Beatles conventions where he sometimes performs ***Maisie***.

Juber also contributed guitar work to Ringo Starr's 1981 album **Stop and Smell The Roses**, and played on the soundtrack version of George Harrison's ***Breath Away From Heaven*** from **Shanghai Surprise** *(see Various Artists - Shanghai Surprise.)* He has released a number of solo albums since his departure from Wings. Jubu has produced and played on recordings for Al Stewart, with whom he has also toured. He has done music for TV's **As The World Turns**, and scores for his father-in-law Sherwood Schwartz, producer of such well-known TV series as Gilligan's Island and The Brady Bunch. Juber musically reunited with Denny Laine and Steve Holly, his fellow members in Wings, at Beatlefest '97 in the New York area.

Bobby Keys

Record 157 title:
Bobby Keys
Label / Catalog number:
Warner Bros / K 46141
Jacket / Inserts:
Unique / Record label inner sleeve
Recording Location / Date:
One or more of the following studios: Command, Island or Olympic, London, U.K. / Jan 72
Media:
Album 12"
Producer:
Bobby Keys, Andy Johns & Jim Gordon

Song 157a title:
Bootleg
Release date / Country:
07 Jul 72 / U.K.
Track details:
Side 1, track 3 / 3 min. 42 sec.
Composer:
C. Axton - D. Dunn - W. Jackson - I. Hayes

One or more of the following: Dave Mason: Guitar; Eric Clapton: Guitar; Klaus Voormann: Bass; Jim Price: Horns; Jim Gordon: Drums; Bobby Keys: Horns; Nicky Hopkins: Keyboards; Leslie West: Guitar; Felix Pappalardi: Keyboards; Corky Laing: Drums &/or Percussion; Jack Bruce: Bass; The Dixie Flyers; George Harrison (probable) Guitar; Ringo Starr: (probable) Drums

Saxophone player Bobby Keys has played on numerous solo Beatles albums including George Harrison's **All Things Must Pass**; John Lennon's **Rock 'N' Roll**, **Sometime In New York City**, and **Walls And Bridges**; and Ringo Starr's **Ringo** and **Goodnight Vienna**. He came to The Beatles' attention by way of Delaney & Bonnie & Friends*. After his stint with Delaney & Bonnie & Friends, Keys joined Joe Cocker's* band Mad Dogs And Englishmen. He has worked extensively with The Rolling Stones* over the last three decades, both on and off the road, and has worked with Keith Richards on some of his solo recordings. Ironically, Keys and Richards happen to share the same day, month and year of birth.

It was reported in the book **All Together Now** that Ringo played drums and Harrison played guitar on the **Bobby Keys** album. According to Wally Podrazik, one of the book's authors, the musician credits were listed on a sticker on a radio station copy of the album that he saw. It is difficult to tell just what songs George and Ringo may have contributed to because of the time that has passed and the style of those who play on the instrumental album. With contributions to the album from musicians like Jack Bruce*, Dave Mason*, Jim Price *(see All Occasion Brass Band)*, Jim Gordon, Nicky Hopkins*, Klaus Voormann *(see Paul Jones)* and Eric Clapton*, the likelihood of Harrison and / or Ringo's involvement increases. Clapton is known to play on ***Bootleg***, ***Command Performance***, ***Crispy Duck*** and ***Steal From A King***. According to Bobby Keys, Harrison and Ringo contributed to his album, but he was not certain on which track. However, Andy Johns (who admitted he was not present for all the sessions) and

Jim Price do not recall any Beatles at the sessions. After listening to the album, they both seriously doubt that Ringo or George contributed to the album. Jack Bruce also does not recall George or Ringo being at any of the sessions he attended. If Ringo and George did contribute to the album, it's probably on the song ***Bootleg***. The other tracks on the album are ***Sand & Foam***, ***Smokefoot***, ***Alter Rock*** and ***Key West***.

In 1972, Keys appeared in a musical scene in Nilsson and Ringo's film **Son Of Dracula**. Keys was one of a small stable of artists signed to Ringo Starr's short-lived Ring O'Records label in 1975, releasing the single ***Gimmie The Key / Honky Tonk (Parts 1 & 2)***. For a time, it was thought highly likely that Ringo was at least involved in the A-side, possibly background vocals and probably on drums and / or percussion. The drummer is listed as one Spider Webb. A promotional extended version of this record was issued (Ring O' / SPRO 8193) running 3 minutes, 54 seconds. Bobby Keys, and the record's producer Trevor Lawrence, seemed quite certain Ringo had nothing to do musically with this single.

Aashish Khan

Record 158 title:
None
Recording Location / Date:
Trident Studios, London, U.K. / 1969 or 1970

Song 158a title:
In Praise Of Lord (We Are All Children Of God)
Release date / Country:
Unreleased
Composer:
A. Khan

George Harrison: Guitar; Ringo Starr: Drums; Eric Clapton: Guitar

Record 159 title:
Young Master Of The Sarod
Media:
Album 12"
Label / Catalog number:
World Pacific / WPS-21444
Producer:
Richard Bock
Jacket / Inserts:
Standard international design with Gatefold with Liner Notes by George Harrison / Record label inner sleeve
Recording Location / Date:
Los Angeles, CA, U.S.A. / Aug 67

Song 159a title:
None
Release date / Country:
(probably) Oct 67 / U.S.A.
Composer:
A. Khan

Aashish Khan was born on December 5, 1939 in Maihar, India. He is the eldest son of Ali Akbar Khan. Aashish, like his famous father and grandfather Ustad Allauddin Khan, is a master of the sarod. Aashish has been featured in a number of performances with his famous father and grandfather since the age of twelve. During his career he has recorded a wide range of music that often fused his north Indian classical music with Western classical, jazz and pop music. He has composed music for a number of Indian and western films including **Breezy**, **The Man Who Would Be King**, **Gandhi** and **Passage To India**. In 1986, he was appointed by the Government of India as a Composer and Conductor for the National Orchestra known as Vadya Vrindya for the All India Radio, New Delhi. Khan has been a member of the Music Faculty of the Long Beach State College, and The Ali Akbar College Of Music in San Rafael, California. He has also served on the Music Faculty of The University Of Washington in Seattle and The University Of Calgary in Alberta, Canada, where he and his brother Pranesh founded the Allauddin School Of Performing Arts.

George Harrison, Aashish Khan and John Barham, Apple Studio, London, 1970, photo courtesy of Aashish Khan

Khan has worked with Ravi Shankar* (an uncle by marriage) and George Harrison. He is featured on the album **Shankar Family & Friends** produced by Harrison, and worked extensively with Harrison on the soundtrack for the film **Wonderwall**. Harrison wrote the liner notes for Khan's instrumental album **Young Master Of The Sarod** during a visit in early August 1967 to Ravi Shankar's Kinnara School of Indian Music in Los Angeles where Aashish taught.

Aashish said Harrison, Ringo Starr, Eric Clapton*, and a keyboard player helped him record a song tentatively titled ***In Praise Of Lord (We Are All Children Of God)*** that was a fusion of rock and Indian music sung in the Hindi language. Khan said the song was recorded at Trident Studios in London in 1969 or 1970, and was intended for a film soundtrack, but was never used.

B.B. King

Record 160 title:
In London
Label / Catalog number:
Beat Goes On / BGOCD42
Jacket / Inserts:
Standard international design in jewel box (printed in U.K.) / 2 page CD insert
Recording Location / Date:
Olympic Studios, London, U.K. / 09-16 Jun 71
Media:
Album 5" CD
Producer:
Ed Michel & Joe Zagarino

Song 160a title:
Ghetto Woman
Release date / Country:
Jan 91 (first issued 11 Oct 71) / France/U.K.
Track details:
Side 1, track 5 / 5 min. 13 sec.
Composer:
B.B. King - D. Clark

B.B. King: Lead Vocals & Guitar; Gary Wright: Piano; Jim Price: Electric Piano; Dr. John: Guitar; Klaus Voormann: Bass; Ringo Starr: Drums; Jim Gordon: Drums; Jimmie Haskell: String Arrangement & Conductor

Song 160b title:
Part-Time Love
Release date / Country:
Jan 91 (first issued 11 Oct 71) / France/U.K.
Track details:
Side 1, track 7 / 3 min. 17 sec.
Composer:
C. Hammond

B.B. King: Lead Vocals & Guitar; Gary Wright: Organ; Jim Price: Trumpet; Klaus Voormann: Bass; Ringo Starr: Drums; Bobby Keys: Tenor Saxophone

Song 160c title:
Wet Hayshark
Track details:
Side 1, track 6 / 2 min. 31 sec.

Release date / Country:
Jan 91 (first issued 11 Oct 71) / France/U.K.

Composer:
G. Wright

B.B. King: Lead Vocals & Guitar; Gary Wright: Piano; Jim Price: Trumpet; Klaus Voormann: Bass; Ringo Starr: Drums; Bobby Keys: Tenor Saxophone; Jim Gordon: Drums

B. B. King, Detroit, MI, mid-1970s, photo courtesy of Tom Bert

B.B. King was born Riley B. King on September 16, 1925 in Itta Bene, Mississippi in the heart of delta blues country. His background and early career were typical of most of America's great delta blues artists – his youth was spent working the cotton fields and singing in his church choir – before moving on to street singing in the mid-1940s. In the early-1950s, he was a DJ on an R&B radio station in Memphis and was dubbed by friends "The Beale Street Blues Boy" before the nickname was shortened to "B.B." King topped the R&B charts with the song ***Three O'Clock Blues*** in 1951. By the mid-1950s, he was playing countless one-night stands on the blues club circuit. By the 1960s, he had a cult following, and soon gained international recognition with R&B hits like ***Paying The Cost To Be The Boss*** and ***Why I Sing The Blues***. King even had a hit in the pop charts with ***The Thrill Is Gone*** in 1970.

In June 1971, King went to London, England to record his album **In London** with many of rock's and blues' elite helping, including among others Ringo Starr. It was reported in Melody Maker magazine that John Lennon was also scheduled to attend the sessions, but did not make it back from the U.S. in time. Portions of the session were also filmed. Unfortunately, the CD issue of this album does not contain the liner notes, detailed credits, or the photo of Ringo Starr that were included in the gatefold of the vinyl LP (ABC / ABCX-730). B.B. King was inducted into the Blues Foundation Hall of Fame in 1984 and the Rock and Roll Hall of Fame in 1987. He continues to tour, record and work with blues and rock artists.

Solomon King

Record 161 title:
A Hundred Years or More

Label / Catalog number:
Capitol / 2622

Recording Location / Date:
EMI-Abbey Road Studios, London, U.K. / 09 Jul 68

Media:
Single 7"

Jacket / Inserts:
Record label sleeve

Song 161a title:
A Hundred Years Or More

Release date / Country:
(probably) Aug 69 / U.S.A.

Track details:
Side 1, track 1 / 2 min. 55 sec.

Composer:
Tobias

Solomon King: Lead Vocals; Ringo Starr: (possible) Tambourine

Record 162 title: Somewhere In The Crowd / Hava Nagila	***Media:*** Single 7" (mono)
Label / Catalog number: Columbia (EMI) / DB 8454	***Jacket / Inserts:*** Record label sleeve
Recording Location / Date: EMI-Abbey Road Studios, London, U.K. / (probably) 09 Jul 68	

Song 162a title:
Hava Nagila
Release date / Country:
1968 / U.K.

Track details:
Side 2, track 1 / 3 min. 10 sec.
Composer:
Trad Arranged by Solomon King

Solomon King: Lead Vocals; Charles Blackwell: Conductor; Ringo Starr: (probable) Hand Claps & (possible) B. Vocals & (possible) Tambourine

Song 162b title:
Somewhere In The Crowd
Release date / Country:
1968 / U.K.

Track details:
Side 1, track 1 / 2 min. 40 sec.
Composer:
L. Reed - Rae

Solomon King: Lead Vocals; Les Reed: Conductor & Arrangement; Ringo Starr: (possible) B. Vocals

Solomon King is a traditional orchestra crooner in the Tom Jones and Engelbert Humperdinck vein, but he is an American. He had a minor hit in 1968 with ***She Wears My Ring***. King is better known in England than in America.

There is much confusion surrounding possible contributions by Ringo Starr to his recordings. Over the years, publications of varying reliability have reported Ringo as possibly contributing background vocals, drums, tambourine and / or hand claps to Kings' recordings of ***A Hundred Years Or More***, ***Hava Nagila*** and ***Somewhere In The Crowd***.

The Beatles Book monthly magazine, a generally reliable source, first reported in its September 1968 issue that Ringo attended a Solomon King recording session on July 9 at EMI's Abbey Road

Solomon King is a traditional orchestra crooner in the Tom Jones and Engelbert Humperdinck vein, but he is an American. He had a minor hit in 1968 with ***She Wears My Ring***. King is better known in England than in America.

There is much confusion surrounding possible contributions by Ringo Starr to his recordings. Over the years, publications of varying reliability have reported Ringo as possibly contributing background vocals, drums, tambourine and / or hand claps to Kings' recordings of ***A Hundred Years Or More***, ***Hava Nagila*** and ***Somewhere In The Crowd***.

The Beatles Book monthly magazine, a generally reliable source, first reported in its September 1968 issue that Ringo attended a Solomon King recording session on July 9 at EMI's Abbey Road Studios, to add a bit of hand clapping while waiting for the rest of The Beatles to arrive. Noted Beatles researcher and author, Mark Lewisohn, checked into Abbey Road Studios' files and found that King recorded the song ***A Hundred Years Or More*** on that that date. There is a prominent tambourine throughout this otherwise heavily orchestrated production leaving one to wonder if Ringo did not play that instrument. However, it contains no audible hand clapping.

King's recording of ***Hava Nagila*** does contain hand clapping, and may also include Ringo playing tambourine and / or singing in the background. The A-side of that single, ***Somewhere In The Crowd***, has been rumored to feature Ringo on background vocals, but it may have been confused with B-side. It's also possible that Ringo added some drumming to these recordings, though it sounds unlikely.

Ringo is probably involved in at least one of these recordings in some capacity. Considering the evidence and repeated listening, it seems likely that Ringo did the hand claps and possibly background vocals and / or tambourine on ***Hava Nagila***, and (possibly) tambourine on ***A Hundred Years Or More***. ***A Hundred Years Or More*** was originally issued in the U.K. as the B-side of King's single ***Goodbye My Old Gal*** (Columbia / DB 8505).

Billy J. Kramer with The Dakotas

Record 163 title:
The Best Of Billy J. Kramer & The Dakotas
Label / Catalog number:
Imperial / CDP-7-96055-2
Jacket / Inserts:
Unique in Jewel box / 12 page CD booklet
Media:
Album 5" CD
Producer:
George Martin

Song 163a title:
Bad To Me
Release date / Country:
08 Oct 91 (first issued 26 Jul 63) / U.S.A.
Recording Location / Date:
EMI-Abbey Road Studios, London, U.K. / 27 Jun 63
Track details:
Side 1, track 3 / 2 min. 18 sec.
Composer:
J. Lennon - P. McCartney

Billy J. Kramer: Lead Vocals; Tony Mansfield: Drums; Mike Maxfield: Lead Guitar; Robin MacDonald: Rhythm Guitar; Ray Jones: Bass

Song 163b title:
Do You Want To Know A Secret?
Release date / Country:
08 Oct 91 (first issued 26 Apr 63) / U.S.A.
Track details:
Side 1, track 1 / 1 min. 59 sec.
Composer:
J. Lennon - P. McCartney

Recording Location / Date:
EMI-Abbey Road Studios, London, U.K. / 21 Mar 63

Billy J. Kramer: Lead Vocals; Tony Mansfield: Drums; Mike Maxfield: Lead Guitar; Robin MacDonald: Rhythm Guitar; Ray Jones: Bass; George Martin: Piano

Song 163c title:
From A Window
Release date / Country:
08 Oct 91 (first issued 17 Jul 64) / U.S.A.
Recording Location / Date:
EMI-Abbey Road Studios, London, U.K. / 29 May 64
Track details:
Side 1, track 12 / 1 min. 53 sec.
Composer:
J. Lennon - P. McCartney

Billy J. Kramer: Lead Vocals; Tony Mansfield: Drums; Mike Maxfield: Lead Guitar; Robin MacDonald: Rhythm Guitar; Ray Jones: Bass; Paul McCartney: B. Vocals

Song 163d title:
I Call Your Name
Release date / Country:
08 Oct 91 (first issued 26 Jul 63) / U.S.A.
Recording Location / Date:
EMI-Abbey Road Studios, London, U.K. / 27 Jun 63
Track details:
Side 1, track 4 / 2 min. 21 sec.
Composer:
J. Lennon - P. McCartney

Billy J. Kramer: Lead Vocals; Tony Mansfield: Drums; Mike Maxfield: Lead Guitar; Robin MacDonald: Rhythm Guitar; Ray Jones: Bass

Song 163e title:
I'll Be On My Way
Release date / Country:
08 Oct 91 (first issued 26 Apr 63) / U.S.A.
Recording Location / Date:
EMI-Abbey Road Studios, London, U.K. / 21 Mar 63
Track details:
Side 1, track 2 / 1 min. 37 sec.
Composer:
J. Lennon - P. McCartney

Billy J. Kramer: Lead Vocals; Tony Mansfield: Drums; Mike Maxfield: Lead Guitar; Robin MacDonald: Rhythm Guitar; Ray Jones: Bass

Song 163f title:
I'll Keep You Satisfied
Release date / Country:
08 Oct 91 (first issued 01 Nov 63) / U.S.A.
Recording Location / Date:
EMI-Abbey Road Studios, London, U.K. / 14 Oct 63
Track details:
Side 1, track 8 / 2 min. 05 sec.
Composer:
J. Lennon - P. McCartney

Billy J. Kramer: Lead Vocals; Tony Mansfield: Drums; Mike Maxfield: Lead Guitar; Robin MacDonald: Rhythm Guitar; Ray Jones: Bass

Song 163g title:
I'm In Love
Release date / Country:
08 Oct 91 (first issued 08 Oct 91) / U.S.A.
Track details:
Side 1, track 9 / 3 min. 40 sec.
Composer:
J. Lennon - P. McCartney

Recording Location / Date:
EMI-Abbey Road Studios, London, U.K. / 14 Oct 63

Billy J. Kramer: Lead Vocals; Tony Mansfield: Drums; Mike Maxfield: Lead Guitar; Robin MacDonald: Rhythm Guitar; Ray Jones: Bass; John Lennon: Voice

Billy J. Kramer was born William Howard Ashton on August 19, 1943 in Bootle (Liverpool), England. His stage name was Billy J. Kramer ("J" for Julian, at the suggestion of John Lennon) *(see Julian Lennon.)* He began his musical career fronting a band called Billy Forde & The Phantoms, who performed regularly around the Liverpool area. Kramer then fronted another local band called The Coasters, but when The Coasters refused to turn professional for new manager, Brian Epstein, Epstein recruited the popular Manchester band The Dakotas. The Dakotas originally consisted of Mike Maxfield, Ray Jones, Robin MacDonald and Tony (Brookbinder) Mansfield. Though usually billed as Billy J. Kramer & The Dakotas the official name was Billy J. Kramer with The Dakotas.

Billy J. Kramer's success was directly linked to The Beatles. He had the same manager, the same producer, the same label, and used the same studio – but, most importantly, four of his five U.K. top tens were composed by Lennon and McCartney. Kramer recorded no less than seven Lennon and McCartney compositions – four of which, ***Bad To Me***, ***I'll Keep You Satisfied***, ***From A Window*** and ***I'm In Love***, have yet to be officially released by The Beatles. The other three are ***Do You Want To Know A Secret?***, ***I Call Your Name*** and ***I'll Be On My Way***. ***I Call Your Name*** was recorded and released by The Beatles nearly a year after Kramer's version. ***I'll Be On My Way*** was officially released by The Beatles on the **Live At The BBC** album in 1994. Acetate demos of John and Paul performing ***Bad To Me*** and ***I'll Be On My Way*** are known to still exist.

In the liner notes to **The Best Of Billy J. Kramer & The Dakotas** CD, Kramer recounted listening to the demo John Lennon made for him of ***Do You Want To Know A Secret?*** – "I had this tape given to me, and it was John Lennon singing it with an acoustic guitar. On the tape he said, 'I'm sorry for the sound quality, but it's the quietest room I could find in the whole building.' Then he flushed the toilet." ***Do You Want To Know A Secret?*** is considered a Beatles' composition contribution to Kramer, even though it was recorded and released after The Beatles version, because there is little dispute that it was specifically intended for Kramer. (Epstein reportedly offered Shane Fenton [aka Alvin Stardust] a chance to record the song first if he signed with Epstein. Fenton was already managed by someone else, and turned down Epstein's offer.) Kramer first recorded the song on March 14, 1963, but had to return to the studio a week later to re-record the song because his voice cracked on the only usable version they had. This, no doubt, delayed the single's release. The take with the crack in Kramer's voice from March 14 was mistakenly released in Holland in the late 1960s on the album **The Mersey And The Beat**, part of EMI's **History Of British Pop** Series, Volume One. It is also noticeable by the absence of George Martin's* piano overdub.

On October 14, 1963, John Lennon joined George Martin in the control room to help Kramer on ***I'll Keep You Satisfied*** and ***I'm In Love***. One can even hear Lennon talking during the false take intro of ***I'm In Love***, and George Martin commenting on how Kramer can shout at Lennon on the upcoming Beatles recording session. Unfortunately, Kramer's version of ***I'm In Love*** was left in the vaults for some eighteen years. The song was instead first released by another Epstein-managed and George Martin-produced group, The Fourmost*, who had a top 20 with it. (***I'll Keep You Satisfied*** has since been covered by Sugar Simone, Swallows, Roger Webb Trio, and The Saltbee; ***I'll Be On My Way*** has since been covered by the Rockin' Ramrods, and The Saltbee; ***From A Window*** has since been covered by Chad & Jeremy, and The Saltbee; ***I'm In Love*** has since been covered by The Saltbee; and ***Bad To Me*** has since been covered by Leif Garrett, Les Challengers, Les Missiles, Liverpool, Lynn, The Saltbee, William Tay, Vince Taylor, and Bobby Vee.)

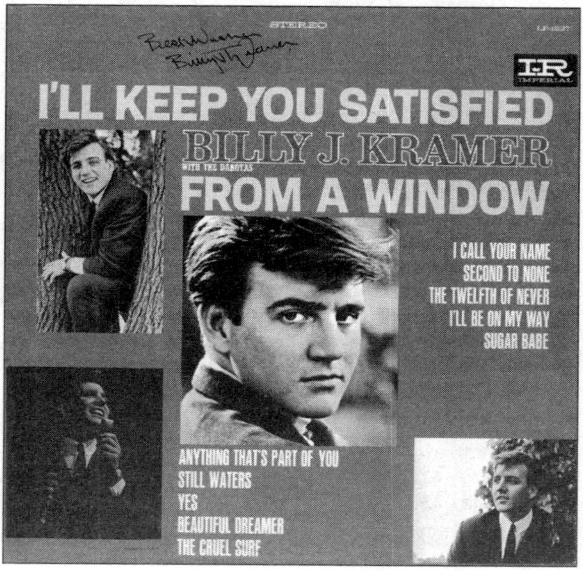

Kramer and The Dakotas were one of the featured acts in The Beatles' 1963 Christmas Shows. The Dakotas also recorded without Kramer and had a U.K. top 20 in 1964 with the instrumental ***The Cruel Sea***. In the latter half of 1964, Jones left the band and was replaced on guitar by Mick Green (who later worked with McCartney on his 1988 album **Choba B CCCP** – the Russian album) from the group Johnny Kidd & The Pirates, with MacDonald moving to bass. Time was not in Billy J. Kramer's favor. The novelty of the British music invasion of 1964 had grown old. Lennon and McCartney were donating less and less music to Epstein's other artists. Kramer would continue to record with The Dakotas until 1967, but without much chart success.

There has always been speculation about whether The Beatles played on any of Kramer's recordings. Lennon and McCartney handed over demos and coached Kramer on the arrangements of their songs, and they did attend some of his sessions. Some publications claim that McCartney plays piano on, and may have helped write, ***Little Children***. The Beatles were performing a three-week engagement in Paris, France at the time the song was supposed to have been recorded. According to Kramer, McCartney had nothing to do with the composition, and the piano was played by George Martin.

John and Paul struggled in their hotel room in Paris, France to compose another song for Kramer called ***One And One Is Two***. Lennon thought so little of the song that upon its completion, that he remarked that if Kramer recorded the song, his career would be finished. Kramer wisely chose to pass on the song, and it was offered to The Strangers with Mike Shannon*, whose version failed in the charts. The song was also offered to The Fourmost*.

The Best Of Billy J. Kramer & The Dakotas claims that Lennon and McCartney contributed background vocals at the end of ***From A Window***. According to Kramer, McCartney sang the high note at the end of the song because he was unable to reach it. McCartney has also confirmed that he sang the high note at the end.

After The Dakotas, Kramer worked with The Remo Four*. Kramer has continued on and off with a solo career over the last three decades, sometimes under his real name, or with a newly formed Dakotas, but there have not been any hits. Kramer has also occasionally made guest appearances at Beatles conventions. The Dakotas regrouped with original members Mansfield and Maxfield around 1990 and worked with Kramer in 1996.

Denny Laine

Record 164 title:
Holly Days
Label / Catalog number:
Capitol / ST 11588
Jacket / Inserts:
Standard international design / Custom inner-sleeve with photos of Paul McCartney
Recording Location / Date:
Rude Studios, Kintyre, Scotland, U.K. / 1976
Media:
Album 12"
Producer:
Paul McCartney

Song 164a title:
Fool's Paradise
Release date / Country:
19 May 77 / U.S.A.
Track details:
Side 1, track 5 / 2 min. 46 sec.
Composer:
N. Petty - S. LeGlaire - H. Linsley

Denny Laine: Lead Vocals; Paul McCartney: (all) Instruments & B. Vocals; Linda McCartney: B. Vocals

Song 164b title:
Heartbeat
Release date / Country:
19 May 77 / U.S.A.
Track details:
Side 1, track 1 / 2 min. 37 sec.
Composer:
B. Montgomery - N. Petty

Denny Laine: Lead Vocals; Paul McCartney: (all) Instruments & B. Vocals

Song 164c title:
I'm Gonna Love You Too
Release date / Country:
19 May 77 / U.S.A.
Track details:
Side 1, track 4 / 2 min. 15 sec.
Composer:
J. Mauldin - N. Petty - N. Sullivan

Denny Laine: Lead Vocals; Paul McCartney: (all) Instruments & B. Vocals

Song 164d title:
I'm Looking For Someone To Love
Release date / Country:
19 May 77 / U.S.A.
Track details:
Side 1, track 4 / 3 min. 57 sec.
Composer:
N. Petty - B. Holly

Paul McCartney: (all) Instruments

Song 164e title:
[Medley] It's So Easy / Listen To Me
Release date / Country:
19 May 77 / U.S.A.
Track details:
Side 2, track 1 / 3 min. 47 sec.
Composer:
B. Holly - N. Petty / N. Petty - C. Hardin

Denny Laine: Lead Vocals; Paul McCartney: (all) Instruments & B. Vocals; Linda McCartney: B. Vocals

Song 164f title:
Lonesome Tears
Release date / Country:
19 May 77 / U.S.A.
Track details:
Side 1, track 6 / 3 min. 05 sec.
Composer:
B. Holly

Paul McCartney: (all) Instruments

Song 164g title:
Look At Me
Release date / Country:
19 May 77 / U.S.A.
Track details:
Side 2, track 2 / 3 min. 10 sec.
Composer:
J.Allison - B. Holly - N. Petty

Denny Laine: Lead Vocals; Paul McCartney: (all) Instruments & B. Vocals

Song 164h title:
Moondreams
Release date / Country:
19 May 77 / U.S.A.
Track details:
Side 1, track 2 / 2 min. 41 sec.
Composer:
N. Petty

Denny Laine: Lead Vocals; Paul McCartney: (all) Instruments & B. Vocals

Song 164i title:
Rave On
Release date / Country:
19 May 77 / U.S.A.
Track details:
Side 1, track 3 / 1 min. 53 sec.
Composer:
N. Petty - B. Tilghman - S. West

Denny Laine: Vocals; Paul McCartney: Vocals & (all) Instruments; Linda McCartney: Vocals

Song 164j title:
Take Your Time
Release date / Country:
19 May 77 / U.S.A.
Track details:
Side 2, track 3 / 3 min. 38 sec.
Composer:
N. Petty - B. Holly

Denny Laine: Lead Vocals; Paul McCartney: (all) Instruments & B. Vocals

Record 165 title:
Japanese Tears
Media:
Album 5" CD
Label / Catalog number:
Intertape / B-80077/500.001
Jacket / Inserts:
Unique in Jewel box (printed in Switzerland) / CD insert (printed in Switzerland)

Song 165a title:
I Would Only Smile
Track details:
Side 1, track 12 / 3 min. 17 sec.
Release date / Country:
1986 (first issued 05 Dec 80) / Japan/Switzerland
Composer:
D. Laine
Producer:
Denny Laine & (probably) Paul McCartney
Recording Location / Date:
(probably) Morgan Studios, London, U.K. / (probably) Mar 72 thru Oct 72 or (possibly) 1973

Denny Laine: Lead Vocals & Guitar; Paul McCartney: Bass & B. Vocals; Henry McCullough: Guitar; Denny Seiwell: Drums; Linda McCartney: B. Vocals & (probable) Keyboards

Song 165b title:
Send Me The Heart
Track details:
Side 1, track 4 / 3 min. 36 sec.
Release date / Country:
1986 (first issued 05 Dec 80) / Japan/Switzerland
Composer:
P. McCartney - D. Laine
Producer:
Denny Laine & (probably) Paul McCartney
Recording Location / Date:
Soundshop Studios, Nashville, TN, U.S.A. / Jun or Jul 74

Denny Laine: Vocals; Paul McCartney: Bass & Vocals; Linda McCartney: B. Vocals; Buddy Emmens: Steel Guitar & Acoustic Guitar; Floyd Cramer: Piano; Geoff Britton: (possible) Drums

Song 165c title:
Weep For Love
Track details:
Side 1, track 13 / 4 min. 29 sec.
Release date / Country:
1986 (first issued 05 Dec 80) / Japan/Switzerland
Composer:
D. Laine
Producer:
Denny Laine, Paul McCartney & (probably) Chris Thomas
Recording Location / Date:
Lympne Castle, Kent, U.K. / 11-29 Sep 78

Denny Laine: Lead Vocals & Guitar; Paul McCartney: B. Vocals & Bass; Laurence Juber: Guitar; Steve Holly: Drums & B. Vocals; Linda McCartney: B. Vocals

Record 166 title:
Somewhere In England
Label / Catalog number:
Pegboy / 1005 [Unauthorized Records]
Jacket / Inserts:
Unique in slipcase in Jewel box / 32 page CD booklet
Recording Location / Date:
National Exhibition Centre in Birmingham, U.K. / 15 Mar 86
Media:
Album 5" CD
Producer:
Unknown-audience recording

Song 166a title:
Johnny B. Goode
Release date / Country:
Jul 96 / Australia
Track details:
Side 1, track 25 / 3 min. 49 sec.
Composer:
C. Berry

Denny Laine: Vocals & Guitar; George Harrison: Vocals & Guitar; Noddy Holder: Vocals; Robert Plant: Vocals; probably the following: Justin Hayward, Ray Thomas, Patrick Moraz, Graeme Edge, John Lodge, Jeff Lynne, Roy Wood, Members of UB40 (Astro, James Brown, Ali Campbell, Robin Campbell, Earl Falconer, Norman Hassan, Brian Travers, Mickey Virtue), Jasper Carrot, Jimmy Tarbuck, Richard Tandy & Bev Bevan

Denny Laine was born Brian Frederick Hines on October 29, 1944 on a boat off Jersey in the Channel Islands, but was raised in Birmingham, England. His father was boxer "Herbo" Hines. His professional name was the result of a childhood nickname, Denny, given to him by his friends due to his fondness for a play den in his parents' garden. Laine was chosen in tribute to Cleo Laine. Laine's first musical inspiration was Buddy Holly, whose music motivated him to take up guitar as a teenager.

Laine first joined a local band Johnny & The Dominators as lead singer. Laine formed the band Denny & The Diplomats in 1960 that shared a bill with The Beatles at the Plaza Ballroom,Old Hill, England on July 5, 1963.

In May 1964 Laine disbanded the Diplomats. He formed The Moody Blues with Ray Thomas, Mike Pinder, Clint Warwick and Graeme Edge. Thomas was a member of El Riot & The Rebels, a band that often opened for The Beatles. Mike Pinder was also a member of El Riot and the band The Crewcats. The Crewcats were a regular act at The Top Ten Club in Hamburg, Germany at the same time as The Beatles. The Moody Blues' first top 10 and a number one in the U.K. was a cover of Bessie Banks' R&B hit ***Go Now*** in 1965, featuring Laine on lead vocals. (Laine would later perform the song along with ***Richard Corey*** on Wings' 1975 / 76 world tour.) The group was briefly signed with Brian Epstein's management company NEMS Enterprises, and was one of the acts billed on The Beatles' British tour in December 1965. The Moody Blues broke up on October 13, 1966, but quickly reformed, replacing Denny Laine and Clint Warwick with John Lodge from El Riot and Justin Hayward. The Moody Blues transformed themselves into a heavily orchestrated psychedelic band, radically different and more successful than their previous incarnation.

Laine signed a solo deal and wrote and released a single, ***Say You Don't Mind*** (a song he sometimes performed in concert with Wings), in April 1967. It failed to ignite his solo career, though it would later become a hit for Colin Blunstone. Soon after, Laine formed The Electric String Band. In 1969, he joined ex-Move member Trevor Burton in the band Balls.

In July 1971, Laine got a call from an old admirer, Paul McCartney, asking if he would like to join his new band Wings. It was not a difficult decision; he had known and liked The Beatles both personally and professionally for years. His flight with Wings would last a decade, and he was the only original member left when McCartney decided to break up the band. Laine was instrumental in recruiting fellow Wings members Laurence Juber*, Steve Holly and Henry McCullough. Laine stuck by McCartney while other members came and departed.

Laine composed and sang lead vocals on the Wings' songs ***Time To Hide*** and ***Again And Again And***

Again, and sang lead vocals on ***I Lie Around*** and ***The Note You Never Wrote***. He co-composed and sang lead or duet vocals on several of the following – ***No Words***, ***London Town***, ***Children Children***, ***Mull Of Kintyre***, ***Deliver Your Children***, ***Don't Let It Bring You Down***, ***Morse Moose And The Grey Goose*** and ***Rainclouds***. McCartney and Wings' live and studio recordings featuring Laine on lead vocals are not considered contributions by McCartney to Laine unless those recordings were released as Denny Laine recordings. Laine played guitar on most of Wings' recordings, including those under a variety of pseudonyms. He would guest with McCartney on several other artists' recordings including Paul's brother Mike (McCartney) McGear's album. Denny also contributed to ***All Those Years Ago***, George Harrison's 1981 tribute song to John Lennon. On November 30, 1973, Denny Laine issued his first solo album titled **Ahh...Laine!**. The jacket featured a photo of him wearing a Wings T-shirt but, according to Denny, McCartney did not contribute to the album.

In 1977, McCartney, having recently acquired most of Buddy Holly's publishing catalogue, began recording the instrumental backing tracks for an album of Holly songs at his home studio in Kintyre, Scotland. Laine supplied the lead vocals with Paul and Linda *(see Linda McCartney)* harmonizing on what would be Laine's second solo album, **Holly Days**. McCartney produced the album, but according to Laine, it was originally scheduled to be produced by Ray Stevens, best known for his novelty songs, and recorded in Nashville, Tennessee with local musicians. Laine recalled, "Ray Stevens couldn't do the session at the time we wanted, and I think Paul was just bored up in Scotland one day and had a go at the tracks." Laine said McCartney played all the instruments on the album. A bootleg CD titled **2 Buddies On Holly Days** (Library / 2323) contains slightly different (unfinished) versions of the **Holly Days** album.

A number of bootleg CDs contain unreleased Paul McCartney And Wings songs featuring Laine on lead vocals including ***Takin' On A Woman***, ***Old Man Loving'***, the old Moody Blues' number ***I've Got A Dream***, ***Find A Way Somehow*** from **Ahh...Laine!**, and ***Luxi***, an ode to Radio Luxenburg. These songs probably represent only a small portion of the recordings that exist in the McCartney tape archives that prominently feature Laine. It's difficult to say whether any of these recordings were ever considered for a solo release by Laine.

Laine reportedly began to harbor some resentment towards McCartney because he felt he was being underpaid, especially for his writing contribution to Wings' 1977 smash hit ***Mull Of Kintyre***. The real split began as a result of McCartney's arrest for marijuana possession in Japan on January 16, 1980, which forced the cancellation of the Wings' world tour. While McCartney remained in a Japanese jail cell, the male members of the band returned to England, no doubt concerned about lost revenues and their future. Shortly after McCartney's return to England, he released his second full-fledged solo album, **McCartney II**, recorded the previous year. Wings members' worst fears were realized when McCartney decided to use a vast array of famous musicians for his next album **Tug Of War**, mostly recorded at George Martin's* AIR Studios in Montserrat, West Indies in early 1981. Although Denny Laine participated in the recordings (some of which were included on McCartney's album **Pipes Of Peace**), tensions mounted, and Laine decided to sever his uncertain association with McCartney.

McCartney became reluctant to tour after John Lennon's death in December 1980. He also had difficulties securing visas as a result of his numerous arrests for marijuana, and desired to rid himself of the restraints and responsibilities of a band. On April 27, 1981, McCartney officially ended the Wings chapter of his career.

During 1980, Denny Laine wrote and recorded the song ***Japanese Tears***, inspired by the aborted tour earlier in the year, and helped his wife Jo Jo launch a recording career. Laine was also preparing his solo album **Japanese Tears** (since reissued under numerous titles, including **In Flight**). The album was a compilation of Wings' leftovers ***I Would Only Smile*** (from the **Red Rose Speedway** album sessions), ***Send Me The Heart*** (from sessions in Nashville in 1974) and ***Weep For Love*** (a track from the **Back To The Egg** album sessions). These particular recordings are considered McCartney contributions to Laine because they were officially released first under Laine's name. The album also included some re-recorded material with his new touring band (consisting of wife Jo Jo, Steve Holly, Mike Piggott, Andy Richards, and Gordon Sellar) and solo tracks, some recorded at Ringo Starr's home, Startling Studios (formerly John Lennon's Ascot Sound Studios). Though the album credits Laine as the sole producer, McCartney had a hand in the original production of the numbers involving Wings. Chris Thomas, who helped produce the album **The Beatles** (white album), was probably also involved in the production of ***Weep For Love***. Unfortunately, the CD issue of **Japanese Tears** does not include a photo insert sheet with pictures of Paul McCartney found on the U.K. LP (Scratch / SCR L 5001.)

Laine Hines, David Peel, Denny Laine and Jo Jo Laine, Beatlefest NY/NJ, 1997, photo by Kristofer Engelhardt

Chances for a Laine and McCartney reunion may have been dashed forever when a series of less than flattering remarks about McCartney that were attributed to Laine turned up in the tabloids in 1983 and 1984. Denny refutes, stating "I have never said anything publicly that would imply that there were disagreements over money, or that I didn't have the greatest respect and love for the McCartneys. We were very close friends, and I blame certain so-called friends in the media for turning us into enemies."

In 1985, Laine contributed to **The Crowd*** single in aid of the Bradford City Disaster Fund. Paul McCartney also contributed to **The Crowd** single.

On March 15, 1986, George Harrison joined Laine, The Moody Blues and Robert Plant onstage for renditions of ***Johnny B. Goode*** and ***Money (That's What I Want)*** at the National Exhibition Centre in Birmingham, U.K. for the charity concert **Heartbeat '86**. The concert was organized by ELO's *(see Jeff Lynne)* drummer Bev Bevan. The performance was broadcast December 10, 1986 in the U.S. on MTV. ***Johnny B. Goode*** has appeared on a number of bootleg records. Laine employed Ringo's son, drummer Zak Starkey, on one of his recordings in the late 1980s.

McCartney, probably feeling some regrets, and knowing how the tabloid press can greatly distort and exploit, sent out an invitation to Laine to attend his performance in Worcester, Massachusetts during his 1990 would tour. Laine said, "I went to visit the tour in Boston. I arrived late and didn't get a chance to go backstage. I waited around afterwards, but they had left early to miss the crowds, which was always the normal procedure."

Laine is in the process of writing his side of the story of why Wings broke up, and said there are many more reasons than those usually mentioned. Laine continues to write, record, and release recordings. In 1997 he released **Wings At The Speed Of Denny Laine**, an album that consists mostly of covers of Wings songs with which he is associated. Laine has also been a guest at several Beatles conventions, but he has yet to recapture the level of success he enjoyed during his years with Paul McCartney.

Billy Lawrie

Record 167 title:
Ship Imagination
Label / Catalog number:
RCA / SF 8395
Jacket / Inserts:
Unique with Gatefold / 4 page lyric insert
Recording Location / Date:
Startling Studios, Ascot, U.K. / (probably) May 73

Media:
Album 12"
Producer:
Gary Osborne & Billy Lawrie

Song 167a title:
Rock & Roller
Release date / Country:
29 Oct 73 / U.K.

Track details:
Side 1, track 2 / 3 min. 35 sec.
Composer:
B. Lawrie - R. Starkey

Billy Lawrie: Lead Vocals; Ronnie Leahy: Keyboards; Jimmy McCulloch; Colin Allen: Drums; Steve Thompson: Bass; Roger Ball: Horns; Malcolm Duncan: Horns; Ray Cooper: Percussion: Mags Maclint: B. Vocals; Lulu: B. Vocals; Liza Strike: B. Vocals

Billy Lawrie is the brother of British songstress Lulu. Lawrie and Ringo worked together for a time during the early 1970s. They composed an unreleased song called ***Where Are You Going***, and another song called ***Rock & Roller*** that was included on Lawrie's album **Ship Imagination**. The album also included a cover of The Beatles' song ***I Feel Fine***. Jimmy McCulloch, who was a member of Paul McCartney's band Wings in the mid-1970s, performs on the album under the pseudonym, Jimmy McAnonymous. (Lawrie's brother-in-law at the time was Maurice Gibb, one of the three brothers in the trio The Bee Gees. Gibb reportedly recorded an album's worth of synthesizer music around 1969 with Ringo, including a song called ***Modulating Maurice***, but apparently none of these recordings have ever surfaced.)

Alvin Lee

Record 168 title:
Detroit Diesel
Label / Catalog number:
Bellaphon / 290.07.093
Jacket / Inserts:
Standard international design in jewel box / 4 page CD booklet
Recording Location / Date:
Space Studios, Buckinghamshire, U.K.
Media:
Album 5" CD
Producer:
Alvin Lee

Song 168a title:
Talk Don't Bother Me
Release date / Country:
1987 (first issued 1986) / Germany
Track details:
Side 1, track 4 / 3 min. 36 sec.
Composer:
A. Lee

Alvin Lee: Lead Vocals, Guitar, Drums & Bass; Tim Hinkley: Hammond Organ; George Harrison: Slide Guitar

Record 169 title:
Nineteeninetyfour
Label / Catalog number:
Thunderbolt/Magnum Music Group / CDTB 150
Jacket / Inserts:
Unique / 4 page CD booklet
Recording Location / Date:
(probably) Space Studios, Buckinghamshire, U.K. / (probably) 1993
Media:
Album 5" CD
Producer:
Nigel Molden (Executive Producer)

Song 169a title:
I Want You (She's So Heavy)
Release date / Country:
Dec 93 / U.K.
Track details:
Side 1, track 12 / 9 min. 52 sec.
Composer:
J. Lennon - P. McCartney

Alvin Lee: Lead Vocals & Guitar; Steve Gould: Bass & B. Vocals; George Harrison: Slide Guitar; Alan Young: Drums; Steve Grant: Keyboards & B. Vocals

Song 169b title:
The Bluest Blues
Release date / Country:
Dec 93 / U.K.
Track details:
Side 1, track 5 / 7 min. 27 sec.
Composer:
A Lee

Alvin Lee: Lead Vocals & Guitar; Steve Gould: Bass; George Harrison: Slide Guitar; Alan Young: Drums; Tim Hinkley: Keyboards; Steve Grant: Keyboards

Record 170 title:
Zoom
Label / Catalog number:
Domino / 8003-2
Jacket / Inserts:
Standard international design in jewel box / 16 page CD booklet
Recording Location / Date:
Space Studios, Buckinghamshire, U.K. / (probably) 1991 or 1992
Media:
Album 5" CD
Producer:
Alvin Lee

Song 170a title:
Real Life Blues
Release date / Country:
25 Aug 92 / Singapore
Track details:
Side 1, track 2 / 4 min. 33 sec.
Composer:
A. Lee

Alvin Lee: Lead Vocals & Guitar; George Harrison: Slide Guitar; Jon Lord: Hammond Organ; Steve Grant: Bass, Keyboards & B. Vocals

Alvin Lee & Mylon Le Fevre

Record 171 title:
On The Road To Freedom
Label / Catalog number:
Columbia / KC 32729
Jacket / Inserts:
Standard international design with Gatefold / Record label inner sleeve
Recording Location / Date:
(possibly) Space Studios, Buckinghamshire, U.K. / Aug 73
Media:
Album 12"
Producer:
Alvin Lee

Song 171a title:
So Sad (No Love Of His Own)
Release date / Country:
02 Nov 73 / U.S.A.
Track details:
Side 1, track 3 / 4 min. 37 sec.
Composer:
G. Harrison

Mylon Le Fevre: Vocals; George Harrison: Slide Guitar, Guitar, Bass & B. Vocals; Alvin Lee: Guitar, B. Vocals; Ron Wood: 12 String Guitar; Mick Fleetwood: Drums

Graham "Alvin" Lee, was born December 19, 1944 in Nottingham, England. He started out playing the clarinet as an adolescent, but changed to guitar. By the age of thirteen he was playing in local groups. He served in such blues and rock bands as The Squarecaps, The Jail Breakers, and The Atomites. Lee, like so many others of his time (including The Beatles), developed his skills in the clubs of Hamburg, Germany as a member of The Jaymen, who later became known as The Jaycats, and finally The Jaybirds.

Alvin Lee, however, is best remembered as the leader of the band Ten Years After, who gained international recognition as a result of their appearance at the **Woodstock Music And Art Fair** in 1969. The name Ten Years After was derived from the fact they were formed approximately ten years after Elvis Presley's rise to stardom. The groups' only U.S. top 40 song was ***I'd Love To Change The World*** in 1971, though they had a number of successful albums, including **Cricklewood Green** and **A Space In Time**. The band slowly drifted towards solo projects in the early 1970s, but has occasionally reformed. Lee formed a band in the late 1970s called Ten Years Later. However, Alvin Lee is the only member of either group who has been able to maintain any amount of commercial success.

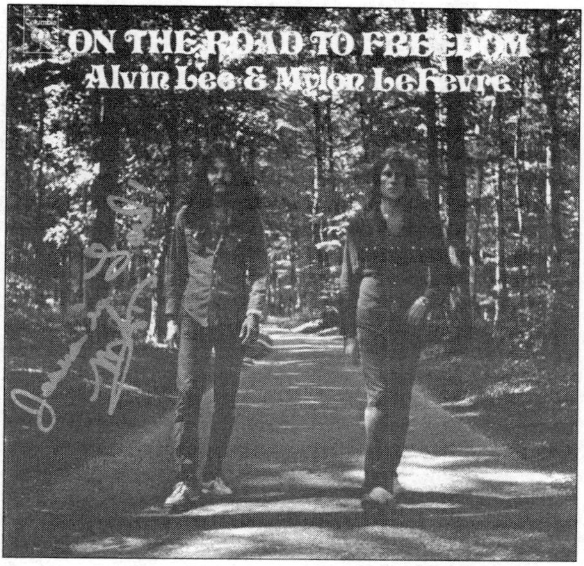

Lee and George Harrison have long been friends, and admirers of each other's work. The two have been neighbors, and they often worked with other musicians in their neighborhood including Gary Moore*, Joe Brown, *(see Vicki Brown)*, Mick Ralphs, Dave Gilmour and Jon Lord. Lee played guitar on Harrison's song ***Ding Dong; Ding Dong***. Harrison contributed to Lee his composition ***So Sad*** (to which he added some guitars and backing vocals), which is included on Lee's album **On The Road To Freedom**, with Mylon LeFevre in 1973. Harrison released his version of the song on his album **Dark Horse** a year later. Harrison and Lee wrote a song called ***Shelter In Your Love***, recorded in March 1985, which has yet to be released. Harrison played slide guitar on ***Talk Don't Bother Me*** on Lee's 1986 album **Detroit Diesel**. Harrison's slide guitar was also featured on ***Real Life Blues*** on Lee's 1992 album **Zoom**. Lee released the album **Nineteenninetyfour** (titled **I Hear You Rockin'** in the U.S.) just before the dawn of that year, an album which included Harrison playing slide guitar on ***The Bluest Blues*** and on Lee's cover of The Beatles' ***I Want You (She's So Heavy)***.

Peggy Lee

Record 172 title:
Let's Love
Label / Catalog number:
Atlantic / SD 18108
Jacket / Inserts:
Standard international design / Record label inner sleeve
Recording Location / Date:
Record Plant (West) Studios, Los Angeles, CA, U.S.A. / Jun 74
Media:
Album 12"
Producer:
Paul McCartney

Song 172a title:
Let's Love
Release date / Country:
01 Oct 74 / U.S.A.
Track details:
Side 1, track 1 / 2 min. 58 sec.
Composer:
P. McCartney

Peggy Lee: Lead Vocals; Paul McCartney: (probable) Piano & (probable) Conductor; additionally, one or more of the following: Dave Grusin: Piano & Synthesizer; Harvey Mason: Drums & Percussion; Gene Cipriano: Oboe; Peter Christlieb: Flute; Chuck Rainey: Bass; Erno Neufeld: Concert Master

Peggy Lee was born Norma Egstrom on May 27, 1920 in Jamestown, North Dakota. Talent would draw this Midwestern teenage girl, who lost her mother at a tender age, off the farm and on to fame. She worked with Benny Goodman's Orchestra and became one of America's foremost female pop vocalists. She also had much success writing lyrics to her husband David Barbour's melodies. Lee is probably best remembered for her 1958 hit ***Fever***, written by Little Willie John, and for her work in the Disney film **Lady And The Tramp**. She has been the recipient of numerous music industry awards throughout her career.

Peggy Lee was one of the first of her generation of musicians to publicly acknowledge the talents of The Beatles, who regularly performed and recorded her 1961 version of ***Till There Was You***. She covered The Beatles' songs ***A Hard Day's Night*** and ***Something***. She has long been a favorite of Paul McCartney – so much so that he wrote and produced ***Let's Love*** as a gift for her in 1974. More recently, Lee recounted the event, but has added a new twist to the story, stating that "He (McCartney) and Linda *(see Linda McCartney)* came over to help record it with me, which was lovely. Later in the studio he played on the song for me and even conducted it; that whole side was all his." DJ Rodney Bingenheimer, who attended the session, also recalls McCartney conducting the orchestra and playing piano on ***Let's Love***. However, there is nothing in the credits to suggest McCartney's involvement goes beyond producer and composer of ***Let's Love***, but it would not be the first time he has conducted an orchestra, or played piano, without being credited. The album finishes with a 1 minute, 20 second reprise of ***Let's Love***, that seems to be edited from the full-length version.

Julian Lennon

Record 173 title:
Help Yourself
Label / Catalog number:
Atlantic / 82280-2
Media:
Album 5" CD
Producer:
Bob Ezrin
Jacket / Inserts:
Standard international design in jewel box / 16 page CD booklet
Recording Location / Date:
Amigo & The Enterprise Studios, CA, U.S.A. / (probably) 1991

Song 173a title:
Saltwater
Release date / Country:
20 Aug 91 / U.S.A.
Track details:
Side 1, track 2 / 4 min. 07 sec.
Composer:
Julian Lennon - M. Spiro - L. Spiro

Julian Lennon: Lead Vocals; Guitars, Keyboards, Mandolin, Percussion, Bass, & Drum Programming; Steve Hunter: Slide Guitar; George Harrison: Slide Guitar Arrangement; additionally, one or more of the following: Scott Humphrey: Keyboards, B. Vocals, Computer & Synthesizer Programming; John McCurry: Guitars; Justin Clayton: Guitars; Louis Molino: Drums; Matt Bissonette: Bass; Bob Ezrin: B. Vocals, Keyboards, Percussion, & Programming; Bobbye Hall: Percussion; Allan Schwartzberg: Drums; Paul Winger: B. Vocals; Peter Fletcher: B. Vocals; Carmen Twillie: B. Vocals; Clydene Jackson-Edwards: B. Vocals; Maxine Anderson: B. Vocals; Bobette Jamison-Harrison: B. Vocals; Clarise Wilkins: B. Vocals; Kim Edwards-Brown: B. Vocals; San Fernando Valley Girl Scout Troop 592: B. Vocals; Olivia D'Abo: B. Vocals; Mark Spiro: B. Vocals

John Charles Julian Lennon was born April 8, 1963 in Liverpool, England. He is the first son of John Lennon and his first wife Cynthia (Powell) Lennon. The name Julian was taken from John's mother, Julia, and would be the inspiration for the "J" in Billy J. Kramer & The Dakotas*. Julian was a great source of guilt to John Lennon, who had barely noticed him growing up during the height of Beatlemania. However, a drawing of Julian's inspired John to write ***Lucy In The Sky With Diamonds***. Another drawing of his was featured on **The Beatles 1968 Christmas Record**, an annual gift to members of The Beatles Fan-Club. John also wrote The Beatles' song ***Goodnight*** for Julian.

At a time when John was able to give more attention to his family, he divorced Cynthia and married Yoko Ono*. Yoko had a daughter Kyoko, the same age as Julian, and the two would occasionally play at John's sprawling English estate, but the new-age family was not to be. Kyoko ended up with her father through a series of abductions and legal maneuvers, and the Lennons' permanently left England to live in New York City.

Julian stayed behind in England to be raised to adulthood by his thrice-married mother. John was unable to leave the United States between 1972 and 1976 for fear of not being re-admitted due to a deportation order stemming from his 1968 arrest for cannabis possession in England. Julian made occasional visits to see his father in the U.S. Unfortunately, the relationship was always a strained one for John, who could never quite forgive himself for abandoning his son, much as John's parents had done to him. The situation was further complicated by John's uneasiness around his ex-wife.

John did encourage Julian to become involved in music, and featured him playing drums on a brief rendition of ***Ya Ya*** included on John's **Walls And Bridges** album in 1974. The relationship did seem to improve some with the birth of John and Yoko's son Sean. Julian played big brother with Sean and guitar with dad, but just as the two were beginning to establish a deeper relationship, John was murdered.

The death of his father put young Julian in the spotlight – suddenly the world expected him to fill his father's shoes. He formed a band called Lennon Drops in 1982, and briefly joined the group Quasar the following year. Julian rose to the occasion with his debut album **Valotte** in 1984, which produced several successful singles. Julian's vocals were hauntingly similar to those of both his dad, and his grandfather Freddie Lennon. Julian tried to record some of his father's unreleased compositions, but apparently Yoko Ono (who held the rights) vetoed the idea. There have been reports that the relationship between Julian and Yoko has often been difficult, but he, Sean, and Yoko have been seen together on numerous occasions over the years.

Unfortunately, Julian's career stalled with the release of his second and third albums, but his fourth release, **Help Yourself** in 1991, received favorable reviews and produced the successful single ***Saltwater***. An acoustic version of ***Saltwater*** was issued in the U.K., and a Spanish language dubbed version was also issued, presumably to tie in with the Summer Olympics held in Spain the following year. When **Help Yourself** was released, it gave special thanks to Mum [Cynthia] and George Harrison, among others.

For years it has been suggested that Julian could fill the role of his father in a Beatles reunion, but as absurd an idea as that is, it seemed inevitable that Julian's and The Beatles' musical paths would cross at some point in the future. Early on in Julian's career, Paul McCartney (who wrote ***Hey Jude*** about him) and George Harrison publicly acknowledged Julian's talents.

According to Julian Lennon and his producer Bob Ezrin, Harrison was sent the tapes of ***Saltwater*** and recorded several slide guitar solos, but they decided not to use them. Instead, they combined both Julian's and George's slide guitar styles, and had guitarist Steve Hunter play it on the released version. Later reports seemed to indicate that George's guitar bit was indeed used, but this was probably a misinterpretation of Julian's initial explanation. At the very least, George helped with the slide guitar arrangement for ***Saltwater***.

Julian contributed to **Dave Clark's Time – The Musical** in 1986. Julian recently made his acting debut in the film **Leaving Las Vegas**, and has begun to produce music for film and television. He wrote and performed with Michael Kamen the closing theme to the 1995 film **Mr. Holland's Opus**, which featured several John Lennon songs. Growing up the son of John Lennon has rarely been easy for Julian.

Little Richard

Record 174 title:
Good Golly Miss Molly [Various Artists]
Label / Catalog number:
Polydor / CDP 399 (promotional)
Jacket / Inserts:
Unique in Jewel box / CD insert
Recording Location / Date:
Rumbo Recorders, Los Angeles, CA, U.S.A. / 1990
Media:
Single 5" CD
Producer:
Jeff Lynne

Song 174a title:
Good Golly Miss Molly
Release date / Country:
(probably) Feb 91 / U.S.A.
Track details:
Side 1, track 1 / 2 min. 10 sec.
Composer:
R. Blackwell - J. Marascalco

Little Richard: Lead Vocals & Piano; Ringo Starr: Drums; Jeff Lynne: Guitars & Bass; Jim Horn: Saxophone

Little Richard was born Richard Penniman in Macon, Georgia on December 5, 1932. Richard was influenced at an early age by religion and gospel music. His father and grandfather were preachers, and Richard sang in church with the Penniman Family Singers before hitting the road in Dr. Hudson's Medicine Show and then Sugarfoot Sam's Minstrel Show. This carnival atmosphere no doubt contributed to Richard's stage show. Little Richard was the first male rock performer to sport heavy make-up and outlandish costumes, a trend that decades later would be dubbed "glitter rock." Richard boasts that he is "the architect of rock 'n' roll," and there is plenty of evidence to support his claim.

Richard had several of his recordings released through RCA beginning in 1951. At the suggestion of Lloyd Price, he contacted Specialty Records who signed him to a contract in 1955. He recorded ***Tutti Frutti***, which went on to sell over three million copies. His next chart success was ***Long Tall Sally*** in March 1956, backed with ***Slippin' And Slidin'***. However, the white controlled entertainment industry in the U.S. at the time was, no doubt, reluctant to heavily promote a black version of Liberace singing sexually suggestive, raunchy rock 'n' roll. His songs were successfully covered (and sanitized) by white artists like Pat Boone. Richard continued to write rock classics like ***Lucille; Jenny, Jenny; Miss Ann***; ***Ooh! My Soul*** and ***Hey Hey Hey Hey***, released between 1957 and 1959, all of which were regulars in The Beatles' early stage repertoire. Richard abandoned rock 'n' roll at what would prove to be the height of his career to study for the ministry.

Richard dedicated several years to preaching and recording gospel music before returning to rock 'n' roll in 1962. He began touring Europe extensively with a band that included, among others, Billy Preston*. He first met The Beatles at the Star-Club in Hamburg, Germany in the spring of 1962. On October 12, 1962, Brian Epstein booked Little Richard to top the bill along with The Beatles at the Tower Ballroom in Liverpool, and again on October 28 at the Empire Theatre. These were memorable occasions for The Beatles, especially Paul McCartney, who idolized and copied much of his rock vocal style from Little Richard, particularly on his song ***I'm Down***. McCartney closed many of The Beatles' live performances with ***Long Tall Sally*** or ***I'm Down***. The Beatles considered signing Richard to their Apple Records label in the late 1960s. Years later McCartney would write the forward to Richard's biography, and Richard would typically brag that he taught The Beatles everything they knew and was responsible for their success. Richard continued to tour throughout the latter half of the 1960s, and on September 13, 1969, he appeared on the same bill with John Lennon and The Plastic Ono Band *(see Yoko Ono, Eric Clapton)* at a rock 'n' roll revival in Toronto.

Richard paid a little tribute to Paul McCartney and The Beatles by covering their song ***I Saw Her Standing There*** in 1969. By the mid-1970s, Little Richard re-embraced Christianity and his gospel career and renounced the wilder side of his rock 'n' roll life-style. Richard has spent the last four decades trying to restart his career with new material and public appearances, but has not had much chart success. He was inducted into the Rock and Roll Hall of Fame in 1986.

In 1990, Richard re-recorded ***Good Golly Miss Molly***, produced by Jeff Lynne*, with Ringo Starr on drums. According to Lynne, the recording originally featured Benmont Tench on piano, who was replaced by Little Richard. The song was featured in the soundtrack of the film **King Ralph** starring John Goodman, but the recording's release was limited to an obscure U.S. cassette single (Polydor / 879 678), and a European CD single (Polydor / 879 678-2). The U.S. promotional CD single is listed because it seems to be the easiest to find.

In 1991 Richard was part of The Peace Choir, organized by Yoko Ono and John Lennon's son Sean, who made a recording of Lennon's ***Give Peace A Chance***. He made a guest appearance, and his music was featured, on Paul McCartney's 1995 radio series **Oobu Joobu**. Little Richard continues to play his role as the undisputed greatest and prettiest rock 'n' roll star of all time!

The Royal Liverpool Philharmonic Orchestra & Choir & Choristers Of Liverpool

Record 175 title:
Liverpool Oratorio

Media:
Album 12" LVD

Label / Catalog number:
Pioneer Artists / PA-91-417

Producer:
Chips Chipperfield (film); John Fraser (music); Paul McCartney (executive-music) & Richard Ogden (music)

Jacket / Inserts:
Standard international design with Gatefold with photos of Paul McCartney / 16 page booklet

Recording Location / Date:
On location at Liverpool Cathedral, Liverpool, U.K. / 28-29 Jun 91

Also available on EMI Classics / CDC 7 54372 2 / Album 5" CD [2 CD set] / CD1: I-IV / CD2: V-VIII / (approx. 1 hr. 37 min.)/ Standard international design in double Jewel box / 40 page CD booklet.

Song 175a title:
Paul McCartney's Liverpool Oratorio:
(Movement: I. War / II. School / III. Crypt
/ IV. Father / V. Wedding / VI. Work
/ VII. Crisis / VIII. Peace) [live]

Track details:
Disk 1: I-IV / Disk 2: V-VIII
/ (Total time of film approx. 1 hr. 41 min.)

Release date / Country:
10 Feb 92 (first issued 22 Feb 91) / U.S.A.

Composer:
P. McCartney - C. Davis

The Royal Liverpool Philharmonic Orchestra & Choir & Choristers Of Liverpool Cathedral Conducted by Carl Davis, (with Guest Solos by: Kiri Te Kanawa, Sally Burgess, Jerry Hadley & Willard White)

Kiri Te Kanawa: Soprano; Sally Burgess: Mezzo-Soprano; Jerry Hadley: Tenor; Willard White: Bass; Jeremy Budd: Boy Soloist; Paul McCartney: Introduction; Carl Davis: Conductor of Royal Liverpool Philharmonic Orchestra & Choir & Choristers; Nic Raine: Assistant to Carl Davis; The Royal Liverpool Philharmonic Orchestra includes: Malcolm Stewart: Leader-First Solo Violin; Nicholas Wood: Associate Leader-First Violin; Irene Pearce: Principal-First Violin; Nicolette Brown: First Violin; Lesley Gwyther: First Violin; Clifford Bibby: First Violin; Alexander Marks: First Violin; Donald Turnbull: First Violin; Ian Bone: First Violin; John Hebbron: First Violin; Duncan Atherton: First Violin; Sonia Nash: First Violin; Johathan Pigott: First Violin; Valerie Leary: First Violin; Susan Henderson: Principal-Second Violin; Gerald Adamson: Associate Principal-Second Violin; James Hutton: Second-Violin; Justin Evans: Second Violin; Kenneth Johnson: Second Violin; Martin Burrage:

Second Violin; Wynford Andrews: Second Violin; Richard Gordon-Smith: Second Violin; Helen Cookson: Second Violin; Peter Leach: Second Violin; Celia Goodwin: Second Violin; Ian Flower: Second Violin; Wendy Cochran: Second Violin; Roger Benedict: Principal-Viola; Robert Shepley: Viola; Andrea Creech: Viola; David Ruby: Viola; Richard Wallace: Viola; Alexander Ferguson: Viola; Anne Forshaw: Viola; Juliet Brien: Viola; Angela Berreen: Viola; Audrey Henning: Viola; Christopher Balmer: Viola; Avril Schepens: Viola; Timothy Walden: Principal-Flute; Anthony Ovenell: Flute; Myra Bennett: Piccolo; Jonathan Small: Principal-Oboe; Nigel Roberts: Oboe; Anna Cooper: Cor Anglais; Christopher Swann: Clarinet; Andrew Roberts: Clarinet; Colin Pownall: Bass Clarinet; Alan Pendlebury: Principal-Bassoon; Alison Lee-Browne: Bassoon; Nicholas Lander: Contra Bassoon; David Pigott: Associate Principal-Horn; Martin Taggart: Horn; Michael Ogonovsky: Horn; John Thornton: Horn; Chris Morley: Horn; Ian Blamain: Principal-Trumpet; Alan Stringer: (MBE) Principal Emeritus-Trumpet; Desmond Worthington: Trumpet; Blyth Lindsay: Tenor Trombone; Philip Goodwin: Tenor Trombone; John Langford: Bass Trombone; George Smith: Tuba; Ian Wright: Timpani; Graham Johns: Principal-Percussion; Jean Webster: Percussion; Dawn Mace: Percussion; Mair Jones: Harp; Stephen Disley: Organ; The Royal Liverpool Philharmonic Choir includes: Ian Tracey: Chorusmaster & Master Of The Choristers; Jennifer Allcock: Soprano; Kate Banbury: Soprano; Sylvia Bawden: Soprano; Ruth Bennett: Soprano; Ann Bone: Soprano; Angela Brodbelt: Soprano; Nicola Brooks: Soprano; Ruth Brown: Soprano; Jill Carlson: Soprano; Maria Casstles: Soprano; Shelagh Crosbie: Soprano; Mary Daley: Soprano; Janet Eastwood: Soprano; Carolyn Eddowes: Soprano; Ruth Greening-Jackson: Soprano; Sarah Gregory: Soprano; Janet Hare: Soprano; Joyce Hill: Soprano; Jean Hocknell: Soprano; Patricia Howley: Soprano; Anne Hughes: Soprano; Gillian Jones: Soprano; Louise Jones: Soprano; Alfreda Kennedy: Soprano; Margaret Kershaw: Soprano; Lindsey McDonald: Soprano; Margaret Marks: Soprano; Carey Marsden: Soprano; Helen McClorry: Soprano; Claudia McConnell: Soprano; Geraldine McGinity: Soprano; Elizabeth McIlwaine: Soprano; Maura McWatt: Soprano; Frankie Moor: Soprano; Margaret Morton: Soprano; Anne-Marie Obaje: Soprano; Alison Parker: Soprano; Ann Paver: Soprano; Anne Pigott: Soprano; Jane Pitts: Soprano; Margaretta Price: Soprano; Evelyn Randles: Soprano; Brenda Redmond: Soprano; Sian Roberts: Soprano; Carol Ryan: Soprano; Margaret Satterthwaite: Soprano; Kate Sharp: Soprano; Jillian Simms: Soprano; Margaret Smith: Soprano; Deborah Tate: Soprano; Eunice Theobald: Soprano; Diana Walkden: Soprano; Barbara Wall: Soprano; Janet Wareing: Soprano; Brenda Waterson: Soprano; Gillian Winstanley: Soprano; Eleanor Wright: Soprano; Kathleen Zimak: Soprano; Carolyn Allcock: Alto; Heather Barrett: Alto; Yvonne Bieniek: Alto; Andrina Boyle: Alto; Anne Broe: Alto; Susan Carver: Alto; Joan Childe-Harmer: Alto; Sylvia Church: Alto; Maureen Clarke: Alto; Sally Daunt: Alto; Dorthy Davis: Alto; Helen Dingle: Alto; Alma Bootson: Alto; Catherine Duke: Alto; Patrica Feeney: Alto; Hilary Flett: Alto; Anne Garden: Alto; Florence Gersten: Alto; Wendy Hadfield: Alto; Pamela Hankin: Alto; Jackie Hine: Alto; Patricia Hulme: Alto; Barbara Jackson: Alto; Mavis Jenkins: Alto; Joyce Jones: Alto; Margaret Kay: Alto; Marion Kilshaw: Alto; Judith Laity: Alto; Joyce Lowdon: Alto; Veronica Maguire: Alto; Valerie McGraw: Alto; Janice Perkins: Alto; Rowena Preston: Alto; Margaret Smith: Alto; Rona Smith: Alto; Susan Smith: Alto; Olga South: Alto; Carol Stone-Williams: Alto; Norma Taylor: Alto; Mary Tew: Alto; Olive Walker: Alto; Aileen Ward: Alto; Jules Waring: Alto; Dorthy Watt: Alto; Anne Wheaton: Alto; Patrica Wheeler: Alto; Alison White: Alto; Daphne Wigmore: Alto; Eryl Williams: Alto; Lorna Winstanley: Alto; Ann Woodward: Alto; Peter Bates: Tenor; Barry Butcher: Tenor; Ian Crinyion: Tenor; John Davies: Tenor; Stephen Davies: Tenor; Fred Gilliver: Tenor; John Gilmore: Tenor; Niel Heritage: Tenor; Jim Hetherington: Tenor; Harry Holmes: Tenor; Christopher Hull: Tenor; Gwyn Jenkins: Tenor; Brian Jones: Tenor; Brian H Jones: Tenor; Stuart Keen: Tenor; Norman Kidd: Tenor; Richard Marks: Tenor; Bruce Marsden: Tenor; John Martin: Tenor; Christopher McCurry: Tenor; Francis Morris: Tenor; Ian Naylor: Tenor; Hugh Peate: Tenor; Gordon Wilkinson: Tenor; Robert Williams: Tenor; Kenneth Wynn: Tenor: Peter Zacharias: Tenor; Noel Andrews: Bass; Timothy Atkinson: Bass; Stuart Christie: Bass; Jim Cooke: Bass; Howard Cox: Bass; Kevin Dennett: Bass; John Dingle: Bass; Alistair Doxat-Pratt: Bass; Peter Drury: Bass; Clive Eames: Bass; David Eddowes: Bass; William Gould: Bass; Gary Jones: Bass; Keith Jones: Bass; Robert Jones: Bass; David Kruger: Bass; Dennis Lavelle: Bass; Michael Lind: Bass; Robert Lowdon: Bass; Alec Mackinnon: Bass; Andrew McGowan: Bass; Robin Moor: Bass; Michael Olver: Bass; Michael Pitts: Bass; Richard Rushworth: Bass; David Scott: Bass; Toby Screech: Bass; Frank Seddon: Bass; Colin Smith: Bass; Phil Snelling: Bass; John Spielgelbert: Bass; Miles Tew: Bass; Tony Twemlow: Bass; Geoff Wells: Bass; David Wetherell: Bass; John White: Bass; Paul Whitefoot: Bass; Colin Yates: Bass; The Liverpool Cathedral Choristers include: Christopher Ambler: Chorister; Benjamin Appleton: Chorister; Andrew Berkeley: Chorister; Benjamin Bridson: Chorister; Stuart Christie: Chorister; Geoffrey Coombe: Chorister; Mark Crotty: Chorister; Michael Evans: Chorister; Stuart Gilbert: Chorister; Martin Gratton: Chorister; Austin Hewitt: Chorister; Alexander

Hornby: Chorister; Michael Horton: Chorister; Benjamin Humphries: Chorister; Paul Jones: Chorister; Stuart Jones: Chorister; Andrew Kay: Chorister; Paul Kelly: Chorister; Joseph Lalgee: Chorister; David Leahey: Chorister; Neil Leahey: Chorister; Cliff Jenkinson: Chorister; Jonathan McDonald: Chorister; Ian Middlehurst: Chorister; Jeffrey Moore: Chorister; Robin Panter: Chorister; Julian Pigott: Chorister; Matthew Polglase: Chorister; Stephen Quirk: Chorister; Peter Rimmer: Chorister; Peter Shephard: Chorister; Paul Taylor: Chorister; Nicholas Thomas: Chorister; Ian Upton: Chorister; Philip White-Jones: Chorister

In the late 1830s, Mr. William Sudlow, an amateur organist, and a group of friends regularly met at Liverpool's St. Martin's Church to perform choral music. On January 10, 1840, they formed the Liverpool Philharmonic Society. In 1988, Carl Davis was conducting the Royal Liverpool Philharmonic Orchestra's performance of his and Carla Lane's ***Pigeon's Progress*** *(see Linda McCartney)*. Paul McCartney, impressed with the composer / conductor, who had moved to Britain some thirty years earlier from his native New York, sent Davis a good luck message via the Philharmonic's General Manager, Brian Pidgeon. Shortly thereafter, Davis approached McCartney with the idea of contributing something for the culmination of the Philharmonic's year-long celebration of their 150th anniversary. They came up with the idea of composing an Oratorio loosely based on McCartney's childhood and life in war time Liverpool. (Davis had an earlier Beatles connection, composing and conducting the original score for Dick Clark's made-for-TV film **Birth Of The Beatles**. He later contributed to McCartney's 1993 album **Off The Ground**.)

Program from Liverpool performance

At age eleven, McCartney had auditioned for the Choristers of Liverpool Cathedral, but was turned down, much to his, and ultimately their, embarrassment. Thirty-eight years later, the hometown boy made his triumphant return to the cathedral as the classical composer of the Liverpool Oratorio. The Oratorio has since been performed in many major cities across the globe, where McCartney has received generally favorable reviews on his first major classical work. Singles with excerpts from **Paul McCartney's Liverpool Oratorio** were issued containing the following titles ***Save The Child***, ***The Drinking Song***, ***The World You're Coming Into*** and ***Tres Conejos***.

Nils Lofgren

Record 176 title:
Live From Montreaux (Ringo Starr And His All-Starr Band)
Media:
Album 12" LVD
Label / Catalog number:
Videoarts / VALJ-3369
Producer:
Jim Beach & Louise Velazquez (film); Ringo Starr (music)
Jacket / Inserts:
Unique / Lyric insert & translation
Recording Location / Date:
On location at Montreaux Jazz Festival, Montreaux, Switzerland / 13 Jul 92

Song 176a title:
Shine Silently [live]
Track details:
Side 1, track 8 / 6 min. 29 sec.
Release date / Country:
(probably) Nov 93 / Japan
Composer:
N. Lofgren - D. Wagner

Nils Lofgren: Lead Vocals & Guitar; Ringo Starr: Drums; Joe Walsh: Acoustic Guitar; Todd Rundgren: Acoustic Guitar & B. Vocals; Burton Cummings: Keyboards; Dave Edmunds: Guitar & B. Vocals; Timothy B. Schmit: Bass & B. Vocals; Tim Cappello: Percussion; Zak Starkey: Drums

Song 176b title:
Walkin' Nerve [live]
Track details:
Side 2, track 6 / 4 min. 00 sec.
Release date / Country:
(probably) Nov 93 / Japan
Composer:
N. Lofgren

Nils Lofgren: Lead Vocals & Guitar; Ringo Starr: Drums; Joe Walsh: Guitar; Todd Rundgren: Guitar; Burton Cummings: Keyboards & Percussion; Dave Edmunds: Guitar; Timothy B. Schmit: Bass; Tim Cappello: Percussion; Zak Starkey: Drums

This song is also included on Rykodisc / RCD 20264 / Album 5" CD / Side 1, track 10 / released 14 Sep 93 in the U.S.A. / Standard international design in jewel box / 12 page CD booklet.

Record 177 title:
Ringo Starr And His All-Starr Band
Media:
Album 12" LVD
Label / Catalog number:
Pioneer Artists / PA-090-007
Producer:
Tim Snow (film); Joe Walsh & Jim Nipar (music)
Jacket / Inserts:
Standard international design / Record label inner sleeve
Recording Location / Date:
On location at Greek Theatre, Los Angeles, CA, U.S.A. / 03 Sep 89

Song 177a title:
Bein Angry [live]
Track details:
Side 2, track 3 (15) / 4 min. 34 sec.
Release date / Country:
Jul 90 / U.S.A.
Composer:
N. Lofgren

Nils Lofgren: Lead Vocals & Guitar; Billy Preston: Keyboards & B. Vocals; Jim Keltner: Drums; Ringo Starr: Drums; Levon Helm: Drums & B. Vocals; Joe Walsh: Guitar & B. Vocals; Rick Danko: Bass; Clarence Clemons: Saxophone; Dr. John: Keyboards

Record 178 title:
Ringo Starr And His All-Starr Band
Label / Catalog number:
Rykodisc / RCD 10190 & RCD5-1019
Media:
Album 5" [2 CD set]
Producer:
Tim Snow (film); Joe Walsh & Jim Nipar (music)
Jacket / Inserts:
Unique in Jewel box in box set / 6 page CD booklet, sticker postcard & Rykodisc info. postcard / CD insert
Recording Location / Date:
On location at Greek Theatre, Los Angeles, CA, U.S.A. / 03 Sep 89

Song 178a title:
Shine Silently [live]
Release date / Country:
12 Oct 90 / U.S.A.
Track details:
Side 1, track 5 / 6 min. 39 sec.
Composer:
N. Lofgren - D. Wagner

Nils Lofgren: Lead Vocals & Guitar; Billy Preston: Keyboards; Jim Keltner: Drums; Ringo Starr: Drums; Levon Helm: Drums; Joe Walsh: Guitar; Rick Danko: Bass; Clarence Clemons: Tambourine; Dr. John: Keyboards

Record 179 title:
Silver Lining
Label / Catalog number:
Rykodisc / RCD 10170
Media:
Album 5" CD
Producer:
Kevin McCormick & Nils Lofgren
Jacket / Inserts:
Standard international design in jewel box / 14 page CD booklet with photo of Ringo Starr
Recording Location / Date:
Ocean Way Studios, Los Angeles, CA, U.S.A. / 1990

Song 179a title:
Bein' Angry
Release date / Country:
06 Mar 91 / U.S.A.
Track details:
Side 1, track 8 / 5 min. 52 sec.
Composer:
N. Lofgren

Nils Lofgren: Lead Vocals & Guitar; Kevin McCormick: Fretless Bass; Andy Newmark: Drums; Billy Preston: Organ; Ringo Starr: B. Vocal

Song 179b title:
Walkin' Nerve
Track details:
Side 1, track 3 / 3 min. 53 sec.
Release date / Country:
06 Mar 91 / U.S.A.
Composer:
N. Lofgren

Nils Lofgren: Lead Vocals & Guitar; Kevin McCormick: Bass; Ringo Starr: Drums

Nils Lofgren was born on June 21, 1951 in Chicago, Illinois. Lofgren studied classical accordion from age six to fifteen, and then switched to keyboards and guitar. He was the leader of the band Grin in the early 1970s. He first gained recognition playing on Neil Young's **After The Gold Rush** album, and joined his backup band Crazy Horse shortly thereafter. Lofgren made a brief cameo appearance in Robert Stigwood's 1978 film **Sgt. Pepper's Lonely Hearts Club Band**. He was soon in demand as a top backup and session player, and had mild success as a solo artist. Lofgren became internationally famous in the mid-1980s as a member of Bruce Springsteen's E Street Band. He also did a cover of The Beatles' ***Anytime At All*** on his 1981 album **Night Fades Away**.

Lofgren was a member of Ringo Starr's All-Starr Band tour in 1989. During the tour, he performed ***Bein' Angry*** and ***Shine Silently*** with Ringo backing him on drums. Ringo was thanked on Lofgren's 1991 album **Silver Lining**, to which he provided drums and backing vocals. Ringo also made a cameo appearance in the video for the album's single ***Valentine***, even though he did not do the drumming on the actual recording. On May 31, 1991, Ringo joined Lofgren onstage at the Roxy in Los Angeles to play drums on ***Walkin' Nerve***. He played drums again on ***Walkin' Nerve*** about a year later during a Lofgren performance in London. Lofgren was also a member of Ringo's All-Starr Band tour in 1992 performing ***Shine Silently*** and ***Walkin' Nerve*** with Ringo backing him on drums. Another song performed by Lofgren during the 1992 tour that featured Ringo on drums was a cover of the Beau Brummels' ***Just A Little***, though it has not been included on any official releases. Lofgren said Ringo did not contribute to his 1992 CD ***Crooked Line***, but was thanked in the credits for his general support and encouragement. Lofgren was unable to join Ringo's All-Starr Band tour in 1995 due to previous commitments, but did fill in for several dates as the opening act and joined the band for the encores. Lofgren, a D.C. area resident, opened for Ringo's All-Starr Band performance outside D.C. in 1997.

Jackie Lomax

Record 180 title:
Is This What You Want?
Media:
Album 5" CD
Label / Catalog number:
Apple / CDP 7975812
Jacket / Inserts:
Standard international design in jewel box / 8 page CD booklet with photo of Paul McCartney

Song 180a title:
Baby You're A lover
Track details:
Side 1, track 10 / 3 min. 02 sec.
Release date / Country:
19 Nov 91 (first issued 21 Mar 69) / Germany
Composer:
J. Lomax
Producer:
George Harrison
Recording Location / Date:
Sound Recorders, Los Angeles, CA, U.S.A. / Oct - Nov 68

Jackie Lomax: Lead Vocals & Guitar; Hal Blaine: Drums; George Harrison: Guitar; Larry Knechtel: Keyboards; Joe Osborne: Bass; Paul Beaver: Synthesizers; Bernie Krause: Synthesizers

Song 180b title:
(I) Fall Inside Your Eyes
Track details:
Side 1, track 6 / 3 min. 08 sec.
Release date / Country:
19 Nov 91 (first issued 21 Mar 69) / Germany
Composer:
J. Lomax
Producer:
George Harrison
Recording Location / Date:
Sound Recorders, Los Angeles, CA., U.S.A. / Oct - Nov 68

Jackie Lomax: Lead Vocals & Guitar; Joe Osborn: Bass; Hal Blaine: Drums; Larry Knechtel: Keyboards; Paul Beaver: Synthesizer; Bernie Krause: Synthesizer

Song 180c title:
Going Back To Liverpool
Track details:
Side 1, track 15 / 3 min. 07 sec.
Release date / Country:
19 Nov 91 / Germany
Composer:
J. Lomax
Producer:
Paul McCartney & (probably) George Harrison

Recording Location / Date:
Apple Studios, London, U.K. / 11 Mar 69 & (probably) 12 Mar 69

Jackie Lomax: Lead Vocals; George Harrison: Guitar & B. Vocals; Billy Preston: Keyboards & B. Vocals; Pete Clark: Drums; Billy Kinsley: Bass; Tim Renick: Guitar

Song 180d title:
How Can You Say Goodbye
Release date / Country:
19 Nov 91 (first issued 21 Mar 69) / Germany
Producer:
George Harrison
Recording Location / Date:
Sound Recorders, Los Angeles, CA., U.S.A. / Oct - Nov 68
Track details:
Side 1, track 3 / 4 min. 11 sec.
Composer:
J. Lomax

Jackie Lomax: Lead Vocals & Guitar; George Harrison: Guitar; Hal Blaine: Drums; Joe Osborn: Bass; Larry Knechtel: Keyboards

Song 180e title:
How The Web Was Woven
Release date / Country:
19 Nov 91 (first issued 06 Feb 70) / Germany
Producer:
George Harrison
Recording Location / Date:
Trident Studios, London, U.K. / Oct &/or Nov 69
Track details:
Side 1, track 17 / 3 min. 50 sec.
Composer:
C. Westlake - D. Most

Jackie Lomax: Lead Vocals; Leon Russell: (all) Keyboards & Guitar

Song 180f title:
I Just Don't Know
Release date / Country:
19 Nov 91 (first issued 21 Mar 69) / Germany
Producer:
George Harrison
Recording Location / Date:
Sound Recorders, Los Angeles, CA., U.S.A. / Oct - Nov 68
Track details:
Side 1, track 12 / 2 min. 52 sec.
Composer:
J. Lomax

Jackie Lomax: Lead Vocals & Guitar; Hal Blaine: Drums; Joe Osborn: Bass; Larry Knechtel: Piano

Song 180g title:
Is This What You Want?
Release date / Country:
19 Nov 91 (first issued 21 Mar 69) / Germany
Producer:
George Harrison
Recording Location / Date:
Sound Recorders, Los Angeles, CA, U.S.A. & EMI-Abbey Road Studios, London, U.K. / Oct - Nov 68
Track details:
Side 1, track 2 / 2 min. 44 sec.
Composer:
J. Lomax

Jackie Lomax: Lead Vocals & Guitar; George Harrison: Guitar; Hal Blaine: Drums; Larry Knechtel: Piano; Joe Osborn: Bass; John Barham: String Arrangements

Song 180h title:
Little Yellow Pills
Release date / Country:
19 Nov 91 (first issued 21 Mar 69) / Germany
Producer:
George Harrison
Track details:
Side 1, track 7 / 4 min. 02 sec.
Composer:
J. Lomax

Recording Location / Date:
Sound Recorders, Los Angeles, CA, U.S.A. / Oct - Nov 68

Jackie Lomax: Lead Vocals & Guitar; Hal Blaine: Drums; Larry Knechtel: Keyboards; Joe Osborne: Bass

Song 180i title:
New Day [CD version]
Track details:
Side 1, track 13 / 3 min. 15 sec.
Release date / Country:
19 Nov 91 / Germany
Composer:
J. Lomax
Producer:
Jackie Lomax & Mal Evans
Recording Location / Date:
Olympic Studios, London, U.K. / Mar - Apr 69

Jackie Lomax: Lead Vocals & Guitar; Billy Kinsley: Bass; Tim Renick: Guitar, Chris Hatfield: Keyboards; Pete Clark: Drums; George Harrison: Guitar

Song 180j title:
Sour Milk Sea
Track details:
Side 1, track 5 / 3 min. 52 sec.
Release date / Country:
19 Nov 91 (first issued 26 Aug 68) / Germany
Composer:
G. Harrison
Producer:
George Harrison
Recording Location / Date:
EMI-Abbey Road† & Trident Studios, London, U.K. / 24†-26 Jun 68

Jackie Lomax: Lead Vocals & Rhythm Guitar; George Harrison: Rhythm Guitar; Paul McCartney: Bass; Eric Clapton: Lead Guitar; Ringo Starr: Drums; Nicky Hopkins: Piano; Eddie Clayton: Congas

Song 180k title:
Speak To Me
Track details:
Side 1, track 1 / 3 min. 08 sec.
Release date / Country:
19 Nov 91 (first issued 21 Mar 69) / Germany
Composer:
J. Lomax

Producer:
George Harrison
Recording Location / Date:
Sound Recorders, Los Angeles, CA, U.S.A. & (probably) EMI-Abbey Road Studios, London, U.K. / Oct - Nov 68

Jackie Lomax: Lead Vocals & Guitar; Hal Blaine: Drums; George Harrison: Guitar; Joe Osborn: Bass; Larry Knechtel: Keyboards; John Barham: String Arrangements

Song 180l title:
Sunset
Track details:
Side 1, track 4 / 3 min. 54 sec.
Release date / Country:
19 Nov 91 (first issued 21 Mar 69) / Germany
Composer:
J. Lomax
Producer:
George Harrison
Recording Location / Date:
EMI-Abbey Road Studios, London, U.K. / (probably) Jul 68

Jackie Lomax: Lead Vocals & Guitar; Spike Heatley: Bass; Alan Branscombe: Piano; John Barham: String Arrangement

Song 180m title:
Take My Word
Track details:
Side 1, track 8 / 3 min. 55 sec.
Release date / Country:
19 Nov 91 (first issued 21 Mar 69) / Germany
Composer:
J. Lomax

Brian Wilson, of the Beach Boys, Saginaw, MI, 1980
photo by Kristofer Engelhardt

Thursday

3. Saville Row.
LONDON. W.1.

Dear Brute,

You have got a great name and a lovely voice and a beautiful Record on Apple called King of Fish. I felt I should make some contact with you, (until we meet someplace when we will really make contact), as I have been involved with it all so, HELLO!
I dig the 'Nobody Knows' side too.
Thanks for being patient with us and for Being: George Harrison.

Letter from George Harrison to Brute Force, 1969,
photo courtesy of Steve Friedland

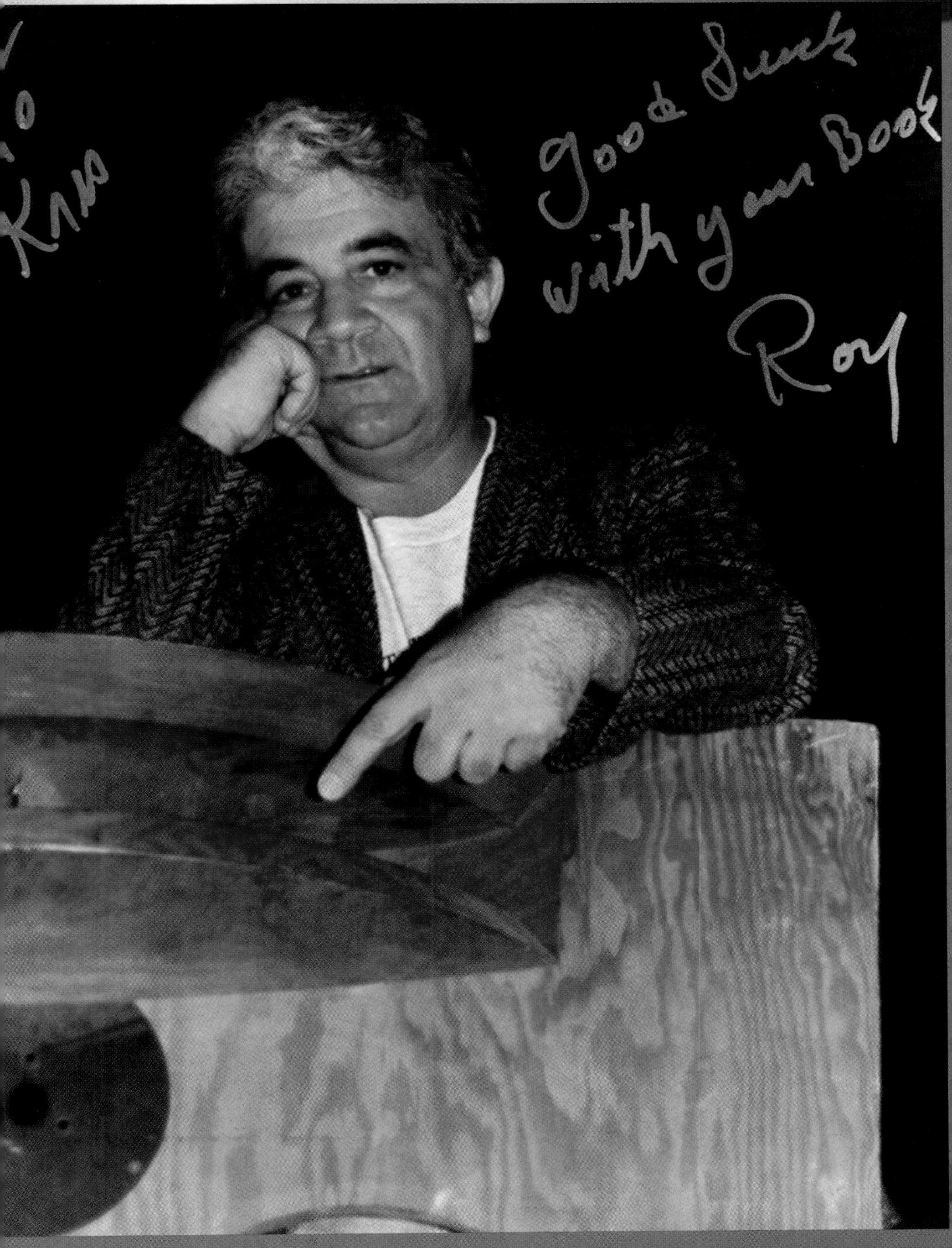

Roy Cicala, photo courtesy of Roy Cicala

Eric Clapton, Saginaw, MI, 1979, photo by Kristofer Engelhardt

Daryl Hall and John Oates. Saginaw, MI, 1978,
photos by Kristofer Engelhardt

Paul McCartney, Detroit, MI, 1990, photo by Kristofer Engelhardt,
(autographed by the entire band)

Carl Perkins, Detroit, MI, 1994,
photo by Kristofer Engelhardt

Mike Campbell, Tom Petty, Ringo Starr, Jeff Lynne and George Harrison,
photo card from the U.K. limited edition 7" single "I Won't Back Down - MCA Records

Producer:
George Harrison
Recording Location / Date:
Sound Recorders, Los Angeles, CA, U.S.A. & (probably) Trident &/or EMI-Abbey Road Studios, London, U.K. / Oct - Nov 68

Jackie Lomax: Lead Vocals & Guitar; George Harrison: Guitar; Hal Blaine: Drums; Joe Osborn: Bass; John Barham: String Arrangements; Paul Beaver: Synthesizers; Bernie Krause: Synthesizers

Song 180n title:
The Eagle Laughs At You
Track details:
Side 1, track 9 / 2 min. 24 sec.
Release date / Country:
19 Nov 91 (first issued 26 Aug 68) / Germany
Composer:
J. Lomax
Producer:
George Harrison
Recording Location / Date:
Trident Studios, London, U.K. / 24-26 Jun 68

Jackie Lomax: Lead Vocals, Bass & Guitar; Eric Clapton: Lead Guitar; George Harrison: Guitar; Tony Newman: Drums

Song 180o title:
Thumbin' A Ride
Track details:
Side 1, track 16 / 3 min. 56 sec.
Release date / Country:
19 Nov 91 (first issued 02 Jun 69) / Germany
Composer:
J. Leiber - M. Stoller
Producer:
Paul McCartney
Recording Location / Date:
Apple Studios, London, U.K. / 11 Mar 69 & (probably) 12 Mar 69

Jackie Lomax: Lead Vocals & Guitar; George Harrison: Guitar & B. Vocals; Pete Clark: Drums; Billy Kinsley: Bass; Tim Renick: Guitar; Chris Hatfield: Keyboards; Pattie (Boyd) Harrison/Clapton: B. Vocals

Song 180p title:
Won't You Come Back
Track details:
Side 1, track 14 / 4 min. 10 sec.
Release date / Country:
19 Nov 91 / Germany
Composer:
J. Lomax
Producer:
George Harrison
Recording Location / Date:
EMI-Abbey Road Studios, London, U.K. / 1968

Jackie Lomax: Lead Vocals & (probable) Guitar; probably one or more of the following: Alan Branscombe: Keyboards; Pete Clark: Drums; George Harrison: Guitar; Spike Heatley: Bass; Nicky Hopkins: Keyboards; Bishop O'Brien: Drums; Tony Newman: Drums; Klaus Voormann: Bass; Billy Kinsley: Bass; Tim Renick: Guitar; Chris Hatfield: Keyboards

Song 181p title:
You've Got Me Thinking
Track details:
Side 1, track 11 / 2 min. 53 sec.
Release date / Country:
19 Nov 91 (first issued 21 Mar 69) / Germany
Composer:
J. Lomax
Producer:
George Harrison
Recording Location / Date:
EMI-Abbey Road Studios, London, U.K. / (probably) Jun or Sep 68

Jackie Lomax: Lead Vocals & Guitar; George Harrison: (possible) Guitar; Ringo Starr: Drums; Klaus Voormann: Bass; Eric Clapton: Guitar

Record 182 title:
New Day / Thumbin' A Ride
Label / Catalog number:
Apple / 1807
Jacket / Inserts:
Record label sleeve
Recording Location / Date:
Olympic Studios, London, U.K. / Mar - Apr 69
Media:
Single 7"
Producer:
Jackie Lomax & Mal Evans

Song 182a title:
New Day [single version]
Release date / Country:
09 May 69 / U.S.A.
Track details:
Side 1, track 1 / 2 min. 50 sec.
Composer:
J. Lomax

Jackie Lomax: Lead Vocals & Guitar; Billy Kinsley: Bass; Tim Renick: Guitar, Chris Hatfield: Keyboards; Pete Clark: Drums; George Harrison: Guitar

John "Jackie" Lomax was born on May 10, 1944 in Liverpool (Wallasey), England and, like so many others of his generation in Liverpool, became involved in the pop music scene during the late 1950s and early 1960s. He was the bass guitarist and lead singer of the popular Liverpool band The Undertakers, who frequently shared the same bill with The Beatles in Liverpool and Hamburg. During the mid-1960s, his group Lomax Alliance was signed to Brian Epstein's management.

Following the death of Epstein, Lomax was signed to Apple Publishing and The Beatles' then-embryonic Apple Records label. He was put under the guidance of George Harrison, who recruited some of the best musicians on both sides of the Atlantic to record with Lomax. Lomax's first single, the Harrison-penned ***Sour Milk Sea*** (written during George's stay at the Maharishi's camp in India), premiered as one of Apple's first four releases. Harrison recorded a home demo of the song with The Beatles following their return from India. Sadly, The Beatles never properly recorded it – or did they? Lomax's is backed by The Beatles (excluding Lennon) on his recording of the song. ***Sour Milk Sea*** failed to be the chart success it deserved to be, but, in fairness to Lomax, it was overshadowed in the charts by two of Apple's other debut singles ***Hey Jude*** by The Beatles, and ***Those Were The Days*** by Mary Hopkin*. Lomax and Harrison continued to record between sessions for **The Beatles** (the white album), to which Lomax contributed backing vocals and hand claps on ***Dear Prudence***.

Harrison and Lomax resumed recording during October and November 1968 at Sound Recorders Studio in Los Angeles. Backing Lomax during these sessions were Hal Blaine, Larry Knechtel and Joe Osborn, who were part of a group of session players known as the "wrecking crew" used extensively by producers Phil Spector* and Lou Adler. Beaver & Krause also contributed to the album on a revolutionary new instrument known as the synthesizer. (Bernie Krause would later claim that side two of George Harrison's album ***Electronic Sounds*** was actually a recording of Krause. His claim is given credence by the fact that Krause's name was painted over-but faintly visible-on the front of the album jacket). According to Lomax, eight basic tracks were recorded in Los Angeles, but the CD booklet claims only six tracks were recorded there. Harrison continued recording, remixing and overdubbing Lomax's debut album for Apple, adding John Barham's string arrangements, horns and backing vocalists to tracks previously recorded in Los Angeles and elsewhere.

Lomax's album **Is This What You Want?** was released on March 21, 1969. It initially failed to gain much notice, leaving its producer somewhat disillusioned. The album has sold fairly well over the ensuing years, and is regarded by many as one of Apple's best non-Beatles albums. Lomax's second single for Apple was ***New Day***, produced by The Beatles' assistant, Mal Evans.

Jackie Lomax's Apple releases fail to give a detailed or always accurate account of each of his recordings. The CD reissue of his Apple album credits ***Little Yellow Pills*** and ***Won't You Come Back*** as being recorded and produced by Harrison in March 1968. This is incorrect, as Harrison was halfway around the world in India for the entire month of March. The CD notes seem to indicate (as do many other sources) that ***The Eagle Laughs At You*** (the B-side to the ***Sour Milk Sea*** single) also includes

Harrison, McCartney, and Starr – though Lomax denies Paul's and Ringo's involvement. Information in Marc Roberty's reference books on Eric Clapton is at odds with previously published information concerning the Lomax sessions. Several reliable publications list both Ringo and Eric Clapton as playing on ***New Day***, while others list only Harrison's involvement. Lomax said Harrison plays on ***New Day***, but that Clapton and Ringo do not.

Fortunately, Lomax recalls most of the studios and musicians used for each of his recordings for Apple. However, he did not attend most of sessions held to overdub the backing vocals and horns, and does not know who was involved, except for singer Madeline Bell. Lomax said Harrison played guitar on most of his Apple recordings. He is uncertain whether Harrison played guitar on ***You've Got Me Thinking***. He does not remember who played on ***Won't You Come Back***.

Lomax also drew a complete blank on a song labeled as ***The Millionaire*** by Jackie Lomax on an Apple Records' acetate that apparently exists. Perhaps the acetate was incorrectly identified, and may be The Iveys doing the song ***And Her Daddy's A Millionaire*** *(see Badfinger)*. ***The Millionaire*** may be nothing more than an early working title for another Lomax song. If ***The Millionaire*** is an unreleased Lomax recording, there is a good chance Harrison contributed to it in some way.

The B-side of ***New Day*** was a cover of The Coasters' song ***Thumbin' A Ride***. Lomax said, "It was McCartney's idea to record ***Thumbin' A Ride***. McCartney produced it because Harrison was away at the time." All evidence indicates that ***Thumbin' A Ride*** and ***Going Back To Liverpool*** were probably recorded on March 11, 1969 and / or possibly March 12. Harrison was at Apple on the March 12, but was called away that evening when police raided his home for drugs. March 12 was also the day McCartney was married, though it would not be unlike McCartney to work on his wedding night. The March 15, 1969 issue of New Musical Express (NME) magazine reported that at least some sessions took place on the March 11. It states "Hours after announcing that he was to marry the following day, he [Paul] spent the evening in Apple's basement studios playing drums for two hours with George Harrison." The CD booklet features a photo of Lomax on guitar and McCartney on drums in Apple Studios. Lomax said McCartney did not end up playing drums on any of his released recordings, but other sources claim McCartney played drums on ***Thumbin' A Ride***. Lomax did say Harrison contributed to some of the ***Thumbin' A Ride*** sessions. Harrison certainly sings backing vocals on ***Going Back To Liverpool***, which most likely was recorded at the same sessions as it credits McCartney as producer. Other reliable sources, including an article in NME on March 22, 1969, indicate that Harrison was also involved in the production of ***Going Back To Liverpool***. Lomax also seems to think George produced the song.

The third and last Lomax single (except for foreign reissues) for Apple Records was ***How The Web Was Woven***, recorded the following fall and released on February 6, 1970. It was produced by Harrison and featured Leon Russell on all the instruments. With the arrival of Allen Klein at Apple, and the bitterness and controversy surrounding the breakup of The Beatles, Jackie Lomax, like most all of Apple's other artists, was neglected. Lomax said Harrison nearly gave him his song ***Something*** to record, and that he turned down John Lennon's offer to record ***Across The Universe***.

Lomax moved to the United States and the Warner Bros. record label, releasing his second album, ***Home Is In My Head***, in 1971. The record's musical credits list Rickie Redstreak on rhythm guitar and Frank Furter on slide and second guitar, fueling speculation that these were pseudonyms for old

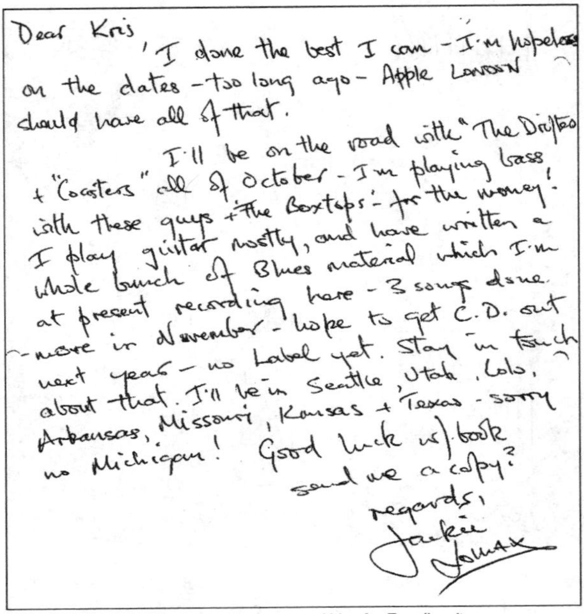

Dear Kris,
I done the best I can - I'm hopeless on the dates - too long ago - Apple London should have all of that.
I'll be on the road with "The Drifters + "Coasters" all of October - I'm playing bass with these guys + The Boxtops - for the money! I play guitar mostly, and have written a whole bunch of Blues material which I'm at present recording here - 3 songs done - more in November - hope to get C.D. out next year - no Label yet. Stay in touch about that. I'll be in Seattle, Utah, Colo, Arkansas, Missouri, Kansas + Texas - sorry no Michigan! Good luck w/ book send me a copy?
regards,
Jackie Lomax

Letter from Jackie Lomax toKristofer Engelhardt

Lomax buddies Paul McCartney and George Harrison. In fact, they were Lomax and Bryn Haworth. Lomax had to use the pseudonyms to avoid U.S. immigration and working permit violations, which technically allowed him to sing on recordings but not to play on them.

Lomax would release another album for Warner Bros. in 1972, but, lacking chart success, he was dropped by the label and returned to his native England. In 1974, he joined the band Badger, but by 1975 he was back in the U.S., this time recording for Capitol Records. After two more commercially disappointing albums, he was dropped by that label. He made a brief cameo appearance in Robert Stigwood's 1978 film **Sgt. Pepper's Lonely Hearts Club Band**. Lomax continues to write songs and perform near his home in southern California. He recently toured with an updated version of The Drifters, The Coasters and The Box Tops, playing bass and guitar.

The London Symphony Orchestra & Chorus

Record 183 title:
Paul McCartney's Standing Stone
Label / Catalog number:
EMI Classics / 7243 5 56484 2 6
Jacket / Inserts:
Standard international design in jewel box / 1 page CD insert & 48 page CD booklet with photos of Paul McCartney
Recording Location / Date:
EMI-Abbey Road Studios, London, U.K. / 30 Apr 97 & 1-2 May 97
Media:
Album 5" CD
Producer:
John Fraser

Song 183a title:
Movement I After heavy light years
(1 Fire/rain. Allegro energico) (2 Cell growth. Semplice) (3 `Human' theme. Maestoso)
Release date / Country:
25 Sep 97 / U.S.A.
Track details:
Side 1, track 1-3 / 16 min. 33 sec.
Composer:
P. McCartney

The London Symphony Chorus: Vocals; The London Symphony Orchestra; Lawrence Foster: Conductor; Janice Graham: Leader; Stephen Westrop: Chorusmaster

Song 183b title:
Movement II He awoke startled
(4 Meditation. Contemplativo) (5 Crystal ship. Con noto scherzando) (6 Sea voyage. Pulsating, with cool jazz feel) (7 Lost at sea. Sognando) (8 Release. Allegro con spirito)
Track details:
Side 1, track 4-8 / 16 min. 14 sec.

Release date / Country:
25 Sep 97 / U.S.A.

Composer:
P. McCartney

The London Symphony Chorus: Vocals; The London Symphony Orchestra; Lawrence Foster: Conductor; Janice Graham: Leader; Stephen Westrop: Chorusmaster

Song 183c title:
Movement III Subtle colours merged soft contours (9 Safe haven/standing stone. Pastorale con moto) (10 Peaceful moment. Andante tranquillo) (11 Messenger. Energico) (12 Lament. Lamentoso) (13 Trance. Misterioso) (14 Eclipse. Eroico)

Track details:
Side 1, track 9-14 / 22 min. 56 sec.

Release date / Country:
25 Sep 97 / U.S.A.

Composer:
P. McCartney

The London Symphony Chorus: Vocals; The London Symphony Orchestra; Lawrence Foster: Conductor; Janice Graham: Leader; Stephen Westrop: Chorusmaster

Song 183d title:
Movement IV Strings pluck, horns blow, drums beat (15 Glory tales. Trionfale) (16 Fugal celebration. L'istesso tempo. Fresco) (17 Rustic dance. Rustico) (18 Love duet. Andante intimo) (19 Celebration. Andante)

Track details:
Side 1, track 15-19 / 19 min. 08 sec.

Release date / Country:
25 Sep 97 / U.S.A.

Composer:
P. McCartney

The London Symphony Chorus: Vocals; The London Symphony Orchestra; Lawrence Foster: Conductor; Janice Graham: Leader; Stephen Westrop: Chorusmaster

The London Symphony Orchestra was founded in London, England in 1904. It has attracted some of the world's most prestigious conductors including Hans Richter, Artur Nikisch, Andre Previn and Claudio Abbado. In 1993, Paul McCartney was commissioned by Richard Lyttelton, president of EMI Classics, to contribute a work to help celebrate EMI's 100th anniversary in 1997. (In 1991, the label had released **Liverpool Oratorio** *[see The Royal Liverpool Philharmonic Orchestra & Choir & Choristers Of Liverpool Cathedral]*, McCartney's first major foray into the world of classical music.) McCartney dedicated much time over the next four years to the creation of ***Standing Stone***, a symphonic poem in four movements performed and recorded by over 300 members of The London Symphony Orchestra & Chorus.

McCartney began by writing the music, and then wrote the story as a poem, to help structure the four movements. He used an Apple PowerMac computer, programmed with *QBase* software, to aid him in composing and annotating the music. He also employed the help of several musicians and composers, including Steve Lodder, Richard Rodney Bennett, John Harle and David Matthews, who are credited as Musical Associates. They helped McCartney translate his composition and ideas into a symphony by assisting with the structuring, arrangement, orchestration and notation of **Standing Stone**. John Fraser produced the recordings at EMI's Abbey Road Studios in London with McCartney in attendance and acting as Executive Producer. Lawrence Foster, an American, conducted the Orchestra & Chorus. Final mixing and editing by McCartney and Fraser took place at The Mill (McCartney's private studio) several weeks later.

Standing Stone is an allegory of the development of life on earth in all of its manifestations from the big bang to the present. The title and initial ideas for **Standing Stone** were taken from two paintings McCartney had done that dealt with the dawn of time and prehistoric Celtic spiral-designs and megaliths. McCartney also felt a need to express in poetry his feelings following the death of Ivan Vaughan, a lifelong friend who had introduced him to John Lennon. McCartney took the advice of Allen Ginsberg*, and sought the help of poet Tom Pichard, who edited the poem.

Standing Stone premiered at the Royal Albert Hall on October 14, 1997, again performed by The

London Symphony Orchestra & Chorus. This date was chosen as it closely marked the 35th Anniversary of EMI's release of ***Love Me Do***, The Beatles first record for the label. (***Love Me Do*** was actually released on October 5.) The premiere also included a symphonic rendering of ***A Leaf*** (see Anya Alexeyev) and ***The Spiral***, and several other classical compositions by McCartney, including ***Inebriation***, performed by The Brodsky Quartet, and ***Stately Horn*** featuring the Mike Thompson Horn Quartet. McCartney was called to the stage a total of six times following the performance. Proceeds from the premiere went to the Music Sound Foundation, a charity founded by EMI to promote music education. The U.S. premiere was held at Carnegie Hall in New York City on November 19, 1997. The record was a major success on both the U.S. and U.K. classical charts. Photos for the CD booklet were provided, in part, by McCartney's wife Linda and daughter Mary. Portions of the making and performance of **Standing Stone** were also filmed.

Kenny Lynch

Record 184 title:
The Stars Sing Lennon & McCartney
Label / Catalog number:
Music For Pleasure / MFP 5755
Jacket / Inserts:
Unique / Record label inner sleeve

Media:
Album 12" (mono)
Recording Location / Date:
U.K. / (probably) Feb or Mar 63

Song 184a title:
Misery
Release date / Country:
23 Jun 86 (first issued 22 Mar 63) / U.K.

Track details:
Side 2, track 5 / 2 min. 04 sec.
Composer:
J. Lennon - P. McCartney

Kenny Lynch: Lead Vocals; Burt Weedon: Guitar; Harry Robinson: Conductor

Kenny Lynch, who is of West Indian descent, was born on March 18, 1939 in London. He first appeared onstage at the age of twelve. Lynch had his first U.K. top 40 with ***Mountain Of Love*** in 1960. In 1962, he made his screen debut in the film **Just For Fun**. In 1963, he had two U.K. top 10s with covers of ***Up On The Roof*** and ***You Can Never Stop Me Loving You***. He co-wrote the Small Faces' *(see Kenney Jones, Ian McLagan, Rod Stewart, Ron Wood)* 1966 hit ***Sha La La La Lee***. In 1983, he returned to the charts with the song ***Half The Day's Gone And We Haven't Earnt A Penny***. He has been a popular entertainer and TV personality in Britain for over three decades, and was awarded an OBE.

Kenny first met The Beatles when they appeared on the same bill at the Liverpool Empire on October 28, 1962. Lynch, along with The Beatles, also appeared on the Helen Shapiro tour in February 1963. Just before the tour, Lennon and McCartney composed the song ***Misery*** with the intention of giving it to Shapiro to record. Her producer, Norrie Paramor, turned it down before Shapiro ever had a chance to hear it. However, Lynch liked the song, performed it on the tour, and became the first artist, other than The Beatles, to record a Lennon and McCartney composition. Unfortunately, it failed in the charts. Some may argue that this song is really a cover version, as it was released on the same day as The Beatles' version, but The Beatles had specifically given it to Lynch to record and release as a single, and it was given much press and airplay before its release. Lynch continued to appear with The Beatles on a number of occasions over the next year. In 1973, Paul McCartney asked Lynch to appear on the cover of his highly successful album **Band On The Run**.

Vera Lynn

Record 185 title:
Don't You Remember When
Label / Catalog number:
EMI / 2413
Jacket / Inserts:
Record label sleeve
Recording Location / Date:
Marquee Studios, London, U.K. / (probably) late 1975

Media:
Single 7"
Producer:
Lynsey de Paul

Song 185a title:
Don't You Remember When
Release date / Country:
20 Feb 76 / U.K.

Track details:
Side 1, track 1 / 5 min. 00 sec.
Composer:
L. de Paul - B. Blue

Vera Lynn: Lead Vocals; Ringo Starr: Tambourine; Tony Hymas: Arrangement

Famed British singer (Dame) Vera Lynn was born on March 20, 1917 in London, England. By the age of fifteen, she had her own dance troupe. She toured England for several years for a variety of song and dance bands before hosting a series of weekly radio broadcasts called **Sincerely Yours** during World War II. She quickly became known as the "Forces Sweetheart," regularly entertaining allied troops. Following the war she maintained a successful worldwide career on stage, screen and television. She was the first British artist to have a number one in the U.S. with the song ***Auf Wiedersehen***, for which she is best remembered. She also wrote two books – **Vocal Refrain** and **We'll Meet Again**. In 1969, she was made an O.B.E (officer of the order of the British Empire) and, in 1975, D.B.E. (Dame Commander of the Order of the British Empire). Vera Lynn, like The Beatles, was a regular visitor to EMI's Abbey Road Studios. She was a fan of The Beatles and recorded cover versions of their songs ***Yesterday*** and ***Good Night***. Her music was featured in The Beatles' **Anthology** film.

Lynn's single ***Don't You Remember When*** featured Ringo Starr on tambourine. It was produced by singer / songwriter Lynsey de Paul, who was dating Ringo Starr at the time. She said, "Ringo turned up to collect me from the studio, we put a tambourine in his hand for a photo-shoot and he ended up playing on the track."

Lynsey recounted how her 1976 single ***If I Don't Get You The Next One Will*** was inspired by Ringo: "We had arranged to go to dinner, and instead he slept through the evening in his offices, so the song relates to revenge."

Lynsey recalled how she did some recording at Ringo's home studio with help from George Harrison: "Ringo had a recording studio in his house, but he was not technologically minded at the time, insofar as he could not even turn on the equipment. George came to his house, which had written above the front door 'This is not here,' [left by John and Yoko when they owned the house], and the three of us jammed from midnight to three o'clock in the morning. As we could not record on the proper desk, Ringo placed a little cassette player, driven by batteries, on a chair in between all of us. Unfortunately, the batteries were running low, and the tape was slowing down as it recorded. When we played it back the result was that it sounded as if we were all getting faster and faster, and higher and higher in pitch. It was very funny. Ringo played drums, George the guitar, and I played piano."

De Paul has written over a dozen songs that have reached the top 10 in the U.K., and has had several hits of her own, including ***Sugar Me*** and ***Won't Somebody Dance With Me***. She also recorded a cover of The Beatles' ***Because*** for the soundtrack to the 1976 film **All This And World War II**. Along with her songwriting, De Paul has acted and worked in radio and television.

Jeff Lynne

Record 186 title:
Armchair Theatre
Label / Catalog number:
Reprise / 9 26184-2
Jacket / Inserts:
Standard international design in jewel box / 8 page CD booklet
Recording Location / Date:
Posh Studios, Warwickshire, U.K. / late 1989 - early 1990
Media:
Album 5" CD
Producer:
Jeff Lynne

Song 185a title:
Every Little Thing
Release date / Country:
11 Jun 90 / U.S.A.
Track details:
Side 1, track 1 / 3 min. 41 sec.
Composer:
J. Lynne

Jeff Lynne: Lead Vocals, Electric & Acoustic Guitars; Jim Horn: Saxophones; Mette Mathiesen: Drums & Percussion; George Harrison: Acoustic Guitar & B. Vocals; Richard Tandy: Acoustic Guitar; Phil Hatton: B. Vocals; Hema Desai: Operatic Voice; Michael Kamen: Strings

Song 186b title:
Lift Me Up
Release date / Country:
11 Jun 90 / U.S.A.
Track details:
Side 1, track 3 / 3 min. 36 sec.
Composer:
J. Lynne

Jeff Lynne: Lead Vocals, Keyboards, Electric & Acoustic Guitars, Piano, Bass & Chair; George Harrison: Slide & Acoustic Guitar, Harmony & B. Vocals; Mette Mathiesen: Drums; Vikram A. Patil: Percussion; Nellai D. Kanan: Percussion; Fateh Singh Gangani: Percussion; Sureesh K. Lalwani: Percussion; Dave Morgan: B. Vocals; Phil Hatton: B. Vocals; Richard Tandy: Acoustic Guitar

Song 186c title:
September Song
Release date / Country:
11 Jun 90 / U.S.A.
Track details:
Side 1, track 5 / 2 min. 57 sec.
Composer:
M. Anderson - K. Weill

Jeff Lynne: Lead Vocals, Electric Guitars, Drums, Keyboards, Bass, Choir & B. Vocals; George Harrison: Slide & Acoustic Guitar; Richard Tandy: Piano & Choir; Rita: Saw; Mette Mathiesen: Choir; Sheila Tandy: Choir; Jake Commander: Choir; Phil Hatton: Choir; Dave Morgan: Choir

Song 186d title:
Stormy Weather
Release date / Country:
11 Jun 90 / U.S.A.
Track details:
Side 1, track 9 / 3 min. 42 sec.
Composer:
T. Koehler - H. Arlen

Jeff Lynne: Lead Vocals, Footsteps, Bass & Keyboards; George Harrison: Slide & Acoustic Guitar; Mette Mathiesen: Drums; Richard Tandy: Piano & Choir; Michael Kamen: Arrangement & Conductor of Strings; Phil Hatton: Choir; Jake Commander: Choir; Sheila Tandy: Choir; Dave Morgan: Choir

Record 187 title:
Every Little Thing
Label / Catalog number:
Reprise / W 9799 (7599-21584-2)
Media:
Extended Play 5" CD
Producer:
Jeff Lynne
Jacket / Inserts:
Standard international design in Single Jewel box / Photo (same as LP) Insert
Recording Location / Date:
Posh Studios, Warwickshire, U.K. / late 1989 - early 1990

Song 187a title:
Every Little Thing (12" Remix)
Release date / Country:
Jun 90 / Germany
Track details:
Side 1, track 1 / 7 min. 46 sec.
Composer:
J. Lynne

Jeff Lynne: Lead Vocals, Electric & Acoustic Guitars; Jim Horn: Saxophones; Mette Mathiesen: Drums & Percussion; George Harrison: Acoustic Guitar & B. Vocals; Richard Tandy: Acoustic Guitar; Phil Hatton: B. Vocals; Hema Desai: Operatic Voice; Michael Kamen: Strings

Jeff Lynne, born on December 30, 1947 in Birmingham, England, began his rise to musical stardom in the Birmingham band Idle Race. He soon joined forces with its former member Roy Wood, in his band The Move, which separately evolved into Electric Light Orchestra in 1972. Wood soon left to form the band Wizzard. Despite a dozen personnel changes over the years, ELO's three founding members, and core personnel, were Jeff Lynne, the group's singer, songwriter, lead guitarist and producer; Richard Tandy (who joined the band shortly after its inception) on keyboards and guitar; and drummer Bev Bevan.

ELO was often compared to The Beatles because they continued to evolve a style of classical orchestra rock first credited to The Beatles on their album **Sgt. Pepper's Lonely Hearts Club Band**. They seemed to appeal to an audience that longed for a lavish, live Beatles reunion. They released a live version of The Beatles' ***Day Tripper*** in 1974. Among their biggest hits in either the U.S. or U.K. were ***Can't Get It Out Of My Head***, ***Evil Woman***, ***Strange Magic***, ***Mr. Blue Sky***, ***Sweet Talkin' Woman***, ***The Diary Of Horace Wimp***, ***Don't Bring Me Down*** and ***Hold On Tight***, most using a massive production of synthesizers and symphony instruments. Jeff Lynne recorded covers of The Beatles' ***With A Little Help From My Friends*** and ***Nowhere Man*** for the soundtrack to the 1976 film **All This And World War II**. ELO seemed to have run its course with the advent of the anti-production and minimalist styles of punk and new wave music in the early 1980s. Their last album was **Balance Of Power** in 1986.

During the mid-1980s, Lynne began producing mainstream pop artists like Dave Edmunds*. Edmunds forwarded a message to Lynne from George Harrison, who expressed his desire to collaborate with Lynne. The two got together and quickly became friends. Lynne helped Harrison write and produce the song ***Zig Zag*** for the soundtrack for George's HandMade Films production of the ill-fated **Shanghai Surprise** starring Madonna and Sean Penn *(see Various Artists - Shanghai Surprise)*. Over the course of the following year, Lynne produced and played on Harrison's highly successful album **Cloud Nine**.

Lynne made an appearance with Bevan and Tandy on March 15, 1986 for the rock charity **Heartbeat '86** in Birmingham, England. George Harrison and Denny Laine* also made guest appearances during the performance. On June 5 and 6, 1987, Lynne, along with Harrison, Ringo Starr, Elton John*, Eric Clapton* and Phil Collins, made appearances at London's Wembley Arena for **The Prince's Trust Rock Concert** (McCartney had appeared the previous year).

Lynne and Harrison also worked together on the album **Duane Eddy** *(see Duane Eddy)*. On

February 10, 1988, George and Jeff showed up at KLOS FM Studios in Los Angeles for the live phone-in radio show **Rockline**. During the course of the show, they performed on acoustic guitar impromptu versions of ***Here Comes The Sun***, ***Bells Of Rhymney***, ***Mr. Tambourine Man***, ***Take Me As I Am***, ***That's All Right***, ***Let It Be Me***, ***Something*** and ***Every Grain Of Sand***.

Lynne has produced some of rock's elite, including Brian Wilson *(see The Beach Boys)*, Del Shannon*, Roy Orbison* and Tom Petty*. His association with the latter two artists would lead to the formation of one of the greatest "supergroups" of all time, the Traveling Wilburys, featuring Lynne, Harrison, Bob Dylan*, Tom Petty, and Roy Orbison, along with Harrison-backing veterans Jim Keltner *(see Attitudes)*, Ray Cooper and Jim Horn*.

After all of Jeff Lynne's successes with other artists, he decided to spend some time producing his solo album titled **Armchair Theatre**, with musical help from George Harrison, Jim Horn and Del Shannon, among others. According to Lynne, he has no other finished recordings, other than those that ended up on the album **Armchair Theatre**, that include contributions by Harrison. Lynne said, "There are lots of jams of George and me, but nothing that's finished." Obviously, Lynne and Harrison have been of great benefit to each other, and a whole host of other artists, as a result of their partnership. Lynne, Tom Petty, Jim Keltner and Joe Walsh* backed Ringo singing ***I Call Your Name*** as a contribution to **The John Lennon Scholarship Concert** held on May 5, 1990 in Liverpool and included on the 1991 laser videodisk **The World's Greatest Artists Sing LENNON A Tribute**.

Jeff Lynne, Los Angeles, CA, late 1980s, photo courtesy of Tom Bert

Nothing could have prepared Jeff Lynne for the task he was asked to perform by George Harrison in early 1994. Only a handful of people have ever produced The Beatles, and Jeff Lynne was about to become one of them. This was no ordinary recording session (not that any Beatles' recording sessions are), this was The Beatles' reunion recording, or at least as close to a reunion as they are ever going to get. Though at least three of The Beatles had recorded together on several occasions following their breakup in 1970, it was always for another Beatles' solo recording and not for a new Beatles recording. The chance of all four Beatles reuniting for new recordings was thought to have died along with John Lennon on December 8, 1980. Amazingly, with the help of Yoko Ono* and modern technology, all of that changed.

Yoko Ono revealed in an interview with Philip Norman in the British newspaper Daily Mail in November 1995 that George Harrison and longtime Beatles assistant Neil Aspinall first approached her about the idea of the three surviving Beatles adding to John's unreleased recordings for use in The Beatles' **Anthology** project. Not surprisingly, Paul McCartney thinks he first approached Yoko about the idea, but he is not sure. In all likelihood, the three surviving Beatles discussed the idea with each other before anyone approached Yoko. On January 19, 1994, Ono and McCartney took part in ceremonies in New York to induct John Lennon into the Rock and Roll Hall of Fame. Following the ceremonies, Yoko turned over some of John's unreleased demos to McCartney.

George Martin*, who had produced nearly all the Beatles' recordings, was busy reproducing recordings to be included in The Beatles' **Anthology** project. George Harrison wanted his friend Jeff Lynne to produce the new Beatles' single. McCartney was reluctant, but finally agreed to Harrison's recommendation. Several weeks after McCartney received the tapes, the three surviving Beatles were at Paul McCartney's private studio contributing to the recordings to create a new single. With production assistance from Paul, George and Ringo, Jeff Lynne was able to turn the demo of John Lennon's song ***Free As A Bird*** into a highly polished new Beatles' single. Lynne was invited back to McCartney's studio in February 1995 to produce The Beatles' follow-up single ***Real Love***. Nearly a year later he was back again, this time to produce some of Paul McCartney's recordings for his 1997 album **Flaming Pie**. It was reported in 1998 that Ringo contributed to recordings for Lynne's second solo album.

Taj Mahal & The Graffiti Band

Record 188 title:
Live! The Silver Wilburys
Label / Catalog number:
[none] / SWP 87-2 [Unauthorized Record]
Jacket / Inserts:
Unique in Jewel box / 2 page CD insert
Recording Location / Date:
On location at Palomino Club, Los Angeles, CA, U.S.A. / 19 Feb 87
Media:
Album 5" CD (mono)
Producer:
(probably) Palomino Club

Song 188a title:
Johnny B. Goode [live]
Release date / Country:
1988 / Korea
Track details:
Side 1, track 10 / 4 min. 33 sec.
Composer:
C. Berry

Taj Mahal: Lead Vocals; Jesse Ed Davis: Guitar; George Harrison: Guitar; Bob Dylan: Guitar; John Fogerty: Guitar; Jim Ehinger: Keyboards; Bobby Tsukamoto: Bass; Mark Shark: Guitar; Gary Ray: Drums

Song 188b title:
Lucille [live]
Release date / Country:
1988 / Korea
Track details:
Side 1, track 14 / 5 min. 54 sec.
Composer:
A. Collins - R. Penniman

Taj Mahal: Lead Vocals & Harmonica; Jesse Ed Davis: Guitar; George Harrison: Guitar; Bob Dylan: Guitar; John Fogerty: Guitar; Jim Ehinger: Keyboards; Bobby Tsukamoto: Bass; Mark Shark: Guitar; Gary Ray: Drums

Song 188c title:
Matchbox [live]
Release date / Country:
1988 / Korea
Track details:
Side 1, track 2-3 / 7 min. 11 sec.
Composer:
C. Perkins - [Trad]

Taj Mahal: Vocals & Harmonica; George Harrison: Vocals & Guitar; Jesse Ed Davis: Guitar; Bob Dylan: Guitar; Jim Ehinger: Keyboards; Bobby Tsukamoto: Bass; Mark Shark: Guitar; Gary Ray: Drums

Song 188d title:
Twist And Shout [live]
Release date / Country:
1988 / Korea
Track details:
Side 1, track 15 / 3 min. 21 sec.
Composer:
P. Medley - B. Russell

Taj Mahal: Vocals; John Fogerty: Vocals & Guitar; Jesse Ed Davis: Guitar & B. Vocals; George Harrison: Guitar & B. Vocals; Bob Dylan: Guitar & B. Vocals; Jim Ehinger: Keyboards; Bobby

Tsukamoto: Bass; Mark Shark: Guitar; Gary Ray: Drums

Song 188e title:
Willie And The Hand Jive [live]
Release date / Country:
1988 / Korea
Track details:
Side 1, track 11 / 5 min. 38 sec.
Composer:
J. Otis

Taj Mahal: Lead Vocals; Jesse Ed Davis: Guitar; George Harrison: Guitar & B. Vocals; Bob Dylan: Guitar & B. Vocals; John Fogerty: Guitar & B. Vocals; Jim Ehinger: Keyboards; Bobby Tsukamoto: Bass; Mark Shark: Guitar; Gary Ray: Drums

Taj Mahal was born Henry Fredericks on May 17, 1942 in New York City, New York. His father was a well-known "be-bop" jazz musician. Henry was playing guitar by the age of five. His main musical influence came from his Pan-African and multi-ethnic neighborhood. By age twelve he was learning basic blues from Linwood Perry. Henry Fredericks changed his name to Taj Mahal in 1958. He studied animal husbandry and veterinary science, but settled on a career in music. He has had much critical and some commercial success, primarily with blues-rock bands, including one with well-known session guitarist Jesse Ed Davis*. Though he has never had any major chart successes, he continues to record, tour and gain the respect of his peers.

Taj Mahal, Detroit, MI, photo courtesy of Pat Henry

On February 19, 1987, Taj, along with the Graffiti Band featuring Jesse Ed Davis, were performing at Hollywood's Palomino Club when George Harrison, John Fogerty* and Bob Dylan* joined them onstage. The result was a more than an hour-and-a-half hour jam. Copies of the house video were soon circulating among collectors. A bootleg CD titled **Live! The Silver Wilburys** has also surfaced, including most of the superstar performance. The Silver Wilburys title is a play on The Silver Beatles, as this concert was recorded more than a year before the formation of the Harrison "supergroup" Traveling Wilburys *(see Bob Dylan, Jeff Lynne, Roy Orbison, Tom Petty And The Heartbreakers)*. In reality, it's nothing more than Harrison and Dylan joining Taj Mahal onstage after hours to jam.

Songs omitted from the CD that include Harrison on guitar were ***Checkin' Up On My Baby***, ***She Caught The Katy***, ***You're Going To Need Somebody On Your Bond***, ***Bacon Fat*** and ***Crosscut Saw***, all sung by Taj. Songs with lead vocals sung primarily by Harrison were ***Honey Don't***, ***Dizzy***, ***Miss Lizzy***, ***Peggy Sue*** (all favorite oldies of The Beatles), and Dylan's ***Watching The River Flow***. These are more properly considered Harrison performances, and not contributions to another artist's recordings, because he is the main vocalist.

In Beatlefan magazine (vol. 12, No. 6 / vol. 13, No. 1 - Dec 90 - Jan 91), an article about Ringo signing with the Private Music record label mentioned that he had participated in recordings for Taj Mahal's forthcoming U.S. album **Like Never Before** (Private Music / 2081-2-P) at Los Angeles' Studio 55. However, when the album was released, there was no mention of Starr in the very detailed credits. According to Taj, Starr did attend sessions for the album **Like Never Before**, but he did not contribute to any of Taj's recordings.

The Manhattan Transfer

Record 189 title:
Coming Out
Label / Catalog number:
Atlantic / 18183-2
Jacket / Inserts:
Standard international design in jewel box / 8 page CD booklet
Recording Location / Date:
Studio 55, Los Angeles, CA, U.S.A. / (probably) 1975
Media:
Album 5" CD
Producer:
Richard Perry

Song 189a title:
S.O.S.
Release date / Country:
27 Aug 90 (first issued 30 Aug 76) / U.S.A.
Track details:
Side 1, track 8 / 3 min. 10 sec.
Composer:
G. Shury - P. Swern

Tim Hauser: Vocals & Vocal Arrangement; Laurel Masse: Vocals; Alan Paul: Vocals; Janis Siegel: Vocals & Vocal Arrangement; Ringo Starr: Drums; Jim Keltner: Drums; Clarence MacDonald: Piano; Andy Muson: Bass; Ira Newbom: Guitar; Jackie Kelso: Tenor Saxophone

Song 189b title:
Zindy Lou
Release date / Country:
27 Aug 90 (first issued 30 Aug 76) / U.S.A.
Track details:
Side 1, track 2 / 2 min. 50 sec.
Composer:
J. Moore - E. Smith

Tim Hauser: Vocals & Vocal Arrangement; Laurel Masse: Vocals; Alan Paul: Vocals; Janis Siegel: Vocals & Vocal Arrangement; Ringo Starr: Drums; Jim Keltner: Drums; Dr. John: Piano; Andy Muson: Bass; Ira Newbom: Guitar; Doug Throngren: Percussion

The Manhattan Transfer was formed in 1969 in New York City, originally performing jug band music, but essentially broke up after a short time. Tim Hauser (the only original member), born in Troy, New York in 1940, reformed the group in 1972 with Laurel Masse, born in 1954; Alan Paul, born in Newark, New Jersey in 1949; and Janis Siegel, born in Brooklyn, NY in 1953. They enjoyed modest success, mostly as a New York cabaret act that specialized in "doo-wop," swing, jazz, "scat," and ballads. In 1979, Laurel Masse left the group and was replaced by Cheryl Bentyne. Their biggest hit was a remake of the Ad Libs classic ***Boy From New York City***. The group has earned 10 Grammy Awards. In 1986, their album **Vocalese** received 12 Grammy nominations. The Manhattan Transfer continues to record and perform and remains one of the world's most popular jazz vocal groups.

Ringo became involved in The Manhattan Transfer's recording sessions for **Coming Out** as a result of his friendship with the album's producer, Richard Perry. Perry said, "I asked him if he would play, and he's a great guy, and he never turned me down." Tim Hauser recalls, "Ringo and Jim Keltner produced a particular sound that was very unusual. Ringo played straight time, and Jim played time as well as fills. It had to do with the 'flamming' that was produced by the simultaneity of their snares, coupled with their ability to get in the same groove. I personally loved it. That was the only time we played with Ringo. The session was done at Richard Perry's Studio 55 on Melrose Avenue in Hollywood. That studio was originally built in the 1940s for Bing Crosby as a convenience, as it was right next door to Paramount. It was the studio where he recorded 'White Christmas.'"

Gerry Marsden

Record 190 title:
Lennon / McCartney Songbook
Media:
Album 12"
Label / Catalog number:
K-Tel / ONE 1274
Jacket / Inserts:
Unique with Liner Notes by Paul McCartney

Song 190a title:
[various]
Composer:
J. Lennon - P. McCartney
Release date / Country:
1985 / U.K.

Gerry Marsden *(See Gerry And The Pacemakers.)*

George Martin

Record 191 title:
Love In The Open Air (The soundtrack theme from "The Family Way") / A Theme From "The Family Way"
Media:
Single 7" (mono)
Label / Catalog number:
Decca / F. 12536
Producer:
George Martin
Jacket / Inserts:
Record label sleeve
Recording Location / Date:
(probably) CTS or Decca Studios, London, U.K. / Nov - Dec 66

Song 191a title:
Love In The Open Air (The soundtrack theme from "The Family Way") [single version]
Track details:
Side 1, track 1 / 2 min. 54 sec.
Release date / Country:
23 Dec 66 / U.K.
Composer:
P. McCartney

Neville Marriner: Leader of String Quartet (aka Tudor Minstrels)

Song 191b title:
A Theme From "The Family Way" [single version]
Track details:
Side 2, track 1 / 2 min. 35 sec.
Release date / Country:
23 Dec 66 / U.K.
Composer:
P. McCartney

Neville Marriner: Leader of String Quartet (aka Tudor Minstrels)

Record 192 title:
Love In The Open Air
/ Theme From "The Family Way"
Label / Catalog number:
United Artists / UP 1165
Jacket / Inserts:
Record label sleeve
Recording Location / Date:
EMI-Abbey Road Studios, London, U.K. / 10 Dec 66
Media:
Single 7" (mono)
Producer:
A.I.R. (London)

Song 192a title:
Love In The Open Air
Release date / Country:
23 Dec 66 / U.K.
Track details:
Side 1, track 1 / 3 min. 07 sec.
Composer:
P. McCartney

The George Martin Orchestra

Song 192b title:
Theme from "The Family Way"
Release date / Country:
23 Dec 66 / U.K.
Track details:
Side 2, track 1 / 2 min. 12 sec.
Composer:
P. McCartney

The George Martin Orchestra

Record 193 title:
Love In The Open Air
Label / Catalog number:
United Artists / UA 50,148
Jacket / Inserts:
Record label sleeve
Recording Location / Date:
(probably) EMI-Abbey Road Studios, London, U.K. / (probably) 10 Dec 66
Media:
Single 7" (mono)
Producer:
A.I.R. (London)

Song 193a title:
Love In The Open Air [alternate version]
Release date / Country:
24 Apr 67 / U.S.A.
Track details:
Side 1, track 1 / 2 min. 18 sec.
Composer:
P. McCartney - G. Martin

The George Martin Orchestra

Record 194 title:
Off The Beatle Track
Label / Catalog number:
United Artists / UAS 6377
Jacket / Inserts:
Standard international design W/photos of The Beatles on front & back of jacket & liner notes by The Beatles / Record label inner sleeve
Recording Location / Date:
EMI-Abbey Road Studios, London, U.K. / mid-1964
Media:
Album 12"
Producer:
George Martin and Ron Richards

Song 194a title:
[various]
Release date / Country:
10 Jul 64 / U.S.A.
Composer:
J. Lennon - P. McCartney - G. Harrison

George Martin & His Orchestra

Record 195 title:
The Family Way (Original Soundtrack)
Media:
Album 12”
Label / Catalog number:
Decca / SKLA-4847
Producer:
George Martin
Jacket / Inserts:
Standard international design / Record label inner sleeve
Recording Location / Date:
CTS Studios, London, U.K. / Nov - Dec 66

Song 195a title:
The Family Way (“Love In The Open Air”)
Track details:
Side 1, track 1-6 & Side 2, track 1-7 / 24 min. 19 sec.
Release date / Country:
1967 (first issued 06 Jan 67) / Australia
Composer:
P. McCartney

Neville Marriner: Leader of String Quartet (aka Tudor Minstrels)

George Martin was born January 3, 1926 in London, England. Martin began playing the piano at a young age, and by sixteen had formed a school dance band. He served in the Fleet Air Arm during World War II, and later entered the Guildhall School of Music where he also began playing the oboe. His teacher at Guildhall was Margaret Asher, the mother of Jane and Peter Asher *(see Peter & Gordon.)* Shortly after graduation, he was hired by Parlophone Records, a subsidiary label of EMI. He eventually became a producer and A&R (Artist and Repertoire) man for the label. His first real successes with the label came with his production of comedy records, most notably Peter Ustinov and Peter Sellers *(see Peter Sellers, Terry Southern & Ringo Starr)* of The Goons. Martin seemed to be attracted to the off-beat.

It was little wonder that Martin would take notice of the soft spoken, well-groomed Brian Epstein, who was hardly typical of rock group managers. He was also intrigued, though not overly impressed, by the recordings of The Beatles, which Epstein had brought for him to hear. Other EMI labels had already turned down The Beatles. Epstein, however, did not hesitate to use his leverage as the owner of several major record shops in trying to persuade EMI to sign The Beatles.

After a subsequent meeting with Epstein, Martin arranged for a recording session for The Beatles on June 6, 1962. The London-established, classically trained Martin took an immediate liking to the scruffy Northern scousers, particularly their keen sense of humor and raw talent, and formally signed the group. He set about cultivating

them musically in much the same way that Brian Epstein had done with their public appearance. Martin gained the respect of The Beatles when they learned he had produced records for Sellers and Ustinov of their favorite comedy team, The Goons.

A number of people have claimed to be the "fifth" Beatle. Pete Best and Stu Sutcliffe actually were bona fide "fifth" Beatles; and assistants / road managers, Neil Aspinall and Mal Evans were as close to The Beatles' inner circle as anyone. But in terms of their phenomenal success, only Epstein and Martin qualify as "fifth" Beatles. Epstein was largely responsible for The Beatles successful promotion. Martin, in essence, took a bar band from northern England and helped develop them into credible recording artists and songwriters. The Beatles and Martin were in every sense of the word a musical team from 1962 through to at least **Sgt. Pepper**. Toward the end of The Beatles' career, when they were more knowledgeable and skilled in production, they relied less on George Martin.

Martin's contribution to The Beatles' early success cannot be understated. He selected many of their songs, played keyboards on a good number of their recordings, and arranged many of their ideas into written music. He also exposed The Beatles to classical music, and in doing so, greatly contributed to its fusion with rock music. Martin was flexible and open to experimentation, allowing The Beatles more freedom in the studio than most of his contemporaries would have tolerated.

In 1964, Martin and his orchestra contributed the instrumental music for the soundtrack of The Beatles' first film **A Hard Day's Night**. Two singles from it were issued in the U.S. with picture sleeves that featured photos of The Beatles which today are highly sought after collector's items. Martin also released an album of instrumental arrangements of Beatles songs in 1964 titled **Off The Beatle Track** that featured liner notes by, and black & white photos of, The Beatles on the front and back of the jacket.

In 1965, Martin released a single with an instrumental version of ***I Feel Fine*** and an album of instrumental cover versions of The Beatles' album **Help!**. Martin was the obvious choice for doing the instrumental soundtrack to the Beatles' second film, as he had done it with their first. But the **Help!** instrumental soundtrack was scored by Ken Thorne. Thorne got the job because of his friendship with the film's director, Richard Lester, who did not get on particularly well with Martin. Martin, contrary to many discographies, had nothing to do with the instrumental soundtrack music to **Help!** (Thorne also scored the soundtracks for Lester's 1967 film **How I Won The War**, co-starring John Lennon, and **The Magic Christian** *[see Peter Sellers, Terry Southern & Ringo Starr]*.) Martin's U.S. and U.K. releases of **Help!** (like The Beatles) varied both in jacket design and content. Though the contents were identical, except for the additional song ***Bahama Sound*** on the U.K. version, three songs on the U.S. version featured their original working titles: ***Auntie Gin's Theme*** [***I've Just Seen A Face***], ***That's A Nice Hat*** [***It's Only Love***], and ***Scrambled Egg*** [***Yesterday***]. The front jacket of the U.S. version featured a unique color photo of The Beatles in the Alps from the film **Help!**. The U.K. version only featured black and white photos of The Beatles on the back of the jacket.

In August 1965, Martin, along with several other employees, left EMI to form a production company called AIR (Associated Independent Recording). He had long been a successful producer for other artists besides The Beatles *(see Billy J. Kramer & The Dakotas, The Fourmost, Gerry And The Pacemakers, Cilla Black, The Scaffold)*. Martin was also a successful songwriter, arranger, conductor and musician. Though he continued to produce and record The Beatles at EMI, he was a free agent working for himself and AIR. Martin's next Beatles-related project was the album **The Beatle Girls**, featuring covers of Beatles songs from 1965 and 1966, but without any photos or liner note contributions by The Beatles.

Toward the end of 1966, Martin helped McCartney with his instrumental soundtrack for the film **The Family Way**, essentially doing everything but composing McCartney's two basic themes, ***The Theme From The Family Way*** and ***Love In The Open Air***. The soundtrack album contained a total of 13 variations on the two themes. It was released on Decca in the U.K. and its subsidiary label, London, in the U.S. Due to the soundtrack's limited release, it soon became a collector's item. The Australian album release is currently the most available issue. The credit on the album reads "supervised and orchestrations arranged by George Martin," but no producer is credited on the soundtrack album. However, according to McCartney's fan-club magazine Club Sandwich issue No. 77, Martin did produce the soundtrack album.

It is generally assumed that the soundtrack music was performed by The George Martin Orchestra, as it is usually credited. In fact, it was performed with a string Quartet led by Neville Marriner, and a small brass section that was later dubbed the Tudor Minstrels by Decca when they released the single ***Love In The Open Air / Theme From The Family Way***. ***Love In The Open Air*** was completely remixed for the single and ***Theme From The Family Way*** consisted of two separate edits from the soundtrack album. George Martin and His Orchestra recorded a more up-tempo single version of ***Love In The Open Air / Theme From The Family Way*** for United Artists Records, whom Martin was contracted to at the time. Martin's U.S. single release of ***Love In The Open Air*** is completely different from the version used on the U.K. single, and substituted ***Bahama Sound*** on the B-side. (Yet another single version of ***Love In The Open Air*** was also released by Sounds Sensational, with The Mike Sammes Singers, who later sang background vocals on The Beatles' recordings ***I Am The Walrus*** and ***Good Night***. The theme was also covered by The Casino Royales and the Brass Ring.) The motion picture **The Family Way** premiered in London on December 18, 1966, and was made available on VHS in the U.K. in 1989.

In 1995, Canadian guitarist Carl Aubut released the album **Paul McCartney: The Family Way** (Philips / 314 528 922-2) with McCartney's blessing. It was initially reported that McCartney had contributed to the album's liner notes, but that proved not to be the case. A photograph of McCartney, Aubut and producer Michel Laverdiere together appears on the back of the CD booklet. The recording features guitar, flute, clarinet and a string quartet performing variations on ***The Family Way***. George Martin and music from **The Family Way** were also included in Paul McCartney's 1995 radio series **Oobu Joobu**.

Martin finished out 1966 beginning work with The Beatles on an album that would prove to be their greatest collaboration, **Sgt. Pepper's Lonely Hearts Club Band**. Though not under the influence of mind-altering drugs as were The Beatles, Martin's receptive state of mind was able to interpret and guide The Beatles through their psychedelic vision of **Sgt. Pepper**, becoming the pen of their cosmic muse. Following **Sgt. Pepper**, Martin and The Beatles relied on each other less often. Like Brian Epstein, he had begun to outlive his usefulness to them. He was no longer necessary to their success or their individual pursuits, and he too, now successful with AIR, no longer needed The Beatles.

Martin was employed to do another film soundtrack for The Beatles, this time for the full-length animated film **Yellow Submarine**. It was a film that the late Brian Epstein had allowed to be made. The Beatles were not enthusiastic about the project, and distanced themselves from it. Martin took the project more seriously. By the time the film was ready for release, The Beatles realized it was no ordinary cartoon, but a relevant period piece appropriate for the closing of the psychedelic '60s that would entertain children for generations to come. What began as the outgrowth of an exploitive Saturday morning cartoon series in the U.S., ironically turned out to be one of The Beatles' greatest critical successes! The soundtrack album was a sort of compromise between the previous U.S. and U.K. formats. It includes The Beatles' recordings on side one, and all George Martin's instrumental soundtrack music on side two. The Beatles' side contained the previously released ***All You Need Is Love*** and the title track ***Yellow Submarine***, but most of the other songs were not up to Beatles' usual standard due to their initial lack of interest in the project. The George Martin side of the soundtrack was far more appropriate and inspired.

Martin released his last album of Beatles covers, ***London, By George!***, in late 1968 that centered on the Beatles' **Sgt. Pepper** period. Throughout much of 1968 and 1969, Martin found working with The Beatles difficult. He could no longer bear to watch them bicker and fight. He was often absent or delegating duties to subordinates during many of the final weeks of recording for **The Beatles** (white album).

Martin's early production work in January of 1969 on **Get Back**, later to become the **Let It Be** album, was eventually handed over to Glyn Johns and finally Phil Spector* to re-produce. Following the abortive **Get Back** project, McCartney pleaded with Martin to produce what would prove to be the last album The Beatles' recorded, **Abbey Road**. Martin agreed on the condition that he have full control, and that some rules be followed and order maintained! The Beatles behaved and, with Martin's help pulled off their swan song.

In December 1969, Ringo was filmed performing a prerecorded version (without The Beatles) of ***Octopus's Garden*** for a BBC-TV special on George Martin titled **With A Little Help From My Friends**. Martin was producing Ringo's **Sentimental Journey** album of old standards at the time. It would essentially be the last time The Beatles, except Paul McCartney, would employ the services of George Martin as producer for their solo recordings.

Martin continued to produce a number of successful acts following the breakup of The Beatles including America, Jeff Beck, Gary Brooker*, Billy Preston*, Cheap Trick, John Williams*, Jimmy Webb*, Seatrain, The Little River Band, and Ultravox, among others. Martin reluctantly agreed to arrange and produce the soundtrack for the 1978 film **Sgt. Pepper's Lonely Hearts Club Band**. His autobiography titled **All You Need Is Ears** was published in 1979, he edited the book **Making Music**, published in 1983, and he wrote a companion book to the TV special **The Making of Sgt. Pepper** in 1994.

Of The Beatles, Paul McCartney probably had the most in common with George Martin musically. Following their breakup, all of the Beatles were anxious for musical independence, not only from their seven-year association with each other, but from Martin as well. Though there was never any genuine personal animosity toward him by any members of the group, he represented and reminded them of something that, at the time, they were all very sensitive about and trying to forget – The Beatles. McCartney briefly employed his services for some of the orchestrations on his 1971 album **Ram**, though Martin was not credited. McCartney wisely chose Martin to produce **Live And Let Die**, the title song to the James Bond film, which led to Martin doing the entire soundtrack. It was not until 1981 that McCartney employed Martin full-time and recorded at Martin's AIR Studios at Montserrat in the West Indies. The two worked together steadily up to 1984, with Martin producing the McCartney albums **Tug Of War**, **Pipes Of Peace** and the soundtrack to McCartney's film **Give My Regards To Broad Street**. McCartney has since used a variety of producers, but still utilizes Martin on occasion (primarily for string arrangements and conducting), even as recently as on his 1997 album **Flaming Pie**.

The independently produced album **The Beatles In The Studio – A Conversation With George Martin** features photographs of The Beatles on the jacket and on the picture disc, though they did not contribute to the interview that obviously pertains to them. **Off The Beatle Track** was recently issued on CD (One Way Records / 2117793) in the U.S., and EMI is considering issuing all of its

George Martin albums on CD in the future.

George Martin has continued to act as The Beatles' official producer, re-mastering all of their unreleased and re-released recordings over the years. However, he did not produce The Beatles' recording of **Free As A Bird** in 1994, nor ***Real Love*** the following year, reportedly in part, because his hearing was beginning to fail.

Martin has served as an officer of the Chrysalis Records group that now controls AIR. In June of 1996, he became Sir George Martin. Though essentially retired in recent years, Martin continues to lend his talents to a number of projects. He produced Elton John's* 1997 re-recording of ***Candle In The Wind*** in memory of Diana, Princess of Wales, which became the biggest selling single recording in history. Martin next organized the benefit concert **Music For Montserrat** to aid the volcano ravaged island. The concert was held on September 15, 1997 at the Royal Albert Hall and featured artists who had recorded at Martin's studio on the island including McCartney, Elton John, Carl Perkins* and Eric Clapton*. Martin recently produced an album of various artists covering The Beatles' recordings and contributed to Ringo Starr's album **Vertical Man** in 1998.

Dave Mason

Record 196 title:
It's Like You Never Left
Label / Catalog number:
One Way / A 26077
Jacket / Inserts:
Standard international design in jewel box / 4 page CD booklet
Recording Location / Date:
Record Plant (West) &/or Sunset Sound Studios, Los Angeles, CA, U.S.A. / May 73
Media:
Album 5" CD
Producer:
Dave Mason

Song 196a title:
If You've Got Love
Release date / Country:
18 Jul 95 (first issued 29 Oct 73) / U.S.A.
Track details:
Side 1, track 3 / 3 min. 25 sec.
Composer:
D. Mason

Dave Mason: Lead Vocals & Guitar; Mark Jordan: Piano; Jim Keltner: Drums; Carl Radle: Bass; Maxine Willard: B. Vocals; Clydie King: B. Vocals; Julia Tillman: B. Vocals; Kathleen Saroyan: B. Vocals; George Harrison: Guitar

Dave Mason was born May 10, 1944 in Worcester, England. He rose to prominence in the band Traffic in 1967 which included Steve Winwood *(see Blind Faith)*, Jim Capaldi*, and Chris Wood. Later members of the band briefly included, among others, Rick Grech and Jim Gordon. Mason departed and rejoined Traffic several times before he briefly joined forces with Delaney & Bonnie & Friends*. Mason is probably best remembered for writing Traffic's hit ***Feelin' Alright?***, and Delaney & Bonnie's hit ***Only You Know And I Know***. He has worked with countless artists, including Mama Cass Elliot, Jimi Hendrix and The Rolling Stones*. Mason was also one of many well-known guest musicians on Mike McGear's (McCartney) album **McGough & McGear**, and on The Scaffold* albums *(see McGear, Roger McGough & Mike McGear)*. Mason has been doing a fair bit of session work over the years. He had a top 20 in the U.S. with the song ***We Just Disagree*** in 1977. He was a member of Fleetwood Mac *(see Mick Fleetwood)* between 1993 and 1995. Mason was selected as a member of Ringo Starr's All-Starr Band tour in 1997, but dropped out during rehearsals.

In a 1996 article in Goldmine record collector's magazine (issue # 406), Mason recalled attending several of The Beatles' recording sessions, and said he sang backing vocals on ***Across The Universe***. However, it is not known if his backing vocals survived the final mix of any of the released versions of ***Across The Universe***.

Mason's brief membership in Derek And The Dominos *(see Eric Clapton)* in 1970 led to work on George Harrison's album **All Things Must Pass**. In May 1973, Harrison was in Los Angeles to promote his album **Living In The Material World**. While there, he played on Mason's album **It's Like You Never Left**, under the thinly veiled pseudonym of "Son Of Harry." Contrary to rumors and reports, to the best of Dave Mason's recollection, this is the only contribution by any of The Beatles to his recordings.

Dave Mason, Detroit, MI, photo courtesy of Pat Henry

While appearing in New Orleans in January 1975, Mason was visited backstage by guitarist and fan Jimmy McCulloch, who was a member of Paul McCartney's band Wings. McCulloch invited Mason to Wings' recording sessions for their **Venus And Mars** album later that evening. Upon arrival, Mason was recruited to play guitar on ***Listen To What The Man Said*** and the as-yet-unreleased song ***The Crawl Of The Wild***.

Linda McCartney

Record 197 title:
Animal Magnetism [Various Artists]
Label / Catalog number:
Kingsnake / KS2024

Jacket / Inserts:
Unique in Jewel box / 8 page CD booklet
Recording Location / Date:
The Mill Studios, Sussex, U.K. / 1988

Media:
Album 5" CD
Producer:
Suzy And The Red Stripes
& (probably) Paul McCartney

Song 197a title:
The White Coated Man
Release date / Country:
09 Jan 95 / U.S.A.

Track details:
Side 1, track 3 / 2 min. 18 sec.
Composer:
L. McCartney - C. Lane [P. McCartney]

Linda McCartney: Lead Vocals; Carla Lane: Voice; Paul McCartney (probable) B. Vocals & (probable) Instruments

Record 198 title:
Cold Cuts Vol. 2
Label / Catalog number:
Orange / Five [Unauthorized Record]
Jacket / Inserts:
Unique in Jewel box / 4 page insert
Recording Location / Date:
Good Earth Studios, London, U.K. / (probably) late 1982 or early 1983
Media:
Album 5" CD
Producer:
Tony Visconti

Song 198a title:
Love's Full Glory
Release date / Country:
1994 / Mexico
Track details:
Side 1, track 14 / 3 min. 59 sec.
Composer:
L. McCartney

Linda McCartney: Lead Vocals; Paul McCartney (probable) Involvement

Record 199 title:
Oobu Joobu with Paul McCartney
Jacket / Inserts:
Westwood One paper CD sleeve / Cue Sheet
Media:
Album 5" CD

Song 199a title:
Endless Days And Lonely Nights
Release date / Country:
14 Aug 95 / U.S.A.
Label / Catalog number:
Westwood One Entertainment
/ Show # 95-34 (promotional only)
Track details:
Side 1, track 3-1 / 2 min. 58 sec.
Composer:
(probably) L. McCartney
Producer:
(probably) Paul McCartney

Linda McCartney: Lead Vocals; Paul McCartney: (probable) Involvement

Song 199b title:
New Orleans [segment]
Release date / Country:
27 May 95 / U.S.A.
Label / Catalog number:
Westwood One Entertainment
/ Show # 95-22 (promotional only)
Track details:
CD1, track 2-4 / 2 min. 05 sec.
Composer:
L. McCartney
Producer:
(probably) Paul McCartney

Linda McCartney: Lead Vocals; Paul McCartney: B. Vocals & (probable) Instruments

Song 199c title:
Peacocks
Release date / Country:
10 Jul 95 / U.S.A.
Label / Catalog number:
Westwood One Entertainment
/ Show # 95-29 (promotional only)
Track details:
Side 1, track 3-3 / 3 min. 25 sec.
Composer:
L. McCartney
Producer:
(probably) Paul McCartney

Linda McCartney: Lead Vocals; Paul McCartney: B. Vocals & (probable) Instruments

Song 199d title:
Sugar Time
Track details:
Side 1, track 3-3 / 2 min. 20 sec.

Release date / Country:
29 May 95 / U.S.A.
Label / Catalog number:
Westwood One Entertainment
/ Show # 95-23 (promotional only)
Recording Location / Date:
Rude Studios, U.K. / (probably) 1980
Composer:
Phillips - Echols
Producer:
Lee "Scratch" Perry (instrumental backing) & (probably) Paul McCartney

Linda McCartney: Lead Vocals; Paul McCartney: B. Vocals

Song 199e title:
The White Coated Man [alternate version]
Release date / Country:
05 Jun 95 / U.S.A.
Label / Catalog number:
Westwood One Entertainment
/ Show # 95-24 (promotional only)
Recording Location / Date:
The Mill Studios, Sussex, U.K. / 1988
Track details:
Side 1, track 3-3 / 2 min. 36 sec.
Composer:
L. McCartney - C. Lane [P. McCartney]
Producer:
Suzy And The Red Stripes
& (probably) Paul McCartney

Linda McCartney: Lead Vocals; Carla Lane: Voice; Paul McCartney: (probable) B. Vocals & (probable) Instruments

Song 199f title:
Wide Prairie [segment]
Release date / Country:
26 Jun 95 / U.S.A.
Label / Catalog number:
Westwood One Entertainment
/ Show # 95-27 (promotional only)
Recording Location / Date:
(probably) Paris Olympia Studios, Paris, France / (probably) 12-17 Nov 73
Track details:
Side 1, track 3-2 / 4 min. 33 sec.
Composer:
(probably) P. McCartney - L.McCartney
Producer:
(probably) Paul McCartney

Linda McCartney: Vocals; Paul McCartney: Vocals & (probable) Involvement

Record 200 title:
Oobu Joobu-Ecology
Label / Catalog number:
Best Buy/Mastertone/MPL
/ [matrix #] SA0200 878-02 (promotional only)
Jacket / Inserts:
Unique in Jewel box / 4 page CD insert
Recording Location / Date:
The Mill Studios, Sussex, U.K. / 1988
Media:
Album 5" CD
Producer:
Paul McCartney

Song 200a title:
Cow
Release date / Country:
17 May 97 (first issued 19 Jun 95) / U.S.A.
Track details:
Side 1, track 7 / 3 min. 52 sec.
Composer:
L. McCartney - C. Laine - [P. McCartney]

Linda McCartney: Lead Vocals; Paul McCartney: Keyboards; Carla Lane: Voice

Record 201 title:
Paul McCartney's Rupert And The Frog Song also Linda McCartney's Seaside Woman/The Oriental Nightfish & Seaside Woman / B-Side To Seaside
Media:
Single LVD 8"
Label / Catalog number:
Pioneer Artists / PA-86-MO37
Producer:
Paul McCartney
Jacket / Inserts:
Standard international design with variations
Recording Location / Date:
Paris Olympia Studios, Paris, France / 12-17 Nov 73

Song 201a title:
Seaside Woman
Track details:
Side 2, track 1/ 3 min. 36 sec.
Release date / Country:
14 Nov 85/ U.K.
Composer:
L. McCartney

Linda McCartney: Lead Vocals & Keyboards; Paul McCartney: B. Vocals, Bass & Piano; Denny Laine: Guitar; Davy Lutton: Drums; Jimmy McCulloch: Guitar

This song is also included on A&M / AMSP 7548 / Single 12" / Side 2, track 1 / released 18 Jul 80 in the U.S.A. (first issued 31 May 77) / Unique / Record label inner sleeve.

Song 201b title:
The Oriental Nightfish
Track details:
Side 2, track 2 / 2 min. 38 sec.
Release date / Country:
14 Nov 85 / U.S.A.
Composer:
L. McCartney

Linda McCartney: Lead Vocals & Keyboards; Paul McCartney: Bass; Davy Lutton: Drums; Jimmy McCulloch: Guitar; Denny Laine: Guitar

Record 202 title:
Seaside Woman / B-Side To Seaside
Media:
Single 12"
Label / Catalog number:
A&M / AMSP 7548
Producer:
Paul McCartney
Jacket / Inserts:
Unique / Record label inner sleeve
Recording Location / Date:
Paris Olympia Studios, Paris, France / 12-17 Nov 73

Song 202a title:
B-Side To Seaside
Track details:
Side 2, track 1 / 2 min. 36 sec.
Release date / Country:
18 Jul 80 (first issued 31 May 77) / U.K.
Composer:
P. McCartney

Linda McCartney: Lead Vocals & Keyboards; Paul McCartney: B. Vocals, Bass & Piano; Denny Laine: Banjo; Davy Lutton: Drums

Record 203 title:
Seaside Woman / B-Side To Seaside
Media:
Single 12"
Label / Catalog number:
Capitol / V-15244
Producer:
Super Weed [Paul McCartney]
remixed by: Alvin Clark
Jacket / Inserts:
Record label sleeve with ID sticker / Record label inner sleeve
Recording Location / Date:
Paris Olympia Studios, Paris, France / 12-17 Nov 73 & (probably) remixed: 1986

Song 203a title:
B-Side To Seaside (remixed by Alvin Clark)
Track details:
Side 2, track 1 / 4 min. 38 sec.
Release date / Country:
13 Aug 86 / U.S.A.
Composer:
P. McCartney

Linda McCartney: Lead Vocals & Keyboards; Paul McCartney: B. Vocals, Bass & Piano; Denny Laine: Banjo; Davy Lutton: Drums

Song 203b title:
Seaside Woman (remixed by: Alvin Clark)
Track details:
Side 1, track 1 / 5 min. 18 sec.
Release date / Country:
13 Aug 86 / U.S.A.
Composer:
L. McCartney

Linda McCartney: Lead Vocals & Keyboards; Paul McCartney: B. Vocals, Bass & Piano; Denny Laine: Guitar; Davy Lutton: Drums; Jimmy McCulloch: Guitar

Record 204 title:
Unsurpassed Masters Vol. 2
Media:
Album 5" CD
Label / Catalog number:
Strawberry / STR 003 [Unauthorized Record]
Producer:
(probably) Paul McCartney
Jacket / Inserts:
Unique in Jewel box / 2 page CD insert
Recording Location / Date:
(probably) Morgan Studios, London, U.K. / (probably) Mar 72 thru Oct 72 or (possibly) 1973

Song 204a title:
Seaside Woman (out-take)
Track details:
Side 1, track 13 / 3 min. 54 sec.
Release date / Country:
1994 / (supposedly) Israel
Composer:
L. McCartney

Linda McCartney: Lead Vocals & Keyboards; Paul McCartney: B. Vocals & Bass; Denny Laine: Guitar; Henry McCullough: Guitar; Denny Seiwell: Drums

Linda McCartney was born Linda Louise Eastman on September 24, 1941 in Scarsdale, New York. She was the daughter of Lee Eastman (whose family name was originally Epstein), a prominent New York attorney who specialized in copyright law pertaining to the entertainment industry. Linda's mother, Louise, was the daughter of the wealthy Linder family, who owned a chain of department stores in Cleveland.

Lee's profession put him in the company of the rich and famous from the worlds of film, art and music. One of his clients was Jack Lawrence, who wrote ***Linda***, first recorded by Ray Noble with Buddy Clark in 1947, inspired by Eastman's daughter. Lawrence later signed the copyright of the song over to Eastman in payment for legal services. The song would become a major hit in 1963 for the southern California surf and hot rod duo, Jan & Dean.

Linda's affluent surroundings and exposure to the music world had a great influence on her as a youth. She was quickly swept up by the glitter and rebelliousness of the rock 'n' roll craze of the 1950s. Linda's ordered world was shattered at the age of eighteen when her mother was killed in a plane crash. Linda did not, as has been previously reported, attend Sarah Lawrence College. She did briefly attend college studying history and art. She married a fellow student named Bob See, and the two lived in Colorado for a time. The marriage lasted less than a year but resulted in the birth of a daughter named Heather.

Linda relocated to Arizona with young Heather, and enrolled in a photography class at the Tucson Art Center, taught by Hazel Archer. With a passion for photography in her heart, and a camera in hand, Linda returned to New York determined to make her mark as a professional photographer. She got her foot in the door by taking a position as a receptionist at Town & Country magazine, where she seized the magazine's invitation to do a photo shoot of The Rolling Stones*. Her photos of The Rolling Stones received high marks, providing her with a resume as a rock photographer. She made her way to the foot of the stage of New York's legendary Fillmore East, and soon became its unofficial resident photographer. Her beauty, talent and association with rock's elite saddled her with the unfair label of a groupie.

The Beatles were the prize catch for most photographers in the mid-1960s. Linda admits she was initially taken by John Lennon, but after a close-up photo assignment with The Beatles at Shea Stadium in 1966, she took a greater interest in Paul McCartney. On May 15, 1967, Linda was formally introduced to Paul McCartney at the Bag O'Nails nightclub in London. Linda was invited to attend a press reception to premiere The Beatles' **Sgt. Pepper's Lonely Hearts Club Band** album several days later at Brian Epstein's house, where she and Paul exchanged further glances. One year later, the two would meet again, this time in New York at a press conference where Lennon and McCartney discussed the formation of The Beatles company, Apple.

During the press conference, Linda slipped Paul her phone number and the two spent the next few days together in New York. A month later, McCartney summoned Linda to Los Angeles where he was attending a Capitol Records sales conference to announce that The Beatles would appear on their Apple Records label. Shortly after Paul's return to England, his five-year relationship with his fiancee, actress Jane Asher *(see Peter & Gordon)* ended. In the fall of 1968, he asked Linda to move into his home in London. She began accompanying Paul to the recording sessions for **The Beatles** (white album), and she contributed her photos to the poster included with the album. The following spring Linda took the photos that were used on the U.S. picture sleeve of The Beatles' single ***The Ballad Of John And Yoko***.

The beginning of 1969 saw Linda Eastman, as well as the ever-present Yoko Ono, frequently attending The Beatles' recording sessions. Linda even contributed backing vocals to The Beatles' song ***Let It Be***. In February, Allen Klein became involved in The Beatles' financial affairs. McCartney distrusted Klein, and was represented by the firm of Eastman and Eastman (Linda's father and brother John). Early 1969 brought Paul the news that Linda was pregnant with what would be the first of the couple's three children. On March 12, 1969, Paul and Linda were married. About a year later Paul McCartney, with vocal help from Linda, released his first bona fide solo album, and announced to the world that he had effectively left The Beatles. On the final day of 1970, Paul filed a lawsuit in the London High Court seeking legal dissolution of The Beatles & Co partnership, and the appointment of a receiver to handle the groups' financial affairs. (The court appointed a receiver several months later but the partnership would not be legally dissolved until 1975.) The dream was over, the long and winding road had come to an end, and Paul was beginning a new career and life with the lovely Linda.

Linda made her songwriting debut with the release of Paul's first solo single, ***Another Day***, in early 1971. As was the case with Yoko Ono when she was listed as co-composer on John Lennon's releases, eyebrows were raised by their song publishers (Yoko and Linda were not under contract to Lennon & McCartney's publisher) as to whether Linda had actually helped Paul compose his songs. The McCartneys were generally accused by the press and others of trying to "keep up with the Lennons" in their artistic, personal and legal battles. But Linda continued to receive credit for helping Paul on many of his compositions.

Wings publicity photo, 1971, courtesy of Danny Seiwell

On August 3, 1971, Paul announced the formation of his new group Wings, that included his wife Linda on keyboards and backing vocals. Fans and musicians alike, including those in McCartney's band, were skeptical. But while Yoko Ono's worldly avant garde music was often in stark contrast to that of her husband John Lennon, Linda's 1950s American musical background and soothing vocals easily complemented those of Paul McCartney. She sang backing vocals on much of the Paul and Linda McCartney album **Ram**. She also sang duet vocals with Paul on the song ***I Am Your Singer*** from Wings' 1971 debut album **Wings Wild Life**. Linda continued to contribute backing vocals to many of her husband's solo recordings.

Additionally, Linda sang backing vocals on George Harrison's tribute song to John Lennon, ***All Those Years Ago***. She also sang backing vocals on a number of Ringo Starr's recordings, including ***Six O'Clock***, which she co-wrote with Paul. Her backing vocals can be heard on the following artists' recordings as well: Johnny Cash*, Eddie & The Hot Rods, Adam Faith*, Roy Harper*, Kenney Jones*, Denny Laine*, Mike McGear*, Yoko Ono*, Carly Simon*, James Taylor* and Thornton, Fradkin & Unger And The Big Band*. She also played keyboards on some of Mike McGear's and The Scaffold's* recordings. She has been a member of all of Paul's touring bands in spite of criticism concerning her musical abilities.

Linda has served as the photographer for many of her husband's records and projects. Her photographs have been exhibited on numerous occasions and reproduced in a number of calendars and books, including **Linda's Pictures** in 1976, **Photographs** in 1982, **Sun Prints** in 1989, **Sixties** in 1992, and **Roadworks** in 1996. Linda always had a great love for animals, especially horses, and had been a strong advocate for animal rights. She and Paul became vegetarians in the early 1970s. Linda began her line of vegetarian frozen foods, and wrote several vegetarian cook books. In late 1995, Linda was diagnosed with breast cancer (which took the life of Paul's mother) and lost her long battle with the disease on April 17, 1998.

Almost from the start of their musical relationship, Paul McCartney had begun helping and encouraging Linda to release a solo album. A number of McCartney's and Wings' album sessions were devoted to recording songs featuring Linda. Following the dissolution of Wings, there were reports that Linda was going to do a solo album with help from Lene Lovich and Mary Hopkin*. Over the years, a number of Linda's recordings have appeared on bootleg records, and in films made by the McCartneys. Unfortunately, most of Linda's recordings remain officially unreleased. Only a handful of her recordings have been released as Linda McCartney (Suzy And The Red Stripes), and specific details of Paul's involvement are sketchy. It's a safe assumption that nearly all of Linda's recordings contain some contribution by Paul. The vocal and instrumental backing for most of her recordings was probably provided by Paul and other members of his backing bands, including Wings. Paul's instrumental contributions probably consist of, though are not necessarily limited to, guitar, bass, keyboards and possibly drums. He almost certainly had a hand in the production of most, if not all of her recordings, and probably helped compose many of them as well. Unfortunately, for one reason or another, most of her recordings have yet to be released. Many recordings featuring Linda on lead vocals are technically Wings recordings. However, those recordings commonly identified or released as Suzy And The Red Stripes or Linda McCartney recordings are considered as such. This does not include any songs featuring her on lead vocals from live performances with McCartney and Wings, or any Wings recordings so identified.

Since the early 1970s the McCartneys have been frequent visitors to the Caribbean island nation of Jamaica and have developed a deep admiration for its reggae music. (Paul made a very brief cameo appearance in the posthumous video for the song *One Love* that was included in **Legend**, the 1984 video retrospective of reggae master Bob Marley's career. McCartney's 1995 radio series **Oobu Joobu** was heavily laced with reggae music.) The McCartney's decided to record some reggae music featuring Linda on lead vocals under the moniker of Suzy And The Red Stripes. The name and concept were probably based in part on an idea McCartney had during The Beatles waning days to have the group do unscheduled performances under a name like Rikki And The Red Streaks. Rikki And The Red Streaks was the name of a Liverpool group in the early 1960s; Suzy was a Jamaican nickname; and Red Stripe is the name of its popular beer. McCartney initially planned for Wings' second album, **Red Rose Speedway** released in 1973, to be a two-record set. One of the songs that apparently was considered for inclusion before it was pared down to a single record was a reggae-flavored song Linda wrote and sang called *Seaside Woman*. Linda was often featured performing the song during Wings' tours in 1972 and 1973. According to Denny Laine, *Seaside Woman* was recorded in Paris in late 1973 with help from guitarist Jimmy McCulloch, who joined Wings some six months later. However, the song was almost certainly attempted during the recording sessions for *Red Rose Speedway* nearly a year earlier.

Seaside Woman, by Suzy And The Red Stripes, was released first in the U.S. in 1977 on Epic Records, and reached the top 60 in the charts. At the time, McCartney was negotiating with Epic's parent company, Columbia, with whom he signed a record contract for his releases in the U.S. and Canada in 1979. The song was coupled with the cleverly titled *B-Side To Seaside* written by Paul. Apparently, a 4 minute, 3 second version of the original single version of *Seaside Woman* was issued in Germany. The single has seen numerous reissues on several different labels, in different countries, and in a variety of formats, including color vinyl, box sets, and 12" extended remixes.

The McCartneys commissioned Oscar Grillo to animate and direct a film for *Seaside Woman*, which took first place as the official British entry for the short film category at the 1980 **Cannes Film Festival**. The film was included, along with two other animated films set to the McCartney's music, on the 8" laser video disk **Paul McCartney's Rupert And The Frog Song also Linda McCartney's Seaside Woman / The Oriental Nightfish** issued in 1985. *Oriental Nightfish* was also animated by Grillo, and entered in the **Cannes Film Festival** in 1978.

The 1976 album, **Wings At The Speed Of Sound**, included Linda singing her self-penned *Cook Of The House*. She performed the song during Wings' 1979 U.K. tour. It was also used as the theme song for Linda's vegetarian cooking segment on Paul McCartney's 1995 Westwood One U.S. radio series **Oobu Joobu**. The fifteen-week show also featured a number of Linda's other songs, including six that have yet to be released commercially. They are: a segment of *New Orleans*, recorded about, and probably during, Wings' sessions there in 1975; a segment of *Wide Prairie* (an 11 minute, 28 second version is available on bootlegs) that was probably recorded during the Olympia Studios sessions in Paris in late 1973; *Endless Days And Lonely Nights*; *Peacocks*; *Cow (see below);* and a cover of the McGuire Sisters' 1957 hit *Sugar Time*, with a reggae backing track produced by Lee "Scratch" Perry. It's unclear whether these songs were intended to be released as Wings' songs, or as Linda McCartney (Suzy And the Red Stripes) songs. **Oobu Joobu** also featured a Heather McCartney song called **S.M.A.**, which likely included some assistance from Paul. Linda provided the repetitive dialogue vocal to an out-take from the 1980 **McCartney II** album called *Mr. H Atom*. There are, in all likelihood, more than enough Linda McCartney recordings for two albums.

Tony Visconti stated he that produced a version of the song *"ove's Full Glory* for Linda at his Good Earth Studios in London in the early 1980s which has recently turned up on a number of bootleg record releases. Portions of two versions of *Love's Full Glory* were used in the 1992 film **Appaloosa** that the McCartneys made about a horse of Linda's named Blankit. One version was recorded during sessions Paul produced for Ringo's album **Stop And Smell The Roses** at Super Bear Studios in the south of France in July 1980. It featured Linda on piano, Paul on bass, Ringo on drums, Lloyd Green on pedal steel guitar and Wings' Laurence Juber* on acoustic guitar. The other version included help from Mick Bolton and Ian Maidman.

ANIMAL MAGNETISM
Linda Ronstadt ★ Chrissie Hynde ★ Linda McCartney
Edgar Winter ★ Jimi Jamison ★ Lonesome Dave Peverett
Steve Morse ★ C.F. Turner ★ Leon Russell ★ Brian Howe
Pat Travers ★ Riff West ★ Lester Chambers

The film **Appaloosa** also features ***Appaloosa Jam***, composed by Linda, and recorded with help from Blair Cunningham, Paul's drummer from 1991 - 1993. The centerpiece of the film was the title track ***Appaloosa***, written by Linda. The song was divided into two movements between which Paul added a composition of his subtitled ***Meditation***. The entire suite was recorded on January 29, 1992 at EMI's Abbey Road Studios, with the help of the London Symphony Orchestra. Paul produced the recording with John Fraser, and conducted the orchestra with Carl Davis. McCartney has worked with Davis and Fraser on several classical music projects *(see London Symphony Orchestra & Chorus; The Royal Liverpool Philharmonic Orchestra & Choir and Choristers of Liverpool Cathedral; Anya Alexeyev).* The Boston Pops Orchestra premiered ***Appaloosa*** at Symphony Hall in Boston on May 12, 1992 during **A Tribute To Paul McCartney** concert, conducted by Carl Davis. The performance was aired on PBS-TV that August.

In early 1995, a third Suzy And The Red Stripes song, ***White-Coated Man***, was released on the U.S. CD **Animal Magnetism**. Proceeds from the **Animal Magnetism** CD go to benefit PETA (People for the Ethical Treatment of Animals) and the Paws in Harmony Foundation. ***White-Coated Man***, as well as the song ***Cow***, began as animal right poems written by Carla Lane in 1988 and sent to Linda. Lane is a British TV-comedy writer of shows like **Bread**, **The Liver Birds**, **Butterflies**, **Solo**, **The Mistress** and others. She is also a close friend of the McCartneys, and an animal rights activist. Paul and Linda asked Lane to come to their private recording studio, and when she arrived, Paul was playing the music he had set to ***Cow***. The three spent the day recording ***Cow*** and ***White-Coated Man***. Both songs were included in McCartney's **Oobu Joobu** radio series. ***Cow*** was also included on the promotional-only CD **Oobu Joobu - Ecology**. **Oobu Joobu - Ecology** was given away free, for a limited time, by the Best Buy chain of stores in the U.S. as a tie-in promotion for McCartney's Town Hall Meeting on VH1-TV, and for buying McCartney's 1997 album **Flaming Pie**. Lane claimed in a 1988 interview that she, Paul, country singers Johnny Cash and Tom T. Hall had written a country song about animal rights. It was expected at the time that Cash would record the song, but to date nothing has surfaced.

Mike McGear

Record 205 title:
*McGear

Label / Catalog number:
See For Miles / SEECD 339

Jacket / Inserts:
Standard international design in jewel box / 8 page CD booklet with photos of Paul McCartney

Media:
Album 5" CD

Producer:
Paul McCartney

Song 205a title:
Dance The Do [alternate CD version]

Release date / Country:
06 Apr 92 / U.K.

Track details:
Side 1, track 6 / 3 min. 53 sec.

Composer:
P. McCartney - M. McGear

Recording Location / Date:
Strawberry Studios, Stockport, U.K. / Jan - May 74

Mike McGear: Lead Vocals; Paul McCartney: Synthesizer, Bass & B. Vocals; Denny Laine: Guitar & (probable) B. Vocals; Jimmy McCulloch: Guitar; Linda McCartney: B. Vocals & (possible) Percussion; Gerry Conway: Drums; Brian Jones: Saxophone; (probable) Gysmorchestra (invented by: Lol Cream & Kevin Godley, 10CC)

Song 205b title:
Givin' Grease A Ride
Release date / Country:
06 Apr 92 (first issued 27 Sep 74) / U.K.
Track details:
Side 1, track 11 / 5 min. 33 sec.
Composer:
P. McCartney - M. McGear
Recording Location / Date:
Strawberry Studios, Stockport, U.K. / Jan - May 74

Mike McGear: Lead Vocals; Eric Stewart: Guitar; Paul McCartney: Guitar, B. Vocals, Piano, (probable) Bass & (possibly) Synthesizer; Jimmy McCulloch: Guitar; Linda McCartney: (possible) Keyboards; Denny Laine: (probable) Guitar; Gerry Conway: Drums; (probable) Gysmorchestra (invented by: Lol Cream & Kevin Godley, 10CC)

Song 205c title:
Have You Got Problems?
Release date / Country:
06 Apr 92 (first issued 27 Sep 74) / U.K.
Track details:
Side 1, track 5 / 6 min. 15 sec.
Composer:
P. McCartney - M. McGear
Recording Location / Date:
Strawberry Studios, Stockport, U.K. / Jan - May 74

Mike McGear: Lead Vocals; Paul McCartney B. Vocals, Piano, Bass & (probable) Guitar; Jimmy McCulloch: (possible) Guitar; Gerry Conway: Drums; Brian Jones: Saxophone; Linda McCartney: B. Vocals; Denny Laine: B. Vocals & (probable) Guitar

Song 205d title:
Leave It
Release date / Country:
06 Apr 92 (first issued 06 Sep 74) / U.K.
Track details:
Side 1, track 4 / 3 min. 41 sec.
Composer:
P. McCartney
Recording Location / Date:
EMI-Abbey Road Studios, London & (possibly) Strawberry Studios, Stockport, U.K. / Apr 73 & (possibly) Jan - May 74

Mike McGear: Lead Vocals; Denny Laine: Guitar & B. Vocals; Paul McCartney: B. Vocals, Bass, Piano & (probable) Acoustic Guitar; Tony Coe: Saxophone; Denny Seiwell: Drums; Linda McCartney: B. Vocals & (possible) Keyboards

Song 205e title:
Norton
Release date / Country:
06 Apr 92 (first issued 27 Sep 74) / U.K.
Track details:
Side 1, track 3 / 2 min. 35 sec.
Composer:
P. McCartney - M. McGear
Recording Location / Date:
Strawberry Studios, Stockport, U.K. / Jan - May 74

Mike McGear: Lead Vocals; Denny Laine: (probable) Guitar & (probable) B. Vocals; Gerry Conway: Drums; Eric Stewart: (possible) Guitar; Brian Jones: Saxophone; Derek Taylor: Voice; Jimmy McCulloch: Lead Guitar; Paul McCartney: B. Vocals, Piano, (possible) Bass, (possible) Keyboards & (possible) Guitar; Linda McCartney: B. Vocals & (possible) Keyboards

Song 205f title:
Rainbow Lady
Release date / Country:
06 Apr 92 (first issued 27 Sep 74) / U.K.
Track details:
Side 1, track 9 / 3 min. 26 sec.
Composer:
P. McCartney - M. McGear

Recording Location / Date:
Strawberry Studios, Stockport, U.K. / Jan - May 74

Mike McGear: Lead Vocals; Denny Laine: (probable) Guitar & (possible) B. Vocals; Jimmy McCulloch: (probable) Guitar; Gerry Conway: Drums; Eric Stewart: (possible) Guitar; (probable) Gysmorchestra (invented by: Lol Cream & Kevin Godley, 10CC); Paul McCartney: Bass, B. Vocals, (probable) Acoustic Guitar, (probable) Synthesizer & (probable) Piano; Linda McCartney B. Vocals & (probable) Keyboards

Song 205g title:
Sea Breezes
Release date / Country:
06 Apr 92 (first issued 27 Sep 74) / U.K.
Recording Location / Date:
Strawberry Studios, Stockport, U.K. / Jan - May 74
Track details:
Side 1, track 1 / 4 min. 50 sec.
Composer:
B. Ferry

Mike McGear: Lead Vocals; Paul McCartney: Bass, Keyboards; Strings and Brass Arrangements (probable) Guitar; Linda McCartney: (possible) Keyboards & (possible) Percussion; Denny Laine: (probable) Guitar; Jimmy McCulloch: (probable) Guitar; Gerry Conway: Drums; Eric Stewart: (possible) Guitar; Brian Jones: Saxophone; Gerry Allison: Strings And Brass Arrangement; The Halte Orchestra and Oboe Lady; Gysmorchestra (invented by: Lol Cream & Kevin Godley, 10CC)

Song 205h title:
Simply Love You
Release date / Country:
06 Apr 92 (first issued 27 Sep 74) / U.K.
Recording Location / Date:
Strawberry Studios, Stockport, U.K. / Jan - May 74
Track details:
Side 1, track 10 / 2 min. 47 sec.
Composer:
P. McCartney - M. McGear

Mike McGear: Lead Vocals; Paul McCartney: B. Vocals, Keyboards, Piano, (probable) Bass & (possible) Guitar; Linda McCartney: B. Vocals & (probable) Keyboards; Denny Laine: B. Vocals & (probable) Guitar; Jimmy McCulloch: (possible) Guitar; Gerry Conway: Drums; Eric Stewart: (possible) Guitar; (probable) Gysmorchestra (invented by: Lol Cream & Kevin Godley, 10CC)

Song 205i title:
Sweet Baby
Release date / Country:
06 Apr 92 (first issued 06 Sep 74) / U.K.
Recording Location / Date:
Mike McCartney's Home & (probably) Strawberry Studios, Stockport, U.K. / Jan - May 74
Track details:
Side 1, track 8 / 3 min. 49 sec.
Composer:
P. McCartney - M. McGear

Mike McGear: Lead Vocals; Paul McCartney: Acoustic Guitar, B. Vocals, Keyboards & (probable) Bass; Denny Laine: (probable) Guitar & (probable) B. Vocals; Jimmy McCulloch: (possible) Guitar; Gerry Conway: Drums; Eric Stewart: (possible) Guitar; Linda McCartney: Piano & B. Vocals

Song 205j title:
The Casket
Release date / Country:
06 Apr 92 (first issued 27 Sep 74) / U.K.
Recording Location / Date:
Strawberry Studios, Stockport, U.K. / Jan - May 74
Track details:
Side 1, track 7 / 4 min. 18 sec.
Composer:
P. McCartney - R. McGough

Mike McGear: Lead Vocals; Paul McCartney: Piano; (possible) Guitar & (probable) Keyboards; Linda McCartney: (possible) Keyboards; Denny Laine: (possible) Guitar; Jimmy McCulloch: (possible) Guitar; Eric Stewart: (possible) Guitar; (possible) Gysmorchestra (invented by: Lol Cream & Kevin Godley, 10CC); Paddy Moloney: Aeolian Pipes

Song 205k title:
The Man Who Found God On The Moon
Track details:
Side 1, track 12 / 6 min. 32 sec.

Release date / Country:
06 Apr 92 (first issued 27 Sep 74) / U.K.
Composer:
P. McCartney - M. McGear
Recording Location / Date:
Strawberry Studios, Stockport, U.K. / Jan - May 74

Mike McGear: Lead Vocals; Paul McCartney: Piano, B. Vocals & (possible) Acoustic Guitar, (probable) Bass & (probable) Brass Arrangement; Linda McCartney: B. Vocals & (possible) Keyboards; Denny Laine: (probable) Guitar & B. Vocals; Jimmy McCulloch: (possible) Guitar; Gerry Conway: Drums; Brian Jones: Saxophone; Gerry Allison: (possible) Brass Arrangement; (probably) The Halte Orchestra and Oboe Lady; (probable) Gysmorchestra (invented by: Lol Cream & Kevin Godley, 10CC); Eric Stewart: Guitar; Benna McCartney and Theran McCartney: B. Vocals; Buzz Aldrin & Mission Control on Moon

Song 205l title:
What Do We Really Know?
Track details:
Side 1, track 2 / 3 min. 26 sec.
Release date / Country:
06 Apr 92 (first issued 27 Sep 74) / U.K.
Composer:
P. McCartney
Recording Location / Date:
Strawberry Studios, Stockport, U.K. / Jan - May 74

Mike McGear: Lead Vocals; Denny Laine: (possible) Guitar & B. Vocals; Gerry Conway: Drums; Brian Jones: Saxophone; Jimmy McCulloch: Lead Guitar; Paul McCartney: Keyboards, B. Vocals, Bass & (probable) Guitar; Linda McCartney: B. Vocals, (possible) Percussion & (possible) Keyboards

Record 206 title:
Dance The Do / /Norton
Media:
Single 7"
Label / Catalog number:
Warner Bros / K 16573
Producer:
Paul McCartney
Jacket / Inserts:
Record label sleeve
Recording Location / Date:
Strawberry Studios, Stockport, U.K. / Jan - May 74

Song 206a title:
Dance The Do [single version]
Track details:
Side 1, track 1 / 2 min. 59 sec.
Release date / Country:
04 Jul 75 / U.K.
Composer:
P. McCartney - M. McGear

Mike McGear: Lead Vocals; Paul McCartney: Synthesizer, Bass & B. Vocals; Denny Laine: Guitar & (probable) B. Vocals; Jimmy McCulloch: Guitar; Linda McCartney: B. Vocals & (possible) Percussion; Gerry Conway: Drums; Brian Jones: Saxophone; (probable) Gysmorchestra (invented by: Lol Cream & Kevin Godley, 10CC); Kate Robbins: B. Vocals; Viv Stanshall: B. Vocals

Record 207 title:
Woman
Media:
Album 5" CD
Label / Catalog number:
Edsel/Island / EDCD 507
Producer:
Mike McGear
Jacket / Inserts:
Standard international design in jewel box / 12 page CD booklet
Recording Location / Date:
Strawberry Studios, Stockport &/or EMI-Abbey Road Studios, London, U.K. / 1971 &/or 1972

Song 207a title:
Bored As Butterscotch
Release date / Country:
Feb 97 (first issued 21 Apr 72) / Germany

Track details:
Side 1, track 9 / 2 min. 52 sec.
Composer:
R. McGough - M. McGear & Friend [P.McCartney]

Mike McGear; Lead Vocals; John Megginson: Keyboards; Gerry Conway: Drums; Dave Richards: Bass

Mike McGear was born Peter Michael McCartney on January 7, 1944 in Liverpool, England, and is the younger brother of Paul McCartney. Paul was quoted as saying, "I first met my brother at a very early age." Mother Mary, of ***Let It Be*** fame, was born Mary Mohin on Sept 29, 1909 and married James McCartney, born July 7, 1902, both in Liverpool. Mary was a Catholic nurse and midwife, and Jim was a cotton salesman who also doubled as leader of Jim Mac's Band. Mary McCartney died of breast cancer on October 31, 1956. Jim, who did not remarry until 1964, raised sons Paul and Mike. He died on March 13, 1976.

Michael McCartney gave his first public performance with brother Paul at a talent contest at Butlins, a popular holiday camp in the U.K., in the summer of 1957. Mike's early interests centered on photography, but he took a series of odd jobs including tailor, Catholic Bible salesman and hairdresser.

In 1962 Mike was asked by Merseyside Arts Festival organizers John Gorman and poet Roger McGough to take part in a comedy sketch, and help to organize the festival. Following the festival, the three teamed up with several other artists to form a musical / poetry / comedy act called The Liverpool One Fat Lady All Electric Show. By the end of 1963, the group was pared down to McCartney, McGough and Gorman for a British TV series. The group renamed themselves The Scaffold*.

Mike renamed himself McGear ("gear" was Liverpool slang for cool or great) in an attempt to maintain a separate identity, and to avoid accusations that he was trying to cash in on the McCartney name. But it was inevitable that brother Paul would contribute his influence, associations and talent to Mike's recordings throughout much of his career.

Paul was at Dick James Music in London (The Beatles' Music Publisher) on June 18, 1967 (his birthday and the day he announced to the world he had taken LSD) to begin work on what would become the album **McGough & McGear** *(see Roger McGough & Mike McGear)*. Several days later, sessions for the album took place at De Lane Lea Studios, Kingsway, London. Most of the recordings took place in the summer of 1967, but it took nearly a year before the album was completed and released. It was hoped to be issued on The Beatles' Apple Records label, but was issued on Parlophone because the Apple Records label was not operational yet.

McGough & McGear featured a number of well-known groups and musicians including The Jimi Hendrix Experience, Dave Mason*, Zoot Money* Graham Nash *(see Stephen Stills)*, Gary Leeds, John Mayall, Spencer Davis and brother Paul, among others. Though specific musical credits for each song have never been made available, it's known that Paul sings background vocals and plays a number of keyboards on the album. He probably also plays bass, percussion and acoustic guitar.

Mike recalls that Paul played piano and sang on ***Do You Remember?***. According to Zoot Money, the album's primary producer was Andy Roberts, and Paul McCartney's involvement was limited more to "suggestions." The album credits list the producer as "All of Us." The album also features McGough reading poetry, including ***Summer With Monika*** – also the title of one of his book of poems about his wife, Thelma Pickles, a former girlfriend of John Lennon and Paul McCartney. One song from the sessions, ***Oh To Be A Child (Haydn's Toy Symphony)***, featured most of the superstars, but was left off the album and remains unreleased. The liner notes for **McGough & McGear** were written by The Beatles authorized biographer Hunter Davis. Mike and several of the musicians from the **McGough & McGear** sessions were present during The Beatles' live telecast, via satellite, performance of ***All You Need Is Love*** for the BBC's program **Our World** on June 25, 1967. Mike also made a cameo appearance at the end of The Beatles' made-for-TV film **Magical Mystery Tour**.

Mike "McGear" McCartney and Charlie Engelhardt, Beatlefest Chicago, 1987, photo by Kristofer Engelhardt

In 1971, the members of The Scaffold took a break to pursue solo projects. Mike recorded his first real solo album, **Woman**, with help from Paul (under the name "friend") to compose the song ***Bored As Butterscotch***. The album's front jacket features a photo of the McCartneys' mother, Mary, in her nursing uniform.

In 1973, John Gorman, Andy Roberts, Neil Innes, Roger McGough, Mike McGear and Viv Stanshall formed the loosely knit band Grimms *(see The Bonzo Dog Band)*. The name was taken from the first initials of each band member's surnames. Grimms released two albums in 1973, during which time The Scaffold reunited to record the album **Fresh Liver**. Grimms added poets Adrian Henri and Brian Patten. (McGough and Henri are now recognized as two of Britain's finest poets.) Mike temporarily abandoned his music career after ten years of ups and downs in show business and disillusionment with Grimms and its management. He turned instead to writing the children's book **Roger Bear**.

Following Mike's departure from Grimms, brother Paul lured him back into the recording studio with his song ***Leave It***, which Paul played on and produced for Mike. Mike claims in his book **Thank U Very Much** (as do the liner notes to the U.K. ***McGear** CD, which also revised the artist's name to Mike McGear McCartney) that the song was recorded following Paul's recordings for the album

Band On The Run in Lagos, Nigeria in August 1973. According to the song's drummer Denny Seiwell, it had to be recorded before the trip to Lagos that signaled his departure from McCartney's band Wings.

Paul's band was down to wife Linda *(see Linda McCartney)* and Denny Laine* by the end of 1973. With the **Band On The Run** album out of the way, and no band to tour with, Paul and Mike collaborated during the first half of 1974 on what would become Mike's showcase solo album titled ***McGear**. It featured Paul as composer, producer, arranger, background singer and musician. The album also included help from Linda, Denny Laine, and a lead guitarist named Jimmy McCulloch who ended up joining Wings following the sessions. It's a fairly safe bet that Paul plays most of the bass, piano, and probably a good bit of guitar, keyboards and synthesizer. There is even the possibility that Paul plays some drums. Paul, Linda and Denny's background vocals are recognizable throughout the album. Laine probably plays some acoustic and electric guitar, and possibly plays some bass as well. Linda's instrumental role is probably limited to keyboard work and percussion. Most of the album was recorded at, and with contributions from, 10cc's* Strawberry Studios. Eric Stewart (who would work extensively with McCartney years later) plays guitar and may sing background vocals. His co-members in 10cc, Kevin Godley and Lol Creme, are probably limited to playing their unique invention called the Gysmorchestra. There are also a number of guest cameos. The Brian Jones listed as playing saxophone on the album was a member of the early 1960s Liverpool band The Undertakers *(see Jackie Lomax)*.

Though ***McGear** was a critical success, none of its well-crafted pop/rock tracks were significant chart successes. Toward the end of the ***McGear** sessions, Paul suggested that The Scaffold record the Dominic Behan ode ***Liverpool Lou***, and arranged and produced the recording. Ironically, this regionally styled folk ballad became a top 10 song in the U.K. The Scaffold then went on to record the album **Sold Out**, which would prove to be their last album. The single ***Dance The Do***, a leftover from the ***McGear** sessions omitted from the original album, was released in 1975, but fared no better than other singles taken from the album.

In 1976, Mike released the single ***Do Nothing All Day / A to Z***. That year he was also involved in a couple of singles with The Scaffold and with Grimms. In 1977, Mike talked brother Paul into opening up what remained of the long-closed Apple Studios to record a demo of a song called ***Knocking Down Walls Of Ignorance*** with Zoot Money, Denny Laine and Viv Stanshall. Paul played drums on the track, but when Mike submitted it to EMI for approval, it was rejected in part because they didn't like the drumming! In all likelihood, it's the last song ever recorded at Apple. In April 1977, The Scaffold released a single, their last record to date, and essentially retired for good that month.

Mike has released only three records since The Scaffold's breakup. In 1980, he released the single ***All The Whales In The Ocean / I Juz Want What You Got - Money***. Its credits list "help from Paul", but according to Mike, Paul did not contribute to the recordings. It's known that Paul found ***All The Whales In The Ocean*** so infectious that he constantly sang it during his brief imprisonment in Japan for possession of marijuana. Mike released the single ***No Lar Di Dar (Is Lady Di) / God Bless The Gracious Queen*** in 1981. In 1996 he was part of the charity single ***Take It Into Your Heart*** recorded to benefit the young homeless in Liverpool. There is always the possibility that Mike and / or The Scaffold may at some point in the future return to the recording studio. It is also quite possible that unreleased McGear and Scaffold recordings containing contributions by Paul may someday be released.

In 1981, Mike released his autobiography **Thank U Very Much** (titled **The MACS** in the U.S.) and again preferred to be known as a McCartney. He has since released two books of his photographs that include intimate shots of The Beatles from the early 1960s – **Mike Mac's Whites And Blacks (plus one color)** released in 1986, and **Remember** released in 1992. He has also written another children's book titled **Sonny Joe And The Ringdom Rhymes**, and has produced a video about Liverpool. Mike has also been a guest at Beatles conventions in the past.

Roger McGough & Mike McGear

Record 208 title:
McGough & McGear
Media:
Album 5" CD
Label / Catalog number:
EMI / CDP 7 91877 2
Jacket / Inserts:
Unique in Jewel box / 8 page CD booklet

Song 208a title:
Basement Flat
Track details:
Side 1, track 3 / 2 min. 42 sec.
Release date / Country:
10 Apr 89 (first issued 17 May 68) / U.K.
Composer:
R. McGough - M. McGear
Producer:
Paul McCartney, &/or Andy Roberts, &/or Roger McGough &/or Mike McGear
Recording Location / Date:
(probably) De Lane Lea Studios, Kingsway, London, U.K. / Jun 67 - Apr 68

Mike McGear: Lead Vocals; probably one or more of the following: Dave Mason: B. Vocals; Mitch Mitchell: Drums; John Mayall: Harpsichord; Barry Fantoni: Saxophone; Roger McGough: B. Vocals; Gary Leeds: Drums; Paul McCartney: (possible) Percussion & (possible) B. Vocals; Jane Asher: B. Vocals; Margaret Asher: B. Vocals; Zoot Money: Keyboards; William Bennet, Mike Hart, Vera Kantrovitch, Carol Mason, Viv Prince, Martin Wilkinson, Paul Samwell Smith: Bass, Rosie, Prince Stanislaus Klossowiski de Rola & Baron de Wattevill

Song 208b title:
Come Close And Sleep Now
Track details:
Side 1, track 6 / 2 min. 20 sec.
Release date / Country:
10 Apr 89 (first issued 17 May 68) / U.K.
Composer:
R. McGough
Producer:
Paul McCartney, &/or Andy Roberts, &/or Roger McGough &/or Mike McGear
Recording Location / Date:
(probably) De Lane Lea Studios, Kingsway, London, U.K. / Jun 67 - Apr 68

Roger McGough: Lead Vocals; probably one or more of the following: Spencer Davis: Guitar; Dave Mason: Guitar; Andy Roberts: Guitar; John Mayall: Keyboards; Paul McCartney: (possible) Piano & (possible) Guitar; Graham Nash: Guitar; Zoot Money: Keyboards & Guitar; William Bennet, Mike Hart, Vera Kantrovitch, Carol Mason, Viv Prince, Martin Wilkinson, Rosie, Prince Stanislaus Klossowiski de Rola & Baron de Wattevill

Song 208c title:
Do You Remember?
Track details:
Side 1, track 11 / 3 min. 17 sec.
Release date / Country:
10 Apr 89 (first issued 17 May 68) / U.K.
Composer:
R. McGough - M. McGear
& (possibly) P. McCartney
Producer:
Paul McCartney & (probably) Roger McGough, Mike McGear & (possibly) Andy Roberts
Recording Location / Date:
(probably) De Lane Lea Studios, Kingsway, London, U.K. / (probably) Jun 67

Mike McGear: Lead Vocals; Paul McCartney: B. Vocals, Piano, (probable) Mellotron; probably one or more of the following: Spencer Davis: Guitar; Graham Nash: Guitar & B. Vocals; John Mayall: Harpsichord; Roger McGough: B. Vocals; Gary Leeds: Drums; Zoot Money: Keyboards; Paul Samwell Smith: Bass; William Bennet, Mike Hart, Vera Kantrovitch, Carol Mason, Viv Prince, Martin Wilkinson, Rosie, Prince Stanislaus Klossowiski de Rola & Baron de Wattevill

Song 208d title:
Ex Art Student

Track details:
Side 1, track 13 / 6 min. 29 sec.

Release date / Country:
10 Apr 89 (first issued 17 May 68) / U.K.

Composer:
R. McGough

Producer:
Paul McCartney, (probably) Roger McGough, Mike McGear & (possibly) Andy Roberts

Recording Location / Date:
De Lane Lea Studios, Kingsway, London, U.K. / 20 Jun 67

Mike McGear: Vocals; Jane Asher: Vocals; Roger McGough: Vocals; Graham Nash: Vocals & (probable) Guitar; Jimi Hendrix: Guitar & Sitar; probably one or more of the following: Spencer Davis: Guitar; Dave Mason: Guitar & B. Vocals; Mitch Mitchell: Drums; Noel Redding: Bass; Paul McCartney: (possible) B. Vocals; John Mayall: Harpsichord; William Bennet, Mike Hart, Vera Kantrovitch, Carol Mason, Viv Prince, Martin Wilkinson, Paul Samwell Smith: Bass; Rosie, Prince Stanislaus Klossowiski de Rola & Baron de Wattevill

Song 208e title:
From: "Frink, A Life In The Day Of" And "Summer With Monika"-Prologue Introducing a) Moanin' b) Anji

Track details:
Side 1, track 4 / 9 min. 00 sec.

Release date / Country:
10 Apr 89 (first issued 17 May 68) / U.K.

Composer:
R. McGough - Roberts - Timmons - Graham

Producer:
Paul McCartney, Andy Roberts, &/or Roger McGough &/or Mike McGear

Recording Location / Date:
(probably) De Lane Lea Studios, Kingsway, London, U.K. / Jun 67 - Apr 68

Roger McGough: Lead Vocals; Zoot Money: Keyboards; Andy Roberts: Guitar; probably one or more of the following: John Mayall: Harpsichord; Barry Fantoni: Saxophone; Gary Leeds: Drums; Paul McCartney: Voice, Mellotron & (possible) B. Vocals; William Bennet, Mike Hart, Vera Kantrovitch, Carol Mason, Viv Prince, Martin Wilkinson, Paul Samwell Smith: Bass; Rosie, Prince Stanislaus Klossowiski de Rola & Baron de Wattevill

Song 208f title:
From: "Frink, A Life In The Day Of" And "Summer With Monika" - Epilogue

Track details:
Side 1, track 5 / 1 min. 55 sec.

Release date / Country:
10 Apr 89 (first issued 17 May 68) / U.K.

Composer:
R. McGough - Roberts

Producer:
Paul McCartney, Andy Roberts, &/or Roger McGough &/or Mike McGear

Recording Location / Date:
(probably) De Lane Lea Studios, Kingsway, London, U.K. / Jun 67 - Apr 68

Roger McGough: Lead Vocals; Andy Roberts: Guitar

Song 208g title:
House In My Head

Track details:
Side 1, track 8 / 3 min. 34 sec.

Release date / Country:
10 Apr 89 (first issued 17 May 68) / U.K.

Composer:
R. McGough - M. McGear

Producer:
Paul McCartney, &/or Andy Roberts, &/or Roger McGough &/or Mike McGear

Recording Location / Date:
(probably) De Lane Lea Studios, Kingsway, London, U.K. / Jun 67 - Apr 68

Mike McGear: Lead Vocals; probably one or more of the following: Dave Mason: B. Vocals; Andy Roberts: Guitar; Roger McGough: B. Vocals; Gary Leeds: Drums; Paul McCartney: Piano, (possible) B. Vocals & (possible) Percussion; Jane Asher: B. Vocals; Margaret Asher: B. Vocals; Zoot Money: Keyboards & Guitar; Paul Samwell Smith: Bass; William Bennet, Mike Hart, Vera Kantrovitch, Carol Mason, Viv Prince, Martin Wilkinson, Rosie, Prince Stanislaus Klossowiski de Rola & Baron de Wattevill

Song 208h title:
Little Bit Of Heaven
Release date / Country:
10 Apr 89 (first issued 17 May 68) / U.K.
Track details:
Side 1, track 2 / 1 min. 46 sec.
Composer:
R. McGough
Producer:
Paul McCartney, &/or Andy Roberts, &/or Roger McGough &/or Mike McGear
Recording Location / Date:
(probably) De Lane Lea Studios, Kingsway, London, U.K. / Jun 67 - Apr 68

Mike McGear: Vocals; Roger McGough: Vocals; probably one or more of the following: John Mayall: Keyboards; Paul McCartney: (possible) Keyboards; William Bennet, Mike Hart, Vera Kantrovitch, Carol Mason, Viv Prince, Martin Wilkinson, Rosie, Prince Stanislaus Klossowiski de Rola & Baron de Wattevill

Song 208i title:
Living Room
Release date / Country:
10 Apr 89 (first issued 17 May 68) / U.K.
Track details:
Side 1, track 10 / 2 min. 44 sec.
Composer:
M. McGear
Producer:
Paul McCartney, (probably) Roger McGough, Mike McGear & (possibly) Andy Roberts
Recording Location / Date:
(probably) De Lane Lea Studios, Kingsway, London, U.K. / Jun 67 - Apr 68

Mike McGear: Lead Vocals; Paul McCartney: Voice, B. Vocals, (probable) Bass & (possible) Percussion; Zoot Money: Keyboards & Guitar; probably one or more of the following: Dave Mason: B. Vocals; Andy Roberts: Guitar; John Mayall: Harpsichord; Roger McGough: B. Vocals; Gary Leeds: Drums; Graham Nash: Vocals; Jane Asher: B. Vocals; Margaret Asher: B. Vocals; Paul Samwell Smith: Bass; William Bennet, Mike Hart, Vera Kantrovitch, Carol Mason, Viv Prince, Martin Wilkinson, Rosie, Prince Stanislaus Klossowiski de Rola & Baron de Wattevill

Song 208j title:
Mr. Tickle
Release date / Country:
10 Apr 89 (first issued 17 May 68) / U.K.
Track details:
Side 1, track 9 / 3 min. 20 sec.
Composer:
M. McGear
Producer:
Paul McCartney, &/or Roger McGough, &/or Mike McGear &/or Andy Roberts
Recording Location / Date:
(probably) De Lane Lea Studios, Kingsway, London, U.K. / Jun 67 - Apr 68

Mike McGear: Lead Vocals; probably one of the following: John Mayall: Piano; Paul McCartney: Piano; Zoot Money: Piano

Song 208k title:
Please Don't Run Too Fast
Release date / Country:
10 Apr 89 (first issued 17 May 68) / U.K.
Track details:
Side 1, track 12 / 1 min. 33 sec.
Composer:
M. McGear
Producer:
Paul McCartney, &/or Roger McGough, &/or Mike McGear &/or Andy Roberts
Recording Location / Date:
(probably) De Lane Lea Studios, Kingsway, London, U.K. / Jun 67 - Apr 68

Mike McGear: Lead Vocals; probably one or more of the following: Spencer Davis: Guitar; Paul McCartney: (possible) Keyboards (possible) Guitar; Dave Mason: Guitar; Andy Roberts: Guitar; John Mayall: Keyboards; Zoot Money: Keyboards

Song 208l title:
So Much
Track details:
Side 1, track 1 / 3 min. 58 sec.

Release date / Country:
10 Apr 89 (first issued 17 May 68) / U.K.
Composer:
R. McGough - M. McGear
Producer:
Paul McCartney, (probably) Roger McGough & Mike McGear & (possibly) Andy Roberts
Recording Location / Date:
De Lane Lea Studios, Kingsway, London, U.K. / 20 Jun 67

Mike McGear: Lead Vocals; Jimi Hendrix: Guitar; Graham Nash: B. Vocals & (possible) Guitar; probably one or more of the following: Spencer Davis: Guitar; Dave Mason: Guitar & B. Vocals; Mitch Mitchell: Drums; Noel Redding: Bass; Barry Fantoni: Saxophone; Andy Roberts: Guitar; Roger McGough: B. Vocals; Jane Asher: B. Vocals; Margaret Asher: B. Vocals; Paul Samwell Smith: Bass; Zoot Money: Keyboards & Guitar; William Bennet, Mike Hart, Vera Kantrovitch, Carol Mason, Viv Prince, Martin Wilkinson, Rosie, Prince Stanislaus Klossowiski de Rola & Baron de Wattevill

Song 208m title:
Yellow Book
Track details:
Side 1, track 7 / 2 min. 15 sec.
Release date / Country:
10 Apr 89 (first issued 17 May 68) / U.K.
Composer:
R. McGough - M. McGear
Producer:
Paul McCartney, &/or Roger McGough, &/or Mike McGear &/or Andy Roberts
Recording Location / Date:
(probably) De Lane Lea Studios, Kingsway, London, U.K. / Jun 67 - Apr 68

Mike McGear: Lead Vocals; probably one or more of the following: Dave Mason: B. Vocals; John Mayall: Piano; Roger McGough: B. Vocals; Gary Leeds: Drums; Paul McCartney: (possible) Piano; Graham Nash: B. Vocals; Paul Samwell Smith: Bass; Zoot Money: Piano; William Bennet, Mike Hart, Vera Kantrovitch, Carol Mason, Viv Prince, Martin Wilkinson, Rosie, Prince Stanislaus Klossowiski de Rola & Baron de Wattevill
See Mike McGear, and The Scaffold.

Ian McLagan

Record 209 title:
Troublemaker
Media:
Album 5" CD
Label / Catalog number:
Mercury / PHCR-4152
Producer:
Geoff Workman
Jacket / Inserts:
Standard international design in jewel box / 16 page CD translation & lyric booklet
Recording Location / Date:
Cherokee & Shangri La Studios, Los Angeles, CA U.S.A. & Paris, France / Feb 79

Song 209a title:
Hold On
Track details:
Side 1, track 9 / 3 min. 43 sec.
Release date / Country:
(probably) 20 Nov 93
(first issued 10 Dec 79) / Japan
Composer:
I. McLagan

Ian McLagan: Lead Vocals & (probable) Guitar; Ringo Starr: Drums; additionally, one or more of the following: Johnny Lee Schell: Guitar; Ron Wood: Guitar; Keith Richards: Guitar; Jim Keltner: Drums; Zigaboo Modeliste: Drums; Paul Stallworth: Bass; Stanley Clarke: Bass; Ian McLagan; Keyboards; Flap Workman: Accordion; Bobby Keys: Horns; Ron Wood: Horns; Steve Madaio: Horns

Ian McLagan was born May 12, 1946 in London, England. He is best known as one of the members of Small Faces, which originally included Steve Marriott, Ronnie Lane, Kenney Jones* and Jimmy Winston, whom McLagan replaced in 1965. In 1969, the group underwent a major reorganization. Marriott left to form Humble Pie with Peter Frampton*, and Ron Wood* and Rod Stewart* of the Jeff

Beck Group joined the band, now simply renamed The Faces. Shortly after his joining, Rod Stewart's solo career took off, shifting the focus of the group. Stewart's divided attention and Lane's departure in 1973 left the band as little more than a backup for superstar Stewart, who moved to the U.S. in 1975. Meanwhile, Ron Wood joined The Rolling Stones*, and the remnants of the band, aided by Jesse Ed Davis*, backed Stewart for the last time in 1975. In 1976, Marriott rejoined Jones and McLagan to reform Small Faces. The following year Jimmy McCulloch, who had just quit Paul McCartney's band Wings, joined. In 1978, the band dissolved again. Jones replaced Keith Moon* in The Who, and Ian McLagan augmented Ron Wood on Rolling Stones' tours. Marriott died in a house fire in 1991. According to Kenney Jones, The Faces are planning to reform as a tribute to Ronnie Lane, who suffered from multiple sclerosis for years and died on June 3, 1997.

In 1979, McLagan issued his first solo album and Ringo Starr was listed in the general musical credits. According to Ian, Ringo played drums on the song ***Hold On***. McLagan also helped write the song ***Tonight***, featured on Ringo's 1978 album **Bad Boy**.

Carlos Mendes

Record 210 title:
The Songs Lennon & McCartney Gave Away
Media:
Album 12"
Label / Catalog number:
EMI / NUT 18 (0C 054-07 003)
Jacket / Inserts:
Standard international design with sketches of John Lennon, Paul McCartney & Ringo Starr / Record label inner sleeve
Recording Location / Date:
(probably) Portugal / Dec 68

Song 210a title:
Penina
Release date / Country:
13 Apr 79 (probably first issued: 18 Jul 69) / U.K.
Track details:
Side 2, track 4 / 2 min. 34 sec.
Composer:
P. McCartney

Carlos Mendes: Lead Vocals

In the winter 1994 issue No. 72 of Paul McCartney's Club Sandwich fan magazine, Paul answered questions sent in by subscribers. One fan asked: What is the story behind a song called ***Penina*** which I believe you wrote for a Portuguese band leader in 1968? Might you ever record it yourself? McCartney replied, "I went to Portugal on holiday and returned to the hotel one night slightly the worse for a few drinks. There was a band playing and I ended up on the drums. The hotel was called Penina, I made up a song with that name, someone made inquiries about it and I gave it to them. And, no, I shouldn't think I'd ever record it myself!" The composition was given to a then relatively unknown artist named Carlos Mendes. Apparently, at the time McCartney did not even inform his publishing company about the composition. Issue No. 74 of Club Sandwich lists the Mendes single as being issued in March 1969, while other sources list the date more specifically as July 18, 1969. The song also failed to chart internationally the following year when the Dutch group Jotta Herre issued it as a single (Philips / 369002 PF) in the Netherlands. It has been reported in several publications that McCartney recorded the song, but to date the only version that has surfaced is a brief piano rendition from the **Get Back / Let It Be** rehearsals in January, 1969 which has appeared on several bootleg records.

The Steve Miller Band

Record 211 title:
Brave New World
Label / Catalog number:
Capitol / CDP 7 91246 2
Jacket / Inserts:
Standard international design in jewel box / 2 page CD insert
Recording Location / Date:
Olympic Studio, London, U.K. / 09 May 69
Media:
Album 5" CD
Producer:
Glyn Johns and Steve Miller

Song 211a title:
My Dark Hour
Release date / Country:
Feb 89 (first issued 16 Jun 69) / U.S.A.
Track details:
Side 1, track 9 / 3 min. 05 sec.
Composer:
S. Miller - [P. McCartney]

Steve Miller: Lead Vocals & Guitar; Paul McCartney: Bass, Drums, B. Vocals & Guitar

The Steve Miller Band has gone through numerous personnel changes over the years, including among others, Boz Scaggs and Nicky Hopkins*, but it has always been the band of its namesake, Steve Miller. Born October 5, 1943 in Milwaukee, Wisconsin, Miller spent most of his childhood in Texas. His parents were musically inclined. His father was a physician and part-time amateur recording engineer. His close friends, Les Paul and Mary Ford, gave his five-year-old son Steve a few pointers on the guitar.

When Steve was twelve, he formed a band called The Marksmen whose membership would later include Steve's high school friend Boz Scaggs. By age fourteen, Miller had backed blues legend Jimmy Reed, and in 1961, while attending college at the University of Wisconsin, he formed a band called The Ardells with Scaggs. Miller spent most of the early 1960s in and out of bands and college across the country and in Europe, backing a number of blues legends including Howlin' Wolf*. He relocated to San Francisco in 1966 where he formed what eventually became known as The Steve Miller Band. Miller broke into the charts in late 1968 with the song ***Living In The U.S.A.***

Steve Miller, Detroit, MI, 1970s, photo courtesy of Tom Bert

In June 1969, the Steve Miller album **Brave New World** was released which contained a song called ***My Dark Hour***, with special thanks to Paul Ramon. In the spring 1992 issue No. 61 of Club Sandwich, Paul McCartney's fan-club magazine, McCartney's memory seems particularly vivid about what he describes as a day of painful, historic events. "That was during the tense Apple time. We had a Friday night session at Olympic Studio in Barnes, and

Allen Klein showed up with all the guys. It was a big showdown. And my lawyer was Jewish, so he didn't work on Friday nights. But there was Klein – he was Jewish, and he was working – so he had a big advantage. Maybe he knew my lawyer was Jewish. Anyway, they all showed up at Olympic and there was a big row – they all accused me of stalling. In my mind I was actually trying to save our future, and I was vindicated later, but at the time I was definitely 'the dark horse, the problem.' And that was actually the night we broke The Beatles. That was the big crack in the liberty bell – it never came back together after that one. So we were stuck, the session was over, and the studio was free. I hung around a little bit and met Steve Miller, who was in one of the other studios. We got chatting and he was an 'up.' After the big downer, I needed an up, so he was my security blanket. I stayed chatting for a while and then he suggested cutting something. I asked what, and he said, 'We'll make something up!' I asked if I could play drums and just thrashed around. He called it ***My Dark Hour***, and we recorded it – just the two of us. I overdubbed a bit of bass and some guitar, and we sang it all. We stayed there all night. We just had to do something. I said 'just put me down as Paul Ramon.'" (Paul Ramon was a stage name McCartney briefly used when The Beatles, then known as The Silver Beetles, backed Johnny Gentle *[see Darren Young]* on his tour of Scotland in May 1960.)

Steve Miller was briefly signed to Apple Publishing in the U.K. Towards the end of 1973, Miller reached the top of the charts with what would become his trademark song, ***The Joker***. The songs ***Fly Like An Eagle***, ***Take The Money And Run***, ***Rock 'N' Me***, ***Jet Airliner*** and ***Swingtown*** kept him in the top 20 of the charts throughout the second half of the 1970s. He also had a bit part in Robert Stigwood's film **Sgt. Pepper's Lonely Hearts Club Band**. In 1982, Miller topped the charts with the song ***Abracadabra***. Miller has continued to release new recordings over the last two decades and is popular on the summer tour circuit.

In the spring of 1995, Paul McCartney contacted Miller and the two worked together on a number of songs that appear on McCartney's 1997 album **Flaming Pie**. Miller performs one of the songs from the album, ***Young Boy***, in his concerts. His music was featured on McCartney's 1995 radio series **Oobu Joobu**.

Adrian Mitchell

Record 212 title:
Rehearsals For The New World Tour 1993

Label / Catalog number:
Music With Love / MWL 21/22
[Unauthorized Record]

Jacket / Inserts:
Unique in Jewel box

Recording Location / Date:
On location at Cliffs Pavilion, Westcliff-on Sea, England / 19 Jul 91

Media:
Album 5" CD [2 CD set]

Producer:
Unknown-audience recording

Song 212a title:
Hot Pursuit [live]

Release date / Country:
1993

Track details:
CD2, track 20 / 1 min. 44 sec.

Composer:
(probably) P. McCartney - B. Cunningham - R. McIntosh - P. Wickens - H. Stuart - L. McCartney

Adrian Mitchell: Voice; probably one or more of the following: Paul McCartney: Bass, Guitar or Keyboards; Blair Cunningham: Drums; Robbie McIntosh: Guitar; Paul "Wix" Wickens: Keyboards; Hamish Stuart: Bass; Linda McCartney: Keyboards

Song 212b title:
Maybe Maytime (Singalong Junk) [live]

Track details:
CD2, track 19 / 1 min. 52 sec.

Release date / Country:
1993

Composer:
P. McCartney

Adrian Mitchell: Voice; probably one or more of the following: Paul McCartney: Bass, Guitar or Keyboards; Blair Cunningham: Drums; Robbie McIntosh: Guitar; Paul "Wix" Wickens: Keyboards; Hamish Stuart: Bass; Linda McCartney: Keyboards

Song 212c title:
Song In Space [live]

Release date / Country:
1993

Track details:
CD2, track 17 / 0 min. 59 sec.

Composer:
(probably) P. McCartney - B. Cunningham - R. McIntosh - P. Wickens - H. Stuart - L. McCartney

Adrian Mitchell: Voice; probably one or more of the following: Paul McCartney: Bass, Guitar or Keyboards; Robbie McIntosh: Guitar; Paul "Wix" Wickens: Keyboards; Hamish Stuart: Bass; Linda McCartney: Keyboards

Adrian Mitchell (aka Volcano Jones, Apeman Mudgeon) was born on October 24, 1932 in London, England. His father was a scientist and his mother was a teacher. Adrian attended Oxford University in the early 1950s, and worked as a reporter for the Oxford Mail before taking the same position at London's Evening Standard. Later he became a columnist and reviewer for London's Daily Mail and the Sunday Times. In 1961, he won the prestigious Gregory Award for Poetry. He taught at a number of universities including the University of Iowa in the U.S. between 1963 and 1964, and University of Lancaster in the U.K. between 1967 and 1969.

Mitchell is now regarded as one of England's leading popular contemporary poets (**Out Loud** and **The Apeman Cometh**), novelists (**The Bodyguard**) and playwrights (**Animals Can't Laugh** and **Tyger**). He has given over a thousand poetry recitals throughout the world. His writings are often charged with social commentary. Among his most recent collections of poems is **Love Songs Of World War Three - collected stage lyrics**. Mitchell has adapted a number of foreign classics for the stage which have been presented by the National Theatre and the Royal Shakespeare Company. He currently spends most of his time writing plays, all of them with songs, for children and adult audiences alike.

In 1963, Mitchell was writing the weekly pop column for the Daily Mail. He recalls, "I went to interview The Beatles in February after receiving a scruffy mimeographed press handout explaining how The Beatles got their name (A man came unto us on a flaming pie - etc.) and I thought, I want to interview whoever wrote this...I enjoyed interviewing them over glasses of whisky and Coke. I was the first journalist to interview them for a national newspaper. That day I saw The Beatles play to a BBC Radio audience and thought they were great, especially their friendly attitude toward the audience. [Mitchell is almost certainly referring to The Beatles' appearance at London's Playhouse Theatre on February 20 for the radio show **Parade of The Pops**, which was broadcast live on the BBC Light Program.] I interviewed them several times in the ensuing months. I guess Paul was always the most friendly to me; he knew I was a published poet (and novelist) and named me as his favorite poet in Honey magazine."

McCartney appeared, along with Mitchell, Allen Ginsberg* and others, in the TV special **It's So Far Out It's Straight Down** broadcast on Granada TV in the U.K. on March 7, 1967. Mitchell lamented, "Paul and I lost touch for a bit over the years, but occasionally he'd phone me and we'd talk.

"Lately we've seen more of each other. I've become quite fond of Paul and Linda, who often invite me and my wife to their parties. Following the rehearsals of the **Liverpool Oratorio** *(see The Royal Liverpool Philharmonic Orchestra & Choir & Choristers Of Liverpool Cathedral)*, he asked if I'd like to do some poems at a 'small gig' [at Cliffs Pavilion, Westcliff-on Sea, in England on July 19, 1991] he and his band were doing. I was scheduled to be on holiday in France at the time. 'Oh we'd fly you over,' he said. I was thrilled, so I flew over and went for rehearsals at his private studio by his home in Sussex. Paul picked out four poems – ***Hot Pursuit*** (about singer James Brown), ***Song In Space*** (about the environment), ***Maybe Maytime*** (for my wife Celia) and ***I Like That Stuff*** (a children's riddle I nearly always perform). The gig was great for me – I enjoyed it tremendously. I've performed poems for anti-bomb and anti-Vietnam war rallies of 100,000, but it was a gas to be backed by that right little, tight little band and my hero Paul. I came off stage feeling I'd been covered in stardust. I had my own dressing room with a refrigerator packed with wine and veggie treats. There was a limo to fetch me...wow, a bit unlike poetry gigs where you walk from the station to the venue through the English rain."

Maybe Maytime was performed to the backing of McCartney's song ***Singalong Junk***. The only backing on ***I Like That Stuff*** is a guitar chord at the end, probably played by either McCartney or Robbie McIntosh, though Mitchell cannot recall exactly who played what because he was facing the audience. A portion of ***Song In Space*** was reprinted in McCartney's New World Tour program in 1993.

McCartney sought Mitchell's advice on the lyrics to his 1993 album **Off The Ground**. Mitchell said, "Paul and I sat together in his studio and one by one he played and sang the songs from a few feet away. It was very exciting, and I found it hard to do instant comments on the lyrics; but I did make a few and some I think were incorporated." Mitchell, as well as McCartney, is an advocate for animal rights and vegetarianism.

Zoot Money

Record 213 title:
Mr. Money

Media:
Album 12"

Label / Catalog number:
Magic Moon / LUNE 1

Producer:
Jim Diamond

Jacket / Inserts:
Unique with designed by Paul McCartney / Custom inner-sleeve

Recording Location / Date:
Island (Basing Street) Studios, London, U.K. / (probably) 1980

Release date / Country:
25 Sep 80 / U.K.

Composer:
G. Money - C. Allen - A. Benson - F. Fisher - J. Mercer - H. Arlen - S. Jones - D. Chessler - B. Hilliard - C. Sigman - L. Brown - B. Homer - B. Green

Zoot Money: Lead Vocals

Zoot Money was born George Bruno on July 17, 1942 of Italian parents who moved to England just before World War II. He started out in jazz and skiffle during the 1950s, and became a popular blues musician in the U.K. during the 1960s. His Big Roll Band, which included Andy Somers (later changed to Summers and a member of the popular '80s' band The Police), had only one hit, ***Big Time Operator,*** which reached the U.K. top 30 in 1966. In 1967, he disbanded the Big Roll Band and formed Dantalian's Chariot, which broke up two years later. Zoot and Andy joined Eric Burdon and The New New Animals in 1969.

Money had a long running musical relationship with Paul McCartney's brother Mike *(see McGear, McGough & McGear, The Scaffold)* and was a brief member of The Scaffold before it evolved into Grimms. In 1980, his album **Mr. Money** was released on the obscure London-based record label Magic Moon Records, and was listed as an MPL (McCartney Productions Limited) production.

According to Zoot, McCartney conceived the idea of having him record songs to which Paul owned the music publishing rights after hearing Money's cover version of McCartney's Beatles song ***Blackbird***. The entire project, which was commissioned and financed by McCartney, was subject to McCartney's approval. McCartney did not contribute to the album's recordings in any way. However, he was given special thanks and listed as contributing to the album's jacket design. Zoot said, "It was a general discussion between Paul and I about all the album during which we explored the different 'ages of Zoot' for the album jacket's back, which I personally wanted for the front." Only minor changes were made to the basic design submitted by Money and the photographer to MPL. Money has since involved himself in acting and TV commercials.

Matt Monro

Record 214 title:
By Request

Media:
Album 5" CD

Label / Catalog number:
EMI / CDP 7482752 CZ 8

Jacket / Inserts:
Unique in Jewel box / CD booklet with Liner Notes by Paul McCartney

Recording Location / Date:
(probably) EMI-Abbey Road Studios, London, U.K.

Release date / Country:
19 Oct 87 (first issued 19 Nov 86) / U.K.

Matt Monro: Lead Vocals

Matt Monro was born Terrence Parsons on December 1, 1932 in London, England. He also was known professionally as Al Jordan when he was not driving a bus to supplement his income. His singing style was typical of what is termed easy listening. Monro got his first big break singing a pseudo-Frank Sinatra version of ***You Keep Me Swingin'***. The song was issued under the name Fred Flange and appeared on the Peter Sellers' *(see Peter Sellers, Terry Southern & Ringo Starr)* comedy album **Songs For Swingin' Sellers** produced by George Martin*. Monro was signed to Parlophone Records and produced by Martin.

Monro had his first top 10 in the U.K. with the song ***Portrait Of My Love*** in 1960. During the next five years, Monro had chart success in the U.K. with a number of songs including ***My Kind Of Girl*** (his only U.S. top 20), ***Why Not Now***, ***Gonna Build A Mountain***, ***Softly As I Leave You***, ***When Love Comes Along*** and a cover of the theme from the James Bond Film ***From Russia With Love***.

Paul McCartney got to know Matt Monro at EMI's Abbey Road Studios where Matt usually recorded. Monro was also represented by Brian Epstein for a time. His cover of McCartney's Beatles song ***Yesterday***, released on October 8, reached the U.K. top 10 in the fall of 1965. (He also recorded covers of McCartney's Beatles songs ***Michelle***, ***All My Loving***, ***Here, There And Everywhere*** and ***The Long And Winding Road***.) That year, he relocated to the U.S. where he worked the nightclub circuit and Las Vegas. Monro died of cancer on February 7, 1985. Paul McCartney contributed the liner notes to EMI Records' 1986 retrospective album of Monro's career titled **By Request**.

Monty Python

Record 215 title:
Life Of Brian
Label / Catalog number:
Paramount / LV 12871
Media:
Album 12" LVD
Producer:
Eric Idle & Graham Chapman & Mixed by: George Harrison & Phil MacDonald (music)
Jacket / Inserts:
Standard international design / Record label inner sleeve
Recording Location / Date:
Unit Hotel, Tunisia & Chappell Studios, London & mixed at FPSHOT (Friar Park Studios, Henley-on-Thames), U.K. / 08 Sep 78

Song 215a title:
Always Look On The Bright Side Of Life (reprise)
Release date / Country:
1991 / U.S.A.
Track details:
Side 2, track 1 [end] / 0 min. 51 sec.
Composer:
E. Idle

John Altman: Arrangement

Record 216 title:
Monty Python Examines "The Life Of Brian" (A Conversation with Monty Python conducted by Dave Herman)
Label / Catalog number:
Warner Bros. (The Warner Bros. Music Show) / WBMS 110 (promotional only)
Media:
Album 12"
Producer:
Drea Besch
Jacket / Inserts:
Unique (Warner Bros. Music Show) / Record label inner sleeve
Recording Location / Date:
(probably) Los Angeles, CA, U.S.A. / 1979

Song 216a title:
Monty Python Examines "The Life Of Brian" (A Conversation with Monty Python conducted by Dave Herman)
Release date / Country:
1979 / U.S.A.
Track details:
Side 2, track 1 / 28 min. 45 sec. (total time of LP)
Composer:
Monty Python

Dave Herman: Interviewer; Monty Python: Dialogue; George Harrison: Dialogue

Record 217 title:
Monty Python Sings
Media:
Album 5" CD
Label / Catalog number:
Virgin / MONT D1
Jacket / Inserts:
Standard international design in jewel box / 20 page CD booklet
Recording Location / Date:
Unit Hotel, Tunisia & Chappell Studios, London & mixed at FPSHOT (Friar Park Studios, Henley-on-Thames), U.K. / 08 Sep 78

Song 217a title:
Always Look On The Bright Side Of Life
Track details:
Side 1, track 1 / 3 min. 33 sec.
Release date / Country:
11 Dec 89 (first issued 08 Oct 79) / U.K.
Composer:
E. Idle
Producer:
Eric Idle & Graham Chapman & Mixed by: George Harrison & Phil MacDonald

Eric Idle: Lead Vocals; John Altman: Arrangement

Song 217b title:
Lumberjack Song
Track details:
Side 1, track 3 / 3 min. 20 sec.
Release date / Country:
11 Dec 89 (first issued 14 Nov 75) / U.K.
Composer:
T. Jones - M. Palin - F. Tomlinson
Producer:
George Harrison

Michael Palin: Lead Vocals; probably The Fred Tomlinson Singers: B. Vocals

The Monty Python comedy team consisted of five Brits: Graham Chapman (born January 8, 1941, in Leicester), John Cleese (born October 27, 1939, in Weston-Super-Mare), Eric Idle (born on March 29, 1943, in South Shields), Terry Jones (born February 1, 1942, in Colwyn Bay, Wales), Michael Palin (born May 5, 1943, in Sheffield), and one American, Terry Gilliam (born November 22, 1940, in Medicine Lake, Minnesota). All of its members were highly educated. They first came to the public's attention with their British TV show **Monty Python's Flying Circus**, which aired in Britain between 1969 and 1974.

All the Beatles were big fans of the show. In 1972, Ringo Starr appeared in an episode titled **It's** included on the 1987 VHS release **The Fourth Eagerly Awaited, Impatiently Anticipated, Ardently Sought After, Raring-To-Go And Real Good**. Before Monty Python's Flying Circus, Chapman and Cleese co-wrote and had cameo roles in the Peter Sellers'* film **The Magic Christian**, co-starring Ringo Starr.

George Harrison seemed particularly fond of their brand of humor and struck up a friendship with the group, especially members Michael Palin and Eric Idle. Harrison broadcast a version of the Python's ***Lumberjack Song*** through the P.A. system at the beginning of his shows during his 1974 U.S. tour. He produced a studio version of the song for the Pythons released in 1975, credited as George "Onothimagen" Harrison, a self-deprecating nickname he used for a time after his critically panned **Dark Horse** album and tour in 1974. On Harrison's album **Extra Texture**, the liner notes state "Also not appearing on this record: Eric Idle." Idle claims he did contribute a voice to the album, and apparently did some radio ads for the album in England.

On December 26, 1975, Harrison appeared on Eric Idle's and Neil Innes' *(see Bonzo Dog Band)* BBC-TV show **Rutland Weekend Television** performing ***The Pirate Song***. It was a parody of Harrison's legal troubles, written by Idle and Harrison, using part of the melody of ***My Sweet Lord***, which he'd been accused of lifting from The Chiffons' song ***He's So Fine*** *(see Delaney & Bonnie & Friends)*.

On April 20, 1976, Harrison joined the Pythons onstage at the Civic Center in New York to sing the ***Lumberjack Song***, but unfortunately it was not the same performance that appeared on the album **Monty Python Live At The Civic Center.** That year, Eric Idle sang on Harrison's ***This Song***, written in response to his loss of a plagiarism law suit filed against his song ***My Sweet Lord***. Idle directed the music videos for Harrison's ***True Love*** and ***Crackerbox Palace***, which co-starred Neil Innes.

In 1978, Harrison came to the rescue of Monty Python's film **Life Of Brian**, a biblical comedy about a person named Brian who is mistaken for a messiah-like Jesus Christ. EMI, the film's original producer, backed out at the last minute due to the controversial nature of the film. Harrison, who wanted to see the film made, stepped in and acted as executive producer, assuring the film's financial backing. The film was a major box office success and launched Harrison's HandMade Films company into the forefront of the industry. Harrison made a very brief cameo appearance in the film as Mr. Papadopoulis and helped mix its closing track, ***Always Look On The Bright Side Of Life***, at his home studio in Henley. He also contributed dialogue to the 1979 promotional interview album **Monty Python Examines The Life Of Brian (A Conversation with Monty Python conducted by Dave Herman)**.

Harrison's HandMade Films also released **Monty Python – Live At The Hollywood Bowl** in 1982. In 1981, HandMade released Terry Gilliam's highly successful **Time Bandits** *(see Various Artists - Time Bandits)*, to which Harrison contributed his song ***Dream Away*** for the film's closing. Michael Palin starred in HandMade's **The Missionary** in 1982, and **A Private Function** in 1985. John Cleese starred in **Privates On Parade** in 1982, and Eric Idle starred in **Nuns On The Run**, for the company, in 1990.

HandMade struggled to duplicate its early successes, but the company suffered low box-office receipts from big-budget films like **Water** *(see Billy Connolly/Chris Tummings & The Singing Rebel's Band, Jimmy Helms)* and **Shanghai Surprise** *(see Varioius Artists - Shanghai Surprise)*. George Harrison sold HandMade Films in 1994 after several lawsuits involving distribution. Harrison was successful in a major lawsuit which he filed in 1995 against his HandMade Films partner, Dennis O'Brien, for fraud and mismanagement.

The Monty Python members have since drifted into successful solo projects, and it looks unlikely, since the death of Graham Champan on October 4, 1989, that there will be any significant group reunion. Ringo Starr was originally considered for a role in another Python spin-off film, **Yellowbeard**. Harrison was originally scheduled to write the music for Terry Gilliam's film **Brazil**. Palin wrote the liner notes for Harrison's "supergroup" Traveling Wilburys' *(see Bob Dylan, Jeff Lynne, Roy Orbison, Tom Petty And The Heartbreakers)* first album, while Idle wrote the liner notes for the second (**Volume 3**) Wilburys' album. The CD **Monty Python Sings**, which gives special thanks to George Harrison, has since been released in the U.S.A. (Virgin/Capitol catalogue # V2-86253 2) in its original format.

Keith Moon

Record 218 title:
Two Sides Of The Moon

Media:
Album 5" CD

Label / Catalog number:
Mausoleum Classix/BMG / 60038-2

Jacket / Inserts:
Standard international design in jewel box / 8 page CD booklet

Song 218a title:
Do Me Good

Release date / Country:
01 Jul 97 / U.S.A.

Producer:
Steve Cropper

Track details:
Side 1, track 14 / 2 min. 44 sec.

Composer:
S. Cropper

Recording Location / Date:
Clover Recorders, Los Angeles, CA, U.S.A. / Sep 75

Keith Moon: Lead Vocals; probably one or more of the following: Ringo Starr: Drums & B. Vocals; Steve Cropper: Guitar; Klaus Voormann: Bass; Ronnie Wood: Guitar; David Bowie: Keyboards &/or B. Vocals; Jim Horn: (probable) Saxophone; Chuck Findley: (probable) Horns

Song 218b title:
Move Over Ms. L
Release date / Country:
01 Jul 97 (first issued 17 Mar 75) / U.S.A.
Producer:
Mal Evans, Skip Taylor & John Stronach
Recording Location / Date:
Record Plant (West) Studios, Los Angeles, CA, U.S.A. / Sep - Dec 74
Track details:
Side 1, track 6 / 3 min. 11 sec.
Composer:
J. Lennon

Keith Moon: Lead Vocals; Paul Stallworth: Bass; Joe Walsh: Guitar; Jesse Ed Davis: Guitar; Keith Moon: Drums; Ron Grinel: Drums; David Foster: Piano; Ollie Mitchell: Horns; Steve Douglas: Horns; Mal Evans: Horn Arrangements

Song 218c title:
Naked Man
Release date / Country:
01 Jul 97 / U.S.A.
Producer:
Steve Cropper
Recording Location / Date:
Clover Recorders, Los Angeles, CA, U.S.A. / Sep 75
Track details:
Side 1, track 13 / 3 min. 18 sec.
Composer:
R. Newman

Keith Moon: Lead Vocals; probably one or more of the following: Ringo Starr: Drums & B. Vocals; Steve Cropper: Guitar; Klaus Voormann: Bass; Ronnie Wood: Guitar; David Bowie: B. Vocals &/or Keyboards; Brooks Honeycut: (probable) B. Vocals; Maxine Waters: (probable) B. Vocals; Julia Waters: (probable) B. Vocals; Jim Horn: (probable) Saxophone; Chuck Findley: (probable) Horns

Song 218d title:
Real Emotion
Release date / Country:
01 Jul 97 / U.S.A.
Producer:
Steve Cropper
Recording Location / Date:
Clover Recorders, Los Angeles, CA, U.S.A. / Sep 75
Track details:
Side 1, track 15 / 2 min. 56 sec.
Composer:
S. Cropper

Keith Moon: Lead Vocals; probably one or more of the following: Ringo Starr: Drums & B. Vocals; Steve Cropper: Guitar; Klaus Voormann: Bass; Ronnie Wood: Guitar; David Bowie: B. Vocals &/or Keyboards

Song 218e title:
Solid Gold
Release date / Country:
01 Jul 97 (first issued 17 Mar 75) / U.S.A.
Producer:
Mal Evans, Skip Taylor & John Stronach
Recording Location / Date:
Record Plant (West) Studios, Los Angeles, CA, U.S.A. / Sep - Dec 74
Track details:
Side 1, track 2 / 2 min. 47 sec.
Composer:
N. Barclay

Keith Moon: Lead Vocals; Ringo Starr: Announcer; Cam Davis: B. Vocals & Drums; Paul Stallworth: Bass; Jean Millington: B. Vocals & Bass; Nickey Barclay: B. Vocals & Piano; Patti Quatro: B. Vocals & Guitar; Joe Walsh: Guitar and Arp Synthesizer; Beau Guss; Guitar (solo); Sherlie Matthews: B. Vocals; Lorna Willard: B. Vocals; Julia Tillman: B. Vocals

Song 218f title:
Together
Release date / Country:
01 Jul 97 (first issued 17 Mar 75) / U.S.A.
Producer:
Skip Taylor & John Stronach
Recording Location / Date:
Record Plant (West) Studios, Los Angeles, CA, U.S.A. / Sep - Dec 74
Track details:
Side 1, track 10 / 3 min. 01 sec.
Composer:
H. Nilsson

Keith Moon: Vocals; Harry Nilsson: Vocals; Ringo Starr: Drums and "Rap"; Jim Keltner: Drums; Klaus Voormann: Bass; Jesse Ed Davis: Guitar; Danny "Kootch" Kortchmar; Paul Lenart: Guitar; Robert Greenridge: Steel Drums; Jimmy Haskell: Arrangement and Conductor of Strings

Song 218g title:
Together Rap
Release date / Country:
01 Jul 97 / U.S.A.
Producer:
Skip Taylor & John Stronach
Recording Location / Date:
Record Plant (West) Studios, Los Angeles, CA, U.S.A. / Sep - Dec 74
Track details:
Side 1, track 18 / 1 min. 59 sec.
Composer:
H. Nilsson

Keith Moon: "Rap"; Ringo Starr: Drums and "Rap"; Jim Keltner: Drums; Klaus Voormann: Bass; Jesse Ed Davis: Guitar; Danny "Kootch" Kortchmar; Paul Lenart: Guitar

Song 218h title:
U.S. Radio Spot (contains portions of: Crazy Like A Fox / Solid Gold / Together/ In My Life)
Release date / Country:
01 Jul 97 / U.S.A.
Producer:
Mal Evans, Skip Taylor & John Stronach
Recording Location / Date:
Record Plant (West) Studios, Los Angeles, CA, U.S.A. / Sep - Dec 74 thru Feb 75
Track details:
Side 1, track 11 / 1 min. 02 sec.
Composer:
(A. Staehely - N. Barclay - H. Nilsson - J. Lennon - P. McCartney) - [K. Moon]

Keith Moon: Lead Vocals & Drums; Ringo Starr: Drums, Announcer & "Rap"; Cam Davis: B. Vocals & Drums; Paul Stallworth: Bass; Jean Millington: B. Vocals & Bass; Nickey Barclay: B. Vocals & Piano; Patti Quatro: B. Vocals & Guitar; Joe Walsh: Guitar and Arp Synthesizer; Beau Guss; Guitar (solo); Sherlie Matthews: B. Vocals; Lorna Willard: B. Vocals; Julia Tillman: B. Vocals; Jim Keltner: Drums; Klaus Voormann: Bass; Jesse Ed Davis: Guitar; Danny "Kootch" Kortchmar; Paul Lenart: Guitar; Robert Greenridge: Steel Drums; Jimmy Haskell: Arrangement and Conductor of Strings; Curly Smith: Drums; Jimmie Randall: Bass; Spencer Davis: Acoustic Guitar; Al Staehely: Acoustic Guitar; John Staehely: Electric Guitar; Jay Ferguson: Piano; Norman Kurban: Piano; Ron Hicklin: B. Vocals; August Johnson: B. Vocals; Greg Matta: B. Vocals; Irma Routen: B. Vocals; Andra Willis: B. Vocals; Clydie King: B. Vocals; Ira Hawkins: B. Vocals; James Gilstrap: B. Vocals; Gerald Garrett: B. Vocals; Carolyn Willis: B. Vocals

Keith Moon was born on August 23, 1947 in London, England. Moon, alternately known as "Moon The Loon" or "Moonie," earned his reputation as one of rock's most outrageous personalities in the group The Who *(see Roger Daltrey, John Entwistle)*. Moon was a member of a surf music band called The Beachcombers when, in 1964, he challenged The Who's drummer during a public performance, demolishing the drummer's kit (and membership in the group) in the process. Moon ended up sitting in with The Who for the rest of his life. He made a habit of destroying his kit, which became his trademark, even going so far as to plant explosives in his dual bass drums. However, his destructive nature was not confined to the stage, as the world soon learned when many of his rock contemporaries began trying to out-do his hotel room bashing.

In spite of all of his excesses, Keith Moon was loved and respected by his peers, including all of The

Beatles. He was the only member of The Who present during The Beatles' live telecast, via satellite, performance of ***All You Need Is Love*** for the BBC's program **Our World**, on June 25, 1967.

Keith moon, Los Angeles, CA, 1974, photo courtesy of Tom Bert

On December 15, 1969, John Lennon performed at the Lyceum Ballroom in London at the **Peace For Christmas** charity concert on behalf of UNICEF with what was called The Plastic Ono Supergroup (with a cast of 1000's). It included the same line-up of musicians John and Yoko used at the **Live Peace In Toronto 1969 Concert** *(see Yoko Ono)*, the Delaney & Bonnie & Friends* tour line-up with George Harrison and Keith Moon among others. Lennon referred to Moon in the **Some Time In New York City** album credits as "Kief Spoon." Moon appeared onstage playing drums along with his chauffeur, Neil Boland, on percussion. Weeks later, Boland was accidentally run over and killed by Moon while the two were trying to escape an attack outside a club in England.

Unfortunately Moon was self-destructive as well, becoming a regular on the rock party circuit that included, among others, Ringo Starr. Moon soon formed a mutual friendship and working relationship with Ringo, whom he affectionately referred to as Bongo. In the first half of the 1970s, Moon and Starr appeared together in the films **200 Motels** *(see Frank Zappa)*, **That'll Be The Day**, **Born To Boogie** *(see T. Rex)*, **Son Of Dracula** *(see Harry Nilsson)*, and in the 1978 film **Sextette**. Ringo appears in The Who's 1979 film **The Kids Are Alright** at Moon's invitation. Ringo even did a promotional radio spot for the film contained on a one-sided promotional single (New World Pictures / CR 3926).

In 1974, John Lennon was spending his nearly year-long "lost weekend" in Los Angeles, during which time he recorded part of his **Rock 'N' Roll** album and produced Harry Nilsson's album **Pussy Cats**. Ringo was in Los Angeles preparing to record his album **Goodnight Vienna**. Keith Moon was also staying in Los Angeles when he, Lennon, Nilsson and Starr decided to move into a house together. While in Los Angeles, Moon recorded his first and only solo album using a cast of well-known session players and rock stars, including Ringo. The Beatles' road manager, Mal Evans, was put in charge of producing the session's party madness. Ringo supplied the title **Two Sides Of The Moon** for the album, and provided some drumming and dialogue. The album, like **Pussy Cats**, which Moon and Ringo also contributed to, consisted of covers of some of Moon's favorite songs, including The Beach Boys'* ***Don't Worry Baby***. Moon, who had never lost his love for surf music, performed with The Beach Boys on a number of occasions.

The album also contained two Lennon compositions - The Beatles' ***In My Life***, and ***Move Over Ms. L***, which Lennon first released as the B-side to ***Stand By Me*** a week before Moon's release. It can be argued whether ***Move Over Ms. L*** qualifies as a composition contribution. The following scenario is likely: Moon heard Lennon playing the song during the time they lived together in L.A. and may have shown an interest in it; Lennon recorded the song (it's not really about Yoko) intending to include it on his **Walls And Bridges** album, but changed his mind. He then offered the composition as a contribution to his pal Moon's album. When Lennon was forced into prematurely releasing his **Rock 'N' Roll** album, he decided to use his leftover recording of ***Move Over Ms. L*** as the B-side of the single.

Whether Moon was forced to delay the release of his version until Lennon's version was released, or whether it was just coincidence that his version came out a week later, is not clear. Because Lennon gave the song to Moon after he had initially passed on it, and a considerable amount of time passed before his release of it, it should be considered as a composition contribution.

There is no indication from the credits that Lennon, who had essentially returned to living in New York City, was directly involved in any of the recordings on Moon's album. Jim Keltner, who also drummed on some of **Two Sides Of The Moon**, does not recall Lennon being involved in any of the sessions for the album, nor does May Pang, Lennon's companion at the time, or the album's engineer, Lee Kiefer.

When **Two Sides Of The Moon** was released on CD in 1997, it contained several bonus tracks, including drumming contributions from Ringo, an alternate take of Ringo's speaking part in the song ***Together***, and the promotional ***U.S. Radio Spot*** for **Two Sides Of The Moon** that included Ringo's speaking part from the song ***Solid Gold***. Moon asks at the beginning of the bonus track ***Do Me Good***, "Do you think The Beatles will get back together?" Unfortunately, the CD did not include any detailed credits for the bonus tracks. Steve Cropper, who wrote two of three bonus tracks that he produced for Moon, said Ringo played on the sessions, but he was not certain if he played on all the tracks. He said the tracks were recorded for a second album that Moon never completed. Cropper and others at the session also recall a song called ***My Rubbereem***, on which Ringo and British comedian Peter Cook played drums.

Moon recorded a cover of The Beatles' ***When I'm 64*** for the soundtrack to the 1976 film **All This And World War II**. Keith Moon's self-destructive life-style caught up with him on September 8, 1978, when he died as a result of a mixture of prescription drugs and alcohol. Ironically, he passed away in a London apartment owned by his friend, Harry Nilsson, where Mama Cass Elliot died four years earlier. Hours before his death, Moon attended Paul McCartney's annual Buddy Holly Week birthday celebration *(see The Crickets)*. Keith Moon was not only rock's most outrageous drummer, but, arguably, one of its best.

The Who quickly replaced Moon with Kenney Jones*. The Who have worked together very little since Moon's death. They enlisted Ringo Starr's son Zak to play drums for their 1996 tour. Moon had been a major influence in Zak's learning to play the drums.

Gary Moore

Record 219 title:
Still Got The Blues
Label / Catalog number:
Virgin / CDV 2612
Media:
Album 5" CD
Producer:
Gary Moore, Ian Taylor & [George Harrison]
Jacket / Inserts:
Standard international design / 8 page CD booklet
Recording Location / Date:
FPSHOT (Friar Park Studio, Henley-on-Thames)
& (probably) Sarm West Studio, London, U.K. / 1989 or 1990

Song 219a title:
That Kind Of Woman
Release date / Country:
26 Mar 90 / U.K.
Track details:
Side 1, track 10 / 4 min. 30 sec.
Composer:
G. Harrison

Gary Moore: Lead Vocals & Guitar; George Harrison: B. Vocals, Slide & Rhythm Guitar; Nicky Hopkins: Piano; Bob Daisley: Bass; Graham Walker: Drums; Martin Drover: Trumpet; Frank Mead: Alto Saxophone; Nick Pentelow: Tenor Saxophone; Nick Payn: Baritone Saxophone

Gary Moore was born on April 4, 1952 in Belfast, Northern Ireland. Moore was a founding member of the band Skid Row in the early 1970s, but left by 1972. In 1974, Moore joined Thin Lizzy, but left after several months to join Colosseum II. He sat in with Thin Lizzy on selected dates, and rejoined the band from 1977 through 1979. Moore has worked with a wide range of musicians including Andrew Lloyd Webber, Ginger Baker *(see Blind Faith, Eric Clapton)*, Jack Bruce* and B.B. King*, among many others. Moore spent most of the 1980s working on solo projects and contributing to other artists' recordings, while honing his skills as one of the leading and most in-demand blues guitarists of the 1990s.

Moore's most successful project to date is the album **Still Got The Blues**. The album features the George Harrison composition ***That Kind Of Woman***, which was originally written for and recorded by Eric Clapton*. Clapton shelved the song (Clapton's version was released after Moore's version) and Harrison gave Moore a crack at the song. Harrison often cites Moore as one of his favorite guitarists. He not only contributed guitar and background vocals to Moore's version, but also helped with the production, though he is not credited.

According to Moore's manager John Martin, Harrison and Moore also recorded an untitled jam. Moore played guitar on Harrison's "supergroup" Traveling Wilburys' *(see Bob Dylan, Jeff Lynne, Roy Orbison, Tom Petty And The Heartbreakers)* song ***She's My Baby***, and joined Harrison onstage during Harrison's Royal Albert Hall performance fund-raiser for the Natural Law Political Party on April 6, 1992. Harrison joined in on the encore of Moore's performance at London's Royal Albert Hall on October 5, 1992. The two performed ***That Kind Of Woman*** and ***While My Guitar Gently Weeps***. The credits of Moore's album **Blues Alive** give special thanks to Harrison (for the encore appearance at Albert Hall). Though Harrison's performance was not included on the album, it was recorded and may be released in the future. It's a safe bet, especially since they are neighbors, that there will be plenty of Harrison and Moore to come.

Eddie Murphy

Record 220 title:
Love's Alright

Label / Catalog number:
Motown / 374636354-2

Media:
Album 5" CD

Producer:
Eddie Murphy, David Allen Jones & Trenten Gumbs

Jacket / Inserts:
Standard international design in jewel box / 16 page CD booklet

Recording Location / Date:
The following studios: Air, London & Hog Hill, Sussex, U.K., Bubblehill, Can Am Recorders, Capitol, Larrabee North, One On One, Record One & Aire, Los Angeles, CA, Woodland Digital, Nashville, TN; Compass Point, Bahamas & Cajun Recorders / Mar 92

Song 220a title:
Yeah

Release date / Country:
23 Feb 93 / U.S.A.

Track details:
Side 1, track 1 / 4 min. 44 sec.

Composer:
E. Murphy - D. Jones - T. Gumbs

Eddie Murphy: Vocals; Audrey Wheeler: Vocals; Sandi Barber: Vocals; Babyface: Vocals; Bon Jovi: Vocals; Garth Brooks: Vocals; En Vogue: Vocals; Johnny Gill: Vocals; Amy Grant: Vocals; Aaron Hall: Vocals; Hammer: Vocals; Heavy D: Vocals; Howard Hewitt: Vocals; Julio Iglesias: Vocals; Janet Jackson: Vocals; Michael Jackson: Vocals; Elton John: Vocals; Patti LaBelle: Vocals; Emmanuel Lewis: Vocals; Paul McCartney: Vocals; Teddy Pendergrass: Vocals; Richie Sambora: Vocals; Luther Vandross: Vocals; Barry White: Vocals; Stevie Wonder: Vocals & Harmonica; Herbie Hancock: Piano; Stanley Clarke: Bass; David Allen Jones: Drum Programming; Trenten Gumbs: Drum Programming

Eddie Murphy was born on April 3, 1961 in Brooklyn, New York. Murphy rose to prominence in the early 1980s on NBC-TV's **Saturday Night Live**, creating such comic characters as "Velvet Jones" and "Mister Robinson", and impersonating "Buckwheat" and "Gumby." Like his successful predecessors, Murphy soon outgrew **SNL** and branched out into films like **Trading Places**, **Beverly Hills Cop**, **Coming To America**, and, most recently, **The Nutty Professor**. He has also ventured into popular music with the albums **How Could It Be**, **So Happy** and **Love's Alright**.

In early 1992, Murphy approached McCartney to contribute to ***Yeah***, a song he was recording with an all-star guest line-up, with proceeds going to a U.S. educational trust charity. McCartney said "yeah" on the condition that Murphy try going meatless for a week. Murphy said "yeah" and, in March, arrived at Paul's private studio in Sussex, England.

Jimmy Nail

Record 221 title:
Growing Up In Public

Media:
Album 5" CD

Label / Catalog number:
Atlantic / 7 82433-2

Producer:
Danny Schogger, Guy Pratt & Jimmy Nail

Jacket / Inserts:
Standard international design in jewel box / 8 page CD booklet

Recording Location / Date:
Livingstone Studios, London, U.K. / (probably) early 1992

Song 221a title:
Real Love

Track details:
Side 1, track 5 / 4 min. 33 sec.

Release date / Country:
29 Sep 92 (first issued Jun 92) / U.S.A.

Composer:
G. Pratt - D. Schogger - J. Nail

Jimmy Nail: Lead Vocals; Guy Pratt: Guitar & Drum Programming; Danny Schogger: Keyboards, Synthesizer, Bass & Drum Programming; Katie Kissoon: B. Vocals; Linda Taylor: B. Vocals; Andy Caine: B. Vocals; Marc Fox: Percussion; George Harrison: Guitar; Graham Ward: Drums

Jimmy Nail was born on March 16, 1954 in Newcastle-upon-Tyne, England. Nail, the son of a professional football (soccer) player, had ambitions of becoming a teacher, but his extensive musical education led him to front a number of local bands in the 1970s. Motown and the British blues-rock scene of the late 1960s were his major musical influences. Though virtually unknown in the U.S., Nail has become a major recording artist, composer, actor and author in the U.K. He has been the nominee and recipient of numerous British entertainment industry awards during the last two decades.

In the 1980s he starred in the hit TV series **Auf Wiedersehen Pet**, and later in **Spender**, which he wrote, directed and helped produce. He also wrote a best-selling novel about **Spender**. His current TV series success is called **Crocodile Shoes**. Nail recently landed a role in the film version of Andrew Lloyd Webber and Tim Rice's musical **Evita**.

In 1985, Nail had his first hit with a remake of Rose Royce's soul classic ***Love Don't Live Here Anymore***. Nail performed with George Harrison at a George Formby convention on March 2, 1991. The following year his **Growing Up In Public** album was released. The special thanks to George Harrison in the albums' credits is no doubt due to Harrison's guitar work on ***Real Love***. The album also included contributions from friends Dave Gilmour (of Pink Floyd fame) and blues guitarist Gary Moore*. It contained ***Ain't No Doubt***, which reached the top of the U.K. charts.

Nail has had a number of other hits, including the title track from his country-flavored platinum **Crocodile Shoes** album, which he co-produced, and **Cowboy Dreams** in 1994. Nail's autobiographical title track from his **Big River** album in 1995 was also a major hit. The album also included a cover of Nail's favorite John Lennon song, ***Love***. There seems little doubt that the multi-talented Jimmy Nail will continue to have a major impact on the British entertainment industry.

Nervous

Record 222 title:
None
Recording Location / Date:
Hog Hill Studios, East Sussex, U.K. / Jul 94
Producer:
Nervous & Michael Brook

Song 222a title:
The Chain Saw Song
Release date / Country:
[Unreleased]
Composer:
Nervous

Justin Travis: Lead Vocals; Paul McCartney: Chain Saw & B. Vocals; James McCartney: Tubular Bells; Mary McCartney: Whistling; Dickie Lorraine: Acoustic Guitar & B. Vocals; Dean Watkyn: Bass & B. Vocals; Paul Codish: Jew's Harp; Oscar O'Lochlinn: Drums; William Drake: Keyboards; Keith Holden: Harmonica & B. Vocals; Bernie Holden: Clarinet; Michael Brook: B. Vocals; some firemen: B. Vocals

Justin Travis, lead singer of the group Nervous, was born on September 26, 1965 in Portsmouth, England. He attributes his interest in music to his parents, both veterans of skiffle bands in England during the 1950s. He was also greatly influenced by artists like Jimi Hendrix, The Doors, The Byrds, Nick Drake, Tom Waits, Bob Dylan* and Paul McCartney.

Travis began playing in a variety of garage bands in his early teens. After years in bands with names like Baby Lemonade and Flik Spatula, and some bad experiences, he became disillusioned with the music business. He moved to Spain, as he puts it, "to chill out and do a little gardening." He sent a couple of songs he had written there to a publisher friend back home who encouraged him to return to England and form a new band.

Travis took his friend's advice and formed the band Nervous. Nervous currently consists of Travis, Dickie Lorraine (aka Richard Cripps), William Drake, Dean Watkyn, Melvin Duffy and Barney C. Rockford. According to their press release, members of the band first met alongside a highway in England while changing a tire. Travis said, "It's an absolute lie, but we like to think it's true."

According to Travis, "Dickie Lorraine had known Ringo's son Jason and, through him, got to know McCartney's daughters Stella and Mary quite well. We've been friends with McCartney and his family for years. Paul called me up and asked if we'd fancy coming down to his studio and making an album. So I said yeah, sure! We high-tailed it down there for a couple of weeks in July of 1994 and had a great time. We were given full facilities, technicians and instruments, including the mellotron with the flute reel from ***Strawberry Fields Forever*** on it.

"One day Paul was out clearing a path for his horses through the forest with his chain saw. We were doing this track in the studio on which everybody was going to be playing something, and he wandered in with his chain saw so we asked him to play it! It's probably the most unusual instrument he has ever been asked to play. His technicians miked up the chain saw, but the exhaust fumes set the fire alarm off. The next thing we knew we had two fire engines coming up the road, so we got the firemen to sing on the recording! It was a classic rock 'n' roll moment.

"Paul is a very, very encouraging person to us and a great person to hang out with. He's our mate, we love him! McCartney's son James and daughter Mary play on the recording as well. The song was originally called ***The Mental Song***, but we have appropriately retitled it ***The Chain Saw Song***." Nervous hope to have their second album out in 1998, and will probably release ***The Chain Saw Song*** as the B-side of a single.

Harry Nilsson

Record 223 title:
Daybreak (from The Soundtrack Album of The Apple Film "Son Of Dracula"
Media:
Single 7"
Label / Catalog number:
RCA / APBO-0246
Producer:
Harry Nilsson
Jacket / Inserts:
Standard international design PS with photo of Ringo Starr (two variations of this sleeve exist)

Recording Location / Date:
London, U.K. / Sep 72
Song 223a title:
Daybreak [single version]
Track details:
Side 1, track 1 / 3 min. 03 sec.
Release date / Country:
25 Mar 74 / U.S.A.
Composer:
H. Nilsson

Harry Nilsson: Lead Vocals & Piano; Ringo Starr: Drums; George Harrison: Cow Bell; Jim Price: Organ; Bobby Keys: High Saxophone; Klaus Voormann: Bass; Peter Frampton: Guitar; Ray Cooper: Percussion; Chris Spedding: Bouzouki; Gene Cipriano: Horns

Record 224 title:
Duit On Mon Dei
Media:
Album 5" CD
Label / Catalog number:
RCA / BVCP-7315
Producer:
Harry Nilsson & Richie Schmitt
Jacket / Inserts:
Standard international design in jewel box / 2 page CD insert with photos of Ringo Starr & 16 page lyric & translation booklet

Song 224a title:
Good For God
Track details:
Side 1, track 11 / 3 min. 23 sec.
Release date / Country:
21 Jan 95 (first issued 21 Mar 75) / Japan
Composer:
H. Nilsson
Recording Location / Date:
RCA's Music Center of the World, Los Angeles, CA, U.S.A. / 04 Oct 74

Harry Nilsson: Lead Vocals; Jim Keltner: Drums; Robert Greenidge: Steel Drums; Jesse Ed Davis: Guitar; Danny "Kootch" Kortchmar: Guitar; Klaus Voormann; Bass; Trevor Lawrence: Saxophone: Bobby Keys: Saxophone; Gene Cipriano: Tenor Saxophone; Carl McKnight: Percussion; Pat Murphy: Percussion; Ringo Starr: Voice

Song 224b title:
Kojak Columbo
Track details:
Side 1, track 4 / 3 min. 30 sec.
Release date / Country:
21 Jan 95 (first issued 21 Mar 75) / Japan
Composer:
H. Nilsson
Recording Location / Date:
RCA's Music Center of the World, Los Angeles, CA, U.S.A. / Sep - Oct 74

Harry Nilsson: Lead Vocals; Jim Keltner: Drums; Jesse Ed Davis: Guitar; Danny "Kootch" Kortchmar: Guitar; Klaus Voormann; Bass; Trevor Lawrence: Saxophone: Bobby Keys: Saxophone; Gene Cipriano: Saxophone; Pat Murphy: Congas; Ringo Starr: Drums; Doug Dillard: Banjo; Dr. John: Piano; Emmett Kennedy: Percussion; Milt Holland: Percussion; Joe De Aguero: Marimba

Record 225 title: Flash Harry
Label / Catalog number: Mercury / 6302 022
Jacket / Inserts: Standard international design / Custom inner-sleeve
Recording Location / Date: Cherokee Studios, Los Angeles, CA, U.S.A. / Dec 79 - Mar 80
Media: Album 12"
Producer: Steve Cropper & Bruce Robb

Song 225a title: Harry
Release date / Country: 05 Sep 80 / U.K.
Track details: Side 1, track 1 / 2 min. 22 sec.
Composer: E. Idle

Eric Idle: Vocals; Charlie Dore: Vocals; Ringo Starr: (possible) Drums; additionally, one or more of the following: Bobby Keys: Saxophone; Danny Kortchmar: Guitar; Donald "Duck" Dunn: Bass; Fred Tackett: Guitar; Jerome Jumonville: Horns; Jim Horn: Horns; Jim Keltner: Drums; Keith Allison: Bass; Klaus Voormann: Bass; Malcolm Rebennack (aka Dr. John): Piano &/or Guitar; Paul Stallworth: Bass; Ritchie Zito: Guitar; Steve Cropper: Guitar; Van Dyke Parks: Keyboards; Lowell George: Guitar; Arthur Gerst, Den Denay, Bill Payne, Jimmy Roberts, John Jarvis, Luis Damian, Rick Shlosser, Ricky Lawson, Scott Edwards, Tony Martin Jr., Fred Staehle, Wilton Felder & Jim Gordon

Song 225b title: How Long Can Disco On
Release date / Country: 05 Sep 80 / U.K.
Track details: Side 2, track 4 / 2 min. 54 sec.
Composer: R. Starkey - H. Nilsson

Harry Nilsson: Lead Vocals; Ringo Starr: Drums; additionally, one or more of the following: Bobby Keys: Saxophone; Danny Kortchmar: Guitar; Donald "Duck" Dunn: Bass; Fred Tackett: Guitar; Jerome Jumonville: Horns; Jim Horn: Horns; Jim Keltner: Drums; Keith Allison: Bass; Klaus Voormann: Bass; Malcolm Rebennack (aka Dr. John): Piano &/or Guitar; Paul Stallworth: Bass; Ritchie Zito: Guitar; Steve Cropper: Guitar; Van Dyke Parks: Keyboards; Lowell George: Guitar; Arthur Gerst, Den Denay, Bill Payne, Jimmy Roberts, John Jarvis, Luis Damian, Rick Shlosser, Ricky Lawson, Scott Edwards, Tony Martin Jr., Fred Staehle, Wilton Felder & Jim Gordon

Song 225c title: I've Got It
Release date / Country: 05 Sep 80 / U.K.
Track details: Side 2, track 2 / 3 min. 42 sec.
Composer: H. Nilsson - P. Botkin Jr.

Harry Nilsson: Lead Vocals; Ringo Starr: Drums; additionally, one or more of the following: Bobby Keys: Saxophone; Danny Kortchmar: Guitar; Donald "Duck" Dunn: Bass; Fred Tackett: Guitar; Jerome Jumonville: Horns; Jim Horn: Horns; Jim Keltner: Drums; Keith Allison: Bass; Klaus Voormann: Bass; Malcolm Rebennack (aka Dr. John): Piano &/or Guitar; Paul Stallworth: Bass; Ritchie Zito: Guitar; Steve Cropper: Guitar; Van Dyke Parks: Keyboards; Lowell George: Guitar; Arthur Gerst, Den Denay, Bill Payne, Jimmy Roberts, John Jarvis, Luis Damian, Rick Shlosser, Ricky Lawson, Scott Edwards, Tony Martin Jr., Fred Staehle, Wilton Felder & Jim Gordon

Song 225d title: Old Dirt Road
Release date / Country: 05 Sep 80 / U.K.
Track details: Side 1, track 4 / 4 min. 26 sec.
Composer: J. Lennon - H. Nilsson

Harry Nilsson: Lead Vocals; Ringo Starr: (probable) Drums; additionally, one or more of the following: Bobby Keys: Saxophone; Danny Kortchmar: Guitar; Donald "Duck" Dunn: Bass; Fred Tackett: Guitar; Jerome Jumonville: Horns; Jim Horn: Horns; Jim Keltner: Drums; Keith Allison: Bass; Klaus Voormann: Bass; Malcolm Rebennack (aka Dr. John): Piano &/or Guitar; Paul Stallworth: Bass;

Ritchie Zito: Guitar; Steve Cropper: Guitar; Van Dyke Parks: Keyboards; Lowell George: Guitar; Arthur Gerst, Den Denay, Bill Payne, Jimmy Roberts, John Jarvis, Luis Damian, Rick Shlosser, Ricky Lawson, Scott Edwards, Tony Martin Jr., Fred Staehle, Wilton Felder & Jim Gordon

Record 226 title:
Pussy Cats
Media:
Album 5" CD
Label / Catalog number:
RCA / 50570-2
Producer:
John Lennon
Jacket / Inserts:
Standard international design in jewel box with photo of John Lennon on the front / 12 page CD booklet with photos of John Lennon & Ringo Starr
Recording Location / Date:
One or more of the following studios: Burbank, Record Plant (West), Los Angeles, CA &/or Record Plant (East)†, New York, NY, U.S.A. / 04 Apr 74 & May or Jun 74† except where noted

Song 226a title:
All My Life
Track details:
Side 1, track 4 / 3 min. 10 sec.
Release date / Country:
29 Aug 95 (first issued 19 Aug 74) / U.S.A.
Composer:
H. Nilsson

Harry Nilsson: Lead Vocals & Arrangement; Ringo Starr: Drums; Jim Keltner: Drums; Bobby Keys: Saxophone; Ken Ascher: Piano, Orchestrations & Conducting The Masked Alberts Orchestra; Klaus Voormann: Bass; Jesse Ed Davis: Guitar; Danny "Kootch" Kortchmar: Guitar; Sneaky Pete Kleinow: Pedal Steel Guitar; Keith Moon: Chinese Wood Blocks; John Lennon: Arrangement

Song 226b title:
Black Sails
Track details:
Side 1, track 9 / 3 min. 13 sec.
Release date / Country:
29 Aug 95 (first issued 19 Aug 74) / U.S.A.
Composer:
H. Nilsson
Recording Location / Date:
Record Plant (East) Studios, New York, NY, U.S.A. / 18 Jun 74

Harry Nilsson: Lead Vocals & Arrangement; Ken Ascher: Orchestrations & Conducting The Masked Alberts Orchestra

Song 226c title:
Don't Forget Me
Track details:
Side 1, track 3 / 3 min. 38 sec.
Release date / Country:
29 Aug 95 (first issued 19 Aug 74) / U.S.A.
Composer:
H. Nilsson

Harry Nilsson: Lead Vocals, Piano & Arrangement; Ken Ascher: Orchestrations & Conducting The Masked Alberts Orchestra

Song 226d title:
Loop De Loop
Track details:
Side 1, track 8 / 2 min. 36 sec.
Release date / Country:
29 Aug 95 (first issued 19 Aug 74) / U.S.A.
Composer:
T. Vann

Harry Nilsson: Lead Vocals, Electric Piano & Arrangement; Keith Moon: Drums; Jim Keltner: Drums; Ringo Starr: Drums; Jim Horn: Saxophone; Bobby Keys: Saxophone; Trevor Lawrence: Saxophone; Jane Getz: Piano; John Lennon: Arrangement; Klaus Voormann: Bass; Danny "Kootch" Kortchmar: Guitar; Jesse Ed Davis: Guitar; Chuck Findley: Trombone; Troy Germano (The Masked Alberts Kids Chorale): B. Vocals; Kristin Turner (The Masked Alberts Kids Chorale): B. Vocals; Erik Mueller (The Masked Alberts Kids Chorale): B. Vocals; Nathalie Altman (The Masked Alberts Kids Chorale): B. Vocals; Peri Prestopino (The Masked Alberts Kids Chorale): B. Vocals; Cantey Turner (The Masked Alberts Kids Chorale): B. Vocals; Phyllida Paterson (The Masked Alberts Kids Chorale): B. Vocals;

Rachel Mueller (The Masked Alberts Kids Chorale): B. Vocals; Damon Vigiano (The Masked Alberts Kids Chorale): B. Vocals; Susie Bell (The Masked Alberts Kids Chorale): David Steinberg (The Masked Alberts Kids Chorale): B. Vocals; Eric Carmen: Handclaps; Michael McBride: Handclaps

Song 226e title:
Many Rivers To Cross
Release date / Country:
29 Aug 95 (first issued 19 Aug 74) / U.S.A.
Track details:
Side 1, track 1 / 4 min. 54 sec.
Composer:
J. Cliff

Harry Nilsson: Lead Vocals; Jim Keltner: Drums; Ringo Starr: Drums; Bobby Keys: Saxophone; Ken Ascher: Piano, Orchestrations & Conducting The Masked Alberts Orchestra; Klaus Voormann; Willie Smith: Organ; Jesse Ed Davis: Guitar; Danny "Kootch" Kortchmar: Guitar; Sneaky Pete Kleinow: Pedal Steel Guitar; John Lennon: B. Vocals & Arrangement; Lori Burton: B. Vocals

Song 226f title:
Mucho Mungo / Mt. Elga
Release date / Country:
29 Aug 95 (first issued 19 Aug 74) / U.S.A.
Track details:
Side 1, track 7 / 3 min. 44 sec.
Composer:
J. Lennon / H. Nilsson (Adpt.)

Harry Nilsson: Lead Vocals & Arrangement; Jim Keltner: Bobby Keys: Saxophone; Trevor Lawrence: Saxophone; Ken Ascher: Piano, Orchestrations & Conducting The Masked Alberts Orchestra; Klaus Voormann: Bass; Jesse Ed Davis: Guitar; Danny "Kootch" Kortchmar; Keith Moon: Congas; Cynthia Webb: Maracas; Ringo Starr: Maracas; John Lennon: Arrangement

Song 226g title:
Old Forgotten Soldier
Release date / Country:
29 Aug 95 (first issued 19 Aug 74) / U.S.A.
Track details:
Side 1, track 5 / 4 min. 15 sec.
Composer:
H. Nilsson

Harry Nilsson: Lead Vocals, Piano & Arrangement; Klaus Voormann: Bass; Jesse Ed Davis: Guitar

Song 226h title:
Rock Around The Clock
Release date / Country:
29 Aug 95 (first issued 19 Aug 74) / U.S.A.
Track details:
Side 1, track 10 / 3 min. 11 sec.
Composer:
J. DeKnight - .M. Freedman

Harry Nilsson: Lead Vocals, Electric Piano & Arrangement; Keith Moon: Drums; Jim Keltner: Drums; Ringo Starr: Drums; Jim Horn: Saxophone; Bobby Keys: Saxophone; Trevor Lawrence: Saxophone; Jane Getz: Piano; John Lennon: Arrangement; Klaus Voormann: Bass; Danny "Kootch" Kortchmar: Guitar; Jesse Ed Davis: Guitar; Chuck Findley: Trombone

Song 226i title:
Save The Last Dance For Me
Release date / Country:
29 Aug 95 (first issued 19 Aug 74) / U.S.A.
Track details:
Side 1, track 6 / 4 min. 29 sec.
Composer:
D. Pomus - M. Shuman

Harry Nilsson: Lead Vocals & Arrangement; Ringo Starr: Drums; Jim Keltner: Drums; Bobby Keys: Saxophone; Trevor Lawrence: Saxophone; Gene Cipriano: Saxophone; Jane Getz: Piano; Klaus Voormann: Bass; Sneaky Pete Kleinow: Pedal Steel Guitar: Jesse Ed Davis: Guitar; Danny "Kootch" Kortchmar: Guitar; John Lennon: Arrangement; Ken Ascher: Piano, Orchestrations & Conducting The Masked Alberts Orchestra

Song 226j title:
Subterranean Homesick Blues
Release date / Country:
29 Aug 95 (first issued 19 Aug 74) / U.S.A.
Track details:
Side 1, track 2 / 3 min. 11 sec.
Composer:
B. Dylan
Recording Location / Date:
One or more of the following studios: Record Plant (East), New York, NY, Burbank &/or Record Plant (West), Los Angeles, CA, U.S.A. / 28 Mar 74

Harry Nilsson: Lead Vocals & Clavinet; Jim Keltner: Drums; Ringo Starr: Snare Drum; Doug Hoefer:

Drums; Bobby Keys: Saxophone; Trevor Lawrence: Saxophone; Ken Ascher: Electric Piano; Jesse Ed Davis: Guitar; Danny "Kootch" Kortchmar; Sneaky Pete Kleinow: Pedal Steel Guitar; Klaus Voormann: Bass; John Lennon: Arrangement

Record 228 title:
Sandman

Media:
Album 5" CD

Label / Catalog number:
RCA / BVCP-7316

Jacket / Inserts:
Standard international design in Jewel box / 2 page CD insert w/photos of RS & 16 page lyric & translation booklet

Recording Location / Date:
(probably) RCA's Music Center of the World, Los Angeles, CA, U.S.A. / 1975

Song 227a title:
[unknown]

Release date / Country:
21 Jan 95 (first issued 19 Jan 76) / Japan

Track details:

Composer:
H. Nilsson - A. Harvey - D. Kortchmar - P. Botkin, Jr.

Harry Nilsson: Lead Vocals; Ringo Starr: "Special Thanks" (possible) Percussion/Drums & (possible) B. Vocals; additionally, one or more of the following: Jim Keltner: Drums; Klaus Voormann: Bass; Van Dyke Parks: Keyboards; Jane Getz: Keyboards; Leon Russell: Keyboards; Joe DeAguero: Percussion; Pat Murphy: Percussion; Gary Coleman: Percussion; Emmett Kennedy: Percussion; Robert Greenidge: Percussion; Emil Richards: Percussion; Jesse Ed Davis: Guitar; Danny "Kootch" Kortchmar: Guitar; Fred Tackett: Guitar; Trevor Lawrence: Horns; Bobby Keys: Horns; Gene Cipriano: Horns; Jim Horn: Horns; Johnny Rotella: Horns; Jay Migliori: Horns; Doug Dillard: Banjo; Bobby Bruce: Strings; Ilene Novog: Strings; Perry Botkin Jr.: Orchestra & Strings; Joe Cocker: "Special Thanks;" J. R. Shanklin: "Special Thanks;" Hillary Gerrard "Special Thanks;" Mike Berniker: "Special Thanks;" Frank Mancini: "Special Thanks"

Record 228 title:
Son Of Dracula (Music from the Apple film)

Media:
Album 5" CD

Label / Catalog number:
RCA/Rapple / BVCP-7315

Jacket / Inserts:
Standard international design in jewel box / 6 page tri-fold CD booklet with photo of Ringo Starr & 16 page lyric & translation booklet

Recording Location / Date:
London, U.K. / Aug - Oct 72 except where noted

Song 228a title:
Count Down Meets Merlin And Amber

Release date / Country:
21 Jan 95 (first issued 01 Apr 74) / Japan

Producer:
Ringo Starr & Harry Nilsson

Track details:
Side 1, track 4 / 2 min. 00 sec.

Composer:
P. Buckmaster

Harry Nilsson: Dialogue; Ringo Starr: Dialogue; Suzanna Leigh: Dialogue; one or more of the following for incidental music by Paul Buckmaster: Morris Pert: Drums; Frank Riccotti: Percussion; Ray Cooper: Percussion; Peter Robinson: Keyboards; Ann O'Dell: Keyboards; Diana Lewis: Keyboards; Barry Guy: Bass; Chris Lawrence: Bass; Martin Ford: Electric French Horn & Orchestral Organization

Song 228b title:
Daybreak
Release date / Country:
21 Jan 95 (first issued 01 Apr 74) / Japan
Producer:
Harry Nilsson
Recording Location / Date:
London, U.K. / Sep 72
Track details:
Side 1, track 2 / 2 min. 42 sec.
Composer:
H. Nilsson

Harry Nilsson: Lead Vocals & Piano; Ringo Starr: Drums; George Harrison: Cow Bell; Jim Price: Organ; Bobby Keys: High Saxophone; Klaus Voormann: Bass; Peter Frampton: Guitar; Ray Cooper: Percussion; Chris Spedding: Bouzouki; Gene Cipriano: Horns

Song 228c title:
Frankenstein, Merlin & The Operation
Release date / Country:
21 Jan 95 (first issued 01 Apr 74) / Japan
Producer:
Ringo Starr & Harry Nilsson
Track details:
Side 1, track 11 / 3 min. 15 sec.
Composer:
J. Tavener

Harry Nilsson: Dialogue; Ringo Starr: Dialogue; Suzanna Leigh: Dialogue; one or more of the following for incidental music by Paul Buckmaster: Morris Pert: Drums; Frank Riccotti: Percussion; Ray Cooper: Percussion; Peter Robinson: Keyboards; Ann O'Dell: Keyboards; Diana Lewis: Keyboards; Barry Guy: Bass; Chris Lawrence: Bass; Martin Ford: Electric French Horn & Orchestral Organization

Song 228d title:
Intro (to "Without You")
Release date / Country:
21 Jan 95 (first issued 01 Apr 74) / Japan
Track details:
Side 1, track 8 / 0 min. 20 sec.
Producer:
Ringo Starr & Harry Nilsson

Harry Nilsson: Dialogue; Freddie Jones: Dialogue

Song 228e title:
It Is He Who Would Be King
Release date / Country:
21 Jan 95 (first issued 01 Apr 74) / Japan
Producer:
Ringo Starr & Harry Nilsson
Track details:
Side 1, track 1 / 3 min. 04 sec.
Composer:
P. Buckmaster

Ringo Starr: Dialogue; one or more of the following for incidental music by Paul Buckmaster: Morris Pert: Drums; Frank Riccotti: Percussion; Ray Cooper: Percussion; Peter Robinson: Keyboards; Ann O'Dell: Keyboards; Diana Lewis: Keyboards; Barry Guy: Bass; Chris Lawrence: Bass; Martin Ford: Electric French Horn & Orchestral Organization

Song 228f title:
Perhaps This Is All A Dream
Release date / Country:
21 Jan 95 (first issued 01 Apr 74) / Japan
Producer:
Ringo Starr & Harry Nilsson
Track details:
Side 1, track 6 / 0 min. 45 sec.
Composer:
P. Buckmaster

Harry Nilsson: Dialogue; Suzanna Leigh: Dialogue; one or more of the following for incidental music by Paul Buckmaster: Morris Pert: Drums; Frank Riccotti: Percussion; Ray Cooper: Percussion; Peter Robinson: Keyboards; Ann O'Dell: Keyboards; Diana Lewis: Keyboards; Barry Guy: Bass; Chris Lawrence: Bass; Martin Ford: Electric French Horn & Orchestral Organization

Song 228g title:
The Abdication Of Count Down
Track details:
Side 1, track 13 / 1 min. 08 sec.

Release date / Country:
21 Jan 95 (first issued 01 Apr 74) / Japan
Producer:
Ringo Starr & Harry Nilsson
Composer:
P. Buckmaster

Harry Nilsson: Lead Vocals; one or more of the following for incidental music by Paul Buckmaster: Morris Pert: Drums; Frank Riccotti: Percussion; Ray Cooper: Percussion; Peter Robinson: Keyboards; Ann O'Dell: Keyboards; Diana Lewis: Keyboards; Barry Guy: Bass; Chris Lawrence: Bass; Martin Ford: Electric French Horn & Orchestral Organization

Song 228h title:
The Count's Vulnerability
Release date / Country:
21 Jan 95 (first issued 01 Apr 74) / Japan
Producer:
Ringo Starr & Harry Nilsson
Track details:
Side 1, track 9 / 2 min. 09 sec.
Composer:
P. Buckmaster

Ringo Starr: Dialogue; Freddie Jones: Dialogue; Suzanna Leigh: Dialogue; Dennis Price: Dialogue; one or more of the following for incidental music by Paul Buckmaster: Morris Pert: Drums; Frank Riccotti: Percussion; Ray Cooper: Percussion; Peter Robinson: Keyboards; Ann O'Dell: Keyboards; Diana Lewis: Keyboards; Barry Guy: Bass; Chris Lawrence: Bass; Martin Ford: Electric French Horn & Orchestral Organization

Song 228i title:
The End (Moonbeam)
Release date / Country:
21 Jan 95 (first issued 01 Apr 74) / Japan
Producer:
Ringo Starr, Harry Nilsson & Richard Perry
Track details:
Side 1, track 14 / 0 min. 48 sec.
Composer:
H. Nilsson

Harry Nilsson: Dialogue & Mellotron; Ringo Starr: Dialogue; Herbie Flowers: Bass; John Uribe: Acoustic Guitar; Klaus Voormann: Acoustic Guitar

Record 229 title:
Son Of Schmilsson
Label / Catalog number:
RCA/BMG / 3812-2-R
Jacket / Inserts:
Standard international design in jewel box / 4 page CD insert
Media:
Album 5" CD
Producer:
Richard Perry

Song 229a title:
Ambush
Release date / Country:
1988 (first issued 10 Jul 72) / U.S.A.
Recording Location / Date:
Trident & (possibly) Apple Studios, London, U.K. / Mar - May 72
Track details:
Side 1, track 9 / 5 min. 22 sec.
Composer:
H. Nilsson

Harry Nilsson: Lead Vocals; Harry Nilsson: Electric Piano; Ringo Starr: Drums; Klaus Voormann: Bass; Nicky Hopkins: Piano; Chris Spedding: Guitar; Peter Frampton: Guitar; John Uribe: Lead Guitar; Ray Cooper: Tambourine; Jim Price: Trumpets, Trombone & Horn Arrangement; Bobby Keys: Saxophone

Song 229b title:
At My Front Door
Release date / Country:
1988 (first issued 10 Jul 72) / U.S.A.
Track details:
Side 1, track 8 / 2 min. 40 sec.
Composer:
E. Abner - J. Moore

Recording Location / Date:
Trident & (possibly) Apple Studios, London, U.K. / Mar - May 72

Harry Nilsson: Lead Vocals; Ringo Starr: Drums; Klaus Voormann: Bass; Piano: Nicky Hopkins: Piano; Peter Frampton: Electric Guitar; Chris Spedding: Electric Guitar; Ray Cooper: Congas; Bobby Keys: Tenor Saxophone

Song 229c title:
Spaceman
Track details:
Side 1, track 6 / 3 min. 34 sec.
Release date / Country:
1988 (first issued 10 Jul 72) / U.S.A.
Composer:
H. Nilsson
Recording Location / Date:
Trident & (possibly) Apple Studios, London, U.K. / Apr - May 72

Harry Nilsson: Lead Vocals & Electric Piano; Ringo Starr: Drums; Klaus Voormann: Bass; John Uribe: Acoustic Guitar; Chris Spedding: Acoustic Guitar; Peter Frampton: Acoustic Guitar: Nicky Hopkins: Piano; Richard Perry: Percussion; Paul Buckmaster: Arrangement & Conductor of Orchestra

Song 229d title:
Take 54
Track details:
Side 1, track 1 / 4 min. 18 sec.
Release date / Country:
1988 (first issued 10 Jul 72) / U.S.A.
Composer:
H. Nilsson
Recording Location / Date:
Trident & (possibly) Apple Studios, London, U.K. / Mar - May 72

Harry Nilsson: Lead Vocals & Electric Piano; Ringo Starr: Drums; Klaus Voormann: Bass & Horns; Nicky Hopkins: Piano; Lowell George: Guitar; Jim Price: Horns; Bobby Keys: Saxophone & Horns; Milt Holland: Percussion

Song 229e title:
The Most Beautiful World In The World
Track details:
Side 1, track 11 / 3 min. 35 sec.
Release date / Country:
1988 (first issued 10 Jul 72) / U.S.A.
Composer:
H. Nilsson
Recording Location / Date:
CTS Studios, London, U.K. / Apr - May 72

Harry Nilsson: Lead Vocals; Ringo Starr: Drums; Klaus Voormann: Bass; Nicky Hopkins: Piano; Paul Keough: Guitar; Les Thatcher: Guitar; Ray Cooper: Percussion; Richard Perry: Percussion, Arrangement & Conductor of Orchestra & Choir; Kirby Johnson: Arrangement of Orchestra & Choir; Del Newman: Additional Orchestration

Song 229f title:
You're Breakin' My Heart
Track details:
Side 1, track 5 / 3 min. 06 sec.
Release date / Country:
1988 (first issued 10 Jul 72) / U.S.A.
Composer:
H. Nilsson
Recording Location / Date:
Trident & (possibly) Apple Studios, London, U.K. / Apr - May 72

Harry Nilsson: Lead Vocals & Electric Piano; Berry Morgan: Drums; Klaus Voormann: Bass & Horns; Nicky Hopkins: Piano; George Harrison: Slide Guitar; Peter Frampton: Electric Guitar; Jim Price: Horns; Bobby Keys: Horns

Record 230 title:
...That's The Way It Is

Media:
Album 5" CD

Label / Catalog number:
RCA / BVCP-7317

Producer:
Trevor Lawrence

Jacket / Inserts:
Standard international design in jewel box / 2 page CD insert & 16 page lyric & translation booklet

Recording Location / Date:
One or more of the following studios: Davlen Sound, Sound Labs &/or RCA's Music Center of the World, Los Angeles, CA, U.S.A. / (probably) Mar 76 &/or (possibly) 1977

Song 230a title:
A Thousand Miles Away

Track details:
Side 1, track 5 / 2 min. 50 sec.

Release date / Country:
21 Jan 95 (first issued 19 Jul 77) / Japan

Composer:
Sheppard - Miller

Recording Location / Date:
One or more of the following studios: Davlen Sound, Sound Labs &/or RCA's Music Center of the World, Los Angeles, CA, U.S.A. / (probably) Mar 76 &/or (possibly) 1977

Harry Nilsson: Vocals; Tony La Peau: Vocals; Ringo Starr: Announcer; additionally, one or more of the following: Jim Keltner: Drums; Chili Charles: Drums; Klaus Voormann: Electric Bass; Malcolm Rebennack (aka Dr. John): Keyboards; Van Dyke Parks: Keyboards; Jane Getz Wilson: Keyboards; David Paich: Keyboards; James Newton Howard: Keyboards; Danny "Kootch" Kortchmar: Guitar; Jesse Ed Davis: Guitar; Fred Tackett: Guitar; Lon Van Eaton: Guitar; Derrek Van Eaton: Guitar; Keith Allison: Guitar; Dennis Budimir: Guitar; Peter Jameson: Guitar; John Morell: Guitar; David Wolfert: Guitar; Michael Anthony: Guitar; Bobby Keys: Saxophone; Gene Cipriano: Saxophone; James Roberts: Saxophone; Buddy Collette: Saxophone; William Green: Saxophone; Jim Horn: Saxophone; Johnny Rotella: Saxophone; Lynda Laurence: Chorus; Abigale Haness: Chorus; John Lehman: Chorus; Monalisa Harrington: Chorus; Sherlie Matthews: Chorus; Joseph Greene: Chorus; William Thedford: Chorus; Deidra Askey: Chorus; Richard Glasser: Chorus

Song 230b title:
Daylight Has Caught Me

Track details:
Side 1, track 8 / 3 min. 49 sec.

Release date / Country:
21 Jan 95 (first issued 19 Jul 77) / Japan

Composer:
H. Nilsson - M. Rebennack

Harry Nilsson: Vocals; Tony La Peau: Vocals; Ringo Starr: (possible) Drums &/or Percussion; additionally, one or more of the following: Jim Keltner: Drums; Chili Charles: Drums; Doug Hoefer: Percussion; Klaus Voormann: Electric Bass; Malcolm Rebennack (aka Dr. John): Keyboards; Van Dyke Parks: Keyboards; Jane Getz Wilson: Keyboards; David Paich: Keyboards; James Newton Howard: Keyboards; Danny "Kootch" Kortchmar: Guitar; Jesse Ed Davis: Guitar; Fred Tackett: Guitar; Lon Van Eaton: Guitar; Derrek Van Eaton: Guitar; Keith Allison: Guitar; Dennis Budimir: Guitar; Peter Jameson: Guitar; John Morell: Guitar; David Wolfert: Guitar; Michael Anthony: Guitar; Robert Greenidge: Steel Drum; Malcolm Cecil: Synthesizer; Bobby Keys: Saxophone; Gene Cipriano: Saxophone; James Roberts: Saxophone; Buddy Collette: Saxophone; William Green: Saxophone; Jim Horn: Saxophone; Johnny Rotella: Saxophone; Steven Madaio: Trumpet; Anthony Terran: Trumpet; Lew McCreary: Trombone; Richard Nash: Trombone; Benny Powell: Trombone

Record 231 title:
The Lost Lennon Tapes
Label / Catalog number:
Westwood One Radio Network / [Matrix #] LT 88-38 (promotional only)
Jacket / Inserts:
Unique "Lost Lennon Tapes" / Cue Sheets
Recording Location / Date:
One or more of the following studios: Record Plant (East), New York, NY, Burbank &/or Record Plant (West), Los Angeles, CA, U.S.A. / Apr 74
Media:
Album 12" [2 LP set]
Producer:
John Lennon

Song 231a title:
Mucho Mungo / Mt. Elga (rehearsal)
Release date / Country:
12 Sep 88 / U.S.A.
Track details:
LP2, Side 2, track 1 / 1 min. 54 sec./1 min. 11 sec.
Composer:
J. Lennon - H. Nilsson (Adpt.)

Harry Nilsson: Lead Vocals & (probable) Keyboards; John Lennon: Arrangement, B. Vocals & (probable) Guitar

Harry Nilsson III was born on June 15, 1941, in Brooklyn, New York. He lived most of his life in southern California, and began working as the supervisor of computer processing for a bank. Nilsson started his musical career in the mid-1960s doing commercial jingles and TV show theme songs, and selling his compositions to artists such as The Monkees (***Cuddly Toy***), The Ronettes (***Paradise***) *(see Ronnie Spector)* and Three Dog Night (***One***).

Nilsson's recording career took off with the Grammy Award winning song ***Everybody's Talking***, the theme from the film **Midnight Cowboy**. His follow-up hit was ***I Guess The Lord Must Be In New York City***, which was originally intended as the theme for **Midnight Cowboy**. American audiences also heard him weekly singing the opening theme to the TV show **The Courtship Of Eddie's Father**.

Nilsson's association with The Beatles, especially John Lennon and Ringo Starr, was a fun-filled one. His first album, **Pandemonium Shadow Show**, contained covers of The Beatles' songs ***You Can't Do That*** (actually a medley of a number of Beatles' songs) and ***She's Leaving Home***. The critically acclaimed album attracted the attention (via The Beatles' press officer and Apple publicist Derek Taylor) of Lennon and McCartney, who declared in 1968 that Nilsson was their favorite "group." They even tried to sign him to their Apple Records label, but he remained contracted to RCA throughout most of his career. He did contribute his composition ***The Puppy Song***, at McCartney's request, to Mary Hopkin's* debut Apple album **Postcard**. In 1971, Nilsson expanded his talents to include writing and scoring the critically acclaimed animated film for TV **The Point**, which would later be re-recorded with a new narration featuring Ringo Starr.

Nilsson's biggest success came in late 1971 with the release of the album **Nilsson Schmilsson**, and the Badfinger-penned *(see Badfinger)* song ***Without You***. Its follow-up album was **Son Of Schmilsson**, featuring both George Harrison and Ringo Starr (who used the thinly veiled pseudonyms "George Harrysong" and "Richie Snare"). Ringo's involvement in the Nilsson sessions was the result of his previous work with the album's producer Richard Perry, who produced both Ringo's and Nilsson's most successful albums. (Nilsson appeared on the two Perry-produced Ringo albums, **Ringo** in 1973, and **Goodnight Vienna** the following year. He also contributed to Starr's albums **Rotogravure** in 1976, and **Stop And Smell The Roses** in 1981.) According to Perry, the bulk of **Son Of Schmilsson** was recorded at Trident Studios and was filmed for a documentary that remains unreleased. The album's credits also list additional recording and remixing at The Beatles' Apple Studios. The album jacket's gatefold features a photo (omitted from CD releases) of Harrison and Ringo, as well as special thanks to Derek Taylor. Taylor produced Nilsson's 1973 album **A Little Touch Of Schmilsson In The Night**.

In 1974, the soundtrack album and the long awaited film **Son Of Dracula**, starring Nilsson as Count

Down (or Downe) and Ringo Starr as Merlin, were released. The film was produced by Ringo and mostly shot in London. The screenplay was written by Jay Fairbanks with much revision by Ringo. The plot centers around the Count's rejection of the netherworld, and his desire to become mortal and have the ability to love. The film was reminiscent of an Ed Wood production accompanied by some of Nilsson's better music. Today the film is a highly sought-after cult classic.

The single ***Daybreak*** from the **Son Of Dracula** soundtrack album included contributions from both Ringo and Harrison, and a photo of Ringo on the picture sleeve. It would be Nilsson's last hit. The original vinyl album release included an instruction bag and iron-on transfer that included a photo of Ringo as Merlin. The album is on "Rapple" Records (a sort of merger between RCA and the Apple Records label) – no doubt because **Son Of Dracula** was an Apple Films release and Nilsson was still contracted to RCA. Ringo and Harry are listed as the overall producers of the album which links the music with dialogue from the film.

The pair attempted yet another film in 1974 titled **Harry & Ringo's Night Out** that apparently was nothing more than the title suggested and was never released. Nilsson also appeared in the video for Ringo's single ***Only You***.

Fortunately, there was no film of Harry and Lennon's night out on March 12, 1974, when the two heckled the Smothers Brothers' comeback performance at Los Angeles' Troubadour Club. The intoxicated pair was eventually expelled. Several days later, Lennon sent an apology and flowers to Dick and Tom Smothers. (The Beatles had been fans of the politically charged **Smothers Brothers' Comedy Hour** on CBS-TV. Harrison made a brief cameo appearance on an episode broadcast on November 17, 1968. The previous month the show premiered The Beatles' videos for ***Hey Jude*** and ***Revolution*** in the U.S. Tom was recruited by Lennon to perform on the Plastic Ono Band's *[see Yoko Ono]* 1969 single ***Give Peace A Chance***. Ringo appeared on the Smothers Brothers' NBC-TV Special broadcast on April 28, 1975 singing ***No No Song*** accompanied by Tom and Dick Smothers. Ringo, along with other members of the cast, also sang backing vocals on John Stewart's performance of ***Survivors [Can You Hear Me]***. A picture sleeve for Stewart's single [RCA / JB - 10268] used a photo of the performance with Ringo. However, Ringo did not contribute to any of Stewart's recordings.)

Lennon first met Nilsson in England shortly after he publicly praised Nilsson, but their professional partnership began in Los Angeles in early 1974 when the two were reintroduced by Ringo. At the time, Lennon was separated from his wife Yoko Ono, and was in Los Angeles to record his oldies album **"Rock 'N' Roll**. The album's producer, Phil Spector*, suddenly disappeared along with the master tapes. Lennon remained in Los Angeles while trying to recover the tapes, and decided to move into a rented house with Ringo, Keith Moon* and Nilsson. Lennon later referred to his stay in Los Angeles as his "Sindbad's Voyage" and "lost weekend."

Lennon offered to produce Nilsson, who anxiously accepted, and the two were soon off and recording. Lennon decided to pick up where he had left off with his **Rock 'N' Roll** album and produce an album of Nilsson singing rock oldies. The sessions began on the evening of March 28, 1974, with Nilsson doing a cover of Dylan's ***Subterranean Homesick Blues*** arranged by John. The evening ended with an historic jam session that included John Lennon, Danny Kortchmar *(see Attitudes)* and Jesse Ed Davis* on guitars, May Pang and Mal Evans on tambourine, Harry Nilsson on backing vocals, Stevie Wonder on electric piano, a producer named Ed on bass, Linda McCartney* on Hammond

organ, and Paul McCartney on drums. It was the first and only time Paul and John played together in a studio after the breakup of The Beatles. Some of the fragments of songs performed were ***Lucille***, ***Sleepwalk***, ***Stand By Me***, ***Cupid***, ***Chain Gang***, ***Take This Hammer*** and ***Midnight Special***.

Unfortunately, Nilsson had ruptured one of his vocal cords at the outset of the recordings produced by Lennon and soon lost his voice. Lennon and Nilsson fled the Los Angeles madness, retreating to New York to salvage what they could of an album they planned to call **Strange Pussies** (the inoffensive title **Pussy Cats** was wisely substituted instead). Most of the album's basic tracks were recorded in Los Angeles. Additional mixing, overdubbing, and some completely new recordings were done at the Record Plant in New York. According to May Pang and assistant producer and recording engineer Roy Cicala, almost all of Nilsson's vocals were re-recorded in New York.

While finishing **Pussy Cats** in New York, Lennon helped persuade RCA not to back out of a $5 million contract they were negotiating with Nilsson. Meanwhile, Lennon recorded his album **Walls And Bridges** (which included the Lennon - Nilsson composition ***Old Dirt Road*** featuring backing vocals by Nilsson).

Though **Pussy Cats'** first single (a cover of Jimmy Cliff's ***Many Rivers To Cross***) sounded more like Lennon than Nilsson, it failed to chart. The high point of the album, as far as Beatles fans were concerned, was the Lennon penned ***Mucho Mungo***. Lennon guitarist Jesse Ed Davis claimed the song was originally titled ***Mucho Macho***, in reference to him. However, May Pang, Lennon's companion at the time, claims Davis' story is false. Nilsson also claimed that he and Lennon co-composed another song titled ***You Are Here***. (Lennon wrote and recorded a song called ***You Are Here*** that appeared on his **Mind Games** album prior to his collaborations with Nilsson.)

Ironically, **Pussy Cats** was the beginning of a string of unsuccessful releases that essentially ended Nilsson's once-successful recording career. Lennon reunited with Yoko shortly after **Pussy Cats'** release, avoided the party scene and began his retreat from the music world for the next five years.

Nilsson's follow-up album was originally titled **God's Greatest Hits**, but it was retitled **Duit On Mon Dei**. ("Duit On Mon Dei" was apparently a favorite expression of Ringo's [and later Nilsson's] for putting things off, and was printed on the front jacket of his **Ringo** album. The slogan also became part of the logo of an in-house newsletter at Apple). The front cover with its original title was reproduced inside the gatefold of the jacket, however. Ringo contributed to two songs on **Duit On Mon Dei**. The album also carried the message "If You Care About 'You Know Who's' Immigration Status – Write Your 'You Know What,'" in obvious reference to John Lennon's deportation difficulties at the time.

In 1976, Nilsson released another no-hitter titled **Sandman**. The front photo of the album jacket was taken by Beatles' roadie Mal Evans, with a sketch of Ringo inside the gatefold. Ringo is listed under "Special Thanks To" possibly for backing vocals, though they are not evident on any of the tracks. He may have also provided drums or some kind of percussion. Nilsson and Ringo co-composed a song called ***Party*** that was scheduled for inclusion on Ringo's 1976 album **Rotogravure**, but remains unreleased.

Kristofer Engelhardt and Harry Nilsson, Beatlefest Chicago, 1992, photo by Charles Engelhardt

Nilsson quickly followed up **Sandman** with another album that failed in the charts aptly titled **That's The Way It Is**, again with "A Very Special Thanks To Ringo Starr." No specific credits are listed for Ringo, but he can clearly be heard announcing Tony La Peau on ***A Thousand Miles Away***. He may also play drums on ***Daylight Has Caught Me***. The album also featured a cover of George Harrison's song ***That Is All***.

And that's the way it would be until 1980 when Nilsson, like John Lennon, signed a new record contract and released the album **Flash Harry** on Mercury/Phonogram Records. Like Lennon's album **Double Fantasy**, **Flash Harry** would prove to be Nilsson's last album released during his lifetime. The album included many of Nilsson's usual gang of sidemen, including Ringo. Also along for the ride was Eric Idle *(see Monty Python)*, who opened the album with a tribute he had written to Nilsson. Nilsson in turn included a cover of Idle's ***Always Look On The Bright Side Of Life***. Also included on the album are the Nilsson-Starr composition ***How Long Can Disco On***, and Harry's version of the Lennon-Nilsson composition ***Old Dirt Road***. Again no specific musical credits for each track are listed, but it's generally accepted that Ringo plays drums on both tracks. He may also contribute to the tracks ***I've Got It*** and ***Harry***. The liner notes to **Flash Harry** were written by old pal Derek Taylor, but its release was limited to Europe, reducing any chance of it reviving his career in the U.S.

On April 27, 1981, Nilsson, along with others including McCartney and Harrison, attended Ringo's wedding to actress Barbara Bach. Following the tragic murder of John Lennon, Nilsson became an active spokesman for gun control and wrote and recorded the single ***With A Bullet***, along with **Beatlefest** promoter Mark Lapidos. Harry then began promoting the record at **Beatlefest** Conventions across the country, with proceeds going to the National Coalition To Ban Handguns. Not surprisingly, Ringo recorded several radio spot promotions for Nilsson's anti-handgun campaign in 1981 that were included as bonus tracks on the 1994 CD release of Ringo's **Stop And Smell The Roses** album.

In 1984, the guest-star Yoko Ono-tribute album **Every Man Has A Woman** *(see Spirit Choir)* was released featuring three covers of Yoko Ono songs by Nilsson – ***Loneliness***, ***Silver Horse*** and ***Dream Love***. Nilsson also recorded the Ono songs ***Never Say Goodbye***, ***Yang Yang***, ***Men, Men, Men*** and ***Listen, The Snow Is Falling*** for the album, but they were not used and remain unreleased.

Nilsson contributed to Ringo's 1992 album release **Time Takes Time**. He wrote the "middleword" for **Songs By George Harrison 2**, a limited edition book published by Genesis. He gave one of his few public performances singing ***Without You*** during Ringo's September 4, 1992 All Starr Band performance at Caesar's Palace in Las Vegas. He also appeared in a 1994 anti-drunk-driving video that featured Ringo and Paul McCartney contributing to an all-star cover of The Beatles' ***Drive My Car*** *(see R.A.D.D.)*.

Nilsson died of a heart attack on January 15, 1994, nearly a year after his first attack. Ringo reportedly paid many of Nilsson's bills towards the end of his life. George Harrison and Ringo's wife Barbara attended his funeral. At the time of his death, Nilsson had been working on his autobiography, his first new studio album in almost fourteen years, and was selecting songs for a CD anthology. The anthology, **Personal Best**, was released a year later, with a booklet that included photos of Lennon, McCartney, and Starr. Unfortunately it did not contain any previously unreleased material that included contributions by any of The Beatles.

Several weeks later, a CD titled **For The Love Of Harry: Everybody Sings Nilsson** (MusicMasters / 01612-65127-2) was released. It featured some of rock's biggest names covering twenty-three Nilsson compositions including ***Lay Down Your Arms*** performed by Ringo Starr with Stevie Nicks. The CD booklet included photos of Ringo and John Lennon.

Don Nix

Record 232 title:
Hobos, Heroes And Street Corner Clowns
Media:
Album 12"
Label / Catalog number:
Enterprise/Stax / ENS 1032
Jacket / Inserts:
Standard international design with Gatefold / Record label inner sleeve
Recording Location / Date:
Apple Studios, London, U.K. / Feb or Mar 73

Song 232a title:
I Need You
Release date / Country:
Oct 73 / U.S.A.
Producer:
Don Nix
Track details:
Side 2, track 4 / 2 min. 52 sec.
Composer:
D. Nix

Don Nix: Lead Vocals & Acoustic Guitar; George Harrison: Guitar; probably one or more of the following: Pete Carr, Eddie Hinton, Roger Hawkins, David Hood, Klaus Voormann: Bass; Wayne Perkins: Guitar; Jeanie Greene: B. Vocals; Claudia Lennear: B. Vocals

Song 232b title:
The Train Don't Stop Here No More
Release date / Country:
1973 / U.S.A.
Producer:
Don Nix & [George Harrison]
Track details:
Side 1, track 2 / 2 min. 26 sec.
Composer:
D. Nix

Don Nix: Lead Vocals, Acoustic Guitar & Harmonica; George Harrison: Voice; probably the following: Klaus Voormann: Bass; Wayne Perkins: Acoustic Guitar

Don Nix was born on September 27, 1941 in Memphis, Tennessee. Nix and classmates Donald "Duck" Dunn and Steve Cropper, along with Terry Johnson, Jerry Smith, Charlie Freeman, Charles Axton and Wayne Jackson, formed the legendary Stax-Volt recording group The Mar-Keys. Their song ***Last Night*** reached the top 10 in 1961.

George Harrison and Don Nix off Santa Catalina Island, CA, 1971, photo by Patti Boyd Harrison, courtesy of Don Nix

Nix left The Mar-Keys in 1963 and went on to a fairly successful solo career as a top session guitarist, saxophonist, songwriter, producer and recording artist. He has worked with John Mayall, Leon Russell*, Delaney & Bonnie *(see Delaney & Bonnie & Friends)* and many musicians in the Stax-Volt Records

stable in Memphis. Dunn and Cropper later joined Booker T. to form Booker T. And The MG's.

Nix first met George Harrison in Los Angeles in 1971 through Chris O'Dell. O'Dell, his girlfriend at the time, had worked for Apple Records in London. O'Dell had also dated Leon Russell*, who wrote the song ***Pisces Apple Lady*** about her. Harrison wrote the song ***Miss O'Dell***, also about her. Harrison struck up a friendship with Nix and called upon him to help assemble and be one of the background vocalists for **The Concert For Bangla Desh**. Nix was also a frequent guest at Harrison's home, Friar Park, during the early 1970s.

Don's album **Hobos, Heroes And Street Corner Clowns** has long been rumored to feature both George Harrison and Ringo Starr, primarily because the album was partially recorded at Apple Studios, and credits, among others, Beatles' sideman Klaus Voormann *(see Paul Jones)*. In the October 11, 1973 issue of Rolling Stone magazine, an ad was taken out for the album that noted the record "was recorded in part at Apple Studios in London, and if you're listening you'll pick up on guest artists not mentioned in the liner notes."

George Harrison at his Friar Park home in Henley, England, 1973, photo courtesy of Don Nix

It's surprising that Harrison's involvement in **Hobos, Heroes And Street Corner Clowns** was never confirmed, for even a casual listen reveals his voice and distinctive guitar style. Apparently both Harrison and Ringo have publicly acknowledged their involvement with the album, but the specific musical credits have long been forgotten by Nix. Nix is certain that Harrison plays guitar on ***I Need You*** (ironically also the title of a Harrison Beatles' song).

Harrison is also heard saying "That's great Bob, come and hear it," at the end of ***The Train Don't Stop Here No More***. Nix said, "Harrison just sort of took over the production of the song." But just who is the "Bob" at the end of the very familiar style of Harmonica playing? Actually, the "Bob" is Don Nix, and Harrison is teasing him about the similarity of his harmonica playing to Dylan's.

Nix cannot remember if Harrison played on any other tracks, but thinks it's possible. It has also been reported that Ringo plays drums on ***Black Cat Moan***, but Nix is certain that song was recorded in Memphis, ruling out any involvement by Ringo. Nix did confirm that Ringo was at the Apple sessions, though he doubts he contributed to any of the songs. Don thinks that ***I Need You*** and ***The Train Don't Stop Here No More*** were probably the only tracks recorded at Apple, and that the rest were done in Alabama or France, also ruling out any involvement by Harrison or Ringo. Additional tracks on the album are ***She's A Friend Of Mine***, ***Rainy Night In Paris*** (Memphis Reject), ***Sweet Sweet Surrender***, ***We Gotta Move (Keep On Rolling)***, ***When I Lay My Burden Down*** (Traditional), ***Miss Eleana***, ***Look What The Years Have Done***.

In the March 1994 issue of ICE magazine, it was reported that George Harrison's slide guitar was in evidence on both of Don Nix's albums **Gone Too Long** and **Skyrider**. Nix is certain Harrison did not contribute to either album. The only credits on **Gone Too Long** read "This album was recorded in France, England, Muscle Shoals, Memphis and Dallas with spiritual guidance from George Harrison and help from a lot of good friends." According to Nix, the note about spiritual guidance from George Harrison means just that and nothing more.

Don Nix exited the fast lane of the rock 'n' roll life-style nearly a decade ago, and now lives outside Nashville. He still writes songs and released an album appropriately titled **Back To The Well** in 1993. He keeps in touch with many of his old music buddies, but spends most of his time at home with his wife and children, and deals in antique toys. He admits that what he still loves most is producing the right song with the right musicians in the right studio.

Phil Ochs

Record 233 title:
The Lost Lennon Tapes
Label / Catalog number:
Westwood One Radio Network
/ [Matrix #] LT 90-47 (promotional only)
Jacket / Inserts:
Unique "Lost Lennon Tapes" / Cue Sheets
Recording Location / Date:
Ann Arbor, MI, U.S.A. / 10 Dec 71

Media:
Album 12" [2 LP set]
Producer:
(probably) John Lennon

Song 233a title:
Chords Of Fame
Release date / Country:
19 Nov 71 / U.S.A.

Track details:
LP2, Side 2, track 2 / (intro 1 min. 44 sec.) 2 min. 25 sec.
Composer:
P. Ochs

Phil Ochs: Lead Vocals & Guitar; John Lennon: Slide Guitar

Phil Ochs was born December 19, 1940 in El Paso, Texas. He attended military school, and studied journalism at Ohio State University. In the late '50s he was part of a folk duo known as the Singing Socialists before moving to New York's Greenwich Village. There, he earned a reputation as a blunt, confrontational folk singer and activist. He was a gifted songwriter, but his political message limited his commercial success. He was virtually blacklisted from TV and radio. His songs were anthems for the anti-war movement, and inspirations to his contemporaries like Dylan* and Joan Baez, who had a minor hit with his ***There But For Fortune***. He is best remembered for his anti-war song ***I Ain't Marching Anymore***. Other Ochs classics included ***Outside Of A Small Circle Of Friends***, ***The Party*** and ***Here's To The State Of Richard Nixon***.

Ochs was one of many performers at the **John Sinclair Freedom Rally** headlined by John Lennon, and held in Ann Arbor, Michigan on December 10, 1971 *(see Yoko Ono, David Peel)*. At the hotel either before or following the concert, Lennon joined Ochs on slide guitar on Ochs' song ***Chords Of Fame***, which was taped and ended up being featured on Westwood One's **The Lost Lennon Tapes** radio series. ***Chords Of Fame*** was also the title of Ochs' posthumous album released shortly after his death.

With the end of the Vietnam War, Ochs was little more than a man out of time and out of work. During a visit to Africa, Ochs was attacked by a person who severely damaged his vocal chords, effectively ending his singing career. He lived in London for a time, writing for the magazine Time Out before returning to New York. He gave his last performance there at Folk City in October 1975. On April 9, 1976, he took his life.

Yoko Ono

Record 234 title:
A Chance Operation (The John Cage Tribute) [Various Artists]
Media:
Album 5" [2 CD set]
Label / Catalog number:
Koch International Classics / 3-7238-2 Y6x2
Producer:
Yoko Ono
Jacket / Inserts:
Standard international design in double Jewel box / 88 page CD booklet
Recording Location / Date:
Evergreen Recording Studios New York, NY, U.S.A. / Nov 86 & Jan 87

Song 234a title:
Georgia Stone
Release date / Country:
Oct 93 / U.S.A.
Track details:
CD1, track 70-98 / 20 min. 33 sec.
Composer:
Y. Ono

Yoko Ono: Lead Vocals; John Lennon: Voice

Record 235 title:
Approximately Infinite Universe
Media:
Album 5" CD [2 CD set]
Label / Catalog number:
Rykodisc / RCD 10417/18
Producer:
Yoko Ono & John Lennon
Jacket / Inserts:
Standard international design in jewel box with photo of John Lennon on the back, with outer wraparound advert. / 8 page CD booklet with photos of John Lennon, credit insert & Rykodisc insert
Recording Location / Date:
Record Plant (East) Studios, New York, NY, U.S.A. / Oct - Nov 72 except where noted

Yoko Ono/Plastic Ono Band with Elephants Memory, Endless Strings and Choir Boys

Song 235a title:
Air Talk
Track details:
CD2, track 6 / 3 min. 21 sec.
Release date / Country:
22 Jul 97 (first issued 08 Jan 73) / U.S.A.
Composer:
Y. Ono

Yoko Ono: Lead Vocals; Wayne Gabriel: Guitar; Gary Van Scyoc: Bass; Richard Frank Jr.: Drums & Percussion; Adam Ippolito: Organ; Stan Bronstein: Saxophone; Gary Van Scyoc or Adam Ippolito: Trumpet

Song 235b title:
Approximately Infinite Universe
Track details:
CD1, track 6 / 3 min. 20 sec.
Release date / Country:
22 Jul 97 (first issued 08 Jan 73) / U.S.A.
Composer:
Y. Ono

Yoko Ono: Lead Vocals; Wayne Gabriel: Guitar; Gary Van Scyoc: Bass; Richard Frank Jr.: Drums & Percussion; Adam Ippolito: Piano; Stan Bronstein: Saxophone; Ron Frangipane: String Orchestrations

Song 235c title:
Death Of Samantha
Track details:
CD1, track 2 / 6 min. 22 sec.
Release date / Country:
22 Jul 97 (first issued 08 Jan 73) / U.S.A.
Composer:
Y. Ono

Yoko Ono: Lead Vocals; Wayne Gabriel: Guitar; Gary Van Scyoc: Bass; Richard Frank Jr.: Drums & Percussion; Stan Bronstein: Saxophone; Gary Van Scyoc &/or Adam Ippolito: Trumpet

Song 23d title:
Dogtown
Track details:
CD2, track 13 / 2 min. 49 sec.
Release date / Country:
22 Jul 97 / U.S.A.
Composer:
Y. Ono
Recording Location / Date:
(probably) John Lennon & Yoko Ono's apartment at 105 Bank Street (Greenwich Village) New York, NY, U.S.A. / (probably sometime between) Nov 71 & Apr 73

Yoko Ono: Lead Vocals; John Lennon: Acoustic Guitar & B. Vocals

Song 235e title:
I Felt Like Smashing My Face In A Clear Glass Window
Track details:
CD2, track 1 / 4 min. 07 sec.
Release date / Country:
22 Jul 97 (first issued 08 Jan 73) / U.S.A.
Composer:
Y. Ono

Yoko Ono: Lead Vocals; Wayne Gabriel: Guitar; Gary Van Scyoc: Bass; Richard Frank Jr.: Drums & Percussion; Stan Bronstein: Saxophone; Adam Ippolito: Keyboards

Song 235f title:
I Have A Woman Inside My Soul
Track details:
CD2, track 7 / 5 min. 31 sec.
Release date / Country:
22 Jul 97 (first issued 08 Jan 73) / U.S.A.
Composer:
Y. Ono

Yoko Ono: Lead Vocals; Wayne Gabriel: Guitar; Gary Van Scyoc: Bass; Richard Frank Jr.: Drums & Percussion; Adam Ippolito: Organ; Stan Bronstein: Saxophone; John Lennon: B. Vocals & (probable) Guitar

Song 235g title:
I Want My Love To Rest Tonight
Track details:
CD1, track 3 / 5 min. 11 sec.
Release date / Country:
22 Jul 97 (first issued 08 Jan 73) / U.S.A.
Composer:
Y. Ono

Yoko Ono: Lead Vocals; Gary Van Scyoc: Bass; Richard Frank Jr.: Drums & Percussion; Adam Ippolito: Piano; Ron Frangipane: String Orchestrations; Dennis Ferrante: B. Vocals

Song 235h title:
Is Winter Here To Stay?
Release date / Country:
22 Jul 97 (first issued 08 Jan 73) / U.S.A.
Track details:
CD2, track 10 / 4 min. 20 sec.
Composer:
Y. Ono

Yoko Ono: Lead Vocals; Mick Jagger: Guitar; Gary Van Scyoc: Bass; Richard Frank Jr.: Drums; Adam Ippolito: Organ; Stan Bronstein: Saxophone; John Lennon: Guitar

Song 235i title:
Kite Song
Release date / Country:
22 Jul 97/ U.S.A.
Track details:
CD2, track 3 / 3 min. 19 sec.
Composer:
Y. Ono

Yoko Ono: Lead Vocals; John Lennon: Voice†; Wayne Gabriel: Guitar; Gary Van Scyoc: Bass; Richard Frank Jr.: Drums; Adam Ippolito: Organ; Daria Price: Castanets

Also found on ONOBOX/(New York Rock†) / RCD 10224/29 (RCD 10225) / Album 5" [6 CD set] / CD2, track 12 / 3 min. 09 sec / released 03 Mar 92 (first issued 08 Jan 73) .

Song 235j title:
Looking Over From My Hotel Window
Release date / Country:
22 Jul 97 (first issued 08 Jan 73) / U.S.A.
Track details:
CD2, track 11 / 3 min. 31 sec.
Composer:
Y. Ono

Yoko Ono: Lead Vocals & Piano

Song 235k title:
Move On Fast
Release date / Country:
22 Jul 97 (first issued 13 Nov 72) / U.S.A.
Track details:
CD2, track 8 / 3 min. 43 sec.
Composer:
Y. Ono

Yoko Ono: Lead Vocals; Wayne Gabriel: Guitar; Gary Van Scyoc: Bass; Richard Frank Jr.: Drums & Percussion; Adam Ippolito: Organ; Stan Bronstein: Saxophone; John Lennon: Guitar & (probable) B. Vocals

Song 235l title:
Now Or Never
Release date / Country:
22 Jul 97 (first issued 13 Nov 72) / U.S.A.
Track details:
CD2, track 9 / 4 min. 57 sec.
Composer:
Y. Ono

Yoko Ono: Lead Vocals; John Lennon: Guitar; Gary Van Scyoc: Bass; Adam Ippolito: Organ & Harmonium; Richard Frank Jr.: Drums & Percussion; Stan Bronstein: Saxophone; George Young: Saxophone; Wayne Gabriel: Guitar

Song 235m title:
Shiranakatta (I Didn't Know)
Release date / Country:
22 Jul 97 (first issued 08 Jan 73) / U.S.A.
Track details:
CD2, track 5 / 3 min. 13 sec.
Composer:
Y. Ono

Yoko Ono: Lead Vocals; Wayne Gabriel: Guitar; Gary Van Scyoc: Bass; Richard Frank Jr.: Drums; Adam Ippolito: Piano

Song 235n title:
Song For John
Track details:
CD1, track 8 / 2 min. 05 sec.

Release date / Country:
22 Jul 97 (first issued 08 Jan 73) / U.S.A.
Composer:
Y. Ono

Yoko Ono: Lead Vocals; Gary Van Scyoc: Bass; Richard Frank Jr.: Drums; Adam Ippolito: Piano

Song 235o title:
Waiting For The Sunrise
Track details:
CD1, track 11 / 2 min. 32 sec.
Release date / Country:
22 Jul 97 (first issued 08 Jan 73) / U.S.A.
Composer:
Y. Ono

Yoko Ono: Lead Vocals; Gary Van Scyoc: Bass; Richard Frank Jr.: Drums; Adam Ippolito: Piano; Stan Bronstein: Flute

Song 235p title:
What A Bastard The World Is
Track details:
CD1, track 10 / 4 min. 33 sec.
Release date / Country:
22 Jul 97 (first issued 08 Jan 73) / U.S.A.
Composer:
Y. Ono

Yoko Ono: Lead Vocals; Gary Van Scyoc: Bass; Richard Frank Jr.: Drums & Percussion; Adam Ippolito: Piano; Ron Frangipane: String Orchestrations; Wayne Gabriel: Guitar

Song 235q title:
What A Mess
Track details:
CD2, track 4 / 2 min. 41 sec.
Release date / Country:
22 Jul 97 (first issued 08 Jan 73) / U.S.A.
Composer:
Y. Ono

Yoko Ono: Lead Vocals; Gary Van Scyoc: Bass; Richard Frank Jr.: Drums & Percussion; Adam Ippolito: Piano; John Lennon: B. Vocals

Song 235r title:
What Did I Do!
Track details:
CD1, track 4 / 4 min. 10 sec.
Release date / Country:
22 Jul 97 (first issued 08 Jan 73) / U.S.A.
Composer:
Y. Ono

Yoko Ono: Lead Vocals; Wayne Gabriel: Guitar; Gary Van Scyoc: Bass; Richard Frank Jr.: Drums & Percussion; Adam Ippolito: Piano; Stan Bronstein: Saxophone; Adam Ippolito or Gary Van Scyoc: Trumpet

Song 235s title:
Winter Song
Track details:
CD2, track 2 / 3 min. 36 sec.
Release date / Country:
22 Jul 97 (first issued 08 Jan 73) / U.S.A.
Composer:
Y. Ono
Recording Location / Date:
Butterfly Studios, New York, NY, U.S.A. / Oct - Nov 72

Yoko Ono: Lead Vocals; Gary Van Scyoc: Bass; Richard Frank Jr.: Drums & Percussion; Adam Ippolito: Piano; Ron Frangipane: String Orchestrations; Wayne Gabriel: Guitar; John Lennon: Guitar

Song 235t title:
Yang Yang
Track details:
CD1, track 1 / 3 min. 50 sec.
Release date / Country:
22 Jul 97 (first issued 08 Jan 73) / U.S.A.
Composer:
Y. Ono

Yoko Ono: Lead Vocals; Wayne Gabriel: Guitar; Gary Van Scyoc: Bass; Richard Frank Jr.: Drums; Adam Ippolito: Piano; Stan Bronstein: Clarinet

Record 236 title:
Aspen 7 Magazine /
(The British Box-Spring and Summer)
Media:
Extended Play 8" flexi-disc Soundsheet
(mono)
Label / Catalog number:
Eva Tone / Section 11
(matrix # EV-330707AXT11)
Producer:
John Lennon & Yoko Ono
Jacket / Inserts:
Unique Box Set / Aspen magazine, Record folder with additional flexi-disc Soundsheet by Christopher Logue and Apple artist John Tavener, a John Lennon diary, a twenty four page pamphlet, two art prints, two art flyers, a poster, an eight page art pamphlet, a paper cutout, a poetry (lyric) sheet for the John & Yoko flexi-disc, and an Aspen magazine order form
Recording Location / Date:
(probably) On location at Queen Charlotte Hospital, Second West Ward, Room 1, London or (possibly) John Lennon's temporary residence at 34 Montague Square, London, U.K. / 4-25 Nov 68

Song 236a title:
Song For John: Let's Go On Flying /
Snow Is Falling All The Time / Mum's
Only Looking For Her Hand In The Snow
Track details:
Side 1, track 1 / 4 min. 55 sec.
Release date / Country:
(probably) May 69 / U.S.A.
Composer:
Y. Ono

Yoko Ono: Lead Vocals; John Lennon: Guitar

Record 237 title:
Feeling The Space
Media:
Album 5" CD
Label / Catalog number:
Rykodisc / RCD 10419
Producer:
Yoko Ono & John Lennon
Jacket / Inserts:
Standard international design in jewel box with photo by John Lennon on the front, with outer wraparound advert / 6 page CD booklet, credit insert & Rykodisc insert

Song 237a title:
("I Learned To Stutter") / Coffin Car [live]
Track details:
CD1, track 13 / (2 min. 29 sec.) /
4 min. 22 sec.
Release date / Country:
22 Jul 97 / U.S.A.
Composer:
Y. Ono
Recording Location / Date:
On location at The First International Feminist Planning Conference, Harvard University, Cambridge (Boston), MA, U.S.A. / 03 Jun 73

Yoko Ono: Lead Vocals & Piano; John Lennon: Electric Guitar (with Plastic Ono Band & Something Different)

Song 237b title:
Men, Men, Men
Track details:
CD1, track 11 / 4 min. 05 sec.
Release date / Country:
22 Jul 97 (first issued 24 Sep 73) / U.S.A.
Composer:
Y. Ono
Recording Location / Date:
Record Plant (East) Studios, New York, NY, U.S.A. / Jul 73

Yoko Ono: Lead Vocals; David Spinozza: Guitar; Ken Ascher: Piano; Gordon Edwards: Bass; Jim Keltner: Drums; Arthur Jenkins: Percussion; John Lennon: Voice (with Plastic Ono Band & Something Different)

Song 237c title:
Mildred, Mildred
Release date / Country:
22 Jul 97 / U.S.A.
Track details:
CD1, track 14 / 3 min. 36 sec.
Composer:
Y. Ono
Recording Location / Date:
(probably) John Lennon & Yoko Ono's apartment at 105 Bank Street (Greenwich Village) New York, NY, U.S.A. / (probably sometime between) Nov 71 & Apr 73

Yoko Ono: Lead Vocals; John Lennon: Acoustic Guitar & B. Vocals (with Plastic Ono Band)

Record 238 title:
Fly
Label / Catalog number:
Rykodisc / RCD 10415/16
Media:
Album 5" CD [2 CD set]
Producer:
Yoko Ono & John Lennon
Jacket / Inserts:
Standard international design in jewel box with photo by John Lennon on the front and back inc. outer wraparound advert. / 8 page CD booklet with drawing by John Lennon & photo of John Lennon & Ringo Starr, credit insert & Rykodisc insert

Song 238a title:
Air Male (Tone Deaf Jam)
(also on John Lennon's film "Erection")
Release date / Country:
22 Jul 97 (first issued 20 Sep 71) / U.S.A.
Track details:
CD2, track 1 / 10 min. 43 sec.
Composer:
Y. Ono
Recording Location / Date:
Record Plant (East) Studios, New York, NY, U.S.A. / Jul - Aug 71

Yoko Ono: Lead Vocals & Claves; Joe Jones Tone Deaf Music Co. with John Lennon

Song 238b title:
Between The Takes
Release date / Country:
22 Jul 97 / U.S.A.
Track details:
CD2, track 6 / 1 min. 56 sec.
Composer:
Y. Ono
Recording Location / Date:
EMI-Abbey Road Studios, London, U.K. / Oct 70

Yoko Ono: Lead Vocals; John Lennon: Electric Guitar; Ringo Starr: Drums; Klaus Voormann: Bass

Song 238c title:
Don't Count The Waves
Release date / Country:
22 Jul 97 (first issued 20 Sep 71) / U.S.A.
Track details:
CD2, track 2 / 5 min. 22 sec.
Composer:
Y. Ono
Recording Location / Date:
Ascot Sound Studios, Ascot, U.K. & Record Plant (East) Studios, New York, NY, U.S.A. / Jul - Aug 71

Yoko Ono: Lead Vocals & Claves; Joe Jones Tone Deaf Music Co. with John Lennon; Klaus Voormann: Percussion; Jim Keltner: Tuned Drums

Also included on Imagine / Pioneer Artists / PA-86-164 / Album 12" LVD / Side 1, track 4 / 5 min. 35 sec

Song 238d title:
Don't Worry Kyoko (Mummy's Only Looking For A Hand In The Snow) [single version]
Release date / Country:
22 Jul 97 (first issued 20 Oct 69) / U.S.A.
Recording Location / Date:
Lansdowne Studios, London, U.K. / 03 Oct 69
Track details:
CD1, track 4 / 4 min. 52 sec.
Composer:
Y. Ono

Yoko Ono: Lead Vocals; John Lennon: Guitar; Klaus Voormann: Bass; Eric Clapton: Guitar; Ringo Starr: Drums

Song 238e title:
Fly (also on Yoko Ono's film "Fly")
Release date / Country:
22 Jul 97 (first issued 20 Sep 71) / U.S.A.
Recording Location / Date:
Ascot Sound Studios, Ascot, U.K. / Jul - Aug 71
Track details:
CD2, track 4 / 22 min. 48 sec.
Composer:
Y. Ono

Yoko Ono: Lead Vocals; John Lennon: Guitar

Song 238f title:
Midsummer New York
Release date / Country:
22 Jul 97 (first issued 20 Sep 71) / U.S.A.
Recording Location / Date:
Ascot Sound Studios, Ascot, U.K. / Jul - Aug 71
Track details:
CD1, track 1 / 3 min. 50 sec.
Composer:
Y. Ono

Yoko Ono: Lead Vocals; John Lennon: Guitar & Piano; Klaus Voormann: Bass; Chris Osborne: Dobro Guitar; Jim Keltner: Drums & Percussion

Song 238g title:
Mind Holes
Release date / Country:
22 Jul 97 (first issued 20 Sep 71) / U.S.A.
Recording Location / Date:
Ascot Sound Studios, Ascot, U.K. / Jul - Aug 71
Track details:
CD1, track 3 / 2 min. 46 sec.
Composer:
Y. Ono

Yoko Ono: Lead Vocals; John Lennon: Guitar; Klaus Voormann: Bass; Chris Osborne: Dobro Guitar; Jim Keltner: Drums

Song 238h title:
Mind Train
Release date / Country:
22 Jul 97 (first issued Sep 20/71) / U.S.A.
Recording Location / Date:
Ascot Sound Studios, Ascot, U.K. / Jul - Aug 71
Track details:
CD1, track 2 / 16 min. 50 sec.
Composer:
Y. Ono

Yoko Ono: Lead Vocals; John Lennon: Guitar; Klaus Voormann: Bass; Chris Osborne: Dobro Guitar: Jim Keltner: Drums

Song 238i title:
Mrs. Lennon
Release date / Country:
22 Jul 97 (first issued 20 Sep 71) / U.S.A.
Recording Location / Date:
Ascot Sound Studios, Ascot, U.K. / Jul - Aug 71
Track details:
CD1, track 5 / 4 min. 10 sec.
Composer:
Y. Ono

Yoko Ono: Lead Vocals; John Lennon: Piano & Organ; Klaus Voormann: Guitar, Bass & Bells

Also included on Imagine / Pioneer Artists / PA-86-164 / Album 12" LVD / Side 1, track 4 / 5 min. 35 sec.

Song 238j title:
O' Wind (Body Is The Scar of Your Mind)
Release date / Country:
22 Jul 97 (first issued 20 Sep 71) / U.S.A.
Recording Location / Date:
Ascot Sound Studios, Ascot, U.K. / Jul - Aug 71
Track details:
CD1, track 8 / 5 min. 22 sec.
Composer:
Y. Ono

Yoko Ono: Lead Vocals; John Lennon: Guitar; Jim Keltner: Drums & Tabla; Jim Gordon: Tabla; Klaus Voormann: Cymbal; Bobby Keys: Claves

Song 238k title:
Open Your Box (Hirake)
Release date / Country:
22 Jul 97 (first issued 20 Sep 71) / U.S.A.
Recording Location / Date:
Ascot Sound Studios, Ascot, U.K. / Feb 71
Track details:
CD1, track 6 / 3 min. 31 sec.
Composer:
Y. Ono

Yoko Ono: Lead Vocals; John Lennon: Guitar; Klaus Voormann: Bass; Jim Gordon: Drums

Song 238l title:
Telephone Piece
Release date / Country:
22 Jul 97 (first issued 20 Sep 71) / U.S.A.
Recording Location / Date:
Record Plant (East) Studios, New York, NY, U.S.A. / Jul - Sep 71
Track details:
CD2, track 5 / 0 min. 30 sec.
Composer:
Y. Ono

Yoko Ono: Voice

Song 238m title:
Toilet Piece/Unknown
Release date / Country:
22 Jul 97 (first issued 20 Sep 71) / U.S.A.
Recording Location / Date:
Record Plant (East) Studios, New York, NY, U.S.A. / Jul - Sep 71
Track details:
CD1, track 7 / 0 min. 30 sec.
Composer:
Y. Ono

Song 238n title:
Will You Touch Me
Release date / Country:
22 Jul 97 / U.S.A.
Recording Location / Date:
(probably) John Lennon & Yoko Ono's apartment at 105 Bank Street (Greenwich Village) New York, NY, U.S.A. / (probably sometime between) Nov 71 & Apr 73
Track details:
CD2, track 7 / 2 min. 45 sec.
Composer:
Y. Ono

Yoko Ono: Lead Vocals; John Lennon: Acoustic Guitar & Voice

Song 238o title:
You
Release date / Country:
22 Jul 97 (first issued 20 Sep 71) / U.S.A.
Recording Location / Date:
Record Plant (East) Studios, New York, NY, U.S.A. / Jul - Aug 71
Track details:
CD2, track 3 / 8 min. 57 sec.
Composer:
Y. Ono

Yoko Ono: Lead Vocals; Joe Jones Tone Deaf Music Co.

Record 239 title:
Free As A Bird
Label / Catalog number:
FAB / FAB 1 [Unauthorized Record]
Jacket / Inserts:
Unique / 8 page CD booklet
Media:
Album 5" CD

Song 239a title:
Greenfield Morning I Pushed An Empty Baby Carriage All Over The City [alternate mix]
Release date / Country:
(probably) Jan 96
Producer:
John Lennon & Yoko Ono
Recording Location / Date:
EMI-Abbey Road Studios, London, U.K. / Oct 70
Track details:
Side 1, track 13 / 5 min. 30 sec.
Composer:
Y. Ono

Yoko Ono: Lead Vocals; John Lennon: Guitar; Klaus Voormann: Bass; Ringo Starr: Drums; George Harrison: Sitar

Song 239b title:
Open Your Box (Hirake) [alternate take]
Release date / Country:
(probably) Jan 96
Producer:
Yoko Ono & John Lennon
Recording Location / Date:
Ascot Sound Studios, Ascot, U.K. / Feb 71
Track details:
Side 1, track 12 / 3 min. 32 sec.
Composer:
Y. Ono

Yoko Ono: Lead Vocals; John Lennon: Guitar; Klaus Voormann: Bass; Jim Gordon: Drums

Record 240 title:
Hound Dog
Label / Catalog number:
Contraband Music / CBM 5040 [Unauthorized Record]
Jacket / Inserts:
Unique
Media:
Album 12" (mono)
Producer:
[audience recording] John Lennon & Yoko Ono: Overall Original Production; Bob Fries: Music Producer 1972; Phil Spector: Recording Supervisor 1972
Recording Location / Date:
On location at Madison Square Garden, New York, NY, U.S.A. / 30 Aug 72

Song 240a title:
Move On Fast [live]
Release date / Country:
mid-1970s / U.S.A.
Track details:
Side 2, track 2
Composer:
Y. Ono

Yoko Ono: Lead Vocals; John Lennon: Guitar; Stan Bronstein: Saxophone; Gary Van Scyox: Bass; Adam Ippolito: Keyboards; Rick Frank Drums; Wayne Gabriel: Guitar

Record 241 title:
Imagine
Label / Catalog number:
Pioneer Artists / PA-86-164
Jacket / Inserts:
Standard international design
Media:
Album 12" LVD
Producer:
Yoko Ono & John Lennon

Song 241a title:
Don't Count The Waves
Release date / Country:
1986
Track details:
Side 1, track 4 / 5 min. 35 sec.
Composer:
Y. Ono
Recording Location / Date:
Ascot Sound Studios, Ascot, U.K. & Record Plant (East) Studios, New York, NY, U.S.A. / Jul - Aug 71

Yoko Ono: Lead Vocals & Claves; Joe Jones Tone Deaf Music Co. with John Lennon; Klaus Voormann: Percussion; Jim Keltner: Tuned Drums

Song 241b title:
Mrs. Lennon
Release date / Country:
1986
Track details:
Side 1, track 6 / 4 min. 29 sec.
Composer:
Y. Ono
Recording Location / Date:
Ascot Sound Studios, Ascot, U.K. / Jul - Aug 71

Yoko Ono: Lead Vocals; John Lennon: Piano & Organ; Klaus Voormann: Guitar, Bass & Bells

Record 242 title:
It's Alright (I See Rainbows) An Air Play
Label / Catalog number:
Rykodisc / RCD 10422
Jacket / Inserts:
Standard international design in jewel box with outer wraparound advert / 6 page CD booklet with photo of John Lennon & credit insert
Media:
Album 5" CD

Song 242a title:
Never Say Goodbye
Release date / Country:
26 Aug 97 (first issued 29 Nov 82) / U.S.A.
Track details:
Side 1, track 2 / 4 min. 17 sec.
Composer:
Y. Ono
Producer:
Yoko Ono
Recording Location / Date:
Hit Factory Studios, New York, NY, U.S.A. / 1982

Yoko Ono: Lead Vocals; John Lennon: Voice; Sean Lennon: Voice; additionally, one or more of the following: Neil Jason: Bass; Pete Cannarozzi: Keyboards & Synthesizer; Paul Griffin: Synthesizer; Gordon Grody: B. Vocals; Kurt Yahijan: B. Vocals; Carlos Alomar: B. Vocals; Michael Holmes: Keyboards; Paul Shaffer: Keyboards; Yogi Horton: Drums; Alan Schwartzberg: Drums; Rubens Bassini: Percussion; David A. Friedman: Percussion; Sammy Figeroa: Percussion; Roger Squitero: Percussion

Song 242b title:
You're The One (previously unreleased version)
Track details:
Side 1, track 12 / 4 min. 50 sec.

Release date / Country:
26 Aug 97 (first issued 19 Jan 84) / U.S.A.

Composer:
Y. Ono

Producer:
John Lennon & Yoko Ono

Recording Location / Date:
One or more of the following studios: Hit Factory, Sterling Sound & A&R, New York, NY, &/or Automatt, San Francisco, CA, U.S.A. / Aug - Sep 80 &/or 1983

Yoko Ono: Lead Vocals; John Lennon: Voice & (possible) Guitar; additionally, one or more of the following: Hugh McCracken: Guitar; Earl Slick: Guitar; Tony Levin: Bass; George Small: Keyboards; John Tropea: Guitar; Elliott Randall: Guitar; Steve Love: Guitar; Neil Jason: Bass; Wayne Pedziwiatr: Bass; Paul Griffin: Keyboards; Jimmy Maelen: Percussion; Pete Cannarozzi: Synthesizer; Ed Walsh: Oberheim Synthesizer; Gordon Grody: B. Vocals; Kurt Yahijan: B. Vocals

Record 243 title:
Live In New York City

Label / Catalog number:
Pioneer Artists / PA-86-162

Media:
Album 12" LVD

Producer:
John Lennon & Yoko Ono: Overall Original Production; Yoko Ono: Executive & Music Producer 1985; Bob Fries: Music Producer 1972; Phil Spector: Recording Supervisor 1972; Gerard Meola: Video Producer 1985; Steve Gebhardt: Video Director 1972; Carol Dysinger: Video Director 1985

Jacket / Inserts:
Standard international design

Recording Location / Date:
On location at Madison Square Garden, New York, NY, U.S.A. / 30 Aug 72

Song 243a title:
Born In A Prison [live]

Release date / Country:
1986 / U.S.A.

Track details:
Side 1, track 9 / 3 min. 54 sec.

Composer:
Y. Ono

Yoko Ono: Lead Vocals; John Lennon: Guitar & B. Vocals; Gary Van Scyoc: Bass; Adam Ippolito: Keyboards; Richard Frank Jr.: Drums; Stan Bronstein: Saxophone; Wayne Gabriel: Guitar; Jim Keltner: Drums; John Ward: Bass (with The Elephant's Memory Band)

Song 243b title:
Sisters, O Sisters [live]

Release date / Country:
1986 / U.S.A.

Track details:
Side 1, track 5 / 2 min. 52 sec.

Composer:
Y. Ono

Yoko Ono: Lead Vocals; John Lennon: Guitar; Gary Van Scyoc: Bass; Adam Ippolito: Keyboards; Richard Frank Jr.: Drums; Stan Bronstein: Saxophone; Wayne Gabriel: Guitar; Jim Keltner: Drums; John Ward: Bass (with The Elephant's Memory Band)

Record 244 title:
Miscellaneous Tracks
Label / Catalog number:
Yellow Dog/Orange / YD-Orange 018
[Unauthorized Record]
Jacket / Inserts:
Unique in Jewel box / 4 page CD insert
Recording Location / Date:
Americana Hotel, New York, NY / 06 Sep 72
Media:
Album 5" CD
Producer:
The Jerry Lewis Muscular Dystrophy Telethon

Song 244a title:
Now Or Never
Release date / Country:
Nov 95 / Australia
Track details:
Side 1, track 2 / 4 min. 20 sec.
Composer:
Y. Ono

Yoko Ono: Lead Vocals; John Lennon: Guitar; Gary Van Scyoc: Bass; Adam Ippolito: Organ & Harmonium; Richard Frank Jr.: Drums & Percussion; Stan Bronstein: Saxophone; Wayne Gabriel: Guitar

Record 245 title:
One And One And One Is Three
Label / Catalog number:
Benefit / 001/3 (002) [Unauthorized Record]
Jacket / Inserts:
Unique
Recording Location / Date:
(probably) Butterfly Studios, (possibly) The Fillmore East Theater, New York, NY, U.S.A. / (probably) 22-26 Aug 72 except where noted
Media:
Album 12" [3 record set] (mono)

Song 245a title:
Born In A Prison [rehearsal]
Release date / Country:
1985 / U.S.A.
Track details:
LP2, Side 1, track 3 / 4 min. 05 sec.
Composer:
Y. Ono

Yoko Ono: Lead Vocals; John Lennon: Guitar & B. Vocals; Gary Van Scyoc: Bass; Adam Ippolito: Keyboards; Richard Frank Jr.: Drums; Stan Bronstein: Saxophone; Wayne Gabriel: Guitar; John Ward: (probable) Bass; Jim Keltner: (probable) Drums (with The Elephant's Memory Band)

Song 245b title:
Don't Worry Kyoko (Mummy's Only Looking For Her Hand In The Snow) [rehearsal]
Release date / Country:
1985 / U.S.A.
Recording Location / Date:
Butterfly Studios, The Fillmore East Theater or Record Plant East Studios, New York, NY, U.S.A. / 22-26 Aug 72
Track details:
LP3, Side 1, track 2 / 5 min. 13 sec.
Composer:
Y. Ono

Yoko Ono: Lead Vocals; probably the following: John Lennon: Guitar; Gary Van Scyoc: Bass; Adam Ippolito: Keyboards; Richard Frank Jr.: Drums; Stan Bronstein: Saxophone; Wayne Gabriel: Guitar; John Ward: (probable) Bass; Jim Keltner: (probable) Drums (with The Elephant's Memory Band)

Song 245c title:
Move On Fast [rehearsal]
Track details:
LP1, Side 1, track 4 / 3 min. 41 sec.

Release date / Country:
1985 / U.S.A.
Composer:
Y. Ono

Yoko Ono: Lead Vocals; John Lennon: Guitar; Stan Bronstein: Saxophone; Gary Van Scyox: Bass; Adam Ippolito: Keyboards; Rick Frank Drums; Wayne Gabriel: Guitar; John Ward: (probable) Bass; Jim Keltner: (probable) Drums (with The Elephant's Memory Band)

Song 245d title:
Open Your Box (Hirake) [rehearsal]
Track details:
LP2, Side 2, track 4 / 3 min. 12 sec.
Release date / Country:
1985 / U.S.A.
Composer:
Y. Ono

Yoko Ono: Lead Vocals; John Lennon: Guitar; Gary Van Scyox: Bass; Adam Ippolito: Keyboards; Rick Frank: Drums; Wayne Gabriel: Guitar; John Ward: (probable) Bass; Jim Keltner: (probable) Drums (with The Elephant's Memory Band)

Song 245e title:
Sisters, O Sisters [rehearsal]
Track details:
LP1, Side 2, track 1 / 3 min. 42 sec.
Release date / Country:
1985 / U.S.A.
Composer:
Y. Ono

Yoko Ono: Lead Vocals; John Lennon: Guitar; Gary Van Scyoc: Bass; Adam Ippolito: Keyboards; Richard Frank Jr.: Drums; Stan Bronstein: Saxophone; Wayne Gabriel: Guitar; John Ward: (probable) Bass; Jim Keltner: (probable) Drums (with The Elephant's Memory Band)

Song 245f title:
We're All Water [rehearsal]
Track details:
LP2, Side 2, track 2 / 5 min. 02 sec.
Release date / Country:
1985 / U.S.A.
Composer:
Y. Ono

Yoko Ono: Lead Vocals; Gary Van Scyoc: Bass; Richard Frank Jr.: Drums & Percussion; Adam Ippolito: Keyboards; Stan Bronstein: Saxophone; Wayne Gabriel: Guitar; John Lennon: Guitar; John Ward: (probable) Bass; Jim Keltner: (probable) Drums (with The Elephant's Memory Band)

Record 246 title:
One To One Concert
Media:
Album 12"
Label / Catalog number:
Contraband Music / 3949—AX & R1 3665-A [Unauthorized Record]
Jacket / Inserts:
Unique with cover photo insert

Song 246a title:
Sisters, O Sisters [live]
Track details:
Side 2, track 3
Release date / Country:
U.S.A.
Composer:
Y. Ono
Producer:
[Unknown-audience recording] John Lennon & Yoko Ono: Overall Original Production
Recording Location / Date:
On location at Crisler Arena, Ann Arbor, MI, U.S.A. / 10 Dec 71

Yoko Ono: Lead Vocals; John Lennon: Guitar; Leslie Bacon: B. Vocals; Jerry Rubin: Congas; Frank Lanci: Congas; Billy Minelli: Tambourine; Tom Doyle: 12 String Guitar; Eddie Mottau: Guitar; Chris Osborne: Guitar; David Peel: Washtub Bass; Yoko Ono: Indian Drum

Song 246b title:
We're All Water [live]
Track details:
Side 1, track 4 / 5 min. 12 sec.

Release date / Country:
mid 1970s / U.S.A.
Label / Catalog number:
Contraband Music / 3949—AX & R1 3665-A [Unauthorized Record]
Composer:
Y. Ono
Producer:
[Unknown-audience recording] John Lennon & Yoko Ono: Overall Original Production, Bob Fries: Music Producer 1972; Phil Spector: Recording Supervisor 1972
Recording Location / Date:
On location at Madison Square Garden, New York, NY, U.S.A. / 30 Aug 72

Yoko Ono: Lead Vocals; John Lennon: Guitar; Gary Van Scyoc: Bass; Adam Ippolito: Keyboards; Richard Frank Jr.: Drums; Stan Bronstein: Saxophone; Wayne Gabriel: Guitar; Jim Keltner: Drums; John Ward: Bass

Record 247 title:
ONOBOX/(A Story)
Label / Catalog number:
Rykodisc / RCD 10224/29 (RCD 10229)
Media:
Album 5" [6 CD set]
Producer:
John Lennon, Yoko Ono & Phil Spector
Jacket / Inserts:
Standard international design box set with Jewel box's / 4 page CD insert, Onobox Ultracase Limited Edition flyer & 96 page book with photos of John Lennon
Recording Location / Date:
Record Plant (East) Studios, New York, NY / 01-20 Mar 72

Song 247a title:
Sisters, O Sisters
Release date / Country:
03 Mar 92 (first issued 24 Apr 72) / U.S.A.
Track details:
CD6, track 15 / 3 min. 46 sec.
Composer:
Y. Ono

Yoko Ono: Lead Vocals; Gary Van Scyoc: Bass; Richard Frank Jr. &/or Jim Keltner: Drums & Percussion; Adam Ippolito: Keyboards; Stan Bronstein: Saxophone; Ron Frangipane: String Orchestrations; John Lennon: Voice & Guitar (with Elephant's Memory Plus Invisible Strings)

Record 248 title:
ONOBOX/(Kiss, Kiss, Kiss)
Label / Catalog number:
Rykodisc / RCD 10224/29 (RCD 10227)
Media:
Album 5" [6 CD set]
Jacket / Inserts:
Standard international design box set with Jewel box / 4 page CD insert, Onobox Ultracase Limited Edition flyer & 96 page book with photos of John Lennon

Song 248a title:
Beautiful Boys
Release date / Country:
03 Mar 92 (first issued 17 Nov 80) / U.S.A.
Track details:
CD4, track 6 / 2 min. 54 sec.
Composer:
Y. Ono
Producer:
John Lennon, Yoko Ono & Jack Douglas
Recording Location / Date:
Hit Factory Studios, New York, NY, U.S.A. / 15 Aug 80

Yoko Ono: Lead Vocals; one or more of the following: John Lennon: (possible) Guitar & (possible) Keyboards; Hugh McCracken: Guitar; Earl Slick: Guitar; Tony Levin: Bass; Andy Newmark: Drums; Arthur Jenkins, Jr.: Percussion; Ed Walsh: Oberheim Synthesizer; George Small: Keyboards

Song 248b title:
Don't Be Scared
Release date / Country:
03 Mar 92 (first issued 19 Jan 84) / U.S.A.
Producer:
John Lennon & Yoko Ono
Recording Location / Date:
Hit Factory Studios, &/or A&R Studios, & (probably) Sterling Sound, New York, NY &/or Automatt, San Francisco, CA, U.S.A. / 09 Aug 80 & (probably) 1983
Track details:
CD4, track 10 / 4 min. 35 sec.
Composer:
Y. Ono

Yoko Ono: Lead Vocals; John Lennon: Voice & (possible) Guitar; additionally, one or more of the following: Hugh McCracken: Guitar; Earl Slick: Guitar; Tony Levin: Bass; Andy Newmark: Drums; Ed Walsh: Oberheim Synthesizer; George Small: Keyboards; Howard Johnson: Horns; Grant Hungerford: Horns; John Parran: Horns; Seldon Powell: Horns; George "Young" Opalisky: Horns; Roger Rosenberg: Horns; David Tofani: Horns; Ronald Tooley; Arthur Jenkins, Jr.: Percussion; John Tropea: Guitar; Elliott Randall: Guitar; Steve Love: Guitar; Neil Jason: Bass; Wayne Pedziwiatr: Bass; Yogi Horton: Drums; Allan Schwartzberg: Drums; Paul Griffin: Keyboards; Jimmy Maelen: Percussion; Pete Cannarozzi: Synthesizer; Gordon Grody: B. Vocals; Kurt Yahijan: B. Vocals; Carlos Alomar: B. Vocals; Billy Alessi: B. Vocals; Bob Alessi: B. Vocals; Pete Thom

Song 248c title:
Every Man Has A Woman Who Loves Him
Release date / Country:
03 Mar 92 (first issued 17 Nov 80) / U.S.A.
Producer:
John Lennon, Yoko Ono & Jack Douglas
Recording Location / Date:
Hit Factory Studios, New York, NY, U.S.A. / Sometime between 20 Aug 80 - 03 Sep 80
Track details:
CD4, track 8 / 4 min. 03 sec.
Composer:
Y. Ono

Yoko Ono: Lead Vocals; John Lennon: B. Vocals, Guitar & Keyboards; Hugh McCracken: Guitar; Earl Slick: Guitar; Tony Levin: Bass; Andy Newmark: Drums; Arthur Jenkins, Jr.: Percussion; Ed Walsh: Oberheim Synthesizer; George Small: Keyboards

Song 248d title:
Give Me Something
Release date / Country:
03 Mar 92 (first issued 17 Nov 80) / U.S.A.
Producer:
John Lennon, Yoko Ono & Jack Douglas
Recording Location / Date:
Hit Factory Studios, New York, NY, U.S.A. / Aug - Sep 80
Track details:
CD4, track 3 / 1 min. 34 sec.
Composer:
Y. Ono

Yoko Ono: Lead Vocals; one or more of the following: John Lennon: Guitar & Keyboards; Hugh McCracken: Guitar; Earl Slick: Guitar; Tony Levin: Bass; Andy Newmark: Drums; Ed Walsh: Oberheim Synthesizer; George Small: Keyboards; Howard Johnson: Horns; Grant Hungerford: Horns; John Parran: Horns; Seldon Powell: Horns; George "Young" Opalisky: Horns; Roger Rosenberg: Horns; David Tofani: Horns; Ronald Tooley

Song 248e title:
Hard Times Are Over
Release date / Country:
03 Mar 92 (first issued 17 Nov 80) / U.S.A.
Producer:
John Lennon, Yoko Ono & Jack Douglas
Recording Location / Date:
Hit Factory & A&R Studios, New York, NY, U.S.A. / 19 Aug 80 & 10 Sep 80
Track details:
CD4, track 9 / 3 min. 20 sec.
Composer:
Y. Ono

Yoko Ono: Lead Vocals; John Lennon: Guitar & B. Vocals; Hugh McCracken: Guitar; Earl Slick: Guitar; Tony Levin: Bass; Andy Newmark: Drums; George Small: Keyboards; George "Young" Opalisky: Horns; Roger Rosenberg: Horns; David Tofani: Horns; Ronald Tooley; Benny Cummings

Singers-Kings Temple Choir: Choir; Arthur Jenkins: Percussion

Song 248f title:
Have You Seen A Horizon Lately
Track details:
CD4, track 18 / 2 min. 01 sec.
Release date / Country:
03 Mar 92 (first issued 08 Jan 73) / U.S.A.
Composer:
Y. Ono
Producer:
Yoko Ono & John Lennon
Recording Location / Date:
Record Plant (East) Studios, New York, NY, U.S.A. / Oct - Nov 72

Yoko Ono: Lead Vocals; Wayne Gabriel: Guitar; Gary Van Scyoc: Bass; Richard Frank Jr.: Drums & Percussion; Adam Ippolito: Organ; Stan Bronstein: Saxophone; John Lennon: Voice (with Elephants Memory, Endless Strings and Choir Boys)

Song 248g title:
I'm Moving On
Track details:
CD4, track 4 / 2 min. 21 sec.
Release date / Country:
03 Mar 92 (first issued 17 Nov 80) / U.S.A.
Composer:
Y. Ono
Producer:
John Lennon, Yoko Ono & Jack Douglas
Recording Location / Date:
Hit Factory Studios, New York, NY, U.S.A. / Aug - Sep 80

Yoko Ono: Lead Vocals; one or more of the following: John Lennon: Lead Guitar & Keyboards; Hugh McCracken: Rhythm Guitar; Earl Slick: Rhythm Guitar; Tony Levin: Bass; Andy Newmark: Drums; George Small: Keyboards

Song 248h title:
Kiss, Kiss, Kiss
Track details:
CD4, track 2 / 2 min. 40 sec.
Release date / Country:
03 Mar 92 (first issued 23 Oct 80) / U.S.A.
Composer:
Y. Ono
Producer:
John Lennon, Yoko Ono & Jack Douglas
Recording Location / Date:
Hit Factory Studios, New York, NY / 08 Aug 80

Yoko Ono: Lead Vocals; one or more of the following: John Lennon: Guitar & Keyboards; Hugh McCracken: Guitar; Earl Slick: Guitar; Tony Levin: Bass; Andy Newmark: Drums; Arthur Jenkins, Jr.: Percussion; Ed Walsh: Oberheim Synthesizer; George Small: Keyboards

Song 248i title:
Let Me Count The Ways
Track details:
CD4, track 14 / 3 min. 03 sec.
Release date / Country:
03 Mar 92 (first issued 19 Jan 84) / U.S.A.
Composer:
Y. Ono
Producer:
John Lennon & Yoko Ono
Recording Location / Date:
John and Yoko's home at Dakota Apartments, New York, NY, U.S.A. / (probably) Jun 80

Yoko Ono: Lead Vocals & Piano

Song 248j title:
O' Sanity
Track details:
CD4, track 12 / 1 min. 04 sec.
Release date / Country:
03 Mar 92 (first issued 05 Jan 84) / U.S.A.
Composer:
Y. Ono
Producer:
John Lennon & Yoko Ono

Recording Location / Date:
One or more of the following studios: Hit Factory, Sterling Sound & A&R,
New York, NY &/or Automatt, San Francisco, CA, U.S.A. / Aug - Sep 80 &/or 1983

Yoko Ono: Lead Vocals; one or more of the following: John Lennon: (possible) Guitar; Hugh McCracken: Guitar; Earl Slick: Guitar; Tony Levin: Bass; Andy Newmark: Drums; George Small: Keyboards; Arthur Jenkins, Jr.: Percussion; John Tropea: Guitar; Elliott Randall: Guitar; Steve Love: Guitar; Neil Jason: Bass; Wayne Pedziwiatr: Bass; Yogi Horton: Drums; Allan Schwartzberg: Drums; Paul Griffin: Keyboards; Jimmy Maelen: Percussion

Song 248k title:
Sleepless Night
Track details:
CD4, track 11 / 3 min. 53 sec.
Release date / Country:
03 Mar 92 (first issued 19 Jan 84) / U.S.A.
Composer:
Y. Ono
Producer:
John Lennon & Yoko Ono
Recording Location / Date:
One or more of the following studios: Hit Factory, Sterling Sound & A&R,
New York, NY &/or Automatt, San Francisco, CA, U.S.A. / Aug - Sep 80 &/or 1983

Yoko Ono: Lead Vocals; one or more of the following: John Lennon: (possible) Guitar; Hugh McCracken: Guitar; Earl Slick: Guitar; Tony Levin: Bass; Andy Newmark: Drums; Ed Walsh: Oberheim Synthesizer; George Small: Keyboards; Arthur Jenkins, Jr.: Percussion; John Tropea: Guitar; Elliott Randall: Guitar; Steve Love: Guitar; Neil Jason: Bass; Wayne Pedziwiatr: Bass; Yogi Horton: Drums; Allan Schwartzberg: Drums; Paul Griffin: Keyboards; Jimmy Maelen: Percussion; Pete Cannarozzi: Synthesizer

Song 248l title:
Walking On Thin Ice - For John
Track details:
CD4, track 1 / 6 min. 02 sec.
Release date / Country:
03 Mar 92 (first issued 06 Feb 81) / U.S.A.
Composer:
Y. Ono
Producer:
John Lennon, Yoko Ono & Jack Douglas
Recording Location / Date:
Hit Factory Studios, New York, NY, U.S.A. / Nov 80 & 06-08 Dec 80

Yoko Ono: Lead Vocals; John Lennon: Voice, Lead Guitar & Keyboards; Hugh McCracken: Rhythm Guitar; Earl Slick: Rhythm Guitar; Tony Levin: Bass; Andy Newmark: Drums; Jack Douglas: Percussion

Song 248m title:
Yes, I'm Your Angel
Track details:
CD4, track 5 / 3 min. 35 sec.
Release date / Country:
03 Mar 92 (first issued 17 Nov 80) / U.S.A.
Composer:
Y. Ono
Producer:
John Lennon, Yoko Ono & Jack Douglas
Recording Location / Date:
Hit Factory Studios, New York, NY, U.S.A. / 05 Sep 80

Yoko Ono: Lead Vocals; John Lennon: Voice; additionally, one or more of the following: Tony Levin: Bass; Andy Newmark: Drums; Ed Walsh: Oberheim Synthesizer; George Small: Keyboards; Howard Johnson: Horns; Grant Hungerford: Horns; John Parran: Horns; Seldon Powell: Horns; George "Young" Opalisky: Horns; Roger Rosenberg: Horns; David Tofani: Horns; Ronald Tooley; Arthur Jenkins, Jr.: Percussion; Tony Davilio: Horn Arrangement

Song 248n title:
You're The One
Track details:
CD4, track 16 / 4 min. 35 sec.
Release date / Country:
03 Mar 92 (first issued 19 Jan 84) / U.S.A.
Composer:
Y. Ono

Producer:
John Lennon & Yoko Ono
Recording Location / Date:
One or more of the following studios: Hit Factory, Sterling Sound & A&R, New York, NY, &/or Automatt, San Francisco, CA, U.S.A. / Aug - Sep 80 &/or 1983

Yoko Ono: Lead Vocals; John Lennon: Voice & (possible) Guitar; additionally, one or more of the following: Hugh McCracken: Guitar; Earl Slick: Guitar; Tony Levin: Bass; George Small: Keyboards; John Tropea: Guitar; Elliott Randall: Guitar; Steve Love: Guitar; Neil Jason: Bass; Wayne Pedziwiatr: Bass; Paul Griffin: Keyboards; Jimmy Maelen: Percussion; Pete Cannarozzi: Synthesizer; Ed Walsh: Oberheim Synthesizer; Gordon Grody: B. Vocals; Kurt Yahijan: B. Vocals

Song 248o title:
Your Hands
Release date / Country:
03 Mar 92 (first issued 19 Jan 84) / U.S.A.
Track details:
CD4, track 13 / 3 min. 13 sec.
Composer:
Y. Ono
Producer:
John Lennon & Yoko Ono
Recording Location / Date:
One or more of the following studios: Hit Factory, Sterling Sound & A&R, New York, NY &/or Automatt, San Francisco, CA, U.S.A. / Aug - Sep 80 & (probably) 1983

Yoko Ono: Lead Vocals; one or more of the following: John Lennon: (possible) Guitar; Hugh McCracken: Guitar; Earl Slick: Guitar; Tony Levin: Bass; George Small: Keyboards; John Tropea: Guitar; Elliott Randall: Guitar; Steve Love: Guitar; Neil Jason: Bass; Wayne Pedziwiatr: Bass; Paul Griffin: Keyboards; Jimmy Maelen: Percussion; Pete Cannarozzi: Synthesizer; Ed Walsh: Oberheim

Record 249 title:
ONOBOX/(London Jam)
Media:
Album 5" [6 CD set]
Label / Catalog number:
Rykodisc / RCD 10224/29 (RCD 10224)
Producer:
Yoko Ono & John Lennon
Jacket / Inserts:
Standard international design box set with Jewel box's / 4 page CD insert, Onobox Ultracase Limited Edition flyer & 96 page book with photos of John Lennon
Recording Location / Date:
Ascot Sound Studios, Ascot, U.K. / 1971

Song 249a title:
The Path
Release date / Country:
03 Mar 92 / U.S.A.
Track details:
CD1, track 15 / 5 min. 43 sec.
Composer:
Y. Ono

Yoko Ono: Lead Vocals; John Lennon: Keyboards

Record 250 title:
ONOBOX/(New York Rock)
Media:
Album 5" CD [6 CD set]
Label / Catalog number:
Rykodisc / RCD 10224/29 (RCD 10225)
Producer:
Yoko Ono & John Lennon
Jacket / Inserts:
Standard international design box set with Jewel box / 4 page CD insert, Onobox Ultracase Limited Edition flyer & 96 page book with photos of John Lennon

Song 250a title:
Catman (The Rosies Are Coming)
Track details:
CD2, track 6 / 5 min. 44 sec.

Release date / Country: 03 Mar 92 (first issued 08 Jan 73) / U.S.A.
Composer: Y. Ono
Recording Location / Date: Butterfly Studios, New York, NY, U.S.A. / Oct - Nov 72

Yoko Ono: Lead Vocals; Wayne Gabriel: Guitar; Gary Van Scyoc: Bass; Richard Frank Jr.: Drums & Percussion; Adam Ippolito: Organ; Stan Bronstein: Saxophone (with Elephants Memory, Endless Strings and Choir Boys)

Song 250b title: Peter The Dealer
Track details: CD2, track 9 / 4 min. 58 sec.
Release date / Country: 03 Mar 92 (first issued 08 Jan 73) / U.S.A.
Composer: Y. Ono
Recording Location / Date: Record Plant (East) Studios, New York, NY, U.S.A. / Oct - Nov 72

Yoko Ono: Lead Vocals; Wayne Gabriel: Guitar; Gary Van Scyoc: Bass; Richard Frank Jr.: Drums; Adam Ippolito: Piano; Stan Bronstein: Saxophone (with Elephants Memory, Endless Strings and Choir Boys)

Record 251 title: ONOBOX/(Run, Run, Run)
Media: Album 5" [6 CD set]
Label / Catalog number: Rykodisc / RCD 10224/29 (RCD 10226)
Producer: Yoko Ono
Jacket / Inserts: Standard international design box set with Jewel box's / 4 page CD insert, Onobox Ultracase Limited Edition flyer & 96 page book with photos of John Lennon

Recording Location / Date: Record Plant (East) Studios, New York, NY, U.S.A. / Jul 73
Song 251a title: She Hits Back
Track details: CD3, track 12 / 4 min. 04 sec.
Release date / Country: 03 Mar 92 (first issued 02 Nov 73) / U.S.A.
Composer: Y. Ono

Yoko Ono: Lead Vocals; David Spinozza: Guitar; Ken Ascher: Piano; Gordon Edwards: Bass; Jim Keltner: Drums; Arthur Jenkins: Percussion; John Lennon: Guitar; Something Different: Chorus (Plastic Ono Band & Something Different)

Record 251b title: ONOBOX/(Run, Run, Run)
Media: Album 5" [6 CD set]
Label / Catalog number: Rykodisc / RCD 10224/29 (RCD 10226)
Producer: Yoko Ono
Jacket / Inserts: Standard international design box set with Jewel box's / 4 page CD insert, Onobox Ultracase Limited Edition flyer & 96 page book with photos of John Lennon
Recording Location / Date: Record Plant (East) Studios, New York, NY, U.S.A. / Jul 73
Song 251c title: Woman Power
Track details: CD3, track 14 / 5 min. 37 sec.
Release date / Country: 03 Mar 92 (first issued 24 Sep 73) / U.S.A.
Composer: Y. Ono

Yoko Ono: Lead Vocals; David Spinozza: Guitar; Ken Ascher: Piano; Gordon Edwards: Bass; Jim Keltner: Drums; Arthur Jenkins: Percussion; John Lennon: Guitar; Something Different: Chorus; Sneaky Pete Kleinow: Pedal Steel Guitar (Plastic Ono Band & Something Different)

Record 252 title:
Open Your Box
Label / Catalog number:
Apple / R 5892
Jacket / Inserts:
Standard international design PS
Recording Location / Date:
Ascot Sound Studios, Ascot & EMI-Abbey Road Studios†, London, U.K. / Feb 71 & 04 Mar 71†
Media:
Single 7"
Producer:
Yoko Ono & John Lennon

Song 252a title:
Open Your Box (Hirake) [remixed version]
Release date / Country:
12 Mar 71 / U.K.
Track details:
Side 1, track 1 / 3 min. 31 sec.
Composer:
Y. Ono

Yoko Ono: Lead Vocals; John Lennon: Guitar; Klaus Voormann: Bass; Jim Gordon: Drums

Record 253 title:
Rock And Roll Circus [Various Artists]
Label / Catalog number:
Abkco / 1268-2
Jacket / Inserts:
Standard international design in jewel box in slip cover / 42 page CD booklet with photos of John Lennon
Recording Location / Date:
InterTel Studios, Stonebridge House, London, U.K. / 10 Dec 68
Media:
Album 5" CD
Producer:
Jimmy Miller, Jody Klein & Lenne Allik

Song 253a title:
Whole Lotta Yoko
Release date / Country:
15 Oct 96 / U.S.A.
Track details:
Side 1, track 13 / 4 min. 48 sec.
Composer:
Y. Ono

Yoko Ono: Lead Vocals; John Lennon: Rhythm Guitar & B. Vocals; Eric Clapton: Lead Guitar; Keith Richards: Bass; Mitch Mitchell: Drums; Ivry Gitlis: Violin with (Ivry Gitlas with The Dirty Mac)

Also available on Abkco / 1003-1 / Album 12" LVD / Side 1, track 11 / Standard international design.

Record 254 title:
S.I.R. John Winston Ono Lennon
Label / Catalog number:
Moonlight / ML 9506 [Unauthorized Record]
Jacket / Inserts:
Unique in Jewel box / 4 page CD booklet
Media:
Album 5" CD

Song 254a title:
Mind Train [rehearsal]
Release date / Country:
Aug 95 / Czech Republic
Producer:
(probably) John Lennon & Yoko Ono
Track details:
Side 1, track 12 / 6 min. 22 sec.
Composer:
Y. Ono

Recording Location / Date:
Butterfly Studios, New York, NY / 21-22 Aug 72

Yoko Ono: Lead Vocals; John Lennon: Guitar & Voice; Gary Van Scyoc: Bass; Adam Ippolito: Keyboards; Richard Frank Jr.: Drums; Stan Bronstein: Saxophone; Wayne Gabriel: Guitar; Jim Keltner: Drums; John Ward: Bass

Song 254b title:
[untitled "Jam"]
Track details:
Side 1, track 6 / 2 min. 21 sec.
Release date / Country:
Aug 95 / Czech Republic
Composer:
Y. Ono
Producer:
John Lennon, Yoko Ono & Phil Spector
Recording Location / Date:
Record Plant (East) Studios, New York, NY / 01-20 Mar 72

Yoko Ono: Lead Vocals; Gary Van Scyoc: Bass; Richard Frank Jr. &/or Jim Keltner: Drums & Percussion; Adam Ippolito: Keyboards; Stan Bronstein: Saxophone; Wayne Gabriel: Guitar; John Lennon: Guitar & Voice

Song 254c title:
We're All Water [rehearsal]
Track details:
Side 1, track 14 / 11 min. 55 sec.
Release date / Country:
Aug 95 / Czech Republic
Composer:
Y. Ono
Producer:
(probably) John Lennon & Yoko Ono
Recording Location / Date:
Butterfly Studios, New York, NY, U.S.A. / 21-22 Aug 72

Yoko Ono: Lead Vocals; John Lennon: Guitar & Voice; Gary Van Scyoc: Bass; Adam Ippolito: Keyboards; Richard Frank Jr.: Drums; Stan Bronstein: Saxophone; Wayne Gabriel: Guitar; John Ward: Bass; Jim Keltner: Drums

Record 255 title:
Sometime In New York City
Media:
Album 5" CD [2 CD set]
Label / Catalog number:
Capitol / C2 93850
Jacket / Inserts:
Standard international design in jewel box with photos of John Lennon on front and back / 16 page CD booklet with photos of John Lennon & 1 page insert

Song 255a title:
Au [aka A Small Eternity With Yoko Ono] [live]
Track details:
CD2, track 6 / 6 min. 37 sec.
Release date / Country:
01 May 90 (first issued 12 Jun 72) / U.S.A.
Composer:
J. Lennon - Y. Ono
Producer:
John Lennon, Yoko Ono & Phil Spector
Recording Location / Date:
On location at Fillmore East Theater, New York, NY, U.S.A. / 06 Jun 71

Yoko Ono: Lead Vocals; John Lennon: Feedback Guitar & Voice; Frank Zappa: Feedback Guitar; Don Preston: Mini Moog (with The Mothers of Invention)

Song 255b title:
Born In A Prison
Track details:
CD1, track 4 / 4 min. 02 sec.
Release date / Country:
01 May 90 (first issued 12 Jun 72) / U.S.A.
Composer:
Y. Ono

Producer:
John Lennon, Yoko Ono & Phil Spector
Recording Location / Date:
Record Plant (East) Studios, New York, NY / 01-20 Mar 72

Yoko Ono: Lead Vocals; Gary Van Scyoc: Bass; Richard Frank Jr. &/or Jim Keltner: Drums & Percussion; John LaBosca: Piano; Stan Bronstein: Saxophone; Ron Frangipane: String Orchestrations; John Lennon: Guitar & B. Vocals (with Elephant's Memory Plus Invisible Strings)

Song 255c title:
Don't Worry Kyoko (Mummy's Only Looking For Her Hand In The Snow) [live]
Track details:
CD2, track 2 / 1 min. :00 sec.
Release date / Country:
01 May 90 (first issued 12 Jun 72) / U.S.A.
Composer:
Y. Ono
Producer:
John Lennon & Yoko Ono & [Geoff Emerick]
Recording Location / Date:
On location at Lyceum Ballroom, London, U.K. / 15 Dec 69

Yoko Ono: Lead Vocals; John Lennon: Guitar; Jim Gordon: Drums; George Harrison: Guitar; Eric Clapton: Guitar; Klaus Voormann: Bass; Bobby Keys: Saxophone; Keith Moon: Drums; Alan White Drums: Billy Preston: Organ; Nicky Hopkins: (overdubbed) Electric Piano; Delaney Bramlett: Guitar: Bonnie Bramlett: Percussion; Jim Price: Horns; "Legs" Larry Smith: Percussion; Chris Wood: Percussion; Neil Boland: Percussion

Song 255d title:
Jamrag [aka Say Please, & Aaawk] [live]
Track details:
CD2, track 4 / 5 min. 36 sec.
Release date / Country:
01 May 90 (first issued 12 Jun 72) / U.S.A.
Composer:
J. Lennon - Y. Ono - [F. Zappa]
Producer:
John Lennon, Yoko Ono & Phil Spector
Recording Location / Date:
On location at The Fillmore East, New York, NY, U.S.A. / 06 Jun 71

Yoko Ono: Lead Vocals; John Lennon: Voice, B. Vocals & Guitar; Frank Zappa: Guitar; Mark Volman: B. Vocals; Howard Kaylan: B. Vocals; Ian Underwood: Winds B. Vocals & Keyboards; Aynsley Dunbar: Drums; Jim Pons: Bass; Bob Harris: Keyboards & B. Vocals; Don Preston: Mini Moog (with The Mothers of Invention)

Song 255e title:
We're All Water
Track details:
CD1, track 10 / 7 min. 13 sec.
Release date / Country:
01 May 90 (first issued 12 Jun 72) / U.S.A.
Composer:
Y. Ono
Producer:
John Lennon, Yoko Ono & Phil Spector
Recording Location / Date:
Record Plant (East) Studios, New York, NY / 01-20 Mar 72

Yoko Ono: Lead Vocals; Gary Van Scyoc: Bass; Richard Frank Jr. &/or Jim Keltner: Drums & Percussion; Adam Ippolito: Keyboards; Stan Bronstein: Saxophone; Wayne Gabriel: Guitar; John Lennon: Guitar (with Elephant's Memory Plus Invisible Strings)

Record 256 title:
Telecasts
Label / Catalog number:
[none] / [Matrix #] BS-63 601739X [Unauthorized Record]
Jacket / Inserts:
Unique / 1 page CD Insert
Recording Location / Date:
New York, NY, U.S.A. / 11 May 72
Media:
Album 5" CD (mono)
Producer:
[audience recording] (The Dick Cavett Show)

Song 256a title:
We're All Water [live]
Release date / Country:
1996
Track details:
Side 1, track 5 / 4 min. 15 sec.
Composer:
Y. Ono

Yoko Ono: Lead Vocals; Gary Van Scyoc: Bass; Richard Frank Jr.: Drums & Percussion; Adam Ippolito: Keyboards; Stan Bronstein: Saxophone; Wayne Gabriel: Guitar; John Lennon: Guitar

Record 257 title:
The Lost Lennon Tapes
Label / Catalog number:
Westwood One / [Matrix #] LT90-26 (promotional only)
Jacket / Inserts:
Unique "Lost Lennon Tapes" / Cue Sheets
Media:
Album 12 [2 LP set]

Song 257a title:
John, John (Let's Hope For Peace)
Release date / Country:
25 Jun 90 / U.S.A.
Producer:
Glyn Johns &/or George Martin
Recording Location / Date:
Apple Studios, London, U.K. / 23 Jan 69
Track details:
Side 3, track 1 / 0 min. 50 sec.
Composer:
Y. Ono

Yoko Ono: Lead Vocals; John Lennon: Guitar; Paul McCartney: Drums

Song 257b title:
No One [Nobody] Sees Me Like You Do
Release date / Country:
15 Jul 91 / U.S.A.
Producer:
John Lennon, Yoko Ono & Jack Douglas
Recording Location / Date:
The Hit Factory Studios, New York, NY, U.S.A. / Aug or Sep 80
Track details:
Side 3, track 1 / 3 min. 44 sec.
Composer:
Y. Ono

Yoko Ono: Lead Vocals; John Lennon: Rhythm Guitar; Tony Levin: Bass; Andy Newmark: Drums; George Small: Keyboards; Arthur Jenkins, Jr.: Percussion; Earl Slick &/or Hugh McCracken: Guitar

Song 257c title:
Oh My Love
Release date / Country:
15 Jul 91 / U.S.A.
Producer:
John Lennon & Yoko Ono
Track details:
Side 1, track 2 / 2 min. 08 sec.
Composer:
Y. Ono

Recording Location / Date:
(probably) U.K. / (probably) 1969

Yoko Ono: Lead Vocals; John Lennon: Rhythm Guitar

Record 258 title:
The Mike Douglas Show with John Lennon & Yoko Ono
Media:
VHS [5 VHS set]
Release date / Country:
26 May 98 / U.S.A.
Producer:
WBS in association with Mike Douglas Entertainments Inc. & Michael Krauss
Jacket / Inserts:
Unique in box set / 48 page hard bound book with photos of John Lennon

Song 258a title:
Midsummer New York [live]
Label / Catalog number:
Rhino R32438 (2429)
Recording Location / Date:
Philadelphia, PA, U.S.A. / 15 Feb 72
Song details:
Tape 2 / 2 min. 51 sec.
Composer:
Y. Ono

Yoko Ono: Lead Vocals; John Lennon: Guitar; Gary Van Scyoc: Bass; Adam Ippolito: Keyboards; Richard Frank Jr.: Drums; Stan Bronstein: Saxophone; Wayne Gabriel: Guitar; Jerry Rubin: African Drum; Barbara Loden: African Drum

Song 258b title:
Sakura (Cherry Blossoms) [live]
Label / Catalog number:
Rhino R3 2438 (2432)
Recording Location / Date:
Philadelphia, PA, U.S.A. / 18 Feb 72
Song details:
Tape 5 / 1 min. 34 sec.
Composer:
Trad Arr: Y. Ono

Yoko Ono: Lead Vocals; John Lennon: Guitar & Voice; Adam Ippolito: Keyboards

Song 258c title:
Sisters, O Sisters [live]
Label / Catalog number:
Rhino R3 2438 (2430)
Recording Location / Date:
Philadelphia, PA, U.S.A. / 16 Feb 72
Song details:
Tape 3 / 2 min. 48 sec.
Composer:
Y. Ono

Yoko Ono: Lead Vocals; John Lennon: Guitar & B. Vocals

Record 259 title:
The Plastic Ono Band - Live Peace In Toronto 1969
Media:
Album 5" CD
Label / Catalog number:
7 Apple/Capitol / CDP 0777 7 90428 2 1
Producer:
John Lennon & Yoko Ono (music)
Jacket / Inserts:
Standard international design in jewel box / 32 page CD booklet with calendar with photos of John Lennon
Recording Location / Date:
On location at Varsity Stadium, Toronto, Ontario, Canada / 13 Sep 69

Song 259a title:
Don't Worry Kyoko (Mummy's Only Looking For Her Hand In The Snow) [live]
Release date / Country:
18 Jul 95 / U.S.A.
Track details:
Side 1, track 7 / 4 min. 44 sec.
Composer:
Y. Ono

Yoko Ono: Lead Vocals; John Lennon: Guitar, Eric Clapton: Guitar; Alan White: Drums; Klaus Voormann: Bass

This song is also included on Live Rock & Roll Revival, Toronto / Image Entertainment / ID6582HB / Album 12" LVD / Side 1, track 12 / released 1989 in the U.S.A. (first issued 12 Dec 69) / Standard international design with photos of John Lennon on front / produced by Kenneth C. Walker, Thor Eaton & Frazer Pennebaker for Pennebaker Assoc. & Alan Douglas for Douglas Corp

Song 259b title:
John, John (Let's Hope For Peace) [live]
Release date / Country:
18 Jul 95 / U.S.A.
Track details:
Side 1, track 8 / 12 min. 54 sec.
Composer:
Y. Ono

Yoko Ono: Lead Vocals; John Lennon: Feedback Guitar, Eric Clapton: Feedback Guitar; Alan White: Drums; Klaus Voormann: Feedback Bass

This song is also included on Live Rock & Roll Revival, Toronto / Image Entertainment / ID6582HB / Album 12" LVD / Side 1, track 13 / 11 min. 20 sec. / released 1989 in the U.S.A. (first issued 12 Dec 69) / Standard international design with photos of John Lennon on front / produced by Kenneth C. Walker, Thor Eaton & Frazer Pennebaker for Pennebaker Assoc. & Alan Douglas for Douglas Corp

Record 260 title:
Then & Now
Label / Catalog number:
Pioneer / PA-85-116
Media:
Album 12" LVD
Producer:
Glyn Johns & George Martin; Barbara Graustark (overall film)
Jacket / Inserts:
Standard international design with photos of John Lennon
Recording Location / Date:
Twickenham Films Studios, London, U.K. / 10 Jan 69

Song 260a title:
[untitled jam]
Release date / Country:
Dec 84 / U.S.A.
Track details:
0 min. 10 sec. / Side 1, track 4
Composer:
Y. Ono

Yoko Ono: Lead Vocals; John Lennon: Guitar; Paul McCartney: Bass; Ringo Starr: Drums

Record 261 title:
Unfinished Music No. 1. Two Virgins
Label / Catalog number:
Rykodisc / RCD 10411
Media:
Album 5" CD
Producer:
John Lennon & Yoko Ono
Jacket / Inserts:
Standard international design in jewel box with photo of & by John Lennon on the front and back inc. outer wraparound advert / 4 page CD booklet with drawing by John Lennon, credit insert with photo of & by John Lennon & Rykodisc insert

Song 261a title:
Remember Love
Track details:
Side 1, track 3 / 4 min. 05 sec.
Release date / Country:
03 Jun 97 (first issued 04 Jul 69) / U.S.A.
Composer:
Y. Ono
Recording Location / Date:
Room 1742, Hotel La Reine, Elizabeth, Montreal, Canada / 01 Jun 69

Yoko Ono: Lead Vocals; John Lennon: Acoustic Guitar

Song 261b title:
Two Virgins Side One (Two Virgins No. 1 / Together†/Two Virgins No. 2/Two Virgins No. 3 / Two Virgins No. 4/Two Virgins No. 5)
Track details:
Side 1, track 1 / 14 min. 14 sec.
Release date / Country:
03 Jun 97 (first issued 11 Nov 68) / U.S.A.
Composer:
J. Lennon & Y. Ono (De Silva - Brown - Henderson†)
Recording Location / Date:
John Lennon's home studio at Kenwood, Weybridge, Surrey, U.K. / (probably) 20 May 68

Yoko Ono: Lead Vocals & Instruments; John Lennon: B. Vocals, Voice & Instruments

Song 261c title:
Two Virgins Side Two (Two Virgins No. 6 / Hushabye Hushabye/Two Virgins No. 7 / Two Virgins No. 8/Two Virgins No. 9/Two Virgins No. 10)
Track details:
Side 1, track 2 / 14 min. 40 sec.
Release date / Country:
03 Jun 97 (first issued 11 Nov 68) / U.S.A.
Composer:
J. Lennon & Y. Ono
Recording Location / Date:
John Lennon's home studio at Kenwood, Weybridge, Surrey, U.K. / (probably) 20 May 68

Yoko Ono: Lead Vocals & Instruments; John Lennon: B. Vocals, Voice & Instruments

Record 262 title:
Unfinished Music No. 2: Life With The Lions
Media:
Album 5" CD
Label / Catalog number:
Rykodisc / RCD 10412
Producer:
John Lennon & Yoko Ono
Jacket / Inserts:
Standard international design in jewel box with photo of John Lennon on the front and back inc. outer wraparound advert / 8 page CD booklet, credit insert with photo of John Lennon & Rykodisc insert

Song 262a title:
Cambridge 1969 [live]
Track details:
Side 1, track 1 / 26 min. 28 sec.
Release date / Country:
03 Jun 97 (first issued 09 May 69) / U.S.A.
Composer:
J.Lennon - Y. Ono
Recording Location / Date:
On location at Lady Mitchell Hall, Cambridge, U.K. / 02 Mar 69

Yoko Ono: Lead Vocals; John Lennon: Feedback Guitar; John Tchikai: Saxophone; John Stevens: Percussion; Mal Evans: Watch

Song 262b title:
Mulberry
Track details:
Side 1, track 7 / 8 min. 57 sec.
Release date / Country:
03 Jun 97 / U.S.A.
Composer:
Y. Ono

Recording Location / Date:
(probably) On location at Queen Charlotte Hospital, Second West Ward, Room 1, London or (possibly) John Lennon's temporary residence at 34 Montague Square, London, U.K. / (probably) 4-25 Nov 68

Yoko Ono: Lead Vocals; John Lennon: Acoustic Guitar

Song 262c title:
No Bed For Beatle John
Track details:
Side 1, track 2 / 4 min. 40 sec.
Release date / Country:
03 Jun 97 (first issued 09 May 69) / U.S.A.
Composer:
J.Lennon - Y. Ono
Recording Location / Date:
On location at Queen Charlotte Hospital, Second West Ward, Room 1, London, U.K. / 4-25 Nov 68

Yoko Ono: Lead Vocals; John Lennon: B. Vocals

Song 262d title:
Song For John
Track details:
Side 1, track 6 / 1 min. 29 sec.
Release date / Country:
03 Jun 97 / U.S.A.
Composer:
Y. Ono
Recording Location / Date:
(probably) On location at Queen Charlotte Hospital, Second West Ward, Room 1, London or (possibly) John Lennon's temporary residence at 34 Montague Square, London, U.K. / (probably) 4-25 Nov 68

Yoko Ono: Lead Vocals; John Lennon: Acoustic Guitar

Record 263 title:
Walking On Thin Ice-For John (Re-Edit†)
Media:
Single 12"
Label / Catalog number:
Polydor / 883 872-1
Producer:
John Lennon, Yoko Ono & Jack Douglas; Joseph Watt†
Jacket / Inserts:
PolyGram 12" open center jacket / Record label inner sleeve
Recording Location / Date:
Hit Factory Studios, New York, NY, U.S.A. / Nov 80 & 06-08 Dec 80 & 1986

Song 263a title:
Walking On Thin Ice-For John (Re-Edit†)
Track details:
Side 2, track 1 / 7 min. 17 sec.
Release date / Country:
Apr 86 / U.S.A.
Composer:
Y. Ono

Yoko Ono: Lead Vocals; John Lennon: Lead Guitar & Keyboards; Hugh McCracken: Rhythm Guitar; Earl Slick: Rhythm Guitar; Tony Levin: Bass; Andy Newmark: Drums; Jack Douglas: Percussion

Record 264 title:
Walking On Thin Ice / It Happened
Label / Catalog number:
Geffen / GEF 49683
Jacket / Inserts:
Standard international design PS / Credit Insert
Recording Location / Date:
Record Plant (East) Studios, New York, NY, U.S.A. / 1973 & 1980†
Media:
Single 7"
Producer:
John Lennon† & Editor† & Remixer,† Yoko Ono & David Spinozza

Song 264a title:
It Happened [edited & remixed version]
Release date / Country:
06 Feb 81 / U.S.A.
Track details:
Side 2, track 1 / 5 min. 06 sec.
Composer:
Y. Ono

Yoko Ono: Lead Vocals; David Spinozza: Guitar; Hugh McCracken: Guitar; Gordon Edwards: Bass; Kenny Asher: Keyboards; Arthur Jenkins, Jr.: Percussion; Rick Marotta: Drums; John Lennon: Voice

Record 265 title:
Wedding Album
Label / Catalog number:
Apple /SMAX 3361
Jacket / Inserts:
Standard international design with Gatefold in box set with photos of John Lennon / Copy of Marriage Certificate, The Press (20 page booklet with photos of John Lennon), Bagism (white plastic bag), 4 do-it-yourself photos with John Lennon, postcard with photo of John Lennon, piece of wedding cake (photo), 6 page fold-out with photo and drawings by John Lennon, The Wedding (12 page fold-out poster with photos of John Lennon)
Recording Location / Date:
On location at Hilton Hotel, Amsterdam, Netherlands / 26 Mar 69
Media:
Album 12"
Producer:
John Lennon & Yoko Ono

Song 265a title:
[John, John (Let's Hope For Peace)]
Release date / Country:
20 Oct 69 / U.S.A.
Track details:
Side 2, track 1 (beginning) / 5 min. 14 sec.
Composer:
Y. Ono

Yoko Ono: Lead Vocals; John Lennon: Voice

Song 265b title:
[Stay In Bed]
Release date / Country:
20 Oct 69 / U.S.A.
Track details:
Side 2, track 1 (end) / 0 min. 48 sec.
Composer:
Y. Ono

Yoko Ono: Lead Vocals; John Lennon: Guitar & Vocals

Record 266 title:
Wedding Album
Label / Catalog number:
Rykodisc / RCD 10413
Jacket / Inserts:
Standard international design in jewel box with photo of John Lennon inc. outer wraparound advert / 28 page CD booklet with photos of John Lennon, credit insert & Rykodisc insert
Media:
Album 5" CD

Song 266a title:
Don't Worry Kyoko (Mummy's Only Looking For Her Hand In The Snow)
Release date / Country:
03 Jun 97 (first issued (probably) May 69) / U.S.A.
Producer:
John Lennon & Yoko Ono
Recording Location / Date:
(probably) On location at Queen Charlotte Hospital, Second West Ward, Room 1, London or (possibly) John Lennon's temporary residence at 34 Montague Square, London, U.K. / (probably) 4-25 Nov 68
Track details:
Side 1, track 5 / 2 min. 14 sec.
Composer:
Y. Ono

Yoko Ono: Lead Vocals; John Lennon: Acoustic Guitar

Song 266b title:
Listen, The Snow Is Falling
Release date / Country:
03 Jun 97 (first issued 01 Dec 71) / U.S.A.
Recording Location / Date:
Record Plant (East) Studios, New York, NY / 29 Oct 71
Track details:
Side 1, track 4 / 3 min. 22 sec.
Composer:
Y. Ono
Producer:
John Lennon, Yoko Ono & Phil Spector

Yoko Ono: Lead Vocals; John Lennon: Guitar; Klaus Voormann: Guitar; Hugh McCracken: Guitar; Nicky Hopkins: Keyboards & Chimes

Song 266c title:
Who Has Seen The Wind?
Release date / Country:
03 Jun 97 (first issued 06 Feb 70) / U.S.A.
Recording Location / Date:
Trident Studios, London, U.K. / (probably) 27 Jan 70
Track details:
Side 1, track 3 / 2 min. 03 sec.
Composer:
J. Lennon - Y. Ono
Producer:
John Lennon

Yoko Ono: Lead Vocals & Flute; John Lennon: (probable) Guitar; George Harrison: (probable) Guitar; John Barham: Harpsichord

Record 267 title:
Yoko Ono/Plastic Ono Band
Label / Catalog number:
Rykodisc / RCD 10414
Jacket / Inserts:
Standard international design in jewel box with photo of John Lennon inc. outer wraparound advert / 8 page CD booklet with photos of John Lennon, credit insert & Rykodisc insert
Media:
Album 5" CD
Producer:
John Lennon & Yoko Ono

Song 267a title:
AOS [rehearsal]
Release date / Country:
03 Jun 97 (first issued 11 Dec 70) / U.S.A.
Recording Location / Date:
On location at Albert Hall, London, U.K. / 29 Feb 68
Track details:
Side 1, track 4 / 7 min. 06 sec.
Composer:
Y. Ono

Yoko Ono: Lead Vocals; Ornette Coleman: Trumpet; Edward Blackwell: Drums; David Izenzon: Bass; Charles Haden: Bass

Song 267b title:
Greenfield Morning I Pushed An Empty Baby Carriage All Over The City
Release date / Country:
03 Jun 97 (first issued 11 Dec 70) / U.S.A.
Recording Location / Date:
EMI-Abbey Road Studios, London, U.K. / 26 Sep 70 - 27 Oct 70
Track details:
Side 1, track 3 / 5 min. 38 sec.
Composer:
Y. Ono

Yoko Ono: Lead Vocals; John Lennon: Guitar; Klaus Voormann: Bass; Ringo Starr: Drums; George Harrison: Sitar

Song 267c title:
Open Your Box [previously unreleased version]
Release date / Country:
03 Jun 97 / U.S.A.
Recording Location / Date:
Trident Studios, London, U.K. / (probably) Oct 70 or (possibly) Feb 71
Track details:
Side 1, track 7 / 7 min. 35 sec.
Composer:
Y. Ono

Yoko Ono: Lead Vocals; John Lennon: Guitar; Klaus Voormann: Bass; Ringo Starr: Drums

Song 267d title:
Paper Shoes
Release date / Country:
03 Jun 97 (first issued 11 Dec 70) / U.S.A.
Recording Location / Date:
EMI-Abbey Road Studios, London, U.K. / 26 Sep 70 - 27 Oct 70
Track details:
Side 1, track 6 / 7 min. 26 sec.
Composer:
Y. Ono

Yoko Ono: Lead Vocals; John Lennon: Guitar; Klaus Voormann: Bass; Ringo Starr: Drums

Song 267e title:
Something More Abstract
Release date / Country:
03 Jun 97 / U.S.A.
Recording Location / Date:
EMI-Abbey Road Studios, London, U.K. / Oct 70
Track details:
Side 1, track 8 / 0 min. 44 sec.
Composer:
Y. Ono

Yoko Ono: Lead Vocals; John Lennon: Guitar; Klaus Voormann: Bass; Ringo Starr: Drums

Song 267f title:
The South Wind
Release date / Country:
03 Jun 97 / U.S.A.
Recording Location / Date:
New York, NY, U.S.A. / (probably) Sep - Dec 70 or Jun - Jul 71
Track details:
Side 1, track 9 / 16 min. 38 sec.
Composer:
Y. Ono

Yoko Ono: Lead Vocals; John Lennon: Acoustic Guitar

Song 267g title:
Touch Me
Track details:
Side 1, track 5 / 4 min. 37 sec.

Release date / Country:
03 Jun 97 (first issued 11 Dec 70) / U.S.A.
Composer:
Y. Ono
Recording Location / Date:
EMI-Abbey Road Studios, London, U.K. / 26 Sep 70 - 27 Oct 70

Yoko Ono: Lead Vocals; John Lennon: Guitar; Klaus Voormann: Bass; Ringo Starr: Drums

Song 267h title:
Why
Track details:
Side 1, track 1 / 5 min. 37 sec.
Release date / Country:
03 Jun 97 (first issued 11 Dec 70) / U.S.A.
Composer:
Y. Ono
Recording Location / Date:
EMI-Abbey Road Studios, London, U.K. / 26 Sep 70 - 27 Oct 70

Yoko Ono: Lead Vocals; John Lennon: Guitar & B. Vocals; Klaus Voormann: Bass; Ringo Starr: Drums

Song 267i title:
Why Not
Track details:
Side 1, track 2 / 9 min. 55 sec.
Release date / Country:
03 Jun 97 (first issued 11 Dec 70) / U.S.A.
Composer:
Y. Ono
Recording Location / Date:
EMI-Abbey Road Studios, London, U.K. / 26 Sep 70 - 27 Oct 70

Yoko Ono: Lead Vocals; John Lennon: Guitar; Klaus Voormann: Bass; Ringo Starr: Drums

Yoko Ono often draws ridicule, and occasionally sympathy, but rarely praise. It is impossible to ignore John Lennon when talking about Yoko Ono – only The Beatles played as big a role in his life. She was his friend, his lover and his creative partner. John supported and defended his love for Yoko, and her art and music, at great expense and risk to his popularity, and that of The Beatles. He believed in her when few others would. She gave him an artistic freedom he had never known in The Beatles, curbed his aggressive behavior, and softened his heart. Despite all the criticism she has received, she has never publicly damaged John's name or reputation. Far too many volumes (mostly negative) have been written on their relationship that do little to expose the full extent of their influence on each other's music.

In most cases it's clear what is a Lennon contribution to a Yoko Ono recording, especially with respect to recordings listed solely under her name. Truly collaborative efforts where both the lead vocals and the writing credits are equally shared, as in the case of songs like ***The Luck Of The Irish*** and ***Angela***, are generally classified as John Lennon recordings. The **Two Virgins** album, though a collaborative effort, contains mostly Ono vocals, and is generally considered a Yoko Ono recording to which John contributed, though the recording is as much a John and Yoko collaboration as **Revolution 9**, (technically) by The Beatles. John and Yoko's **Wedding Album** and **Life With The Lions** also consist mostly of what are best classified as Yoko Ono recordings to which John contributed. Most of Yoko's recordings before John's death contain contributions by John, mainly in the form of production and, to a lesser degree, guitar, backing vocals, keyboards and composition.

Yoko Ono was born on February 18, 1933 in Tokyo, Japan. She was the eldest daughter of a prominent upper-class banking family, and was afforded all its attendant privileges, including a childhood shuttled between the U.S. and Japan. Yoko had been interested in music since her childhood piano instructions. She suffered the same classless deprivations of World War II in Japan as her future husband John Lennon did in England.

After the war, Yoko returned to the U.S. and attended Sarah Lawrence College in the mid-1950s. She studied fine arts and philosophy, but dropped out after several years. She married Japanese musician Toshi Ichiyanagi in 1956, who helped expose her to New York's avant-garde art and music scene. The marriage lasted several years before Yoko met artist, musician and avant-garde filmmaker Tony Cox, by whom she had one child, a daughter named Kyoko. Cox began promoting Ono's unique brand of conceptual art, films, and participatory happenings from **Cut Piece** (allowing people to cut a piece of clothing from the artist) to **Bagism** (placing the artist inside a bag). Her most notable work up to the time was a book of poems published in 1964, titled **Grapefruit** *(see Grapefruit).*

In September 1966, the couple moved to London and arranged an exhibit titled **Unfinished Paintings and Objects** in November at the Indica Art Gallery operated by John Dunbar *(see Marianne Faithfull).* Dunbar was a close friend of Peter Asher *(see Peter & Gordon),* who also happened to be the brother of Paul McCartney's girlfriend, Jane. McCartney was the first Beatle to meet Ono, and suggested to her that his partner John might be more interested in her activities. Lennon attended a preview of the exhibit on November 9, and was pleasantly amused by the off-beat humor of Ono's conceptual art.

For the next year and a half, Ono pursued Lennon for patronization of her art projects. In October 1967, Lennon sponsored Yoko's exhibit titled **Yoko Plus Me.** Lennon, who was becoming increasingly bored with his wife and life in the upscale suburbs, began taking greater interest in the eccentric artist.

In May 1968, he invited her to his home while his wife was away on vacation. The two began experimenting in John's home studio, Lennon at the controls with sound effects and Yoko with her distinctive warbling vocals, resulting in the recording **Two Virgins**. By morning, as the official version goes, they were not . . ., though many claim the actual consummation of their relationship took place months before. When John's wife Cynthia returned home, she found the couple comfortably settled in her home, effectively ending her six-year marriage.

John immediately went public with Yoko in attendance at almost all Beatles-related functions. The two were now virtually inseparable, staging "happenings" and media events almost weekly. Lennon's relationship with Ono quickly shattered his "mop-top" image; fans were bewildered, and the press was outraged, at Lennon's outlandish behavior and mockery of his marriage to Cynthia.

Though Beatles' wives and friends had occasionally dropped by for their recording sessions, they never participated or dared offer suggestions. Yoko Ono was a different matter – both she and John felt that the other Beatles should immediately accept her both as the love of John's life, and his new musical partner. McCartney was initially tolerant of her avant-garde ideas, but soon both he and Harrison deeply resented Ono's presence, and felt she was driving a wedge between John and The Beatles. Yoko soon began lending her ideas and vocals to the recordings for **The Beatles** (white album) on such songs as ***Revolution 9***, ***The Continuing Story Of Bungalow Bill***, ***Birthday*** and ***What's The New Mary Jane***. She even enlisted The Beatles in jams of her compositions during the rehearsals for the album and film **Let It Be**, and contributed to The Beatles' 1969 Christmas message record sent to fan-club members. However, the continued resentment of the other Beatles towards Ono made Lennon all the more defensive, pushing him even further towards solo activities with Yoko.

In October 1968, the couple, both still married, but not to each other, announced that they were expecting a baby in February. The following month, Yoko would suffer her first of several miscarriages during her relationship with Lennon. John moved into Yoko's Queen Charlotte's Hospital room in London to stay beside her, during which time the two recorded much of what became their second album together, **Life With The Lions**. The album included such bizarre and off-beat tracks as a recording of the unborn (later miscarried) child's heartbeat and two minutes of silence. Yoko would later write a poem about the miscarriage titled ***Oh My Love***, with John on guitar. The song was featured on Westwood One's **The Lost Lennon Tapes** radio series. John later re-wrote the song and recorded it for his **Imagine** album.

During the fall of 1968, their first album, **Two Virgins**, was being refused distribution by EMI because it featured full frontal and rear nude photos of the couple. The album was finally distributed by other record labels (Tetragrammaton Records in the U.S. and Track in the U.K.) using a brown "paper bag" slip cover. These original issues have since become collector's items. The album was reissued on vinyl in 1985 by Out Of The Past Records, and in 1991 on CD (taken from vinyl) by Creative Sounds. Rykodisc Records issued, under Yoko's supervision, her entire Apple Records' album catalogue on CD in 1997 (including **Two Virgins**), which contained alternate versions and previously unreleased bonus tracks to which John Lennon contributed.

Shortly after Yoko's miscarriage, she and John agreed to take part in The Rolling Stones'* **Rock And Roll Circus**, a made-for-TV-film that included a performance featuring Yoko with John backing her on guitar on a jam called ***Whole Lotta Yoko*** (aka ***Her Blues***).

On March 2, 1969, John played feedback guitar behind Yoko at an avant-garde jazz concert at The Lady Mitchell Hall in Cambridge, England. It was his first genuine public performance since The Beatles quit touring in 1966. The performance was recorded and appeared on side one of **Life With The Lions** (a Lennon word play on one of his favorite childhood radio shows, **Life With The Lyons**), released two months later, with the Queen Charlotte's Hospital recordings on side two. The album's back jacket featured a photo of the couple leaving court after Lennon's arrest for possession of hashish (marijuana). Rather than fight what Lennon maintained was a set-up, he agreed to plead guilty if charges against Yoko (she could have faced deportation) were dropped, and he was sentenced to a small fine. It was a decision the Lennons would live to regret for years to come.

Not included on **Life With The Lions** was a medley of acoustic demos apparently recorded during the Lennon's hospital stay, and later featured on a flexi-disc included in **Aspen**, a box magazine that included a variety of art objects. The record and box with its complete contents has become quite valuable. One of the songs on the flexi, titled ***Song For John: Let's Go On Flying, Snow Is Falling All The Time, Mum's Only Looking For Her Hand In The Snow***, features an early acoustic version of ***Don't Worry Kyoko***. These songs feature Lennon's unmistakable acoustic guitar. Apparently John and Yoko also planned a third **Unfinished Music** album that reportedly included lengthy portions of people laughing.

On March 20, 1969, John Lennon and Yoko Ono, now both legally divorced from their previous spouses, were married in Gibraltar. Like almost all of John and Yoko's activities throughout their career, the wedding and honeymoon were filmed and recorded and turned into a media event, later released as the **Wedding Album**. Unfortunately, Rykodisc's 1997 CD was unable to reproduce all the miscellaneous items included in the original **Wedding Album** package. John and Yoko's "bed-in for peace" honeymoon set the stage for their campaign for world peace.

On May 26, 1969, The Lennons, still unable to secure a U.S. visa, arrived in Montreal, Canada to hold their second "bed-in for peace." The entire saga was filmed, and released as the documentary, **John and Yoko: The Bed-in**, in 1991. From their Queen Elizabeth Hotel room bed, they recorded ***Give Peace A Chance***. Though there were many guests who visited the Lennons in their room, the only participants in the recording of ***Give Peace A Chance*** were political activists Timothy and Rosemary Leary, Tommy Smothers of the musical comedy duo The Smothers Brothers, journalist Paul Williams, The Beatles' press officer and Apple publicist Derek Taylor, and members of the Hari Krsna Temple of Canada *(see Radha Krsna Temple)*. It was to be the first of many incarnations of the loose membership of the Plastic Ono Band. The B-side, ***Remember Love***, was the first of many Lennon singles that featured a Yoko Ono song on the flip side. The song has been reported as being recorded at EMI's Abbey Road Studios, Apple Studios, or at the Lennons' home studio in England. However, Ono's Rykodisc catalogue credited it as being recorded during the "bed-in for peace" in Montreal.

Throughout the summer of 1969, the Lennons tried to live the life of a normal family. They spent time with John's son Julian, and Yoko's daughter Kyoko, who was caught in the middle of a custody battle. They bought a mansion, Tittenhurst Park, Ascot, and installed a home studio (Ascot Sound Studio, later renamed Startling Studio when the home was bought by Ringo Starr). The Beatles returned to EMI Studios for what would prove to be their final recordings together, the album **Abbey Road**.

With the completion of recordings for **Abbey Road**, John and Yoko accepted an offer to perform at a rock 'n' roll revival in Toronto, Canada on September 13, 1969. The revival featured many of

Lennon's early rock heroes including Jerry Lee Lewis, Bo Diddley, Chuck Berry* and Little Richard*. The Lennons hastily assembled a band consisting of Eric Clapton* *(see also Blind Faith)*, Klaus Voormann *(see Paul Jones)* and Alan White (later a member of the group Yes). They rehearsed about a half-dozen numbers during the plane flight to Canada. Lennon opened the Plastic Ono Band set with a few well-known oldies The Beatles used to perform, and showcased what was to be the Plastic Ono Band's new single, ***Cold Turkey***. Lennon had lobbied for The Beatles to record ***Cold Turkey***, but they turned it down fearing the controversy that a song about heroin withdrawal would create for their image. Yoko performed ***Don't Worry Kyoko*** towards the end of the Lennons' set, which marked her first performance backed by a rock band, drawing a mixed reaction from the audience. The Lennons' performance was released on the album **Live Peace In Toronto 1969**, and on VHS and laser video disk some twenty years later. A studio recording of ***Don't Worry Kyoko*** served as the B-side of the ***Cold Turkey*** single.

Lennon planned to issue his then-unreleased Beatles' recordings ***You Know My Name (Look Up The Number)*** and ***What's The New Mary Jane*** as the Plastic Ono Band's third single (Apples / 1002) on December 5, 1969. The release was canceled due to objections by some of The Beatles over the use of their group recordings being issued as Plastic Ono Band recordings.

The Beatles were rapidly coming apart at the seams over personal and business differences, and Lennon had previously made it known to the others of his intention to leave the group – though it was decided that no official announcement should be made. When Paul McCartney released his first solo in April 1970, he used the opportunity to be the first to publicly announce he was leaving The Beatles, an act that left Lennon distrustful and embittered towards McCartney for years.

On December 15, 1969, John and Yoko made another live appearance, this time at London's Lyceum Ballroom at a **Peace For Christmas** concert for UNICEF. Backing Lennon were the Delaney & Bonnie & Friends tour group, including George Harrison. Once again the performance concluded with Yoko Ono, this time doing a sixteen-minute version of ***Don't Worry Kyoko*** with an enthusiastic response. The Beatles' engineer Geoff Emerick produced a recording of the event. However, two years later when the recording of the performance was finally released, John and Yoko were listed as the producers. Phil Spector, who was not even at the performance, was also listed (in error) on the record label as one of the producers.

While The Beatles were trying to salvage an album and movie (**Let It Be**), out of the previous year's filmed recordings, with the help of legendary producer Phil Spector, the Plastic Ono Band released its third single ***Instant Karma / Who Has Seen The Wind***, with Spector helping out on productions. (Spector would work on and off with John and Yoko on numerous projects over the years.) Though many reliable sources list ***Who Has Seen The Wind*** as being recorded the same evening as ***Instant Karma***, The Beatles' archivist Mark Lewisohn has been unable to find any evidence that it was recorded during those sessions. Consequently, there is little information about exactly who played on it. The single credits Yoko Ono as the sole composer; however Ono's Rykodisc catalogue credits it as being written by Lennon and Ono.

The Lennons spent much of 1970 in England doing battle with Paul McCartney, the press, and the British Government. Shortly after the highly publicized breakup of The Beatles, John and Yoko sought psychotherapy at Dr. Arthur Janov's Primal Institute in Los Angeles. It was a radical sort of regression therapy that exorcised one's pain and neurosis through screaming. One result of the therapy was the album **John Lennon / Plastic Ono Band**, and its companion album **Yoko Ono / Plastic Ono Band**, using the same musicians. The couple's first true solo albums, considered by many to be their finest, set the pattern for their future releases. Despite Lennon's defense and promotion of Yoko's work, he and his record company were aware that sales of his records could suffer if combined with Yoko's less commercially appealing recordings. Except for the **Some Time In New York City** period, John and Yoko's work would be released as separate solo records until their final joint recordings shortly before Lennon's death.

Controversy surrounded the release of John and Yoko's next single ***Power To The People / Open Your Box***. Apparently, in the U.K., the single was intended as a double A-side, as the whole green Apple was used for both songs. Later copies put Lennon's political anthem ***Power To The People*** on the split Apple B-side. The sexually suggestive lyrics of Yoko's ***Open Your Box*** had to be remixed to be unrecognizable before EMI would release the song in the U.K. In the U.S., Yoko's song ***Touch Me*** had to be substituted for the B-side. When the song was issued on the album **Fly** in the U.S., it was retitled ***Hirake***.

Yoko's next companion album, this time to Lennon's **Imagine**, was the double album **Fly**, again using the same basic musicians as John's album. Additionally, it included most of Yoko's B-sides up to that point. The two-record set's higher price initially made it a hard sell, but today it fetches a good price among collectors if its elaborate package is intact. Unfortunately, the booklet in Rykodisc's 1997 CD issue of **Fly** did not reproduce the poster with a photo of Lennon that was contained in the original LP package. A promotional film titled **Imagine** included portions of both albums. The film also included cameo appearances by George Harrison, Dick Cavett, Fred Astaire, and Andy Warhol, among other notables. Two of Yoko's songs were omitted from the VHS and laser laser video disk that were released in 1986.

Few who appreciate John's classic song ***Imagine*** realize that Yoko's book, **Grapefruit**, was its major lyrical inspiration. The inspiration for the song's melody may be even more unusual. In late 1965, John's father Freddie teamed up with a record producer and manager named Tony Cartwright. The two wrote and recorded an autobiographical song called ***That's My Life (My Love And My Home)***. It was released just weeks after John's autobiographical song ***In My Life***. Parts of ***That's My Life*** sound hauntingly like ***Imagine***. John was known to amuse friends by playing ***That's My Life***. It is conceivable that Freddie may have based his song on an early version of ***Imagine*** that John played for him or perhaps John, consciously or subconsciously, wrote ***Imagine*** based on ***That's My Life***. It would be more than a little ironic if the melody to one of John's biggest hits was actually borrowed from his wayward father.

On June 6, 1971, John and Yoko joined Frank Zappa And The Mothers Of Invention* for a jam onstage at New York's Fillmore East Theater. The performance was a combination of John and Yoko's experimental music fused with Zappa's free-form jazz and comedy. Much of **Jamrag** consisted of bits and pieces of well-known Zappa compositions. Due to the nature of the jam, song times for each "title" vary widely from release to release, and are an approximation at best. Some twenty years later, Zappa released his version of the performance with alternate titles that had a substantially different mix from the Lennon-Ono-Spector production.

By the fall of 1971, John and Yoko had taken up permanent residence in an apartment on Bank Street in the artist district of Greenwich Village in New York City. John referred to New York as the new Rome or Paris (the center of the world) and, being a seaport, it reminded him of his native Liverpool. To Yoko, New York was the place she called home much of her life. She was known and appreciated by the art community there, and could more effectively fight to secure custody of her daughter Kyoko.

On arrival in the Village, the Lennons were set upon by the vanguard of New York's radical-left political underground, from Ed Sanders (The Fugs) and Allen Ginsberg* to Jerry Rubin. John was also introduced to a politically active street musician named David Peel*, whose comical approach to protest songs appealed to the Lennons. Political message now took priority over music, resulting in a year's worth of mostly now-dated slogan songs that were John and Yoko's only true pop music collaborations. The first was the single ***Happy Xmas (War Is Over) / Listen, The Snow Is Falling***, originally issued on green vinyl for Christmas.

John and Yoko had been persuaded by their "new-left" friends to perform at the **John Sinclair Freedom Rally** benefit concert on December 10, 1971, in Ann Arbor, Michigan, to free Sinclair from prison. Sinclair was an underground newspaper editor, rock promoter, and manager of the Detroit rock group, The MC5 (Motor City Five). He was also organizer of Michigan's radical White Panther Party. Sinclair was sentenced to jail for ten years for selling two marijuana cigarettes to undercover police. John and Yoko could sympathize with the legal injustice obviously imposed because of Sinclair's political activities, something the Lennons would soon experience themselves.

Yoko Ono and Kristofer Engelhardt at the press reception for Ono's art exhibit at Crambrook Acadamy of Art Museum, Detroit, MI, 1993, photo by George Heritier

Taking the stage of Crisler Arena in Ann Arbor was a who's who of the radical, political left. A figure somewhat resembling John Lennon (actually David Peel) took the stage at about three in the morning to perform. John and Yoko, along with Rubin and others, soon took center stage in front of Peel. Lennon performed the song ***John Sinclair***, specially written for the performance, along with his and Yoko's political songs ***Luck Of The Irish*** and ***Attica State***. Yoko performed ***Sisters, O Sisters***, her newly written anthem to feminism and the women's movement. Within fifty-five hours of John and Yoko leaving the stage, Sinclair was free from prison.

The Lennons returned to the Record Plant (East) in New York to record overdubs on the tapes of the Ann Arbor show and to produce an album for Peel. Fueled by their political power through performance, John and Yoko appeared on December 17, 1971 at the famed Apollo Theater in New York at a benefit concert for the families of victims of the Attica State Prison riots. John performed ***Attica State*** and ***Imagine***, and Yoko performed ***Sisters, O Sisters***.

John and Yoko were in political high gear by the beginning of 1972. The couple began joining demonstrations and using national TV to spread their political message. Their first appearance was on **The David Frost Show** on January 13 (taped December 16, '71), backed by David Peel And The Lower East Side, performing the same set of political anthems they had on previous outings, including ***Sisters, O Sisters***.

During the week of February 14-18, John and Yoko were co-hosts of **Mike Douglas'** daytime-TV talk show. The Lennons were given free rein to do their thing, from musical performances, to cooking, biofeedback, participatory art, and heated political discussions. It was one of the most intimate and revealing views of the couple in public. They were backed by the New York hard-rock band Elephant's Memory*, for whom the Lennons would later produce an album on Apple. John performed his current solo songs and a historic jam with his childhood hero Chuck Berry*. Yoko performed ***Midsummer New York***, ***Sakura***, and ***Sisters, O Sisters***.

The couple's next major TV appearance was on the **Dick Cavett Show**, again backed by Elephant's Memory, with Yoko singing ***We're All Water*** and John singing the A-side of the couple's only single release of 1972, ***Woman Is The Nigger Of The World / Sisters, O Sisters***. The A-side's title and refrain were misconstrued and deemed highly offensive by most U.S. DJs. The single was included on John and Yoko's most collaborative and political work, the 1972 double album **Sometime In New York City**. The album's jacket featured highly controversial slogans and photos, including one with the heads of Richard Nixon and Chairman Mao superimposed on nude dancers. The album also featured a second "free" disc of the couple's performances with Zappa in New York the previous year and for UNICEF in London in 1969. The U.K. release of the single was canceled, and the album was delayed in the U.K. by several months due to a dispute with Lennon's music publishing company, Northern Songs, over the validity of Yoko's co-composing contributions. Unlike a similar dispute over Linda McCartney's co-composing contributions with Paul, Yoko's contributions were unmistakable. Yoko was also listed in the general credits as playing drums (congas), probably on ***We're All Water***.

Several months of Lennon's nationwide political attacks on his newly adopted homeland were more than President Nixon's administration would tolerate. Nixon's advisors feared Lennon would play his "Beatle card" and carry his anti-Nixon administration message in song all the way to the Republican National Convention in San Diego. On March 6, 1972, Lennon's visa extension was canceled by U.S. Immigrations, paving the way for his deportation. The official reason given was that he was an undesirable alien due to his drug conviction in England in 1968 – though, in fact, it was due to his leftist politics. The Lennons, on the advice of attorneys fighting John's deportation order, began taking a less offensive political tack.

The Lennons staged their first full-length performance for the **One-to-One** concert at Madison Square Garden on August 30, 1972, to benefit the mentally retarded. **One-to-One** was a charitable foundation fronted by TV commentator Geraldo Rivera, who at the time was exposing the deplorable conditions at New York State's Willowbrook home for the retarded. Yoko performed the following numbers during the two shows – ***Sisters O Sisters***, ***Born In A Prison***, ***We're All Water***, ***Open Your Box***, ***Move On Fast*** and ***Don't Worry Kyoko (Mummy's Only Looking For A Hand In The Snow)***." According to Gary Van Scyoc and Wayne Gabriel of Elephant's Memory, the rehearsals took place in New York City beginning at Butterfly Studios and finishing at the Fillmore East Theater. Some bootleg records of the rehearsals claim they were recorded at S.I.R. Studios, but S.I.R. first opened two years after the rehearsals. Other bootleg records of these rehearsals and the performance feature additional songs not on the official live album release. John and Yoko struck another charitable note the following week on the annual Labor Day weekend **Jerry Lewis Muscular Dystrophy Telethon** with Yoko performing ***Now Or Never***.

With Lennon effectively taken out of the anti-war / Nixon political picture, Yoko was free to pursue the less threatening fight for women's rights and feminism. She released a single ***Josei Joi Banzai / Josei Joi Banzai (Part 2)***, exclusive to Japan, and another double album set **Approximately Infinite Universe**, this time without benefit of a companion Lennon release. With the excellent backing of Elephant's Memory, and her blunt, reasoned and unique feminist message, the album gained Yoko many positive reviews. John was credited as playing guitar on two songs under the thinly veiled pseudonym of Joel Nohnn (John Lennon, rearranged), but it was obvious to the casual listener that Lennon made additional uncredited musical and vocal (Choir Boys) contributions to the album. According to Wayne Gabriel, Elephant's Memory (though not credited) was responsible for arranging all the songs on **Approximately Infinite Universe**. The album, like Ono's previous Apple releases, has become somewhat of a collector's item. During this period Elephant's Memory backed up Yoko on New York City's local PBS-TV musical program **Flip Side**.

On June 3, 1973, Yoko and John attended **The First International Feminist Planning Conference** at Harvard University. Yoko addressed the conference and performed a half-dozen or so songs accompanied by John on guitar. (Rykodisc released a portion of the address ***I Learned To Stutter*** and ***Coffin Car*** as bonus tracks on their CD release of **Feeling The Space**.)

While Yoko released several more singles in 1973, John maintained his necessary lower profile, but his confinement, and Yoko's increasing independence and feminist-activism were taking their toll on the marriage. With little musical activity, Elephant's Memory was let go.

Toward the end of 1973, Yoko issued an album of frustrated and bitter feminist songs titled **Feeling The Space** that she produced without John's help. The album did include contributions from John under the pseudonym of "John O'cean," and a photo of him was featured on the album's jacket. The Lennons' assistant, May Pang, seems to think that all of John's contributions to **Feeling The Space** were recorded during his one and only visit to the sessions. John went through the motions of recording a companion album, using the same backing musicians Yoko had gathered for her album. The album **Mind Games** and its title single were a welcome pop relief from a highly political period, but they would be John's only record releases of 1973.

Unused ticket for performance in Budapest, Hungary, 1985, courtesy of Ernoe Tihanui

John and Yoko decided to separate shortly after the completion of recordings for the album **Mind Games**. Lennon headed for the West Coast with May Pang, whom Yoko had instructed to accompany John. Once in Los Angeles, Lennon persuaded Phil Spector to produce an album of John singing his favorite rock 'n' roll oldies. Though Lennon describes this often over-intoxicated year-long period as his "lost weekend" or "Sindbad's Voyage," it proved to be the most productive period of his solo career.

This period was also a highly productive time for Yoko. She assembled a band, performing in New York clubs before embarking on a tour of Japan in August 1974. A promotional-only album, **Welcome: The Many Sides Of Yoko Ono**, was issued earlier in the year in Japan. It was a sort of current greatest hits album, with side one subtitled **Gentle and Emotional Yoko**, and side two **Rockin' and Driving Yoko**. Though the record did not contain any Lennon contributions that had not already been released elsewhere, the unique jacket photo included John. Yoko also recorded enough material for another solo album, tentatively titled **A Story**, using the same musicians as on **Feeling The Space**, but the album remained unreleased until 1992 when it was included as a part of **ONOBOX**.

In mid-1974, John returned to New York to finish up production on Harry Nilsson's* album **Pussy Cats**, and to record his album **Walls And Bridges**, chronicling his "lost weekend." Helping out on the single ***Whatever Gets You Through The Night*** was Elton John*, who convinced a skeptical Lennon that the song was a number one, and made him promise that if it topped the charts he would perform the number onstage with Elton. Much to Lennon's delight the song did go number one, but, to his horror, Elton made him keep his promise. On November 28, 1974, Lennon strolled out onstage to perform three numbers with Elton. In attendance was Yoko Ono, who met Lennon backstage. According to John and Yoko's version of the story, it rekindled their love. It sounds romantic, but in reality John and Yoko had maintained almost daily contact during their separation. Though John's relationship with Yoko did seem to improve in the last quarter of 1974, he was still living with May Pang, and, because of legal obligations, was determined to finish up recording his **Rock 'N' Roll** oldies album begun the previous year with Phil Spector in Los Angeles.

Yoko's Japanese single ***Yume O Moto / It Happened*** proved to be her last release of the decade. The B-side credited production to Yoko and studio musician, Dave Spinozza, her companion during much of her separation from John. The song was released for the first time elsewhere as the B-Side of ***Walking On Thin Ice*** in 1981.

Shortly after the dawn of 1975, John went back to live with Yoko at their Dakota Apartments in New York City, which was home for the remainder of his life. Yoko soon became pregnant with the only child she would bear for John, Sean Ono Lennon, born on his father's birthday, October 9, 1975. It was a momentous time for the Lennons – just two days earlier John's deportation order was permanently dropped, and some nine months later John was granted U.S. residence.

These events marked the beginning of what would become John and Yoko's nearly five-year retirement from public life and recording. John adopted a role reversal, becoming a "house husband," and Yoko took on the task of managing the Lennons' financial affairs. With John now able to leave the U.S. without fear of being denied readmission, the couple was free to travel, and used the opportunity to make extended visits to Yoko's family in Japan. Save for the occasional news article about the sale of one of Yoko's prized cows or the couple's move into the high society of Palm Beach, Florida, little else of John and Yoko's life behind the gates of the Dakota was known to the eager public. It was quite an about-face for a couple that had promoted their entire relationship in public. This period in John and Yoko's life is the least understood, and the subject of great speculation, spawning a number of negative, kiss-and-tell-all books.

In early June 1980, John was part of a small crew sailing from New York to Bermuda. The journey proved perilous, and the experience gave Lennon the confidence he seemed to be lacking to step back into the public spotlight. John phoned Yoko from Bermuda with renditions of several new songs, along with the numbers he had written from the bits and pieces of unfinished material during his nearly five years of retirement. This in turn inspired Yoko to record, under the name "friends," over a dozen-and-a-half of her songs in late June and early July 1980 at the Record Plant (East) Studios. These recordings, produced by Roy Cicala *(see Lori Burton)* were never used. Most of the songs (some with new titles) were re-recorded elsewhere and subsequently released. Like John's songs, some were leftovers, including ***Hard Times Are Over***, that dated back to 1973.

Following John's return to New York, the two booked time at New York's Hit Factory Studios with the idea of combining the best of each artist's recordings for a John and Yoko album to be titled **Double Fantasy**. The remainder of the tracks would be refined at a later date for a follow-up album to be titled **Milk And Honey**. As happened early in their partnership, the singles from both albums would feature John on the A-side and Yoko on the B-side. Critics, happy to finally have a new release from John, were kind in their reviews, especially of Yoko's material. According to Jack Douglas, John contributed guitar to all of Yoko's songs from the sessions that he helped the couple produce.

By 1980, artists like The B-52's, whose style was reminiscent of Yoko's early experimental recordings, were making a "new wave" in the musical charts. John felt certain the musical times had finally caught up with Yoko, and that the time was right to promote her as a solo artist. On December 8, 1980, time caught up with John Lennon as he stopped to sign what proved to be his death warrant for a deranged "fan" patiently hanging around the entrance to the Dakota building. The couple were on their way to the studio to finish work on what John felt sure was Yoko's first number one, a song called ***Walking On Thin Ice***. When John returned to the Dakota that night, the same deranged individual gunned him down in the entrance way. It was the day the music died. The dream was over.

Yoko, like Paul McCartney, seemed best able to cope with grief by turning to her work. On February 6, 1981, ***Walking On Thin Ice / It Happened*** was released to sympathetic, if not favorable, reviews and was her biggest success, especially on the Disco charts. The B-side was a remixed version of the Japanese-only release from 1974, but its credit insert lists John and Yoko as producer in 1973, and additionally lists Jack Douglas as co-producer on the record label. The insert also lists John, Yoko and Douglas as editors and re-mixers.

Yoko's first album following John's death was appropriately titled **Season Of Glass**. Many felt the album photo of John's bloodstained glasses from the night he was killed, and the inclusion of gun shots on one song, were in poor taste. The album was a reflection of Yoko's grief and anger over the loss of John. It used the same studio and musicians that were used on the **Double Fantasy / Milk And Honey** sessions. In fact, several of the songs had originally been recorded during the **Double Fantasy / Milk And Honey** sessions. Of these, ***No One Sees Me Like You Do***, featuring John on rhythm guitar, was included on one of **The Lost Lennon Tapes** radio series promotional albums. The song was written in 1973, but was re-recorded and retitled ***Nobody Sees Me Like You Do***, without Lennon's guitar work for **Season Of Glass**. Though the album fared well in the charts, the singles released from it did not.

In June 1981, Yoko was sued for plagiarism by the publishers of the song ***Makin' Whoopee***, claiming Yoko's song, ***Yes, I'm Your Angel***, from **Double Fantasy**, was copied from it. It probably was not intentional, but it signaled the beginning of a period of personnel and legal attacks on Yoko following John's death. Yoko's next album release, **It's Alright**, came a year and a half later and featured a ghost-like photo of John on the jacket's back and his voice mixed into the song ***Never Say Goodbye***.

Yoko, having proclaimed herself the "keeper of the wishing well," now began portioning out the remainder of the couple's unreleased material, starting with an interview album titled **Heart Play-unfinished dialogue**, on December 5, 1983. It was designed to promote the January 1984 release of the long promised **Milk And Honey** album, the cover of which was a colored version of the **Double Fantasy** format. The majority of the basic tracks were recorded during the August / September 1980 sessions for **Double Fantasy**, though, due to a dispute with Ono, co-producer Jack Douglas was not credited.

The years immediately following John's death were not easy ones for Yoko. Several books, some by former employees and associates, were highly critical of her character, and many of her and John's personal belongings were stolen by an ex-employee – though fortunately most of them were recovered. One diversion from her problems was the release of a 50th birthday tribute album of her compositions performed by a number of well-known guest artists including Harry Nilsson*, Elvis Costello*, Spirit Choir*, John Lennon (singing his version of ***Every Man Has A Woman Who Loves Him***), and the Lennons' son Sean (singing ***It's Alright***).

Yoko Ono, photo courtesy of Tom Bert

In late 1984, Yoko joined forces with Paul McCartney in an attempt to buy back Northern Songs Publishing, the Lennon and McCartney songwriting catalogue, but they were out-bid by Michael Jackson*. Toward the end of 1984, a documentary film titled **Yoko Ono Then And Now** was aired and released on laser video disk, featuring footage of Lennon and The Beatles.

Yoko released the album **Starpeace** in the fall of 1985, and backed up the release with a brief world tour several months later. On February 21, 1986, she released the album **John Lennon – Live In New York City** from the **One-to-One** concert. The companion laser video disk (and VHS) contained two of her songs from the performance. Yoko continued to release Lennon-related material throughout the later half of the 1980s including books, films, videos, and recordings, the most ambitious being the nearly five-year long Westwood One Radio series **The Lost Lennon Tapes**. The series featured unreleased Lennon rarities including home demos, out-takes, interviews, and poetry readings by John. In 1989, Yoko began holding exhibits of three decades of her art.

In 1990, a five-song benefit CD titled **Happy Birthday, John** was given a limited release in Japan only. It included three mixes of Yoko singing John's song ***Love***. The CD also included Sean's cover of his father's Beatles song ***Dear Prudence***, also included on the 1991 laser video disk **The World's Greatest Artists Sing LENNON A Tribute**.

A six-CD box-set retrospective of Yoko's career titled **ONOBOX** was released in March 1992. It includes edited and unedited versions of most of her recordings, along with the previously unreleased album **A Story** from 1974. (**A Story** was also released by Rykodisc separately in 1997.) The set also includes a previously unreleased John and Yoko composition titled ***The Path***. Included in the set is a booklet that sheds additional light on Lennon's involvement with Yoko's recordings. (The box set was also available as a mail-order-only limited edition of 350 **ONOBOX ULTRACASE** that additionally included the separately released **Walking On Thin Ice** compilation CD of highlights from the **ONOBOX** set and the sculpture **A Key To Open A Universe**, numbered and signed by Yoko.)

Yoko toured with exhibitions of new artwork in 1993. She contributed a three-movement, 20-minute song called ***Georgia Stone*** that spanned 28 tracks on a double CD titled **A Chance Operation (The John Cage Tribute)**. Track 73 contained an excerpt of John Lennon talking.

On January 19, 1994, Ono and McCartney embraced at ceremonies in New York to induct John

Lennon into the Rock and Roll Hall of Fame. Following the ceremonies, Yoko turned over some of John's unreleased demos to McCartney, to be used for the creation of a new Beatles' recording. That year, an album was issued featuring Yoko's music from the off-Broadway musical **New York Rock**, loosely based on the lives of John and Yoko.

Yoko and Sean visited Paul McCartney at his home in East Sussex, England on March 11, 1995. While at the McCartneys, Yoko recorded her song ***Hiroshima, Sky is Always Blue***, with Sean on guitar; Paul on bass, backing vocals and probably production; Linda on celeste; their son James on guitar; and daughters Heather, Stella and Mary on percussion and backing vocals. Though the song has yet to be officially released, it was premiered on August 6, 1995 on Japanese television to observe the 50th anniversary of the dropping of the atomic bomb.

In November 1995, Ono released her first album in ten years, titled **Rising**, recorded with backing by son Sean and his band IMA. That year she reestablished contact with her daughter Kyoko. Yoko toured with IMA in the spring of 1996.

Yoko still resides at the Dakota Apartments, managing the Lennon estate and archives. She promises future Lennon releases, including recordings that were aired on **The Lost Lennon Tapes** radio series. One thing is certain – Yoko Ono will not quietly fade away, but will continue to champion causes, be artistically creative, and keep John's music and message alive.

Roy Orbison

Record 268 title:
Mystery Girl
Media:
Album 5" CD
Label / Catalog number:
Virgin / 2-91058
Producer:
Jeff Lynne
Jacket / Inserts:
Standard international design in jewel box / 12 booklet
Recording Location / Date:
A&M, Rumbo Recorders &/or Chapel Studios, Los Angeles, CA & FPSHOT (Friar Park Studio, Henley-on-Thames)†, U.K. / 1988

Song 268a title:
A Love So Beautiful
Track details:
Side 1, track 4 / 3 min. 30 sec.
Release date / Country:
02 Feb 89 / U.S.A.
Composer:
J. Lynne & R. Orbison

Roy Orbison: Lead Vocals & Acoustic Guitar; Jeff Lynne: Acoustic Guitar, Keyboards, B. Vocals & Bass; George Harrison: Acoustic Guitar;† Ray Cooper: Drums; Louis Clark: String Conductor

Record 269 title:
The Very Best of Roy Orbison
Media:
Album 5"
Label / Catalog number:
Virgin / 7243 8 42350 2 4
Producer:
Mike Utley, Roy Orbison, Jeff Lynne, T. Bone Burnett, David Lynch, Don Was, David Was, Peter Anderson & N. Petty
Jacket / Inserts:
Standard international design in jewel box / 12 CD booklet with Liner note by George Harrison
Recording Location / Date:
1955 - 1988

Release date / Country:
Mar 97 / U.S.A.

Roy Orbison: Lead Vocals

Composer:
R. Orbison - J. Melson - J. Lynne - T. Petty - W. Dees - J. Williams - C. Walker - C. Demetrius - W. Moore - D. Penner - W. Nelson - B. Steinberg - T. Kelly

Roy Orbison was born April 23, 1936 in Vernon, but was raised in Wink, Texas. Orbison began his musical career in 1954 with the country and western group The Wink Westerners. Orbison and his group, now called The Teen Kings, sent their 1955 release ***Ooby Dooby***, on the Je-Wel label, to Sam Phillips of Sun Records in Memphis. Phillips signed Roy Orbison & The Teen Kings, who re-recorded ***Ooby Dooby*** for Sun, making it a hit in 1956. At the time, Sun was fostering the talents of rock legends Elvis Presley, Jerry Lee Lewis, Johnny Cash* and Carl Perkins*. The Teen Kings disbanded, but Sun issued several singles by Orbison, though none were successful.

Orbison began to concentrate more on writing sophisticated love ballads and pop-rock songs, highlighting his wide vocal range. In 1957 he left Sun, moved to Nashville, and began writing for the prestigious Acuff-Rose Song Publishing Co. His song ***Claudette***, written for his wife, became a B-side hit for The Everly Brothers* in 1958. Orbison signed with RCA records in 1959, but his Chet Atkins* produced recordings met with little success. In 1960, he signed with the newly formed Monument Records label and began his four-year string of top 10 songs that included ***Only The Lonely***, ***Blue Angel***, ***Running Scared***, ***Crying***, ***Dream Baby***, ***In Dreams***, ***Mean Woman Blues***, ***It's Over*** and finally ***Oh, Pretty Woman*** in 1964.

Orbison was one of the few American rock stars to thrive in the charts during the height of Beatlemania and the British music invasion. Orbison was no stranger to Beatlemania. During his 1963 U.K. tour he had to give up his top billing to The Beatles. At the beginning of the tour he recalled asking those around him who The Beatles were, only to be reminded by John Lennon who was standing behind him. Ironically, The Beatles were big fans of his and performed his song ***Dream Baby*** on their first BBC radio performance broadcast on March 8, 1962. During that tour, Orbison praised The Beatles in the U.K. music press and began wearing the dark sunglasses that would become his trademark.

When The Beatles first brought ***Please Please Me*** to their producer George Martin, he thought it could be a hit, but that it sounded too much like a Roy Orbison song. Not surprising – as Lennon later admitted that his writing of ***Please Please Me*** was a deliberate attempt at writing a Roy Orbison-styled song. The Beatles reworked it into the more up-tempo version that became their first number-one song in the U.K. Orbison was also on the set of The Beatles' first film **A Hard Day's Night**, egging John Lennon on during his famous bathtub scene.

Roy Orbison's successes were suddenly followed by a lengthy period of failures and tragedies. His divorce from Claudette, and his signing with MGM Records, in 1965 seemed to sound the death knell of his career. Though he would quickly re-marry Claudette, the marriage ended in tragedy on June 6, 1966, when she was hit and killed by a truck while she and Roy were riding their motorcycles. Two years later on August 5, 1968, while on tour, Orbison's house caught fire killing two of his three sons. Shortly after the tragedy, Orbison married German-born Barbara Wellhonen and moved to Germany for several years. Unfortunately, the tragic events of the past began to take a toll on his health, and he began suffering from ulcers and heart disease. In 1978, he underwent heart by-pass surgery.

In 1986, Orbison moved to Malibu, California and began making successful live appearances again. During the **Sgt. Pepper** 20th anniversary party at Abbey Road Studios on June 1, 1987, Paul McCartney recounted to Orbison how ***Please Please Me*** was originally rejected for sounding too much like an Orbison number. Orbison found McCartney receptive to the idea of producing Orbison recording the song as it was originally intended to sound. Orbison also considered approaching George Harrison to give him a hand recording the song.

In 1987, Roy Orbison was inducted into the Rock and Roll Hall of Fame, but 1988 would be the year of his come back. Jeff Lynne*, who had just produced George Harrison's comeback album **Cloud Nine**, was recruited to produce albums for Tom Petty* and Roy Orbison. Harrison was looking for some help in recording a new B-side for a single, and Lynne suggested Orbison and Petty. Bob

Dylan's* home studio was suggested as the meeting place, and along with veteran studio drummer Jim Keltner *(see Attitudes)*, they formed what would become the "supergroup," Traveling Wilburys.

The ultimate tragedy struck on December 6, 1988, when Roy Orbison died of a massive heart attack while visiting his mother. Harrison, Lynne and Petty were pallbearers at Orbison's funeral. Fortunately, the album that Orbison was recording with Lynne during breaks in recordings for Traveling Wilburys was essentially completed, and posthumously released as **Mystery Girl**. It contained ***You Got It***, Orbison's last top 10 song.

The album credits ***You Got It*** as being mixed at Harrison's home studio, but Lynne seems certain it was mixed at Rumbo Recorders in Los Angeles. Lynne said, "We did so many sessions at that point with all the Wilburys that George may have played acoustic guitar on ***You Got It***." However, Lynne thinks, based on the rest of the album's credits, which he believes to be correct, that Harrison probably did not contribute to ***You Got It***. Fellow Wilbury Harrison is credited as playing guitar on ***A Love So Beautiful*** from the album. Lynne is not aware of Harrison contributing to any other of Roy Orbison's recordings.

A brief clip of Orbison singing ***Help!*** was included on the 1991 laser videodisk **The World's Greatest Artists Sing LENNON A Tribute**. In 1997, Virgin Records issued (mail order only in the U.S.) **The Very Best Of Roy Orbison** which contains a brief ode in the liner notes from, among others, George Harrison.

Buck Owens Duet with Ringo Starr

Record 270 title:
Act Naturally
Label / Catalog number:
Capitol / CDP 7 92893 2
Jacket / Inserts:
Standard international design in jewel box / 8 page CD booklet with photo of Ringo Starr
Recording Location / Date:
EMI-Abbey Road Studios, London, U.K. / 27 Mar 89

Media:
Album 5" CD
Producer:
Jerry Crutchfield & Jim Shaw

Song 270a title:
Act Naturally
Release date / Country:
04 Oct 89 (first issued 21 Jun 89) / U.S.A.

Track details:
Side 1, track 5 / 2 min. 59 sec.
Composer:
J. Russell - V. Morrison

Buck Owens: Vocals; Ringo Starr: Vocals; Terry Christoffersen: Rhythm Guitar; Reggie Young: Lead Guitar; Jim McCarty: Drums; Doyle Curtsinger: Bass; Jim Shaw: Piano

Buck Owens was born Alvis Edgar Owens Jr. on August 12, 1929 in Sherman, Texas. When Buck, as he preferred to be called, was eight his family moved to Mesa, Arizona. By the time Buck was a teenager, he had developed a passionate interest in the guitar, and was playing in country bands by age sixteen. He soon married and moved to Bakersfield, California, a town made up largely of Southern and Midwestern transplants from the Dust-Bowl era. It was in this environment that Owens and others, such as Ferlin Husky and Merle Haggard, developed a more urban, western style of country music, making Bakersfield its western capitol.

Owens began turning out number-one country hits in rapid-fire succession starting with ***Under Your Spell Again*** in 1959 and ***Excuse Me (I Think I've Got A Heartache)*** the following year. In 1963 he had one of his biggest hits with the song ***Act Naturally***, that created quite a controversy in country music because it included a pronounced drum track.

In 1965, The Beatles recorded ***Act Naturally*** as their song-per-album that featured Ringo on vocals.

The song took on added significance because Ringo was considered by many critics to be the most natural actor of The Beatles, making it as much Ringo's theme song as Buck's. Not surprisingly, The Beatles (and Ringo in particular) were fans of Buck Owens. The admiration was mutual. Owens had long been a professed Beatles fan, and took more than a little criticism from some of his peers in country music because of it.

Throughout the later half of the 1960s, he and his backing band, The Buckaroos, became one of country music's most popular acts. Owens became a familiar household name between 1969 and 1986 when he co-hosted the country music comedy TV show **Hee Haw**. He returned to the top of the country charts in 1988 on a duet with Dwight Yoakam of ***Streets Of Bakersfield***, which Owens had also recorded in 1972.

In 1989, Ringo teamed up with Owens to record a duet of ***Act Naturally***. It was released as a single and appeared on Owens' album of the same name. Ringo also appeared in the music video for the song. The ***Act Naturally*** promotional CD single has become a rare collector's item. Today, even in semi-retirement, Buck Owens continues to be one of the reigning kings of country music.

David Peel & The Lower East Side

Record 271 title:
John Lennon For President
Label / Catalog number:
Orange / ORA 005
Jacket / Inserts:
Unique with photos of John Lennon on front & back jacket
Recording Location / Date:
Record Plant (East) Studios, New York, NY, U.S.A. / (probably) Jun 72
Media:
Album 12"
Producer:
John Lennon & Yoko Ono

Song 271a title:
Amerika
Release date / Country:
11 Nov 80 / U.S.A.
Track details:
Side 1, track 4 / 9 min. 29 sec.
Composer:
D. Peel

David Peel: Lead Vocals & Guitar; Yoko Ono: B. Vocals & Percussion; The Lower East Side: Instruments

Record 272 title:
The Pope Smokes Dope
Label / Catalog number:
Apple / SW 3391
Jacket / Inserts:
Unique / Custom inner-sleeve
Media:
Album 12"

Song 272a title:
Everybody's Smoking Marijuana
Release date / Country:
17 Apr 72 / U.S.A.
Track details:
Side 1, track 2 / 4 min. 06 sec.
Composer:
D. Peel
Producer:
John Lennon & Yoko Ono & (probably) David Peel
Recording Location / Date:
Record Plant (East) & (probably) Audio Techniques Studios†, New York, NY, U.S.A. / 13 Dec 71 & (probably) spring or summer 1971†

David Peel: Lead Vocals & (probable) Guitar; additionally, one or more of the following: Eddie

Mottau: Guitar; Chris Osborne: Guitar; Eddie Ryan: Drums; The Lower East Side Friends: Chorus; Tom Doyle: Guitar & B. Vocals; Bruce Bierman: B. Vocals; John Robertson: Guitar; Billy Minelli: Bass; Frank Lanci: Drums

Song 272b title:
F Is Not A Dirty Word
Release date / Country:
17 Apr 72 / U.S.A.
Producer:
John Lennon & Yoko Ono
Recording Location / Date:
Record Plant (East) Studios, New York, NY, U.S.A. / 13 Dec 71
Track details:
Side 1, track 3 / 3 min. 12 sec.
Composer:
D. Peel - Trad

David Peel: Lead Vocals & (probable) Guitar; additionally, one or more of the following: Eddie Mottau: Guitar; Chris Osborne: Guitar; Eddie Ryan: Drums; The Lower East Side Friends: Chorus; Tom Doyle: Guitar & B. Vocals; Bruce Bierman: B. Vocals; John Robertson: Guitar; Billy Minelli: Bass; Frank Lanci: Drums

Song 272c title:
I'm A Runaway
Release date / Country:
17 Apr 72 / U.S.A.
Producer:
John Lennon & Yoko Ono
Recording Location / Date:
Record Plant (East) Studios, New York, NY, U.S.A. / 13 Dec 71
Track details:
Side 1, track 1 / 3 min. 39 sec.
Composer:
D. Peel

David Peel: Lead Vocals & (probable) Guitar; Lenny Mars: Flute, Percussion & Banjo; Yoko Ono: Percussion; additionally, one or more of the following: Eddie Mottau: Guitar; Chris Osborne: Guitar; Eddie Ryan: Drums; The Lower East Side Friends: Chorus; Tom Doyle: Guitar & B. Vocals; Bruce Bierman: B. Vocals; John Robertson: Guitar; Billy Minelli: Bass; Frank Lanci: Drums

Song 272d title:
I'm Gonna Start Another Riot
Release date / Country:
17 Apr 72 / U.S.A.
Producer:
John Lennon & Yoko Ono & (probably) David Peel
Recording Location / Date:
Record Plant (East) & (probably) Audio Techniques Studios†, New York, NY, U.S.A. / 13 & 22 Dec 71 & (probably) spring or summer 1971†
Track details:
Side 2, track 4 / 2 min. 37 sec.
Composer:
D. Peel

David Peel: Lead Vocals & (probable) Guitar; Lenny Mars: Percussion & Mandolin; additionally, one or more of the following: Eddie Mottau: Guitar; Chris Osborne: Guitar; Eddie Ryan: Drums; The Lower East Side Friends: Chorus; Tom Doyle: Guitar & B. Vocals; Bruce Bierman: B. Vocals; John Robertson: Guitar; Billy Minelli: Bass; Frank Lanci: Drums

Song 272e title:
McDonald's Farm
Release date / Country:
17 Apr 72 / U.S.A.
Producer:
John Lennon & Yoko Ono
Recording Location / Date:
Record Plant (East) Studios, New York, NY, U.S.A. / 13 Dec 71
Track details:
Side 1, track 5 / 3 min. 13 sec.
Composer:
D. Peel

David Peel: Lead Vocals & (probable) Guitar; additionally, one or more of the following: Eddie Mottau: Guitar; Chris Osborne: Guitar; Eddie Ryan: Drums; The Lower East Side Friends: Chorus; Tom Doyle: Guitar & B. Vocals; Bruce Bierman: B. Vocals; John Robertson: Guitar; Billy Minelli: Bass; Frank Lanci: Drums

Song 272f title:
The Ballad Of Bob Dylan
Release date / Country:
17 Apr 72 / U.S.A.
Producer:
John Lennon & Yoko Ono
Recording Location / Date:
Record Plant (East) Studios, New York, NY, U.S.A. / 22 Dec 71
Track details:
Side 2, track 1 / 3 min. 19 sec.
Composer:
D. Peel

David Peel: Lead Vocals & (probable) Guitar; Lenny Mars: Harp, Piano, Banjo & Mandolin; Eddie Mottau: Guitar; Chris Osborne: Guitar; additionally, one or more of the following: Eddie Ryan: Drums; The Lower East Side Friends: Chorus; Tom Doyle: Guitar & B. Vocals; Bruce Bierman: B. Vocals; John Robertson: Guitar; Billy Minelli: Bass; Frank Lanci: Drums

Song 272g title:
The Ballad of New York City /
John Lennon-Yoko Ono
Release date / Country:
17 Apr 72 / U.S.A.
Producer:
John Lennon & Yoko Ono
Recording Location / Date:
Record Plant (East) Studios, New York, NY, U.S.A. / 13 Dec 71
Track details:
Side 1, track 6 / 3 min. 19 sec.
Composer:
D. Peel

David Peel: Lead Vocals & (probable) Guitar; Lenny Mars: Flutes; Eddie Mottau: Guitar; Chris Osborne: Guitar; John Lennon: Voice; Yoko Ono: Voice; additionally, one or more of the following: Eddie Ryan: Drums; The Lower East Side Friends: Chorus; Tom Doyle: Guitar & B. Vocals; Bruce Bierman: B. Vocals; John Robertson: Guitar; Billy Minelli: Bass; Frank Lanci: Drums

Song 272h title:
The Birth Control Blues
Release date / Country:
17 Apr 72 / U.S.A.
Track details:
Side 2, track 5 / 4 min. 48 sec.
Composer:
D. Peel [E. Sanders - T. Kupferberg - K. Weaver]
Producer:
John Lennon & Yoko Ono & (probably) David Peel
Recording Location / Date:
Record Plant (East) & (probably) Audio Techniques Studios†, New York, NY, U.S.A. / 13 & 22 Dec 71 & (probably) spring or summer 1971†

David Peel: Lead Vocals & (probable) Guitar; additionally, one or more of the following: Eddie Mottau: Guitar; Chris Osborne: Guitar; Eddie Ryan: Drums; The Lower East Side Friends: Chorus; Tom Doyle: Guitar & B. Vocals; Bruce Bierman: B. Vocals; John Robertson: Guitar; Billy Minelli: Bass; Frank Lanci: Drums

Song 272i title:
The Chicago Conspiracy
Release date / Country:
17 Apr 72 / U.S.A.
Track details:
Side 2, track 2 / 3 min. 47 sec.
Composer:
D. Peel
Producer:
John Lennon & Yoko Ono & (probably) David Peel
Recording Location / Date:
Record Plant (East) & (probably) Audio Techniques Studios†, New York, NY, U.S.A. / 13 & 22 Dec 71 & (probably) spring or summer 1971†

David Peel: Lead Vocals & (probable) Guitar; Lenny Mars: Flute & Percussion; additionally, one or more of the following: Eddie Mottau: Guitar; Chris Osborne: Guitar; Eddie Ryan: Drums; The Lower East Side Friends: Chorus; Tom Doyle: Guitar & B. Vocals; Bruce Bierman: B. Vocals; John Robertson: Guitar; Billy Minelli: Bass; Frank Lanci: Drums

Song 272j title:
The Hip Generation
Release date / Country:
17 Apr 72 / U.S.A.
Producer:
John Lennon & Yoko Ono
Recording Location / Date:
Record Plant (East) Studios, New York, NY, U.S.A. / 13 & 22 Dec 71
Track details:
Side 2, track 3 / 1 min. 50 sec.
Composer:
D. Peel

David Peel: Lead Vocals & (probable) Guitar; additionally, one or more of the following: Eddie Mottau: Guitar; Chris Osborne: Guitar; Eddie Ryan: Drums; The Lower East Side Friends: Chorus; Tom Doyle: Guitar & B. Vocals; Bruce Bierman: B. Vocals; John Robertson: Guitar; Billy Minelli: Bass; Frank Lanci: Drums

Song 272k title:
The Hippie From New York City
Release date / Country:
17 Apr 72 / U.S.A.
Producer:
John Lennon & Yoko Ono
Recording Location / Date:
Record Plant (East) Studios, New York, NY, U.S.A. / 14 Dec 71
Track details:
Side 1, track 4 / 3 min. 01 sec.
Composer:
D. Peel

David Peel: Lead Vocals & (probable) Guitar; Lenny Mars: Harp, Flute & Banjo; additionally, one or more of the following: Eddie Mottau: Guitar; Chris Osborne: Guitar; Eddie Ryan: Drums; The Lower East Side Friends: Chorus; Tom Doyle: Guitar & B. Vocals; Bruce Bierman: B. Vocals; John Robertson: Guitar; Billy Minelli: Bass; Frank Lanci: Drums

Song 272l title:
The Pope Smokes Dope
Release date / Country:
17 Apr 72 / U.S.A.
Producer:
John Lennon & Yoko Ono
Recording Location / Date:
Record Plant (East) Studios, New York, NY, U.S.A. / (probably) Nov &/or Dec 71
Track details:
Side 1, track 6 / 2 min. 15 sec.
Composer:
D. Peel

David Peel: Lead Vocals & (probable) Guitar; John Lennon: Voice & (possible) B. Vocals; Lenny Mars: Mandolin, Flute & Percussion; additionally, one or more of the following: Eddie Mottau: Guitar; Chris Osborne: Guitar; Eddie Ryan: Drums; The Lower East Side Friends: Chorus; Tom Doyle: Guitar & B. Vocals; Bruce Bierman: B. Vocals; John Robertson: Guitar; Billy Minelli: Bass; Frank Lanci: Drums

David Peel was born David Rosario in New York City, New York on August 3, 1942. He gained notoriety in the 1960s as one of Greenwich Village's most visible and outrageous street singers. He recorded two albums for Elektra Records, **Have A Marijuana** in 1968, and **The American Revolution** in 1970. He has also long been one of America's most outspoken activists for the legalization of marijuana.

In 1971, New York's radical activists introduced David Peel to the Village's newest resident, John Lennon. Lennon admired Peel's raw, street-wise political message and outrageous humor, and offered to record Peel for Apple Records. John and Yoko *(see Yoko Ono)* began producing Peel's album **The Pope Smokes Dope** at the Record Plant (East) in New York City just days after their performance with Peel at the John Sinclair Freedom Rally held in Ann Arbor, Michigan on December 10, 1971.

According to Peel, he began recording and producing the songs ***I'm Gonna Start Another Riot***, ***The Chicago Conspiracy***, ***Birth Control Blues***, and probably ***Everybody's Smoking Marijuana*** in the spring or summer of 1971, at what was then called Audio Techniques Studios in New York City. These songs were finished up or completely re-recorded and produced by John Lennon at Record Plant. The

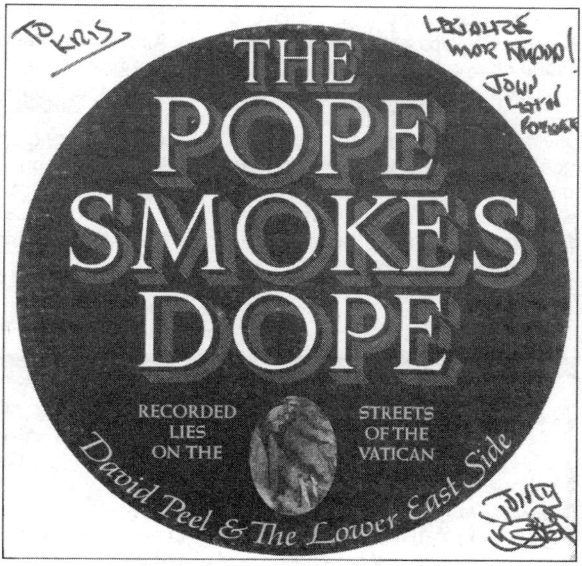

album's controversial title and lyrics, and the promotional single, ***F [Fuck] Is Not A Dirty Word***, could hardly have expected to receive airplay. Not surprisingly, the song was left off the lyric insert of the album.

It has been reported in a number of publications that John Lennon contributed backing vocals or played Dobro guitar on several of the songs on **The Pope Smokes Dope**. Author John Robertson (not the John Robertson who played on the album), in his book **The Art & Music Of John Lennon** lists Lennon as playing Dobro guitar and singing backing vocals on ***The Ballad of New York City / John Lennon - Yoko Ono*** and ***The Pope Smokes Dope***. Perhaps Robertson is referring to John talking at the beginning of these songs. Lower East Side guitarist Tom Doyle, and engineer Dennis Ferrante, who were present for some of the recordings, think John may have sung backing vocals on ***Hippie From New York City***, and possibly ***I'm A Runaway***. However, David Peel said, "I wish I could say John sang and played on my album, but I'm not aware of it and nobody told me he did. I'd never forget something like that! I know there are books that say he did, but it's never been confirmed. With 16 tracks I wasn't in control of everything; maybe they added something when I wasn't there, I don't know." Peel remains highly skeptical about claims that John Lennon played or sang backing vocals on **The Pope Smokes Dope** album. Lenny Rothbart, known at the time of the recordings as Lenny Mars, said Eddie Mottau and Chris Osborne played guitar on ***The Ballad of New York City / John Lennon - Yoko Ono***. (Though Peel is credited as having written all the tracks on the album, the song ***The Birth Control Blues*** contains portions of The Fugs' songs ***Saran Wrap***, ***Slum Goddess***, and ***Nothing***.)

On December 16, 1971, John Lennon and Yoko Ono taped their appearance on **The David Frost Show** broadcast on January 13, 1972. The Lennons arranged for David Peel And The Lower East Side to perform on the show. John, accompanied by Yoko on percussion, played washtub bass on ***The Ballad Of New York City / John Lennon - Yoko Ono*** and ***The Hippie From New York City***, on which he also sang backing vocals.

The following month, the Lennons teamed up with the group Elephant's Memory* who acted as their backup band for their album **Some Time In New York City**. The album included the song ***New York City***, that chronicles Lennon's introduction to Peel, and features a photo of Peel in performance with Lennon in Ann Arbor on its cover.

Peel was instrumental in helping Lennon organize the **One-To-One** benefit concert on August 30, 1972 at Madison Square Garden, and joined in the ***Give Peace A Chance*** encore. It was during this period that Lennon, in a battle with immigration to stay in the U.S., was advised to avoid radicals like Peel, and adopt a lower political profile.

Peel has since released several recordings highlighting his association with Lennon. One record, Peel's 1977 album **Bring Back The Beatles** (Orange / 6001), includes ***My Fat Budgie*** that appends a Peel melody to Lennon's **A Spaniard In The Works** poem ***The Fat Budgie***. The album also includes Peel's cover of The Beatles' song ***With A Little Help From My Friends***, and a cover of Lennon's song ***Imagine***. Among those in Peel's backing band on the album was Leslie Fradkin *(see Thornton, Fradkin & Unger And The Big Band)*.

Peel's 1980 album **John Lennon For President** features interviews with John and Yoko. The album also contains the Lennon-produced song ***Amerika***, recorded following the sessions for **The Pope**

Smokes Dope, and first released on the soundtrack for the motion picture **Please Stand By**. ***Amerika*** was also issued in Jeff Levy's book **Apple Log IV** as a single, featuring a picture of Lennon on the sleeve. Peel also issued a picture disc single, ***In My Life***, (not the Lennon and McCartney song) with a photo of John, Yoko and Peel and an interview with Lennon on the other side.

David Peel is still active in the New York City music scene and plans to issue some of his recordings on CD, including his performance with the Lennons on **The David Frost Show**. He continues to promote the memory of The Beatles and his admiration for John Lennon by attending the annual song rally held every October 9 in a portion of New York's Central Park called Strawberry Fields, dedicated to Lennon. He was featured in the 1989 Japanese made-for-TV documentary **John Lennon - Love & Peace**.

Carl Perkins

Record 273 title:
Artifacts III (Free As A Bird: 1981-1994)
Label / Catalog number:
Big Music / 9 BIGBX 009.4 (BIG 4036) [unauthorized release]
Jacket / Inserts:
Unique in Jewel box in box set with photos of The Beatles / 24 page box set booklet & (4) 2 page CD inserts
Recording Location / Date:
AIR Studios, Montserrat, West Indies / (probably) 24 Feb 81

Media:
Album 5" CD [4 CD set]
Producer:
George Martin

Song 273a title:
My Old Friend [original version]
Release date / Country:
(probably) Feb 95 / Italy

Track details:
CD4, track 1 / 3 min. 20 sec.
Composer:
C. Perkins

Carl Perkins: Lead Vocals; Paul McCartney: Keyboards, Guitar, Drums, Bass & B. Vocals

Record 274 title:
Blue Suede Shoes (A Rockabilly Session with Carl Perkins and Friends Starring George Harrison, Ringo Starr, Eric Clapton, Rosanne Cash & Dave Edmunds)
Label / Catalog number:
Pioneer Artists / PA 87194
Jacket / Inserts:
Standard international design with photo of George Harrison & Ringo Starr on front and back of jacket
Recording Location / Date:
Limehouse Studios, London, U.K. / 21 Oct 85

Media:
Album 12" LVD
Producer:
Dave Edmunds (music)
Stephanie Bennett (film)

Song 274a title:
Blue Moon Of Kentucky [live]
Release date / Country:
1986 / U.S.A.

Track details:
Side 1, track 12-2 / 1 min. 23 sec.
Composer:
M. Monroe

Carl Perkins: Lead Vocals & Guitar; Eric Clapton: Guitar & B. Vocals; Earl Slick: Acoustic Guitar; Dave Charles: Drums; Greg Perkins: Acoustic Guitar; Ringo Starr: Tambourine; Lee Rocker: Bass; John David: Bass; Mickey Gee: Guitar; Dave Edmunds: Acoustic Guitar & B. Vocals; George

Harrison: Guitar & B. Vocals; Rosanne Cash: Percussion & B. Vocals; Slim Jim Phantom: Percussion; Geraint Watkins: Piano

Song 274b title:
Blue Suede Shoes [live]
Release date / Country:
1986 / U.S.A.
Track details:
Side 1, track 16-1 / 3 min. 10 sec.
Composer:
C. Perkins

Carl Perkins: Lead Vocals & Guitar; Mickey Gee: Guitar; Ringo Starr: Drums; Earl Slick: Acoustic Guitar; Dave Edmunds: Acoustic Guitar; Vocals & B. Vocals; George Harrison: Guitar & B. Vocals; Eric Clapton: Guitar & B. Vocals; Dave Charles: Drums; Geraint Watkins: Piano; Slim Jim Phantom: Drums; Lee Rocker on Bass; Rosanne Cash: Percussion

Song 274c title:
Blue Suede Shoes/Gone Gone Gone (Reprise) [live]
Release date / Country:
1986 / U.S.A.
Track details:
Side 1, track 16-2 / 3 min. 45 sec.
Composer:
C. Perkins

Carl Perkins: Vocals & Guitar; Mickey Gee: Guitar; Ringo Starr: Drums; Earl Slick: Acoustic Guitar; Dave Edmunds: Vocals & Acoustic Guitar; George Harrison: Vocals & Guitar; Eric Clapton: Guitar & B. Vocals; Dave Charles: Drums; Geraint Watkins: Piano; Slim Jim Phantom: Drums; Lee Rocker on Bass; Rosanne Cash: Percussion

Song 274d title:
Glad All Over [live]
Release date / Country:
1986 / U.S.A.
Track details:
Side 1, track 13 / 2 min. 03 sec.
Composer:
Schroeder - Tepper - Bennett

Carl Perkins: Vocals & Guitar; George Harrison: Vocals & Guitar; Eric Clapton: Guitar & B. Vocals; Earl Slick: Acoustic Guitar; Dave Charles: Drums; Greg Perkins: Acoustic Guitar; Ringo Starr: Tambourine; Lee Rocker: Bass; John David: Bass; Mickey Gee: Guitar; Dave Edmunds: Acoustic Guitar & B. Vocals; Rosanne Cash: Percussion & B. Vocals; Slim Jim Phantom: Percussion; Geraint Watkins: Piano

Song 274e title:
Gone Gone Gone [live]
Release date / Country:
1986 / U.S.A.
Track details:
Side 1, track 15 / 2 min. 39 sec.
Composer:
C. Perkins

Carl Perkins: Lead Vocals & Guitar; Mickey Gee: Guitar; Ringo Starr: Drums; Earl Slick: Acoustic Guitar; Dave Edmunds: Acoustic Guitar; Vocals & B. Vocals; George Harrison: Guitar & B. Vocals; Eric Clapton: Guitar & B. Vocals; Dave Charles: Drums; Geraint Watkins: Piano; Slim Jim Phantom: Drums; Lee Rocker on Bass; Rosanne Cash: Percussion

Song 274f title:
Matchbox [live]
Release date / Country:
1986 / U.S.A.
Track details:
Side 1, track 4 / 3 min. 48 sec.
Composer:
C. Perkins - [Trad]

Carl Perkins: Vocals & Guitar; Ringo Starr: Vocals & Drums; Eric Clapton: Vocals & Guitar; Dave Edmunds: Acoustic Guitar; Geraint Watkins: Piano; Mickey Gee: Guitar; John David: Bass

Song 274g title:
Night Train To Memphis / Amen [live]
Release date / Country:
1986 / U.S.A.
Track details:
Side 1, track 12-3 / 2 min. 15 sec.
Composer:
B. Smith - M. Hughes - O. Bradley

Carl Perkins: Lead Vocals & Guitar; Eric Clapton: Guitar & B. Vocals; Earl Slick: Acoustic Guitar; Dave Charles: Drums; Greg Perkins: Acoustic Guitar; Ringo Starr: Tambourine; Lee Rocker: Bass;

John David: Bass; Mickey Gee: Guitar; Dave Edmunds: Acoustic Guitar & B. Vocals; George Harrison: Guitar & B. Vocals; Rosanne Cash: Percussion & B. Vocals; Slim Jim Phantom: Percussion; Geraint Watkins: Piano

Song 274h title:
That's All Right (Mama) [live]
Release date / Country:
1986 / U.S.A.
Track details:
Side 1, track 12-1 / 2 min. 15 sec.
Composer:
A. Crudup

Carl Perkins: Lead Vocals & Guitar; Eric Clapton: Guitar & B. Vocals; Earl Slick: Acoustic Guitar; Dave Charles: Drums; Greg Perkins: Acoustic Guitar; Ringo Starr: Tambourine; Lee Rocker: Bass; John David: Bass; Mickey Gee: Guitar; Dave Edmunds: Acoustic Guitar & B. Vocals; George Harrison: Guitar & B. Vocals; Rosanne Cash: Percussion & B. Vocals; Slim Jim Phantom: Percussion; Geraint Watkins: Piano

Song 274i title:
The World Is Waiting For The Sunrise [live]
Release date / Country:
1986 / U.S.A.
Track details:
Side 1, track 11 / 2 min. 48 sec.
Composer:
E. Lockhart - E. Seitz

Carl Perkins: Lead Guitar; George Harrison: Guitar Percussion & B. Vocals

Song 274j title:
Whole Lotta Shakin' Goin' On [live]
Release date / Country:
1986 / U.S.A.
Track details:
Side 1, track 14 / 3 min. 07 sec.
Composer:
Williams - David

Carl Perkins: Lead Vocals & Guitar; Eric Clapton: Guitar & B. Vocals; Earl Slick: Acoustic Guitar; Dave Charles: Drums; Greg Perkins: Acoustic Guitar; Ringo Starr: Tambourine; Lee Rocker: Bass; John David: Bass; Mickey Gee: Guitar; Dave Edmunds: Acoustic Guitar & B. Vocals; George Harrison: Guitar & B. Vocals; Rosanne Cash: Percussion & B. Vocals; Slim Jim Phantom: Percussion; Geraint Watkins: Piano

Song 274k title:
Your True Love [live]
Release date / Country:
1986 / U.S.A.
Track details:
Side 1, track 10 / 3 min. 22 sec.
Composer:
C. Perkins

Carl Perkins: Vocals & Guitar; George Harrison: Vocals & Guitar; John David: Bass; David Charles: Drums; Dave Edmunds: Acoustic Guitar & B. Vocals; Geraint Watkins: Piano; Mickey Gee: Guitar

Record 275 title:
Go Cat Go
Media:
Album 5" CD
Label / Catalog number:
Dinosaur Entertainment / 76401-84508-2
Jacket / Inserts:
Standard international design in jewel box / 8 page CD booklet

Song 275a title:
Distance Makes No Difference With Love
Release date / Country:
15 Oct 96 / U.S.A.
Track details:
Side 1, track 4 / 4 min. 12 sec.
Composer:
C. Perkins
Producer:
George Harrison & Mixer
Recording Location / Date:
FPSHOT (Friar Park Studio, Henley-on-Thames) U.K. / 18, 19 & 22 Jun 96

Carl Perkins: Lead Vocals & Lead Guitar; George Harrison: Slide Guitar, Bass & B. Vocals; Jim Capaldi: Drums

Song 275b title:
Honey Don't
Track details:
Side 1, track 12 / 2 min. 43 sec.
Release date / Country:
15 Oct 96 / U.S.A.
Composer:
C. Perkins
Producer:
Joe Walsh & Jim Nipar
Recording Location / Date:
(probably) On location at various venues in the U.S.A. or (possibly) On location at Greek Theatre, Los Angeles, CA StarStruck Studios, Nashville, TN U.S.A.† / (probably) 23 Jul - 04 Sep 89 (possibly) 03 Sep 89 & 1996

Carl Perkins: Vocals†; Ringo Starr: Vocals; Billy Preston: Keyboards & B. Vocals; Jim Keltner: Drums; Levon Helm: B. Vocals & Drums; Nils Lofgren: Guitar & B. Vocals; Joe Walsh: Guitar; Rick Danko: Bass & B. Vocals; Clarence Clemons: Saxophone; Dr. John: Keyboards

Song 275c title:
My Old Friend [duet version†]
Track details:
Side 1, track 16 / 3 min. 21 sec.
Release date / Country:
15 Oct 96 / U.S.A.
Composer:
C. Perkins
Label / Catalog number:
Dinosaur Entertainment / 76401-84508-2
Producer:
Paul McCartney & George Martin
Recording Location / Date:
AIR Studios, Montserrat, West Indies & (probably) The Mill, Sussex, or AIR Studios, London, U.K.† / (probably) 24 Feb 81 & Apr 96†

Carl Perkins: Lead Vocals & Guitar; Paul McCartney: Piano, Guitar, Drums & Bass; George Martin: String Arrangement

Record 276 title:
Go Cat Go
Media:
VHS
Label / Catalog number:
Unapix / UPX 70131
Producer:
Bob Maklevitch
Jacket / Inserts:
Standard international design / Post card mailer
Recording Location / Date:
On location backstage at Liberty Bowl, Memphis, TN, U.S.A. / 27 Apr 93

Song 276a title:
Blue Suede Shoes
Track details:
Side 1, track 6 / 1 min. 38 sec.
Release date / Country:
Feb 97 / U.S.A.
Composer:
C. Perkins

Carl Perkins: Vocals & Electric Guitar; Paul McCartney: Vocals & Acoustic Guitar

Song 276b title:
Lend Me Your Comb
Track details:
Side 1, track 4 / 1 min. 02 sec.
Release date / Country:
Feb 97 / U.S.A.
Composer:
K. Twamey - F. Wise - B. Weisman

Carl Perkins: Vocals & Electric Guitar; Paul McCartney: Vocals & Acoustic Guitar

Song 276c title:
Matchbox
Track details:
Side 1, track 5 / 1 min. 15 sec.

Release date / Country:
Feb 97 / U.S.A.

Composer:
C. Perkins - [Trad]

Carl Perkins: Vocals & Electric Guitar; Paul McCartney: Vocals & Acoustic Guitar

Song 276d title:
Maybellene
Release date / Country:
Feb 97 / U.S.A.

Track details:
Side 1, track 3 / 0 min. 46 sec.
Composer:
Berry - Freed - Fratto

Carl Perkins: Lead Vocals & Electric Guitar; Paul McCartney: B. Vocals & Acoustic Guitar

Song 276e title:
My Old Friend
Release date / Country:
Feb 97 / U.S.A.

Track details:
Side 1, track 2 / 3 min. 23 sec.
Composer:
C. Perkins

Carl Perkins: Lead Vocals & Electric Guitar; Paul McCartney: Acoustic Guitar & B. Vocals

Song 276f title:
The World Is Waiting For The Sunrise
Release date / Country:
Feb 97 / U.S.A.

Track details:
Side 1, track 7 / 1 min. 08 sec.
Composer:
E. Lockhart - E. Seitz

Paul McCartney: B. Vocals; Carl Perkins: Electric Guitar

Record 277 title:
Oobu Joobu [Various Artists]
Label / Catalog number:
Westwood One / Show # 95-32
(promotional only)
Jacket / Inserts:
Westwood One CD sleeves / cue sheet
Recording Location / Date:
On location backstage at Liberty Bowl, Memphis, TN, U.S.A. / 27 Apr 93

Media:
Album 5" CD
Producer:
Bob Maklevitch (film producer) &
Eddy Pumer (overall production)

Song 277a title:
Your True Love
Release date / Country:
31 Jul 95 / U.S.A.

Track details:
Side 1, track 4-2 / 2 min. 03 sec.
Composer:
C. Perkins

Carl Perkins: Lead Vocals & Electric Guitar; Paul McCartney: B. Vocals & Acoustic Guitar

Carl Perkins, the son of a cotton sharecropper, was born on April 9, 1932 in Lake County near Tiptonville, Tennessee. The songs he heard black cotton workers sing while he worked the fields as a boy played a major role in his love for music. He began his recording career in the mid-1950s at Sam Phillips' Sun Records and toured with Johnny Cash* and Elvis Presley, his label mates at Sun, along with Jerry Lee Lewis. Perkins is regarded as one of the founding fathers of rockabilly. His first real hit for Sun was ***Blue Suede Shoes*** in 1956, the label's first million selling record, but shortly after its release, Perkins was hospitalized as a result of a serious auto accident. Meanwhile, Elvis released a cover of ***Blue Suede Shoes***. These events stifled Perkins' chances for even greater success. During Perkins' recording session for ***Matchbox***, Cash, Presley and Lewis joined in a jam that would be released decades later and billed as the Million Dollar Quartet. Perkins' last song to chart for Sun was ***Your True Love*** in 1957.

Perkins' recordings for other record labels proved less successful, and by the early 1960s he had fallen on hard times. During his revival tour of England in mid-1964, he met The Beatles, who had

Carl Perkins, photo courtesy of Tom Bert

included nearly a dozen songs of his in their repertoire over the years. George Harrison was a particularly big fan, who fashioned much of his guitar style after Perkins. Harrison even adopted the stage name of Carl (after Perkins) during a tour of Scotland in 1960. (Harrison still considers ***Blue Suede Shoes*** one of his top 10 favorite songs.) The Beatles performed Perkins' song ***Sure To Fall*** during their audition for Decca Records in 1962.

On June 1, 1964, Perkins arrived at EMI Studios to watch The Beatles record his song ***Matchbox***. Perkins has claimed in interviews that, while he was in attendance at the sessions, The Beatles did covers of his songs ***Sawdust Dance Floor***, ***Your True Love*** and ***Sure To Fall***. If they were recorded, they apparently no longer exist. Several months later, The Beatles recorded Perkins' ***Honey Don't*** and ***Everybody's Trying To Be My Baby***, virtually guaranteeing Perkins a fat royalty check. The Beatles released their versions of ***Sure To Fall*** and ***Blue Suede Shoes***, as well ***Glad All Over*** and ***Lend Me Your Comb*** made popular by Perkins, on their albums **Live At The BBC** (1994), **Anthology 1** (1995), and **Anthology 3** (1996).

Perkins backed Johnny Cash during much of the '60s and '70s, but at the time was unable to revive his career. In 1969, John Lennon chose to open his first major rock performance without The Beatles at the **Toronto Rock 'n' Roll Revival** with a cover of ***Blue Suede Shoes***. Ringo Starr's 1981 album **Stop And Smell The Roses** contained a cover of ***Sure To Fall***.

Perkins traveled to AIR Studios in Montserrat for a week's stay in February 1981 at the invitation of Paul McCartney. While there, the two warmed up on a number of Perkins classics, including ***Honey Don't***, ***Boppin' The Blues*** and ***Lend Me Your Comb***. Perkins shared vocals with McCartney and played his distinctive rockabilly guitar on Paul's song ***Get It***.

The night before Perkins departed Montserrat, he wrote a song of thanks to McCartney called ***My Old Friend***. McCartney was said to have been moved to tears by the song and Perkins' gesture. The two proceeded to record the song, though it would remain officially unreleased until 1996. The original recording is available on the bootleg release **Artifacts III**. Shortly after his work with McCartney, Perkins teamed up again with old buddies Jerry Lee Lewis and Johnny Cash for an album appropriately titled **Survivors**, for, unlike Elvis, they had managed to survive numerous personal problems and tragedies.

In 1985, Perkins re-recorded ***Blue Suede Shoes*** with Lee Rocker and Slim Jim Phantom of the neo-rockabilly band The Stray Cats for inclusion on the Dave Edmunds* soundtrack for **Porky's Revenge**. The soundtrack also included ***I Don't Want To Do It***, an unreleased Bob Dylan* song recorded by Edmunds' good friend George Harrison.

Edmunds was instrumental in putting together **Blue Suede Shoes (A Rockabilly Session with Carl Perkins and Friends Starring George Harrison, Ringo Starr, Eric Clapton, Rosanne Cash and Dave Edmunds)**, which first aired on New Year's Day, 1986. Along with their backing contributions to **A Rockabilly Session**, Harrison sang ***Everybody's Trying To Be My Baby*** and Ringo sang ***Honey Don't*** – not considered contributions, but more rightly classified as solo Beatle recordings. Also performed, but not aired, were ***Right String (But The Wrong Yo-Yo)*** and ***Sure To Fall***. Perkins had also sent out invitations to Paul McCartney, who declined possibly fearing the spectacle of a Beatles reunion.

Perkins was inducted into the Rock and Roll Hall of Fame in 1987, one year before The Beatles! He performed ***Honey Don't*** and ***That's All Right (Mama)*** with George Harrison and Joe Brown *(see Vicki Brown)* at HandMade Film's 10th anniversary celebration in London in October 1988. Harrison also joined Perkins onstage at London's Hard Rock Cafe on June 15, 1992, in celebration of the restaurant's twenty-first birthday. Harrison was scheduled to produce an album for Perkins, but Perkins became ill with throat cancer. Perkins beat the disease and resumed his career.

Paul McCartney had just finished his sound check for his performance at the Liberty Bowl in Memphis, Tennessee on April 27, 1993, when he was greeted backstage by Carl Perkins and his film crew who were working on a possible TV special. Perkins correctly predicted that Paul would be eager to jam with him for the cameras. The following songs were taped: ***Your True Love*** and ***Get It*** (featured on McCartney's 1995 radio series **Oobu Joobu**), ***Blue Suede Shoes***, ***Lend Me Your Comb***, ***Maybellene***, ***Matchbox***, and ***The World Is Waiting For The Sunrise*** (available only on the 1997 Carl Perkins' VHS release **Go Cat Go**.) According to Perkins' son Stan, McCartney also jammed on ***Movie Magg***, ***Right String (But The Wrong Yo-Yo)*** and a couple of gospel songs with Carl. (***Get It***, is not considered a contribution to Perkins' recordings because McCartney is the composer and primary vocalist.) Perkins performed ***Rave On*** with Paul McCartney at Paul's annual Buddy Holly birthday celebration in London on September 7, 1995.

Perkins was a guest speaker and performer at the **BeatleDays** Convention, in Nashville, in June 1996. Later that month, he recorded a song he had written called ***Distance Makes No Difference With Love*** with help from Harrison at George's Friar Park Studios. The song was included on Perkins' album **Go Cat Go**, released in October 1996. Also included on the album was the 1981 recording of ***My Old Friend*** that featured duet vocals by McCartney recorded in 1996. Ringo contributed a previously unreleased alternate live version of ***Honey Don't*** from his 1989 All-Starr Band tour to the album, with vocal overdubs supplied by Carl. Perkins' vocals last little more than fifteen seconds, but because Ringo specifically donated the recording to Carl's project, it is considered a contribution. The album also included Lennon's recording of ***Blue Suede Shoes*** from his **Live Peace In Toronto 1969** album *(see Yoko Ono)*. Obviously The Beatles, who performed many of the songs made popular by Perkins in their early repertoire, are still able to play most of them with ease.

Perkins performed at the **Music For Montserrat** benefit concert organized by George Martin*, held on September 15, 1997, at London's Royal Albert Hall. The benefit also included a performance by McCartney whom Perkins backed during the encore.

In the weeks following the performance, Perkins suffered a series of strokes that led to his death on January 19, 1998. George Harrison performed ***Your True Love*** at Perkins' funeral. He was one of the most highly respected and admired people in music during his nearly half-century long career.

Peter & Gordon

Record 278 title:
The Best Of Peter & Gordon

Media:
Album 5" CD

Label / Catalog number:
Rhino / R2-70748

Jacket / Inserts:
Unique in Jewel box / 12 page CD booklet

Song 278a title:
A World Without Love

Track details:
Side 1, track 1 / 2 min. 38 sec.

Release date / Country:
30 Jul 91 (first issued 28 Feb 64) / U.S.A.
Composer:
J. Lennon - P. McCartney
Producer:
Norman Newell
Recording Location / Date:
EMI-Abbey Road Studios, London, U.K. / 21 Jan 64

Peter Asher: Vocals; Gordon Waller: Vocals; Vic Flick: Guitar; Geoff Love: Arrangement

Song 278b title:
I Don't Want To See You Again
Track details:
Side 1, track 4 / 1 min. 59 sec.
Release date / Country:
30 Jul 91 (first issued 11 Sep 64) / U.S.A.
Composer:
J. Lennon - P. McCartney
Label / Catalog number:
Rhino / R2-70748
Producer:
Norman Newell
Recording Location / Date:
EMI-Abbey Road Studios, London, U.K. / Aug 64

Peter Asher: Vocals; Gordon Waller: Vocals

Song 278c title:
Nobody I Know
Track details:
Side 1, track 3 / 2 min. 29 sec.
Release date / Country:
30 Jul 91 (first issued 29 May 64) / U.S.A.
Composer:
J. Lennon - P. McCartney
Label / Catalog number:
Rhino / R2-70748
Producer:
Norman Newell
Recording Location / Date:
EMI-Abbey Road Studios, London, U.K. / Apr 64

Peter Asher: Vocals; Gordon Waller: Vocals; Eddie King: Guitar; Geoff Love: Arrangement

Song 278d title:
Woman
Track details:
Side 1, track 11 / 2 min. 24 sec.
Release date / Country:
30 Jul 91 (first issued 10 Jan 66) / U.S.A.
Composer:
B. Webb [aka J. Lennon - P. McCartney]
Label / Catalog number:
Rhino / R2-70748
Producer:
John Burgess
Recording Location / Date:
EMI-Abbey Road Studios, London, U.K. / Dec 65

Peter Asher: Vocals; Gordon Waller: Vocals; Bob Leaper: Arrangement & Conductor; Paul McCartney: Arrangement

Peter & Gordon were Peter Asher (born June 22, 1944 in London, England), and Gordon Waller (born June 4, 1945 in Braemar, Scotland). The two met while in a private boy's school as a result of their mutual interest in music, and began to develop a style reminiscent of The Everly Brothers*.

In January 1964, the duo landed a recording contract with EMI. Asher took up an offer by his sister Jane's boyfriend, Paul McCartney, to record one of his compositions, ***A World Without Love***, rejected by The Beatles and originally intended for Billy J. Kramer *(see Billy J. Kramer & The Dakotas)*. Their recording of the song was a number one on both sides of the Atlantic, and the first of four major hits written by McCartney for the duo. A live version of the song was released on the U.K. various artists album **Tribute To Michael Holiday** (Columbia / 33SX 1635). Peter Asher says he still possesses McCartney's demo acetate of ***A World Without Love***.

Several months later the duo released their second McCartney original, ***Nobody I Know***, and in September their third, ***I Don't Want To See You Again***. (***Nobody I Know*** has since been covered by Petula Clark, and The Saltbee; ***World Without Love*** has since been covered by The Angeles, Anita Bryant, Diahann Carroll, Patty Duke, Bobby Goldsboro, Bobby Rydell, Sheila, and The Saltbee; ***I Don't Want To See You Again*** has since been covered by The Saltbee.) McCartney moved into the

Asher family home in London in late 1963 and lived there for over two years, rooming next to Peter.

By the end of 1964, the Lennon and McCartney songwriting team had drastically reduced the number of compositions they handed out to other artists. Peter & Gordon's first hit not written by McCartney was ***I Go To Pieces***, given to them by Del Shannon* while they were on tour with him in 1964. The duo, who were also big Buddy Holly fans (check out Peter's glasses at the time), followed that up with a memorable version of Holly's ***True Love Ways***.

McCartney, tired of criticism that the Lennon and McCartney songwriting moniker virtually guaranteed chart success, decided to use a pseudonym for his next and last contribution to Peter & Gordon. The song ***Woman*** was a top 20 and was credited to Bernard Webb. The song was also credited to an A. Smith, though copies with this name are less common. Asher said he and McCartney invented the name Bernard Webb. If asked why the song was published by Northern Songs, McCartney's publishing company, they were to say that Webb was an old schoolmate of Paul's and he did it as a favor. It was not long before the poorly kept secret was out though – but not before McCartney had made his point.

According to Peter Asher, none of The Beatles contributed directly to any of Peter & Gordon's recordings, but McCartney did attend an early session for ***Woman***. Asher said, "We ended up cutting the song twice for some reason and Paul and I weren't crazy about the way it ended up. We didn't like the Bob Leaper arrangement too much. We started cutting it; he was there for day one. Paul had some arrangement ideas, some of which our producer ignored, and I think that's why he didn't come back. Paul wanted the song to be much smaller, and what John Burgess did was take Paul's ideas, and then have Bob Leaper turn them into a very big orchestration which Paul wasn't crazy about. I think in retrospect Paul was right. We could have made a better record, it was a great song." During The Beatles' **Let It Be** rehearsals, McCartney discussed his preference for Peter & Gordon's earlier take of ***Woman***, and wondered if Asher still had The Beatles acetate of it. (***Woman*** has since been covered by David Wills.)

Peter & Gordon's last two major hits, ***Lady Godiva*** and ***Knight In Rusty Armour*** in late 1966, were uncharacteristically commercial "British." The two songs were written, in part, by Mike Leander. (Leander was later called upon by Paul McCartney to arrange the strings for his Beatles' song ***She's Leaving Home***.) The duo was also on the same bill as The Beatles during their German and Far East tour in 1966, and recorded a cover of John Lennon's Beatles song ***If I Fell***.

Peter & Gordon's folk style floundered during the psychedelic era between 1967 and 1968. The duo gradually drifted apart during this period. Gordon began recording as a solo artist, and Peter produced his first recording, ***And The Sun Will Shine***, for Paul Jones*.

Peter then took a job as A&R (Artist and Repertoire) manager at The Beatles' Apple Records, effectively ending the partnership of Peter & Gordon. Peter soon left Apple along with James Taylor* and became Taylor's full-time producer and manager. According to Asher, his leaving Apple had nothing to do with his sister Jane and McCartney ending their relationship, and everything to do with the arrival of Allen Klein.

Asher used his success with Taylor as a springboard to a highly successful career, producing and / or managing such artists as Linda Ronstadt, Carole King, Randy Newman, Little Feat, Joni Mitchell, Diana Ross, Cher, Bonnie Raitt, and many others. Asher has twice received a Grammy Award for Producer Of The Year. He produced a song on Ringo's 1992 album **Time Takes Time**.

Peter's sister, Jane Asher, continues to be a successful actress in Great Britain. Gordon Waller briefly continued on as a solo artist with little success before taking some acting roles during the early 1970s. He was last reported to be operating a gift and repair shop in England.

Tom Petty

Record 279 title:
A Bunch Of Videos And Some Other Stuff
Media:
Album 12" LVD
Label / Catalog number:
Image / ID6832TP
Producer:
Joanne Sellar (film); Jeff Lynne, with Tom Petty & Mike Campbell (music)
Jacket / Inserts:
Standard international design
Recording Location / Date:
Pinewood Studios, London, U.K. (film), M.C. Studios, Los Angeles, CA, U.S.A. (music) / 1988 or 1989

Song 279a title:
I Won't Back Down
Release date / Country:
Dec 89 / U.S.A.
Track details:
Side 2, track 3 / 3 min. 00 sec.
Composer:
T. Petty - J. Lynne

Tom Petty: Lead Vocals, Acoustic & Electric Guitar; George Harrison: Acoustic Guitar & B. Vocals; Howie Epstein: B. Vocals; Mike Campbell: Acoustic & Electric Guitars; Jeff Lynne: Keyboards, B. Vocals, Bass, Acoustic & Electric Guitar; Phil Jones: Drums

This song is also included on Full Moon Fever / MCA / MCAD-6253 / Album 5" CD / Side 1, track 2 / first issued 24 Apr 89 / Standard international design in jewel box / 12 page CD booklet.

Record 280 title:
Wildflowers
Media:
Album 5" CD
Label / Catalog number:
Warner Bros / 9 45759-2
Producer:
Rick Rubin, Tom Petty & Mike Campbell
Jacket / Inserts:
Standard international design in jewel box with cardboard slip cover / 16 page CD booklet
Recording Location / Date:
Ocean Way Recording &/or Sound City, Los Angeles, CA, U.S.A. / (summer) 1994

Song 280a title:
To Find A Friend
Release date / Country:
01 Nov 94 / U.S.A.
Track details:
Side 1, track 11 / 3 min. 21 sec.
Composer:
T. Petty

Tom Petty: Lead Vocals & Acoustic Guitars; Mike Campbell: Electric Guitar, Coral Sitar & Bass; Ringo Starr: Drums; Lenny Castro: Percussion; Benmont Tench: Tack Piano & Zenon

Record 281 title:
Songs And Music From The Motion Picture SHE'S THE ONE
Media:
Album 5" CD
Label / Catalog number:
Warner Bros / 9 46285-2
Producer:
Rick Rubin, Tom Petty & Mike Campbell
Jacket / Inserts:
Standard international design in jewel box / 8 page CD booklet
Recording Location / Date:
Sound City &/or Village Recorders &/or Andora Studios, Los Angeles, CA, U.S.A. / 1996

Song 281a title:
Hung Up And Over Due
Release date / Country:
06 Aug 96 / U.S.A.
Track details:
Side 1, track 14 / 5 min. 48 sec.
Composer:
T. Petty

Tom Petty: Lead Vocals & probably one or more of the following: Guitar, Bass, Harmonica, Tambourine, Harpsichord & Piano; Mike Campbell: probably one or more of the following: Marxophone, Guitar, Bass & Piano; Benmont Tench: Keyboards; Howie Epstein: Bass, B. Vocals; Ringo Starr: Drums; Carl Wilson: B. Vocals (Tom Petty And The Heartbreakers)

Tom Petty was born on October 20 1950 in Gainesville, Florida. Petty played in local-high-school rock bands, as many young American males did in the '60s. He began playing dates in the South with the band Mudcrutch before heading to Los Angeles to secure a contract with Shelter Records.

Petty, and fellow Mudcrutch members Benmont Tench and Mike Campbell joined forces with Ron Blair and Stan Lynch and released their first album, **Tom Petty And The Heartbreakers**, in 1976. The band soon acquired a cult following by echoing the styles of Bob Dylan* and The Byrds. Their second album, **You're Gonna Get It!**, went gold in 1978. Their third album, **Damn The Torpedoes** in 1979, went platinum.

Petty's fierce independence and stubborn determination led to disputes with his record company, stalling new releases. In 1982 Howie Epstein replaced Blair. In 1983 Petty produced Del Shannon's* album **Drop Down And Get Me**. Two years later, Tom Petty And The Heartbreakers released the album **Southern Accents**. In 1986 and '87, Tom Petty And The Heartbreakers backed Bob Dylan on a world tour.

Some of Tom Petty And The Heartbreakers' better known songs include ***American Girl***, ***Breakdown***, ***Don't Do Me Like That***, ***Refugee***, ***Here Comes My Girl***, ***The Waiting***, ***You Got Lucky***, ***Change Of Heart***, ***Don't Come Around Here No More***, ***Jammin' Me***, ***I Won't Back Down***, ***Runnin' Down A Dream***, ***Free Fallin'***, ***Mary Jane's Last Dance*** and ***You Don't Know How It Feels***.

In 1988, Petty teamed up with George Harrison, Jeff Lynne*, Roy Orbison*, and Bob Dylan to form the "supergroup" Traveling Wilburys. Petty's highly successful 1989 solo album **Full Moon Fever** included contributions from George Harrison on the song ***I Won't Back Down***. The album also included collaborations with Jeff Lynne. The music video for ***I Won't Back Down*** includes appearances by Harrison on acoustic guitar and Ringo on drums, though Starr does not actually play on the recording. The video also features Jeff Lynne on bass, Tom Petty on acoustic guitar, and Mike Campbell on electric guitar. A limited edition 7" single released in the U.K. also included photos of George and Ringo on its picture sleeve. Petty helped Harrison write the lyrics to his 1989 song ***Cheer Down***.

Shortly after the Traveling Wilburys' recording sessions, Petty, Campbell and Jeff Lynne went to work with Del Shannon on what would prove to be Shannon's last album. The following year Traveling Wilburys released their second album and Tom Petty and The Heartbreakers released **Into The Great Wide Open** which thanks "the entire Wilbury family." However, Harrison did not contribute to this album.

Petty, along with Jeff Lynne, Jim Keltner *(see Attitudes)* and Joe Walsh*, backed Ringo singing ***I Call Your Name*** as a contribution to **The John Lennon Scholarship Concert** held on May 5, 1990 in Liverpool. The song is included on the 1991 laser videodisk **The World's Greatest Artists Sing LENNON A Tribute**. In 1991, Petty was part of The Peace Choir, organized by Yoko Ono* and John Lennon's son Sean, who made a recording of Lennon's ***Give Peace A Chance***.

The Heartbreakers contributed to Ringo's 1992 album **Time Takes Time**. However, Petty played on only one track, titled ***Call Me***, that its producer Jeff Lynne claims will never be released. Ringo's first actual musical contribution to a Petty recording was playing drums on ***To Find A Friend*** from his 1994 solo album **Wildflowers**. Ringo also applied his sticks and skins to the song ***Hung Up And Overdue*** from Tom Petty And The Heartbreakers' soundtrack album to the film **She's The One**. Petty contributed to Ringo's 1998 album **Vertical Man**.

On April 24, 1993, Ringo appeared at the **Farm Aid VI** benefit concert at the Ames Cyclone Stadium in Iowa playing drums in a makeshift band led by Don Was called The New Maroons. That summer, Ringo teamed up with Don Was on bass, Mark Goldenberg on guitar, female vocalist Jonell Mosser, and Benmont Tench of The Heartbreakers on keyboards to record as The New Maroons. They recorded the songs ***Dark End Of The Street***, ***John The Revelator***, ***Somethin' Wild***, ***Too Many Memories***, and ***Born To Lose***. Unfortunately, the songs have yet to be released.

Billy Preston

Record 282 title:
Encouraging Words

Media:
Album 5" CD

Label / Catalog number:
Apple / CDP 0777 7 81279 2 5

Producer:
George Harrison & Billy Preston

Jacket / Inserts:
Standard international design in jewel box / 8 page CD booklet with photo of George Harrison

Song 282a title:
All That I've Got (I'm Gonna Give It To You)

Track details:
Side 1, track 15 / 3 min. 35 sec.

Release date / Country:
18 May 93 (first issued 30 Jan 70) / U.S.A.

Composer:
B. Preston - D. Troy

Producer:
George Harrison

Recording Location / Date:
Probably one or more of the following studios: Olympic, Apple, Trident &/or EMI-Abbey Road, London, U.K. / Nov 69

Billy Preston: Lead Vocals & Keyboards; probably one or more of the following: Alan White: Drums; Jim Gordon: Drums & Percussion; Klaus Voormann: Bass; Carl Radle: Bass; Bobby Keys: Horns; Ringo Starr: (possible) Drums

Song 282b title:
All Things Must Pass

Track details:
Side 1, track 12 / 3 min. 41 sec.

Release date / Country:
18 May 93 (first issued 11 Sep 70) / U.S.A.

Composer:
G. Harrison

Recording Location / Date:
Probably one or more of the following studios: Olympic, Apple, Trident &/or EMI-Abbey Road, London, U.K. / Apr - Jun 70

Billy Preston: Lead Vocals & Keyboards; probably one or more of the following: Klaus Voormann: Bass; Carl Radle: Bass; George Harrison: Guitar; Ringo Starr: (possible) Drums; Alan White: Drums; Jim Gordon: Drums; John Barham: Orchestral Arrangements

Song 282c title:
As Long As I Got My Baby
Track details:
Side 1, track 14 / 2 min. 43 sec.
Release date / Country:
18 May 93 / U.K.
Composer:
B. Preston
Recording Location / Date:
Probably one or more of the following studios: Olympic, Apple, Trident &/or EMI-Abbey Road, London, U.K. &/or (possibly) in Gothenburg or Stockholm, Sweden / (probably) Apr - Jun 70 (possibly) 08, 09, 13 or 14 Dec 69

Billy Preston: Lead Vocals & Keyboards; probably one or more of the following: Klaus Voormann: Bass; Carl Radle: Bass; Ringo Starr: (possible) Drums &/or Percussion; Alan White: Drums &/or Percussion; Jim Gordon: Drums &/or Percussion; Otis Williams: B. Vocals; Eddie Kendricks: B. Vocals; Paul Williams: B. Vocals; Melvin Franklin: B. Vocals; Dennis Edwards: B. Vocals

Song 282d title:
Encouraging Words
Track details:
Side 1, track 11 / 3 min. 32 sec.
Release date / Country:
18 May 93 (first issued 11 Sep 70) / U.S.A.
Composer:
B. Preston
Recording Location / Date:
Trident &/or Apple Studios, London, U.K. / Apr 70

Billy Preston: Lead Vocals & Keyboards; Eric Clapton: Guitar; George Harrison: Guitar; Ringo Starr: Drums; Klaus Voormann: Bass; Doris Troy: B. Vocals

Song 282e title:
I Don't Want To Pretend
Track details:
Side 1, track 10 / 2 min. 35 sec.
Release date / Country:
18 May 93 (first issued 11 Sep 70) / U.S.A.
Composer:
B. Preston
Recording Location / Date:
Probably one or more of the following studios: Olympic, Apple, Trident &/or EMI-Abbey Road, London, U.K. / Apr - Jun 70

Billy Preston: Lead Vocals & Keyboards; probably one or more of the following: Ringo Starr: Drums; Alan White: Drums; Jim Gordon: Drums; Klaus Voormann: Bass; Carl Radle: Bass; George Harrison: Guitar

Song 282f title:
I've Got A Feeling
Track details:
Side 1, track 7 / 2 min. 50 sec.
Release date / Country:
18 May 93 (first issued 11 Sep 70) / U.S.A.
Composer:
J. Lennon - P. McCartney
Recording Location / Date:
Probably one or more of the following studios: Olympic, Apple, Trident &/or EMI-Abbey Road, London, U.K. / Apr - Jun 70

Billy Preston: Lead Vocals & Keyboards; probably one or more of the following: Alan White: Drums; Jim Gordon: Drums; Ringo Starr: (possible) Drums; Klaus Voormann: Bass; Carl Radle: Bass

Song 282g title:
Let The Music Play
Track details:
Side 1, track 5 / 2 min. 41 sec.
Release date / Country:
18 May 93 (first issued 11 Sep 70) / U.S.A.
Composer:
B. Preston - J. Greene - J. Kirkland
Recording Location / Date:
Probably one or more of the following studios: Olympic, Apple, Trident &/or EMI-Abbey Road, London, U.K. / Apr - Jun 70

Billy Preston: Lead Vocals & Keyboards; probably one or more of the following: Ringo Starr: (possible) Drums &/or Percussion; Alan White: Drums &/or Percussion; Jim Gordon: Drums & Percussion

Song 282h title:
Little Girl
Track details:
Side 1, track 2 / 3 min. 25 sec.

Release date / Country:
18 May 93 (first issued 11 Sep 70) / U.S.A.
Composer:
B. Preston
Recording Location / Date:
Probably one or more of the following studios: Olympic, Apple, Trident &/or EMI-Abbey Road, London, U.K. / Apr - Jun 70

Billy Preston: Lead Vocals & Keyboards; probably one or more of the following: Ringo Starr: (possible) Drums; Alan White: Drums; Jim Gordon Drums; Klaus Voormann: Bass; Carl Radle: Bass; John Barham: Orchestral Arrangement

Song 282i title:
My Sweet Lord
Track details:
Side 1, track 4 / 3 min. 19 sec.
Release date / Country:
18 May 93 (first issued 11 Sep 70) / U.S.A.
Composer:
G. Harrison
Recording Location / Date:
Probably one or more of the following studios: Olympic, Apple, Trident &/or EMI-Abbey Road, London, U.K. / Apr - Jun 70

Billy Preston: Lead Vocals & Keyboards; probably one or more of the following: Ringo Starr: (possible) Drums: Alan White: Drums; Jim Gordon: Drums; Klaus Voormann: Bass; Carl Radle: Bass; George Harrison: (possible) Guitar; Edwin Hawkins Singers: B. Vocals

Song 282j title:
Right Now
Track details:
Side 1, track 1 / 3 min. 12 sec.
Release date / Country:
18 May 93 (first issued 11 Sep 70) / U.S.A.
Composer:
B. Preston
Recording Location / Date:
Apple &/or Trident Studios, London, U.K / Apr - Jun 70

Billy Preston: Lead Vocals & Keyboards; Eric Clapton: Guitar; George Harrison: Guitar & B. Vocals; Ringo Starr: Drums; Klaus Voormann: Bass; Doris Troy: B. Vocals

Song 282k title:
Sing One For The Lord
Track details:
Side 1, track 8 / 3 min. 46 sec.
Release date / Country:
18 May 93 (first issued 11 Sep 70) / U.S.A.
Composer:
G. Harrison - B. Preston
Recording Location / Date:
Probably one or more of the following studios: Olympic, Apple, Trident or EMI-Abbey Road, London, U.K. / Apr - Jun 70

Billy Preston: Lead Vocals & Keyboards; probably one or more of the following: George Harrison: Guitar & (possibly) Synthesizer; Ringo Starr: Drums; Klaus Voormann: Bass; Carl Radle: Bass

Song 282l title:
The Same Thing Again
Track details:
Side 1, track 6 / 4 min. 30 sec.
Release date / Country:
18 May 93 (first issued 11 Sep 70) / U.S.A.
Composer:
B. Preston - Herndon
Recording Location / Date:
Probably one or more of the following studios: Olympic, Apple, Trident or EMI-Abbey Road, London, U.K. / Apr - Jun 70

Billy Preston: Lead Vocals & Keyboards; probably the following musicians are involved: Bobby Keys: Horns; Klaus Voormann: Bass; Carl Radle: Bass

Song 282m title:
Use What You Got
Track details:
Side 1, track 3 / 4 min. 18 sec.
Release date / Country:
18 May 93 (first issued 11 Sep 70) / U.S.A.
Composer:
B. Preston

Recording Location / Date:
Probably one or more of the following studios: Olympic, Apple, Trident or EMI-Abbey Road, London, U.K. / Apr - Jun 70

Billy Preston: Lead Vocals & Keyboards; probably one or more of the following: Ringo Starr: (possible) Drums; Alan White: Drums; Jim Gordon: Drums; Bobby Keys: Horns; Klaus Voormann: Bass; Carl Radle: Bass; George Harrison: (possible) B. Vocals

Song 282n title:
When You Are Mine
Release date / Country:
18 May 93 (first issued 11 Sep 70) / U.S.A.
Track details:
Side 1, track 9 / 2 min. 42 sec.
Composer:
B. Preston
Recording Location / Date:
Probably one or more of the following studios: Olympic, Apple, Trident or EMI-Abbey Road, London, U.K. / Apr - Jun 70

Billy Preston: Lead Vocals & Keyboards; probably one or more of the following: Ringo Starr: (possible) Drums; Alan White: Drums; Jim Gordon: Drums; Klaus Voormann: Bass; Carl Radle: Bass; Bobby Keys: Horns

Song 282o title:
You've Been Acting Strange
Release date / Country:
18 May 93 (first issued 11 Sep 70) / U.S.A.
Track details:
Side 1, track 13 / 3 min. 22 sec.
Composer:
B. Preston
Recording Location / Date:
Probably one or more of the following studios: Olympic, Apple, Trident or EMI-Abbey Road, London, U.K. / Apr - Jun 70

Billy Preston: Lead Vocals & Keyboards; probably one or more of the following: Ringo Starr: Drums; Alan White: Drums; Jim Gordon: Drums; Klaus Voormann: Bass; Carl Radle: Bass

Record 283 title:
Fort Worth Express
Label / Catalog number:
Hindustani Music / Raga 001-A:B
[Unauthorized Record]
Media:
Album 5" [2 CD set]
Producer:
Unknown-audience recording
Jacket / Inserts:
Unique with slip cover in double Jewel box
Recording Location / Date:
On location at the Tarrant County Convention Center, Fort Worth, TX, U.S.A. / 22 Nov 74

Song 283a title:
Nothing From Nothing [live]
Release date / Country:
1996 / U.S.A
Track details:
CD2, track 8 / 3 min. 40 sec.
Composer:
B. Preston - B. Fisher

Billy Preston: Lead Vocals & Keyboards; Tom Scott: Saxophone; Chuck Findley: Trumpet; Robben Ford: Guitar; Andy Newmark: Drums; Emil Richards: Percussion; Willie Weeks: Bass; Jim Horn: Saxophone; George Harrison: Guitar; Jim Keltner: Drums

Song 283b title:
Outa-Space [live]
Release date / Country:
1996 / U.S.A
Track details:
CD2, track 9 / 4 min. 21 sec.
Composer:
B. Preston - J. Greene

Billy Preston: Keyboards; Tom Scott: Saxophone; Chuck Findley: Trumpet; Robben Ford: Guitar;

Andy Newmark: Drums; Emil Richards: Percussion; Willie Weeks: Bass; Jim Horn: Saxophone; George Harrison: Guitar; Jim Keltner: Drums

Song 283c title:
Will It Go Round In Circles [live]
Release date / Country:
1996 / U.S.A
Track details:
CD1, track 4 / 3 min. 50 sec.
Composer:
B. Preston - B. Fischer

Billy Preston: Lead Vocals & Keyboards; Tom Scott: Saxophone; Chuck Findley: Trumpet; Robben Ford: Guitar; Andy Newmark: Drums; Emil Richards: Percussion; Willie Weeks: Bass; Jim Horn: Saxophone; George Harrison: Guitar; Jim Keltner: Drums

Record 284 title:
It's My Pleasure
Label / Catalog number:
A&M / SP 4532
Media:
Album 12"
Producer:
Malcolm Cecil, Robert Margouleff & Billy Preston
Jacket / Inserts:
Standard international design / Record label inner sleeve & poster
Recording Location / Date:
Kendun Recorders &/or Centaur Electronic Music Center, Los Angeles, CA, U.S.A. / Sep - Oct 74

Song 284a title:
That's Life
Release date / Country:
20 Jun 75 / U.S.A.
Track details:
Side 1, track 3 / 3 min. 41 sec.
Composer:
B. Preston

Billy Preston: Lead Vocals & Keyboards; George Harrison: Guitar; Ollie Brown: Drums; Malcolm Cecil: T.O.N.T.O (The Original New-Timbrel Orchestra consists of twelve synthesizers linked together and played simultaneously); Robert Margouleff: T.O.N.T.O; Lorna Maxine: B. Vocals; Julia Waters: B. Vocals; Oren Waters; B. Vocals; Luther Waters: B. Vocals

Record 285 title:
Ringo Starr And His All-Starr Band
Label / Catalog number:
Pioneer Artists / PA-090-007
Media:
Album 12" LVD
Producer:
Joe Walsh & Jim Nipar
Jacket / Inserts:
Standard international design
Recording Location / Date:
On location at Greek Theatre, Los Angeles, CA, U.S.A. / 03 Sep 89

Song 285a title:
Will It Go 'Round In Circles [live]
Release date / Country:
Jul 90 / U.S.A.
Track details:
Side 1, track 6 / 4 min. 02 sec.
Composer:
B. Preston - B. Fisher

Billy Preston: Lead Vocals & Keyboards; Jim Keltner: Drums; Ringo Starr: Drums; Levon Helm: Drums & B. Vocals; Nils Lofgren: Guitar & B. Vocals; Joe Walsh: Guitar & B. Vocals; Rick Danko: Bass & B. Vocals; Clarence Clemons: Saxophone; Dr. John: Keyboards This song is also included on Rykodisc / RCD 10190 & RCD5-1019 / Albums 5" [2 CD set] / Side 1, track 10 / released 12 Oct 90 / Unique in box set in Jewel box / 6 page CD booklet, sticker postcard, Rykodisc info. postcard & CD insert.

Record 286 title:
Ringo Starr And His Third All-Starr Band Volume 1

Media:
Album 5" CD

Label / Catalog number:
Blockbuster Exclusive / [matrix #] 0ERE4<5297>RINGOSTARR ADFL

Producer:
Greg Delancy (Mixer) Ringo Starr and David Fishof (Executive Producers)

Jacket / Inserts:
Standard international design / 4 page CD insert

Recording Location / Date:
Nippon Budakon Hall, Tokyo, Japan / 27 Jun 95

Song 286a title:
Nothing From Nothing [live]

Track details:
Side 1, track 5 / 3 min. 18 sec.

Release date / Country:
12 Aug 97 / U.S.A.

Composer:
B. Fisher - B. Preston - C. Puckett

Billy Preston: Lead Vocals & Keyboards; Mark Farner: Guitar; Ringo Starr: Drums; Zak Starkey: Drums; John Entwistle: Bass; Randy Bachman: Guitar; Felix Cavaliere: Keyboards; Mark Rivera: Saxophone

Record 287 title:
That's The Way God Planned It

Media:
Album 5" CD

Label / Catalog number:
Apple / CDP 7975802

Producer:
George Harrison

Jacket / Inserts:
Standard international design in jewel box / 8 page CD booklet with photo of George Harrison

Song 287a title:
Do What You Want

Track details:
Side 1, track 1 / 3 min. 41 sec.

Release date / Country:
19 Nov 91 (first issued 22 Aug 69) / Germany

Composer:
B. Preston

Recording Location / Date:
Trident Studios, London, U.K. / Apr 69

Billy Preston: Lead Vocals & Keyboards; George Harrison: Guitar; Eric Clapton: Guitar; Keith Richards: Guitar or Bass; Klaus Voormann: (possible) Bass; Madeline Bell: (probable) B. Vocals; Doris Troy: (probable) B. Vocals; Ringo Starr: (possible) Percussion

Song 287b title:
Everything's All Right

Track details:
Side 1, track 3 / 2 min. 41 sec.

Release date / Country:
19 Nov 91 (first issued 22 Aug 69) / Germany

Composer:
B. Preston - D. Troy

Recording Location / Date:
Probably one or more of the following studios: Olympic, Apple, Trident &/or EMI-Abbey Road, London, U.K. / Apr - Jul 69

Billy Preston: Lead Vocals & Keyboards; probably one or more of the following: Doris Troy: B. Vocals; Klaus Voormann: Bass; Ringo Starr: (possible) Drums; Madeline Bell: B. Vocals

Song 287c title:
It Doesn't Matter

Track details:
Side 1, track 5 / 2 min. 39 sec.

Release date / Country:
19 Nov 91 (first issued 22 Aug 69) / Germany

Composer:
B. Preston

Recording Location / Date:
Probably one or more of the following studios: Olympic, Apple, Trident &/or EMI-Abbey Road, London, U.K. / Apr - Jul 69

Billy Preston: Lead Vocals & Keyboards; probably one or more of the following: Doris Troy: B. Vocals; Ringo Starr: (possible) Drums &/or Percussion; Klaus Voormann: Bass; Madeline Bell: B. Vocals

Song 287d title:
Let Us All Get Together Right Now
Track details:
Side 1, track 9 / 4 min. 06 sec.
Release date / Country:
19 Nov 91 (first issued 22 Aug 69) / Germany
Composer:
B. Preston - D. Troy
Recording Location / Date:
Probably one or more of the following studios: Olympic, Apple, Trident &/or EMI-Abbey Road, London, U.K. / Apr - Jul 69

Billy Preston: Lead Vocals & (probable) Keyboards; probably one or more of the following: Ringo Starr: Drums; George Harrison: Sitar; Madeline Bell: B. Vocals; Doris Troy: B. Vocals

Song 287e title:
Morning Star
Track details:
Side 1, track 6 / 3 min. 16 sec.
Release date / Country:
19 Nov 91 (first issued 22 Aug 69) / Germany
Composer:
W.C. Handy - M. David
Recording Location / Date:
Probably one or more of the following studios: Olympic, Apple, Trident &/or EMI-Abbey Road, London, U.K. / Apr - Jul 69

Billy Preston: Lead Vocals & (probable) Keyboards; John Barham: Strings; probably one or more of the following: Doris Troy: B. Vocals; Madeline Bell: B. Vocals

Song 287f title:
She Belongs To Me
Track details:
Side 1, track 4 / 4 min. 06 sec.
Release date / Country:
19 Nov 91 (first issued 22 Aug 69) / Germany
Composer:
B. Dylan
Recording Location / Date:
Probably one or more of the following studios: Olympic, Apple, Trident or EMI-Abbey Road, London, U.K. / Apr - Jul 69

Billy Preston: Lead Vocals & Keyboards; probably the following musicians are involved: George Harrison: Guitar; Ringo Starr: (possible) Drums; Klaus Voormann: Bass; Doris Troy: B. Vocals; Madeline Bell: B. Vocals

Song 287g title:
That's The Way God Planned It (Parts 1 & 2)
Track details:
Side 1, track 12 / 5 min. 32 sec.
Release date / Country:
19 Nov 91 (first issued 27 Jun 69) / Germany
Composer:
B. Preston
Recording Location / Date:
Trident Studios, London, U.K. / Apr 69

Billy Preston: Lead Vocals & Keyboards; George Harrison: Guitar; Keith Richards: Bass or Guitar, Eric Clapton: Guitar; Klaus Voormann: (possible) Bass; Ginger Baker: Drums; Ringo Starr: (possible) Percussion; Madeline Bell: (probable) B. Vocals; Doris Troy: B. Vocals

Song 287h title:
That's The Way God Planned It [alternate version]
Track details:
Side 1, track 15 / 4 min. 13 sec.
Release date / Country:
19 Nov 91 / Germany
Composer:
B. Preston
Recording Location / Date:
Trident Studios, London, U.K. / Apr 69

Billy Preston: Lead Vocals & Keyboards; George Harrison: Guitar; Keith Richards: Bass or Guitar, Eric Clapton: Guitar; Klaus Voormann: (possible) Bass; Ginger Baker: Drums; Ringo Starr: (possible) Percussion

Song 287i title:
This Is It
Release date / Country:
19 Nov 91 (first issued 22 Aug 69) / Germany
Track details:
Side 1, track 10 / 2 min. 42 sec.
Composer:
B. Preston - D. Troy
Recording Location / Date:
Probably one or more of the following studios: Olympic, Apple, Trident or EMI-Abbey Road, London, U.K. / Apr - Jul 69

Billy Preston: Lead Vocals & Keyboards; probably the following musicians are involved: Ringo Starr: Drums; George Harrison: Guitar; Klaus Voormann: Bass; Madeline Bell: B. Vocals

Song 287j title:
What About You?
Release date / Country:
19 Nov 91 (first issued 27 Jun 69) / Germany
Track details:
Side 1, track 8 / 2 min. 07 sec.
Composer:
B. Preston
Recording Location / Date:
Probably one or more of the following studios: Olympic, Apple, Trident or EMI-Abbey Road, London, U.K. / Apr - Jul 69

Billy Preston: Lead Vocals & Keyboards; possibly one or more of the following: Klaus Voormann: Bass; George Harrison: Guitar; Ringo Starr: (possible) Drums &/or Percussion; Madeline Bell: B. Vocals

Record 288 title:
The Best
Label / Catalog number:
A&M / CD 3205
Media:
Album 5" CD
Producer:
Billy Preston
Jacket / Inserts:
Standard international design in jewel box / 4 page CD booklet
Recording Location / Date:
Aug - Sep 71

Song 288a title:
I Wrote A Simple Song
Release date / Country:
1988 (first issued 08 Nov 71) / U.S.A.
Track details:
Side 1, track 10 / 3 min. 23 sec.
Composer:
B. Preston - J. Greene

Billy Preston: Lead Vocals & Keyboards; George Harrison: Guitar; Rocky Peoples: Tenor Saxophone; Charles Garnette: Trumpet; King Errison: Congas; Manuel Kellough: Drums; Quincy Jones: Strings & Horn Arrangement

Record 289 title:
Concert For Bangla Desh
Label / Catalog number:
FRT / 1001 [Unauthorized Record]
Jacket / Inserts:
Unique / Record label inner sleeve
Media:
Album 12"
Producer:
[Unknown-audience recording]
George Harrison & Phil Spector
Recording Location / Date:
On location at Madison Square Garden, New York, NY, U.S.A. 01 Aug 71 [afternoon]

Song 289a title:
That's The Way God Planned It [live]
Release date / Country:
mid-1970s / U.S.A.

Track details:
Side 2, track 2
Composer:
B. Preston

Billy Preston: Lead Vocals & Keyboards; George Harrison: Rhythm Guitar; Leon Russell: Piano; Ringo Starr: Drums; Jim Keltner: Drums; Eric Clapton: Lead Guitar; Jesse Ed Davis: Rhythm Guitar; Klaus Voormann: Bass; Carl Radle: Bass; Alan Beutler: B. Vocals; Marlin Greene: B. Vocals; Jeanie Greene: B. Vocals; Joe Green: B. Vocals; Dolores Hall: B. Vocals; Jackie Kelso: B. Vocals; Claudia Lennear: B. Vocals; Lou McCreary: B. Vocals; Don Nix: B. Vocals; Don Preston: B. Vocals; Pete Ham: Acoustic Guitar; Joey Molland: Acoustic Guitar; Tom Evans: Acoustic Guitar; Mike Gibbons: Percussion

Record 290 title:
The Concert For Bangla Desh
Label / Catalog number:
Warner Bros / NJL-38583
Media:
Album 12" LVD
Producer:
George Harrison & Allen Klein (film),
George Harrison & Phil Spector (music)
Jacket / Inserts:
Standard international design with variations / 4 page translation insert
Recording Location / Date:
On location at Madison Square Garden, New York, NY, U.S.A. / 01 Aug 71 [evening]

Song 290a title:
That's The Way God Planned It [live]
Release date / Country:
1990 / Japan

Track details:
Side 1, track 6 / 4 min. 30 sec.
Composer:
B. Preston

Billy Preston: Lead Vocals & Keyboards; George Harrison: Rhythm Guitar; Leon Russell: Piano; Ringo Starr: Drums; Jim Keltner: Drums; Eric Clapton: Lead Guitar; Jesse Ed Davis: Rhythm Guitar; Klaus Voormann: Bass; Carl Radle: Bass; Alan Beutler: B. Vocals; Marlin Greene: B. Vocals; Jeanie Greene: B. Vocals; Joe Green: B. Vocals; Dolores Hall: B. Vocals; Jackie Kelso: B. Vocals; Claudia Lennear: B. Vocals; Lou McCreary: B. Vocals; Don Nix: B. Vocals; Don Preston: B. Vocals; Pete Ham: Acoustic Guitar; Joey Molland: Acoustic Guitar; Tom Evans: Acoustic Guitar; Mike Gibbons: Percussion

This song is also included on Capitol/Apple / CDP 7 93265 2 / Album 5" CD [2 CD set] / CD1, track 6 / released 01 Aug 91 (first issued 20 Dec 71) in the U.S.A. / Standard international design in double Jewel box / 34 page CD booklet with photo of George Harrison & Ringo Starr.

Billy Preston was born on Sept 2, 1946 in Houston, Texas, but was raised in Los Angeles. Billy began playing organ at the age of six. His career in show business began at the age of ten when he played the part of W. C. Handy as a child in the film **St. Louis Blues**. His musical roots were firmly planted in gospel, backing such great artists as James Cleveland and Mahalia Jackson.

In 1962 Little Richard* recruited Preston to play on his European tour, including Liverpool and the Star-Club in Hamburg, where he first met The Beatles. He was a member of the house band on the mid-'60s rock-music TV show **Shindig**, and later backed Ray Charles. It was during this period that Billy recorded two solo albums and covered The Beatles' songs ***A Hard Day's Night*** and ***Eight Days A Week***.

Preston traveled to England with Ray Charles to film a BBC-TV special in September 1968. George Harrison contacted him and invited him to stop by Apple Records when he returned to England in January 1969. On January 22, 1969, Preston arrived at Apple and was recruited by George Harrison for the recording sessions that would eventually become the album **Let It Be**. By day's end, Preston was offered a contract with The Beatles' Apple Records. During those sessions, The Beatles backed up Preston on several of his songs, tentatively titled ***Billy's Songs 1 & 2***, though they have never been released in any form. On January 31, Preston joined The Beatles on the roof of

Billy Preston, Detroit, MI, 197, photo courtesy of Tom Bert

Apple for what would be their last live performance. The first single from those sessions, ***Get Back***, was credited as "The Beatles with Billy Preston," the first and only time such a credit was ever given by the group. He also played on ***Something*** and ***I Want You (She's So Heavy)***, which would end up on the album **Abbey Road**.

Following the long and unfinished sessions for **Let It Be**, George Harrison began producing Billy's first album for Apple Records titled **That's The Way God Planned It**. The album featured Eric Clapton*, Doris Troy*, Keith Richards *(see The Rolling Stones)*, Ginger Baker, Madeline Bell, Richie Havens and other musicians frequently used by Harrison during this period. It is likely that Harrison plays on several tracks on the album besides the title track. Ringo Starr probably contributed to the album as well. An edited version of the title track was issued as a single with critical acclaim, and was a top 20 in the U.K. Several of the tracks on the album were leftovers from Preston's recording sessions for Capitol Records and were not produced by Harrison. Early copies of the U.S. version of the album featured an alternate close-up photo of Preston, which has become a rare collector's item.

Preston joined Harrison on the Delaney & Bonnie & Friends* tour. Following the tour, the band backed John Lennon and Yoko Ono's* Plastic Ono Supergroup UNICEF **Peace For Christmas** benefit concert at London's Lyceum Ballroom on December 15, 1969.

At the beginning of 1970, Apple released the single ***All That I've Got (I'm Gonna Give It To You) / As I Get Older***. Harrison produced the A-side and supposedly played guitar on the track. However, there are no audible guitars – though it does sound a lot like Ringo on drums. The B-side was produced by none other than Preston's old mentor, Ray Charles. It sounds as if Ray joined in on piano, and George Harrison might have overdubbed his guitar on the track.

Undaunted by Preston's lack of major success in the charts, Harrison set about producing yet another star-studded album for Preston titled **Encouraging Words**. The album employed many of the same musicians used on **That's The Way God Planned It** and on Harrison's **All Things Must Pass** album, recorded around the same time. It also included contributions from session players Joe Greene and Jesse Kirkland, though exactly which tracks they play on is not known. Ringo also contributed to the **Encouraging Words** album, and Harrison also contributed guitar and his compositions ***All Things Must Pass*** and ***My Sweet Lord***.

The album's first single was to be ***My Sweet Lord / Long As I Got My Baby***, initially scheduled for release before Harrison's release of the song, but it was rescheduled by Apple at the last moment. Apple probably felt that Harrison's version was a hit single, and deserved to be the premiere release. Preston's version was finally issued as a single ten days after Harrison's version (with ***Little Girl*** as the B-side), but it was totally overshadowed by Harrison's million selling version.

Ironically, George's arrangement of ***My Sweet Lord*** for Preston was similar to the Edwin Hawkins Singers' ***Oh Happy Day***, no doubt due in part to their presence on the record as background singers. Harrison first considered the Edwin Hawkins Singers as the artists to do the song as a single for Apple. Harrison claimed in his defense in a plagiarism suit (which he lost) years later that ***My Sweet Lord*** was based on ***Oh Happy Day***, not ***He's So Fine***, as was charged.

As Long As I Got My Baby was reportedly recorded in Sweden using The Temptations as background singers. Harrison and Preston did spend a few days in Sweden during the Delaney & Bonnie tour, but there would have been very little time to book a studio. Bobby Keys*, who was a member of the tour band, recalls ***My Sweet Lord*** being sung on the bus, and said he would have certainly remembered a session including The Temptations if there had been one. Most likely ***As Long As I Got My Baby*** was recorded in London.

Encouraging Words includes the Harrison-penned ***All Things Must Pass***, which George would not release until several months later on his album of the same title. George also wrote ***What Is Life*** for Billy, but ended up recording it himself. Preston also included a cover of ***I've Got A Feeling*** that he had played on for The Beatles. It is not known if Harrison and / or Ringo play on all of these tracks, though it's certainly possible.

With the breakup of The Beatles, session players were needed for their solo recordings. Billy Preston was one of the first, and most frequently used, throughout the first half of the 1970s, playing on George Harrison's albums **All Things Must Pass**, **The Concert For Bangla Desh**, **Dark Horse**, **Extra Texture**, **Gone Troppo**, and **Thirty-Three & 1/3**. Aside from performing at **The Concert For Bangla Desh**, Preston accompanied Harrison on his 1974 U.S. tour. The bootleg CD **Fort Worth Express**, from Harrison's 1974 tour, includes the three songs performed by Preston. Preston also contributed to Starr's studio albums **Sentimental Journey**, **Ringo**, and **Goodnight Vienna**. His studio work with John Lennon was limited to **Instant Karma** and **God**.

In 1971, Preston left Apple and signed with A&M records. Harrison contributed guitar, credited as George H., to the title track of Preston's first A&M album **I Wrote A Simple Song**. Preston expressed in the credits "my deepest appreciation to George Harrison [among others] who played a large part in making this first album possible on A&M." According to an article in the September 16, 1971 issue of Rolling Stone magazine, Harrison also helped mix the album. To what extent, if any, Harrison was involved in the album's mixing is unknown.

Preston's 1972 album **Music Is My Life** contained a cover of The Beatles' ***Blackbird***. He released over a half-dozen albums for A&M, producing four top 10 songs - ***Outa Space***, ***Will It Go Round In Circles***, and ***Nothing From Nothing*** (all of which he performed on the 1974 Harrison tour), and ***Space Race***.

Harrison contributed guitar to ***That's Life*** from Preston's 1975 A&M album **It's My Pleasure** using his familiar pseudonym Hari Georgeson. Billy Preston's **The Best** album, issued in 1982 with thanks to Harrison, included ***I Wrote A Simple Song***. It was issued on CD in 1988. Preston also worked on and off the road with The Rolling Stones, among others. His last major chart success was the duet ***With You I'm Born Again*** with Syreeta Wright in 1979. Preston also appeared in Robert Stigwood's 1978 film **Sgt. Pepper's Lonely Hearts Club Band**.

Preston became a member of Ringo Starr's All-Starr Band tour in 1989, ending a long absence from any activities with members of The Beatles. During the tour he performed ***Will It Go 'Round In Circles*** with Ringo backing him on drums. He was also a member of Ringo's All-Starr Band tour in 1995 performing ***Nothing From Nothing*** with Ringo on drums. Preston was a guest at the 1996 **Beatlefest** in Los Angeles. If Billy Preston leaves the world nothing more, he will always be remembered most for composing Joe Cocker's* ***You Are So Beautiful***.

P.J. Proby

Record 291 title:
The Legendary P.J. Proby 'At His Very Best'
Label / Catalog number:
See For Miles / SEE CD 72
Jacket / Inserts:
Unique / 8 page CD booklet
Recording Location / Date:
EMI-Abbey Road Studios, London, U.K. / 07 Apr 65
Media:
Album 5" CD
Producer:
Ron Richards [George Martin]

Song 291a title:
That Means A Lot

Release date / Country:
1989 (first issued 05 Jul 65) / France

Track details:
Side 1, track 9 / 2 min. 31 sec.

Composer:
J. Lennon - P. McCartney

P.J. Proby: Lead Vocals; George Martin: Arrangement & Conductor

P. J. Proby, photo courtesy of P. J. Proby

P.J. Proby was born James Marcus Smith on November 6, 1938 in Houston, Texas. Smith began his career after moving to Los Angeles where he adopted his first alias, Jett Powers. He took bit acting parts and formed local bands before turning to songwriting. In 1963, he was introduced by songwriter Sharon Sheeley (Eddie Cochran's fiancee) to British rock-TV producer Jack Good, later of **Shindig** fame.

Good invited Smith, then known as P.J. Proby, to appear on the British TV special **Around The Beatles** in the spring of 1964. That is when Proby first met the group. Proby had a string of top 20 hits in the U.K. from mid-1964 through the end of 1965 including ***Hold Me***, ***Together***, ***I Apologize***, ***Let The Water Run Down***, and the songs ***Somewhere*** and ***Maria*** from the musical **West Side Story**. His bookings were affected by the controversy that surrounded him after he accidentally split his trousers onstage a couple of times. Proby recalls, "I just happened to be the first person England had ever seen flesh on before."

On February 20, 1965, The Beatles recorded ***That Means A Lot***, a song written by McCartney. It was initially intended for use in The Beatles' motion picture **Help!**, but was quickly abandoned and offered to P.J. Proby, whose recording of the song became a top 40 in the U.K. several months later. Proby remembers, "I was closest to John Lennon; we were drinking buddies. I ran into Lennon in a nightclub and said write me a song, and he came to me the next week with ***That Means A Lot***. I asked him if I could use George Martin as the producer and he said, 'Damn you, what do you want, my wife, my life and my children too?' So he got me George Martin; that's the only time I ever recorded with George Martin producing. Ron Richard was in charge of me, but George did everything, the arrangement, he worked the boards, everything. Martin had everything set up and ready to record when I got to the studio." Proby said none of The Beatles attended the session. He thought the orchestra that backed him on the recording was either Johnny Spence, or an orchestra hand picked by Martin. (***That Means A Lot*** has since been covered by The Saltbee.) The Beatles' recording of ***That Means A Lot*** was officially released on their album **Anthology 2** in 1996.

Proby had a couple more songs in the top 40 in the U.K. between 1966 and 1968. His only major hit in the U.S. was the song ***Niki Hoeky*** in 1967, which ironically failed to chart in the U.K. He, like a number of others, was briefly a member of the group Canned Heat in the late 1960s.

Proby released several records during the 1970s, but none of them met with any chart success. In 1977 (and again in 1995 and 1996), he played the part of Elvis Presley in his later years in the British musical **Elvis**. Proby has had a couple of record releases in the last two decades. He appeared in the British stage musicals **Good Rockin' Tonight** (Jack Good's life story) in 1993 and 1994, and played himself in **Only The Lonely**, the story of his old friend Roy Orbison*, in 1994 and 1995. He released an album titled **Legend** in 1997, and played the part of the Godfather in The Who's tour of **Quadrophenia** that included Ringo's son Zak.

Tommy Quickly

Record 292 title:
The Songs Lennon & McCartney Gave Away
Media:
Album 12"
Label / Catalog number:
EMI / NUT 18 (0C 054-07 003)
Producer:
Les Reed
Jacket / Inserts:
Standard international design with sketches of John Lennon, Paul McCartney & Ringo Starr
Recording Location / Date:
London, U.K. / Jul 63

Song 292a title:
Tip Of My Tongue
Track details:
Side 1, track 9 / 2 min. 02 sec.
Release date / Country:
13 Apr 79 (first issued 30 Jul 63) / U.K.
Composer:
J. Lennon - P. McCartney

Tommy Quickly

Record 293 title:
None
Producer:
Tony Hatch
Label / Catalog number:
Pye
Recording Location / Date:
Pye Studios, London, U.K. / Jul 64

Song 293a title:
No Reply
Release date / Country:
[Unreleased]
Composer:
J. Lennon - P. McCartney

Tommy Quickly: Lead Vocals; Colin Manley: Lead & Rhythm Guitar; Roy Dyke: Drums; Don Andrew: Bass; Paul McCartney: Tambourine; John Lennon: Percussion

Tommy Quickly was born Tommy Quigley in Liverpool, England on July 7, 1945 or 1943, depending on your source. He fronted a Liverpool band under the name Johnny Quickly and The Challengers. Quickly was yet another singer corralled by The Beatles' manager Brian Epstein into his stable of NEMS Enterprises' artists. Quickly was not signed to an EMI label like most other NEMS artists, but to the rival Decca/Pye/Piccadilly organization.

Epstein had high hopes and major plans for Quickly. He underwent the familiar Epstein make over – suit and tie, and a new stage demeanor. He booked Quickly on several dates with The Beatles in the summer of 1963, and arranged for Lennon and McCartney to donate their song ***Tip Of My Tongue*** for him to record. The Beatles had recorded the song the previous year, but rejected it as their second single in favor of ***Please Please Me***, which became their first number one song in the U.K. Quickly's version confirmed The Beatles' wisdom in passing on the song; it was one of the few unqualified chart failures of a Lennon and McCartney composition. (***Tip Of My Tongue*** was also issued in July 1992 on an obscure U.K. CD titled **The Best of Tommy Quickly, The Remo Four, Johnny Sandon And Gregory Phillips** [See For Miles / SEECD 349]. The song has since been covered by The Badbeats, and The Saltbee.)

Quickly was one of the featured artists in The Beatles' 1963 Christmas Show. In 1964 Epstein arranged for The Remo Four* to act as Quickly's backing band. On June 3, 1964, Lennon, McCartney and Harrison (Ringo was ill at the time) recorded a demo of John's song ***No Reply***, that was included on The Beatles' album **Anthology 1** in 1995. The liner notes suggest that it may have been recorded specifically as a reference demo for Tommy Quickly. Quickly's version was recorded and set for release on Pye Records on August 7, 1964, but was never issued. Colin Manley of the Remo Four, who played lead and rhythm guitar on Quickly's version, vividly remembers: "The song was recorded at Pye Studios in London and produced by Tony Hatch. The Remo Four's Don Andrew played bass and Roy Dyke played drums. Paul McCartney played tambourine and John Lennon banged away on Coke bottles for percussion. Epstein was also there coaching Quickly who was having trouble with the vocals. John said to his chauffeur, Alf, 'Go out and buy a bottle of whiskey, we've done the backing, now let Tommy sing.' We all got pretty stewed.

"I don't think the **Anthology 1** version is the demo we heard; it's too complete. I wish it would have been the one we heard. I'd back my life that the demo we used had no middle eight; it didn't have any clue as to the rhythm we should use. It contained the sound of a toilet flushing at the end which we thought was hilarious because it was typical of John's humor. I think we were told it was recorded in a hotel room. We immediately noticed when The Beatles put it on their album **Beatles For Sale** that it had a middle eight." Manley suspects Quickly's difficulty with the vocals and the incompleteness of the song are the reasons it was never issued.

Epstein, however, refused to admit defeat, and booked Quickly, backed by The Remo Four, on The Beatles' tour of the U.K. in the fall of 1964. His only chart success at the time was a cover of the Hank Williams' song ***The Wild Side Of Life***. Despite everyone's efforts, Tommy was unable to keep pace with the burgeoning British music scene, and quickly faded into obscurity. Any hopes of restarting his career were dashed by a head injury that has left him permanently disabled.

R.A.D.D. (Recording Artists Against Drunk

Record 294 title:
Drive My Car [Various Artists]

Label / Catalog number:
Recording Artists Against Drunk Driving / [none] (promotional only)

Jacket / Inserts:
Plain white with center die cut

Recording Location / Date:
Clear Lake Audio & Ocean Way Studios, Los Angeles, CA, U.S.A. & The Mill, Sussex, U.K. / (between) 14 Dec 93 - 21 Jan 94

Media:
VHS

Producer:
Paul & Dan Rothchild (music); Gary Legon & Marcy Gensic (film)

Song 294a title:
Drive My Car/[hip-hop section "Give Up The Keys"]/Drive My Car

Release date / Country:
07 Feb 94 / U.S.A.

Track details:
Side 1, track 1 / 1 min. 40 sec./0 min. 52 sec./1 min. 51 sec. (Total time of music & film 4 min. 23 sec.)

Composer:
J. Lennon - P.McCartney / [Bally - D. Rothchild] / J. Lennon - P.McCartney

Paul McCartney: Vocals; Phil Collins: Vocals; David Crosby: Vocals; Graham Nash: Vocals; Little Richard: Vocals; Ringo Starr: Vocals; Harry Nilsson: Vocals; Steve Berlin: Vocals; David Hidalgo: Vocals & Guitar; Conrad Lozano: Vocals; Louie Perez: Vocals; Cesar Rosas: Vocals; Weird Al Yancovic: Vocals; Milissa Etheridge: Vocals; Brett Michaels: Vocals; Clint Black: Vocals; Trisha Yearwood: Vocals; Julian Lennon: Vocals; Lisa Hartman Black: Vocals; Travis Tritt: Vocals; Katie Sagal: Vocals; Patti Smyth: Vocals; [Bally]: Vocals; Mike Landau: Guitar; Randy Jacobs: Guitar; Jody Cortez: Drums; Dan Rothchild: Bass; Ray Manzarek: Piano; Eddy Ray Wolffe: Guitar; Clarence Clemons: Saxophone; Taras Prodaniuk or Charles Domanico: Bass; Dean Parks: Acoustic Guitar;

Pete Anderson: Electric Guitar; Jeff Donavan: Drums; Skip Edwards: Keyboards
The American Music Awards premiered the video ***Drive My Car*** by R.A.D.D. (Recording Artists Against Drunk Driving) on February 7, 1994, which also happened to be the 30th anniversary of The Beatles' first visit to the U.S. The video had been in the works for almost a year and recording took place over a period of nine weeks. R.A.D.D. is an anti-drunk driving organization founded in 1986 by David Niven Jr. and Mort Weinstein. The organization, with the help of popular recording artists, attempts to discourage people from driving while drunk.

The ***Drive My Car*** video features some of the top names in country and rock, including Ringo Starr and the song's primary composer Paul McCartney. The full-length music video consists of four musical sections: the traditional Beatles style version of the song, a country version, a "hip-hop" version, and a hard rock version. Each artist's vocal performance was filmed live and edited into the final recording and music video. All the video was shot in Hollywood except for Phil Collins' and McCartney's portion, which were recorded at their private studios in England. McCartney appears and performs in the video for about 20 seconds, and he is also seen very briefly disguised in an afro wig. Only a few seconds of Ringo's performance with Harry Nilsson appears in the video.

The recording was produced by Paul Rothchild along with his son Dan. Paul Rothchild gained notoriety as the producer of The Doors and Janis Joplin. Gary Legon and Marcy Gensic were in charge of the video. Legon also worked on the video **Ringo Starr And His All Star Band Live From Montreaux** from Starr's second tour in 1992 *(see Burton Cummings)*.

The ***Drive My Car*** promotional video, and an audio cassette, were available via mail order for a limited time, but, to date, the recording has never appeared on any record format. The promotional audio cassette also contains a brief message by Paul McCartney. He made it possible for the organization to be able to use the ***Drive My Car*** song as their theme. McCartney headlined R.A.D.D.'s 1997 holiday public service media campaign to promote designated driving with a public service announcement. He received R.A.D.D.'s 1997 Founder's Award for his efforts.

The Radha Krsna [Krishna] Temple (London)

Record 295 title:
The Radha Krsna Temple (London)
Media:
Album 5" CD
Label / Catalog number:
Apple / CDP 0777 7 81255 2 5
Jacket / Inserts:
Standard international design in jewel box
/ 16 page CD booklet with photos of George Harrison

Song 295a title:
Bhaja Bhakata/Arotrika [or "Arati"]
Track details:
Side 1, track 3 / 8 min. 24 sec.
Release date / Country:
18 May 93 (first issued 21 May 71) / U.S.A.
Composer:
Trad arr. Mukunda Das Adkikary
Producer:
George Harrison
Recording Location / Date:
Trident Studios, London, U.K. / Sep 69 - Jan 70

Lilavati devi dasi: Vocals; Jivananda dasa: Vocals; Murari dasa: Mrdanga

Song 295b title:
Bhaja Hure Mana
Track details:
Side 1, track 6 / 8 min. 53 sec.
Release date / Country:
18 May 93 (first issued 21 May 71) / U.S.A.
Composer:
Trad arr. Mukunda Das Adkikary
Producer:
George Harrison

Recording Location / Date:
(possibly) The Radha Krsna Temple, London, U.K. / Sep 69 - Jan 70

Yamuna devi: Lead Vocals & Harmonium

Song 295c title:
Govinda
Release date / Country:
18 May 93 (first issued 06 Mar 70) / U.S.A.
Producer:
George Harrison
Recording Location / Date:
Trident Studios, London, U.K. / Sep 69 - Jan 70
Track details:
Side 1, track 1 / 4 min. 43 sec.
Composer:
Trad arr. Mukunda Das Adkikary

Yamuna devi: Lead Vocals; Mukunda Goswami: Organ; Hari Vilas dasa: Oud; Tamal Krsna Goswami: Flute; Mukunda Goswami: Kartalas; Syamasundar dasa: Kartalas; George Harrison: Guitar; Klaus Voormann: Bass; John Barham: Orchestral Arrangements; Syamasundar dasa: B. Vocals; Lilaviti devi dasi: B. Vocals; Jivananda dasa: B. Vocals; Mondakini devi dasi: B. Vocals; Jyotirmayi devi dasi: B. Vocals; Malati devi dasi: B. Vocals; Janaki devi dasi: B. Vocals; Guru dasa: B. Vocals; Radharaman dasa: B. Vocals; Purandara dasa; B. Vocals; Tirthapada dasa: B. Vocals; Digvijaya dasa: B. Vocals; Prtha devi dasi: B. Vocals; Kulasekhar dasa: B. Vocals; Pantanjili devi dasi: B. Vocals

Song 295d title:
Govinda Jai Jai [or "Govinda Jaya Jaya"]
Release date / Country:
18 May 93 (first issued 06 Mar 70) / U.S.A.
Producer:
George Harrison
Recording Location / Date:
Trident Studios, London, U.K. / Sep 69 - Jan 70
Track details:
Side 1, track 7 / 5 min. 5 sec.
Composer:
Trad arr. Mukunda Das Adkikary

Lilavati devi dasi: Vocals; Jivananda dasa: Vocals

Song 295e title:
Hare Krsna [Krishna] Mantra
Release date / Country:
18 May 93 (first issued 22 Aug 69) / U.S.A.
Producer:
George Harrison & Paul McCartney
Recording Location / Date:
EMI-Abbey Road Studios, London, U.K. / Jul 69 or (possibly) Mar or Apr 69)
Track details:
Side 1, track 4 / 3 min. 33 sec.
Composer:
Trad arr. Mukunda Das Adkikary

Yamuna divi: Vocals; Syamasundar dasa: Vocals; George Harrison: Guitar, Bass & Harmonium; Alan White: Drums; Mukunda Das Adhikary: Mridangam & Guitar; Malati devi dasi: Kartalas, Gong & B. Vocals; Digvijaya dasa: B. Vocals; Tirthapada dasa: B. Vocals; Janaki devi dasi: B. Vocals; Prtha devi dasi: B. Vocals; Kulasekhar dasa: B. Vocals; Pantanjili devi dasi: B. Vocals

Song 295f title:
Prayer To The Spiritual Masters
Release date / Country:
18 May 93 (first issued) 22 Aug 69 / U.S.A.
Producer:
George Harrison & (probable) Paul McCartney
Recording Location / Date:
EMI-Abbey Road Studios, London, U.K. / Jul 69 or (possibly) Mar or Apr 69)
Track details:
Side 1, track 8 / 3 min. 59 sec.
Composer:
Trad arr. Mukunda Das Adkikary

Syamasundar dasa: Vocals; Mukunda Goswami: Vocals, Mrdanga & Kulasekhar; Yamuna devi: Vocals; Malati devi dasi: Vocals; Syamasundar dasa: Esraj; Mel Evans: Piano; Pantanjali devi dasi: B. Vocals; Prtha devi dasi: B. Vocals; Tirthapada dasa: B. Vocals; Digvijaya dasa: B. Vocals; George Harrison: (possible) B. Vocals

Song 295g title:
Sri Guruvastak [or Gurvastakam]
Release date / Country:
18 May 93 (first issued 21 May 71) / U.S.A.
Producer:
George Harrison
Recording Location / Date:
(possibly) The Radha Krsna Temple, London, U.K. / Sep 69 - Jan 70

Track details:
Side 1, track 2 / 3 min. 12 sec.
Composer:
Trad arr. Mukunda Das Adkikary

Jivananda dasa: Vocals & (possible) Guitar; Yogesvara dasa: Vocals; George Harrison: (probable) Guitar & (possible) Tamboura

Song 295h title:
Sri Isopanisad
Release date / Country:
18 May 93 (first issued 21 May 71) / U.S.A.
Producer:
George Harrison
Recording Location / Date:
(possibly) The Radha Krsna Temple, London, U.K. / Sep 69 - Jan 70

Track details:
Side 1, track 5 / 4 min. 03 sec.
Composer:
Trad arr. Mukunda Das Adkikary

Jivananda dasa: Lead Vocals & Guitar; George Harrison: (probable) Guitar

Most people's experience with The Hare Krishna movement has been confined to airports around the world. The movement was founded by A.C. Bhaktivedanta Swami Prabhupada. His missionaries arrived in London to set up a temple in the spring of 1968, and by the fall of that year they had arranged a meeting, through Allen Ginsberg*, with Apple Records' A&R man Peter Asher *(see Peter & Gordon)*. Not surprisingly, they soon became friendly with George Harrison, and even took up residence, along with Prabhupada, for a time at John Lennon's home in Tittenhurst Park, Ascot. During this period, members of the sect roamed the streets of London chanting the ***Hare Krishna Mantra***. The song became so familiar in England that The Beatles did a loose rendition of it during their **Get Back / Let It Be** rehearsals in January 1969. Members of the Hare Krishna movement contributed backing vocals to Lennon's ***Give Peace A Chance***, recorded on June 1, 1969, at the Hotel Reine-Elizabeth in Montreal, during the Lennons' "Bed-In for Peace."

George Harrison played on and produced, with help from Paul McCartney, The Radha Krishna Temple's first Apple single ***Hare Krishna Mantra / Prayer To The Spiritual Masters***. The session probably took place before a scheduled Beatles recording session at EMI for the album **Abbey Road**. ***Hare Krishna Mantra*** became a top 20 in the U.K.

Harrison next set about recording their follow-up single ***Govinda*** that also met with some success. Shortly after, a full album produced by Harrison, titled **The Radha Krsna Temple (London)**, (the spelling of Krishna and Krsna are both correct) was released. The album is sorely lacking in detailed credits. Judging from the photos of Harrison playing guitar and harmonium in the CD booklet (not included in the original vinyl release), it is quite likely he plays those instruments on the album. Though harmonium is present throughout much of the album, it is difficult to know if Harrison plays it on some or all the tracks. There is some guitar on ***Sri Guruvastak*** and ***Sri Isopanisad*** that Harrison may play. There is also a possibility that Harrison might even be buried in the background vocals. Mukunda Goswami of ISKCON (International Society for Krishna Consciousness), who was involved in the recordings, was able to recall some of the other participants.

Following the arrival of Allen Klein, and the breakup of The Beatles, Apple Records concentrated mainly on more marketable artists, and on The Beatles' solo projects, leaving curious novelties like Radha Krsna Temple chanting in the streets. George Harrison continues to lend his support to the movement and in 1973 donated a seventeen-acre manor outside London to ISKCON. In March 1994, the manor was closed for a time by order of the local council after complaints that a large number of worshipers were creating a disturbance in the area.

Several years after Apple had ceased operations, **The Radha Krsna Temple** album was reissued in England under the title **Goddess of Fortune** on the Spiritual Sky label. George Harrison gave a written endorsement for the book **Divine Nature: A Spiritual Perspective On The Environmental Crisis** by Michael A. Cremo and Mukunda Goswami published by ISKCON in 1995.

Leon Redbone

Record 296 title:
Whistling In The Wind
Media:
Album 5" CD
Label / Catalog number:
Private Music / 01005-82117-2
Producer:
Beryl Handler & Leon Redbone
Jacket / Inserts:
Standard international design in jewel box / 4 page CD booklet
Recording Location / Date:
M&I Recording Studios, New York, NY & Ocean Way Recording Studios, Los Angeles, CA,† U.S.A. / 1992 & 07 Jun 93†

Song 296a title:
My Little Grass Shack
Track details:
Side 1, track 7 / 2 min. 41 sec.
Release date / Country:
12 Apr 94 / U.S.A.
Composer:
J. Noble - B. Cogswell - T. Harrison

Leon Redbone: Vocals; Ringo Starr: Vocals†; Giampaolo Biagi: Drums; Cyndi Cashdollar: Dobro Guitar & B. Vocals; Vince Giordano: Bass; Frank Vignola: Guitar & Mandolin; Terry Waldo: Piano; Beryl Handler: B. Vocals; Doug Epstein: B. Vocals; Ira: B. Vocals; Mitch: B. Vocals

Record 297 title:
None
Producer:
Beryl Handler & Leon Redbone
Recording Location / Date:
M&I Recording Studios, New York, NY & Ocean Way Recording Studios, Los Angeles, CA,† U.S.A. / 1992 & 07 Jun 93†

Song 297 title:
Sing Me A Song Of Hawaii
Release date / Country:
[Unreleased]

Leon Redbone: Lead Vocals; Ringo Starr: Drums†

Leon Redbone gained national attention after appearing on NBC-TV's **Saturday Night Live** and **The Tonight Show**. Redbone's baritone crooning is familiar to most Americans through his work on commercials, most notably for Budweiser Beer. His voice is also heard regularly on the theme songs for **Mr. Belvedere** and **Harry And The Hendersons**. One of Redbone's commercials was included several times during Paul McCartney's 1995 radio series **Oobu Joobu**. Redbone has released a total of ten albums in just under twenty years, and regularly tours the U.S. and Europe.

Ringo had met Redbone on several occasions and admired his work. He asked Redbone if he could add his vocals to ***My Little Grass Shack***. Redbone recorded ***Little Grass Shack*** in New York, and Ringo added his duet vocals in Los Angeles. Ringo also played drums on the unreleased Redbone recording ***Sing Me A Song Of Hawaii***.

The Remo Four

Record 298 title:
None
Producer:
George Harrison
Recording Location / Date:
EMI-Abbey Road Studios, London, U.K. / (probably) Dec 67

Song 298 title:
In The First Place
Release date / Country:
[Unreleased]
Composer:
C. Manley - T. Ashton

Colin Manley: Vocals & Acoustic Guitar; George Harrison: Voice & (possible) Guitar; Tony Ashton: Keyboards; Philip Rogers: Bass; Roy Dyke: Drums

The Remo Four initially called themselves The Remo Quartet when they formed in Liverpool, England in 1958, but modified their name in 1961. The Remo Four underwent numerous personnel changes during their career. In 1962 they became known as Johnny Sandon & The Remo Four. They often shared the same bill with The Beatles in and around Liverpool in the early 1960s and, like The Beatles, were a resident band at the Star Club in Hamburg, Germany. The Beatles' manager Brian Epstein initially failed to interest them in becoming the backing band for Billy J. Kramer *(see Billy J. Kramer & The Dakotas)*, but succeeded in getting them to back Tommy Quickly* in 1964. The Remo Four, on their own and backing Quickly, were one of the featured acts on The Beatles' U.K. tour in the fall of 1964.

By 1967, The Remo Four consisted of founding member and guitarist Colin Manley, a schoolmate of Harrison and McCartney (born April 16, 1942 in Liverpool); bass player, Phil Rogers, who joined the group in 1962; drummer, Roy Dyke (born February 13, 1945 in Liverpool, England) who joined the group in 1961; and keyboard player Edward Antony Ashton (born March 1, 1946, in Blackburn, England) who joined the group in 1965. In late 1967, George Harrison enlisted the help of The Remo Four as his session band for the non-Indian portion of his soundtrack album for the film **Wonderwall**. Tony Ashton said Peter Tork, of group The Monkees, walked in on the **Wonderwall** sessions. "We all dropped our instruments and began singing 'hey, hey we're The Monkees.' I think maybe he played tambourine, though I don't know if it's on tape."

Harrison was reported to have produced an album for The Remo Four in 1968, but according to Ashton and Manley, no such album was ever planned or recorded. Manley and Ashton said Harrison did start to produce a recording of Ashton and Manley's composition ***In The First Place*** at EMI's Abbey Road Studios during the sessions for **Wonderwall**. The song was inspired, in part, by the Modern Jazz Quartet's version of ***Adagio From Concierto De Aranjuez***. Ashton and Manley think Harrison may have played guitar on the track. Manley said Harrison's countdown can be heard at the beginning of the recording. Manley recalls Harrison telling him that Paul McCartney offered a few suggestions concerning the song's verses. The Remo Four broke up a short time later. Ashton and Dyke enlisted Kim Gardner to form Ashton, Gardner & Dyke*. Ashton says he wrote a completely new song, again inspired by ***Adagio From Concierto De Aranjuez***, called ***As It Was In The First Place***, which Ashton, Gardner & Dyke recorded and included on their self-titled album in 1969. Manley, Ashton, Dyke and a new bass player named Tony Coates reunited as The Remo Four in 1997.

Kate Robbins

Record 299 title:
Tomorrow
Label / Catalog number:
Anchor
Jacket / Inserts:
Record label sleeve
Recording Location / Date:
EMI Studios, Abbey Road, London, U.K. / (probably) 1978
Media:
Single 7"
Producer:
Del Newman [Paul McCartney Executive Producer & Involvement]

Song 299a title:
Tomorrow
Release date / Country:
30 Jun 78 / U.K.
Track details:
Side 1, track 1 / 3 min. 26 sec.
Composer:
M. Charnin - C. Strouse

Kate Robbins: Lead Vocals

Kate Robbins was born on August 21, 1958 in Margate, Kent, England. She is the daughter of Mike and Elizabeth Robbins. Elizabeth was the first cousin of Paul McCartney on his father's side and helped teach Paul how to play guitar. Kate went into show business and had a hit with the song ***More Than In Love*** in 1981. She is also an accomplished impressionist.

Most reliable publications have stated that Paul produced the song ***Tomorrow*** for Kate. However, the record label states that Del Newman produced the record and its B-side. The record does list production by McCartney's MPL Communications, and the songs are administrated by McCartney Music. That may be the source of all the confusion. According to Kate, McCartney did not produce the recording, but was the executive producer and played a very active role in the record's development. McCartney chose the song (to which he owned the publishing rights) for Kate. Kate thought there was a total of four mixes, and said that McCartney chose the mix that was used for the single. Though the role of executive producer is not considered a contribution, because of the wider scope of McCartney's involvement with record, it is included. Kate also pointed out that McCartney has advised her throughout her career in the music business and helped her set up her publishing company. Kate has also contributed backing vocals to several of Paul McCartney's recordings.

The Rolling Stones

Record 300 title:
Rock And Roll Circus [Various Artists]
Media:
Album 5" CD
Label / Catalog number:
Abkco / 1268-2
Producer:
Jimmy Miller, Jody Klein & Lenne Allik
Jacket / Inserts:
Standard international design in jewel box in slip cover
42 page CD booklet with photos of John Lennon
Recording Location / Date:
InterTel Studios, Stonebridge House, London, U.K. / 11 Dec 68

Song 300a title:
Jumping Jack Flash
Release date / Country:
15 Oct 96 / U.S.A.
Track details:
Side 1, track 14 / 3 min. 35 sec.
Composer:
M. Jagger - K. Richards

Mick Jagger: Lead Vocals; John Lennon: Introduction; Keith Richards: Guitar; Brian Jones: Guitar; Bill Wyman: Bass; Charlie Watts: Drums; Nicky Hopkins: Keyboards; Rocky Dijon: Percussion

This song is also included on Abkco / 1003-1 / Album LVD 12" / Side 2, track 12 / Standard international design.

Song 300b title:
Salt Of The Earth
Release date / Country:
15 Oct 96 / U.S.A.
Track details:
Side 1, track 19 / 4 min. 56 sec.
Composer:
M. Jagger - K. Richards

Mick Jagger: Lead Vocals; Keith Richards: Acoustic Guitar; Brian Jones: Slide Guitar; Bill Wyman: Bass; Charlie Watts: Drums; Nicky Hopkins: Keyboards; Rocky Dijon: Percussion; Audience (inc. John Lennon): B. Vocals

This song is also included on Abkco / 1003-1 / Album LVD 12" / Side 2, track 17/ Standard international design.

Record 301 title:
Singles Collection (The London Years)
Media:
Album 5" CD [3 CD set] (mono)
Label / Catalog number:
Abkco / 1218-2 CD ONE
Jacket / Inserts:
Unique in Jewel box in box set / 4 page CD insert & 72 page box set booklet

Song 301a title:
I Wanna Be Your Man
Release date / Country:
Aug 89 (first issued 01 Nov 63) / U.S.A.
Track details:
CD1, track 3 / 1 min. 43 sec.
Composer:
J. Lennon - P. McCartney
Producer:
Andrew Loog Oldham & Eric Easton
Recording Location / Date:
Kingsway Sound Studios, London, U.K. / 07 Oct 63

Mick Jagger: Lead Vocals; Charlie Watts: Drums; Bill Wyman: Bass; Keith Richards: Guitar; Brian Jones: Guitar

Song 301b title:
We Love You
Release date / Country:
1989 (first issued 18 Aug 67) / U.S.A.
Producer:
Andrew Loog Oldham
Recording Location / Date:
Olympic Studios, London, U.K. / 12-13 Jun 67 (Jul 67† or possibly 18 May 67)
Track details:
CD2, track 13 / 4 min. 19 sec.
Composer:
M. Jagger - K. Richards

Mick Jagger: Lead Vocals; Charlie Watts: Drums; Bill Wyman: Bass; Keith Richards: Guitar; Brian Jones: Mellotron & Horns; Nicky Hopkins &/or Ian Stewart: (probable) Piano; John Lennon: B. Vocals†; Paul McCartney: B. Vocals†

In 1963, The Rolling Stones took shape around five Englishmen: Mick Jagger, Keith Richards, Brian Jones, Bill Wyman and Charlie Watts. The band's lifelong songwriter and lead vocalist was born Michael "Mick" Jagger on July 26, 1943 in Dartford *(see Mick Jagger)*. Keith Richards (over the years he has dropped and added the "s"), the band's primary lead guitarist and songwriter, was born on December 18, 1943, also in Dartford. The band's most versatile musician and second guitarist was Lewis Brian Jones, born on February 28, 1942 in Cheltenham. Bill Wyman, the group's bass player, was born William Perks on October 24, 1936 in London. Drummer Charlie Watts was born on June 2, 1941, also in London. There were two additional people integral to The Rolling Stones: Andrew Loog Oldham, their original manager and producer, who had previously handled public relations for The Beatles for a brief time, and Ian Stewart, the band's studio keyboard player and road manager.

Oldham felt Stewart's appearance onstage did not fit the image he planned for The Rolling Stones. Oldham planned to create an image for The Rolling Stones that would offer people an alternative to The Beatles, who represented a more wholesome image. He transformed the band's conventional blues image to one of hard rocking, naughty boys who would push the boundaries of acceptability in lyrics, behavior and fashion. Though he would find Jagger, Richards, and particularly Brian Jones willing participants in his plans, Watts, Wyman and Stewart remained more conventional and far less controversial.

The Rolling Stones' career is permanently linked to that of The Beatles. By most accounts, The Beatles first saw The Rolling Stones during their performance at the Crawdaddy Club in London on April 14, 1963. Several weeks later, George Harrison recommended the group to Dick Rowe of Decca Records, who, mindful of his rejection of The Beatles the previous year, signed The Rolling Stones to an exclusive contract.

On September 10, 1963, Lennon and McCartney were in London attending a Variety Club lunch and, on their way home, ran into Oldham who invited them to The Rolling Stones' rehearsal at the Ken Colyer Jazz Club. The band was looking for a song to record for their second single, and inquired if John and Paul had anything they could use. Lennon and McCartney offered them their as-yet-unfinished composition ***I Wanna Be Your Man***, which John and Paul finished on the spot. They recorded and released it as their second single three weeks before The Beatles' version was released. The song was a U.K. top 20 for The Rolling Stones. (***I Wanna Be Your Man*** has since been covered by Adam Faith*, Ray Columbus & The Invaders, L.A. Guns, The Rezillos, and The Rockin' Ramrods.)

Though the press tried to paint the picture of a fierce rivalry between The Rolling Stones and The Beatles, the competition was always friendly. The two bands even kept in contact over record release dates so as not to compete with each other's releases. John Lennon later claimed to have resented manager Brian Epstein for insisting The Beatles' success was dependent upon them abandoning their scruffy image in favor of matching suits, while The Rolling Stones were able to capitalize on their scruffy image. Their image made it easier for the public to accept the more controversial aspects of The Beatles, however.

The Rolling Stones often visited The Beatles in the studio. Brian contributed to the chorus of ***Yellow Submarine***, and Mick and Keith appeared in a film documenting the recording of ***A Day In The Life***. The Rolling Stones were often accused, sometimes justifiably, of copying The Beatles. One rather

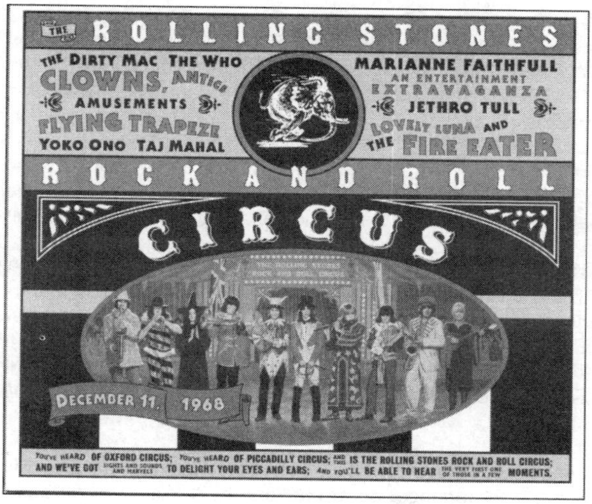

obvious example was their album **Their Satanic Majesties Request**, that bore more than a little resemblance to **Sgt. Pepper's Lonely Heart's Club Band**. The music and the jacket photo, taken by the same photographer as **Sgt. Pepper**, was every bit as psychedelic. The album's 3-D jacket included photos of The Beatles' faces. The Beatles had included the phrase "Welcome The Rolling Stones Good Guys" on **Sgt. Pepper's** cover. A very small number of U.S. copies have been found of **Their Satanic Majesties Request** containing the front and back slick of The Beatles' **Magical Mystery Tour** album on the inside of the gatefold. This is, no doubt, the result of a misprint (possibly deliberate) at an independent pressing plant, which seems likely considering the fact that both albums were big sellers in the U.S. and released at almost the same time, though by different record companies.

During the beginning of 1967's "Summer of Love," Mick Jagger, Keith Richards, and Brian Jones were arrested on drug charges, and the British courts were eager to make an example of them by handing out stiff sentences. The Beatles, who would eventually face similar problems, publicly supported reforms to stiff British drug laws, and came to the support of The Rolling Stones. George Harrison was a guest at Keith Richards' house party hours before Richards was busted there by police.

The two bands' members were seeing each other more often, and continued showing up for each other's recording sessions. On May 11, 1967, Mick Jagger attended The Beatles' recording sessions for ***Baby You're A Rich Man***, and most likely contributed to the background chorus. On June 8, The Beatles invited Brian Jones to play saxophone on their recording of ***You Know My Name (Look Up The Number)***. Keith Richards, along with Mick Jagger and his girl friend Marianne Faithfull*, were some of the many rock-star elite present during The Beatles' live telecast, via satellite, performance of ***All You Need Is Love*** for the BBC's program **Our World**, on June 25, 1967.

Lennon and McCartney sang backing vocals on The Rolling Stones' single ***We Love You*** in a show of support for the unfair treatment The Rolling Stones received following their drug arrests. There is some debate about the actual recording date of ***We Love You***. In Bill Wyman's autobiography **Stone Alone** he states the first initial tracks for ***We Love You*** were recorded June 12 and 13, and that John and Paul added their background vocals in July. The **Singles Collection** simply lists the song as being recorded in July. Other reliable publications list John and Paul's contribution as being recorded in June. Noted Beatles researcher Mark Lewisohn lists the date of John and Paul's contribution as May 18. One thing is certain, John and Paul did not record their background vocals before the song was recorded, and most reliable accounts list the song as being recorded in June and / or July. In August, Mick and Marianne accompanied The Beatles on their trip to Bangor, Wales to study transcendental meditation – the fateful weekend Brian Epstein died.

The release of **Their Satanic Majesties Request** album in late 1967 also marked the departure of Andrew Loog Oldham. Allen Klein, who had handled The Rolling Stones' financial affairs since 1965, now took even greater control of the band's finances. (The Rolling Stones tried desperately to get out from under Klein's control, which they essentially did in 1972, though Klein owns virtually all the Rolling Stones' pre-1970 catalogue.) There was even talk of The Rolling Stones and The Beatles forming some kind of business partnership. (The Beatles were forming Apple Records in 1967, and The Rolling Stones went on to form Rolling Stone Records in 1970.) In 1969, The Beatles hired Klein to manage Apple in spite of The Rolling Stones' warnings.

The Rolling Stones' next album, **Beggars Banquet**, was initially rejected for release by their record company, Decca, because of its proposed cover that depicted a toilet room covered with graffiti that included among other less savory phrases, "John loves Yoko." The album was finally released in late 1968 in a plain white sleeve designed to look like an invitation. There are some who claim there are photos of Lennon, McCartney and Harrison to be found inside the album's gatefold. Again the album cover drew criticism for its similarity to **The Beatles** (plain white album cover). Ironically, Decca would reissue the album in the 1980s with the original banned front cover. During the recording of the album, Brian Jones, the heart of The Rolling Stones' blues and experimental sound, was often absent or ineffective due to mental and physical deterioration from substance abuse.

The Rolling Stones' next project was to be a made-for-TV special titled **Rock And Roll Circus**, filmed on December 10 & 11, 1968 at InterTel Studios, Stonebridge House in London. The film was directed by Michael Lindsay-Hogg who, three weeks later, would begin directing The Beatles' film **Let It Be**. Again The Rolling Stones were following the lead of The Beatles, who had produced the TV special **Magical Mystery Tour** the previous year. Among the performers were Marianne Faithfull, Jethro Tull, Taj Mahal*, The Who *(see John Entwistle, Keith Moon)*, and John Lennon and Yoko Ono*.

Lennon performed ***Yer Blues*** on guitar, along with Eric Clapton* on guitar, Mitch Mitchell (Jimi Hendrix Experience) on drums, and Keith Richards on bass. John also sang along with the audience on the chorus of ***Salt Of The Earth***. During rehearsals, Lennon, Clapton and Jagger played ***Peggy Sue***, and John did a version of Elvis' hit ***It's Now Or Never***. Due to The Rolling Stones' dissatisfaction with their performance and Allen Klein's control, **Rock And Roll Circus** was not released until 1996.

Throughout the first half of 1969, Brian Jones' health continued to deteriorate. In June, Jones announced that he was leaving The Rolling Stones due to musical differences. In fact, Jagger and Richards, who began taking away the leadership role from Jones early on, confronted Jones at his

Mick Jagger and Keith Richards, Detroit, MI, photo courtesy of Pat Henry

home informing him he was being replaced by guitarist Mick Taylor (born January 17, 1948, in Hertfordshire, England). Jones was amicable about the decision, but nearly a month later, on July 3, 1969, he drowned in his swimming pool. The coroner's report concluded that the drowning was probably due to the influence of drugs and alcohol. Many people close to Brian, including members of The Rolling Stones, question that conclusion. Jones was known to be a good swimmer, but was subject to asthma attacks. At the time of his death he had surrounded himself with questionable "friends" and employees who, it is theorized, may have been involved in too much rough horseplay with Jones in the swimming pool.

After The Beatles broke up in 1970, and The Rolling Stones relocated to the south of France as tax exiles in 1971, there was little chance for interaction between the two groups' members. McCartney and Ringo did attend Jagger's wedding in St. Tropez, and Mick frequently dropped in on Lennon when he was in New York. Jagger played guitar on Yoko's 1973 album **Approximately Infinite Universe**. He sang backing vocals on ***Do You Want To Dance*** from Lennon's **Rock 'N' Roll** album. During a break in the recording of the album, Lennon helped produced ***Too Many Cooks***, sung by Jagger, that has yet to be officially released.

In March 1975, Ron Wood* replaced Mick Taylor as The Rolling Stones' new guitarist while still a member of The Faces *(see Kenney Jones, Ian McLagan, Rod Stewart)*. He quit The Faces later in the year, and, to date, remains a full-fledged member of The Rolling Stones. Billy Preston* and Bobby Keys* have also done much session work and backing on tour for The Rolling Stones.

The jacket design of The Rolling Stones' 1978 album **Some Girls**, which contains a photo of George Harrison, was altered shortly after its release due to the unauthorized use of photographs of some famous women. Bill Wyman joined Ringo, Dave Mason, and others in a band that performed on the Jerry Lewis Telethon on September 3, 1979. Ringo also made a cameo appearance in 1985 for a promotional video for Wyman's **Willie And The Poor Boys** project.

In 1985, tragedy again struck The Rolling Stones when founding member and friend Ian Stewart died suddenly of a heart attack while in his doctor's office. For The Rolling Stones, who as a band were perilously close to death themselves, it was the end of an era. Jagger and Richards were about as friendly towards one another as Lennon and McCartney were in the early 1970s. Perhaps the most telling moment of admiration and affection between The Beatles and The Rolling Stones came when Mick Jagger (with George, Ringo and Yoko present) inducted The Beatles into the Rock 'N' Roll Hall Of Fame on January 20, 1988 at New York's Waldorf Astoria Hotel, complete with a jam session following the ceremonies. It was the first time Jagger and Richards had appeared in public in several years. Shortly thereafter, The Rolling Stones decided to give it another try, recorded a new album and backed it with a tour.

In 1989, a twenty-five year retrospective on VHS and laser videodisk titled **25 x 5 The Continuing Adventures Of The Rolling Stones** was issued containing newsreel footage of The Beatles. That year The Rolling Stones were inducted into the Rock and Roll Hall of Fame. Some of the biggest among The Rolling Stones' many hits include ***Not Fade Away***, ***Time Is On My Side***, ***(I Can't Get No) Satisfaction***, ***Paint It Black***, ***Jumpin' Jack Flash***, ***Street Fighting Man***, ***Honky Tonk Woman***, ***Brown Sugar***, ***Angie***, ***Miss You***, ***Start Me Up*** and ***Mixed Emotion***. In 1993 Bill Wyman retired from The Rolling Stones – who keep on rolling!

Todd Rundgren

Record 302 title:
Live From Montreaux (Ringo Starr And His All-Starr Band Volume 2)

Media:
Album 5" CD

Label / Catalog number:
Rykodisc / RCD 20264

Producer:
Jim Beach & Louise Velazquez (Film); Ringo Starr (Music)

Jacket / Inserts:
Standard international design in jewel box / 12 page CD booklet

Recording Location / Date:
On location at Montreaux Jazz Festival, Montreaux, Switzerland / 13 Jul 92

Song 302a title:
Bang The Drum All Day [live]

Track details:
Side 1, track 9 / 3 min. 25 sec.

Release date / Country:
14 Sep 93 / U.S.A.

Composer:
T. Rundgren

Todd Rundgren: Lead Vocals & Drums; Ringo Starr: Drums; Joe Walsh: Keyboards, B. Vocals & Drums; Burton Cummings: Keyboards, B. Vocals & Percussion; Nils Lofgren: Acoustic Guitar; Dave Edmunds: Guitar; Timothy B. Schmit: Bass; Tim Cappello: Percussion; Zak Starkey: Drums

Videoarts / VALJ-3369 / Album 12" LVD / Side 1, track 9 / released (probably) Nov 93 in Japan / Unique / Lyric & translation insert.

Todd Rundgren was born on June 22, 1948 in Philadelphia (Upper Darby), Pennsylvania. Todd was typical of many young American males of the mid-1960s. He was a big fan of The Beatles, seemed to have trouble finding himself or fitting in, and turned to music. He joined a number of bands during and after high school, and in 1967 he formed the short-lived group Nazz. Nazz was a mod-styled band, reminiscent of the pre-**Sgt. Pepper** Beatles, that had two minor hits which have stood the test of time to become rock classics – ***Open My Eyes*** and ***Hello It's Me***.

Todd Rundgren Detroit 1982 Photo by Patrick Henry

Todd Rundgren, Detroit, MI, photo courtesy of Pat Henry

By 1970, Rundgren was essentially a solo artist. His album **Runt**, that also served as a moniker for him, produced the top 20 song ***We Gotta Get You A Woman***. His highly acclaimed 1972 album **Something / Anything?**, which, like many of his works, he recorded almost entirely unassisted, also yielded a top 20 song with ***I Saw The Light***. In the mid-1970s, Rundgren recorded two barely noticed classics – ***A Dream Goes On Forever*** and ***Real Man***. In 1973, Rundgren re-recorded and released ***Hello It's Me***, this time making it his first and only top 10, though he has had a large cult following, and his albums have sold very well over the years.

Rundgren has found praise and commercial success as a studio musician and producer for other acts. He has worked with a number of artists over the years including, among others, Patti Smith, Psychedelic Furs, Meat Loaf, Grand Funk Railroad *(see Mark Farner)*, Cheap Trick, XTC, Hall And Oates* and The Tubes.

In 1974, Rundgren teamed up with Roger Powell, Kasim Sulton and Willie Wilcox to form Utopia, a side-project band with which he frequently, but not always, records. He has recently become heavily involved in video arts, but continues producing, touring and recording with and without Utopia.

Rundgren's association with The Beatles began in 1971 when he was given the task of finishing up production on Badfinger's* album **Straight Up**, which George Harrison had started to produce before becoming tied up with the **Bangla Desh** project. In 1974, Rundgren and John Lennon became involved in a brief, but bitter political / musical shouting match via the music press that would end with Rundgren retreating from some of his previous statements. Rundgren recorded excellent covers of John Lennon's Beatles songs ***Rain*** and ***Strawberry Fields Forever*** for his 1976 album **Faithful**. Todd and Utopia released **Deface The Music**, a sort of Beatles musical parody, in 1980. Their 1981 album **Swing To The Right** featured a jacket photo of a mass burning of Beatles' records in 1966 during protests in the southern U.S. in reaction to John Lennon's statement that The Beatles were more popular than Christ. The photo and title were no doubt about America's recent political swing to the right. In 1989, Rundgren composed the lyrics and music for the off-Broadway production of **Up Against It**, a screenplay written by Joe Orton, which The Beatles considered using for a film following **Help!**.

Rundgren was a member of Ringo Starr's All-Starr Band tour in 1992. During the tour he performed ***Bang The Drum All Day*** with Ringo backing him on drums. Rundgren also performed an acoustic rendition of John Lennon's ***You've Got To Hide Your Love Away*** during the All-Starr's performance in Liverpool.

Leon Russell

Record 303 title:
Leon Russell
Label / Catalog number:
DCC/Shelter / GZS-1049
Jacket / Inserts:
Standard international design in jewel box with die-cut cardboard slip cover / 8 page CD booklet
Media:
Album 5" CD
Producer:
Denny Cordell & Leon Russell

Song 303a title:
Delta Lady
Release date / Country:
18 Nov 93 (first issued 01 Feb 70) / Japan/Canada
Recording Location / Date:
Olympic Sound Studios, London, U.K. / 02 & 05 Sep 69
Track details:
Side 1, track 6 / 4 min. 00 sec.
Composer:
L. Russell

Leon Russell: Lead Vocals & (probable) Guitar; George Harrison: Leslie Guitar; Ringo Starr: Drums; Eric Clapton (possible): Guitar; Bill Wyman: Bass: Steve Winwood: Organ; Bonnie Bramlett: B. Vocals; Clydie King: B. Vocals; Merry Clayton: B. Vocals

Song 303b title:
I Put A Spell On You
Release date / Country:
18 Nov 93 (first issued 01 Feb 70) / Japan/Canada
Recording Location / Date:
Olympic Sound Studios, London, U.K. / Sep - Oct 69
Track details:
Side 1, track 3 / 4 min. 10 sec.
Composer:
L. Russell

Leon Russell: Lead Vocals; George Harrison: Guitar; Bill Wyman: Bass; Charlie Watts: Drums; Chris Stainton: Guitar or Percussion or Keyboards; Steve Winwood: Guitar, or Percussion or Keyboards; Clydie King: (probable) B. Vocals; Merry Clayton: (probable) B. Vocals

Song 303c title:
Indian Girl
Track details:
Side 1, track 15 / 4 min. 08 sec.
Release date / Country:
18 Nov 93 / Japan/Canada
Composer:
L. Russell
Recording Location / Date:
Olympic Sound Studios, London, U.K. / Sep - Oct 69

Leon Russell: Lead Vocals & Piano; George Harrison: Acoustic Guitar; Eric Clapton: Acoustic Guitar; Ringo Starr: Drums; Klaus Voormann: Bass

Song 303d title:
Pisces Apple Lady
Track details:
Side 1, track 11 / 2 min. 50 sec.
Release date / Country:
18 Nov 93 (first issued 02/01/70) / Japan/Canada
Composer:
L. Russell
Recording Location / Date:
Olympic Sound Studios, London, U.K. / Sep - Oct 69

Leon Russell: Lead Vocals & Piano; George Harrison: Guitar; Ringo Starr: Drums; Bill Wyman: Bass; Merry Clayton: (probable) B. Vocals; Clydie King: (probable) B. Vocals

Song 303e title:
Prince Of Peace
Track details:
Side 1, track 7 / 3 min. 05 sec.
Release date / Country:
18 Nov 93 (first issued 01 Feb 70) / Japan/Canada
Composer:
L. Russell - G. Dempsey
Recording Location / Date:
Olympic Sound Studios, London, U.K. / Sep 69 &/or Oct &/or Nov 69

Leon Russell: Lead Vocals & Piano; George Harrison: Acoustic Slide Guitar; Eric Clapton: Lead Guitar; Bill Wyman &/or Klaus Voormann: Bass; B.J. Wilson: (probable) Percussion or Jon Hiseman: (probable) Percussion; Merry Clayton: (probable) B. Vocals; Clydie King: (probable) B. Vocals

Song 303f title:
Roll Away The Stone
Track details:
Side 1, track 12 / 3 min. 06 sec.
Release date / Country:
18 Nov 93 (first issued 01 Feb 70) / Japan/Canada
Composer:
L. Russell - G. Dempsey
Recording Location / Date:
Olympic Sound Studios, London, U.K. / Sep - Oct 69

Leon Russell: Lead Vocals & Keyboards; George Harrison: Guitar; Ringo Starr: Drums; Bill Wyman: Bass; Steve Winwood: Keyboards; Eric Clapton: Guitar; Chris Stainton: Keyboards

Song 303g title:
Shoot Out On The Plantation
Track details:
Side 1, track 4 / 3 min. 10 sec.
Release date / Country:
18 Nov 93 (first issued 01 Feb 70) / Japan/Canada
Composer:
L. Russell
Recording Location / Date:
Olympic Sound Studios, London, U.K. / Sep 69

Leon Russell: Lead Vocals & Piano; George Harrison: Guitar; Ringo Starr: Drums; Klaus Voormann: Bass; Steve Winwood: Piano; Jim Horn: Horns

Song 303h title:
(The New) Sweet Home Chicago
Release date / Country:
18 Nov 93 / Japan/Canada
Recording Location / Date:
Olympic Sound Studios, London, U.K. / Sep - Oct 69

Track details:
Side 1, track 13 / 3 min. 11 sec.
Composer:
L. Russell - M. Benno

Leon Russell: Lead Vocals & Piano &/or Bass; George Harrison: Guitar; Chris Stainton: Guitar, or Bass or Keyboards; Charlie Watts: Percussion; B.J. Wilson: (probable) Percussion; Steve Winwood: Keyboards or Bass or Guitar

Record 304 title:
Concert For Bangla Desh
Label / Catalog number:
FRT / 1001 [Unauthorized Record]
Jacket / Inserts:
Unique / Record label inner sleeve
Recording Location / Date:
On location at Madison Square Garden, New York, NY, U.S.A. / 01 Aug 71 [afternoon]

Media:
Album 12"
Producer:
[unknown-audience recording]
George Harrison & Phil Spector

Song 304a title:
Medley: Jumpin' Jack Flash-Youngblood-Jumpin' Jack Flash [live]
Release date / Country:
mid-1970s / U.S.A.

Track details:
Side 2, track 4
Composer:
M. Jagger - K. Richards — J. Lieber - M. Stoller - D. Pomus

Leon Russell: Vocals & Piano; Don Preston: Vocals & Lead Guitar; George Harrison: Rhythm Guitar & B. Vocals; Ringo Starr: Drums; Billy Preston: Organ; Jim Keltner: Drums; Eric Clapton: Lead Guitar; Jesse Ed Davis: Rhythm Guitar; Klaus Voormann: Bass; Carl Radle: Bass; Alan Beutler: B. Vocals; Marlin Greene: B. Vocals; Jeanie Greene: B. Vocals; Joe Green: B. Vocals; Dolores Hall: B. Vocals; Jackie Kelso: B. Vocals; Claudia Lennear: B. Vocals; Lou McCreary: B. Vocals; Don Nix: B. Vocals; Pete Ham: Acoustic Guitar; Joey Molland: Acoustic Guitar; Tom Evans: Acoustic Guitar; Mike Gibbons: Percussion

Record 305 title:
The Concert For Bangla Desh
Label / Catalog number:
Warner Bros / NJL-38583
Jacket / Inserts:
Standard international design with variations / 4 page translation insert
Recording Location / Date:
On location at Madison Square Garden, New York, NY, U.S.A. / 01 Aug 71 [evening]

Media:
Album 12" LVD
Producer:
George Harrison & Phil Spector

Song 305a title:
Medley: Jumpin' Jack Flash-Youngblood-Jumpin' Jack Flash [live]
Release date / Country:
1990 / Japan

Track details:
Side 2, track 2 / 10 min. 12 sec.
Composer:
M. Jagger - K. Richards — J. Lieber - M. Stoller - D. Pomus

Leon Russell: Vocals & Piano; Don Preston: Vocals & Lead Guitar; George Harrison: Rhythm Guitar & B. Vocals; Ringo Starr: Drums; Billy Preston: Organ; Jim Keltner: Drums; Eric Clapton: Lead

Guitar; Jesse Ed Davis: Rhythm Guitar; Klaus Voormann: Bass; Carl Radle: Bass; Alan Beutler: B. Vocals; Marlin Greene: B. Vocals; Jeanie Greene: B. Vocals; Joe Green: B. Vocals; Dolores Hall: B. Vocals; Jackie Kelso: B. Vocals; Claudia Lennear: B. Vocals; Lou McCreary: B. Vocals; Don Nix: B. Vocals; Pete Ham: Acoustic Guitar; Joey Molland: Acoustic Guitar; Tom Evans: Acoustic Guitar; Mike Gibbons: Percussion

This song is also included on Capitol/Apple / CDP 7 93265 2 / Album 5" CD [2 CD set] / CD2, track 1 / released 01 Aug 91 (first issued 20 Dec 71) in the U.S.A. / Standard international design in double Jewel box / 34 page CD booklet with photo of George Harrison & Ringo Starr.

Leon Russell, Detroit, MI, early 1970s, photo courtesy of Tom Bert

Leon Russell (aka Russell Bridges and Hank Wilson) was born on April 2, 1941 in Lawton, Oklahoma. Early in his career, he worked with Ronnie Hawkins* and The Hawks, who later evolved into The Band* *(see also Rick Danko, Levon Helm)*. Russell's blend of blues, country and gospel, and his musical versatility on guitar, keyboards, horn and percussion, led to session work as a member of Phil Spector's* "Wall Of Sound - Wrecking Crew" *(see Ronnie Spector)*. Over the years, Russell has worked with dozens of well-known artists.

Russell and Delaney Bramlett* *(see also Delaney & Bonnie & Friends)* were friends dating back to the popular mid-1960s music television show **Shindig**. Both were occasional members of the house band, The Shindogs. Russell followed Delaney & Bonnie's migration to England in 1969, capturing the attention of English producer Denny Cordell, who then managed and produced Joe Cocker*. Russell and Cordell teamed up with Cocker and, along with many members of Delaney & Bonnie's "friends," toured as Mad Dogs And Englishmen. Several years later Cordell and Russell founded Shelter Records.

In the fall of 1969, Harrison, Ringo and most of the "friends" contributed to Russell's first album, **Leon Russell**. Harrison and Ringo only contributed to songs recorded at Olympic Studios in England. John Lennon was also present at some of the Olympic Studio sessions, though it's unlikely that he contributed to any of Russell's recordings. Unfortunately, the album did not list the specific musicians for each track. Additional information was revealed in the liner notes of the gold-disc CD reissue of the album in 1993, but the specific musicians for each track were still not included. Fortunately, ICE magazine printed the basic musical line-up for each song just before the CD's release.

Russell probably recorded his version of George Harrison's composition ***Beware Of Darkness*** before Harrison released it. Marc Roberty claims in his book **Eric Clapton The Complete Recordings Sessions 1963 - 1992** that ***Beware Of Darkness*** was recorded in October or November 1969 at Olympic Studios during the recordings for the **Leon Russell** album. Russell's version would not be released until after Harrison's version, on the album **Leon Russell And The Shelter People**. The album mentions the song as being recorded at Island Studios on August 24-26, 1970. Though it lists the musicians involved, it fails to credit Eric Clapton who, by most reliable accounts, was also involved. The album's credits, and Roberty's book, also fail to mention who plays sitar on the song.

This has naturally led to speculation that Harrison may have played sitar and assisted with the production of Russell's version of the song. According to Jim Price, who also played on ***Beware of Darkness***, Harrison did not contribute to Russell's version. He thinks it's likely the musically versatile Russell played sitar on the song. Russell shared vocals with Harrison on ***Beware Of Darkness*** at **The Concert For Bangla Desh**.

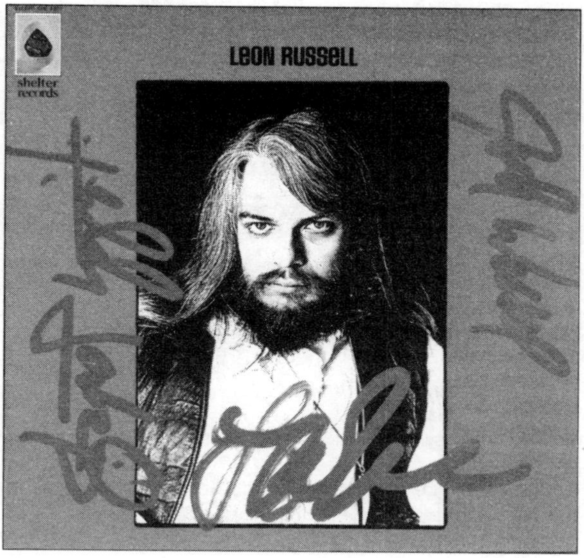

In an interview in Rolling Stone magazine about the album **Leon Russell And The Shelter People**, Russell explained: "I did one session with Ringo and George, but I didn't really have any songs, and we were more or less jamming. I have one track that's really nice, but I haven't gotten around to writing the words for it."

Delta Lady, a 1991 CD release on the Del Rack label (DRZ 918), has more specific musical credits than the **Leon Russell** album. It also includes a fade-out that is sixteen seconds longer on ***Beware Of Darkness***, and fourteen seconds longer on **Delta Lady**. Several other extended versions that this album claims to feature are considerably shorter than the times listed. The Del Rack CD's credits contain other errors and omissions as well.

Russell's solo career hit its peak in 1972 with the release of the highly successful album **Carney**, featuring his biggest hit ***Tight Rope***. Russell was one of the many well-known Los Angeles studio musicians who contributed to sessions in late 1973 for John Lennon's **Rock 'N' Roll** album.

Russell contributed to Harrison's 1975 album **Extra Texture**. Leon and his wife, Mary McCreary, recorded Harrison's composition ***I'll Still Love You*** (originally titled ***When Every Song Is Sung***). Their version remains unreleased, though Ringo recorded a version included on his album **Rotogravure**. (The song was also recorded by Cilla Black* and Ronnie Spector*.) Harrison is rumored to have contributed to the Russell's **Wedding Album** recorded at about the same time. However, neither the music nor the detailed credits suggest any involvement by Harrison. Most likely, Harrison contributed to Russell's version of ***When Every Song Is Sung*** that was intended for inclusion on the **Wedding Album**.

Russell turned more towards country music during the 1970s, and occasionally billed himself as Hank Wilson. He released only two albums in the 1980s, one of which featured a cover of ***I've Just Seen A Face***, during which time he formed a video production company. Russell released the album **Anything Can Happen** in 1992. He continues to record and tour, but has yet to regain the commercial success he enjoyed in the early 1970s.

The Scaffold

Record 306 title:
Singles A's & B's
Label / Catalog number:
Charly/See For Miles / CM 114
Media:
Album 12"
Jacket / Inserts:
Unique

Song 306a title:
(Stop Blowing Those) Charity Bubbles
Release date / Country:
18 Oct 82 (first issued 27 Jun 69) / U.K.
Producer:
Norrie Paramor & Tim Rice
Recording Location / Date:
EMI-Abbey Road Studios, London, U.K. / 1969
Track details:
Side 1, track 7 / 2 min. 34 sec.
Composer:
R. McGough - M. McGear

Mike McGear: Lead Vocals; Paul McCartney: Guitar

Song 306b title:
Goose
Release date / Country:
18 Oct 82 (first issued 27 Jun 69) / U.K.
Producer:
Norrie Paramor & Tim Rice
Recording Location / Date:
EMI-Abbey Road Studios, London, U.K. / 1969
Track details:
Side 2, track 6 / 2 min. 34 sec.
Composer:
R. McGough - M. McGear

Mike McGear: Lead Vocals; Paul McCartney: Guitar; Nicky Hopkins: Piano

Song 306c title:
Lily The Pink
Release date / Country:
18 Oct 82 (first issued 18 Oct 68) / U.K.
Track details:
Side 1, track 6 / 4 min. 15 sec.
Composer:
Trad Arr. J. Gorman - M. McGear - R. McGough
Producer:
Norrie Paramor & Tim Rice [Assistance by Paul McCartney]
Recording Location / Date:
EMI-Abbey Road Studios, London, U.K. / 1968

John Gorman: Vocals; Mike McGear: Vocals; Roger McGough: Vocals; Graham Nash: B. Vocals; Jack: Bruce: Bass; Paul McCartney: (probable) Involvement; Tim Rice: B. Vocals

Song 306d title:
Liverpool Lou
Release date / Country:
18 Oct 82 (24 May 74) / U.K.
Track details:
Side 1, track 11 / 2 min. 58 sec.
Composer:
D. Behan (Trad arr: P. McCartney - L. McCartney)
Producer:
Paul McCartney
Recording Location / Date:
Strawberry Studios, Stockport, U.K. / (probably) May 74

Mike McGear: Lead Vocals; Denny Laine: Gob-Iron; Jimmy McCulloch: Guitar; Gerry Conway: Drums; Paul McCartney: Gyzmo, Bass, Arrangement & (probable) B. Vocals; Linda McCartney: Piano & Arrangement

Song 306e title:
Ten Years After On Strawberry Jam
Release date / Country:
18 Oct 82 (first issued 24 May 74) / U.K.
Producer:
Paul McCartney
Recording Location / Date:
Strawberry Studios, Stockport, U.K. / Jan - May 74

Track details:
Side 2, track 9 / 2 min. 52 sec.
Composer:
P. McCartney - L. McCartney

Mike McGear: Vocals; Roger McGough: Vocals; John Gorman: Vocals; The Stockport Gdansk Band Co-operative; (members of) 10cc; (members of) Wings; Paul McCartney: (probable) Instruments

Song 306f title:
Thank U Very Much
Release date / Country:
18 Oct 82 (first issued 03 Nov 67) / U.K.
Producer:
Tony Palmer [Assistance by Paul McCartney]
Recording Location / Date:
EMI-Abbey Road Studios, London, U.K. / Jul 67

Track details:
Side 1, track 3 / 2 min. 30 sec.
Composer:
M. McGear

Mike McGear: Lead Vocals; John Gorman: B. Vocals; Roger McGough: B. Vocals

The Scaffold was an English trio of musicians / actors / comedians / poets that began to take form in Liverpool, England in late 1962. The members were John Gorman, born on January 4, 1937 in Birkenhead; Roger McGough, born on November 9, 1937 in Liverpool; and Mike McGear*, born Peter Michael McCartney on January 7, 1944 in Liverpool. Michael is the younger brother of Paul McCartney. In 1962, Mike was asked by Merseyside Arts Festival organizers John Gorman and poet Roger McGough to take part in a comedy sketch and help organize the festival. Following the festival, the three teamed up with several other artists to form a musical / poetry / comedy act called The Liverpool One Fat Lady All Electric Show.

By the end of 1963, the group was pared down to Mike, Roger and John for a British TV series. They renamed themselves The Scaffold. Mike renamed himself McGear ("gear" was Liverpool slang for cool or great) in an attempt to maintain his own identity, and avoid accusations that he was trying to cash in on the rising fame of the McCartney name. The trio would spend the next few years touring and doing TV bits, and was represented for a short time by Brian Epstein's NEMS Enterprises, which also handled The Beatles. Being Paul's brother certainly did not hinder Mike in securing a recording contract with Parlophone/EMI, or in recruiting superstar session players. In 1966, The Scaffold released their first single ***2 Days Monday / 3 Blind Jellyfish***.

It was inevitable that brother Paul would lend his influence, associations and talents to The Scaffold's recordings – though for the most part anonymously. According to Mike, Paul assisted in the recording of ***Thank U Very Much***, giving advice, and contributing to the result. The November 1967 issue of The Beatles Book monthly magazine reported that McCartney "helped operate the buttons and levers up in the studio control room." The song was inspired by Mike's thanks to Paul for giving him a Nikon camera. Paul was not particularly fond of the lyric line, "Aintree Iron" (it relates to sexually transmitted diseases), and strongly suggested to Mike that he omit it, or the song would not be a hit! Released in 1967, it became the first of three U.K. top 10 songs for the trio. Paul later admitted to Mike that he had been wrong about the lyrics that actually generated interest.

The Scaffold, always a loosely knit outfit, spawned numerous solo projects. In 1967, Paul produced and played on the **McGough & McGear** *(see Roger McGough & Mike McGear)* album, released in 1968. Prior to the album's release, one of its songs, ***Do You Remember?***, was re-recorded and released as a Scaffold single. Unlike the version on **McGough & McGear**, it does not include Paul McCartney on piano or backing vocals.

Toward the end of 1968, The Scaffold scored their second top 10 song, ***Lily The Pink***. Again Paul dropped by to lend a little assistance. Unfortunately, The Scaffold's brand of Liverpool humor served as a barrier to the U.S. market, where the group had little success. None of their four U.K. albums

were ever released in the U.S. (a U.S.-only compilation album was released), and only four of their 16 singles were released in the U.S.

Apparently, Paul was also present at EMI's Abbey Road Studios on January 12, 1969 during The Scaffold's recording of humor and poetry that made up side two of their **L The P** [Lily The Pink] album, though Mike does not think Paul contributed in any way. The Scaffold recorded several more albums and singles, including the song ***Stop Blowing Those Charity Bubbles***, that they re-recorded and released as the single ***Charity Bubbles / Goose*** featuring Paul on guitar.

In 1971, EMI dropped The Scaffold, whose members resumed work on a number of other projects. Mike, with a little help from Paul, recorded the solo album **Woman**. In 1973 Mike, along with Roger Gorman, Andy Roberts, Neil Innes, Roger McGough and Viv Stanshall, formed the loosely knit band Grimms *(see The Bonzo Dog Band)*. The name was taken from the first initials of each band-member's surnames. The band also included sidemen Zoot Money* and Gerry Conway. Grimms released two albums in 1973, during which time original Scaffold members reunited to record the album **Fresh Liver**.

In 1974, Paul McCartney produced Mike's second solo album, ***McGear**. McCartney also sang, played on, and wrote most of the tracks for Mike's showcase solo album. Wings and members of 10cc also contributed to the album's backing. Toward the end of the ***McGear** sessions, Paul suggested that The Scaffold record the Dominic Behan ode ***Liverpool Lou***, and produced the recording to which wife Linda *(see Linda McCartney)* added piano. Ironically, unlike any of the well-crafted pop songs from ***McGear**, this regionally styled folk ballad became The Scaffold's third and final top 10 in the U.K! Its B-side, ***Ten Years After On Strawberry Jam***, also received Paul's helping hand. It was recorded during sessions for ***McGear**. Judging from Mike's cryptic liner notes on The Scaffold album **Singles A's & B's**, this was the session that the brother and sister duo The Carpenters dropped in on, though they did not contribute to the recording.

The Scaffold then went on to record the appropriately titled album **Sold Out**, that would prove to be their last album. In April 1977, The Scaffold released their last single and essentially retired for good that month. There is always the possibility that Mike and / or The Scaffold may resume their recording career. Perhaps some of their unreleased recordings, possibly containing contributions by Paul, will be issued in the future.

Michael Schenker Group

Record 307 title:
None
Label / Catalog number:
[Unreleased]
Recording Location / Date:
Air Studios, London, U.K. / Apr 81

Producer:
Ron Nevison

Song 307a title:
None
Release date / Country:
[Unreleased]
Composer:
M. Schenker - P. Raymond - C. Powell - C. Glen - G. Barden

Gary Barden: Lead Vocals; Paul McCartney: Bass; Michael Schenker: Guitar; Paul Raymond: Keyboards & Guitar; Cozy Powell: Drums

Mention heavy-metal bands like Scorpions or UFO, and one immediately thinks of Michael Schenker. Schenker was born in Sarstedt, Germany on January 10, 1955. He was a member of his brother's band, Scorpions, from 1970 until 1972, when he joined UFO. He departed UFO in 1979 and rejoined Scorpions. He formed the Michael Schenker Group in the summer of 1980. The group has seen a number of personnel changes over the years, and Schenker has continued to worked with Scorpions and UFO.

The Michael Schenker Group's bass player, Chris Glen, missed a recording session at George Martin's* AIR Studios in April 1981 for the album **MSG**. Paul McCartney, who was working on his **Tug Of War** album at the same studio, was recruited by MSG's drummer Cozy Powell to fill in on bass. According to Schenker, McCartney contributed to one song, the title of which he cannot recall, that was not released. The **MSG** album credits did include thanks to "Paul McCartney (cheques in the post Maca)," a friendly joke, according to Schenker.

Tom Scott

Record 308 title:
Fort Worth Express
Media:
Album 5" [2 CD set]
Label / Catalog number:
Hindustani Music / Raga 001-A:B
[Unauthorized Record]
Producer:
Unknown-audience recording
Jacket / Inserts:
Unique with slip cover in double Jewel box
Recording Location / Date:
On location at the Tarrant County Convention Center, Fort Worth, TX, U.S.A. / 22 Nov 74

Song 308a title:
Tomcat [live]
Release date / Country:
1996 / U.S.A
Track details:
CD2, track 5 / 3 min. 31 sec.
Composer:
T. Scott

Billy Preston: Keyboards; Tom Scott: Saxophone; Chuck Findley: Trumpet; Robben Ford: Guitar; Andy Newmark: Drums; Emil Richards: Percussion; Willie Weeks: Bass; Jim Horn: Saxophone; George Harrison: Guitar; Jim Keltner: Drums

Record 309 title:
New York Connection
Media:
Album 5"
Label / Catalog number:
Ode/Epic/Legacy / EX 64961
Producer:
Tom Scott & Hank Cicalo
Jacket / Inserts:
Standard international design in jewel box / 4 page CD booklet
Recording Location / Date:
Hit Factory Studios, New York, NY & A&M Studios, Los Angeles, CA†, U.S.A. / mid-1975

Song 309a title:
Appolonia (Foxtrata)
Release date / Country:
16 Jul 96 (first issued 08 Dec 75) / U.S.A
Track details:
Side 1, track 8 / 3 min. 59 sec.
Composer:
T. Scott

Tom Scott: Soprano Saxophone, Flute & Lyricon; George Harrison: Slide Guitar†; Richard Tee: Keyboards; Bob James: Electric Piano; Gary King: Bass; Steve Gadd: Drums; Ralph McDonald: Percussion; Eric Gale &/or Hugh McCracken: Guitar

Tom Scott was born on May 19, 1948 in Los Angeles, California. His mother was a classical pianist, and his father was the composer of themes for several successful films and TV. Tom took up saxophone and clarinet in school, and left college to play in jazz clubs in Los Angeles. He began his solo recording career while working as a session player in the mid-1960s. In the latter half of the 1960s, he too became a successful composer of film and TV theme songs.

In 1971, Scott joined A&M records where he began his solo career in earnest, forming his back-up band the L.A. Express. By the early 1970s, he was one of the most in-demand horn players in the world. In 1973 he added his distinctive saxophone to the album **Ringo**. The following year George Harrison recruited Scott for his **Dark Horse** album, and to back him up on his 1974 North America tour. One of the songs performed on the tour was Scott's instrumental song ***Tomcat***. In 1975, Scott played a solo on McCartney's hit ***Listen To What The Man Said***, and continued to work with George Harrison on his albums **Extra Texture** and **Thirty-Three & 1/3**. Harrison's contribution to Scott's instrumental song ***Appolonia*** was probably recorded during the sessions for **Extra Texture**. He also became involved in other artists' recordings for Harrison's Dark Horse Records label. In 1977, Scott issued a medley called ***Beatles Ballads*** featuring ***Blackbird / Julia / I Will***. He worked again with Ringo on his 1978 **Bad Boy** album, and again with Harrison on his 1981 album **Somewhere In England**.

Tom Scott is still one of the most sought-after studio musicians, and continues to issue successful solo jazz records. He recorded a cover of The Beatles' ***Fool On The Hill*** for the jazz tribute album to The Beatles **I Got No Kick Against Modern Jazz**, issued in 1995. Scott has also been the musical director for a number of television shows including the **The Pat Sajak Show** in 1989-90, the short-lived **Chevy Chase Show** in 1993, **Comic Relief** in 1995, and the **Academy Awards** in 1996.

Peter Sellers, Terry Southern & Ringo Starr

Record 310 title:
The Magic Christian
Label / Catalog number:
Commonwealth United/Garrison Systems / 1761 (promotional only)
Media:
Album 12" (mono)
Producer:
Commonwealth United
Jacket / Inserts:
Unique with photos of Ringo Starr on front and back / 2 page script
Recording Location / Date:
(probably) London, U.K. / 1969

Song 310a title:
Ringo Starr
Release date / Country:
Dec 69 / U.S.A.
Track details:
Side 1, track 2
Composer:
R. Starkey

Ringo Starr: Dialogue

Famed actor and comedian Peter Sellers was born on September 8, 1925 in Southsea, England. Sellers began his career in the radio comedy group The Goons, which included Spike Milligan and Harry Secombe. All the Beatles were avid listeners of the show, and big fans of Sellers, who recorded comedy records for Parlophone/EMI under the production of George Martin*. George Martin has

Ringo Starr and Peter Sellers, promotional poster, scene from the movie The Magic Christian

always claimed he was initially more charmed by The Beatles' humor than their music, and The Beatles were more than a little impressed by his work with Sellers. The Beatles chose Richard Lester as the director of their first two films, in part for his work with Sellers. Martin continued to produce the occasional comedy recording for Sellers, including parodies of ***A Hard Day's Night***, ***Help!***, ***Can't Buy Me Love***, ***Yes It Is***, and four versions of ***She Loves You***. The Beatles met Sellers through Martin, and they became lifelong friends, especially George and Ringo. In 1965, Sellers presented The Beatles with their Grammy Awards, and later in the year appeared on the TV special **The Music Of Lennon and McCartney**.

In January 1969, Ringo, living in a house he bought from Peter Sellers, co-starred with Sellers' in the film **The Magic Christian**. The film was based on the novel and screenplay by Terry Southern. Southern, who appeared on the cover of the **Sgt. Pepper's** album, was a favorite author of The Beatles (and in particular Ringo). Starr had previously appeared in the film **Candy** based on Southern's book. **The Magic Christian** was in actuality a Peter Sellers film. Ringo plays the part of Youngman Grand, the adopted son of Sir Guy Grand (Sellers), the world's wealthiest man. Sir Guy sets out to prove that "everyone has his price" and explores the extremes to which people will go to obtain money.

The Magic Christian was produced by Dennis O'Dell, former head of Apple Films. The movie's theme, ***Come And Get It***, performed by Badfinger* and composed by Paul McCartney, was highly appropriate. Its score was composed by Ken Thorne. (Thorne also scored the 1967 film **How I Won The War** co-starring John Lennon.) The film's star-studded cast also included cameo appearances by Graham Chapman and John Cleese, soon to achieve fame with Monty Python*. The film closed with the song ***Something In The Air*** by Thunderclap Newman, which featured a sixteen-year-old guitarist named Jimmy McCulloch. (McCulloch later became Paul McCartney's guitarist in his band Wings from 1974 to 1977.)

A U.S. promotional album **The Magic Christian**, on Commonwealth United Records, included an open end interview with Peter Sellers, Terry Southern and Ringo which was essentially a promo plug for Sellers' film. The jacket of the one-side promotional album included a photo of Ringo and Sellers. A soundtrack album to **The Magic Christian** was also released on Commonwealth United

Records (CU 6004) in the U.S., and featured a different design, but the same photo of Ringo and Sellers. It contained a brief segment of Ringo's dialogue from the "Hunting Scene" in the film.

Sellers made a cameo appearance in The Beatles' film **Let It Be** that was being shot at the same time, and in the same studio as **The Magic Christian**. The subject of drug use in the dialogue no doubt contributed to its being left on the cutting floor. Ringo and Sellers became good partying buddies following the filming of **Magic Christian**. Sellers joined Ringo singing ***Octopus' Garden*** on the **David Frost Show** on December 6, 1969. The film **The Magic Christian** premiered six days later. **The Magic Christian** was issued on VHS in 1989.

Sellers was also a friend and frequent visitor at George Harrison's home. He is featured in the gatefold photo of George's **Dark Horse** album – Sellers' and Harrison's backs are turned along with a quote from the film **The Producers**, a favorite of Sellers and Harrison. Sellers accompanied Harrison through much of his 1974 North American tour and was influential in Harrison's involvement in the film industry. Peter Sellers introduced Harrison to lawyer / accountant Dennis O'Brien. Harrison and O'Brien would later form the HandMade Films Co. Harrison's 1975 album **Extra Texture** specifically mentions Sellers as "not appearing" on the album.

Outside of England, Peter Sellers is remembered most as Inspector Clouseau in his **Pink Panther** movies, and for his title role in **Doctor Strangelove**. Perhaps his best and most prophetic role was in the film **Being There** (which featured the song ***Basketball Jones***, *see Cheech And Chong*). Sellers lost his long battle with heart disease on July 24, 1980, shortly after the film's release. The 1995 television special **The Peter Sellers Story** included an interview with George Harrison.

Paul Shaffer

Record 311 title:
The Worlds's Most Dangerous Party
Media:
Album 5" CD [2 CD set]
Label / Catalog number:
SBK/ERG/EMI / 0777 7 89530 2 9
Producer:
Todd Rundgren
Jacket / Inserts:
Standard international design in jewel box / 8 page CD booklet
Recording Location / Date:
One or more of the following studios: Hit Factory, New York, Utopia Sound (East), NY, Utopia Sound (West), Los Angeles, CA, U.S.A. / 1993

Song 311a title:
Mysterious Ways†
Track details:
Side 1, track 5† / (Intro 0 min. 29 sec.†)
Release date / Country:
13 Jul 93 / U.S.A.
Composer:
A. Clayton - L. Mullen - D. Evans - P. Hewson

Ringo Starr: Voice†; additionally, one or more of the following: Paul Shaffer: Keyboards; Sid McGinnis: Guitars; Will Lee: Bass & Percussion; Anton Fig: Drums & Percussion

Paul Shaffer was born on November 28, 1949 in Thunder Bay, Ontario, Canada. He was a member of the Thunder Bay band The Fabulous Fugitives in the mid-1960s. The musician, composer, producer, band leader and actor has been known primarily to U.S. TV viewing audiences beginning with NBC's sitcom **A Year At The Top** in 1977. He first gained notoriety as the music director of NBC-TV's **Saturday Night Live** comedy show in 1978. He also served as the band leader for The Blues Brothers group featuring Dan Aykroyd and John Belushi during his stint with **SNL**. In 1982, he became the leader of The World's Most Dangerous Band on NBC-TV's **Late Night with David Letterman** show. When Letterman moved to CBS-TV in 1993, the show was renamed **The Late Show with David Letterman**, and Shaffer's band was renamed the CBS Orchestra. He has gained the respect of popular musicians the world over for his innovative cover arrangements of their songs.

Ringo Starr's involvement in Shaffer's album **The Worlds's Most Dangerous Party** is no doubt due to the admiration he has for Shaffer, and because Todd Rundgren*, who toured with Ringo, produced the album. Ringo is introduced by Shaffer at the end of the song ***Burning Down The House***, and is asked by Shaffer "Do you want to sit in with the band?" Ringo's reply is, "Love to!" The song that follows is a cover of U2's ***Mysterious Ways***. The liner notes of the album credit Ringo for "Guest Appearance," and do not specifically credit him as playing drums, while other guests' musical credits are specifically listed. Though the dialogue between Ringo and Shaffer suggests Ringo plays on, or is involved in, ***Mysterious Ways***, it's all part of the party atmosphere of the album. Shaffer confirmed that Ringo's only contribution to the album was his dialogue. Also of note is that Paul McCartney band members Hamish Stuart, Robbie McIntosh and Wix are also listed in the album credits as additional party guests. Shaffer sat in with Ringo Starr's All-Starr Band during both of their performances at Caesar's Atlantic City, New Jersey on July 22, 1995.

Paul Shaffer, New York City, NY, late 1980s, photo courtesy of Tom Bert

Ravi Shankar

Record 312 title:
Chants Of India
Label / Catalog number:
Angel / 7243 8 55948 2 3
Media:
Album 5" CD
Producer:
George Harrison
Jacket / Inserts:
Standard international design in jewel box / 16 page CD booklet with photo of George Harrison

Song 312a title:
Asato Maa
Release date / Country:
06 May 97 / U.S.A.
Recording Location / Date:
Media Artist Studio, Madras, India / Jan & Apr 96
Track details:
Side 1, track 4 / 7 min. 10 sec.
Composer:
Trad/Arr: R. Shankar

George Harrison: B. Vocals; additionally, one or more of the following: Kalyan: Violin & Assistant; Anoushka Shankar: Conductor & Assistant; Veena: Subramaniam; Veena: Devi; Murali: Keyboards; Seenu: Mridangam; Balasai: Flute; Kamalakar: Flute; Ronu Mazumdar: Flute; Shekar: Cello; Biswas: Cello; John: Cello; Murali: Violin; Rex: Violin; Balu: Violin; Sasi: Violin; Girijan: Violin; Narayanan: Tampura; Rebbecca Goodsell: Tampura; Sririam: Venkataraman: Tampura; Gowri Shankar:

Tampura; Babu Parameshwaran: Indian Chorus; Natesan: Indian Chorus; Ramchandran Suresh: Indian Chorus; Sashidran: Indian Chorus; Babu: Indian Chorus; Mani: Indian Chorus; Mani Kiran: Indian Chorus; Shanta Dhananjayan: Indian Chorus; Suhasini: Indian Chorus; Latha: Indian Chorus; Rashmi: Indian Chorus; Sarada: Western Chorus; Martha: Western Chorus; Vimala: Western Chours; Pearl: Western Chorus; Adela: Western Chorus; Dr. Grub: Western Chorus; Billy: Werstern Chorus; Tony: Western Chorus; Arul: Western Chorus; Ranjith: Western Chorus

Song 312b title:
Gaayatri
Track details:
Side 1, track 7 / 3 min. 26 sec.
Release date / Country:
06 May 97 / U.S.A.
Composer:
Trad/Arr: R. Shankar
Recording Location / Date:
Media Artist Studio, Madras, India / Jan & Apr 96

George Harrison: Bass & Glockenspiel; additionally, one or more of the following: Kalyan: Violin & Assistant; Anoushka Shankar: Conductor & Assistant; Veena: Subramaniam; Veena: Devi; Murali: Keyboards; Seenu: Mridangam; Balasai: Flute; Kamalakar: Flute; Ronu Mazumdar: Flute; Shekar: Cello; Biswas: Cello; John: Cello; Murali: Violin; Rex: Violin; Balu: Violin; Sasi: Violin; Girijan: Violin; Narayanan: Tampura; Rebbecca Goodsell: Tampura; Sririam: Venkataraman: Tampura; Gowri Shankar: Tampura; Babu Parameshwaran: Indian Chorus; Natesan: Indian Chorus; Ramchandran Suresh: Indian Chorus; Sashidran: Indian Chorus; Babu: Indian Chorus; Mani: Indian Chorus; Mani Kiran: Indian Chorus; Shanta Dhananjayan: Indian Chorus; Suhasini: Indian Chorus; Latha: Indian Chorus; Rashmi: Indian Chorus; Sarada: Western Chorus; Martha: Western Chorus; Vimala: Western Chours; Pearl: Western Chorus; Adela: Western Chorus; Dr. Grub: Western Chorus; Billy: Werstern Chorus; Tony: Western Chorus; Arul: Western Chorus; Ranjith: Western Chorus

Song 312c title:
Geetaa
Track details:
Side 1, track 10 / 2 min. 15 sec.
Release date / Country:
06 May 97 / U.S.A.
Composer:
Trad/Arr: R. Shankar
Recording Location / Date:
FPSHOT (Friar Park Studio, Henley-on-Thames), U.K. / Jul - Aug 96

One or more of the following musicians are involved: Chandrashekhar: Violin, Chorus & Assistant; Anoushka Shankar: Conductor & Assistant; Balachandar: Mridamgam/Morsing; Bikram Ghosh: Tabla; Tarun Bhatacharaya: Santoor; Ronu Mazumdar: Flute; Jane Lister: Harp; Antonia Paget: Violla; Michael Paget: Viola: Michael Paget; Viola: Stella Page; Isabel Dunn: Cello; Terry Emery: Tuned Percussion; George Harrison: B. Vocals, Acoustic Guitar, Bass, Autoharp, Glockenspiel & Vibraphone; Deepa Singh: Chorus; Hari Sivanesan: Chorus; Sivashakti Sivanesan: Chorus; Gaurav Mazumdar: Chorus; Shyamali Basu: Chorus; Sukanya Shankar: Chorus

Song 312d title:
Hari Om
Track details:
Side 1, track 12 / 3 min. 05 sec.
Release date / Country:
06 May 97 / U.S.A.
Composer:
R. Shankar
Recording Location / Date:
Swara Laya Studio, Madras, India / Jan & Apr 96

George Harrison: B. Vocals; additionally, one or more of the following: Kalyan: Violin & Assistant; Anoushka Shankar: Conductor & Assistant; Veena: Subramaniam; Veena: Devi; Murali: Keyboards; Seenu: Mridangam; Balasai: Flute; Kamalakar: Flute; Ronu Mazumdar: Flute; Shekar: Cello; Biswas: Cello; John: Cello; Murali: Violin; Rex: Violin; Balu: Violin; Sasi: Violin; Girijan: Violin; Narayanan: Tampura; Rebbecca Goodsell: Tampura; Sririam: Venkataraman: Tampura; Gowri Shankar: Tampura; Babu Parameshwaran: Indian Chorus; Natesan: Indian Chorus; Ramchandran Suresh: Indian Chorus; Sashidran: Indian Chorus; Babu: Indian Chorus; Mani: Indian Chorus; Mani Kiran: Indian Chorus; Shanta Dhananjayan: Indian Chorus; Suhasini: Indian Chorus; Latha: Indian Chorus; Rashmi: Indian Chorus; Sarada: Western Chorus; Martha: Western Chorus; Vimala: Western Chours; Pearl: Western Chorus; Adela: Western Chorus; Dr. Grub: Western Chorus; Billy: Werstern Chorus; Tony: Western Chorus; Arul: Western Chorus; Ranjith: Western Chorus

Song 312e title:
Mahaa Mrityunjaya
Release date / Country:
06 May 97 / U.S.A.
Track details:
Side 1, track 8 / 4 min. 41 sec.
Composer:
Trad/Arr: R. Shankar
Recording Location / Date:
FPSHOT (Friar Park Studio, Henley-on-Thames), U.K. / Jul - Aug 96

One or more of the following: Chandrashekhar: Violin, Chorus & Assistant; Anoushka Shankar: Conductor & Assisstant; Balachandar: Mridamgam/Morsing; Bikram Ghosh: Tabla; Tarun Bhatacharaya: Santoor; Ronu Mazumdar: Flute; Jane Lister: Harp; Antonia Paget: Violla; Michael Paget: Viola: Michael Paget; Viola: Stella Page; Isabel Dunn: Cello; Terry Emery: Tuned Percussion; George Harrison: B. Vocals, Acoustic Guitar, Bass, Autoharp, Glockenspiel & Vibraphone; Deepa Singh: Chorus; Hari Sivanesan: Chorus; Sivashakti Sivanesan: Chorus; Gaurav Mazumdar: Chorus; Shyamali Basu: Chorus; Sukanya Shankar: Chorus

Song 312f title:
Mangalam (Tala Mantra)
Release date / Country:
06 May 97 / U.S.A.
Track details:
Side 1, track 11 / 4 min. 10 sec.
Composer:
R. Shankar
Recording Location / Date:
FPSHOT (Friar Park Studio, Henley-on-Thames), U.K. / Jul - Aug 96

One or more of the following: Chandrashekhar: Violin, Chorus & Assistant; Anoushka Shankar: Conductor & Assisstant; Balachandar: Mridamgam/Morsing; Bikram Ghosh: Tabla; Tarun Bhatacharaya: Santoor; Ronu Mazumdar: Flute; Jane Lister: Harp; Antonia Paget: Violla; Michael Paget: Viola: Michael Paget; Viola: Stella Page; Isabel Dunn: Cello; Terry Emery: Tuned Percussion; George Harrison: B. Vocals, Acoustic Guitar, Bass, Autoharp, Glockenspiel & Vibraphone; Deepa Singh: Chorus; Hari Sivanesan: Chorus; Sivashakti Sivanesan: Chorus; Gaurav Mazumdar: Chorus; Shyamali Basu: Chorus; Sukanya Shankar: Chorus

Song 312g title:
Omkaaraaya Namaha
Release date / Country:
06 May 97 / U.S.A.
Track details:
Side 1, track 2 / 1 min. 55 sec.
Composer:
Trad/Arr: R. Shankar
Recording Location / Date:
FPSHOT (Friar Park Studio, Henley-on-Thames), U.K. / Jul - Aug 96

One or more of the following: Chandrashekhar: Violin, Chorus & Assistant; Anoushka Shankar: Conductor & Assisstant; Balachandar: Mridamgam/Morsing; Bikram Ghosh: Tabla; Tarun Bhatacharaya: Santoor; Ronu Mazumdar: Flute; Jane Lister: Harp; Antonia Paget: Violla; Michael Paget: Viola: Michael Paget; Viola: Stella Page; Isabel Dunn: Cello; Terry Emery: Tuned Percussion; George Harrison: B. Vocals, Acoustic Guitar, Bass, Autoharp, Glockenspiel & Vibraphone; Deepa Singh: Chorus; Hari Sivanesan: Chorus; Sivashakti Sivanesan: Chorus; Gaurav Mazumdar: Chorus; Shyamali Basu: Chorus; Sukanya Shankar: Chorus

Song 312h title:
Poornamadah
Release date / Country:
06 May 97 / U.S.A.
Track details:
Side 1, track 6 / 1 min. 23 sec.
Composer:
Trad/Arr: R. Shankar
Recording Location / Date:
Media Artist Studio, Madras, India / Jan & Apr 96

One or more of the following musicians are involved: Kalyan: Violin & Assistant; Anoushka Shankar: Conductor & Assistant; Veena: Subramaniam; Veena: Devi; Murali: Keyboards; Seenu: Mridangam; Balasai: Flute; Kamalakar: Flute; Ronu Mazumdar: Flute; Shekar: Cello; Biswas: Cello; John: Cello; Murali: Violin; Rex: Violin; Balu: Violin; Sasi: Violin; Girijan: Violin; Narayanan: Tampura; Rebbecca Goodsell: Tampura; Sririam: Venkataraman: Tampura; Gowri Shankar: Tampura; Babu Parameshwaran: Indian Chorus; Natesan: Indian Chorus; Ramchandran Suresh: Indian Chorus; Sashidran: Indian Chorus; Babu: Indian Chorus; Mani: Indian Chorus; Mani Kiran: Indian Chorus; Shanta Dhananjayan: Indian Chorus; Suhasini: Indian Chorus; Latha: Indian Chorus; Rashmi: Indian

Chorus; Sarada: Western Chorus; Martha: Western Chorus; Vimala: Western Chours; Pearl: Western Chorus; Adela: Western Chorus; Dr. Grub: Western Chorus; Billy: Werstern Chorus; Tony: Western Chorus; Arul: Western Chorus; Ranjith: Western Chorus; George Harrison: B. Vocals, Acoustic Guitar, Bass, Autoharp, Glockenspiel & Vibraphone

Song 312i title:
Prabhujee
Track details:
Side 1, track 15 / 8 min. 10 sec.
Release date / Country:
06 May 97 / U.S.A.
Composer:
R. Shankar
Recording Location / Date:
FPSHOT (Friar Park Studio, Henley-on-Thames), U.K. / Jul - Aug 96

George Harrison: B. Vocals, Guitar & Bass; additionally, one or more of the following: Chandrashekhar: Violin, Chorus & Assistant; Anoushka Shankar: Conductor & Assisstant; Balachandar: Mridamgam/Morsing; Bikram Ghosh: Tabla; Tarun Bhatacharaya: Santoor; Ronu Mazumdar: Flute; Jane Lister: Harp; Antonia Paget: Violla; Michael Paget: Viola: Michael Paget; Viola: Stella Page; Isabel Dunn: Cello; Terry Emery: Tuned Percussion; Deepa Singh: Chorus; Hari Sivanesan: Chorus; Sivashakti Sivanesan: Chorus; Gaurav Mazumdar: Chorus; Shyamali Basu: Chorus; Sukanya Shankar: Chorus

Song 312j title:
Sahanaa Vavatu
Track details:
Side 1, track 5 / 4 min. 25 sec.
Release date / Country:
06 May 97 / U.S.A.
Composer:
Trad/Arr: R. Shankar
Recording Location / Date:
FPSHOT (Friar Park Studio, Henley-on-Thames), U.K. / Jul - Aug 96

One or more of the following: Chandrashekhar: Violin, Chorus & Assistant; Anoushka Shankar: Conductor & Assisstant; Balachandar: Mridamgam/Morsing; Bikram Ghosh: Tabla; Tarun Bhatacharaya: Santoor; Ronu Mazumdar: Flute; Jane Lister: Harp; Antonia Paget: Violla; Michael Paget: Viola: Michael Paget; Viola: Stella Page; Isabel Dunn: Cello; Terry Emery: Tuned Percussion; George Harrison: B. Vocals, Acoustic Guitar, Bass, Autoharp, Glockenspiel & Vibraphone; Deepa Singh: Chorus; Hari Sivanesan: Chorus; Sivashakti Sivanesan: Chorus; Gaurav Mazumdar: Chorus; Shyamali Basu: Chorus; Sukanya Shankar: Chorus

Song 312k title:
Sarve Shaam
Track details:
Side 1, track 16 / 5 min. 05 sec.
Release date / Country:
06 May 97 / U.S.A.
Composer:
Trad/Arr: R. Shankar
Recording Location / Date:
FPSHOT (Friar Park Studio, Henley-on-Thames), U.K. / Jul - Aug 96

George Harrison: Autoharp & Marimba; additionally, one or more of the following: Chandrashekhar: Violin, Chorus & Assistant; Anoushka Shankar: Conductor & Assisstant; Balachandar: Mridamgam/Morsing; Bikram Ghosh: Tabla; Tarun Bhatacharaya: Santoor; Ronu Mazumdar: Flute; Jane Lister: Harp; Antonia Paget: Violla; Michael Paget: Viola: Michael Paget; Viola: Stella Page; Isabel Dunn: Cello; Terry Emery: Tuned Percussion; Deepa Singh: Chorus; Hari Sivanesan: Chorus; Sivashakti Sivanesan: Chorus; Gaurav Mazumdar: Chorus; Shyamali Basu: Chorus; Sukanya Shankar: Chorus

Song 312l title:
Svara Mantra
Track details:
Side 1, track 13 / 4 min. 36 sec.
Release date / Country:
06 May 97 / U.S.A.
Composer:
R. Shankar
Recording Location / Date:
FPSHOT (Friar Park Studio, Henley-on-Thames), U.K. / Jul - Aug 96

One or more of the following: Chandrashekhar: Violin & Assistant; Anoushka Shankar: Conductor & Assisstant; Balachandar: Mridamgam/Morsing; Bikram Ghosh: Tabla; Tarun Bhatacharaya: Santoor; Ronu Mazumdar: Flute; Jane Lister: Harp; Antonia Paget: Violla; Michael Paget: Viola: Michael

Paget; Viola: Stella Page; Isabel Dunn: Cello; Terry Emery: Tuned Percussion; George Harrison: Acoustic Guitar, Bass, Autoharp, Glockenspiel & Vibraphone

Song 312m title:
Vandanaa Trayee
Release date / Country:
06 May 97 / U.S.A.
Recording Location / Date:
Media Artist Studio, Madras, India / Jan & Apr 96
Track details:
Side 1, track 1 / 4 min. 28 sec.
Composer:
Trad/Arr: R. Shankar

George Harrison: Vibraphone & Acoustic Bass; additionally, one or more of the following: Kalyan: Violin & Assistant; Anoushka Shankar: Conductor & Assistant; Veena: Subramaniam; Veena: Devi; Murali: Keyboards; Seenu: Mridangam; Balasai: Flute; Kamalakar: Flute; Ronu Mazumdar: Flute; Shekar: Cello; Biswas: Cello; John: Cello; Murali: Violin; Rex: Violin; Balu: Violin; Sasi: Violin; Girijan: Violin; Narayanan: Tampura; Rebbecca Goodsell: Tampura; Sririam: Venkataraman: Tampura; Gowri Shankar: Tampura; Babu Parameshwaran: Indian Chorus; Natesan: Indian Chorus; Ramchandran Suresh: Indian Chorus; Sashidran: Indian Chorus; Babu: Indian Chorus; Mani: Indian Chorus; Mani Kiran: Indian Chorus; Shanta Dhananjayan: Indian Chorus; Suhasini: Indian Chorus; Latha: Indian Chorus; Rashmi: Indian Chorus; Sarada: Western Chorus; Martha: Western Chorus; Vimala: Western Chours; Pearl: Western Chorus; Adela: Western Chorus; Dr. Grub: Western Chorus; Billy: Werstern Chorus; Tony: Western Chorus; Arul: Western Chorus; Ranjith: Western Chorus

Song 312n title:
Vedic Chanting (One)
Release date / Country:
06 May 97 / U.S.A.
Recording Location / Date:
Swara Laya Studio, Madras, India / Jan & Apr 96
Track details:
Side 1, track 3 / 3 min. 10 sec.
Composer:
Trad/Arr: R. Shankar

One or more of the following: Kalyan: Violin & Assistant; Anoushka Shankar: Conductor & Assistant; Veena: Subramaniam; Veena: Devi; Murali: Keyboards; Seenu: Mridangam; Balasai: Flute; Kamalakar: Flute; Ronu Mazumdar: Flute; Shekar: Cello; Biswas: Cello; John: Cello; Murali: Violin; Rex: Violin; Balu: Violin; Sasi: Violin; Girijan: Violin; Narayanan: Tampura; Rebbecca Goodsell: Tampura; Sririam: Venkataraman: Tampura; Gowri Shankar: Tampura; Babu Parameshwaran: Indian Chorus; Natesan: Indian Chorus; Ramchandran Suresh: Indian Chorus; Sashidran: Indian Chorus; Babu: Indian Chorus; Mani: Indian Chorus; Mani Kiran: Indian Chorus; Shanta Dhananjayan: Indian Chorus; Suhasini: Indian Chorus; Latha: Indian Chorus; Rashmi: Indian Chorus; Sarada: Western Chorus; Martha: Western Chorus; Vimala: Western Chours; Pearl: Western Chorus; Adela: Western Chorus; Dr. Grub: Western Chorus; Billy: Werstern Chorus; Tony: Western Chorus; Arul: Western Chorus; Ranjith: Western Chorus

Song 312o title:
Vedic Chanting (Two)
Release date / Country:
06 May 97 / U.S.A.
Recording Location / Date:
Swara Laya Studio, Madras, India & FPSHOT (Friar Park Studio, Henley-on-Thames), U.K. / Jan & Apr & Jul - Aug 96
Track details:
Side 1, track 14 / 2 min. 14 sec.
Composer:
Trad/Arr: R. Shankar

Ravi Shankar: Sitar; additionally, one or more of the following: Kalyan: Violin & Assistant; Anoushka Shankar: Conductor & Assistant; Veena: Subramaniam; Veena: Devi; Murali: Keyboards; Seenu: Mridangam; Balasai: Flute; Kamalakar: Flute; Ronu Mazumdar: Flute; Shekar: Cello; Biswas: Cello; John: Cello; Murali: Violin; Rex: Violin; Balu: Violin; Sasi: Violin; Girijan: Violin; Narayanan: Tampura; Rebbecca Goodsell: Tampura; Sririam: Venkataraman: Tampura; Gowri Shankar: Tampura; Babu Parameshwaran: Indian Chorus; Natesan: Indian Chorus; Ramchandran Suresh: Indian Chorus; Sashidran: Indian Chorus; Babu: Indian Chorus; Mani: Indian Chorus; Mani Kiran: Indian Chorus; Shanta Dhananjayan: Indian Chorus; Suhasini: Indian Chorus; Latha: Indian Chorus; Rashmi: Indian Chorus; Sarada: Western Chorus; Martha: Western Chorus; Vimala: Western Chours; Pearl: Western Chorus; Adela: Western Chorus; Dr. Grub: Western Chorus; Billy: Werstern Chorus; Tony: Western Chorus; Arul: Western Chorus; Ranjith: Western Chorus; Chandrashekhar: Violin, Chorus

& Assistant; Anoushka Shankar: Conductor & Assisstant; Balachandar: Mridamgam/Morsing; Bikram Ghosh: Tabla; Tarun Bhatacharaya: Santoor; Ronu Mazumdar: Flute; Jane Lister: Harp; Antonia Paget: Violla; Michael Paget: Viola: Michael Paget; Viola: Stella Page; Isabel Dunn: Cello; Terry Emery: Tuned Percussion; Deepa Singh: Chorus; Hari Sivanesan: Chorus; Sivashakti Sivanesan: Chorus; Gaurav Mazumdar: Chorus; Shyamali Basu: Chorus; Sukanya Shankar: Chorus

Song 312p title:
Veenaa-Murali
Release date / Country:
06 May 97 / U.S.A.
Recording Location / Date:
Swara Laya Studio, Madras, India / Jan & Apr 96
Track details:
Side 1, track 9 / 3 min. 44 sec.
Composer:
Trad/Arr: R. Shankar

One or more of the following: Kalyan: Violin & Assistant; Anoushka Shankar: Conductor & Assistant; Veena: Subramaniam; Veena: Devi; Murali: Keyboards; Seenu: Mridangam; Balasai: Flute; Kamalakar: Flute; Ronu Mazumdar: Flute; Shekar: Cello; Biswas: Cello; John: Cello; Murali: Violin; Rex: Violin; Balu: Violin; Sasi: Violin; Girijan: Violin; Narayanan: Tampura; Rebbecca Goodsell: Tampura; Sririam: Venkataraman: Tampura; Gowri Shankar: Tampura; Babu Parameshwaran: Indian Chorus; Natesan: Indian Chorus; Ramchandran Suresh: Indian Chorus; Sashidran: Indian Chorus; Babu: Indian Chorus; Mani: Indian Chorus; Mani Kiran: Indian Chorus; Shanta Dhananjayan: Indian Chorus; Suhasini: Indian Chorus; Latha: Indian Chorus; Rashmi: Indian Chorus; Sarada: Western Chorus; Martha: Western Chorus; Vimala: Western Chours; Pearl: Western Chorus; Adela: Western Chorus; Dr. Grub: Western Chorus; Billy: Werstern Chorus; Tony: Western Chorus; Arul: Western Chorus; Ranjith: Western Chorus; George Harrison: B. Vocals, Acoustic Guitar, Bass, Autoharp, Glockenspiel & Vibraphone

Record 313 title:
Fort Worth Express
Label / Catalog number:
Hindustani Music / Raga 001-A:B
[Unauthorized Record]
Jacket / Inserts:
Unique with slip cover in double Jewel box
Recording Location / Date:
On location at the Tarrant County Convention Center, Fort Worth, TX, U.S.A. / 22 Nov 74
Media:
Album 5" [2 CD set]
Producer:
Unknown-audience recording

Song 313a title:
Dream, Nightmare & Dawn (Music For A Ballet)
Part Two: Nightmare (Dispute & Violence) [live]
Release date / Country:
1996 / U.S.A
Track details:
CD1, track 11 / 5 min. 08 sec.
Composer:
R. Shankar

Billy Preston: Keyboards; Tom Scott: Saxophone; Chuck Findley: Trumpet; Robben Ford: Guitar; Andy Newmark: Drums; Willie Weeks: Bass; Jim Horn: Saxophone; George Harrison: Guitar; Jim Keltner: Drums; Emil Richards: Marimbas & Percussion; Ravi Shankar: Vocals, Conductor or Sitar; Hariprasad Chaurasia: Bamboo Flute; Rijram Desad: Percusion & Strings; T.V. Gopalkrishnan: Mridangam; Gopal Krishan: Vichitra Veena; Sultan Khan: Sarangi; Kartick Kumar: Sitar; Kamalesh Maitra: Percussion; Satyadev Pawar: North India Violin; Alla Rakha: Tabla; Harihar Rao: Vocals, Sitar or Percussion; Shivkumar Sharma: Santoor; L. Subramaniam: Violin

Song 313b title:
I Am Missing You [live]
Release date / Country:
1996 / U.S.A
Track details:
CD1, track 10 / 4 min. 57 sec.
Composer:
R. Shankar

Lakshmi Shankar: Lead Vocals; Ravi Shankar: Conductor or Sitar; Hariprasad Chaurasia: Bamboo Flute; Rijram Desad: Percussion & Strings; T.V. Gopalkrishnan: Mridangam & Vocals; Gopal Krishan:

Vichitra Veena; Sultan Khan: Sarangi; Kartick Kumar: Sitar; Kamalesh Maitra: Percussion; Satyadev Pawar: North India Violin; Alla Rakha: Tabla; Harihar Rao: Sitar, B. Vocals & Percussion; Viji Shankar: B. Vocals; Shivkumar Sharma: Santoor; L. Subramaniam: Violin; Kumar Shankar: B. Vocals; Tom Scott: Saxophone; Emil Richards: Percussion; George Harrison: Acoustic Guitar & B. Vocals; Willie Weeks: Bass

Song 313c title:
Zoom Zoom Zoom [live]
Release date / Country:
1996 / U.S.A
Track details:
CD1, track 6 / 5 min. 16 sec.
Composer:
R. Shankar

Lakshmi Shankar: Lead Vocals; Ravi Shankar: Conductor; Hariprasad Chaurasia: Bamboo Flute; Rijram Desad: Percussion & Strings; T.V. Gopalkrishnan: Mridangam & Vocals; Gopal Krishan: Vichitra Veena; Sultan Khan: Sarangi; Kartick Kumar: Sitar; Kamalesh Maitra: Percussion; Satyadev Pawar: North India Violin; Alla Rakha: Tabla; Harihar Rao: Sitar, B. Vocals & Percussion; Viji Shankar: B. Vocals; Shivkumar Sharma: Santoor; L. Subramaniam: Violin; Kumar Shankar: B. Vocals; Billy Preston: Keyboards; Robben Ford: Acoustic Guitar; Andy Newmark: Drums; Willie Weeks: Bass; Jim Horn: Saxophone; George Harrison: Electric Guitar; Jim Keltner: Drums; Emil Richards: Marimbas

Record 314 title:
In Celebration (Orchestral And Ensembles)
Label / Catalog number:
Angel/Dark Horse / CDCD 7243 5 55577 2 8 (7243 5 55579 2 8)
Media:
Album 5" [4 CD set]
Producer:
George Harrison
Jacket / Inserts:
Unique book set with CDs / 64 page booklet with Liner Note Introduction by George Harrison with photos of George Harrison
Recording Location / Date:
FPSHOT (Friar Park Studios, Henley-on-Thames), U.K. / 1974

Song 314a title:
(Raga) Jait
Release date / Country:
20 Feb 96 (first issued 06 Feb 76) / U.S.A.
Track details:
CD2, track 2 / 9 min. 42 sec.
Composer:
R. Shankar

Lakshmi Shankar: Lead Vocals; Kartick Kumar: Sitar; Kamlesh Maitra: Sarod & Tabla Tarang; Satyadev Pawar: Violin; Harihar Rao: Manjira; Viji Shankar: Tanpura; Kamala Chakravarty: Tanpura; T.V. Gopalkrishnan: Mridangam; L. Subramaniam: Violin; Gopal Kishan Veenkar: Vichitra Veena; Anantlal: Shahnai; Rijram Desad: Madal Tarang; Alla Rakha: Tabla; Shivkumar Sharma: Santoor; Hariprasad Chaurasia: Flute; Sultan Khan: Sarangi; Ravi Shankar: Arrangement & Conductor

Record 315 title:
In Celebration (Vocal And Experimental)
Label / Catalog number:
Angel/Dark Horse / CDCD 7243 5 55577 2 8 (7243 5 55581 2 8)
Media:
Album 5" [4 CD set]
Producer:
George Harrison
Jacket / Inserts:
Unique book set with CDs / 64 page booklet with Liner Note Introduction by George Harrison with photos of George Harrison

Song 315a title:
Dream, Nightmare & Dawn (Music For A Ballet) Part Two: Nightmare (Dispute & Violence)
Track details:
CD4, track 13 / 2 min. 59 sec.

Release date / Country:
20 Feb 96 (first issued 20 Sep 74) / U.S.A.
Composer:
R. Shankar
Recording Location / Date:
A&M Studios, Los Angeles, CA, U.S.A. / Apr 73 - early 1974

Ravi Shankar: Vocals & Conductor; Harihar Rao: Vocals; Klaus Voormann: Bass; L. Subramaniam: Violin; Tom Scott: Saxophones; Jim Keltner: Percussion; Ed Shaunessey: Drums; Emil Richards: Marimbas & Percussion

Song 315b title:
Friar Park
Track details:
CD4, track 7 / 5 min. 50 sec.
Release date / Country:
20 Feb 96 (first issued Jun 87) / U.S.A.
Composer:
R. Shankar
Recording Location / Date:
FPSHOT (Friar Park Studios, Henley-on-Thames), U.K. / 1986

Ravi Shankar: Sitar & Arrangement; George Harrison: Autoharp & (supposed) Synthesizer; Markandeya Mishra: Tabla; Ray Cooper: Marimba & Percussion

Song 315c title:
I Am Missing You
Track details:
CD4, track 9 / 3 min. 40 sec.
Release date / Country:
20 Feb 96 (first issued 20 Sep 74) / U.S.A.
Composer:
R. Shankar
Recording Location / Date:
A&M Studios, Los Angeles, CA, U.S.A. / (probably) Apr 73

Lakshmi Shankar: Lead Vocals; George Harrison: Autoharp Acoustic Guitar & Arrangement; Viji Shankar: B. Vocals; Kamala Chakravarty: B. Vocals; Klaus Voormann: Bass; Tom Scott: Saxophone; Jim Keltner: Drums; Ringo Starr: Drums; Emil Richards: Percussion & Marimbas; Billy Preston: Keyboards

Song 315d title:
Oh Bhagawan [Oh Bhaugowan]
Track details:
CD4, track 6 / 3 min. 35 sec.
Release date / Country:
20 Feb 96 (first issued 09 Aug 71) / U.S.A.
Composer:
R. Shankar
Recording Location / Date:
The Record Plant (West) Studios, Los Angeles, CA, U.S.A. / Jul 71

Ravi Shankar: Vocals & Sitar; Sanjukta Ghosh: Vocals; Shubho Shankar: Vocals; G. Sachdev: Flute; Harihar Rao: Ek Tara

Song 315e title:
Supaney Mein Aye [Supane Me Aye Preetam Sainya]
Track details:
CD4, track 4 / 4 min. 11 sec.
Release date / Country:
20 Feb 96 (first issued 20 Sep 74) / U.S.A.
Composer:
R. Shankar
Recording Location / Date:
A&M Studios, Los Angeles, CA, U.S.A. / (probably) Apr 73

Lakshmi Shankar: Lead Vocals; Shivkumar Sharma: Santoor; Aashish Khan: Sarod; Shubho Shankar: Sitar; Al Kasey: Mandolin; Ronald Cohen: Sarangi; L. Subramaniam: Violin; Hariprasad Chaurasia: Flute; Alla Rakha: Tabla

Song 315f title:
Ta Na Tom
Track details:
CD4, track 10 / 6 min. 42 sec.
Release date / Country:
20 Feb 96 / U.S.A.
Composer:
R. Shankar
Recording Location / Date:
FPSHOT (Friar Park Studios, Henley-on-Thames), U.K. / 1974

Lakshmi Shankar: Vocals; Viji Shankar: Vocals; Kamala Chakravarty: Vocals; T.V. Gopalkrishnan: Vocals; Rijram Desad: Vocals; Ravi Shankar: Vocals, Conductor & Arrangement; Hariprasad Chaurasia: Flute; L. Subramaniam: Violin; Satyadev Pawar: Violin; Alla Rakha: Pakawaj

Song 315g title:
Vandana
Release date / Country:
20 Feb 96 (first issued 06 Feb 76) / U.S.A.
Recording Location / Date:
FPSHOT (Friar Park Studios, Henley-on-Thames), U.K. / 1974

Track details:
CD4, track 1 / 2 min. 37 sec.
Composer:
R. Shankar

Lakshmi Shankar: Lead Vocals & Swaramandal; Kamlesh Maitra: Sarod & Tabla Tarang, Duggi Tarang & Ek Tara; Satyadev Pawar: Violin; Harihar Rao: Manjira & B. Vocals; Viji Shankar: B. Vocals & Tanpura; Kamala Chakravarty: B. Vocals & Tanpura; T.V. Gopalkrishnan: B. Vocals; L. Subramaniam: Violin; Kartick Kumar: Sitar; Gopal Kishan Veenkar: B. Vocals; Anantlal: Shahnai; Rijram Desad: Pakhawaj; Alla Rakha: Tabla; Shivkumar Sharma: Santoor & B. Vocals; Hariprasad Chaurasia: Flute; Sultan Khan: Sarangi; Ravi Shankar: Arrangement & Conductor

Record 316 title:
In Concert 1972
Label / Catalog number:
Apple / 7243 8 53817 2 0
Jacket / Inserts:
Standard international design in jewel box / 8 page CD booklet
Recording Location / Date:
On location at Philharmonic Hall, New York, NY, U.S.A. / 08 Oct 72

Media:
Album 5" CD [2 CD set]
Producer:
Al Steckler, George Harrison, Zakir Hussein & Phil McDonald

Song 316a title:
Raga-Hem Bihag [live]
Release date / Country:
02 Dec 96 (first issued 22 Jan 73) / U.K.

Track details:
CD1, track 1 / 25 min. 18 sec.
Composer:
R. Shankar - A. Khan

Ravi Shankar: Sitar; Ali Akbar Khan: Sarod; Alla Rakha: Tabla; Ashoka: Tambouras; Susan: Tambouras

Song 316b title:
Raga-Manj Khamaj [live]
Release date / Country:
02 Dec 96 (first issued 22 Jan 73) / U.K.

Track details:
CD1, track 2 / 50 min. 57 sec.
Composer:
R. Shankar - A. Khan

Ravi Shankar: Sitar; Ali Akbar Khan: Sarod; Alla Rakha: Tabla; Ashoka: Tambouras; Susan: Tambouras

Song 316c title:
Raga-Sindhi Bhairavi [live]
Release date / Country:
02 Dec 96 (first issued 22 Jan 73) / U.K.

Track details:
CD2, track 1 / 26 min. 18 sec.
Composer:
R. Shankar - A. Khan

Ravi Shankar: Sitar; Ali Akbar Khan: Sarod; Alla Rakha: Tabla; Ashoka: Tambouras; Susan: Tambouras

Record 317 title:
Joi Bangla/Oh Bhaugowan / Raga Mishra-Jhinjhoti
Media:
Single 7"
Label / Catalog number:
Apple / 1838
Producer:
George Harrison
Jacket / Inserts:
Picture sleeve
Recording Location / Date:
(probably) Record Plant (West) Studios, Los Angeles, CA, U.S.A. / Jul 71

Song 317a title:
Joi Bangla
Track details:
Side 1, track 1 / 3 min. 18 sec.
Release date / Country:
09 Aug 71 / U.S.A.
Composer:
R. Shankar

Probably one or more of the following: Ravi Shankar: Vocals & Sitar; Ali Akbar Khan: Sarod; G. Sachdev: Flute; Harihar Rao: Ek Tara; Alla Rakha: Tabla

Song 317b title:
Raga Mishra-Jhinjhoti (Duet Sitar & Sarod)
Track details:
Side 2, track 1 / 6 min. 52 sec.
Release date / Country:
09 Aug 71 / U.S.A.
Composer:
Trad

Ravi Shankar: Sitar; Ali Akbar Khan: Sarod; Alla Rakah: Tabla

Record 318 title:
Raga
Media:
VHS
Label / Catalog number:
Mystic Fire Video, Island Visual Arts, PolyGram Video & Apple Films / 76239
Producer:
Howard Worth (film) George Harrison: Re-producer (soundtrack only)
Jacket / Inserts:
Standard international design with photo of George Harrison on back / Postcard Mailer
Recording Location / Date:
On location at Big Sur, CA, U.S.A. / 10-11 Jun 68

Song 318a title:
["Sitar Lessons"] [live]
Track details:
4 min. 20 sec.
Release date / Country:
1991 (first issued 23 Nov 71) / U.S.A.
Composer:
R. Shankar

Ravi Shankar: Lead Vocals & Sitar; George Harrison: Sitar, Finger Cymbals & B. Vocals (with Yehudin Menuhin and Bismallah Khan)

Record 319 title:
Raga (Original Sound Track Album)
Label / Catalog number:
Apple / SWAO-3384
Media:
Album 12"
Producer:
[various producers] / Re-produced by George Harrison
Jacket / Inserts:
Unique with Gatefold / 16 page booklet with photo of George Harrison
Recording Location / Date:
[various locations] / [various dates] mostly Apr - Jul 68

Song 319a title:
Baba Teaching
Release date / Country:
07 Dec 71 / U.S.A.
Track details:
Side 1, track 3 / 1 min. 08 sec.
Composer:
Trad

Song 319b title:
Banaras Ghat
Release date / Country:
07 Dec 71 / U.S.A.
Track details:
Side 2, track 2 / 2 min. 45 sec.
Composer:
R. Shankar

Song 319c title:
Birth To Death
Release date / Country:
07 Dec 71 / U.S.A.
Track details:
Side 1, track 4 / 3 min. 10 sec.
Composer:
R. Shankar

Song 319d title:
Bombay Studio
Release date / Country:
07 Dec 71 / U.S.A.
Track details:
Side 2, track 3 / 2 min. 45 sec.
Composer:
R. Shankar

Song 319e title:
Dawn To Dusk
Release date / Country:
07 Dec 71 / U.S.A.
Track details:
Side 1, track 1 / 3 min. 38 sec.
Composer:
R. Shankar

Song 319f title:
Frenzy And Distortion
Release date / Country:
07 Dec 71 / U.S.A.
Track details:
Side 2, track 5 / 1 min. 06 sec.
Composer:
R. Shankar

Mr. Amin: Vocals; [a Collage by Collin Walcot]

Song 319g title:
Gurur Bramha
Release date / Country:
07 Dec 71 / U.S.A.
Track details:
Side 1, track 6 / 1 min. 10 sec.
Composer:
R. Shankar

Song 319h title:
Kinnara School
Release date / Country:
07 Dec 71 / U.S.A.
Track details:
Side 2, track 4 / 1 min. 51 sec.
Composer:
R. Shankar

Song 319i title:
Raga Desh
Release date / Country:
07 Dec 71 / U.S.A.
Track details:
Side 2, track 6 / 8 min. 50 sec.
Composer:
R. Shankar

Song 319j title:
Medley: Raga Parameshwari-Rangeswhart
Release date / Country:
07 Dec 71 / U.S.A.
Track details:
Side 2, track 1 / 4 min. 31 sec.
Composer:
R. Shankar

Song 319k title:
United Nations
Release date / Country:
07 Dec 71 / U.S.A.
Track details:
Side 1, track 7 / 4 min. 33 sec.
Composer:
R. Shankar - Y. Menuhin

Song 319l title:
Vedic Hymns
Release date / Country:
07 Dec 71 / U.S.A.
Track details:
Side 1, track 2 / 1 min. 30 sec.
Composer:
Trad

Song 319m title:
Vinus House
Release date / Country:
07 Dec 71 / U.S.A.
Track details:
Side 1, track 5 / 2 min. 37 sec.
Composer:
R. Shankar

Record 320 title:
Ravi Shankar's Music Festival From India
Label / Catalog number:
Dark Horse / SP 22007
Media:
Album 12"
Producer:
George Harrison
Jacket / Inserts:
Standard international design with photo of George Harrison on front jacket / Custom inner-sleeve
Recording Location / Date:
FPSHOT (Friar Park Studios, Henley-on-Thames), U.K. / 1974

Song 320a title:
Bhajan
Release date / Country:
06 Feb 76 / U.S.A.
Track details:
Side 2, track 2 / 3 min. 50 sec.
Composer:
R. Shankar

Lakshmi Shankar: Lead Vocals; one or more of the following: Kamalesh Maitra: Sarod, Madal, Tabla Tarang, Duggi Tarang & Ek Tara; Satyadev Pawar: Violin; Lakshmi Shankar: Swaramandal; Harihar Rao: Kartal, Manjira, Dholak, B. Vocals & Gub Gubi; Viji Shankar: B. Vocals & Tanpura; Kamala Chakravarty: B. Vocals & Tanpura; T.V. Gopalkrishnan: Mridagam, Khanjira & B. Vocals; L. Subramaniam: Violin; Kartick Kumar: Sitar; Gopal Kishan Veenkar: Vichitra Veena and B. Vocals; Anantlal: Shahnai; Rijram Desad: Pakhawaj, Nal, Nagada, Madal Tarang, Huduk & Duff; Alla Rakha: Tabla; Shivkumar Sharma: Santoor, Kanoon & B. Vocals; Hariprasad Chaurasia: Flutes; Sultan Khan: Sarangi; Ravi Shankar: Arrangement & Conductor

Song 320b title:
Chaturang
Release date / Country:
06 Feb 76 / U.S.A.
Track details:
Side 1, track 4 / 2 min. 00 sec.
Composer:
R. Shankar

Lakshmi Shankar: Lead Vocals; one or more of the following: Kamalesh Maitra: Sarod, Madal, Tabla Tarang, Duggi Tarang & Ek Tara; Satyadev Pawar: Violin; Lakshmi Shankar: Swaramandal; Harihar Rao: Kartal, Manjira, Dholak, B. Vocals & Gub Gubi; Viji Shankar: B. Vocals & Tanpura; Kamala Chakravarty: B. Vocals & Tanpura; T.V. Gopalkrishnan: Mridagam, Khanjira & B. Vocals; L. Subramaniam: Violin; Kartick Kumar: Sitar; Gopal Kishan Veenkar: Vichitra Veena and B. Vocals; Anantlal: Shahnai; Rijram Desad: Pakhawaj, Nal, Nagada, Madal Tarang, Huduk & Duff; Alla Rakha: Tabla; Shivkumar Sharma: Santoor, Kanoon & B. Vocals; Hariprasad Chaurasia: Flutes; Sultan Khan: Sarangi; Ravi Shankar: Arrangement & Conductor

Song 320c title:
Dehati
Release date / Country:
06 Feb 76 / U.S.A.
Track details:
Side 2, track 4 / 10 min. 04 sec.
Composer:
R. Shankar

Lakshmi Shankar: Lead Vocals; one or more of the following: Kamalesh Maitra: Sarod, Madal, Tabla Tarang, Duggi Tarang & Ek Tara; Satyadev Pawar: Violin; Lakshmi Shankar: Swaramandal; Harihar Rao: Kartal, Manjira, Dholak, B. Vocals & Gub Gubi; Viji Shankar: B. Vocals & Tanpura; Kamala Chakravarty: B. Vocals & Tanpura; T.V. Gopalkrishnan: Mridagam, Khanjira & B. Vocals; L. Subramaniam: Violin; Kartick Kumar: Sitar; Gopal Kishan Veenkar: Vichitra Veena and B. Vocals; Anantlal: Shahnai; Rijram Desad: Pakhawaj, Nal, Nagada, Madal Tarang, Huduk & Duff; Alla Rakha: Tabla; Shivkumar Sharma: Santoor, Kanoon & B. Vocals; Hariprasad Chaurasia: Flutes; Sultan Khan: Sarangi; Ravi Shankar: Arrangement & Conductor

Song 320d title:
Dhamar
Release date / Country:
06 Feb 76 / U.S.A.
Track details:
Side 1, track 2 / 5 min. 20 sec.
Composer:
R. Shankar

Lakshmi Shankar: Lead Vocals; one or more of the following: Kamalesh Maitra: Sarod, Madal, Tabla Tarang, Duggi Tarang & Ek Tara; Satyadev Pawar: Violin; Lakshmi Shankar: Swaramandal; Harihar Rao: Kartal, Manjira, Dholak, B. Vocals & Gub Gubi; Viji Shankar: B. Vocals & Tanpura; Kamala Chakravarty: B. Vocals & Tanpura; T.V. Gopalkrishnan: Mridagam, Khanjira & B. Vocals; L. Subramaniam: Violin; Kartick Kumar: Sitar; Gopal Kishan Veenkar: Vichitra Veena and B. Vocals; Anantlal: Shahnai; Rijram Desad: Pakhawaj, Nal, Nagada, Madal Tarang, Huduk & Duff; Alla Rakha: Tabla; Shivkumar Sharma: Santoor, Kanoon & B. Vocals; Hariprasad Chaurasia: Flutes; Sultan Khan: Sarangi; Ravi Shankar: Arrangement & Conductor

Song 320e title:
Kajri
Release date / Country:
06 Feb 76 / U.S.A.
Track details:
Side 2, track 1 / 4 min. 45 sec.
Composer:
R. Shankar

Lakshmi Shankar: Lead Vocals; one or more of the following: Kamalesh Maitra: Sarod, Madal, Tabla Tarang, Duggi Tarang & Ek Tara; Satyadev Pawar: Violin; Lakshmi Shankar: Swaramandal; Harihar Rao: Kartal, Manjira, Dholak, B. Vocals & Gub Gubi; Viji Shankar: B. Vocals & Tanpura; Kamala Chakravarty: B. Vocals & Tanpura; T.V. Gopalkrishnan: Mridagam, Khanjira & B. Vocals; L. Subramaniam: Violin; Kartick Kumar: Sitar; Gopal Kishan Veenkar: Vichitra Veena and B. Vocals; Anantlal: Shahnai; Rijram Desad: Pakhawaj, Nal, Nagada, Madal Tarang, Huduk & Duff; Alla Rakha: Tabla; Shivkumar Sharma: Santoor, Kanoon & B. Vocals; Hariprasad Chaurasia: Flutes; Sultan Khan: Sarangi; Ravi Shankar: Arrangement & Conductor

Song 320f title:
Naderdani
Release date / Country:
06 Feb 76 / U.S.A.
Track details:
Side 2, track 3 / 4 min. 40 sec.
Composer:
R. Shankar

Lakshmi Shankar: Lead Vocals; one or more of the following musicians are involved: Kamalesh Maitra: Sarod, Madal, Tabla Tarang, Duggi Tarang & Ek Tara; Satyadev Pawar: Violin; Lakshmi Shankar: Swaramandal; Harihar Rao: Kartal, Manjira, Dholak, B. Vocals & Gub Gubi; Viji Shankar: B. Vocals & Tanpura; Kamala Chakravarty: B. Vocals & Tanpura; T.V. Gopalkrishnan: Mridagam, Khanjira & B. Vocals; L. Subramaniam: Violin; Kartick Kumar: Sitar; Gopal Kishan Veenkar: Vichitra Veena and B. Vocals; Anantlal: Shahnai; Rijram Desad: Pakhawaj, Nal, Nagada, Madal Tarang, Huduk & Duff; Alla Rakha: Tabla; Shivkumar Sharma: Santoor, Kanoon & B. Vocals; Hariprasad Chaurasia: Flutes; Sultan Khan: Sarangi; Ravi Shankar: Arrangement & Conductor

Song 320g title:
Tarana
Release date / Country:
06 Feb 76 / U.S.A.
Track details:
Side 1, track 3 / 3 min. 50 sec.
Composer:
R. Shankar

Lakshmi Shankar: Lead Vocals & (possible) Swaramandal; one or more of the following: Kamalesh Maitra: Sarod, Madal, Tabla Tarang, Duggi Tarang & Ek Tara; Satyadev Pawar: Violin; Swaramandal; Harihar Rao: Kartal, Manjira, Dholak, B. Vocals & Gub Gubi; Viji Shankar: B. Vocals & Tanpura; Kamala Chakravarty: B. Vocals & Tanpura; T.V. Gopalkrishnan: Mridagam, Khanjira & B. Vocals; L. Subramaniam: Violin; Kartick Kumar: Sitar; Gopal Kishan Veenkar: Vichitra Veena and B. Vocals; Anantlal: Shahnai; Rijram Desad: Pakhawaj, Nal, Nagada, Madal Tarang, Huduk & Duff; Alla Rakha: Tabla; Shivkumar Sharma: Santoor, Kanoon & B. Vocals; Hariprasad Chaurasia: Flutes; Sultan Khan: Sarangi; Ravi Shankar: Arrangement & Conductor

Record 321 title:
Shankar Family & Friends

Media:
Album 12"

Label / Catalog number:
Dark Horse / SP-22002

Producer:
George Harrison

Jacket / Inserts:
Standard international design with photo of George Harrison on front and back / Custom inner-sleeve & 4 page insert

Recording Location / Date:
A&M Studios, Los Angeles, CA, U.S.A. / Apr 73 - early 1974

Except where Noted – One or more of the following: George Harrison: Autoharp, Acoustic Guitar & Electric Guitar; Jitendra Abhisheki: Vocals; Kamala Chakravarty: B. Vocals; Lakshmi Shankar: Swaramandal & Vocals; Shivkumar Sharma: Santoor, Shaker & B. Vocals; Kumar Shankar: B. Vocals; Ravi Shankar: Sitar, Vocals, Synthesizer & Surbahar; Shubho Shankar: Sitar & B. Vocals; Ray Kramer: Cello; W. Webb: Esraj; Dennis Budimir: Acoustic Guitar; Klaus Voormann: Bass; Nodu Mullick: Tambura & Kartal; Krishna Temple: Kartal; Al Kasey: Mandolin; Ronald Cohen: Sarangi; Aashish Khan: Sarod, B. Vocals & Swaramandal; George Ruckert: Sarod; Fakir Muhammad: Tambura; L. Subramaniam: Violin; Bobby Bruce: Electric Violin; Gordon Swift: Electric Violin; Ray Pizzi: Bassoon; Hariprasad Chaurasia: Flute & Cowbells; G. Sachdev: Flute; Sharad Kumar: Flute; Tom Scott: Boehm Flute, Saxophones & Clapper; Gene Cipriano: Oboe; Jim Keltner: Drums; Ed Shaunessey: Drums; Ringo Starr: Drums; Emil Richards: Percussion & Marimbas; Palghat Raghu: Mridingam; Vini Poncia: Tambourine; Alla Rakha: Pakhavaj & Tabla; Harihar Rao: Vocals & Dholak; Pranesh Khan: Dholak; Billy Preston: Organ; Fred Teague: Organ; Nicky Hopkins: Piano; Paul Beaver: Synthesizer; Malcolm Cecil: Synthesizer; Robert Margouleff: Synthesizer

Song 321a title:
Dream, Nightmare & Dawn
(Music For A Ballet) Overture

Track details:
Side 2, track 1 / 2 min. 28 sec.

Release date / Country:
07 Oct 74 (first issued 20 Sep 74) / U.S.A.

Composer:
R. Shankar

One or more of the following: George Harrison: Autoharp, Acoustic Guitar & Electric Guitar; Jitendra Abhisheki: Vocals; Chakravarty: B. Vocals; Lakshmi Shankar: Swaramandal & Vocals; Shivkumar Sharma: Santoor, Shaker & B. Vocals; Kumar Shankar: B. Vocals; Ravi Shankar: Sitar, Vocals, Synthesizer & Surbahar; Shubho Shankar: Sitar & B. Vocals; Ray Kramer: Cello; W. Webb: Esraj; Dennis Budimir: Acoustic Guitar; Klaus Voormann: Bass; Nodu Mullick: Tambura & Kartal; Krishna Temple: Kartal; Al Kasey: Mandolin; Ronald Cohen: Sarangi; Aashish Khan: Sarod, B. Vocals & Swaramandal; George Ruckert: Sarod; Fakir Muhammad: Tambura; L. Subramaniam: Violin; Bobby Bruce: Electric Violin; Gordon Swift: Electric Violin; Ray Pizzi: Bassoon; Hariprasad Chaurasia: Flute & Cowbells; G. Sachdev: Flute; Sharad Kumar: Flute; Tom Scott: Boehm Flute, Saxophones & Clapper; Gene Cipriano: Oboe; Jim Keltner: Drums; Ed Shaunessey: Drums; Ringo Starr: Drums; Emil Richards: Percussion & Marimbas; Palghat Raghu: Mridingam; Vini Poncia: Tambourine; Alla Rakha: Pakhavaj & Tabla; Harihar Rao: Vocals & Dholak; Pranesh Khan: Dholak; Billy Preston: Organ; Fred Teague: Organ; Nicky Hopkins: Piano; Paul Beaver: Synthesizer; Malcolm Cecil: Synthesizer; Robert Margouleff: Synthesizer

Song 321b title: ***Track details:***
Dream, Nightmare & Dawn (Music For A Ballet) Side 2, track 2 / 3 min. 52 sec.
Part One: Dream (Festivity & Joy)
Release date / Country: ***Composer:***
07 Oct 74 (first issued 20 Sep 74) / U.S.A. R. Shankar

Song 321c title: ***Track details:***
Dream, Nightmare & Dawn (Music For A Ballet) Side 2, track 3 / 3 min. 10 sec.
Part One: Dream (Love-Dance Ecstasy)
Release date / Country: ***Composer:***
07 Oct 74 (first issued 20 Sep 74) / U.S.A. R. Shankar

Song 321d title: ***Track details:***
Dream, Nightmare & Dawn (Music For A Ballet) Side 2, track 7 / 3 min. 07 sec.
Part Two: Nightmare (Despair & Sorrow)
Release date / Country: ***Composer:***
07 Oct 74 (first issued 20 Sep 74) / U.S.A. R. Shankar

Song 321e title: ***Track details:***
Dream, Nightmare & Dawn (Music For A Ballet) Side 2, track 6 / 2 min. 51 sec.
Part Two: Nightmare (Disillusionment & Frustration)
Release date / Country: ***Composer:***
07 Oct 74 (first issued 20 Sep 74) / U.S.A. R. Shankar

Song 321f title: ***Track details:***
Dream, Nightmare & Dawn (Music For A Ballet) Side 2, track 4 / 3 min. 12 sec.
Part Two: Nightmare (Lust)
Release date / Country: ***Composer:***
07 Oct 74 (first issued 20 Sep 74) / U.S.A. R. Shankar

Ringo Starr: Drums; George Harrison: Guitar; additionally one or more of the following: George Harrison: Autoharp, Acoustic Guitar & Electric Guitar; Jitendra Abhisheki: Vocals; Kamala Chakravarty: B. Vocals; Lakshmi Shankar: Swaramandal & Vocals; Shivkumar Sharma: Santoor, Shaker & B. Vocals; Kumar Shankar: B. Vocals; Ravi Shankar: Sitar, Vocals, Synthesizer & Surbahar; Shubho Shankar: Sitar & B. Vocals; Ray Kramer: Cello; W. Webb: Esraj; Dennis Budimir: Acoustic Guitar; Klaus Voormann: Bass; Nodu Mullick: Tambura & Kartal; Krishna Temple: Kartal; Al Kasey: Mandolin; Ronald Cohen: Sarangi; Aashish Khan: Sarod, B. Vocals & Swaramandal; George Ruckert: Sarod; Fakir Muhammad: Tambura; L. Subramaniam: Violin; Bobby Bruce: Electric Violin; Gordon Swift: Electric Violin; Ray Pizzi: Bassoon; Hariprasad Chaurasia: Flute & Cowbells; G. Sachdev: Flute; Sharad Kumar: Flute; Tom Scott: Boehm Flute, Saxophones & Clapper; Gene Cipriano: Oboe; Jim Keltner: Drums; Ed Shaunessey: Drums; Ringo Starr: Drums; Emil Richards: Percussion & Marimbas; Palghat Raghu: Mridingam; Vini Poncia: Tambourine; Alla Rakha: Pakhavaj & Tabla; Harihar Rao: Vocals & Dholak; Pranesh Khan: Dholak; Billy Preston: Organ; Fred Teague: Organ; Nicky Hopkins: Piano; Paul Beaver: Synthesizer; Malcolm Cecil: Synthesizer; Robert Margouleff: Synthesizer

Song 321g title: ***Track details:***
Dream, Nightmare & Dawn (Music For A Ballet) Side 2, track 8 / 3 min. 07 sec.
Part Three: Dawn (Awakening)
Release date / Country: ***Composer:***
07 Oct 74 (first issued 20 Sep 74) / U.S.A. R. Shankar

Song 321h title: ***Track details:***
Dream, Nightmare & Dawn (Music For A Ballet) Side 2, track 9 / 4 min. 21 sec.
Part Three: Dawn (Peace & Hope)
Release date / Country: ***Composer:***
07 Oct 74 (first issued 20 Sep 74) / U.S.A. R. Shankar

Song 321i title:
I Am Missing You (Reprise)
Release date / Country:
07 Oct 74 (first issued 20 Sep 74) / U.S.A.
Track details:
Side 1, track 4 / 3 min. 56 sec.
Composer:
R. Shankar

Song 321j title:
Jaya Jagadish Hare
Release date / Country:
07 Oct 74 (first issued 20 Sep 74) / U.S.A.
Track details:
Side 1, track 5 / 4 min. 50 sec.
Composer:
R. Shankar - Trad

Song 321k title:
Kahan Gayelava Shyam Salone
Release date / Country:
07 Oct 74 (first issued 20 Sep 74) / U.S.A.
Track details:
Side 1, track 2 / 3 min. 15 sec.
Composer:
R. Shankar

Record 322 title:
The Concert For Bangla Desh
Label / Catalog number:
Warner Bros / NJL-38583
Media:
Album 12" LVD
Producer:
George Harrison & Phil Spector
Jacket / Inserts:
Standard international design with variations / 4 page translation insert
Recording Location / Date:
On location at Madison Square Garden, New York, NY, U.S.A. / 01 Aug 71 [evening]

Song 322a title:
(Introduction) Bangla Dhun (Sitar & Sarod Duet, Dadra Tal-6 Beats, Teental-16 Beats) [live]
Release date / Country:
1990 / Japan
Track details:
Side 1, track 1 / 23 min. 39 sec.
Composer:
Traditional

Ravi Shankar: Sitar; Ali Akbar Khan: Sarod; Alla Rakah: Tabla; Kamala Chakravarty: Tamboura
This song is also included on Capitol/Apple / CDP 7 93265 2 / Album 5" CD [2 CD set] / CD1, tracks 1-2 / released 01 Aug 91 (first issued 20 Dec 71) in the U.S.A. / Standard international design in double Jewel box / 34 page CD booklet with photo of George Harrison & Ringo Starr.

The honorable Pandit, Ravi Shankar, was born Robindra Shankar on April 7, 1920 in Varanasi (Benares), India. Ravi's father was away from the family most of his life, practicing law in Calcutta and London, and later teaching at Columbia University in New York. His father was also attached to the League of Nations for a time. Ravi's first ambition in life was to be an actor, but he soon developed a love for music. At the age of ten, Ravi moved to Paris with his family, and performed throughout the world in his brother Uday Shan-Kar's Company of Hindu Dancers and Musicians. Touring the world exposed Ravi to a wide variety of musical styles that were later instrumental in his bridging the gap between Eastern and Western music.

In 1935, Ustad Allauddin Khan, India's renowned master of the sarod, joined the dance troope. After several years of artistic wandering, Ravi decided to devote nearly eight years to disciplined and intensive musical training on Indian stringed instruments (sitar) under Ustad. In May 1941, Ravi married Ustad's daughter Annapurna. Ustad's son, Ali Akbar Khan, also became a master of the sarod, as did his son Aashish Khan*. Ali Akbar and Aashish have worked extensively with Ravi through the years.

In 1952, Shankar began a two-decade collaboration with violinist Yehudi Menuhin that culminated in the Grammy Award winning album **West Meets East**. Shankar and Indian music received a major boost in the West with endorsements he received from George Harrison and The Beatles, who, in 1965, began to incorporate Indian music into their recordings. Shankar, however, was not without his critics back in India who felt he had contaminated Indian music.

George Harrison's first real exposure to Indian music and the sitar was on the set of The Beatles' film **Help!** in the spring of 1965. The plot of the film centered on Eastern religion. David Crosby of The Byrds *(see Stephen Stills)* recommended Shankar's album **Portrait Of A Genius** to Harrison at a guest house in Los Angeles during The Beatles' 1965 summer tour. Harrison's first recorded use of the sitar was on the song ***Norwegian Wood***, on the album **Rubber Soul** that fall. It is often cited as the first time a sitar was ever used on a pop/rock record. However, Ken Thorne's ***Another Hard Day's Night***, on The Beatles' **Help!** soundtrack album, is the first known use of a sitar on a pop/rock record, predating ***Norwegian Wood*** by several months.

Harrison met Shankar some months later at a dinner hosted by friends from North London's Asian Music Circle. Members of that group had assisted Harrison with the recording of his Indian-influenced song ***Love You To***, included on The Beatles' album **Revolver**. Ravi said, "George met me and showed interest in learning sitar; I explained how difficult and horrendous it is to learn sitar and play 'properly;' George said he would try!" Shortly thereafter, Shankar arrived at Harrison's home to give him lessons. During one lesson, Shankar admonished Harrison for stepping over the sitar to answer the phone. Harrison quickly learned that to Ravi Shankar the sitar was more than just an instrument.

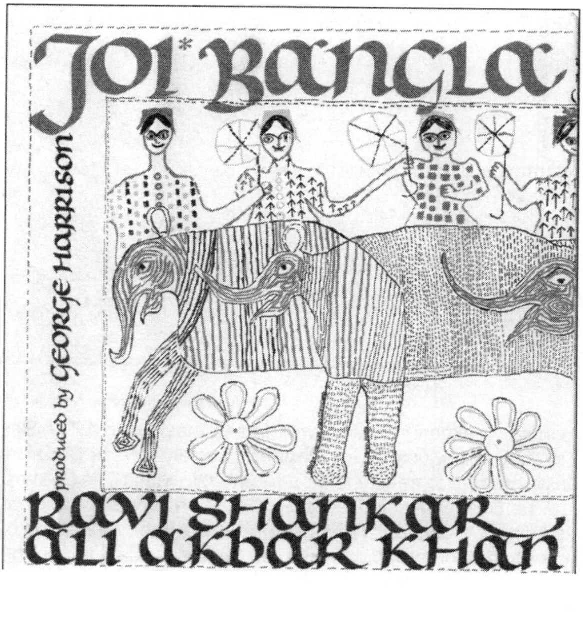

Harrison visited India in September

and October of 1966 to take additional lessons from Shankar. He became equally interested in Indian philosophy and religion, which are inseparable from Indian music. There, the two forged a friendship that lasts to this day. It is unlikely that The Beatles would ever have attended the Maharishi Mahesh Yogi's lectures on Transcendental Meditation, or traveled to his ashram in Rishikesh, India, had it not been for George Harrison's initial interest in Indian music.

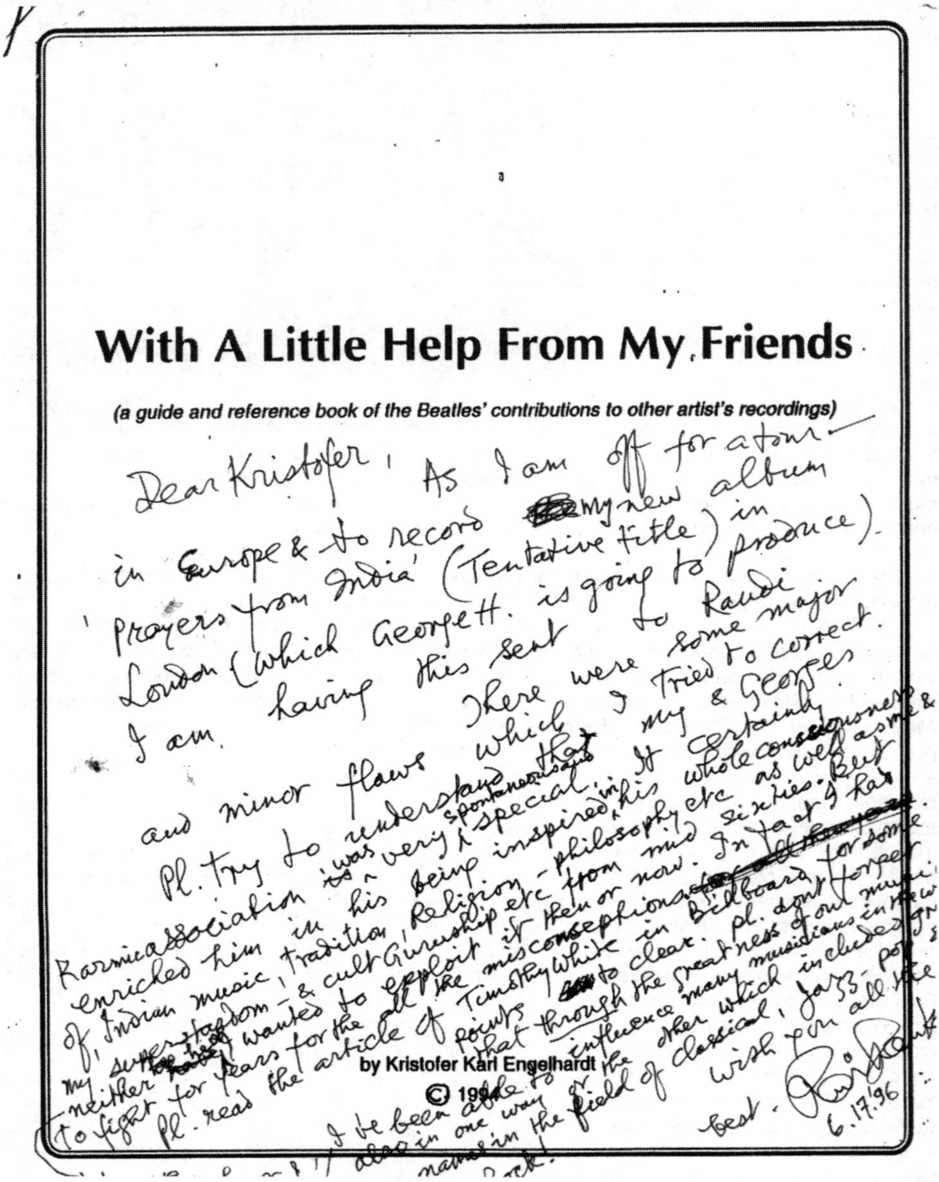

With A Little Help From My Friends

(a guide and reference book of the Beatles' contributions to other artist's recordings)

Dear Kristofer, As I am off for a tour in Europe & to record my new album 'Prayers from India' (Tentative title) in London (which George H. is going to produce). I am having this sent to Randi. There were some major and minor flaws which I tried to correct. Pl. try to understand that my & George's Karmic association was spontaneous & very special. It certainly enriched him in his being inspired in his whole consciousness of Indian music, tradition, Religion - philosophy etc as well as me & my superstardom - & cult Guruship etc from mid sixties. But neither he nor I wanted to exploit it then or now. In fact I had to fight for years for all the misconceptions. pl. read the article of Timothy White in Billboard for some points to clear. pl. don't forget that through the greatness of our music I've been able to influence many musicians in the West also in one way or the other which included great names in the field of classical, jazz-pop & Rock! wish you all the best. Ravi Shankar 6.17.96

by Kristofer Karl Engelhardt

© 199?

Letter from Ravi Shankar to Kristofer Engelhardt

Harrison's experimentation with Indian music within The Beatles culminated with the song ***Within You Without You*** on the **Sgt. Pepper's Lonely Hearts Club Band** album. Thereafter, Harrison essentially returned to traditional pop/rock music within The Beatles. However, Harrison's first solo release for The Beatles' Apple Records label, **Wonderwall Music**, was a film soundtrack he partly recorded in India in January 1968. Several weeks later, an unused backing track from the sessions in India was used to create ***The Inner Light***, Harrison's last Indian-influenced Beatles song.

Ravi had been a well-known Indian musician in the West for some time, but his appearance at the legendary **Monterey Pop Festival** elevated him to the unwilling status of cult hero to the counter-culture movement of the late 1960s. He was encouraged and flattered to be discovered by a new generation of admirers. However, as a classically trained Indian musician he had difficulty performing between sets of rock 'n' roll bands to rowdy, drugged out, Western youth in large sports arenas. Shankar found it especially difficult to accept the destruction of musical instruments by acts like Jimi Hendrix and The Who. Over the years, George Harrison has served as both catalyst and mediator for Shankar in bridging the cultural gap between Eastern and Western music.

In the summer of 1971, Ravi Shankar described to Harrison the appalling situation in Bangla Desh, a newly independent nation born out of the eastern part of divided Pakistan in the Indian subcontinent. Bangla Desh was faced with political strife and a recent natural disaster. Harrison was only too willing to help organize what would become **The Concert for Bangla Desh**, with proceeds going to benefit in the relief of that country's people.

Shankar joined the stable of artists at Apple Records. His first release by the label was the single ***Joi Bangla***, issued to tie in with the Bangla Desh benefit. Next came the soundtrack to the Apple film **Raga**, a project he and Harrison had worked on for over two years that was originally titled **Messenger Out Of The East**. Harrison also made a brief cameo appearance in the film, playing sitar with Shankar. One song on the soundtrack, titled ***Frenzy And Distortion***, sounds suspiciously like it could be The Beatles, or at least Harrison on vocals, circa 1968. According to Ravi, the song was a musical collage done by a student of his and sung by an Indian musician, and containing no musical segments by The Beatles or Harrison. Harrison also helped produce Shankar's album **In Concert 1972** for Apple Records.

George Harrison enlisted a number of his Eastern- and Western-musician friends and produced the critically acclaimed **Shankar Family & Friends** album, released in 1974 on Harrison's newly formed Dark Horse Record's label. Harrison contributed to the album under the pseudonym Hari Georgeson, which he often used during this period. Ringo Starr also contributed to the album under the pseudonym Billy Shears.

Shankar Family & Friends also accompanied Harrison on his 1974 Dark Horse tour of the U.S. George joined in on portions of the Indian music, but, sadly, none of that portion of the show has been officially released. Included in the Indian set were the songs ***Zoom Zoom Zoom***, ***Jai Sri Kalij***, ***Naderdani***, ***Chatpatay***, ***Anurag (Romance)***, ***I Am Missing You*** and ***Dispute And Violence***.

In 1976, Dark Horse released **Ravi Shankar's Music Festival From India**, produced by Harrison at his home studio in Henley. Dark Horse Records filmed **Ravi Shankar's Music Festival From India**, performing in London just before Harrison's 1974 U.S. Tour. The film has yet to be released.

In 1987, Ravi Shankar recorded his album **Tana Mana** in part at Harrison's home studio in Henley. Harrison was listed in the album's general credits as playing autoharp and synthesizer. Ravi and Frank Serafine are also listed as playing synthesizer. Serafine seems fairly sure the only song recorded at Harrison's home studio was ***Friar Park***, and that George plays synthesizer and autoharp on it. According to Ravi, ***Friar Park*** is the only song recorded at George's Friar Park Studios from **Tana Mana**, and Harrison contributed autoharp. In 1988, Ravi also helped George and son Dhani Harrison on ***Ride Rajbun***, a track featured as part of **The Bunbury Tails** album project, finally released in 1992.

In 1996, Dark Horse Records, in association with Angel (EMI) Records, released the four-CD retrospective set **In Celebration**. George Harrison essentially conceived the idea, and, with help from Ravi's friend Alan Kozlowski, selected the tracks and produced the retrospective compilation in celebration of Ravi's 75th birthday. The set contained a total of eight songs that Harrison directly contributed to, one of which (***Ta Na Tom***) was previously unreleased. The credits for these songs are considerably more detailed than in previous releases. For example, Harrison is not listed in the credits of the album **Tana Mana** as one of the producers, but he is credited as producer of the song ***Friar Park*** from that album. The credits of **In Celebration** list Harrison as playing autoharp on ***Friar Park***, but do not credit him as playing synthesizer. No synthesizer is detectable on ***Friar Park***. **In Celebration** also credits Harrison as playing autoharp and guitar on ***I Am Missing You*** and Ringo Starr playing drums. In his book **The Quiet One - A Life Of George Harrison**, author Alan Clayson claims that "George was the slightly throaty vocal refrain – in Hindi – on the title track (*Tana Mana*). No amount of listening adds credibility to his claim. The song *Tana Mana* is also included on **In Celebration**, and the credits correctly list it as being recorded at Serafine's Studios in Los Angeles, and sung by Ravi Shankar and Lakshmi Shankar. Harrison is not credited as contributing to the song.

George Harrison and Ravi Shankar at Los Angeles, CA press conference, photo available from The Beatles (USA) Fan Club

Ravi Shankar continues to be, as George Harrison calls him, "The Godfather of World Music." Shankar admits he loves Harrison like a son. Harrison produced and performed on Shankar's 1997 album **Chants Of India**. The album was recorded in India in January and April, and in England in July and August 1996. A film was made of the album being recorded that included scenes with Harrison. Shankar acted primarily as arranger of the traditional Indian chants and composer of several new pieces. Harrison accompanied Shankar during several promotional appearances for the album. On July 24, 1997, VH1-TV aired a half-hour interview with Shankar and Harrison titled **Ying & Yang** as part of the media promotion for **Chants Of India**. The special included Shankar, his wife Sukanya, and Harrison performing *Prabhujee*, and Harrison performing *All Things Must Pass* on acoustic guitar. George also performed two other songs during the appearance that were not aired. Harrison is also helping edit Shankar's autobiography, as well as writing its introduction, for Genesis Publications.

Del Shannon

Record 323 title:
Callin' Out My Name/Hot Love/When I Had You

Media:
Single 5" CD

Label / Catalog number:
Silvertone / ZD 45104

Producer:
Del Shannon

Jacket / Inserts:
Standard international design in jewel box / CD insert (printed in Germany)

Recording Location / Date:
Weddington Studios (NRG), Los Angeles, CA, U.S.A / 25 May 88

Song 323a title:
Hot Love

Release date / Country:
1991 / Austria

Track details:
Side 1, track 2 / 3 min. 26 sec.

Composer:
D. Shannon

Del Shannon: Lead Vocals & (probable) Acoustic Guitar; Billy Coiffi: B. Vocals, Electric & Acoustic Guitar; Bob Mair: Bass; Mel Watt: Drums; Michael Clark: Keyboards; George Harrison: B. Vocals;

Tom Petty: B. Vocals; Jeff Lynne: B. Vocals

Del Shannon was born Charles Westover in Grand Rapids, Michigan on December 30, 1934, but lived in nearby Coopersville. Shannon took an interest in music early in life and began playing guitar in high school bands. He changed his stage name to Del Shannon after the Cadillac Coupe deVille and a local wrestler friend named Shannon. He continued to perform even while in the army. Following his stay in the army, he became popular playing clubs in the Battle Creek, Michigan area, and began to write songs. Shannon attracted the attention of a local DJ who took his tapes to a Detroit-based music management company. They in turn offered him a contract and a recording session in New York, where he recorded his composition ***Runaway*** in early 1961. ***Runaway*** was followed by the hits ***Hats Off To Larry*** and ***Little Town Flirt***.

At about the same time The Beatles were cutting their first record for EMI, Shannon embarked on his first U.K. tour and took notice of The Beatles' surging popularity. On April 18, 1963, Shannon finally got to see The Beatles in action performing ***From Me To You*** when they shared a bill at the Royal Albert Hall in London. He was so impressed with the song that several weeks later he recorded a cover version of it in England. It made him the first American artist to cover a Lennon and McCartney composition – their first composition to enter the U.S. charts.

Ironically, The Beatles and the onslaught of the British music invasion of America had a devastating effect on artists like Shannon. However, he was able to turn out three hits in 1964 (***Handy Man***, ***Keep Searchin'***, and ***Stranger In Town***). John Lennon admitted that his 1964 composition ***I'll Be Back*** was a rewrite of a Del Shannon song to which he had been listening. Unfortunately, mismanagement, changing musical styles, and personal problems would ultimately lead to Shannon's departure from the charts. It took the British duo Peter & Gordon* to take one of his most beautiful songs, ***I Go To Pieces***, into the top 10. He also recorded a cover version of Peter & Gordon's hit ***A World Without Love***, written by Lennon and McCartney.

Throughout the second half of the 1960s, and into the 1970s, Shannon scored some hits as a producer for other artists (most notably ***Gypsy Woman*** by Brian Hyland), and recorded a wide variety of music. He also worked with, among others, Jeff Lynne* and Dave Edmunds* with some degree of critical acclaim, but without much chart success.

Shannon's 1975 retrospective album **The Vintage Years** features a photo of Del with McCartney and Ringo in their hotel room in Florida during their historic first visit to the U.S. in 1964. Shannon visited The Beatles in their hotel room the following year in New York. Ringo and Lennon attended Del Shannon and Chuck Berry's* performances at Brian Epstein's Saville Theatre in London on February 19, 1967. Shannon made a brief cameo appearance in Robert Stigwood's 1978 film **Sgt. Pepper's Lonely Hearts Club Band**. In the early 1980s, Shannon hooked up with Tom Petty*, who produced his all too appropriately titled album **Drop Down And Get Me**. Shannon recorded a cover of The Beatles' song ***I Should Have Known Better***, that was originally intended to be included on the album, but remains unreleased.

According to Shannon's lifelong friend and song publisher Dan Bourgoise of Bug Music, Shannon recorded a song called ***Hot Love*** backed by the group The Monte Carlos in May of 1988. During the session, Shannon got a call from Tom Petty and / or Jeff Lynne, who stopped by with George Harrison and sang backing vocals on ***Hot Love***. At the time, the three were in the process of forming the "supergroup" Traveling Wilburys *(see Bob Dylan, Roy Orbison)*. These events lead to Lynne's, along with Tom Petty And The Heartbreakers', substantial involvement in the album **Rock On**, that would prove to be Shannon's final recordings, and arguably some of his best work. Following the death of Roy Orbison, The Wilburys released a version of Del's song ***Runaway***, recorded during sessions for their second album. At the time there were reports that Shannon was being considered as Orbison's replacement in the group. Contrary to rumors, Bourgoise said ***Hot Love*** was the only recording of Del's to which Harrison ever contributed. ***Hot Love*** was left off the **Rock On** album, but was released on a CD single in Europe in 1991, and on the 1998 Australian CD release **Del Shannon 1961 - 1990 A Complete Career Anthology** (Raven Records / RVCD 51). Del Shannon, suffering from depression for many years, took his life on February 8, 1990.

Tony Sheridan

Record 324 title:
Ain't She Sweet
Label / Catalog number:
Atco / SD 33-169
Media:
Album 12"
Jacket / Inserts:
Unique

Song 324a title:
Sweet Georgia Brown [revised-lyric version† with guitar & drumming overdub]
Track details:
Side 1, track 2 / 2 min. 03 sec.
Release date / Country:
05 Oct 64 (first issued 01 Jun 64) / U.S.A.
Composer:
B. Bernie - M. Pinkard - K. Casey [revised-lyrics by: P. Murphy†]
Producer:
Bert Kaempfert & [Paul Murphy†]
Recording Location / Date:
Studio Hamburg (aka Rahlstedt/Wandsbek), Hamburg, Germany; (overdubbing probably recorded at Atlantic Studios, New York City, U.S.A.) / 24 May 62; revised-lyric version 04 Jun 64†; guitar & drumming overdub probably early to mid-1964

Tony Sheridan: Lead Vocals & Guitar; Paul McCartney: Bass, Arrangement & B. Vocals; John Lennon: B. Vocals; George Harrison: Guitar & B. Vocals; Pete Best: Drums; Roy Young: Piano; Bernard Purdie: (probable overdubbed) Drums; Cornell Dupree: (probable overdubbed) Guitar

Song 324b title:
Take Out Some Insurance On Me, Baby (If You Love Me Baby) [overdubbed & edited version]
Track details:
Side 1, track 3 / 2 min. 50 sec.
Release date / Country:
05 Oct 64 (first issued Feb 64) / U.S.A.
Composer:
C. Singleton - W. Hall
Producer:
Bert Kaempfert
Recording Location / Date:
Studio Hamburg (aka Rahlstedt/Wandsbek), Hamburg, Germany; (overdubbing probably recorded at Atlantic Studios, New York City, U.S.A.) / 24 Jun 61; overdub & edit spring 1964

Tony Sheridan: Lead Vocals & Guitar; Paul McCartney: Bass; Pete Best: Drums; Bernard Purdie: (probable overdubbed) Drums; Cornell Dupree: (probable overdubbed) Guitar

Record 325 title:
Beatles Oldies
Media:
Album 5" CD
Label / Catalog number:
Polydor / POCP-2306
Jacket / Inserts:
Unique in Jewel box with photo of The Beatles / 4 page CD booklet & 16 page translation insert

Song 325a title:
My Bonnie (Lies Over The Ocean) (Twist) [English Intro]
Track details:
Side 1, track 1 / 2 min. 41 sec.
Release date / Country:
25 Feb 94 (first issued 05 Jan 62) / Japan
Composer:
C. Pratt (also listed as: J.T. Woods or H. J. Fuller)/Arr: T. Sheridan

Producer:
Bert Kaempfert
Recording Location / Date:
Friedrich-Ebert-Halle, (Harburg) Hamburg, Germany / 22-23 Jun 61

Tony Sheridan: Lead Vocals & Lead Guitar; George Harrison: Guitar; Paul McCartney: Bass & B. Vocals; Pete Best: Drums; John Lennon: Hand Claps & B. Vocals

Song 325b title:
Nobody's Child
Release date / Country:
25 Feb 94 (first issued Feb 64) / Japan
Track details:
Side 1, track 24 / 3 min. 55 sec.
Composer:
C. Coben - M. Foree/Arr: T. Sheridan
Producer:
Bert Kaempfert
Recording Location / Date:
Friedrich-Ebert-Halle, (Harburg) Hamburg, Germany / 22-23 Jun 61

Tony Sheridan: Lead Vocals & Lead Guitar; Paul McCartney: Bass; Pete Best: Drums

Song 325c title:
Swanee River
Release date / Country:
25 Feb 94 (first issued: Jun 62) / Japan
Track details:
Side 1, track 22 / 2 min. 54 sec.
Composer:
Trad/Arr. & Ad. Bones
Producer:
Bert Kaempfert
Recording Location / Date:
(probably) Musikhalle (Grosser Saal) or (possibly) Studio Hamburg (aka Rahlstedt/Wandsbek), Hamburg, Germany / (probably) 21 Dec 61 or (possibly) 24 May 62

Tony Sheridan: Lead Vocals & (probable) Lead Guitar; George Harrison: (possible) Guitar; Paul McCartney: (possible) Bass; Colin Melander: (probable) Bass; Pete Best: (possible) Drums; Jimmy Doyle: (possible) Drums; Johnny Watson (possible) Drums; John Lennon: (possible) Guitar; Roy Young: Piano; Rikki Barnes: (probable) Saxophone

Song 325d title:
Sweet Georgia Brown [revised-lyric version†]
Release date / Country:
25 Feb 94 (first issued 08 Apr 64) / Japan
Track details:
Side 1, track 3 / 2 min. 03 sec.
Composer:
B. Bernie - M. Pinkard - K. Casey
[revised-lyrics by: P. Murphy†]
Producer:
Bert Kaempfert & [Paul Murphy†]
Recording Location / Date:
Studio Hamburg (aka Rahlstedt/Wandsbek), Hamburg, Germany / 24 May 62;
(revised-lyrics) 04 Jan 64†

Tony Sheridan: Lead Vocals & Guitar; Paul McCartney: Bass, Arrangement & B. Vocals; John Lennon: B. Vocals; George Harrison: Guitar & B. Vocals; Pete Best: Drums; Roy Young: Piano

Song 325e title:
Take Out Some Insurance On Me, Baby
(If You Love Me Baby) [original-lyric version]
Release date / Country:
25 Feb 94 (first issued 08 Apr 64) / Japan
Track details:
Side 1, track 19 / 2 min. 53 sec.
Composer:
C. Singleton - W. Hall
Producer:
Bert Kaempfert
Recording Location / Date:
Studio Hamburg (aka Rahlstedt/Wandsbek), Hamburg, Germany / 24 Jun 61

Tony Sheridan: Lead Vocals & Lead Guitar; Paul McCartney: Bass; Pete Best: Drums

Song 325f title:
The Saints (When The Saints Go Marching In)
Track details:
Side 1, track 18 / 3 min. 18 sec.
Release date / Country:
25 Feb 94 (recording probably first issued: Oct 61) / Japan
Composer:
Trad/Arr: T. Sheridan
Producer:
Bert Kaempfert
Recording Location / Date:
Friedrich-Ebert-Halle, (Harburg) Hamburg, Germany / 22-23 Jun 61

Tony Sheridan: Lead Vocals & Lead Guitar; Paul McCartney: Bass & B. Vocals; John Lennon: Guitar; George Harrison: Guitar; Pete Best: Drums

Song 325g title:
Why (Can't You Love Me Again)
Track details:
Side 1, track 12 / 2 min. 58 sec.
Release date / Country:
25 Feb 94 (recording first issued Apr 62) / Japan
Composer:
T. Sheridan - Compton
Producer:
Bert Kaempfert
Recording Location / Date:
Friedrich-Ebert-Halle, (Harburg) Hamburg, Germany / 22-23 Jun 61

Tony Sheridan: Lead Vocals & Guitar; John Lennon: Guitar & B. Vocals; Paul McCartney: Bass; Pete Best: Drums; George Harrison: Guitar

Record 326 title:
Hamburg Twist
Media:
Extended Play 7"
Label / Catalog number:
Polydor / PRE 240 003
Producer:
Bert Kaempfert
Jacket / Inserts:
Picture sleeve / Contained exclusively in the book "The Beatles From Cavern To Star-Club" by Hans Gottfridsson
Recording Location / Date:
Studio Hamburg (aka Rahlstedt/Wandsbek), Hamburg, Germany / 24 May 62

Song 326a title:
Sweet Georgia Brown [original-lyric version]
Track details:
Side 1, track 1 / 2 min. 03 sec.
Release date / Country:
Aug 97 (first issued Oct 62) / Sweden
Composer:
B. Bernie - M. Pinkard - K. Casey

Tony Sheridan: Lead Vocals & Guitar; Paul McCartney: Bass & B. Vocals; John Lennon: B. Vocals; George Harrison: Guitar & B. Vocals; Pete Best: Drums; Roy Young: Piano

Record 327 title:
Tony Sheridan Volume I The Singles 1961-1964
Media:
Album 5" CD
Label / Catalog number:
Star-Club / LP 841 141-2
Producer:
Bert Kaempfert
Jacket / Inserts:
Unique / 12 page CD booklet
Recording Location / Date:
Friedrich-Ebert-Halle, (Harburg) Hamburg, Germany / 22-23 Jun 61

Song 327a title:
My Bonnie (Lies Over The Ocean) (Mein Herz Is Bei Dir Nur) (Rock) [German Intro]

Release date / Country:
1991 (first issued 23 Oct 61) / Germany

Track details:
Side 1, track 1 / 2 min. 41 sec.

Composer:
C. Pratt (also listed as: J.T. Woods or H. J. Fuller)/Arr: T. Sheridan - Bertie

Tony Sheridan: Lead Vocals & Lead Guitar; George Harrison: Guitar; Paul McCartney: Bass & B. Vocals; Pete Best: Drums; John Lennon: Hand Claps & B. Vocals

Tony Sheridan was born Anthony Esmond Sheridan McGinnity on May 21, 1940 in Norwich, England. He sang in his church choir, and played violin in grade school, but switched to the guitar. Sheridan has been in a number of bands over the years, starting with The Saints in 1955, Vince Taylor And The Playboys in 1959, and the Jets in 1960. He became known as "The Teacher" because of the influence he had on a number of bands, including The Beatles.

The Beatles first met him at the Top Ten Club in Hamburg in November 1960. They admired the fellow British singer and guitarist, who already had several record releases and TV appearances to his credit. Sheridan had come to Hamburg with his band, the Jets, to headline at the newly opened Top Ten Club. When The Beatles returned to Hamburg for an engagement at the club between March 27 and July 2, 1961, they bunked with Sheridan who had become a solo act backed by a number of house bands. The Beatles and Sheridan's band alternated sets at the club, and, before long, The Beatles were backing Sheridan. Alfred Schacht, who worked for Aberbach Music Publishing, heard Sheridan and The Beatles at the Top Ten Club sometime in late April or early May of 1961. He suggested to his friend Bert Kaempfert that he record them together.

Hamburg native Berthold (Bert) Kaempfert was born on October 16, 1923. He was an internationally known composer, musician, and orchestra leader. Kaempfert is perhaps best remembered for composing and recording such easy-listening songs (many that were hits for other artists) as ***Wonderland By Night***, ***Spanish Eyes*** (Al Martino), ***Danke Shoen*** (Wayne Newton), and the song that re-launched Frank Sinatra's career, ***Strangers In The Night***. Kaempfert was also A&R man for Polydor records in Hamburg, and scouted the Hamburg beat clubs for talent to record. Shortly thereafter, The Beatles signed an agreement with Bert Kaempfert Productions for a one-year exclusive contract that took effect on July 1, 1961. Kaempfert was able to get Deutsche Grammophone Gesellschaft's Polydor Records label to release the recordings with Sheridan and The Beatles.

Tony Sheridan's recordings with The Beatles have been continually reissued on more labels, and in more countries, than any other Beatles-related recordings. They have generally been labeled and classified as Beatles' recordings, almost since their initial release. For the most part, they are Tony Sheridan recordings featuring The Beatles as his backing band. Frequently these records include songs that The Beatles had nothing to do with, or, worse yet, have been mislabeled as being The Beatles. A couple of Sheridan's recordings continue to generate debate over possible uncredited involvement by The Beatles. In spite of over thirty years of confusion surrounding these recordings, it is generally agreed that The Beatles (then consisting of John Lennon on guitar, George Harrison on guitar, Paul McCartney on bass and Pete Best on drums) were involved in eight released record-

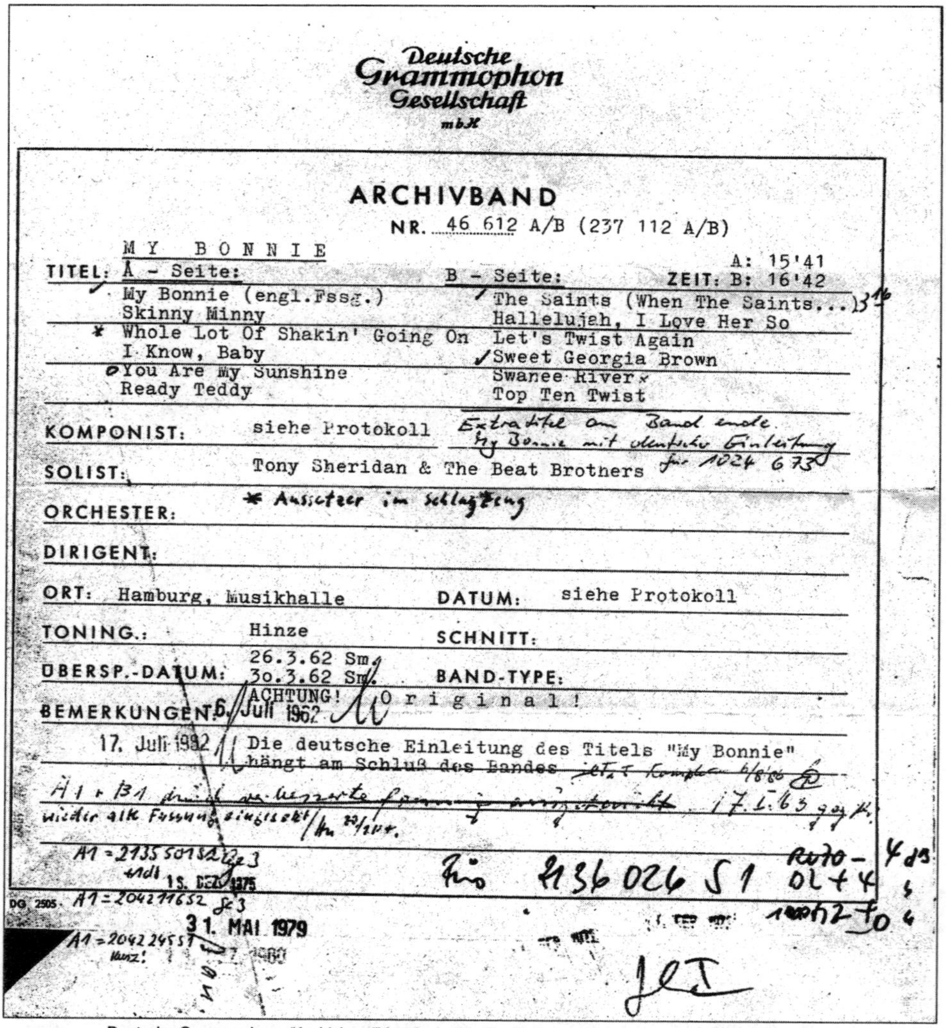

Deutsche Grammophon Gesellschaft mbH

ARCHIVBAND

NR. 46 612 A/B (237 112 A/B)

TITEL: MY BONNIE

ZEIT: A: 15'41 B: 16'42

A - Seite:	B - Seite:
My Bonnie (engl.Fssg.)	The Saints (When The Saints...)
Skinny Minny	Hallelujah, I Love Her So
* Whole Lot Of Shakin' Going On	Let's Twist Again
I Know, Baby	Sweet Georgia Brown
You Are My Sunshine	Swanee River
Ready Teddy	Top Ten Twist

KOMPONIST: siehe Protokoll — Extratitel am Bandende. My Bonnie mit deutscher Einleitung für 1024 673

SOLIST: Tony Sheridan & The Beat Brothers

ORCHESTER: * Aussetzer im Schlagzeug

DIRIGENT:

ORT: Hamburg, Musikhalle — DATUM: siehe Protokoll

TONING.: Hinze — SCHNITT:

ÜBERSP.-DATUM: 26.3.62 Sm. 30.3.62 Sm. — BAND-TYPE:

BEMERKUNGEN: 6. Juli 1962 ACHTUNG! O r i g i n a l !

17. Juli 1962 Die deutsche Einleitung des Titels "My Bonnie" hängt am Schluß des Bandes

A1 = 2135 501 S2

1S. DEZ. 1975

A1 = 204211652

31. MAI 1979

A1 = 2042245S1

Deutsche Grammophone “Archivband” for single “My Bonnie”, notes by and courtesy of Tony Sheridan

ings produced by Kaempfert - ***My Bonnie***, ***Nobody's Child***, ***Sweet Georgia Brown***, ***Take Out Some Insurance On Me, Baby***, ***When The Saints Go Marching In***, ***Why***, and two songs, ***Cry For A Shadow*** and ***Ain't She Sweet***, rightfully classified as Beatles' recordings, because Sheridan did not participate.

Cry For A Shadow (tentatively titled ***Beatle Bop***) is an instrumental originally conceived as a parody of the song ***Apache*** by the British pop group Cliff Richards and The Shadows. It holds the distinction of being the first and only known Harrison-Lennon composition. ***Ain't She Sweet*** features John Lennon on lead vocals. The Beatles performed these songs in their live set at the time.

All of Polydor's documents concerning these recordings are based on information given to them by Bert Kaempfert Productions. While there is no persuasive reason to doubt their accuracy, it is, nonetheless, secondhand information. These documents state that the first sessions with Tony Sheridan and The Beatles took place at Friedrich-Ebert-Halle on June 22-23, 1961 to record ***My Bonnie***, ***Nobody's Child***, ***When The Saints Go Marching In***, ***Why***, and ***Cry For A Shadow***. This was not an actual recording studio but an auditorium with recording equipment off to the side of the stage in a multi-purpose community center and school in the Harburg area of Hamburg. They do, however, represent the first professional recordings The Beatles ever made. According to Tony Sheridan, the

Roy Young at John Lennon's piano, CN Tower, Toronto, Canada, 1996, photo courtesy of Roy Young

Friedrich-Ebert-Halle "studio" was first set up by British Forces, as a make-shift radio station after the war, and later used by German radio.

According to Polydor's notes, The Beatles recorded ***Ain't She Sweet*** and backed Sheridan on ***Take Out Some Insurance On Me, Baby*** on June 24, at Studio Hamburg (aka Rahlstedt/Wandsbek), Hamburg, Germany. In a series of articles in Beatles Book monthly magazine in 1976 and 1977, Iain Hines, a member of Tony Sheridan's band the Jets, makes the startling claim that ***Take Out Some Insurance On Me, Baby*** probably does not include any of The Beatles, but does feature Ringo Starr on drums, not Pete Best, as is generally assumed. It is certainly conceivable, as Ringo's band Rory Storm & The Hurricanes* were regulars in Hamburg during this period. Ringo even joined Sheridan's backing band for a time, and he was certainly no stranger to The Beatles. However, Ringo was not in Germany during the summer of 1961. He and The Hurricanes were playing a summer long engagement at Butlin's, a popular holiday camp in the U.K. No one, including Sheridan, who is certain it was Best on drums, has ever backed up Hines' claim. ***Take Out Some Insurance On Me, Baby*** would not see release until February of 1964.

The first commercially released record that The Beatles ever appeared on was the single ***My Bonnie / When The Saints Go Marching In*** (Polydor / 24 673) issued in Germany, probably in October or November of 1961 (not in the summer of 1961 as has been previously reported). However, this first issue listed them as The Beat Brothers. It was issued as two separate singles – one with a German introduction, and the other with an English introduction. Each release had a picture sleeve. The song was a top 40 in Germany in January 1962. After 1963, it was usually issued as an edited version, without the 35 second German or English introduction. What is more important (if the official story can be believed), is that this was this record that drew Brian Epstein's attention to The Beatles. Epstein even went so far as to have Polydor change The Beat Brothers' name to The Beatles for its U.K. release, and used the record as a demonstration in The Beatles' search for a proper recording contract in their native England. However, Epstein and The Beatles became upset with Polydor's continued attempts to cash in on the remainder of the less than polished recordings once the group had become world famous.

Iain Hines claims that he, not Tony Sheridan (who got the credit), arranged ***When The Saints Go Marching In*** and ***My Bonnie*** for Del Ward. Sheridan flatly denies Hines' contention. "I had the last word in these matters (being the singer), e.g., as far as structure of the songs went. Much of the rhythm (Paul's bass and John's guitar) was meant to compensate for the lack of drive and punch from [Pete Best] the drums. The idea for ***My Bonnie*** – well, I borrowed that from Gene Vincent, whom I had backed on tour in the U.K. prior to Hamburg! ***The Saints*** I had heard from Jerry Lee Lewis."

In April 1962, Polydor issued an EP in France titled ***Mr. Twist***. Besides ***My Bonnie*** and ***When The Saints Go Marching In***, it contained the first known release of ***Cry For A Shadow*** and ***Why***. Polydor had originally scheduled these two songs to be released as a single in Germany in March of 1962. In Germany and England this EP was titled ***My Bonnie***. There seems to be some dispute about its first

Roy Young and Kristofer Engelhardt sitting at John Lennon's piano at press party for Canadian Abuse Prevention Foundation "Imagine Sweepstakes", 1996, CN Tower, Toronto, Canada, photo courtesy of Brad Forder

initial date of release in Germany. Some publications list it as early as September 1961, but a check of record catalogue numbers, and more reliable discographies, indicates it was probably not issued any time in Germany before July 1963. This is further supported by a U.K. interview with The Beatles on October 27, 1962 included in Mark Lewisohn's book **The Beatles Live!**. When asked about their Hamburg recordings, they mention that ***Cry For A Shadow*** was only available on a French EP. If the EP had been issued in Germany before the French EP, The Beatles almost certainly would have been aware of it.

Hines does correctly confirm that Tony Sheridan, not George Harrison, plays lead guitar on most of the tracks. It's an understandable mistake considering the natural assumption that Harrison always played lead, but in 1961 it was Sheridan's style that Harrison was trying to emulate. Hines also implies that Paul McCartney (who had only recently switched from guitar and piano, having taken over on bass from Stuart Sutcliffe) may not play bass on all, if any, tracks. Hines asserts that either Peter Wharton or Colin Melander may be the bass players. But again, this is disputed by Sheridan who said, "Paul was a natural bass player – one told him what was needed and he did it, and more." Sutcliffe had recently quit The Beatles, and decided to live in Germany with Astrid Kirchherr *(see Paul Jones)* and study painting. (Sutcliffe died of a brain hemorrhage in the arms of his fiancee Astrid, on April 10, 1962.) Sheridan said, "Sutcliffe and Astrid attended the recording sessions but did not participate as musicians, but as creative personalities." Sheridan confirmed that The Beatles played their usual instruments (Paul: bass, John: guitar, George: guitar, Pete Best: drums) while backing him. Sheridan said that he played the only guitar on ***Take Out Some Insurance On Me, Baby*** and ***Nobody's Child***. He said that Paul played bass and Pete played drums, but that John and George did not contribute to these songs in any way. (Harrison recorded a version of ***Nobody's Child*** with the "supergroup" Traveling Wilburys, released in 1990.)

Three variations of Sheridan's recording of ***Sweet Georgia Brown*** (he recorded two versions without The Beatles) feature backing by The Beatles. These versions have generated much debate about when and where they were recorded, and who plays piano. The first Beatles-backed version was released in October 1962 on the German EP **Ya Ya** (Polydor EPH 21 485.) The track appears on side two along with ***Skinny Minny***. The original lyric version was first released in stereo as part of an EP called **Hamburg Twist**, contained exclusively in the 1997 book **The Beatles From Cavern To Star-Club** by Hans Gottfridsson. (Gottfridsson is one of the leading experts on The Beatles' activities in Hamburg.) All other Beatles-backed releases (with a handful of exceptions) feature re-recorded vocals with revised lyrics.

On the revised lyrics version, Sheridan refers to The Beatles hair and their fan club and says, "I say this group is absolutely marvelous with a piano, don't you think so?" He warns The Beatles in the lyrics to be "not too commercial boys, not too commercial," after some fancy guitar work in the song. Was Sheridan sending The Beatles a message that he felt they would sound better if they had a piano in their lineup? Was he being openly critical (as were many) that The Beatles had sold out to a more commercial sound and look (as indeed they had) after Brian Epstein had taken over in late 1961? Sheridan admitted there was some truth to the message in the lyrics. He said the revised lyrics were written by Liverpool native Paul Murphy (aka Paul Rogers), a producer and A&R man for Polydor, and Sheridan's producer at the time. (Murphy was also a part-time member of one of Rory Storm's early bands.) Murphy was in charge of re-mixing the recordings The Beatles made for

Kaempfert when Polydor began re-releasing them in 1964. Sheridan also said Murphy knew The Beatles and Brian Epstein, and that the new lyrics were "a joke without malice." According to Sheridan, and Polydor's documents, the revised lyrics were recorded at Studio Hamburg in January of 1964. Obviously, re-releasing the record with revised lyrics referencing The Beatles was done with the intention of capitalizing on the Beatlemania that existed at the time.

It has long been assumed and widely accepted that the original-lyric version and backing was recorded during the June 1961 sessions. However, the 1984 Polydor CD that contains the revised-lyric version lists it being recorded on December 21, 1961. That date is incorrect, as The Beatles were in England the entire month of December. Sheridan correctly identified this as the date his first version of ***Sweet Georgia Brown***, without The Beatles, was recorded. According to Sheridan, and Polydor documents, the bulk of Tony Sheridan and The Beat Brothers' **My Bonnie** album, released in Germany in June 1962, was also recorded on this date. Lewisohn and Gottfridsson have confirmed that Brian Epstein, on the verge of landing a recording contract for The Beatles with EMI Records in England, sought an early release from their contract with Kaempfert due to expire on June 30, 1962. Kaempfert agreed to release The Beatles early on the condition that he be able to use them one last time as a backup band for some Tony Sheridan recordings. The recordings were scheduled to take place between April and May of 1962, when The Beatles would be in Hamburg to help launch the newly opened Star-Club. This session apparently took place on May 24. The following day, The Beatles and Bert Kaempfert Productions signed an agreement to terminate their contract, effective on that date. However, Sheridan says he did not record anything with The Beatles in 1962 because he was being backed by The Beat Brothers that, at the time, included Roy Young *(see Cliff Bennett And The Rebel Rousers)* on keyboards and Rikki Barnes on saxophone. He still maintains The Beatles' backing of ***Sweet Georgia Brown*** was recorded in June of 1961. Gottfridsson included in his book **The Beatles From Cavern To Star-Club** photocopies of Polydor documents that seem to confirm that Kaempfert did indeed produce recordings of ***Sweet Georgia Brown*** and ***Swanee River*** by Tony Sheridan and The Beat Brothers on May 24, 1962 at Hamburg Studio. These documents also list ***Sweet Georgia Brown*** as being arranged by Paul McCartney. On one of the documents the name Beat Brothers is crossed out and replaced with The Beatles! Polydor has previously failed to acknowledged The Beatles taking part in these recording sessions nearly a year after the initial recordings with Sheridan. Perhaps they wished to avoid any possible legal conflicts with EMI.

Sweet Georgia Brown is the only song The Beatles are known to back Sheridan on that features a piano. According to Tony, and Roy Young, Young played piano on ***Sweet Georgia Brown***, not McCartney, as has always been suspected. It certainly sounds like Young's style of playing. Young joined Sheridan's band, The Beat Brothers, in December of 1961, ruling out the possibility that

Roy Young and The Beatles at the Star-Club in Hamburg, Germany, spring 1962, photo courtesy of Roy Young

Young played on any of the June 1961 sessions. Sheridan thinks Young's piano must have been overdubbed later. Young said, "I don't remember dubbing the piano on, I seem to remember recording it all together." Gunther Sorensen, a technician and recording engineer for Polydor, also recalls a session with Sheridan and The Beatles taking place in May of 1962. He said The Beatles recorded two songs, ***Sweet Georgia Brown*** and ***Swanee River***, in one take without playback! If true, it tends to support Young's recollections. If McCartney played piano, then who played bass? Sheridan and others present have also said all the songs with The Beatles were recorded essentially "live" without any overdubbing. If Young's piano was not overdubbed, then ***Sweet Georgia Brown*** was almost certainly recorded in the spring of 1962. Young said Brian Epstein asked him to join The Beatles following his performances with them during their spring 1962 engagement at the Star-Club. Young turned down the offer because he had a more comfortable financial arrangement with the Star-Club at the time.

Pete Best stated in his autobiography **Beatle!** that a second Beatles-backed session with Sheridan for Kaempfert, apparently after they were signed to Epstein in December of 1961, took place. Best stated that The Beatles backed Sheridan on ***Sweet Georgia Brown*** and ***Skinny Minny*** at the second session. It's possible Best was referring to the additional sessions Polydor claims took place on June 23 and 24, 1961. Mersey Beat reportedly mentioned ***Sweet Georgia Brown*** and ***Swanee River*** as having been recorded in the spring of 1962. All three songs ended up on the German album **My Bonnie**, but ***Sweet Georgia Brown*** is not The Beatles-backed version. The album also contained ***My Bonnie*** and ***When The Saints Go Marching In***, both of which appear with asterisks noting "accompanied by The Beatles." This has long led to speculation and doubt as to whether The Beatles are involved in ***Skinny Minny*** and ***Swanee River***.

Polydor and labels in other countries began to release full-length albums of the eight Beatles-backed tracks, padding it out with tracks credited to Tony Sheridan and The Beat Brothers that The Beatles had nothing to do with – or did they? Most authorities are naturally skeptical, considering the amount of mislabeling and misinformation about most of these recordings, due in large part to Sheridan's use of the name The Beat Brothers (regardless of the members). Some accounts claim that it was Kaempfert who initially decided to use the name The Beat Brothers in lieu of Beatles, because it sounded too much like "peedles," which is German slang for penis. Sheridan, however, discounts this theory, and says he used the name Beat Brothers because the Germans had difficulty pronouncing The Beatles' name properly, and adopted the name for his bands until 1964. The first few initial Beatles-backed Sheridan releases were credited to The Beat Brothers. When The Beatles' popularity began to increase, Polydor began to reissue the catalogue – first as Tony Sheridan with The Beatles, and later as The Beatles with Tony Sheridan.

Of the confusion and controversy that has raged over the years, only ***Skinny Minny*** and ***Swanee River*** have remained contenders for possible involvement by The Beatles. There is no evidence, beyond Pete Best's claim, that any of The Beatles contributed to any of Tony Sheridan's versions of ***Skinny Minny***. Sheridan insists he never recorded any versions of ***Skinny Minny*** or ***Swanee River*** with The Beatles. It is unlikely Kaempfert would have had The Beatles record ***Skinny Minny*** and ***Swanee River*** for Polydor without Sheridan being present. There appears to be enough evidence to safely conclude that Sheridan and The Beat Brothers recorded ***Swanee River*** on December 21, 1961, and again on May 24, 1962, with backing from some of The Beatles. Unfortunately only one version of ***Swanee River*** by Sheridan has ever been released, and it is probably the version recorded on December 21 and included on the **My Bonnie** album.

Many questions remain. Polydor's documents indicate that the May 24 versions of ***Sweet Georgia Brown*** and ***Swanee River*** were intended to be issued as a single. Why was the single never released? If instead the May 24 recordings were intended for inclusion on the **My Bonnie** album, why was not the superior version of ***Sweet Georgia Brown*** with The Beatles backing used? If the version of ***Swanee River*** on that album is from the May 24 sessions, why is not the song noted with an asterisk indicating "accompanied by The Beatles," as are the other songs? Was there even enough time to substitute the alternate versions recorded on May 24 for the June release of the **My Bonnie** album? Polydor received these recordings from Bert Kaempfert Productions. Why did it take five months for Polydor to release The Beatles backed version of ***Sweet Georgia Brown***? If there are two versions of ***Swanee River***, why was not the second version released? Plenty of other alternate versions of Sheridan's recordings have been released. Was one version, deliberately or accidentally, destroyed or stolen? Many of the songs on the **My Bonnie** album, including ***Swanee River***, feature a sax-phone, probably played by Rikki Barnes. It seems unlikely that a saxophone player would be employed for one song for a session with The Beatles on May 24. Roy Young's presence at the May 24 sessions is understandable, as he was playing with both The Beatles and Tony Sheridan in Hamburg at the time. The overall sound, and the bass playing and drumming, on ***Swanee River*** are more consistent with the **My Bonnie** album recordings than The Beatles backed version of ***Sweet Georgia Brown***.

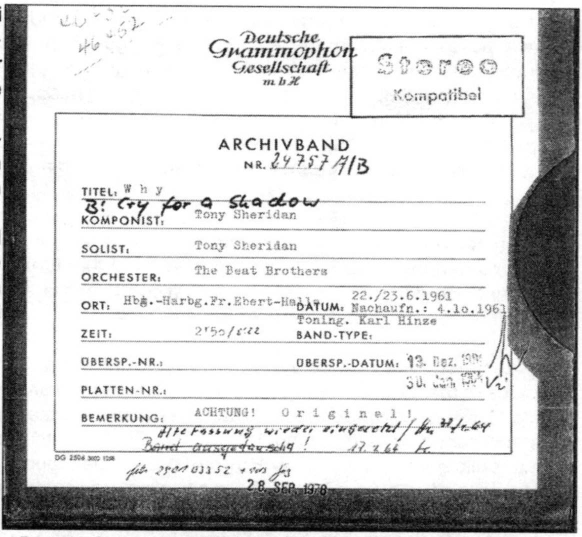
Deutsche Grammophon Gesellschaft mbH

Stereo Kompatibel

ARCHIVBAND

NR. 24757 A/B

TITEL: Why
B: Cry for a Shadow

KOMPONIST: Tony Sheridan

SOLIST: Tony Sheridan

ORCHESTER: The Beat Brothers

ORT: Hbg.-Harbg.Fr.Ebert-Halle

DATUM: 22./23.6.1961 Nachaufn.: 4.1o.1961

Toning. Karl Hinze

ZEIT:

BAND-TYPE:

ÜBERSP.-NR.:

ÜBERSP.-DATUM: 13. Dez.

PLATTEN-NR.:

BEMERKUNG: ACHTUNG! Original!

DG 2506 300 108

28. SEP. 1978

Deutsche Grammophone "Archivband" for single "Why / Cry For A Shadow", courtesy of Tony Sheridan

Another temporary member of The Beat Brothers was Ringo Starr. Ringo quit his position as drummer of the group Rory Storm & The Hurricanes, and joined Sheridan's backing group in Germany in January 1962, but in March he rejoined Rory Storm & The Hurricanes. Here, too, there is some speculation and confusion about whether Ringo contributed to any recordings by Tony Sheridan and The Beat Brothers. Roy Young seemed to think that Ringo may have played drums on Sheridan and The Beat Brothers' recording of ***Ya Ya (part 1 & 2)***. However, it does not sound like Ringo's drumming style on ***Ya Ya***. The 1984 Polydor CD lists ***Ya Ya (parts 1 & 2)*** as being recorded on August 28, 1962. Gottfridsson's book states it was recorded on October 18, 1962. If either date is correct, then Ringo could not have played on ***Ya Ya (parts 1 & 2)***, as he was, at the time, in Liverpool with The Beatles. As has been pointed out, Polydor's published dates have been proven to be less than reliable. Perhaps Young is mistaken, or is referring to live performances of the song, or another (unreleased) version of ***Ya Ya***. Sheridan said Young played organ and Johnny Watson played drums on ***Ya Ya***, and is sure Ringo did not contribute to any of his recordings. Gottfridsson has also concluded that Ringo did not contribute to any of Sheridan's recordings.

In a bizarre postscript to this long and winding story, four of these recordings, released by Atco (Atlantic) Records in the U.S., feature edits and additional overdubs. The revised-lyric version of ***Sweet Georgia Brown*** and ***Take Out Some Insurance On Me, Baby*** featured additional overdubs of guitar and drums by unknown musicians. The "god damned" line is edited out of ***Take Out Some Insurance On Me, Baby***, which also has overdubbed harmonica. Additionally, they edited ***Nobody's Child*** from 3 minutes, 55 seconds, down to 2 minutes, 54 seconds. ***Ain't She Sweet*** was also sweetened with overdubbed drums. Just why Atlantic tampered with the recordings, and who the studio musicians are that added the additional guitar and drums, remain a matter of speculation. The best guess is that the drummer is Bernard Purdie, a well-known veteran session player who had worked extensively for Atlantic. Purdie has long maintained he was contracted to overdub drums on nearly two dozen early Beatles recordings. Purdie's seemingly outrageous claims have never been taken seriously because they were vague and filled with obvious inaccuracies. However, some of his claims do ring true. Purdie recalls a guitar being overdubbed on the sessions, and being paid to keep his mouth shut about his involvement. Atlantic was trying to capitalize on the popularity of The Beatles' name and probably felt that if they gave these earlier recordings a little musical updating they could have a top 10! If Polydor or The Beatles were to find out about this tampering, it might have resulted in legal action. The Beatles' fans also would not have taken kindly to any tampering with the already deceptive releases. Purdie promises he will eventually reveal all, though when he does he will have a lot of explaining to do.

Over the years, various publications have claimed Tony Sheridan and The Beatles may also have recorded ***What'd I Say*** and ***Hully Gully*** during the sessions for Kaempfert. Pete Best claims in his book that The Beatles also auditioned some Lennon and McCartney compositions during the initial recording sessions. In an article in New Musical Express magazine, John Lennon seemed to recall they may have recorded ***Kansas City***, ***Some Other Guy***, and ***Rock And Roll Music*** for Kaempfert. It is certainly possible, as all of these songs were regularly performed by The Beatles and Sheridan at the time. More likely these were some of the songs Sheridan and The Beatles warmed up on in the studio before the start of the recordings. Sheridan does not recall recording any of these songs with The Beatles. Some of these numbers were recorded and released by Sheridan and The Beat Brothers, but none involve The Beatles. It seems inconceivable, given Polydor's track record, that they would not release or promote any additional recordings including The Beatles, if they still existed.

Sheridan said he co-wrote a song with Paul McCartney called ***Tell Me If You Can***. He says he has never recorded the song for "ethical reasons," but that it may be recorded at some later date as a "document." He did perform about fifteen seconds of the song for an Italian radio interview that is making the rounds on underground tapes.

Bert Kaempfert died of a stroke at his home in Majorca, Spain on June 22, 1980. Tony Sheridan continues to reside in Germany. He and Roy Young recently reformed The Beat Brothers which also include Howie Casey *(see Freddie Starr)*. He also makes an occasional appearance at Beatles festivals and conventions throughout the world. On the 25th anniversary of its release, Polydor reissued a replica of the original **My Bonnie** album. The album included a replica of the 1961 Polydor single and picture sleeve of the German introduction version of ***My Bonnie***. The 1994 Japanese release **Beatles Oldies** is the most comprehensive collection of Tony Sheridan recordings on one CD to date. ***My Bonnie***, ***Cry For A Shadow*** and ***Ain't She Sweet*** became part of The Beatles' official catalogue in 1995 with their inclusion on **Anthology 1**. In spite of exhaustive research over the years, some questions are likely to remain unanswered regarding these historic recordings involving The Beatles.

The Silkie

Record 328 title:
Lennon & McCartney Songbook
Label / Catalog number:
Connoisseur Collection / VSOP CD 150
Media:
Album 5" CD
Producer:
John Lennon
Jacket / Inserts:
Standard international design in jewel box with photo of John Lennon & Paul McCartney / 4 page CD booklet with photos of John Lennon & Paul McCartney
Recording Location / Date:
IBC Studios, London, U.K. / 09 Aug 65

Song 328a title:
You've Got To Hide Your Love Away
Release date / Country:
02 Jul 90 (first issued 10 Sep 65) / U.K./E.E.C.
Track details:
Side 1, track 24 / 2 min. 12 sec.
Composer:
J. Lennon - P. McCartney Sylvia

Tatler: Vocals; Mike Ramsden: Vocals & (probable) Guitar; Ivor Aylesbury: Vocals & (probable) Guitar; Paul McCartney: Guitar & Arrangement; George Harrison: Guitar Taps & Tambourine; Kevin Cunningham: Bass

The Silkie were England's answer to American folk groups like Peter, Paul and Mary. Managed by Brian Epstein, the members were Mike Ramsden, Kevin Cunningham, Ivor Aylesbury and Silvia Tatler.

John, Paul and George helped The Silkie record their version of ***You've Got To Hide Your Love Away*** at about the same time as The Beatles' version was being released on their soundtrack album **Help!**. John did most of the producing, while Paul played guitar, and George kept time tapping on the guitar and playing tambourine. Some sources also list Paul as co-producer and George as helping on the arrangement, but no doubt it was primarily John's production. Bill Harry claims in his books **The Ultimate Beatles Encyclopedia** and **The Encyclopedia of Beatles People** that McCartney plays piano on the recording, but even close listening does not reveal any piano. There may, however, be some faint organ in the background. This is the only time anyone has ever suggested that McCartney plays anything other than guitar. There have been unsubstantiated rumors over the years that John Lennon and Paul McCartney may also have helped in the production of The Silkie's single ***The Keys to My Soul / Leave Me to Cry***, though this seems highly unlikely.

Carly Simon

Record 329 title:
Playing Possum
Label / Catalog number:
Elektra / 1033-2
Jacket / Inserts:
Standard international design in jewel box / 12 page CD booklet
Recording Location / Date:
Crystal Studios, Los Angeles, CA, U.S.A. / (probably) summer/fall 1974
Media:
Album 5" CD
Producer:
Richard Perry

Song 329a title:
More And More
Release date / Country:
(first issued 21 Apr 75) / U.S.A.
Track details:
Side 1, track 4 / 4 min. 02 sec.
Composer:
M. Rebennack - A. Robinson

Carly Simon: Lead Vocals; Ringo Starr: Drums; Klaus Voormann: Bass; Dr. John: Piano; Alvin Robinson: Guitar; Jeff Baxter: Guitar; Freddie Staehle: Percussion; Richard Perry: Tambourine; Maxine Willard: B. Vocals; Julia Tillman: B. Vocals; Carolyn Willis: B. Vocals

Record 330 title:
No Secrets
Label / Catalog number:
Elektra / 75049-2
Jacket / Inserts:
Standard international design in jewel box / 6 page CD booklet
Recording Location / Date:
Trident & AIR Studios, London, U.K. / Oct 72
Media:
Album 5" CD
Producer:
Richard Perry

Song 330a title:
Night Owl
Release date / Country:
(first issued 03 Nov 72) / U.S.A.
Track details:
Side 1, track 9 / 3 min. 47 sec.
Composer:
J. Taylor

Carly Simon: Lead Vocals; Nicky Hopkins: Piano; Jim Keltner: Drums; Klaus Voormann: Bass; Jimmy Ryan: Electric Guitar; Ray Cooper: Congas; Bobby Keys: Tenor Saxophone; Bonnie Bramlett: B. Vocals; Doris Troy: B. Vocals; Paul McCartney: B. Vocals; Linda McCartney: B. Vocals

Carly Simon was born on June 25, 1945 in New York City, New York into a highly musical family. Her father was the co-founder of Simon & Schuster publishers, and a classical piano player. Her sister Joanna was an opera singer. Lucy, a folk singer, formed The Simon Sisters with Carly. They had one minor hit in 1964 with the song ***Winken, Blinken And Nod***. When Lucy married, the duo dissolved and Carly went out on her own.

In 1967, Carly briefly teamed up with Albert Grossman, who arranged for her to work with members of The Band* and Bob Dylan*, but the project was aborted over differences with Grossman. She was briefly a member of Elephant's Memory*. Simon spent the next two years singing commercial jingles before being signed to Elektra Records. Her self-titled first album, released in 1971, yielded the top 10 song ***That's The Way I've Always Heard It Should Be***. She also had a top 20 with the title track of her album **Anticipation**, released later that year.

In 1972, Simon hit her career high with ***You're So Vain*** and the album **No Secrets**, which featured a contribution by Paul and Linda McCartney* on the song ***Night Owl***. According to the album's producer, Richard Perry, the backing tracks for ***Night Owl*** were recorded at Trident, but the vocals were recorded at George Martin's* AIR Studios in October 1972. At the time, Paul McCartney was in an adjacent studio recording ***Live And Let Die*** and dropped in on the sessions. Perry and McCartney had become friends who held several things in common, including the same date and year of birth, Old English Sheep Dogs (Desmond and Martha respectively), and wives named Linda who shared nearly identical backgrounds. It was also during this period that Carly Simon met and married James Taylor*, and the two worked together for a time.

The single ***More And More***, from Carly's 1975 album **Playing Possum**, features Ringo Starr on drums. According to Carly, the track was recorded in the winter of 1975. According to the album's producer, Richard Perry, the song was recorded at Crystal Studios in Los Angeles sometime between late summer and late fall of 1974.

Toward the end of the 1970s, Simon recorded the top 10 songs ***You Belong To Me*** and ***Nobody Does It Better***, the theme to the James Bond film **The Spy Who Loved Me**, co-starring none other than Barbara Bach, the future wife of Ringo Starr. In 1980, Simon had a hit with the song ***Jesse***. In 1981, she filed for divorce from Taylor, which was granted in 1983. Simon had a hit with the song ***Coming Around Again*** in 1986. The achievement she is perhaps most proud of was the Grammy, Oscar and Golden Globe award she received in 1990 for the song ***Let The River Run***, from the motion picture **Working Girl**. Simon has spent the last two decades raising her children, composing and recording music, and writing children's books. In 1995 she embarked on her first major concert tour in fifteen years. Carly announced in 1998 that she was battling cancer.

Paul Simon & George Harrison

Record 331 title:
Nobody's Child

Media:
Album 5" CD

Label / Catalog number:
Warner Bros / 9 26280-2

Producer:
Lorne Michaels

Jacket / Inserts:
Standard international design in jewel box / 16 page CD booklet

Recording Location / Date:
NBC-TV Studios-Rockefeller Center, New York, NY / 18 Nov 76

Song 331a title:
Homeward Bound

Track details:
Side 1, track 5 / 2 min. 38 sec.

Release date / Country:
24 Jul 90 / U.S.A.

Composer:
P. Simon

Paul Simon: Vocals & Guitar; George Harrison: Vocals & Guitar

Paul Simon was born on October 13, 1941 in Newark, New Jersey. His father was a bass player and session musician on a number of network TV shows, and his mother was a music teacher. Paul met Art Garfunkel, born November 5, 1941 in New York City, New York, in grade school. The two attended the same high school, forming a folk-duo named Tom & Jerry. They began writing songs and, in 1957, landed a record contract. They released the song ***Hey Schoolgirl***, that made the top 50, and earned them a spot on Dick Clark's **American Bandstand** TV show. The big time, however, lay another half a decade away.

Simon and Garfunkel pursued solo careers after high school and occasionally reformed during the mid-1960s, recording the album **Wednesday Morning, 3 A.M.** The album's producer later overdubbed drums and electric guitar to ***The Sound Of Silence***, without the knowledge of the artists, creating one of the all-time folk-rock classics. The duo quickly reformed in the wake of the song's success and, until their breakup in 1970, established themselves as one of the most popular folk and rock duos of all time. Some of their more successful hits included ***Homeward Bound, I Am A Rock, Hazy Shade of Winter, At The Zoo, Fakin' It, Scarborough Fair / Canticle, Mrs. Robinson, The Boxer, Cecilia, El Condor Pasa (If I Could)***, and their prophetic ***Bridge Over Troubled Water***.

Following their breakup, Garfunkel pursued a singing and acting career. Simon went on writing and recording hit after hit, including ***Mother And Child Reunion, Me And Julio Down By The School Yard, Kodachrome, Loves Me Like A Rock, 50 Ways To Leave Your Lover***, and ***Slip Slidin' Away***.

Simon & Garfunkel re-united occasionally during the 1970s for concerts and guest spots on each other's recordings, such as Simon's ***My Little Town***, billed as Simon & Garfunkel, and Art's ***(What A) Wonderful World***. However, their reunions and solo careers made it apparent that an equal musical partnership was unlikely.

The first half of the decade of the '80s was less than kind to Simon. His personal life was in disarray, and his first and only film, **One-Trick Pony**, went unnoticed, as did most of his recordings. In 1986, Simon turned his floundering image around with his highly successful African-flavored album **Graceland**. Today Simon continues to experiment with African and Latin sounds, and he and Garfunkel still make the occasional appearance together. The duo were inducted into the Rock and Roll Hall of Fame in 1990.

In March 1971, Melody Maker magazine reported that George Harrison was in the studio with Paul Simon. This was probably a friendly visit, as there is no evidence that Harrison contributed to any of Simon's recordings during this period. In 1974 John Lennon, too, had a brief encounter with Simon and Garfunkel, during the final phases of recordings held in New York for Harry Nilsson's* album **Pussy Cats**, which Lennon was producing. Simon & Garfunkel had been asked to the sessions, but Lennon and Nilsson were so intoxicated that the session soon turned into a shouting match, and their contributions were never used. In spite of the evening's events, Simon was apparently left with enough respect for Lennon to write ***The Late Great Johnny Ace***, partly in tribute to John shortly after his death.

On November 20, 1976, NBC-TV's **Saturday Night Live** featured George Harrison and Paul Simon as its musical guests. Harrison was promoting his album **Thirty-Three & 1/3**, and brought along music videos for ***Crackerbox Palace*** and ***This Song***, which were aired. The rehearsal and taping for Harrison and Simon's musical duet took place on November 18, with the following songs or portions of songs performed - ***Dark Horse, Don't Let Me Wait Too Long, That's All Right (Mama), Yesterday, 50 Ways To Leave Your Lover, The Boxer, Bridge Over Troubled Water, Bye Bye Love, Rock Island Line, Here Comes The Sun***, and ***Homeward Bound***. Only the latter two songs were included on the broadcast. During the show, Harrison is seen with producer Lorne Michaels arguing about the amount of money he is to receive. In 1993, McCartney appeared on **Saturday Night Live** and argued about the amount of money he was to be paid. The bit was referring to a previous offer **SNL** had made to pay The Beatles what amounted to standard musician's union scale to appear on the show. This was in parody of then-recent offers of $50 million if The Beatles would reunite. Little did Michaels know that The Beatles nearly took him up on the offer!

To date, the only song from Harrison's appearance with Simon on **SNL** to be officially released is ***Homeward Bound***. It was included on the **Nobody's Child - Romanian Angel Appeal** charity album. The appeal was launched by George Harrison and his wife Olivia, along with Ringo's wife Barbara Bach, Yoko Ono* and Linda McCartney*, in aid of thousands of Romanian orphans. Though ***Homeward Bound*** is a joint performance, it is more appropriate to classify it as a contribution by Harrison to a Paul Simon song. Both ***Bye Bye Love*** and ***Rock Island Line*** have been available on bootleg records, but neither song truly qualifies as a Harrison contribution to a Simon song.

Paul McCartney wrote a review of **The Songs Of Paul Simon** song book for the August 8, 1973 issue of Punch magazine. On several occasions in the 1990s, McCartney has hinted he would like to work with Paul Simon.

Peter Skellern

Record 332 title:
Hard Times
Label / Catalog number:
Island / ILPS 9352
Jacket / Inserts:
Unique / Custom inner-sleeve
Recording Location / Date:
Mayfair Sound Studios, London, U.K. / (probably) Aug 75
Media:
Album 12"
Producer:
Meyer Shagaloff

Song 332a title:
Make Love, Not War
Release date / Country:
26 Sep 75 / U.K.
Track details:
Side 2, track 2 / 3 min. 16 sec.
Composer:
P. Skellern - J. Burrows - J. Harding

Peter Skellern: Lead Vocals & Keyboards; Rob Townsend: Drums; George Ford: Bass; George Harrison: Guitar; Madeline Bell: B. Vocals; Joy Yates: B. Vocals; Joanne Williams: B. Vocals

Peter Skellern was born on March 14, 1947 in Bury, Lancaster, England. He played in school bands, and graduated with honors from the prestigious Guildhall School Of Music in 1968. He played piano with Billy Fury and, as a solo artist, gained a following writing songs in a style reminiscent of Hoagy Carmichael and the brass band sound of the 1930s. He had two major hits in the U.K. in the 1970s - ***You're A Lady*** and ***Hold On To Love***. Another song of his, ***Not Without A Friend***, was produced by longtime Beatles' press officer and Apple publicist Derek Taylor. Skellern has written and performed six autobiographical programs for the BBC, and hosted the talk show **Private Lives** in 1983. In 1984, he formed Oasis with Julian Lloyd Webber, Mary Hopkin* and Bill Lovelady. Skellern continues to work in theater and TV, and in 1995 he released his first album in nearly eight years.

In 1975, Skellern released his album **Hard Times**, that included the song ***Make Love, Not War*** from the musical revue **Loud Reports** by John Burrows, John Harding and Peter Skellern. The song included a guitar contribution by George Harrison. Ringo Starr also covered the album's title track, ***Hard Times***, on his album **Bad Boy**.

"Legs" Larry Smith

Record 333 title:
HandMade Films The 10th Anniversary

Label / Catalog number:
AVM / [matrix #] AVM 1126859 (promotional only)

Jacket / Inserts:
Unique / 4 page CD booklet

Recording Location / Date:
FPSHOT (Friar Park Studios, Henley-on-Thames), U.K. / (probably) 1982 &/or 1983

Media:
Album 5" CD

Producer:
R. Cooper, "Legs" Larry Smith & (G. Harrison) (music)/Ian LaFrenais (film)

Song 333a title:
Bullshot (Theme To The Motion Picture "Bullshot")

Release date / Country:
(probably) Nov 88 / U.K.

Track details:
Side 1, track 8 / 2 min. 21 sec.

Composer:
J. Du Prez - D. Clement - A. Shearman - R. House - [G. Harrison]

"Legs" Larry Smith: Lead Vocals; George Harrison: B. Vocals; Ray Cooper (probable) Percussion

"Legs" Larry Smith was born on January 18, 1944 in Oxford, England. He is a former member of The Bonzo Dog Band*. Smith and George Harrison have been close friends for many years. Harrison wrote a song in tribute to Smith - ***His Name Is Legs (Ladies & Gentlemen)*** on his 1975 album **Extra Texture**. Smith in turn designed the jacket cover for Harrison's 1982 album **Gone Troppo**. Harrison supposedly produced an album for "Legs," though nothing has yet been released.

The 1983 film **Bullshot** was produced by George Harrison's HandMade Films Company. **Bullshot** starred Allen Sherman, Diz White, Ron House, Frances Tomelty, Michael Aldridge, Billy Connolly *(see Billy Connolly/Chris Tummings & The Singing Rebel's Band)* and Mel Smith. The film's title track was sung by "Legs" Larry Smith and included contributions from George Harrison. The song is only available on an in-house promotional CD titled **HandMade Films The 10th Anniversary**, and on the VHS release of **Bullshot** (Thorn EMI/HBO Video/HandMade Films / 9 TVC 2998).

The Smokin' Mojo Filters

Record 334 title:
Come Together [Various Artists]
Media:
Single 5" CD
Label / Catalog number:
Go! Discs / GOD CD 136
Producer:
Brendan Lynch
Jacket / Inserts:
Standard international design in jewel box with photos of Paul McCartney / 2 page CD insert
Recording Location / Date:
EMI-Abbey Road Studios, London, U.K. / 04 Sep 95

Song 334a title:
Come Together
Track details:
Side 1, track 1 / 3 min. 33 sec.
Release date / Country:
04 Dec 95 (first issued 09 Sep 95) / U.K.
Composer:
J. Lennon - P.McCartney

Paul Weller: Lead Vocals & Guitar; Paul McCartney: Guitar, Keyboards & B. Vocals; Noel Gallagher: Guitar; Steve White: Drums; Carleen Anderson: B. Vocals; Steve Craddock: Guitar; Damon Minchella: Bass

The Smokin' Mojo Filters was a Paul Weller project. Paul Weller was born on May 25, 1958 in Woking, England. His parents named him John, but soon took to calling him Paul. Paul began playing guitar at an early age, and grew up to the music of The Beatles which greatly influenced him.

Weller formed the group The Jam, along with Bruce Foxton and Rick Buckler, at the height of the punk-rock movement in the U.K., though their musical and visual style was decidedly mid-1960s "mod" rock. The Jam had a strong following in the U.K. with over a dozen top 20 songs in the late 1970s, including four number ones - ***Going Underground***, ***Start***, ***Town Called Malice***, and ***Beat Surrender***. They also recorded a cover of The Beatles' ***And Your Bird Can Sing***. The Jam were never a force in the U.S. charts. Weller broke up the band at the height of their popularity in 1982.

In 1983, Weller and keyboard player Mick Talbot formed the basis of the rhythm & blues oriented Style Council, which featured a variety of guest vocalists. Like The Jam, Style Council found little success outside the U.K., where they, too, had a dozen top 20 songs, including - ***Speak Like A Child***, ***Long Hot Summer***, ***My Ever Changing Moods***, ***Groovin'***, ***Shout To The Top***, ***The Walls Come Tumbling Down*** and ***It Didn't Matter***, which reached the top 10.

Since 1990, Weller has been primarily a solo act. Weller has long made it known that he is a major fan of The Beatles. He has covered John Lennon's Beatles songs ***Sexy Sadie*** and ***Don't Let Me Down***. The front cover (vinyl only) of his 1995 album **Stanley Road** features a photo of John Lennon. The politically active Weller continues to maintain a high profile on and off the U.K. charts.

A cover of the John Lennon Beatles' song ***Come Together*** was included on the 1995 War Child Charity album **Help**. The charity was set up to aid child victims of war, in this case the former Yugoslavian Republics torn by ethnic fighting. The album included a variety of artists coordinated by Paul Weller's record company, Go! Disc, as a quick response to the victims. The concept was borrowed from John Lennon, who used his ***Instant Karma*** single as an example of how quickly a record could be written, recorded, and released to respond to a given situation.

Apparently, Weller, who reportedly was romantically involved with Paul McCartney's daughter Mary, requested she ask her father if he would contribute to ***Come Together***. McCartney added backing vocals, guitar and keyboards to the session recorded at EMI's Abbey Road Studios on September 4, 1995. (McCartney reportedly later had the assembled band back him on a song he had written the night before, though apparently there was not enough time to record it.) The recording also featured Noel Gallagher from the group Oasis, often cited as a '90s version of The Beatles. (McCartney, and particularly George Harrison, have made a number of less than flattering comments to the media about Oasis in recent years. Oasis members' responses have been volatile.) The session was filmed and included in the **Help** documentary on the making of the album. As a result of the album's rush-release, credits were sparse. There was not even a track listing! However, McCartney's involvement in ***Come Together***, and its inclusion on the album was widely reported with the artists first being identified as Paul Weller & Friends. Several months later, ***Come Together*** was issued as a single credited more specifically as The Smokin' Mojo Filters (Featuring Paul Weller, Paul McCartney and Noel Gallagher). The single's credits also included a quote from John Lennon about his ***Instant Karma*** record concept.

Phil Spector

Record 335 title:
Tandoori Chicken
Label / Catalog number:
Apple
Recording Location / Date:
EMI-Abbey Road &/or Trident Studios, London, U.K. / Feb &/or Mar 71
Media:
Single 7" [Acetate]
Producer:
Phil Spector & George Harrison

Song 335a title:
Tandoori Chicken
Release date / Country:
[Unreleased] / U.K.
Track details:
Side 1, track 1 / 2 min. 14 sec.
Composer:
G. Harrison - P. Spector

Phil Spector: Lead Vocals & Keyboards; George Harrison: Guitar; Leon Russell: Keyboards; Klaus Voormann: Bass; Jim Gordon: Drums; John Lennon: B. Vocals; The Apple Scruffs (Cathy, Lucy & Carol): B. Vocals

Harvey Phillip Spector was born on December 26, 1939 in New York City, New York. His father died when he was nine, and a few years later his mother moved the family to California. Spector learned to play several musical instruments. He took a strong interest in rhythm & blues and the writing and producing team of Leiber and Stoller, with whom he eventually worked.

Spector's real break came in 1958 when he wrote ***To Know Him Is To Love Him***, the title taken from the inscription on his father's tombstone. He recorded the song with Marshall Leib and a high school girl named Annette Kleinbard singing the lead vocals, while Phil provided the balance of the backing. The song became a regular in The Beatles' early repertoire, and they performed it during their audition for Decca Records in 1962. The Beatles first official release of their rendition of the song was on their 1994 album **Live At The BBC**.

Phil formed Philles records with Lester Sill, and was briefly a Brill Building songwriter, and worked with Goffin / King, Mann / Weil and Barry / Greenwich. By age twenty-one, Phil Spector was a millionaire and referred to as the genius boy wonder eccentric producer, admired and emulated by his contemporaries, particularly Brian Wilson *(see The Beach Boys)*.

In 1964, Pete Anders and Vinnie Poncia covered The Beatles' song ***Hold Me Tight*** under the name The Treasures, produced by Spector. That year, Spector produced and co-wrote, along with Anders and Poncia, The Beatles-novelty record ***Ringo, I Love You*** by Bonnie Jo Mason, now better known as Cher. Ironically, years later Poncia and Ringo would become good friends and work extensively together.

By the mid-1960s, Spector had produced hits for such artists as Gene Pitney, Curtis Lee, The Paris Sisters, The Crystals, The Ducanes, Darlene Love, The Righteous Brothers *(see Bobby Hatfield)*, Ike & Tina Turner*, The Checkmates Ltd., and The Ronettes. (Ronnie Bennett of the Ronettes was Spector's girlfriend at the time, and later became his wife *[see Ronnie Spector]*.) Spector's "wall of sound" session players, dubbed the "Wrecking Crew," including, among others, Barney Kessel, Billy Strange, Carole Kaye, Steve Douglas, Nino Tempo, Jack Nitzsche, Glen Campbell, Leon Russell*,

Larry Knechtel, Hal Blaine and Sonny & Cher. The label of eccentric producer was justly earned – his pranks were rarely appreciated, he surrounded himself with security and secrecy, his sessions were budget busters, and his temperament terrified and intimidated many musicians. His results, however, were nearly always chart successes, or, at the very least, rock 'n' roll classics.

Phil, already familiar with the British music scene prior to its invasion of America, attempted to form a musical relationship with The Beatles. The Ronettes had been scheduled to arrive in New York on January 7, 1964, on the same flight as The Beatles, but Phil put them on an earlier flight home and used their seats. The Ronettes were one of the few famous people to get past security at the Plaza Hotel where The Beatles were staying. The Beatles and Spector's paths crossed occasionally over the years, but in spite of their admiration, they had remained loyal to their producer George Martin* until 1970.

Spector's last and perhaps greatest production for the Philles label was Ike & Tina Turner's 1966 recording of ***River Deep - Mountain High***. Though the song was a hit in the U.K., when it failed in the U.S. charts, he scrapped the planned album, destroying what copies had been pressed. When Spector finally allowed the album to be released on A&M records in 1969, George Harrison supplied praise on the jacket sticker. Like Brian Wilson, commercial failure seemed to drive Spector into seclusion, and he all but retired from the music scene during the latter half of the 1960s.

Towards the end of 1969, The Beatles' manager Allen Klein, a long-time acquaintance of Spector's, finally united Phil with The Beatles. In late January 1970, John Lennon, eager to record quickly, grabbed Phil Spector at the suggestion of George Harrison, to produce the single ***Instant Karma***. Lennon was so impressed with Spector that he asked him to re-produce The Beatles' year-old, rough and unfinished **Let It Be** recordings. The recordings were initially produced by George Martin, with much help from recording engineer Glyn Johns. Spector overdubbed a touch of his trademark "wall of sound" to what The Beatles had originally intended to be a bare-bones album. Most of The Beatles, in the midst of breaking up, were pleased with Spector's results, but Paul McCartney later cited Spector's overdubs of an orchestra and chorus to his song ***The Long And Winding Road*** as examples of the group's efforts to sabotage his music.

With The Beatles' camp divided, there was a desire to break away from the past. The groups' only real producer throughout their career had been George Martin, and he seemed to be favored most by McCartney. Pleased with Spector's work on **Let It Be**, George Harrison employed him to co-produce his first genuine solo album, **All Things Must Pass**, and to help record **The Concert For Bangla Desh**.

Phil and George also worked together on recordings for Phil's wife Ronnie. During the sessions, George and Phil had quickly written and recorded a song together in the studio called ***Tandoori Chicken***. Also on hand was John Lennon, who contributed to the backing vocals. Two versions were cut, one with Ronnie on lead vocals, and one with Phil on lead vocals. Ronnie's version was released, but Phil's has yet to see the light of day, except on rare Apple acetates that change hands among collectors. Another version of Phil singing the lead vocals on ***Tandoori Chicken*** can be found on the bootleg CD **John Lennon - Let's Have A Party** (Quality Compact Productions / QCP 72003).

Spector helped produce most of John Lennon and Yoko Ono's* recordings between 1970 and 1973, including John's albums **Lennon / Plastic Ono Band**, **Imagine**, **Sometime In New York City**, and **Rock 'N' Roll**. Without question, **Rock 'N' Roll** was the most infamous production of Phil Spector's career. The album was recorded at the height of both Lennon and Spector's excessive and eccentric behavior and the results reflected it. Spector's attempt to reassemble his "wall of sound" was thwarted by the intoxication of many of the participants. Things got so out of hand that Spector reportedly fired a gun in the studio. Sometime later, Spector disappeared with the album's master tapes. Lennon alleged that, when he tried to recover the tapes, Spector made the outrageous claim that he had been hired by the government to decipher President Nixon's White House (Watergate) tapes and was too busy to return them, or resume work with Lennon. Lennon finally obtained the tapes nearly a year later, but considered them so unusable that he ended up re-recording most of the tracks.

Years later Yoko Ono hired Spector to help her produce **Season Of Glass**, her first album following the death of John Lennon. Yoko also released two posthumous John Lennon albums, **Live In New York City** and **Menlove Avenue**, that included production assistance by Spector. **Menlove Avenue** contained several out-takes from the **Rock 'N' Roll** sessions, including ***To Know Her [Him] Is To Love Her*** and the one and only known Lennon / Spector composition ***Here We Go Again***.

Phil Spector has produced occasionally in the last three decades, and has recently made a number of appearances in public at rock social functions. He was inducted into the Rock and Roll Hall of Fame in 1989.

Ronnie Spector

Record 336 title:
I Love Him Like I Love My Very Life [takes 1, 2, 3, 7 & 8]

Media:
Album 12" [Acetate]

Label / Catalog number:
Apple / RS1/RS2/RS3/RS7/RS8

Producer:
Phil Spector & (probably) George Harrison

Recording Location / Date:
(probably) EMI-Abbey Road, Island &/or Trident Studios, London, U.K. / (probably) Feb 71

Song 336a title:
I Love Him Like I Love My Very Life [takes 1, 2, 3, 7 & 8]

Release date / Country:
[Unreleased] / U.K.

Track details:
Side 1, track 1 / 14 min. 38 sec. [combined time]

Composer:
T. Wine - I. Levine - P. Spector

Ronnie Spector: Lead Vocals; George Harrison: Slide Guitar & (probable) Acoustic Guitar; Jim Gordon: (probable) Drums; Ringo Starr: (possible) Percussion: Phil Spector: (possible) Keyboards; Leon Russell: (probable) Keyboards; Klaus Voormann or Carl Radle: (probable) Bass

Record 337 title:
I Love Him Like I Love My Very Life [takes 9, 10, 16, 17 & 18]

Media:
Album 12" [Acetate]

Label / Catalog number:
Apple / RS9/RS10/RS16/RS17/RS18

Producer:
Phil Spector & (probably) George Harrison

Recording Location / Date:
(probably) EMI-Abbey Road, Island &/or Trident Studios, London, U.K. / (probably) Feb 71

Song 337a title:
I Love Him Like I Love My Very Life

Release date / Country:
[Unreleased] / U.K.

Track details:
Side 1, track 1 / 13 min. 41 sec. [combined time]

Composer:
T. Wine

Ronnie Spector: Lead Vocals; George Harrison: Slide Guitar & (probable) Acoustic Guitar; Jim Gordon: (probable) Drums; Ringo Starr: (possible) Percussion: Phil Spector: (possible) Keyboards; Leon Russell: (probable) Keyboards; Klaus Voormann or Carl Radle: (probable) Bass

Record 338 title:
Lovely La-De-Day
Media:
Single 7" [Acetate]
Label / Catalog number:
Apple / RS3
Producer:
Phil Spector & (probably) George Harrison
Jacket / Inserts:
Recording Location / Date:
(probably) EMI-Abbey Road, Island &/or Trident Studios, London, U.K. / Feb 71

Song 338a title:
Lovely La-De-Day
Track details:
Side 1, track 1 / 3 min. 00 sec.
Release date / Country:
[Unreleased] / U.K.

Ronnie Spector: Lead Vocals; probably one or more of the following: George Harrison: Acoustic Guitar; Jim Gordon: Drums; Leon Russell: Keyboards; Klaus Voormann: Bass; Carl Radle: Bass; Ringo Starr: (possible) Percussion; Phil Spector: (possible) Keyboards

Record 339 title:
Try Some, Buy Some / Tandoori Chicken
Media:
Single 7"
Label / Catalog number:
Apple / 1832
Producer:
Phil Spector & George Harrison
Recording Location / Date:
EMI-Abbey Road &/or Trident Studios, London, U.K. / (probably) Feb 71
Jacket / Inserts:
Picture sleeve

Song 339a title:
Tandoori Chicken
Track details:
Side 2, track 1 / 2 min. 14 sec.
Release date / Country:
19 Apr 71 (first issued 16 Apr 71) / U.S.A.
Composer:
G. Harrison - P. Spector

Ronnie Spector: Lead Vocals; George Harrison: Guitar; Phil Spector: Keyboards; Leon Russell: Keyboards; Klaus Voormann: Bass; Jim Gordon: Drums; John Lennon: B. Vocals; The Apple Scruffs (Cathy, Lucy & Carol): B. Vocals

Song 339b title:
Try Some, Buy Some
Track details:
Side 1, track 1 / 4 min. 08 sec.
Release date / Country:
19 Apr 71 (first issued 16 Apr 71) / U.S.A.
Composer:
G. Harrison

Ronnie Spector: Lead Vocals; George Harrison: Guitar; Gary Wright: Keyboards: Leon Russell: Keyboards; Klaus Voormann: Bass; Jim Gordon: Drums; John Barham: Orchestral & String Arrangements; Pete Ham (probable) Guitar

Record 340 title:
You / You [take 1]
Media:
Single 7" [Acetate]
Label / Catalog number:
Apple / RS1
Producer:
Phil Spector & (probably) George Harrison
Recording Location / Date:
(probably) EMI-Abbey Road, &/or Trident &/or Island Studios, London, U.K. / 09 Feb 71

Song 340a title:
You
Release date / Country:
[Unreleased] / U.K.
Track details:
Side 1, track 1 / 3 min. 48 sec.
Composer:
G. Harrison

Leon Russell: Piano; George Harrison: Guitar; Jim Gordon: Drums; Carl Radle: Bass; Gary Wright: Electric Piano

Record 341 title:
You [take 2]
Label / Catalog number:
Apple / RS2
Media:
Single 7" [Acetate]
Producer:
Phil Spector & (probably) George Harrison
Recording Location / Date:
(probably) EMI-Abbey Road, &/or Trident &/or Island Studios, London, U.K. / 09 Feb 71

Song 341a title:
You
Release date / Country:
[Unreleased] / U.K.
Track details:
Side 1, track 1 / 4 min. 01 sec.
Composer:
G. Harrison

Leon Russell: Piano; George Harrison: Guitar; Jim Gordon: Drums; Carl Radle: Bass; Gary Wright: Electric Piano

Ronnie Spector was born Veronica Bennett on August 10, 1943 in New York City, New York. Ronnie, her sister Estelle, and her cousin Nedra Talley, formed the singing trio The Ronettes. Legendary "wall of sound" producer Phil Spector* signed the group to his Philles record label. Together they turned out such classic early '60s hits as ***Be My Baby***, ***Baby I Love You*** and ***Walking In The Rain***. Before long, Ronnie and Phil became romantically involved, and were married in 1968.

Apple acetate for unreleased Ronnie Spector recording "You"

The Beatles' relationship with Ronnie began in January 1964. The Ronettes embarked on their first U.K. tour with The Rolling Stones*, a band with whom Spector briefly worked. During the tour, The Ronettes met The Beatles. They seemed to show more than musical interest in the three girls, particularly John Lennon, who was attracted to Ronnie. The Beatles offered The Ronettes billing on one of their tours, but Spector would not consent until 1966, and only then with a stand-in for Ronnie.

When Phil Spector became the new (unofficial) A&R man at Apple Records, it allowed him to re-release his legendary Philles **Christmas Album**, and to re-launch his wife Ronnie's career. According to Ronnie, Phil was hired at Apple on the condition that he allow Ronnie to sign with the label. The idea was for Phil and George Harrison to write and produce an album's worth of material for Ronnie. The recordings resulted in only one record release, the single ***Try Some, Buy Some /***

Ronnie Spector, photo courtesy of Ronnie Spector

Tandoori Chicken. A version of the B-side, with Phil on lead vocals, was also recorded, but remains unreleased.

At least three other as-yet-unreleased Ronnie Spector songs were also recorded - ***You***, ***Lovely La-De-Day*** (aka ***Loverly Laddy Day***) and ***I Love Him Like I Love My Very Life***. (The first release of this song was under the title ***I Loved You Like I Love My Very Life*** by Carla Thomas in September 1970. Phil produced a version of the song for Darlene Love a few years later, under the title ***I Loved Him Like I Love My Very Life***.) Ten slightly different takes of ***I Loved Him Like I Love My Very Life*** exist on two 12" one-sided Apple acetates that feature Harrison's distinctive slide guitar. Ronnie reportedly also attempted Harrison's composition ***I'll Still Love You*** (originally titled ***When Every Song Is Sung***). (***I'll Still Love You*** was also attempted by Leon Russell and by Cilla Black*. The song was eventually released by Ringo on his album **Rotogravure**.) There is also a possibility that Ringo may have contributed to some of Ronnie Spector's recording sessions for Apple Records as well. In all likelihood, Harrison also helped Phil with the production of these songs. The plans for an album were abandoned because Ronnie was uncomfortable with the style and direction the recordings were taking. These recordings have yet to see the light of day, except on rare Apple Records' acetates. The Apple acetate (RS 1&2) of ***You*** are backing tracks minus vocals. Several years later, Harrison released ***Try Some, Buy Some*** and ***You***, removing Ronnie's vocal track and substituting his voice, and adding a few instrumental overdubs to the original backing tracks a well.

By 1974, Phil and Ronnie's marriage had ended, and Ronnie restarted her career with a new line-up of Ronettes. She then began a series of cameo appearances with Bruce Springsteen And The E Street Band, and sang with Eddie Money on his top 10 song ***Take Me Home Tonight***, proving she had lost none of her vocal skills. She released two solo albums, and detailed a far from harmonious marriage to Phil Spector in her 1990 autobiography **Be My Baby**.

Spirit Choir

Record 342 title:
Every Man Has A Woman [Various Artists]
Media:
Album 5" CD
Label / Catalog number:
Polydor / 823 490-2
Producer:
Yoko Ono & John Lennon
Jacket / Inserts:
Standard international design with Jewel box / 4 page CD inserts
Recording Location / Date:
Record Plant (East) Studios & (probably) Hit Factory†, New York, NY, U.S.A. / Oct - Nov 72 & 1984†

Song 342a title:
Now Or Never
Release date / Country:
13 Sep 84 / Germany
Track details:
Side 1, track 10 / 3 min. 44 sec.
Composer:
Y. Ono

Spirit Choir: Vocals; John Lennon: Guitar; Gary Van Scyoc: Bass; Adam Ippolito: Organ & Harmonium; Richard Frank Jr.: Drums & Percussion; Stan Bronstein: Saxophone; George Young: Saxophone; Wayne Gabriel: Guitar

Spirit Choir / Plastic Ono Band *(see Yoko Ono)* with Elephants Memory*.

Spirit Of Play

Record 343 title:
Children In Need / Children In Need (Instrumental)
Media:
Single 7"
Label / Catalog number:
Release / KIDS 1988
Producer:
Paul McCartney & Spirit Of Play
Jacket / Inserts:
Picture sleeve
Recording Location / Date:
Hog Hill Studios, Sussex, U.K. / 1988

Song 343a title:
Children In Need
Release date / Country:
Nov 88 / U.K.
Track details:
Side 1, track 1 / 4 min. 45 sec.
Composer:
C. Mathieson - N. Hopkins

Craig Mathieson: Lead Vocals; Paul McCartney: Bass; Ken Wilson: Lead Guitar; Paul Fink: Guitar; Greenfields School Choir: Chorus; Andrew Skirrow: French Horn; London String Quartet: Strings; Woody Woodmansey: Drums; Nicky Hopkins: Piano & Keyboards

Song 343b title:
Children In Need (Instrumental)
Release date / Country:
Nov 88 / U.K.
Track details:
Side 2, track 1 / 4 min. 45 sec.
Composer:
C. Mathieson - N. Hopkins

Paul McCartney: Bass; Ken Wilson: Lead Guitar; Paul Fink: Guitar; Greenfields School Choir: Chorus; Andrew Skirrow: French Horn; London String Quartet: Strings; Woody Woodmansey: Drums; Nicky Hopkins: Piano & Keyboards

Spirit of Play members are Craig Mathieson, vocals; Woody Woodmansey, drums; and Nicky Hopkins*, piano and keyboards. ***Children In Need*** was recorded at Paul McCartney's private studio, and was probably recorded during the period when Hopkins contributed to ***That Day Is Done*** on McCartney's album **Flowers In The Dirt**. Proceeds from the sale of the record went to the BBC's **Children In Need Appeal for 1988**. The B-side instrumental is essentially the same recording as the A-side, minus the lead vocals.

Spirit Of The Forest

Record 344 title:
Spirit Of The Forest
Label / Catalog number:
Virgin / 0-96551
Jacket / Inserts:
Standard international design
Recording Location / Date:
One or more of the following studios: Great Linford Manor, Gt. Linford; Sarm West, Snake Ranch & Eden, London, U.K.; Complex, Los Angeles, CA &/or RCA, New York, NY, U.S.A. / 05 Mar 89
Media:
Single 12"
Producer:
Gentlemen Without Weapons (Kenny Young, Vic Coppersmith-Heaven, Nick Glennie-Smith)

Song 344a title:
Spirit Of The Forest
Release date / Country:
05 Jun 89 / U.S.A.
Track details:
Side 1, track 1 / 5 min. 18 sec.
Composer:
K. Young

Chris Rea: Vocals; Mr. Mister: Vocals; XTC: Vocals; Dave Gilmour: Vocals; Brian Wilson: Vocals; Joni Mitchell: Vocals; Ringo Starr: Vocals; Fish: Vocals; Belinda Carlisle: Vocals; Debbie Harry: Vocals; Bonnie Raitt: Vocals; Kate Bush: Vocals; Little Steven: Vocals; Jon Anderson: Vocals; Sam Brown: Vocals; Escape Club: Vocals; Olivia Newton-John: Vocals; Louise Goffin: Vocals; LL. Cool J: B. Vocals; Afrika Bambaata: B. Vocals; B-52's: B. Vocals; Plasmatics: B. Vocals; Shikisha: B. Vocals; Fleetwood Mac: B. Vocals; Kenny Young: B. Vocals; Vic Coppersmith-Heaven: B. Vocals; Nick Glennie-Smith: B. Vocals; Amy Sky: B. Vocals; Dolette McDonald: B. Vocals; Big Country: B. Vocals; It Bites: B. Vocals; Michael des Barres: B. Vocals; Marc Jordan: B. Vocals; Lisa Bonet: B. Vocals; Lenny Kravitz: B. Vocals; Andy Fairweather Low: B. Vocals; Jungle Brothers: B. Vocals; Raging Hormones: B. Vocals; Johnny Warman: B. Vocals; Bruce Foxton: B. Vocals; David Clayton Thomas: B. Vocals

Spirit Of The Forest was organized by the group Gentlemen Without Weapons for the **Earth Love Fund - Rainforest Appeal** to help bring attention to the destruction of the world's rain forests. An all-star cast, including Ringo Starr, was assembled at several locations to record several variations of the song ***Spirit Of The Forest***. The record's limited release was obscured by a number of charity singles and benefit concerts, and received little radio play. Ringo also appeared in the promotional video for the song. The record's only initial U.S. release on CD was on a Virgin Records' promo (PRCD2795). An edited version clocking in at 4 minutes, 50 seconds was issued on October 18, 1994, on the CD **Earthrise - The Rainforest Album** (Pyramid / R2 71830). (This CD also includes ***How Many People*** by Paul McCartney and ***Saltwater*** by Julian Lennon*.)

Splinter

Record 345 title:
Harder To Live
Media:
Album 12"
Label / Catalog number:
Dark Horse / SP 22006
Jacket / Inserts:
Standard international design with photo of George Harrison on back / Custom inner-sleeve
Recording Location / Date:
FPSHOT (Friar Park Studios, Henley-on-Thames), London, U.K. / 1973

Song 345a title:
After Five Years
Track details:
Side 2, track 2 / 3 min. 08 sec.
Release date / Country:
06 Oct 75 / U.S.A.
Composer:
R. Purvis
Producer:
Tom Scott & (probably) George Harrison

Bill Elliott: Vocals; Bob Purvis: Vocals; probably one or more of the following: George Harrison: (possible) Guitar; Chris Spedding: Guitar; Bill Dickinson: Bass; Klaus Voormann: Bass; Mike Kelly: Drums; Willie Weeks: Bass; Gary Wright: Keyboards; John Taylor: Keyboards; Earl Palmer: Drums; Jim Keltner: Drums; Bill Nuttycombe: String Concertmaster

Song 345b title:
Lonely Man (From the film "Little Malcolm And His Struggle Against The Eunuchs")
Track details:
Side 2, track 4 / 5 min. 29 sec.
Release date / Country:
06 Oct 75 / U.S.A.
Composer:
R. Purvis - M. Evans
Producer:
George Harrison & Tom Scott

Bill Elliott: Vocals; Bob Purvis: Vocals; Billy Preston: Organ; George Harrison: Guitar; Jim Keltner: Drums; Bill Dickinson: Bass; John Taylor: Fender Rhodes

Record 346 title:
Lonely Man [sung in Japanese]
Media:
Single 7"
Label / Catalog number:
Dark Horse / CM 2006
Producer:
George Harrison & Tom Scott
Jacket / Inserts:
Picture sleeve with Sheet music / Advert. flyer
Recording Location / Date:
FPSHOT (Friar Park Studios, Henley-on-Thames), U.K. / 1973 & 1976†

Song 346a title:
Lonely Man [sung in Japanese†]
Track details:
Side 1, track 1 / 4 min. 15 sec.
Release date / Country:
21 May 76 / Japan
Composer:
M. Nakamura (translator) - M. Evans - [R. Purvis]

Bill Elliott: Vocals; Bob Purvis: Vocals; Billy Preston: Organ; George Harrison: Guitar; Jim Keltner: Drums; Bill Dickinson: Bass; John Taylor: Fender Rhodes

Record 347 title:
The Place I Love
Label / Catalog number:
Dark Horse / SP 22001
Jacket / Inserts:
Standard international design with Gatefold / Record label inner sleeve & Lyric insert
Recording Location / Date:
FPSHOT (Friar Park Studios, Henley-on-Thames), U.K. / 1973 or 1974
Media:
Album 12"
Producer:
George Harrison

Song 347a title:
China Light
Release date / Country:
25 Sep 74 (first issued 20 Sep 74) / U.S.A.
Track details:
Side 1, track 3 / 4 min. 35 sec.
Composer:
R. Purvis - W. Elliott

Bill Elliott: Vocals; Bob Purvis: Vocals & Guitar; Willie Weeks: Bass; Mike Kelly: Drums; George Harrison: Acoustic Guitar, Mandolin & Arrangement; Gary Wright: Piano; Billy Preston: Organ

Song 347b title:
Costafine Town
Release date / Country:
25 Sep 74 (first issued 13 Sep 74) / U.S.A.
Track details:
Side 2, track 1 / 3 min. 10 sec.
Composer:
R. Purvis - W. Elliott

Bill Elliott: Vocals; Bob Purvis: Vocals; George Harrison: Bass, Harmonium & Hand Clap Percussion; Mike Kelly: Drums; Gary Wright: Piano; Graham Maitland: Accordion

Song 347c title:
Drink All Day (Got To Find Your Own Way Home)
Release date / Country:
25 Sep 74 (first issued 20 Sep 74) / U.S.A.
Track details:
Side 1, track 2 / 3 min. 20 sec.
Composer:
R. Purvis

Bill Elliott: Vocals; Bob Purvis: Vocals & Guitar; Klaus Voormann: Bass; Jim Keltner: Drums; George Harrison: Harmonium, Jew's Harp, Percussion, Guitars & Dobro Guitar

Song 347d title:
Elly-May
Release date / Country:
25 Sep 74 (first issued 13 Sep 74) / U.S.A.
Track details:
Side 2, track 4 / 2 min. 43 sec.
Composer:
R. Purvis

Bill Elliott: Vocals; Bob Purvis: Vocals; Klaus Voormann: Bass; Mike Kelly: Drums; George Harrison: Guitar & Synthesizer; Gary Wright: Piano

Song 347e title:
Gravy Train
Release date / Country:
25 Sep 74 (first issued 20 Sep 74) / U.S.A.
Track details:
Side 1, track 1 / 4 min. 50 sec.
Composer:
R. Purvis

Bill Elliott: Vocals; Bob Purvis: Vocals; Klaus Voormann: Bass; Mike Kelly: Drums; George Harrison: Guitar; Alvin Lee: Guitar; Mel Collins: Horn Arrangements; Billy Preston: Electric Piano

Song 347f title:
Haven't Got Time
Release date / Country:
25 Sep 74 (first issued 20 Sep 74) / U.S.A.
Track details:
Side 2, track 5 / 3 min. 55 sec.
Composer:
R. Purvis

Bill Elliott: Vocals; Bob Purvis: Vocals; Klaus Voormann: Bass; Mike Kelly: Drums; George Harrison:

Guitar & Percussion; Alvin Lee: Guitar; Mel Collins: Horn Arrangements

Song 347g title:
Situation Vacant
Release date / Country:
25 Sep 74 (first issued 20 Sep 74) / U.S.A.
Track details:
Side 2, track 3 / 4 min. 00 sec.
Composer:
R. Purvis

Bill Elliott: Vocals; Bob Purvis: Vocals & Guitar; Willie Weeks: Bass; Jim Keltner: Drums; George Harrison: Guitars & B. Vocals; Gary Wright: Piano; Mel Collins: Horn Arrangements

Song 347h title:
Somebody's City
Release date / CounTry:
25 Sep 74 (first issued 20 Sep 74) / U.S.A.
Track details:
Side 1, track 4 / 5 min. 20 sec.
Composer:
R. Purvis

Bill Elliott: Vocals; Bob Purvis: Vocals & Guitar; Klaus Voormann: Bass; Mike Kelly: Drums; George Harrison: Percussion & Guitars; Gary Wright: Piano; Mel Collins: Horn Arrangements; Alvin Lee: Guitar

Song 347i title:
The Place I Love
Release date / Country:
25 Sep 74 (first issued 20 Sep 74) / U.S.A.
Track details:
Side 2, track 2 / 4 min. 25 sec.
Composer:
R. Purvis

Bill Elliott: Vocals; Bob Purvis: Vocals; Klaus Voormann: Bass; Mike Kelly: Drums; George Harrison: Percussion & Guitars; Gary Wright: Electric Piano

Record 348 title:
Two Man Band
Label / Catalog number:
Dark Horse / DH 3073
Media:
Album 12"
Producer:
Norbert Putnam
Jacket / Inserts:
Standard international design / Record label inner sleeve
Recording Location / Date:
FPSHOT (Friar Park Studios, Henley-on-Thames), U.K. / mid-1977

Song 348a title:
New York City (Who Am I)
Release date / Country:
03 Oct 77 / U.S.A.
Track details:
Side 2, track 1 / 3 min. 49 sec.
Composer:
R. Purvis

Bill Elliott: Vocals; Bob Purvis: Vocals & Guitar; George Harrison: (probable) Acoustic Guitar; Norbert Putnam: Bass; Kenny Buttrey: Drums & Percussion; David Briggs: String Arrangement; (probably) The Memphis Horns

Song 348b title:
Round & Round
Release date / Country:
03 Oct 77 (first issued 06 Sep 77) / U.S.A.
Track details:
Side 1, track 2 / 3 min. 13 sec.
Composer:
P. McGee

Bill Elliott: Vocals; Bob Purvis: Vocals; George Harrison: Slide Guitar; Norbert Putnam: Bass; Kenny Buttrey: Drums & Percussion; Steve Gibson: Guitar; Rod Argent (probable) Keyboards

Splinter members were Bob Purvis, born on May 31, 1950, and Bill Elliott*, born on July 6, 1950. Both hailed from South Shields (Newcastle upon Tyne), England. The two attended the same school, and began playing music together by age eighteen.

Purvis and Elliott formed the group Halfbreed, who had sent a demo tape to Mal Evans at Apple Records. In 1971, Elliott was recruited by Apple to sing lead vocals on ***God Save Us***. The recording was written and produced by John Lennon for a benefit single to help defend the editors of the underground paper OZ. According to Purvis, Elliott sang his vocals to a finished backing track and never met any of The Beatles.

Purvis departed Halfbreed, and Elliott formed a band called Truth. Purvis (who was managed at the time by The Beatles' road manager, Mal Evans) reunited with Elliott in London, and formed Splinter in August 1972. They began rehearsing at The Beatles' Apple Studios, where they met George Harrison who, along with Pete Ham *(see Badfinger)*, helped them record the song ***Lonely Man***. At the time, Harrison was looking for a song for the Apple Film **Little Malcolm And His Struggle Against The Eunuchs**, of which he was the executive producer. This less than complete version was used for the soundtrack, but was never released on record. Purvis still has an Apple acetate of it that he said had the working title ***Another Chance That I Let Go***. The film, starring John Hurt, was adapted from a play by David Halliwell that Harrison had first seen on February 4, 1966.

Harrison produced a completed version of ***Lonely Man*** for Splinter at his home studio that evolved into the album **The Place I Love**. The album was used to help launch Harrison's Dark Horse Records label. Purvis said, "I have a demo where Billy and I are playing the songs that we're going to put forth on the album, and George is jamming' away in the background. George spent more time on our album than he did on his album! The guy really put himself out for us you know?" Ironically, ***Lonely Man*** was left off **The Place I Love**, but then was included on Splinter's follow-up album **Harder To Live**. According to Purvis, a video of ***Lonely Man*** was made that featured Harrison playing with Splinter.

In an article on the duo in the September 9, 1974 issue of London's paper The Sun, Harrison noted of Splinter: "They are good, honest boys who make good, simple records, and it is a joy for me to help them." Their debut single, ***Costafine Town***, proved to be the only song of theirs that enjoyed any major chart success. Any chance of their follow-up single ***Drink All Day*** being a hit was dashed by a BBC ban of the song, which was withdrawn and replaced by the single ***China Light***.

Harrison saw to it that **The Place I Love** album was played through the public address system at venues during his 1974 U.S. tour. Its success, both musically and commercially, benefited greatly from major contributions by Harrison under the thinly veiled pseudonyms of Hari Georgeson, Jai Raj Harisein and P. Roducer. Purvis proudly admits that, in a way, he and Elliott were the composers and singers for what was essentially a George Harrison album. Purvis said he played rhythm guitar on most of the songs on **The Place I Love**, but, because he was all but mixed out, was not credited. The jacket photos for Splinter's first album were taken at Harrison's home, as was the back jacket photo of Splinter's second album, **Harder To Live**. Purvis said the initial photos for **The Place I Love** were taken by Peter Sellers *(see Peter Sellers, Terry Southern & Ringo Starr)*. "He spent a whole day photographing Billy and me. I had a week's growth on me face and my hair was greasy and I was feelin' rough; Billy was lookin' rough and we both didn't want our photographs taken! Peter took them away and never brought them back. I think he knew we didn't want them taken."

Harrison turned over most of the production of the **Harder To Live** album to Tom Scott* because he was away at the time. Scott admitted that ***Lonely Man*** was already finished, and that he really did not

Bill Elliott, George Harrison, M. Nakamura and Bob Purvis, 1976, photo courtesy of Bob Purvis

add anything to it, although he is credited, along with Harrison, as the producer. He also seems quite sure that George did not contribute to any other songs on **Harder To Live**. However, Bob Purvis seems quite sure the backing for ***After Five Years*** was recorded during the sessions for **The Place I Love** album, and, thus, would have been produced by Harrison. Purvis could not make up his mind whether Harrison played guitar on the song, but was certain Chris Spedding did. He said they also recorded several versions of ***After Five Years*** in Japanese. Purvis suspects these, and the Japanese version of ***Lonely Man***, using the original backing tracks that Harrison contributed to, were recorded at the same time. The duo, who were interested in Japanese culture, had several other Japanese-only releases, though none of these contained contributions by Harrison.

Splinter's third album, **Two Man Band** released in 1977, has credits that are somewhat lacking in specifics, and there are a variety of keyboards and saxophone that are not even mentioned. Parker McGee is credited as playing guitar on the album, but Purvis does not remember him playing on any of the songs on the album. ***I'll Bend For You***, the B-side of the single ***Round And Round***, was not included on the album. Like the album, it lists Norbert Putnam as producer and George Harrison and Dennis Morgan as executive producers – a title that generally implies financial, managerial or superficial, rather than hands-on, involvement. Purvis said, "George did come in and have his say on a few things on certain tracks. He played guitar on ***Round And Round***, and I think acoustic guitar on ***New York City (Who Am I)***."

An alternate version of ***Love Is Not Enough*** to the one included on **Two Man Band** was issued as a single in Japan. It won the outstanding song award at the **World Popular Song Festival** in Tokyo in 1976. Purvis also recalls Harrison playing guitar on three Splinter demos, ***Dreaming***, ***Rush Of Daily Life***, and ***Domingo Bay***, that he thinks were recorded by Phil McDonald at Dark Horse's offices in London around 1976.

Splinter struck out with Dark Horse in spite of three tuneful and well-crafted albums. Purvis laments, "We left George (Dark Horse) under a bit of a cloud. I had a bit of a chip on my shoulder. If I could change any period of time in my life, I would like to change that period because of the things I said and did and because George was a really terrific person. I wish I could turn back the clock and tell him I've grown up! Nobody knows what he's like until they've seen him in the studio and the dedication and how good he is on the guitar; he's got this incredible nature that draws people to him." Harrison released all the artists from his Dark Horse Records stable shortly after his move to Warner Bros., where the label was used exclusively for George Harrison releases.

Splinter released several more albums following their departure from Dark Horse before breaking up in 1984 when Bill Elliott decided to become a shop fitter. Bob Purvis continues to write, record and perform music of the quality he generated with Splinter.

Bruce Springsteen

Record 349 title:
Artifacts III (Free As A Bird: 1981-1994)
[Various Artists]
Label / Catalog number:
Big Music / BIGBX 009.4 (BIG 4036)
[Unauthorized Record]
Jacket / Inserts:
Unique in Jewel box in box set with photos of The Beatles / 24 page box set booklet & 2 page CD inserts
Recording Location / Date:
On location at Garden State Arts Center, Holmdel, NJ, U.S.A. / 11 Aug 89
Media:
Album 5" CD [4 CD set]
Producer:
Unknown-audience recording

Song 349a title:
Get Back [live]
Release date / Country:
(probably) Feb 95 / Italy
Track details:
CD4, track 18 / 4 min. 43 sec.
Composer:
J. Lennon - P. McCartney

Bruce Springsteen: Vocals & Guitar; Billy Preston: Vocals & Keyboards; Jim Keltner: Drums; Ringo Starr: Drums & B. Vocals; Levon Helm: Drums; Nils Lofgren: Guitar & B. Vocals; Joe Walsh: Guitar; Rick Danko: Bass; Clarence Clemons: Saxophone; Dr. John: Keyboards (Ringo Starr And His All-Starr Band)

Bruce Springsteen was born on September 23, 1949 in Freehold, New Jersey. He began playing guitar and writing songs when he was thirteen years old. He joined a band called The Castiles in high school, and other local groups between the mid-1960s and early '70s, playing bars and clubs around the New York and New Jersey area.

It was during his club circuit era that Springsteen met Steve Van Zandt *(see Artists United Against Apartheid)* and Clarence Clemons*, both of whom would later form a part of Springsteen's E Street Band. The E Street Band would also include, among others, Nils Lofgren* and drummer Max Weinberg.

Weinberg has long been a friend and admirer of Ringo Starr, and featured conversations with him in his 1984 book on drumming **The Big Beat**. He put together a series of CDs, issued in 1994, called **Let There Be Drums** that featured a variety of drummers' recordings. Volume 3 included Ringo's recording ***Drumming Is My Madness***. Weinberg has made several guest appearances with Ringo Starr's All-Starr Band. He drummed on ***No No Song*** and ***With A Little Help From My Friends*** during the band's encore performance on July 13, 1995 at Radio City Music Hall in New York City, and on July 18, at the Garden State Arts Center in Holmdel, New Jersey. He also drummed on ***Photograph*** and ***With A Little Help From My Friends*** during the All-Starr Band's encore performance at the Arts Center in Holmdel on June 3, 1997.

In 1972, Springsteen signed with Columbia Records who tried to promote him as the next Bob Dylan*. Though his first two album releases gathered favorable reviews from the critics, they initially failed in the charts. Meanwhile, Springsteen began drawing huge crowds with his energetic performances.

Springsteen's third album, and its title single ***Born To Run***, effectively launched him into superstardom with a legendary cult following. More hit songs followed including ***Hungry Heart***, ***Dancing In The Dark***, ***Born In The U.S.A.***, ***I'm On Fire***, ***Glory Days***, ***Tunnel Of Love***, ***Human Touch***, and his last top 10, ***Streets Of Philadelphia*** in 1994. Springsteen was also able to reach the top of the charts via his compositions ***Blinded By The Light*** by Manfred Mann's Earth Band, ***Because The Night*** by Patti Smith, and ***Fire*** by The Pointer Sisters.

Bruce Springsteen, Detroit, MI, photo courtesy of Pat Henry

On August 11, 1989, Bruce Springsteen joined Ringo Starr's All-Starr Band onstage at the Garden State Arts Center in Holmdel, New Jersey. Springsteen played guitar and sang on ***Get Back*** and ***Long Tall Sally***, with Ringo on drums, and ***Photograph*** and ***With A Little Help From My Friends*** with Ringo on lead vocals. The Little Richard* classic, ***Long Tall Sally***, and ***Get Back***, were not a part of the regular set of songs on the tour. ***Get Back*** was a Beatles' song that originally featured Billy Preston, who shares the vocals with Springsteen on this occasion. So far only ***Get Back*** has become available, and that is on the bootleg CD set **Artifacts III**.

Freddie Starr

Record 350 title:
Freddie Starr
Label / Catalog number:
PVK / PVK 004
Jacket / Inserts:
Unique
Recording Location / Date:
(probably) InterTel Studios, Stonebridge House, London, U.K. / (probably) 1977 &/or 1978

Media:
Album 12"
Producer:
Bruce Baxter & Mike Cooper

Song 350a title:
You've Lost That Lovin' Feelin'
Release date / Country:
19 May 78 / U.K.

Track details:
Side 1, track 3 / 5 min. 08 sec.
Composer:
B. Mann - C. Weil - P. Spector

Freddie Starr: Lead Vocals; Paul McCartney: B. Vocals

Freddie (Starr) Fowell was born in Liverpool, England on January 9, 1943. He won first prize for his singing and impersonations at a talent contest when he was just nine years old. He was a member of the song and comedy act The Hilda Fallon Road Show between 1954 and 1958. He also appeared in the film **Violent Playground**.

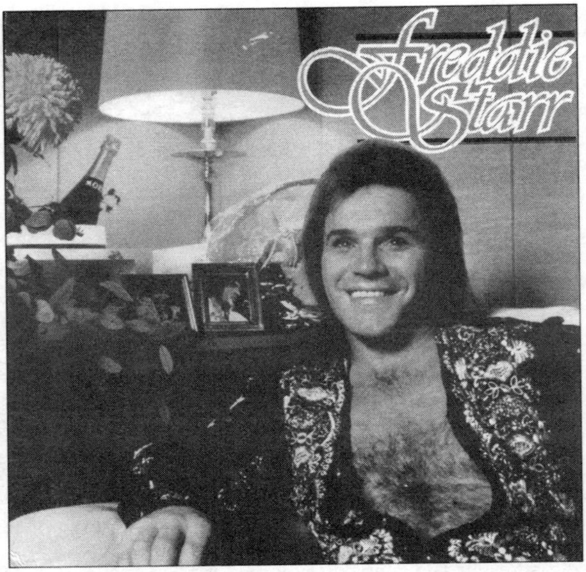

In 1961, Freddie became a member of Howie Casey And The Seniors, a popular Liverpool band originally called Derry And The Seniors before he joined. They were the first Liverpool rock band to appear in Hamburg, Germany. Howie Casey pleaded with Liverpool booking agent Allan Williams not to send The Beatles to Hamburg, because they were lousy and would spoil it for the other groups from Liverpool. Casey admits he has been eating his words ever since.

By June 1962, Howie Casey And The Seniors had disbanded. Casey stuck with his saxophone and got a job with Paul McCartney as part of the horn section of Wings' 1975-76 world tour and their 1979 U.K. tour. He also contributed to the McCartney and Wings albums **Band On The Run**, **At The Speed Of Sound**, **Back To The Egg**, **Wings Over America** and **Concerts For The People Of Kampuchea**.

Fowell changed his stage name to Starr, after another famous Liverpudlin, and formed a group called The Ventures, but in November 1962, he left to form Freddie Starr And The Midnighters. These bands sometimes shared the same bill with their friends The Beatles, and they were briefly managed by Brian Epstein before breaking up in April 1964.

Freddie Starr released three unsuccessful singles for Decca Records. Throughout the mid-1960s, Starr fronted various groups, and became better known as an impersonator (inc. Elvis) in a variety of comedy acts. In 1974 he scored his only U.K. top 10 with the song ***It's You*** and had a hit there the following Christmas with ***White Christmas***. He was the star of British TV's **Who Do You Do**. He currently has a TV series called **The Freddie Starr Show**, and has plans to record an album sometime in 1997. Starr remains virtually unknown in the U.S.

The album **Freddie Starr** gives "special thanks to Paul McCartney for his assistance with vocals." According to Starr, McCartney happened to be at the studio in Wembley where he was recording, and added backing vocals to ***You've Lost That Lovin' Feelin***." Perhaps McCartney was returning an old favor, or maybe his involvement had something to do with the fact that the album consists of covers of early rock standards, including a Buddy Holly song whose publishing catalogue McCartney owns.

Cat Stevens

Record 351 title:
None
Recording Location / Date:
Sweet Silence Studios, Copenhagen, Denmark / 30 Sep 76

Song 351a title:
Blue Monday

Release date / Country:
[Unreleased]

Cat Stevens: Lead Vocals; Ringo Starr: Drums

Song 351b title: I Just Want To Make Love To You
Release date / Country: [Unreleased]

Cat Stevens: Lead Vocals; Ringo Starr: Drums

Cat Stevens was born Steven Georgiou on July 21, 1947 in London, England. His father was Greek and his mother was Swedish. Cat dreamed of being a famous painter, but when he saw how successful The Beatles had become, he decided to pursue music as a profession. He came to the attention of the British public in 1966 with his top 40 song ***I Love My Dog***. His singles ***Matthew And Son*** and ***I'm Gonna Get Me A Gun*** reached the U.K. top 10 in 1967, as did ***Lady D'Arbanville*** in 1970. His first real hit in the U.S. was ***Wild World*** which nearly reached the top 10 in 1971. A string of hit songs followed including ***Moon Shadow***, ***Peace Train*** and ***Morning Has Broken***.

In 1979, Cat Stevens converted to the Muslim faith, changed his name to Yusuf Islam, and all but retired from the music business. He returned to the music scene in late 1997. He released an album titled **I Have No Cannons That Roar**, and performed at Sarajevo's "Night Of Beautiful Songs", an event held to promote peace, and showcase Bosnian culture.

Yusuf said he met Ringo at a hotel in Copenhagen, Denmark, and invited him down to a recording session for his album **Izitso** at Sweet Silence Studios in Copenhagen. He recalled that the party atmosphere of the sessions led to a jam of him singing ***Blue Monday*** and ***I Just Want To Make Love To You***, with Ringo joining in on drums. The tracks were not proper takes, so they were never used, though Yusuf thinks he still has the tapes somewhere. He seems quite sure Ringo did not playing on any of the tracks that ended up being used on the **Izitso** album. Ringo, apparently impressed with Sweet Silence Studios, returned there in July 1978 to do some recordings with producer Russ Ballard.

Rod Stewart

Record 352 title: Oriental Nightfish
Label / Catalog number: Reading Railroad / HAR 169 [Unauthorized Record]
Jacket / Inserts: Unique
Recording Location / Date: On location at Odeon Cinema Theatre, Lewisham, U.K. / 18 Nov 74
Media: Albums 12" [2 LP set] (mono)
Producer: Unknown-audience recording

Song 352a title: Mine For Me [live]
Release date / Country: U.S.A.
Track details: LP1, Side 4, track 1 / 0 min. 29 sec.
Composer: P. McCartney

Rod Stewart: Lead Vocals; Ron Wood: Guitar; Ian McLagen: Keyboards; Tetsu Yamauchi: Bass; Kenney Jones: Drums; Paul McCartney: B. Vocals; Linda McCartney: B. Vocals

Record 353 title:
Smiler
Label / Catalog number:
Mercury / 832 056-2
Jacket / Inserts:
Standard international design in jewel box / 4 page CD insert
Recording Location / Date:
Morgan Studios, London, U.K. / Jan or Feb 74
Media:
Album 5" CD
Producer:
Rod Stewart

Song 353a title:
Mine For Me
Release date / Country:
1989 (first issued 27 Sep 74) / Germany
Track details:
Side 1, track 12 / 4 min. 02 sec.
Composer:
P. McCartney

Rod Stewart: Lead Vocals; Ron Wood: Guitar; Martin Quittenton: Guitar; Ian McLagen: Organ; Spike Heatley: Bass; Kenney Jones: Drums; Ray Cooper: Percussion; The Tropic Isle Steel Band: Steel Drums; Paul McCartney: B. Vocals

Roderick David Stewart was born January 10, 1945 in London, England, and is of Scottish descent. He began his musical career in 1961, after giving up as a professional soccer player. He spent the next three years honing his musical act before landing a recording contract with Decca in 1964. Between 1964 and 1968, Stewart dropped in and out of a number of bands, including The Shotgun Express and The Jeff Beck Group, before settling in with The Faces *(see Kenney Jones, Ron Wood)*, while maintaining a solo career. Stewart's breakthrough came in 1971 with the release of ***Maggie May***, a song that never seemed to leave the charts.

In 1974 Stewart released his solo album **Smiler**, that included the Paul McCartney composition, ***Mine For Me***, on which Paul sang backing vocals. On November 18, 1974, (not November 27 as most publications claim), Paul and Linda *(see Linda McCartney)* joined Stewart onstage at the Odeon Cinema Theatre in Lewisham, England to sing ***Mine For Me***. The performance was broadcast on April 25, 1975 on the U.S. TV show **Midnight Special**, and included on the bootleg album **Oriental Nightfish**. Stewart and The Faces recorded covers of McCartney's ***Maybe I'm Amazed*** and Lennon's ***Jealous Guy***.

By 1975, Stewart was an international star and sex symbol. He took up U.S. residence as a British tax exile. Solo hits like ***Tonight's The Night (Gonna Be Alright)***, ***The First Cut Is The Deepest***, ***Hot Legs***, ***You're In My Heart***, and ***Da Ya Think I'm Sexy*** followed, during which time The Faces disintegrated. In 1976, Stewart contributed a cover of The Beatles' ***Get Back*** for the soundtrack to the 1976 film **All This And World War II**. Stewart has been less active in the charts in recent years, but remains successful on the tour circuit. He released a cover of The Beatles' song ***In My Life*** in 1986. Rod Stewart was inducted into the Rock and Roll Hall of Fame in 1994.

Stephen Stills

Record 354 title:
Stephen Stills
Label / Catalog number:
Atlantic / 7202-2
Jacket / Inserts:
Standard international design in jewel box / 4 page CD booklet
Recording Location / Date:
Island Studios, London, U.K. / (probably) Mar 70
Media:
Album 5" CD
Producer:
Stephen Stills & Bill Halverson

Song 354a title:
To A Flame
Release date / Country:
1988 (first issued 16 Nov 70) / U.S.A.

Track details:
Side 1, track 7 / 3 min. 10 sec.
Composer:
S. Stills

Stephen Stills: Lead Vocals, Guitar, Arrangement & Piano; Ringo Starr: Drums; Arif Mardin: Arrangement & Conductor

Song 354b title:
We Are Not Helpless
Release date / Country:
1988 (first issued 16 Nov 70) / U.S.A.

Track details:
Side 1, track 10 / 4 min. 17 sec.
Composer:
S. Stills

Stephen Stills: Lead Vocals, Guitar, Keyboards & Bass; Ringo Starr: Drums; Rita Coolidge: B. Vocals; Priscilla Coolidge-Jones: B. Vocals; Claudia Lennear: B. Vocals; John Sebastian: B. Vocals; Cass Elliot: B. Vocals; David Crosby: B. Vocals; Graham Nash: B. Vocals; Shirley Matthews Chorus: B. Vocals; Booker T. Jones: B. Vocals

Record 355 title:
Stills
Label / Catalog number:
Sony / SRCS 6189

Media:
Album 5" CD
Producer:
Stephen Stills, Bill Halverson, Ron Albert & Howie Albert

Jacket / Inserts:
Standard international design in jewel box / 4 page CD insert & 16 page translation insert
Recording Location / Date:
Island Studios, London, U.K. / (probably) Mar 70 & early 1974

Song 355a title:
As I Come Of Age
Release date / Country:
1992 (first issued 17 Jun 75) / Japan

Track details:
Side 1, track 9 / 2 min. 36 sec.
Composer:
S. Stills

Stephen Stills: Lead Vocals; Piano, Bass & Organ; Ringo Starr: Drums; Donnie Dacus: Guitar; Graham Nash: B. Vocals; David Crosby: B. Vocals

The name Stills is inseparable from Crosby, Nash and (sometimes) Young, not to mention the group Buffalo Springfield. Born January 3, 1945 in Dallas, Texas, Stephen Stills began his musical career following the same familiar path to stardom as most of his rock contemporaries. His first brush with success was as writer of The Mojo Men's hit ***Sit Down, I Think I Love You***. He auditioned for the group The Monkees, but reportedly was passed over because his teeth were not right for TV!

Stills thrust himself into the musical spotlight in the turbulent year of 1967 with his Buffalo Springfield song ***For What It's Worth***, inspired by recent social unrest between young people and the authorities in Los Angeles. The sleeve of the album **Buffalo Springfield Again** thanked a number of people who inspired the group, including "The Nerk Twins" (Lennon & McCartney) and George and Ringo. In no way were the thanks meant to imply The Beatles contributed to any of Buffalo Springfield's recordings. Buffalo Springfield began to disintegrate shortly after their brief success, due in part to conflicts between Stills and fellow band member Neil Young.

During the summer of 1967, Stills began to work with David Crosby (born David Van Cortlandt Crosby on August 14, 1941 in Los Angeles, California), who was in the midst of departing from The Byrds. The Byrds, with the help of songs written by Bob Dylan*, pioneered a sound known as folk-rock. The unusual spelling of Byrds, and their dress, and the use of Rickenbacker guitars were, admittedly, inspired by The Beatles. The Beatles also had great admiration for The Byrds, and went to see them perform during their first British tour. At the time, Derek Taylor, The Beatles' former and future press officer and Apple publicist, worked for The Byrds, and introduced the two groups. The Byrds also visited The Beatles, who were holed up in Los Angeles between August 23 and 31, during their 1965 U.S. tour. It was during this visit that Crosby told Harrison about Ravi Shankar* and Indian music. The Beatles also visited The Byrds during one of their recording sessions. The dates most often listed for the visit are August 24 and / or 27, 1965. Most sources list ***The Times They Are A-Changin'*** as the track The Byrds were recording during the visit. The visitors (according to Byrds leader Jim / Roger McGuinn) were George and Paul, and the sessions were for the song ***She Don't Care About Time***. According to The Byrds' producer Terry Melcher, none of The Beatles contributed to any of The Byrds' recordings. Nonetheless, the two groups admitted they often borrowed many musical ideas from each other. Crosby officially departed The Byrds in late 1967. In 1989 he released his cover of The Beatles' song ***Drive My Car***. The Beatles included a brief portion of The Byrds' music in their 1996 **Anthology** film.

Stephen Stills, Detroit, MI, mid-1970s, photo courtesy of Tom Bert

According to Peter Asher *(see Peter & Gordon)*, in June 1968, he and Harrison went to Peter Tork's (of The Monkees) house in California, and had a jam session along with David Crosby, Stephen Stills, and probably Russ Kunkel (other reports claim Ringo also attended). Unfortunately, the session was never recorded. Peter Asher recalled that most of the participants (Harrison excluded) were not clothed.

Following Crosby's departure from The Byrds, McGuinn tightened his control of the group. He led a flock of joining and departing members on a musical migration through country and Christian rock, and back to a number of reunions with the original members. Years later, McGuinn's name would be mentioned as a possible recruit for Harrison's part-time "supergroup," Traveling Wilburys *(see Jeff Lynne, Roy Orbison, Tom Petty And The Heartbreakers)*. McGuinn, Harrison, and Petty joined Bob Dylan for his **30th Anniversary Concert Celebration** onstage at Madison Square Garden in New York on October 16, 1992.

Shortly after the final breakup of Buffalo Springfield in the spring of 1968, Crosby introduced Stephen Stills to Graham Nash of The Hollies, one of England's most popular groups. The Hollies and The Beatles often shared the same spotlight throughout northern England early in their careers. Both groups were signed to the same record company, and visited each other during their recording sessions at EMI's Abbey Road Studios. The Hollies even covered Harrison's Beatles song ***If I Needed Someone***, that took its inspiration from one of Harrison's all time favorite songs ***The Bells Of Rhymney***, by The Byrds. It was, after all, a mutual admiration society, even though Harrison was critical of The Hollies' version of his song in the press.

Nash, joined by Stills and Crosby, returned to England in the summer of 1968. He announced his departure from the Hollies that fall. While in England, the three rehearsed together and auditioned for several record labels, including Apple, who rejected them. During this period Stills wrote, but apparently never recorded, the song ***The Doctor Will See You Now Mr. L*** about John Lennon. They were finally signed to Atlantic in 1969. Their first album, the classic **Crosby, Stills & Nash**, launched them as the first of many "supergroups." The group's second album, **Deja Vu**, added the name (Neil) "Young," but their chemistry was as delicate and fragile as their harmonies, and solo projects took priority over group efforts throughout much of their careers. Crosby, Stills & Nash recorded a cover of The Beatles' song ***Blackbird*** in 1971 that was included in their 1991 retrospective box set, and a live version of the song is included on their 1983 album **Allies**.

In late 1969, Stills bought Ringo Starr's home in England, formerly owned by Peter Sellers *(see Peter Sellers, Terry Southern & Ringo Starr)*. Within months, he was recording his first solo album, **Stephen Stills**. It featured a host of superstars including Ringo Starr (credited as "Richie" on two tracks). The album spawned the hit ***Love The One You're With***. During Stills' stay in England, he also participated in the recordings for Apple Records' artist Doris Troy*. In 1975, Stills released an album titled **Stills** containing ***As I Come Of Age***, that credits "English Richie" on drums.

There seems to be some confusion concerning when the three tracks that involve Ringo were recorded. Many reliable publications, including the **Stills** credits, have listed ***As I Come Of Age*** as being recorded in 1971, but most likely it was recorded during the sessions for **Stephen Stills**, with overdubs probably recorded in early 1974. ***To A Flame*** and ***We Are Not Helpless*** are usually listed as having been recorded in London in June or July 1970. However, Stills was on tour in the U.S. at the time. The majority of **Stephen Stills** was recorded in March 1970, and that is probably when all the sessions with Ringo took place. Ringo did not contribute to an alternate version of ***As I Come Of Age***, included on Crosby, Stills & Nash's retrospective box set.

Stills' and Ringo's paths have crossed many times, including appearances at The Band's* **Last Waltz** concert, and Bob Dylan's Rolling Thunder **Night Of The Hurricane 2** benefit concert. He also contributed to Ringo's 1981 album **Stop And Smell The Roses**. Stills released a cover of The Beatles' song ***In My Life*** in 1991. Crosby, Stills and Nash released their version of the song in 1994. Stephen Stills continues to record, with and without the on again, off again Crosby, Stills, Nash and occasionally Neil Young.

Rory Storm & The Hurricanes

Record 356 title:
Liverpool 1963-1968 [Various Artists]
Label / Catalog number:
See For Miles/Charly / CM 118
Jacket / Inserts:
Unique
Recording Location / Date:
EMI-Abbey Road, London, U.K. / 30 Sep 64

Media:
Album 12" (mono)
Producer:
Brian Epstein

Song 356a title:
America
Release date / Country:
15 Mar 83 (first issued 13 Nov 64) / U.K.

Track details:
Side 1, track 7 / 2 min. 32 sec.
Composer:
Bernstein - Sondheim

Rory Storm: Lead Vocals; Ringo Starr: Percussion & B. Vocals; Shane Fenton [aka Alvin Stardust]: Percussion & B. Vocals; Lou Walters: Bass & B. Vocals; Ty Brian: Guitar & B. Vocals; Johnny Guitar: Guitar & B. Vocals; Jimmy Tushingham: Drums & B. Vocals

Record 357 title:
Summertime / Fever / September Song / [Advertising Commercial]
Media:
Single 10"
Label / Catalog number:
Akustik
Producer:
Allan Williams (Executive Producer)
Recording Location / Date:
Akustik Studio, Hamburg, Germany / 15 Oct 60

Song 357a title:
Fever
Track details:
Side 1, track 2
Release date / Country:
[Unreleased] / Germany
Composer:
Davenport - Cooley

Lou Walters: Lead Vocals; John Lennon: (possible) Guitar; George Harrison: (possible) Guitar; Ringo Starr: Drums; Paul McCartney: (probable) Guitar or Bass; Ty Brian: (possible) Guitar

Song 357b title:
September Song
Track details:
Side 1, track 3
Release date / Country:
[Unreleased] / Germany
Composer:
Anderson - Weill

Lou Walters: Lead Vocals; John Lennon: (possible) Guitar; George Harrison: (possible) Guitar; Ringo Starr: Drums; Paul McCartney: (possible) Bass

Song 357c title:
Summertime
Track details:
Side 1, track 1
Release date / Country:
[Unreleased] / Germany
Composer:
Gershwin

Lou Walters: Lead Vocals; John Lennon: Guitar; Paul McCartney: Guitar or Bass; George Harrison: Guitar; Ringo Starr: Drums

Richard Starkey joined the popular Liverpool band Rory Storm & The Hurricanes around March 1959, eventually adopting a stage name (like other members of the group) of Ringo Starr. The Hurricanes also included (among others over the years) Lou "Wally" Walters, born Walter Eymond, on bass; Ty Brian, born Charles O'Brien, on guitar; Johnny Guitar born John Byrne, on guitar; and Rory Storm, born Alan Caldwell, on lead vocals. Storm was known for his outlandish costumes and acrobatics on stage, and for a persistent stutter. The Hurricanes were one of Liverpool's most popular bands during the early '60s. They were initially influenced by skiffle and country & western music, and, in a previous incarnation, were known as the Raving Texans. The Hurricanes were also a regular at Butlins, a popular holiday camp in the U.K. Band members often sat in with other Liverpool groups, including Derry And The Seniors *(see Freddie Starr)*, and The Beatles.

Rory Storm & The Hurricanes, like The Beatles, took up residency at several of Hamburg, Germany's music clubs. On October 15, 1960, Wally cut a record in a small rudimentary studio near Hamburg's central rail station to demonstrate his versatile vocal talents. There seems to be some dispute as to who backed him on what songs, and how many copies were cut. Allan Williams, who paid for the sessions, recounted in his book **The Man Who Gave The Beatles Away**, that Wally, backed by Lennon, McCartney, Harrison and The Hurricanes' drummer, Ringo Starr, recorded two songs – ***Summertime***, and then ***Fever***. Williams recalled that The Beatles also wanted to record a song by themselves, but that time did not permit it. The initial record was cut at 78 RPM, with a left-over radio commercial on the other side. Williams thought four additional discs were cut. In an interview conducted by Mark Lewisohn in 1984, Wally maintained that the three Beatles and Ringo only back him on ***Summertime***, and that only Ty Brian, Johnny "Guitar" Byrne and Ringo backed him on ***Fever*** and the number ***September Song***. Wally thought that nine discs were cut. Byrne said he went along to the sessions, but neither he, nor, does he now think, Brian plays on any of the recordings!

(Byrne has stated in previous interviews, conducted by others, that he thought Brian might have been involved in these recordings.) He recalled Lennon and Harrison playing guitar, Ringo playing drums, and seemed sure McCartney was playing bass while Wally sang ***Summertime*** and ***September Song***, but said that only McCartney and Ringo backed Wally on ***Fever***. Byrne thought six discs were cut and said, "I never got a copy because I didn't play on the recordings." Supposedly, one copy still exists, but determining who is involved has been made more difficult by the fact that the recordings have never surfaced. The musical credits listed for these songs are based on a composite of the available information, and some deductions. The recordings had no producer, in the technical sense, other than the group and the recording studio engineer. However, booking agent Allan Williams, who represented The Beatles at the time, paid for the sessions, so he is credited as (executive) producer.

The Beatles and Rory Storm, long in friendly competition with each other, were linked by more than their common background. Storm's sister Iris was the steady girlfriend of Paul McCartney during the early '60s. Iris would later marry Shane Fenton, aka Alvin Stardust. The Hurricanes, like The Beatles, also backed Tony Sheridan in Hamburg. One of the most popular portions of Rory Storm And The Hurricanes' live act was called "Ringo Starrtime", featuring Ringo Starr on a half dozen numbers.

Ringo's drumming and deadpan humor won him the friendship of The Beatles, who occasionally used him as a substitute when Pete Best was unavailable. On August 16, 1962, Brian Epstein informed Pete Best that the other Beatles had decided to replace him with Ringo Starr. Needless to say, Rory Storm was no happier than Pete Best. Storm replaced Ringo with Gibson Kemp *(see The Escorts, Paul Jones).* The Beatles began to conquer the world shortly after Starr joined the group. Rory Storm & The Hurricanes somehow missed the wave that swept many Liverpool bands across the Atlantic in the British music invasion of America.

In 1964, Brian Epstein decided to help the fledgling Rory Storm & The Hurricanes, offering to personally produce the band in a recording of the **West Side Story** hit ***America***. On hand to help was old band member Ringo Starr. Byrne said, "Ringo played tambourine or maracas, or something like that – some kind of percussion. He probably sang backing vocals, because all the musicians sang in the chorus." Some reference books claim Ringo was clapping in the background. The 1995 CD release of Rory Storm & The Hurricanes' **The Complete Works** (Street Records / RS01) claims, for the first time, that Brian Epstein also sings backing vocals on ***America***, but Byrne disputes this.

Ray Coleman's biography of Brian Epstein lists the session for ***America*** as taking place at IBC Studios in London. Bill Harry also listed IBC Studios in his books **Ultimate Beatles Encyclopedia** and **The Encyclopedia Of Beatles People** (Coleman's book probably is his source). Byrne said, "I'm certain ***America*** was recorded in studio number 2 at Abbey Road." He said the song was recorded on September 30, 1964, and released in November on Friday the 13th. Harry's more recent books list the single (Parlophone / R 5197) as being released on December 20. In a prior book, he listed the release date as November 13, which is the date all other sources list. The Beatles' single ***I Feel Fine*** (Parlophone / R 5200), was released on November 27, 1964. These catalogue numbers would seem to indicate that the ***America*** single was released on November 13. Unfortunately, the song was as unlucky as Brian Epstein was as a record producer, and quickly faded from the charts.

Rory Storm returned to Liverpool, and the band eventually disintegrated. Storm struggled on the outer fringes of the music business for several years. In 1972, following the death of his father, he and his mother apparently committed suicide together. However, there is some evidence to suggest that Rory may not have committed suicide but died of an accidental overdose, prompting his mother to take her life after finding him dead.

Following Storm's death, his sister Iris took possession of a tape apparently identified as containing rehearsals and live recordings of Rory Storm & The Hurricanes (with Ringo) at the Cavern Club and the Jive Hive in Liverpool in 1962. Unfortunately, according to Byrne, the entire rehearsal and live performance had been recorded over with a variety of unrelated and unimportant recordings through the years, rendering the tape useless. Ty Brian died from complications after an operation in 1967. Lou Walters pursued a career in health care, and Johnny Guitar formed a group called Johnny Guitar & The Hurricanes in the 1990s.

The Strangers with Mike Shannon

Record 358 title:
Lennon & McCartney Song Book Volume 2
Media:
Album 5" CD (mono)
Label / Catalog number:
Connoisseur Collection / VSOP CD 162
Jacket / Inserts:
Standard international design in jewel box with photo of John Lennon & Paul McCartney / 8 page CD booklet with photo of John Lennon & Paul McCartney
Recording Location / Date:
20 Mar 64

Song 358a title:
One And One Is Two
Track details:
Side 1, track 17 / 2 min. 11 sec.
Release date / Country:
31 May 91 (first issued 08 May 64) / U.K./E.E.C.
Composer:
J. Lennon - P. McCartney

Mike Shannon: Lead Vocals

The Strangers with Mike Shannon were apparently from South Africa. They were the first group to release the John Lennon and Paul McCartney composition ***One And One Is Two***. Lennon and McCartney recorded several demo versions of the song in their George V Hotel room during The Beatles' engagement in Paris in January 1964. One of The Beatles' demos is available on several bootleg records. The song was originally intended for Billy J. Kramer *(see Billy J. Kramer & The Dakotas)*. It was briefly attempted by The Fourmost*. ***One And One Is Two*** has since been covered by The Beatbads and The Saltbee.

Bernie Taupin

Record 359 title:
[None]
Media:
Album 12"
Label / Catalog number:
Rocket
Producer:
Robert Appere
Recording Location / Date:
(probably) Eastern Studios, Toronto, Ontario, Canada / 1-14 Nov 76

Song 359a title:
Cryin' Time
Release date / Country:
[Unreleased]
Composer:
B. Owens

Bernie Taupin: Vocals; Ringo Starr: Vocals

Bernie Taupin was born on May 22, 1950 in Sleaford, Lincolnshire, England. In 1967, Elton John* failed an audition for Ray Williams of Liberty Records, but Williams gave John lyrics sent to him by Taupin. John corresponded with Taupin, and the two eventually became one of the world's most successful songwriting teams. Taupin also involved himself with side projects that included recording solo albums, producing, and writing lyrics for other artists.

In 1976, John announced that he was retiring from performing, and began working with other lyricists. Fortunately, the retirement, and separation from Taupin, were short-lived, and the two reunited in a partnership that has lasted well into the 1990s. Before their brief separation, Taupin recorded a solo album planned for release on Elton John's Rocket Record label. Unfortunately, the untitled solo album, which contained a duet vocal with Ringo Starr of the Buck Owens' song ***Cryin' Time***, was never released.

Taupin did release a book in 1976 of his lyrics titled **The One Who Writes The Words For Elton John**, edited by Alan Aldridge, which included illustrations by John Lennon and Ringo Starr. (Aldridge had also edited and Illustrated the books **The Beatles Illustrated Lyrics**, and **The Beatles Illustrated Lyrics 2**.) Taupin teamed up with the group Farm Dogs in 1996.

John Tavener

Record 360 title:
The Whale

Media:
Album 5" CD

Label / Catalog number:
Apple / CD SAPCOR 15 (0777 7 98497 2 7)

Producer:
Michael Bremner

Jacket / Inserts:
Standard international design in jewel box / 12 page CD booklet

Recording Location / Date:
On location at the Church Of St. John The Evangelist, Islington, London, U.K. / 22-24 Jul 70

Song 360a title:
The Whale (Part One)

Track details:
Side 1, track 1 / 18 min. 23 sec.

Release date / Country:
19 Oct 92 (first issued 25 Sep 70) / U.K.

Composer:
John Tavener

Anna Reynolds: Vocals; Raimund Herincx: Vocals; Alvar Lidell: Vocals; Ringo Starr: Voices & Percussion; John Tavener: Keyboards; The London Sinfonietta: Orchestra; The London Sinfonietta Chorus: Chorus; David Atherton: Conductor

Song 360b title:
The Whale (Part Two)

Track details:
Side 1, track 2 / 13 min. 15 sec.

Release date / Country:
19 Oct 92 (first issued 25 Sep 70) / U.K.

Composer:
John Tavener

Anna Reynolds: Vocals; Raimund Herincx: Vocals; Alvar Lidell: Vocals; Ringo Starr: Voices & Percussion; John Tavener: Keyboards; The London Sinfonietta: Orchestra; The London Sinfonietta Chorus: Chorus; David Atherton: Conductor

John Tavener was born in London, England on January 28, 1944. He is a classical composer, conductor, pianist and organist. He was interested in music from a very early age, and later attended the Royal Academy of Music, where he was cited for his compositions. In 1966 he wrote **The Whale**. The work was first performed on January 24, 1968, and recorded for broadcast by the BBC on March 8, 1968.

In 1969, Tavener met John Lennon and Yoko Ono*. Lennon's relationship with Yoko had introduced him to the world of experimental music, and Lennon, now looking to broaden Apple Records' artist roster with more avant-garde music, offered Tavener a contract with Apple.

Ringo Starr, with no real artist of his own to back at Apple, ended up in charge of Tavener during his stay with the label. Ringo was present throughout the recording of Tavener's first album **The Whale**, lending his voice along with noises and percussion. The recording was made at the Church of St. John The Evangelist in London.

The following year, Tavener released **Celtic Requiem**, his second and last album on Apple, also recorded at St. John. Again, Ringo was present but, according to Tavener, did not contribute to the recording. Tavener was surprised to learn that some of his music was used for the film **Son Of Dracula**, starring Harry Nilsson* and Ringo Starr. In 1978, **The Whale**, then deleted by Apple, was released on Ringo's Ring O'Records.

Tavener's work has taken on a decidedly religious direction since becoming a member of the Russian Orthodox Church in 1977. Over the years his compositions have been widely recorded and favorably received, including ***The Akathist Of Thanksgiving***, ***The Protecting Veil***, ***Resurrection***, ***The Lamb***, ***Innocence*** and ***Prayer To The Holy Trinity***.

James Taylor

Record 361 title:
James Taylor
Label / Catalog number:
Apple / CDP 7975772
Jacket / Inserts:
Standard international design in jewel box / 16 page CD booklet
Recording Location / Date:
Trident Studios, London, U.K. / Jul - Oct 68
Media:
Album 5" CD"
Producer:
Peter Asher

Song 361a title:
Carolina In My Mind
Release date / Country:
19 Nov 91 (first issued 06 Dec 68) / Germany
Track details:
Side 1, track 7 / 3 min. 37 sec.
Composer:
J. Taylor

James Taylor: Lead Vocals & Guitar; Mick Wayne: Guitar; Paul McCartney: Bass; Peter Asher: Tambourine & B. Vocals; Freddie Redd: Organ; Bishop O'Brien: Drums; Richard Hewson: String Arrangement & Conductor; George Harrison (supposed) B. Vocals

Record 362 title:
Walking Man
Label / Catalog number:
Warner Bros / 2794-2
Jacket / Inserts:
Standard international design in jewel box / 12 page CD booklet
Recording Location / Date:
Hit Factory, New York, NY, U.S.A. / Jan - Apr 74
Media:
Album 5" CD
Producer:
David Spinozza

Song 362a title:
Let It Fall Down
Release date / Country:
Sep 88 (first issued 28 Jun 74) / U.S.A.
Track details:
Side 1, track 3 / 3 min. 30 sec.
Composer:
J. Taylor

James Taylor: Lead Vocals & Acoustic Guitar; Rick Marotta: Drums; Andy Muson: Bass; Hugh McCracken: Electric Guitar; Ralph MacDonald: Percussion; Kenny Ascher: Electric Piano; Paul McCartney: B. Vocals; Linda McCartney: B. Vocals; Carly Simon: B. Vocals

Song 362b title:
Rock 'N' Roll Is Music Now
Release date / Country:
1988 (first issued 28 Jun 74) / U.S.A.
Track details:
Side 1, track 2 / 3 min. 25 sec.
Composer:
J. Taylor

James Taylor: Lead Vocals & Acoustic Guitar; Rick Marotta: Drums & B. Vocals; Andy Muson: Bass; Hugh McCracken: Electric Guitar; David Spinozza: Electric Piano; Kenny Ascher: Piano; Paul McCartney: B. Vocals; Linda McCartney: B. Vocals; Carly Simon: B. Vocals; Howard Johnson: Tuba; Kenny Berger: Baritone Saxophone; Barry Rogers; Trombone; Michael Brecker: Tenor Saxophone;

George Young: Alto Saxophone; Alan Rubin: Trumpet; Randy Brecker: Trumpet

James Taylor, Detroit, MI, mid-1970s, photo courtesy of Tom Bert

James Taylor was born on March 12, 1948 in Boston, Massachusetts. His mother encouraged James, and his brothers Alex and Livingston, and sister Kate to take up music early in life. All would later have varying degrees of success in music, though none would approach that of brother James. His father took a position as Dean of the Medical School at the University of North Carolina in Chapel Hill. James' family also established a summer home on Martha's Vineyard off the coast of Cape Cod, MA.

It was on Martha's Vineyard that Taylor first met guitarist Danny Kortchmar *(see Attitudes)*, forming a musical association that has endured over the years. In 1964, James joined his older brother Alex's band, before moving to New York to join Kortchmar's band The Flying Machine. The group released one single, and recorded additional material that was issued shortly after Taylor's rise to stardom.

Taylor moved to London, England in early 1968. Kortchmar, who had backed Peter & Gordon* on a U.S. tour, urged Taylor to send a tape of his music to Peter, who was A&R man at Apple Records. Peter Asher persuaded Paul McCartney to sign Taylor to Apple. In the summer and fall of 1968, Taylor recorded his first and only album for Apple, produced by Asher and self-titled **James Taylor**. One song, ***Carolina In My Mind***, features Paul McCartney on bass. Taylor has stated in interviews that George Harrison sings backing vocals on the song. Asher, who produced and sings backing vocals on ***Carolina In My Mind***, stated, "No, I have read that too, but it's not true, I'm certain." Richard Hewson, who was the string arranger and conductor for the song, also does not remember Harrison being present. A line in the song about "a holy host of others" apparently refers to The Beatles. The title of another song from Taylor's album, ***Something In The Way She Moves***, was used by George Harrison as part of the lyrics and inspiration for his song ***Something***.

Taylor returned to the U.S. shortly after his Apple album was released. The Beatles and Apple Records were quickly disintegrating, and most of its artists, including Taylor, were being neglected. Asher left Apple to become Taylor's full-time manager and producer, negotiating a contract for Taylor with Warner Bros.

Taylor's first post-Apple album release, **Sweet Baby James**, in the spring of 1970, contained his signature song ***Fire And Rain***, which launched James Taylor to stardom. An earlier version of ***Fire And Rain*** was recorded for inclusion on Taylor's Apple album, but was rejected by the artist and producer.

In 1971, Taylor met singer Carly Simon*. The two shared similar backgrounds, and were married the following year. It was a musical marriage as well, with the couple contributing to each other's recordings. Paul and Linda McCartney* sang backing vocals on two songs from Taylor's 1974 album **Walking Man**. Unfortunately, the Taylors' marriage was troubled, and in 1982 Carly filed for divorce from James. Taylor turned briefly to acting, co-starring with Dennis Wilson *(see The Beach Boys)* in the appropriately titled film **Two Lane Blacktop**. Taylor and Simon performed together at a concert on Martha's Vineyard on August 30, 1995.

Taylor retains a solid following, especially on the concert circuit performing such hits as ***Don't Let Me Be Lonely Tonight***, ***You've Got A Friend***, ***Country Road***, ***How Sweet It Is***, ***Mexico***, ***Shower The People***, ***Her Town Too***, ***Night Owl***, and of course ***Fire And Rain***. James Taylor is a true survivor, who ultimately proved to be Apple's most successful discovery, and one of contemporary music's greatest assets.

10cc

Record 363 title:
Meanwhile
Label / Catalog number:
Polydor / 513279-2
Jacket / Inserts:
Standard international design in jewel box / 12 page CD booklet
Recording Location / Date:
Bearsville Sound, Bearsville, NY, River Sound, New York, NY & Village Recorders, Los Angeles, CA, U.S.A. / Feb - Mar 91
Media:
Album 5" CD
Producer:
Gary Katz & 10cc

Song 363a title:
Don't Break The Promises
Release date / Country:
11 May 92 / U.K.
Track details:
Side 1, track 10 / 6 min. 22 sec.
Composer:
E. Stewart - P. McCartney - G. Gouldman

Eric Stewart: Lead Vocals & Keyboards; Graham Gouldman: Electric & Acoustic Guitars; Jeff Porcaro: Drums & Percussion; Freddie Washington: Bass; Michael Landau: Lead Guitar; David Paitch: String Synthesizer

Record 364 title:
Mirror Mirror
Label / Catalog number:
AVEX/ZYX / ZYX 20350-2
Jacket / Inserts:
Standard international design in jewel box / 20 page CD booklet
Media:
Album 5" CD
Producer:
Eric Stewart & Adrian Lee

Song 364a title:
Code Of Silence
Release date / Country:
Jun 95 (first issued 28 Mar 95) / Germany
Track details:
Side 1, track 2 / 5 min. 41 sec.
Composer:
E. Stewart - [P. McCartney]
Recording Location / Date:
Eric Stewart's home studios in Wittersham & Bethersden, Kent, U.K. & Templar Studios, Lot et Garonne, France / fall 1987, Mar 89 & 1994

Eric Stewart: Lead Vocals, Lead Guitar & Percussion; Paul McCartney: Strings, Electric Piano, Frog Crickets & Percussion; Adrian Lee: all Programming

Song 364b title:
Yvonne's The One
Release date / Country:
Jun 95 / Germany
Track details:
Side 1, track 1 / 4 min. 26 sec.
Composer:
P. McCartney - E. Stewart
Recording Location / Date:
Templar Studios, France / 1993

Eric Stewart: Lead Vocals, Lead & Rhythm Guitar, Keyboards & Percussion; Adrian Lee: Bass, Programming & Arrangements

10cc originally consisted of Kevin Godley, born October 7, 1945, Lawrence "Lol" Creme, born September 17, 1947 *(see Godley & Creme)*, Eric Stewart, born January 20, 1945 and Graham Gouldman, born May 10, 1946 – all from Manchester, England. Gouldman, Creme and Godley attended the same school, and were members of a local Jewish Alliance Brigade.

Stewart was a member of the group Wayne Fontana & The Mindbenders. The group earned New Musical Express magazine's Annual Poll-Winners' Award for their hit song ***The Game Of Love***. It was during their appearance at the Poll-Winners' All-Star Concert at Empire Pool, Wembley (London) on April 11, 1965, that they formally met The Beatles. Fontana left the group before The Mindbenders' 1966 international smash hit ***Groovy Kind Of Love***, on which Stewart sang lead vocals.

Graham Gouldman sat in with The Mindbenders briefly during their final days in 1968, though he never considered himself a member of the group. Gouldman is best known as a successful songwriter, with a number of top 10 songs to his credit including ***For Your Love*** and ***Heart Full Of Soul*** (The Yardbirds), ***Look Through Any Window*** and ***Bus Stop*** (The Hollies), and ***No Milk Today*** (Herman's Hermits). Stewart, along with Godley and Creme, formed the band Hotlegs, who had a big hit with the song ***Neanderthal Man*** in 1970. They later teamed up with Gouldman and renamed themselves 10cc (1cc more than the amount in a typical male ejaculation) to indicate they were above average.

10cc's first hit was the song ***Donna*** (which sounds more than a little like The Beatles' song ***Oh! Darling***) for Jonathan King's UK Records. Stewart says the song is actually based on, and a tribute to, "doo-wop" groups from the 1950s. The Beatles' Apple Records label had previously considered signing the group, but they were apparently turned down by Ringo. Their well-crafted albums – along with hit songs like ***Wall Street Shuffle*** and ***I'm Not In Love*** – earned them a cult following. Godley and Creme left 10cc in 1976 to concentrate on inventing new musical devices (the "Gizmo"). They were also pioneers in the production of music videos.

The "Gizmo," or "Gysmorchestra" as it was apparently called in 1974, was used on Mike "McGear" McCartney's album ***McGear** *(see Mike McGear, The Scaffold)*, produced by Paul McCartney. The album was recorded at 10cc's Strawberry Studios in Stockport, U.K. (The studio was so named because ***Strawberry Fields Forever*** was one of Stewart's favorite Beatles songs.) Helping out were members of 10cc, who were recording their album ***Sheet Music*** at the studio. The Autumn 1994 issue No. 71 of Paul McCartney's Club Sandwich fan-club magazine stated that Paul made no official contribution to the album, and that no one could remember if he gave any unofficial assistance. Stewart remembers, "We had the studio during the day and Paul had it at night. Paul did not contribute to any of our recordings then, but it was very inspiring to have him around." Graham Gouldman also said McCartney did not contribute to any of 10cc's recordings during the ***McGear** sessions, but they did share each other's instruments.

Stewart and Gouldman carried on as 10cc with added personnel making the top 10 with the songs ***The Things We Do For Love*** in 1977 and ***Dreadlock Holiday*** the following year. In early 1981, Stewart did session work on Paul McCartney's album **Tug Of War**. He essentially became a band member for five years, helping McCartney record the album **Pipes Of Peace** and the soundtrack to **Give My Regards To Broad Street**, as well as appearing in the film. Stewart helped compose many of the songs for McCartney's 1986 album **Press To Play**.

By 1983, 10cc had fallen apart, but in 1991 Stewart and Gouldman reunited and recorded the album **Meanwhile**, which included guest appearances by Godley and Creme, and gave special thanks to Paul McCartney. The album featured the song ***Don't Break The Promises***, originally written by McCartney and Stewart during the **Press To Play** period, and later rewritten by Gouldman. McCartney featured a portion of his and Stewart's reggae-styled demo of the song, along with 10cc's version, on his 1995 radio series **Oobu Joobu**. McCartney finally released the full version of the demo, titled as ***Don't Break The Promise***, in 1997.

In 1995, 10cc toured to support their album of odds and ends titled **Mirror Mirror**, that included the song ***Code Of Silence***, to which McCartney contributed. Stewart said, "In the fall of 1987 I was living in Wittersham, Kent not far from McCartney's residence. After a very heavy lunch with Paul, he felt like doing some recording in my home studio and we ended up with the backing track of ***Code Of Silence*** that is pure McCartney. He played some cricket sounds and things like that; it was all Midi instruments. I was really excited about the song. In March of '89, I was living in a house in Bethersden, Kent and Paul dropped in and sang lead vocals on a version of the song. (By then, I had written lyrics for the song.) We never used the song on anything at the time so I used the backing for the **Mirror Mirror** album and recorded new vocals at my home studio in France. I rang Paul up and said I was going to release ***Code Of Silence*** and would like to give him credit as one of the writers but he told me to take full credit." The U.K. and Japanese versions additionally included ***Yvonne's The One***, also written by McCartney and Stewart during the **Press To Play** period. Stewart said McCartney did not play rhythm guitar on 10cc's recording of ***Yvonne's The One***, as credited. The song was inspired by a postcard Pink Floyd's drummer Nick Mason had sent Stewart. McCartney and Stewart's version of the recording is available on several bootleg CDs.

Guthrie Thomas

Record 365 title:
Hobo Eagle Thief
Media:
Album 5" CD
Label / Catalog number:
Sawdust/Line / SDCD 9.00915
Producer:
Guthrie Thomas & Larry Hirsch for Sarah Maris Productions
Jacket / Inserts:
Unique / 8 page CD booklet
Recording Location / Date:
(probably) Cherokee or (possibly) Paramount Studios, Los Angeles, CA, U.S.A. / (probably) 1977

Song 365a title:
Captain Jack
Track details:
Side 1, track 2 / 4 min. 19 sec.
Release date / Country:
1990 (first issued 1985) / Germany
Composer:
G. Thomas

Guthrie Thomas: Lead Vocals & Acoustic Guitars; Marc Edelsen: Guitar & B. Vocals; Mark Dawson: Harmonica & B. Vocals; Byron Berline: Mandolin; Jim Keltner (probable) Drums; Ringo Starr: Drums; Lee Montgomery: B. Vocals; Lyle Ritz or Bob Glob: Bass; David Foster: Organ; Sonny Garrish: Pedal Steel Guitar; Larry Hirsch: Percussion or Celeste or Glockenspiel

Song 365b title:
Carolyn And Benjamin
Track details:
Side 1, track 1 / 3 min. 56 sec.
Release date / Country:
1990 (first issued 1985) / Germany
Composer:
G. Thomas - M. Edelsen

Guthrie Thomas: Vocals & Acoustic Guitar; Marc Edelsen: Vocals; Jesse Ed Davis: Guitar; Byron Berline: Mandolin; Jim Keltner (probable) Drums; Ringo Starr: (probable) Drums; Lee Montgomery: B. Vocals; Lyle Ritz or Bob Glob: Bass; Sonny Garrish: Pedal Steel Guitar; Larry Hirsch: Synthesizer

Song 365c title:
If You Want Me To
Track details:
Side 1, track 8 / 4 min. 05 sec.
Release date / Country:
1990 (first issued 1985) / Germany
Composer:
G. Thomas

Guthrie Thomas: Lead Vocals & Acoustic Guitar; Marc Edelsen: Rhythm Guitar & B. Vocals; Mark Dawson: Harmonica; Jim Keltner: Drums; Ringo Starr: (possible) Drums; Lyle Ritz: Bass; Bob Glob: Bass; Jesse Ed Davis: Electric Guitar; Sonny Garrish: Pedal Steel Guitar; Skip Conover: Dobro Guitar

Song 365d title:
Ship Of Fools
Track details:
Side 1, track 4 / 3 min. 59 sec.
Release date / Country:
1990 (first issued 1985) / Germany
Composer:
G. Thomas

Guthrie Thomas: Lead Vocals & Acoustic Guitar; Marc Edelsen: Rhythm Guitar & B. Vocals; Mark Dawson: Harmonica & B. Vocals; John Hartford: Fiddle; Byron Berline: Fiddle; Jim Keltner: Drums; Ringo Starr: Drums; Lee Montgomery: B. Vocals; Lyle Ritz: Bass; Bob Glob: Bass; David Paich:

Piano; Jesse Ed Davis: Electric Guitar; Sonny Garrish: Pedal Steel Guitar; Nicolette Larson: B. Vocals

Song 365e title: Wake Up
Release date / Country: 1990 (first issued 1985) / Germany
Track details: Side 1, track 3 / 4 min. 11 sec.
Composer: G. Thomas - M. Edelsen

Guthrie Thomas: Lead Vocals & Acoustic Guitar; Jesse Ed Davis: Guitar; Marc Edelsen: (probable) B. Vocals; Mark Dawson: (probable) B. Vocals; Ringo Starr: Drums; Jim Keltner: (probable) Drums; Lee Montgomery: B. Vocals; Lyle Ritz or Bob Glob: Bass; David Paich &/or David Foster: Keyboards; Tom Cherry: Tenor Saxophone

Record 366 title: Lies And Alibis
Label / Catalog number: Capitol / ST-11519
Jacket / Inserts: Unique / Custom inner-sleeve with photos of Ringo Starr
Recording Location / Date: Capitol Records Studios, Los Angeles, CA, U.S.A. / Feb 76
Media: Album 12"
Producer: Guthrie Thomas & John Carter

Song 366a title: Band Of Steel
Release date / Country: 03 May 76 / U.S.A.
Track details: Side 1, track 3 / 5 min. 20 sec.
Composer: R. [Starkey] Starr

Guthrie Thomas: Lead Vocals & Acoustic Guitar; Ringo Starr: Drums & B. Vocals; Jim Keltner: Drums; Lyle Ritz: Bass; John Hartford: Fiddle; Roger Johnson: Electric Guitar; David Paich: Piano; Steve Cropper: B. Vocals; Lee Montgomery: B. Vocals; Tom Brumley: Pedal Steel

Song 366b title: Fifty-Five
Release date / Country: 03 May 76 / U.S.A.
Track details: Side 1, track 1 / 3 min. 55 sec.
Composer: G. Thomas - M. Edelsen

Guthrie Thomas: Lead Vocals & Lead Acoustic Guitar; John Hartford: Fiddles; David Foster: Piano; Ringo Starr: Drums; Jim Keltner: Drums; David Paich: Organ; Roger Johnson: Electric Guitar; Mark Dawson: Harmonica & B. Vocals; Lyle Ritz: Bass; Marc Edelsen: Acoustic Guitar; Renee Armand: B. Vocals; Brooks Cropper: B. Vocals; Lee Montgomery: B. Vocals

Song 366c title: For Awhile
Release date / Country: 03 May 76 / U.S.A.
Track details: Side 1, track 4 / 4 min. 42 sec.
Composer: G. Thomas

Guthrie Thomas: Lead Vocals & Lead Acoustic Guitar; David Foster: Organ; Ringo Starr: (probable) Drums; Jim Keltner: Drums; David Paich: Piano; Roger Johnson: Electric Guitar; Mark Dawson: Harmonica; Lyle Ritz: Bass; Marc Edelsen: Acoustic Guitar; Renee Armand: B. Vocals; Brooks Cropper: B. Vocals; Lee Montgomery: B. Vocals

Song 366d title: Good Days Are Rollin' In
Release date / Country: 03 May 76 / U.S.A.
Track details: Side 1, track 2 / 3 min. 24 sec.
Composer: G. Thomas

Guthrie Thomas: Lead Vocals & Lead Acoustic Guitar; Ringo Starr: Drums; Jim Keltner: Drums; Lyle

Ritz: Bass; Roger Johnson: Electric Guitar; Marc Edelsen: Acoustic Rhythm Guitar; David Foster: Piano; David Paich: Organ; Mark Dawson: B. Vocals; Brooks Cropper: B. Vocals; Renee Armand: B. Vocals

Song 366e title:
Ramblin' Cocaine Blues
Release date / Country:
03 May 76 / U.S.A.
Track details:
Side 2, track 5 / 4 min. 42 sec.
Composer:
L. Jordan - G. Thomas

Guthrie Thomas: Lead Vocals & Acoustic Guitar; Ringo Starr: Drums & (probable) B. Vocals; Jim Keltner: Drums; Lyle Ritz: Bass; John Hartford: Fiddle; Roger Johnson: Electric Guitar; David Paich: Organ; Dave Foster: Piano; Lee Montgomery: B. Vocals; Mark Dawson: B. Vocals; Nicolette Larson: B. Vocals; Bill Herring: B. Vocals; David Jackson: B. Vocals; Denny Brooks: B. Vocals; Ginny Vick: B. Vocals

Song 366f title:
Yesterdays & Tomorrows
Release date / Country:
03 May 76 / U.S.A.
Track details:
Side 2, track 2 / 3 min. 38 sec.
Composer:
G. Thomas

Guthrie Thomas: Lead Vocals & Acoustic Guitar; John Hartford: Fiddles; David Foster: Piano; Ringo Starr: Drums; Jim Keltner: Drums; Mark Dawson: Harmonica; Lyle Ritz: Bass; Ginny Vick: Tambourine; Tom Brumley: Pedal Steel Guitar

Guthrie Thomas was born on January 6, 1952 in Wichita Falls, Texas, but was raised in Oklahoma. Thomas began making guitars at the age of fifteen. His heroes were Dylan Thomas and Woody Guthrie, so he adopted their names. Thomas is a traditional folk singer whose musical style is sometimes described as a cross between Gordon Lightfoot's folk and Waylon Jennings' country. His musical mentor was Ramblin' Jack Elliott. The two became friends when Elliott fell in love with one of Thomas' guitars. Thomas self-depreciatingly refers to himself as a dumb Okie. Guthrie however, is anything but dumb. He has recorded over two dozen albums, and when he is not touring Europe where he is still in demand, he is a practicing pharmacologist.

Thomas had become acquainted with Hoyt Axton in the mid-1970s through their mutual friend Jack Elliott. It was during the taping of a Hoyt Axton TV special in Los Angeles that Guthrie first met Ringo. Guthrie handed Ringo a copy of his album **Sittin' Crooked** following the taping. Subsequently, Arlo Guthrie (Woody Gutherie's son) and Hoyt Axton put in a good word to Ringo about Thomas. Ringo was impressed with Thomas' simple country and folk songwriting, and, within weeks, Ringo contacted Capitol Records and arranged for Thomas to be signed to the label. The two became good friends, and Thomas became a regular guest at Ringo's home in Los Angeles.

Thomas asked Ringo to play drums on **Guthrie Thomas I**, but Ringo was busy at the time. Ringo, without whose help the album would not have been possible, was given special thanks in the credits. Ironically, the album was shelved by Capitol two days after its release, according to Thomas, because he was hired as the musical director for the film **Bound For Glory**, about the life of Woody Guthrie. Thomas also played the role of Woody Guthrie's brother in the film.

Guthrie asked Ringo if he would be interested in drumming on his second album for Capitol, **Lies And Alibis**. Ringo gladly accepted, and was credited as playing drums on ***Band of Steel***, ***Good Days Are Rollin' In*** and ***Ramblin' Cocaine Blues***. According to Thomas, Ringo also played drums on ***Yesterdays & Tomorrows***. Guthrie also thought Ringo probably played on ***For Awhile*** and sang backing vocals on ***Ramblin' Cocaine Blues***. ***Band Of Steel***, written by Ringo, was originally intended for Starr's country album **Beaucoups Of Blues**. Ringo was also given thanks in the album's credits.

The only other Guthrie Thomas album that Ringo contributed to was **Hobo Eagle Thief**. (The album was titled **Like No Other** in Italy, and **Once In Awhile** in Germany.) On **Like No Other** there is a picture of Ringo in the album booklet, along with the quote "I hope you are for me too." **Hobo Eagle Thief** was issued on CD in Germany in 1990. Though specific musical credits for each song are not given, Guthrie seems quite certain Ringo drummed on ***Captain Jack***, ***Ship Of Fools***, ***Wake Up*** and probably ***Carolyn And Benjamin*** and ***If You Want Me To***. Again Jim Keltner was on board for the sessions, as well as veteran session drummer Jim Gordon.

Ringo is also thanked on Guthrie Thomas' albums **Kidnapped** and **This One's For Sarah**. According to Thomas, Ringo did not play on these albums but is thanked for his support and friendship over the years. Guthrie Thomas summed up his thoughts on Ringo saying "One of the nicest people I ever met in the business, and certainly the most generous, was Richard Starkey."

Thornton, Fradkin & Unger And The Big Band

Record 367 title:
Godz Bless California [originally titled - Pass On This Side]

Label / Catalog number:
ESP-DISK/ZYX-Music / ESP 3019-2

Jacket / Inserts:
Unique in Jewel box / 20 page CD booklet

Recording Location / Date:
Sound Exchange or (possibly) A&R Studios, New York, NY, U.S.A. / Jan 71

Media:
Album 5" CD

Producer:
Leslie Fradkin

Song 367a title:
God Bless California

Release date / Country:
(probably) 1993 (first issued 17 Jun 74) / Germany

Track details:
Side 1, track 1 / 3 min. 36 sec.

Composer:
L. Fradkin

Leslie Fradkin: Lead Vocals & Guitar; Paul Thornton: Guitar & B. Vocals; Bob Unger: B. Vocals; Paul McCartney: Bass & B. Vocals; Randy Edelman: Piano & B. Vocals; Denny Seiwell: Drums; Linda McCartney: B. Vocals

Paul McCartney was in New York in January 1971 to record some songs for what would evolve into his album **Ram**. McCartney's first task was to look for some musicians to back him. He began auditioning some of the city's top studio musicians, among them drummer Denny Seiwell.

It was reported that Seiwell brought Paul and Linda *(see Linda McCartney)* to Leslie Fradkin's recording session. Apparently, two songs were recorded, ***God Bless California*** and ***Black Gypsy***. Both recordings reportedly include contributions by McCartney on bass and on backing vocals along with wife Linda. The recording's credits list Seiwell and Paul and Linda as contributing to ***God Bless California***. Seiwell, however, said, "I did not take Paul and Linda to Leslie Fradkin's session. I don't remember Leslie Fradkin, but it sounds like me on drums on ***God Bless California***." Bob Unger, Randy Edelman and Paul Thornton, from the pre-punk group Godz, are also credited as contributing to ***God Bless California***. The song was not released until three years later on an obscure album titled **Pass On This Side** (ESP-DISK / ESP 63019), reissued on CD in Germany in 1993. ***Black Gypsy*** has yet to see the light of day. In 1977, Fradkin played the part of George Harrison in the Broadway stage musical **Beatlemania**. Leslie Fradkin was also a member of David Peel's* Apple Band.

Tibetan Chants

Record 368 title:
[None]
Label / Catalog number:
Apple
Producer:
John Lennon
Recording Location / Date:
Record Plant (East) Studios, New York, NY, USA / 16 Dec 71

Song 368a title:
Tantric Lamas Part I
Release date / Country:
[Unreleased]
Composer:
(probably) Tibetan Chants

Tibetan Chants: Vocals

Song 368b title:
Tantric Lamas Part II
Release date / Country:
[Unreleased]
Composer:
(probably) Tibetan Chants

Tibetan Chants: Vocals

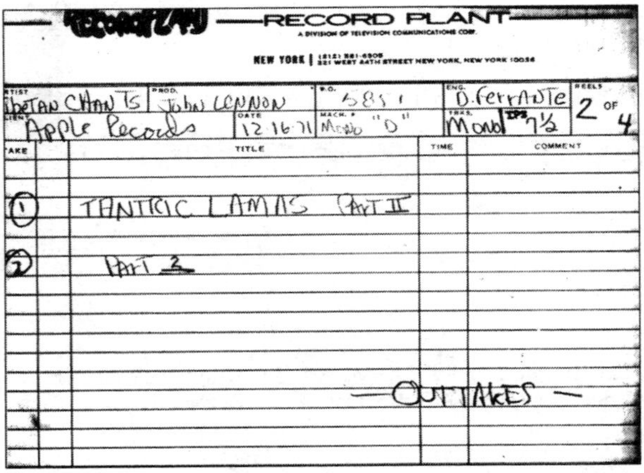

Record Plant Studios tape box cover for "Tantric Lamas", courtesy of Roy Cicala

Yet another unreleased recording found in the old Record Plant's (East) tape library with John Lennon's name listed on it as producer. The client is listed as Apple Records. Dennis Ferrante, the recording engineer for these sessions, seems to think they are an outgrowth of the David Peel* sessions for the LP **The Pope Smokes Dope**. He said Tibetan Chants consisted of a group of about 25-30 people that David had brought in off the streets of New York City to sing chants. That was about as much as Ferrante could remember. David Peel, however, knows nothing about these sessions, or who Tibetan Chants were. These recordings, which are marked "out-takes" on the tape box, may have been nothing more than incidental sounds scheduled for use on **The Pope Smokes Dope** LP. Other tapes marked "David Peel Talk Tracks" and "David Peel Laugh Tracks," probably intended for use on his album, were also discovered in the old Record Plant (East) tape library. Lenny Mars, who played extensively on the sessions for Peel, also remembers one of the studio's recording engineers spending a full day wandering around the streets of New York City trying to get traffic sounds for use on the Peel album. Mars said they ended up using a sound effects record. According to May Pang, John and Yoko put their names to many things during this period that they did not have hands-on involvement in producing *(see Indian Mosk)*.

Timon

Record 369 title:
[None]
Label / Catalog number:
Apple
Producer:
Peter Asher
Recording Location / Date:
(possibly) Trident Studios, London / (probably) 1968

Song 369a title:
Something New Everyday
Release date / Country:
[Unreleased]

Timon: Lead Vocals; Paul McCartney: (possible) Piano

Bill Harry's book **The Encyclopedia Of Beatles People** states a Liverpool area singer who went by the name of Timon recorded a song produced by Peter Asher *(see Peter & Gordon)* for Apple Records called ***Something New Everyday***, on which Paul McCartney played piano. Asher said, "I did produce a couple of tracks with Timon, but I don't remember much about it. I just went in and cut a couple of demos with the guy to decide whether we (Apple) were going to sign him, and we didn't. I don't remember the studio, but it might have been Trident. I'm not sure who played on it, but I don't recall McCartney being involved; it's possible but I think would have remembered that!" Harry's book says George Harrison was not impressed with Timon's recordings so they were never released.

T. Rex

Record 370 title:
Born To Boogie
Media:
Album 12" LVD
Label / Catalog number:
VAP / VPRL-70161
Producer:
Tony Visconti (music); Ringo Starr: Production & Director (film)
Jacket / Inserts:
Standard international design with variations / Credit insert

Song 370a title:
Children Of The Revolution
Track details:
Side 1, track 5 / 3 min. 40 sec.
Release date / Country:
1991 (first issued 18 Dec 72) / Japan
Composer:
M. Bolan
Recording Location / Date:
Apple Studios, London, U.K. / Mar - Apr 72

Marc Bolan: Lead Vocals, Electric & Acoustic Guitar; Ringo Starr: Drums; Elton John: Piano; Steve Currie: Bass; Mickey Finn: Percussion; Bill (Fifield) Legend: Drums; Tony Visconti: B. Vocals

Song 370b title:
I Looked To The Left
Track details:
Side 1, track 5 / 0 min. 18 sec.
Release date / Country:
1991 (first issued 18 Dec 72) / Japan
Composer:
M. Bolan
Recording Location / Date:
On location at Tittenhurst Park, Ascot, U.K. / Mar - Apr 72

Marc Bolan: Lead Vocals & Acoustic Guitar; Ringo Starr: B. Vocals

Also available on (The Soundtrack Of The Motion Picture) Born To Boogie / Marc On Wax / MARC LP 514 / Album 12" [2 LP set] / L2P Side 4, track 2 / issued 04 Nov 91 / U.K. / Unique with Gatefold with photo of Ringo Starr / 16 page booklet

Song 370c title:
Tutti-Frutti
Release date / Country:
1991 (first issued 18 Dec 72) / Japan
Recording Location / Date:
Apple Studios, London, U.K. / Mar - Apr 72

Track details:
Side 1, track 4 / 1 min. 20 sec.
Composer:
M. Bolan

Marc Bolan: Lead Vocals & Electric Guitar; Ringo Starr: Drums; Elton John: Piano; Steve Currie: Bass; Mickey Finn: Percussion; Bill (Fifield) Legend: Drums; Tony Visconti: B. Vocals

Marc Bolan was born Mark Feld on September 30, 1947 in London, England. He began his show business career as a child actor, but first gained notice as a male model on the mod scene in England in the early 1960s. He was also part poet, painter, performer, and songwriter. After several name changes, he settled on Marc Bolan, recording as a solo artist for Decca before moving to EMI Records. Failing as a solo artist, he joined the psychedelic / glam-rock band John's Children, but the band was short-lived. He also caught the attention of The Beatles with his paintings in their Apple Boutique.

Bolan next formed the poetic and folk-oriented Tyrannosaurus Rex, with Steve Took on percussion, and hooked up with producer Tony Visconti *(see Mary Hopkin)*. Though they appealed to the flower power crowd, they had limited commercial success, especially in the U.S. Took was replaced in late 1969 by Mickey Finn, born June 3, 1947 in Thornton Heath, England. Bolan shortened the group's name to T. Rex in 1970, and they had a number two hit in the U.K. with ***Ride A White Swan*** toward the end of the year. By 1971, T. Rex also included Steve Curry, born May 20, 1947 in Grimsby, England, on bass and drummer Bill (Fifield) Legend, born on May 8, 1944 in Barking, England. In 1971, their songs ***Hot Love*** and ***Get It On*** topped the charts in the U.K., and ***Jeepster*** was a number two there.

1972 was the year of "T. Rextasy" in the U.K. The band played to record crowds, and scored on the charts with the songs ***Metal Guru***, ***Telegram Sam***, ***Children Of The Revolution*** and ***Bang A Gong (Get It On)***, which was their only major hit in the U.S. Bolan was the darling of the glitter rock scene, and the heartthrob of U.K. teeny-boppers. His party buddy, Ringo Starr, offered to document the mini Beatlemania-like atmosphere surrounding Bolan. The result was **Born To Boogie**, the Apple Film that premiered in London on December 18, 1972 with Ringo in attendance. Not only did Starr produce the project, he directed it, appeared and performed in it, and personally shot some of the footage! The film had a limited release, and became a cult classic among T. Rex fans.

Marc Bolan, Detroit, MI, mid-1970s, photo courtesy of Tom Bert

In 1992, Apple released **Born To Boogie** on video. An accompanying soundtrack album was released by Marc On Wax Records. The vinyl album featured Ringo singing backing vocals on ***I Look To The Left***, some of his dialogue with Bolan from the film, and a photo of Ringo. Unfortunately, it omitted the Apple Studio jam recordings of ***Tutti-Frutti*** and ***Children Of The Revolution*** that included Ringo on drums and Elton John* on keyboards. It was also released on CD (MARCCD / 514), but without the photo of Ringo. The film also included a cameo by Keith Moon*. Most of the film and soundtrack were recorded at a T-Rex concert at Wembley Empire Pool on March 18, 1972; the grounds of Tittenhurst Park, Ascot, a home of both John Lennon and Ringo Starr; and at Apple Records recording studios in London. Ringo was also in costume to play the part of the mouse in the picture. The total time of Ringo's appearances in the approximately 75-minute film is a little over ten minutes.

Bolan and T. Rex's most successful album, **The Slider**, featured front and back jacket photographs credited to Ringo. However, T. Rex producer Tony Visconti maintains he took the photographs! Visconti recalls, "**The Slider** photos were taken by me during a long day of shooting the Mad Hatter's tea party sequence (from **Born To Boogie**) at John Lennon's house. Ringo was very busy organizing each new shot, and of course we were all bored with nothing to do. During one of the long shot setups, Marc handed me his new Nikon 35mm camera. He was wearing his leather top hat and asked me to shoot a couple of rolls of him wearing the hat, front and back shots. Ringo never went near that Nikon that day; he was too busy! Months later **The Slider** came out with my photos on the front and back cover. But Marc, conveniently 'remembered' that Ringo took those photos, always the opportunist! I did confront him too late, but I never saw the art work until the album was on the market! He apologized, but it was too late to change credits. That's the story. I would be interested to hear Ringo's version." Bolan sings about John Lennon on ***Ballrooms Of Mars*** from **The Slider**.

Ringo's 1972 hit, ***Back Off Boogaloo*** ("Boogaloo" is not a nickname for Paul McCartney), was rumored to have been written by Bolan. Though the lyrics were inspired by a conversation with Bolan, the song was written by Ringo. By 1973, the fame and fortune that had struck so quickly began to fade, and Bolan was a little too preoccupied enjoying the excesses of the rock 'n' roll lifestyle. He contributed guitar on the song ***Have You Seen My Baby (Hold On)***, from the highly successful album **Ringo**. Several personnel changes were made in T. Rex, including the addition of three female backing vocalists. One of them, American soul singer Gloria Jones, became Bolan's girlfriend until his death in a car she was driving on September 16, 1977.

There has been speculation over the years concerning possible contributions by Ringo to other Bolan recordings. **Zinc Alloy And The Hidden Riders Of Tomorrow** and the U.S. compilation album release titled **Light Of Love** thank "Bingo Ringo." The album **Tanx** includes a photo of Ringo. Visconti (who produced the vast majority of Bolan's recordings during this period) said, "Marc was such an opportunist, he would have screamed it from the rooftops if Ringo played on his albums; it never happened!" In 1983, Ringo made an appearance in a TV retrospective on the career of Bolan.

Doris Troy

Record 371 title:
Doris Troy

Media:
Album 5" CD

Label / Catalog number:
Apple / CDP 7 98701 2

Jacket / Inserts:
Standard international design in jewel box / 8 page CD booklet

Song 371a title:
Ain't That Cute

Track details:
Side 1, track 1 / 3 min. 52 sec.

Release date / Country:
30 Jun 92 (first issued 13 Feb 70) / U.S.A.

Composer:
G. Harrison - D. Troy

Producer:
George Harrison

Recording Location / Date:
Trident & (possibly) Apple Studios, London, U.K. / Oct 69

Doris Troy: Lead Vocals; Eric Clapton: (possible) Guitar; George Harrison: Guitar; Bill Moody: (probable) Drums; Berry Morgan (possible) Drums; Ringo Starr: (possible) Drums; Daryl Runswick: (probable) Bass; Klaus Voormann: (possible) Bass; Bobby Keys: Saxophone; Jim Price: Trumpet; Reg Powell: Piano; Billy Preston: Keyboards & B. Vocals; Peter Frampton: Guitar; Delaney Bramlett: (probable) B. Vocals; Madeline Bell: (probable) B. Vocals; Eliza Strike: (probable) B. Vocals; Nanette Workman: (probable) B. Vocals

Song 371b title:
All That I've Got
Release date / Country:
30 Jun 92 / U.S.A.
Producer:
Doris Troy & (possibly) George Harrison
Recording Location / Date:
One or more of the following studios: Trident, Apple &/or EMI-Abbey Road, London, U.K. / Oct 69 - Jul 70
Track details:
Side 1, track 14 / 3 min. 55 sec.
Composer:
D. Troy - B. Preston

Doris Troy: Lead Vocals & (probable) Keyboards; probably one or more of the following: Keyboards; Leon Russell: Keyboards; Gary Wright: Keyboards; Klaus Voormann: Bass; Carl Radle: Bass; Ringo Starr: Drums; Alan White: Drums; Jim Gordon: Drums

Song 371c title:
Dearest Darling
Release date / Country:
30 Jun 92 / U.S.A.
Producer:
Doris Troy & (possibly) George Harrison
Recording Location / Date:
One or more of the following studios: Trident, Apple &/or EMI-Abbey Road, London, U.K. / Oct 69 - Jul 70
Track details:
Side 1, track 16 / 2 min. 50 sec.
Composer:
D. Troy

Doris Troy: Lead Vocals & (probable) Keyboards; probably one or more of the following: George Harrison: Guitar; Ringo Starr; Drums; Alan White: Drums; Jim Gordon: Drums; Klaus Voormann: Bass; Carl Radle: Bass; Gary Wright: Keyboards; Leon Russell: Keyboards; Billy Preston: Keyboards; Bobby Keys: Saxophone; Jim Price: Horns

Song 371d title:
Don't Call Me No More
Release date / Country:
30 Jun 92 (first issued 11 Sep 70) / U.S.A.
Producer:
Doris Troy & (possibly) George Harrison
Recording Location / Date:
Trident &/or Apple Studios, London, U.K. / Oct 69
Track details:
Side 1, track 12 / 2 min. 05 sec.
Composer:
D. Troy - R. Schinnery

Doris Troy: Vocals & (probable) Keyboards; Ray Schinnery: Vocals; Eric Clapton: Guitar; George Harrison: Guitar; Billy Preston (probable) Keyboards & B. Vocals; Ringo Starr: Drums; Klaus Voormann: Bass

Song 371e title:
Exactly Like You
Release date / Country:
30 Jun 92 (first issued 11 Sep 70) / U.S.A.
Producer:
Doris Troy & (possibly) George Harrison
Recording Location / Date:
One or more of the following studios: Trident, Apple &/or EMI-Abbey Road, London, U.K. / Oct 69 - Jul 70
Track details:
Side 1, track 10 / 3 min. 06 sec.
Composer:
J. McHugh - D. Fields

Doris Troy: Lead Vocals; Bill Moody: Drums; Reg Powell: Keyboards; Billy Preston: Keyboards;

Bobby Keys: (probable) Saxophone; Jim Price: (probable) Horns; Daryl Runswick: Bass

Song 371f title:
Games People Play
Release date / Country:
30 Jun 92 (first issued 11 Sep 70) / U.S.A.
Producer:
Doris Troy & (possibly) George Harrison
Recording Location / Date:
One or more of the following studios: Trident, Apple &/or EMI-Abbey Road, London, U.K. / Oct 69 - Jul 70
Track details:
Side 1, track 5 / 3 min. 04 sec.
Composer:
J. South

Doris Troy: Lead Vocals; Reg Powell: Keyboards; Billy Preston: Organ; George Harrison: (probable) B. Vocals; Delaney Bramlett: (probable) B. Vocals; Bill Moody: Drums; Daryl Runswick: Bass; Madeline Bell (probable) B. Vocals; Eliza Strike (probable) B. Vocals; Nanette Workman: (probable) B. Vocals

Song 371g title:
Get Back
Release date / Country:
30 Jun 92 (first issued 28 Aug 70) / U.S.A.
Producer:
Doris Troy & (possibly) George Harrison
Recording Location / Date:
One or more of the following studios: Trident, Apple &/or EMI-Abbey Road, London, U.K. / Oct 69
Track details:
Side 1, track 15 / 3 min. 06 sec.
Composer:
J. Lennon - P. McCartney

Doris Troy: Lead Vocals; Eric Clapton: Guitar; George Harrison: Guitar; Billy Preston: Keyboards; Klaus Voormann: Bass; Bobby Keys: Saxophone; Jim Price: Horns; Ringo Starr: Drums

Song 371h title:
Give Me Back My Dynamite
Release date / Country:
30 Jun 92 (first issued 11 Sep 70) / U.S.A.
Producer:
Doris Troy & (probably) George Harrison
Recording Location / Date:
Trident &/or Apple Studios, London, U.K. / Oct 69
Track details:
Side 1, track 3 / 4 min. 54 sec.
Composer:
G. Harrison - D. Troy

Doris Troy: Lead Vocals; Eric Clapton: Guitar; George Harrison: Guitar; Ringo Starr: Drums; Billy Preston: Keyboards; Klaus Voormann: Bass

Song 371i title:
Gonna Get My Baby Back
Release date / Country:
30 Jun 92 (first issued 11 Sep 70) / U.S.A.
Producer:
Doris Troy & (probably) George Harrison
Recording Location / Date:
One or more of the following studios: Trident, Apple &/or EMI-Abbey Road, London, U.K. / Oct 69 - Jul 70
Track details:
Side 1, track 6 / 2 min. 17 sec.
Composer:
G. Harrison - R. Starkey - D. Troy - S. Stills

Doris Troy: Lead Vocals; probably one or more of the following: Billy Preston: Keyboards; Klaus Voormann: Bass; Carl Radle: Bass; Jim Price: Horns; Bobby Keys: Saxophone; Ringo Starr: Drums; George Harrison: Guitar; Peter Frampton: Guitar; Stephen Stills: Guitar

Song 371j title:
I've Got To Be Strong
Release date / Country:
30 Jun 92 (first issued 11 Sep 70) / U.S.A.
Track details:
Side 1, track 7 / 2 min. 34 sec.
Composer:
J. Lomax - D. Troy

Producer:
Doris Troy & (possibly) George Harrison
Recording Location / Date:
Trident &/or Apple Studios, London, U.K. / Oct 69

Doris Troy: Lead Vocals; Eric Clapton: Guitar; George Harrison: Guitar; Ringo Starr: Drums; Billy Preston: Keyboards & B. Vocals; Gary Wright: Keyboards; Jim Price: (probable) Horns; Bobby Keys: Saxophone; Madeline Bell: (probable) B. Vocals; Eliza Strike: (probable) B. Vocals; Nanette Workman: (probable) B. Vocals

Song 371k title:
Jacob's Ladder [aka Soldier Of The Cross]
Track details:
Side 2, track 57 / 1 min. 13 sec.
Release date / Country:
30 Jun 92 (first issued 28 Aug 70) / U.S.A.
Composer:
Trad/Arr: G. Harrison - D. Troy
Producer:
Doris Troy & [George Harrison]
Recording Location / Date:
One or more of the following studios: Trident, Apple &/or EMI-Abbey Road, London, U.K. / Oct 69 - Jul 70

Doris Troy: Vocals & (probable) Keyboards; Delaney Bramlett: Vocals & (probable) Guitar; George Harrison: Arrangement & (possible) Guitar; probably one or more of the following: Leon Russell: Piano; Billy Preston: Keyboards; Madeline Bell: B. Vocals; Eliza Strike: B. Vocals; Nanette Workman: B. Vocals; Klaus Voormann: Bass; Carl Radle: Bass; Jim Gordon: Drums; Bobby Keys: Saxophone

Song 371l title:
So Far
Track details:
Side 1, track 9 / 4 min. 25 sec.
Release date / Country:
30 Jun 92 (first issued 11 Sep 70) / U.S.A.
Composer:
K. Voormann - D. Troy
Producer:
Doris Troy & (possibly) George Harrison
Recording Location / Date:
One or more of the following studios: Trident, Apple &/or EMI-Abbey Road, London, U.K. / Oct 69 - Jul 70

Doris Troy: Lead Vocals & (probable) Keyboards; probably one or more of the following: George Harrison: Guitar; Klaus Voormann: Bass; Ringo Starr: Drums; John Barham: Orchestral Arrangements; Billy Preston: Keyboards; Leon Russell: Keyboards; Peter Frampton: Guitar; Stephen Stills: Guitar; Jim Price: Horns; Madeline Bell: B. Vocals; Eliza Strike: B. Vocals; Nanette Workman: B. Vocals

Song 371m title:
Special Care
Track details:
Side 1, track 2 / 2 min. 57 sec.
Release date / Country:
30 Jun 92 (first issued 11 Sep 70) / U.S.A.
Composer:
S. Stills
Producer:
Doris Troy & (possibly) George Harrison
Recording Location / Date:
One or more of the following studios: Trident, Apple &/or EMI-Abbey Road, London, U.K. / Oct 69 - Jul 70

Doris Troy: Lead Vocals & (probable) Keyboards; probably one or more of the following: Stephen Stills: Guitar; Peter Frampton: Guitar; Jim Price: Horns; Bobby Keys: Saxophone; Leon Russell: Keyboards; Billy Preston: Keyboards & B. Vocals; Ringo Starr: Drums; Alan White: Drums; Jim Gordon: Drums; Klaus Voormann: Bass; Carl Radle: Bass

Song 371n title:
Vaya Con Dios
Track details:
Side 1, track 18 / 3 min. 29 sec.
Release date / Country:
30 Jun 92 (first issued 13 Feb 70) / U.S.A.
Composer:
L. Russell - James - Pepper

Producer:
Doris Troy & (possibly) George Harrison
Recording Location / Date:
One or more of the following studios: Trident, Apple &/or EMI-Abbey Road, London, U.K. / Oct 69 - Jul 70

Doris Troy: Lead Vocals; Billy Preston: Keyboards; Bill Moody: Drums; Daryl Runswick: Bass; Reg Powell: Keyboards; George Harrison (supposed) Guitar

Song 371o title:
What You Will Blues [Give Me Back My Dynamite (early backing track)]
Release date / Country:
30 Jun 92 / U.S.A.
Track details:
Side 1, track 17 / 4 min. 57 sec.
Composer:
D. Troy
Producer:
Doris Troy & (probably) George Harrison
Recording Location / Date:
One or more of the following studios: Trident, Apple &/or EMI-Abbey Road, London, U.K. / Oct 69 - Jul 70

Doris Troy: Lead Vocals; George Harrison: Voice & Guitar; Eric Clapton: Guitar; Ringo Starr: Drums; Billy Preston: Keyboards; Klaus Voormann: Bass

Song 371p title:
You Give Me Joy Joy
Release date / Country:
30 Jun 92 (first issued 11 Sep 70) / U.S.A.
Track details:
Side 1, track 11 / 3 min. 38 sec.
Composer:
D. Troy - G. Harrison - R. Starkey - S. Stills
Producer:
Doris Troy & (probably) George Harrison
Recording Location / Date:
Trident & (possibly) Apple Studios, London, U.K. / Oct 69

Doris Troy: Lead Vocals & Keyboards; Eric Clapton: Guitar; George Harrison: Guitar; Stephen Stills: Guitar; Peter Frampton: Guitar; Bobby Keys: Saxophone; Jim Price Horns; Klaus Voormann: Bass; Ringo Starr: Drums

Doris Troy was born Doris Higgensen in the Harlem district of New York City, New York on January 6, 1937. She is the daughter of a well-known Pentecostal minister who came to the U.S. from the island of Barbados, West Indies. Doris worked as an usherette at the famous Apollo Theater, and formed a musical nightclub act called the Halos. She also worked as a background singer for artists like Dionne Warwick, Cissy Houston, The Drifters, Solomon Burke, and Chuck Jackson. Her first love was jazz, though her successes came with West Indian-flavored R&B. She changed her last name to Troy after Helen Of Troy. She joined Atlantic Records in 1963, and in June of that year she had her claim-to-fame hit ***Just One Look***, that she co-wrote. In later years the song would also be a major hit for The Hollies and Linda Ronstadt, and be used extensively in commercials.

Troy made several trips to England in the mid-1960s, and appeared on a telecast of the popular-music TV show **Ready, Steady, Goes Live!** on April 16, 1965. Also appearing on that show were guests John Lennon, George Harrison and Adam Faith*, who sang together with Troy at the end of the show.

Troy moved to England in 1969. She, along with Madeline Bell, Eliza Strike and Nanette Workman, formed a group of back-up singers that were highly sought after by artists like Joe Cocker*, Eric Clapton*, The Scaffold*, Stephen Stills*, Carly Simon*, Billy Preston* and Gary Wright*.

It was her association with Preston, and her involvement on his first Apple album, produced by George Harrison, that landed her a deal with Apple Records as a staff songwriter, producer, and artist. Troy's first project for Apple was composing the music for an animated film titled **Timothy's Travels** that, according to Troy, contained no contributions by any of The Beatles. Troy appeared as a back-up singer in the promotional video for Ringo's ***Sentimental Journey***, and she sang on John

Lennon's ***Power To The People***.

The Beatles were together in name only by the end of 1969. Harrison, who had just finished touring with Delaney & Bonnie & Friends*, found much of their blue-eyed gospel band to be the perfect backing for Troy (and Harrison's album ***All Things Must Pass***). Not surprisingly, there is much debate and confusion concerning the exact musical line-up for each song on the **Doris Troy** album. The original vinyl album release did not list any of the musicians involved. A little more information was revealed with the CD release that states Delaney & Bonnie Bramlett were involved in the sessions. Doris vividly remembers Delaney's involvement, but seems fairly sure Bonnie was not present. Bonnie also does not recall being involved in the sessions. The CD liner notes also acknowledge contributions from Eric Clapton, Leon Russell*, Peter Frampton*, and Stephen Stills. According to Troy, the background vocals were supplied by Madeline Bell, Eliza Strike, and Nanette Workman, and other participants of the album's recordings that included Harrison. Drummer Alan White, who was also working with John Lennon and The Plastic Ono Band during this period, recalls drumming on many of the tracks for the album. However, White is fairly sure Jim Gordon drummed on ***Jacob's Ladder***. He also recalls Gary Wright and Klaus Voormann *(see Paul Jones)* playing on the sessions, and thinks Carl Radle played on one track. Troy wanted to do a Beatles' song and chose ***Get Back***, that she thinks George is probably on, as well as most of the other tracks on the album. To the best of her recollection, Klaus Voormann was on bass, Ringo was on drums, Billy Preston was on keyboards on most of the songs, and Stephen Stills played on a few tracks.

Mark Roberty states in his book **Eric Clapton The Complete Recording Sessions, 1963 - 1992**, that Clapton and Harrison play guitar, and Ringo plays drums on the following tracks recorded at Apple and Trident Studios in London – ***Ain't That Cute***, ***Give Me Back My Dynamite***, ***I've Got To Be Strong***, ***You Give Me Joy Joy***, ***Don't Call Me No More***, and ***Get Back***. Eric Clapton's guitar – especially on ***Give Me Back My Dynamite*** (aka ***What You Will Blues***), ***I've Got To Be Strong***, and ***You Give Me Joy Joy*** – is unmistakable. Harrison's guitar contributions are far less identifiable.

The CD liner notes state Peter Frampton plays guitar on the single ***Ain't That Cute***, while George Harrison plays guitar on the B-side, ***Vaya Con Dios***, however, the closest listen reveals no guitar on the B-side except for bass. It's certainly possible that Harrison might have played bass given that this was Troy's first record release for Apple, and that the A-side was co-written and produced by Harrison. Peter Frampton said, "It was my first meeting with a Beatle and I was walking on air. I walked into the control room at Trident Studios and George looked me straight in the eye and said, 'hello Pete.' I'd never met him before, but I was in The Herd and he knew who I was and said 'do you want to play?' He gave me a Les Paul guitar and I started playing rhythm on ***Ain't That Cute***. George stopped me and said, 'Pete, you don't understand; I play rhythm, you play lead!' That's when I developed the lead riff for that; that's not Clapton, that's me! Eric wasn't there when I was. George played rhythm and, as I remember, it was Berry Morgan of Morgan Studios on drums, but I'm not sure." (Frampton also recalls playing on about a half-dozen other songs on the album along with Klaus Voormann at Trident Studios, including ***You Give Me Joy Joy*** and probably ***Special Care***.) Troy recalls that during work on ***Ain't That Cute***, Harrison's mother died, and he left her to continue work on it, and other songs for the album. However, the song was one of the first worked on, and was released five months before Harrison's mother died!

According to Troy, the following musicians played on ***Ain't That Cute***, ***Vaya Con Dios***, ***Games People Play***, and ***Exactly Like You***: Bill Moody on drums, Daryl Runswick on bass and Reg Powell on piano. Bill Moody's recollections of the sessions left little doubt that he and these other musicians did indeed play on the **Doris Troy** album. However, Marc Roberty's book does not mention these musicians, or Frampton for that matter, on ***Ain't That Cute***, and lists a completely different line-up.

The CD liner notes claim (as do other sources including Troy) that Harrison plays guitar on ***Get Back***, though it sounds like Clapton playing both the lead and the rhythm break. It is possible that Harrison is buried in the mix or is doing a fairly good job of imitating Clapton in a trade-off. Troy insists that ***You Tore Me Up Inside***, and ***Hurry*** were recorded in the U.S. before her move to the U.K., which excludes any Beatles' involvement. (The CD liner notes only list ***Hurry*** as being recorded in the U.S.) She said the two songs were included on the album with George's blessing.

The overall credibility of the CD liner notes has to be questioned as a result of its attempt to pass off an early backing track of ***Give Me Back My Dynamite*** as a previously unreleased bonus track titled

What You Will Blues. The only bonus is that one can clearly hear Harrison counting off the song, confirming his presence during the recording of *Give Me Back My Dynamite*. *What You Will Blues* is credited as being composed solely by Troy, who confirmed that Harrison only helped write a few of the lyrics to *Give Me Back My Dynamite*.

It is probably safe to assume that George and Ringo play on those tracks that they helped compose. However, not all the drumming sounds like Ringo: if it is, this is one of his stronger and more diverse efforts. The songs that Harrison and Starr are listed as playing on are based on extensive listening, research, and interviews, but their presence cannot be verified with certainty. The musicians listed are not all-inclusive, or exclusive, for each song.

Doris Troy publicity photo, courtesy of Doris Troy

Doris Troy is listed as producer on all tracks except *Ain't That Cute*, produced by George Harrison. However, Doris recalls Harrison having a hand in much of the album's production, though she could not remember the specific tracks beyond *Jacob's Ladder*. George probably helped with the production of the songs he wrote, or on which he played. Doris said that Delaney Bramlett handled the duet vocals on *Jacob's Ladder*, though it's difficult to tell where Doris ends and Delaney begins. Delaney also thinks it sounds like him singing on *Jacob's Ladder*, and that he probably plays guitar on it because "it's too sloppy to be Eric Clapton." Delaney & Bonnie's version of *Soldier Of The Cross* (aka *Jacob's Ladder*), appears on their album **The Original Delaney & Bonnie – Accept No Substitute**. Doris said that Ray Schinnery, who helped her compose *Don't Call Me No More*, sang duet vocals with her on that song. Roberty's book does not list Schinnery, but does list Billy Preston on backing vocals.

Troy felt it was time to leave Apple records amidst all the chaos and changes that were taking place. Apple Records was brilliant at signing talent *(see Badfinger, Mary Hopkin, James Taylor, Jackie Lomax)*, but poor on follow-up promotion. Following the arrival of business manager Allen Klein, and the breakup of The Beatles, Apple became little more than a holding company and record label used exclusively for The Beatles.

Had Apple included the star-studded line-up on the jackets of the Doris Troy and Jackie Lomax albums, for example, they probably would have received the notice and chart success they justly deserved. Perhaps George Harrison, who was responsible for these albums, felt they should stand on their own merits without the benefit of promoting their superstar involvement. Aside from the Beatles' and their solo recordings, the **Doris Troy** album showcases arguably the best musicianship of Apple Records' recordings.

Following her departure from Apple, Troy continued to be in demand as a back-up session singer, and formed a group called The Gospel Truth, before returning to the U.S. in 1973. She continued to record, and worked extensively with Lola Falana in Las Vegas, where she now currently lives and performs. In 1984, she played the role of her mother in a stage production of her life story called **Mama I Want To Sing**. It has become one of the longest-running off-Broadway musicals with a black cast since the 1930s. Doris continues to tour with that musical. In 1994, a CD collection titled **Just One Look / The Best of Doris Troy** was released.

Ike & Tina Turner

Record 372 title:
River Deep And Mountain High
Label / Catalog number:
A&M / SP-4178
Jacket / Inserts:
Unique with George Harrison: Sticker message
Recording Location / Date:
Gold Star Studios, Los Angeles, CA, U.S.A. / Mar 66
Release date / Country:
13 Sep 69 / U.S.A.

Media:
Album 12"
Producer:
Phil Spector

Tina Turner: Lead Vocals

Ike and Tina Turner were a popular husband-and-wife rhythm & blues act in the 1960s. Ike was born Izear Turner Jr. on November 5, 1931 in Clarksdale, Mississippi. Ike spent his formative years in music backing blues players like Sonny Boy Williamson, Howlin' Wolf*, and B.B. King*. He played on the record ***Rocket 88***, often referred to as the first real rock 'n' roll song recorded at Sun Studios in Memphis, in 1951.

Ike met Tina (born Anna Mae Bullock on November 26, 1939 in Brownsville, Tennessee) while playing an engagement at a club in St. Louis in 1956. Several nights later, Tina got up and sang with the band. By 1958, Tina (as she was now called) fronted her new husband Ike's band. Their first single together was ***A Fool In Love***, which reached the top 40 in 1960. The following year they had a top 20 song, ***It's Gonna Work Out Fine***. Though they continued to be successful as a major rhythm & blues act during the first half of the 1960s, they failed to make much impact on the pop charts.

In 1966, Ike signed an agreement to turn over production of his act to legendary producer Phil Spector*. Not surprisingly, Spector, who produced primarily black female artists, was far more interested in the talents of Tina than Ike. He had her record the song ***River Deep, Mountain High***, then one of his most costly and ambitious productions. Spector was confident that the song would be his biggest success to date. Unfortunately, when the song barely broke the top 100 on the U.S. charts, Spector virtually shut down his Philles record label and went into temporary retirement. He ordered that all the pressings of the **River Deep Mountain High** album be destroyed.

The album would remain unreleased in the U.S. until 1969, when it was issued on A&M Records with a jacket sticker that read "'River Deep-Mountain High' is a perfect record from start to finish. You couldn't improve on it – George Harrison." However, the song reached the top 10 in the U.K. and, with the help of a spot on The Rolling Stones'* tour there, Ike and Tina Turner became major stars across Europe.

Tina Turner, Detroit, MI, 1970s, photo courtesy of Tom Bert

Ike and Tina continued to be a popular R&B stage act throughout the second half of the 1960s, and in 1969 they recorded covers of The Beatles' songs ***Come Together*** and ***Get Back***. Their big break on the U.S. charts did not come until 1971 with a cover of Creedence Clearwater Revival's *(see John Fogerty)* ***Proud Mary***. Ironically, the song was a flop in the U.K. where they were still very popular. The following year they released a cover of The Beatles' song ***With A Little Help From My Friends***. Their next big hit, 1973's ***Nutbush City Limits***, composed by Tina, was their last together.

Tina began trying to forge a solo career. She starred as the Acid Queen in the 1975 film adaptation of The Who's rock opera **Tommy**, and released her first solo album, **The Acid Queen**. Tina split from Ike in 1976, after years of physical abuse, and the two were later divorced. Tina recorded a solo version of ***Come Together*** for the soundtrack to the 1976 film **All This And World War II**. She also made a brief cameo appearance in Robert Stigwood's 1978 film **Sgt. Pepper's Lonely Hearts Club Band**.

The first few years after her split from Ike were a struggle, but old friends The Rolling Stones came to her rescue, and put her on their tour. She signed with Capitol Records, whose 1983 release of her cover of Al Green's song ***Let's Stay Together***, reached the top 10 in the U.K., and was a top 40 in the U.S. the following year. Her cover of The Beatles' song ***Help!*** reached the U.K. top 40 in 1984. That year her single ***What's Love Got To Do With It?***, and album **Private Dancer**, were both multi-million sellers. It marked the return of Tina Turner, and the height of her successful solo career.

The second half of the 1980s and beyond saw Tina doing duets with a number of rock legends, including Mick Jagger, Bryan Adams, Eric Clapton*, Rod Stewart* and Paul McCartney. Her duet with McCartney took place on June 20, 1986, at Wembley Arena for the annual **Prince's Trust All - Star Rock Concert**, when she joined Paul onstage to sing ***Get Back***. In 1989, Tina inducted Phil Spector into the Rock and Roll Hall of Fame, and in 1991 Ike (who was in jail at the time) and Tina were inducted as well. Tina's 1986 autobiography, **I Tina**, was adapted into the successful motion picture, **What's Love Got To Do With It**, in 1993. Since their split, Ike Turner has not enjoyed much success, though his 1997 album **My Bluescountry** received favorable reviews.

Lon & Derrek Van Eaton

Record 373 title:
Black & White
Label / Catalog number:
IBW / 398D
Jacket / Inserts:
Unique in Jewel box / 8 page CD booklet
Media:
Album 5" CD

Song 373a title:
Hold On
Release date / Country:
09 May 98 / U.S.A.
Producer:
Klaus Voormann
Recording Location / Date:
Sunset Sound Studios, Los Angeles, CA, U.S.A. / 1978
Track details:
Side 1, track 12 / 3 min. 19 sec.
Composer:
L. Van Eaton - D. Van Eaton

Derrek Van Eaton: Lead Vocals; Klaus Voormann: Bass, Guitar & B. Vocals; Cynthia Webb: B. Vocals; Ringo Starr: Drums; Lon Van Eaton: Keyboards, B. Vocals & Guitar; Carlos de la Paz: Guitar

Song 373b title:
My World Is Empty Without You
Release date / Country:
09 May 98 / U.S.A.
Producer:
Klaus Voormann
Recording Location / Date:
Sunset Sound Studios, Los Angeles, CA, U.S.A. / 1978
Track details:
Side 1, track 1 / 2 min. 41 sec.
Composer:
B. Holland - L. Dozier - E. Holland

Derrek Van Eaton: Lead Vocals; Klaus Voormann: Bass, Keyboards & Guitar; Ringo Starr: Drums; Lon Van Eaton: Keyboards & Guitar; Tom Seifert: Guitar

Song 373c title:
Ringo Ad (contains portions of: Sun Song/Maybe There's Another/Sweet Music)
Track details:
Side 1, track 1 / 0 min. 60 sec.
Release date / Country:
09 May 98 / U.S.A.
Recording Location / Date:
1972

Ringo: Dialogue; Derrek Van Eaton: Lead Vocals & Guitar; Ringo Starr: Drums & Tambourine; Jim Gordon: Drums; Mike Hugg: Harmonium; Peter Frampton: Guitar; Lon Van Eaton: Guitar, Saxophone, B. Vocals & Keyboards; Klaus Voormann: Bass

Record 374 title:
Brother
Media:
Album 12"
Label / Catalog number:
Apple / SMAS 3390
Jacket / Inserts:
Standard international design with Gatefold / Black inner sleeve & cutout assembly

Song 374a title:
Another Thought
Track details:
Side 2, track 5 / 3 min. 41 sec.
Release date / Country:
22 Sep 72 / U.S.A.
Composer:
L. Van Eaton - D. Van Eaton
Producer:
Klaus Voormann
Recording Location / Date:
Apple Studios, London, U.K. / Oct - Dec 71

Derrek Van Eaton: Lead Vocals; Ringo Starr: Drums; Klaus Voormann: Bass; T. J. Tindall: Guitar; Lon Van Eaton: Piano & Horn & String Arrangements

Song 374b title:
Sweet Music
Track details:
Side 1, track 6 / 3 min. 41 sec.
Release date / Country:
22 Sep 72 (first issued 06 Mar 72) / U.S.A.
Composer:
L. Van Eaton - D. Van Eaton
Producer:
George Harrison
Recording Location / Date:
EMI-Abbey Road & Apple Studios, London, U.K. / early Oct 71

Derrek Van Eaton: Lead Vocals & Guitar; Ringo Starr: Drums & Tambourine; Jim Gordon: Drums; Mike Hugg: Harmonium; Peter Frampton: Guitar; Lon Van Eaton: Guitar, Saxophone, B. Vocals &

Record 375 title:
Give A Little Love (Boy Scouts Of America) [Various Artists]
Media:
Album 5" CD
Label / Catalog number:
Comin / CMN 1187-002
Producer:
Klaus Voormann
Jacket / Inserts:
Unique in Jewel box / 12 page CD booklet
Recording Location / Date:
Sunset Sound Studios, Los Angeles, CA, U.S.A. / 1978

Song 375a title:
Get Happy
Track details:
Side 1, track 4 / 3 min. 25 sec.
Release date / Country:
1988 / U.S.A.
Composer:
L. Van Eaton - D. Van Eaton

Derrek Van Eaton: Lead Vocals & Vibra-Slap; Ringo Starr: Drums & Percussion; Klaus Voormann: Bass & Sleigh Bells; Lon Van Eaton: Keyboards & Horns; Carlos de la Paz: Guitar

Record 376 title:
None
Label / Catalog number:
Apple
Producer:
Klaus Voormann
Recording Location / Date:
Media Sound Studios, New York, NY, U.S.A. / 1972

Song 376a title:
Don't You Know That It's Over
Track details:
3 min. 35 sec.
Release date / Country:
[Unreleased]
Composer:
L. Van Eaton - D. Van Eaton

Derrek Van Eaton: Lead Vocals; George Harrison: Slide Guitar; Lon Van Eaton: Guitar & Keyboards; Klaus Voormann: Bass; Steve Moseley: Drums

Record 377 title:
None
Label / Catalog number:
Apple
Producer:
Klaus Voormann
Recording Location / Date:
Apple Studios, London, U.K. / Oct - Dec 71

Song 377a title:
The Sea
Track details:
4 min. 12 sec.
Release date / Country:
[Unreleased]
Composer:
L. Van Eaton - D. Van Eaton - J. Tavener

Derrek Van Eaton: Lead Vocals; John Tavener: Conductor & String & Horn Arrangements; Ringo Starr: Drums; Klaus Voormann: Bass; Lon Van Eaton: Keyboards

Record 378 title:
None
Label / Catalog number:
Apple
Producer:
Klaus Voormann
Recording Location / Date:
Apple Studios, London, U.K. / Oct - Dec 71

Song 378a title:
Warm Woman [alternate version]
Release date / Country:
[Unreleased]
Track details:
3 min. 10 sec.
Composer:
L. Van Eaton - D. Van Eaton

Derrek Van Eaton: Lead Vocals; Lon Van Eaton: Keyboards; Klaus Voormann: Bass; Ringo Starr: Drums

Record 379 title:
None
Label / Catalog number:
Portrait
Producer:
Klaus Voormann
Recording Location / Date:
Sunset Sound Studios, Los Angeles, CA, U.S.A. / 1978

Song 379a title:
Bye Baby
Release date / Country:
[Unreleased]
Track details:
3 min. 25 sec.
Composer:
L. Van Eaton - D. Van Eaton

Derrek Van Eaton: Lead Vocals; Klaus Voormann: Bass & Guitar; Ringo Starr: Drums; Lon Van Eaton: Keyboards

Song 379b title:
Keep It Up
Release date / Country:
[Unreleased]
Track details:
3 min. 23 sec.
Composer:
L. Van Eaton - D. Van Eaton

Derrek Van Eaton: Lead Vocals; Klaus Voormann: Bass & Guitar; Ringo Starr: Drums; Lon Van Eaton: Keyboards; Carlos de la Paz: Guitar

Lon Van Eaton was born on March 12, 1948; Derrek Van Eaton on August 12, 1950, in Trenton, New Jersey. The brothers had been part of the group Jacob's Creek that broke up in March 1971 after releasing one album for Columbia Records.

The two brothers then spent time recording their own material at home, and sent a tape to numerous record companies including Apple, with whom they signed on September 15, 1971. On September 19, they flew to England, and were escorted to the home of George Harrison. Within days they were recording their first Apple single ***Sweet Music***, produced by Harrison at EMI's Abbey Road Studios. Several days later, Lon and Derrek began recording their debut album (which was not released until almost a year after it was recorded) at Apple Studios. By then, Apple was little more than an exclusive label for solo Beatles' releases. The album included ***Sweet Music*** and featured Ringo Starr drumming on the song ***Another Thought***. The album also included the song ***Warm Woman***. According to the Van Eatons, an album's worth of unreleased recordings, some that Ringo and Harrison contributed to, were done during their stay at Apple. An alternate version of ***Warm Woman***, featuring Ringo on drums, remains in the vaults, as does ***Don't You Know That It's Over***, recorded in New York in 1972, on which Harrison plays slide guitar. Another song, recorded in the

U.K. and titled ***The Sea***, features Ringo on drums, and includes assistance from Apple artist John Tavener*.

Lon and Derrek moved to the Los Angeles area and did some session work on the superstar-studded albums **Ringo** and **Goodnight Vienna** for Ringo Starr. In 1974, they contributed to George Harrison's song **Dark Horse**, and, with his help, were signed with A&M records. In 1975, they released one album for the label, **Who Do You Out Do**, produced by Richard Perry. However, none of The Beatles contributed to the album in any way. The brothers also worked as songwriters for Screen Gems in the mid-1970s.

Lon also played on Ringo's 1976 album **Rotogravure**, and his 1977 album **Ringo The 4th**. Lon was a member of Ringo's Roadside Attraction, a makeshift band put together for Ringo's 1978 album **Bad Boy**, and his TV special **Ringo**. The special, narrated by George Harrison, was a modern-day version of Mark Twain's **The Prince And The Pauper** set in Hollywood. It concluded with a live performance by Ringo's Roadside Attraction.

In 1978, Lon and Derrek also recorded the songs ***Hold On***, ***Get Happy***, ***Bye Baby***, ***Keep It Up***, and a cover of The Supremes' ***My World Is Empty Without You*** for Portrait Records, on which Ringo played drums. ***Get Happy*** was released on the 1988 various artists CD **Give A Little Love (Boy Scouts Of America)**. The CD also featured ***Sweet Music***, and a cover of The Beatles' ***Getting Better***, from their days with A&M. ***Hold On*** and ***My World Is Empty Without You*** were released by the Van Eatons on their 1998 CD **Black & White**. **Black & White** also included a 60 second radio spot by Ringo that was made for the **Brother** album, and the demo version of ***Sweet Music*** that was sent to Apple Records.

Derrek Van Eaton has spent much of his time in recent years working in the funeral business. Lon Van Eaton has been very active in musical projects for a wide range of community and charitable organizations through his Comin Inc. / Imagine a Better World Company. He owns and operates Angels Ranch Recordings Studios. Lon and Derrek officially resurfaced on the various artists album **Come And Get it: A Tribute To Badfinger** *(see Badfinger)* released in 1996.

Record 380 title:
(Adventure): Ring Of Fire (An Indonesian Odyssey) Volume 1: Spice Island Saga; Volume 2: Dance Of The Warriors; Volume 3: East Of Krakatoa; Volume 4: Dream Wanderers Of Borneo

Media:
VHS [4 VHS set]

Label / Catalog number:
Mystic Fire Video/Island/PolyGram / 76057 (M113/76061/76063/76065)

Producer:
Lawrence & Lorne Blair; Hilary Gerrard & Ringo Starr (Associate Producers)

Jacket / Inserts:
Unique in box set / Order form

Recording Location / Date:
On location in Indonesia / mid-1970s thru mid-1980s

Song 380a title:
[unknown]

Track details:
Approx. 4 hrs.

Release date / Country:
1989 (first aired: 1988) / U.S.A.

Composer:
Lawrence Blair

Lawrence Blair: Narration; Lorne Blair: Narration; Mason Daring And The People Of Indonesia; George Harrison: (possible) Involvement

In 1972 Ringo Starr, through Apple Films, put up the money for brothers Lorne and Lawrence Blair to make a documentary of the Indonesia archipelago that form part of a region known as the Ring of Fire, due to its volcanic activity. At the time of Ringo's involvement, it was reported that George Harrison was contributing incidental music to the film. When the film was finally released in 1988, Ringo was given credit as associate producer. Harrison may indeed have contributed to the incidental music in some way, though it is unlikely, as there was no mention of him in the credits.

Various Artists - Shanghai Surprise

Record 381 title:
Shanghai Surprise

Media:
Album 12" LVD

Label / Catalog number:
Vestron Video / VL5181

Producer:
Malcolm Rose (music); John Kohn (film)

Jacket / Inserts:
Standard international design

Recording Location / Date:
Lee International Studios, Shepperton, U.K., Shaw Studios, Hong Kong, and on Location in Hong Kong and Macau (film); FPSHOT (Friar Park Studios, Henley-on-Thames), De Lane Lea Sound Studio & EMI-Abbey Road Studios; London, U.K. (music) / Jan - Mar 86

Track details:
Sides 1 & 2 / 0 min. 45 sec.

Release date / Country:
1987 (premiered: 29 Aug 86) / U.S.A.

Composer:
G. Harrison - M. Kamen (Music-Score) From The Novel: "Faraday's Flowers," by Tony Kenrick; Screenplay by: John Kohn & Robert Bentley (film)

Madonna Louise Ciccone was born on August 16, 1958 in Bay City, Michigan, but her family moved to the Detroit area when she was six. Much like The Beatles, Madonna's long-lived success lies in part with her multi-talented, and ever changing, persona. Her performing arts career was rooted in drama and dance, but she began fronting bands singing dance club material in the early 1980s, and had her first commercial success on the disco charts with ***Everybody***.

In 1984, Madonna had her first top 10 song with ***Borderline***, and her first number one with ***Like A Virgin***. In 1985 she followed up with the hits ***Material Girl***, ***Crazy For You***, ***Into The Groove*** and ***Dress You Up***. Madonna dominated the charts again in 1986 with ***Live To Tell***, ***Papa Don't Preach***, ***True Blue***, and ***Open Your Heart***. Thus began her meteoric rise to fame and fortune. Madonna has since had over a dozen more hits including ***Who's That Girl***, ***Causing That Commotion***, ***Express Yourself***, ***Cherish***, ***Justify My Love*** and ***Take A Bow***, enough to place her in the same category as The Beatles and Elvis Presley.

In 1985, Madonna met actor Sean Penn who had recent successes in the films **Fast Times At Ridgemont High**, **Bad Boys** and **The Falcon And The Snowman**. Within six months of their first meeting, the couple was joined in a turbulent marriage. It ended with Madonna filing for divorce for a second time in early 1989. Penn continues to successfully fill leading roles. Madonna continues to pursue nearly every form of entertainment, and redefine the modern rock star with her usual high dose of shock value.

In 1986, George Harrison's HandMade Films Co., looking for its first major Hollywood box office success, cast Sean Penn and his new bride Madonna in the starring roles for the film **Shanghai Surprise**. Though Penn was an accomplished actor, Madonna's acting experience was fairly limited. Her name, however, was a guaranteed box office draw. Penn was apparently angered by the presence of photographers and the press on the set hounding his wife. He and Madonna reportedly fought with each other and the crew, which threatened the film's completion. Executive producer George Harrison flew to the filming location in Hong Kong in an attempt to patch things up with the press, actors and crew. He later held a press conference with Madonna.

Harrison scored the film's music with Michael Kamen. Harrison met Kamen through Terry Gilliam *(see Monty Python)* and well-known percussionist Ray Cooper. This led to Kamen working on a number of George Harrison's HandMade Films productions including **Mona Lisa** and **The Raggedy Rawney**. Harrison is given thanks on Kamen's **Concerto For Saxophone** CD for the brief interview he gave for Kamen's 1991 video **Concerto For Saxophone**. Harrison has yet to contribute musically to any of Michael Kamen's recordings.

Harrison also contributed six new songs to the soundtrack **Shanghai Surprise**: an officially unreleased duet with Vicki Brown* of the title theme, that reportedly was originally intended to be done with Madonna; ***12 Bar Bali*** (not even listed in the film's credits); alternate versions of ***Someplace Else*** and ***Breath Away From Heaven*** from those that later appeared on Harrison's album **Cloud Nine**; ***Hottest Gong In Town***, only available on record in the high-priced, limited-edition book **Songs By George Harrison 2** from Genesis Publications; and ***Zig-Zag***, later issued as the B-side of ***When We Was Fab***.

Despite Harrison's efforts, **Shanghai Surprise** opened to caustic reviews, and was HandMade's first unintentional "disaster film." It was a personal embarrassment, as well as a financial loss to Harrison. Though Harrison defended the couple throughout the filming, his comments were more candid after the film's failure. The closing credits to **Shanghai Surprise** claimed that the original soundtrack album was available on Dark Horse Records, but no album was ever issued, no doubt due to the film's lack of success.

Various Artists - The Celebrity Selection Of Childrens Stories

Record 382 title:
The Celebrity Selection Of Childrens Stories

Media:
Album 12"

Label / Catalog number:
Warwick / STMP 9030

Jacket / Inserts:
Unique with Liner Notes by Paul McCartney

Release date / Country:
01 Sep 83 / U.K.

Paul and his wife Linda penned some liner notes on the jacket of this children's record with proceeds going to the N.S.P.C.C.

Various Artists - Time Bandits

Record 383 title:
Time Bandits

Media:
12" LVD

Label / Catalog number:
Paramount / LV 2310-WS

Producer:
Ray Cooper (music); Terry Gilliam (Producer & Director) (film)

Jacket / Inserts:
Standard international design / Record label inner sleeve

Recording Location / Date:
Lee International Studios and on location in England, Wales & Morocco (film); CTS Studios, London (music) / 1980 &/or 1981

Song 383a title:
Time Bandits (Musical Score)
Release date / Country:
21 Feb 95 (premiered: Jul 81) / U.S.A.
Track details:
Sides 1 & 2 / Approx. 1 hr. 56 min.
Composer:
M. Moran (music); M. Palin & T. Gilliam (film)

Starring: David Rappaport, Kenny Baker, Malcolm Dixon, Mike Edmonds, Jack Purvis, Tiny Ross & Craig Warnock; Co-starring: John Cleese, Sean Connery, Shelley Duvall, Katherine Helmond, Ian Holm, Michael Palin, Ralph Richardson, David Warner & Peter Vaughn George Harrison: Songs & Additional Material

George Harrison took a greater-than-the-usual executive producer involvement in this HandMade Films production, primarily in its music. He provided his song ***Dream Away***, played over the closing credits of the film. ***Dream Away*** is not a proper contribution, but an actual Harrison recording that later appeared on his album **Gone Troppo**. A quick look at the credits reveals names often musically associated with Harrison, such as the film's musical producer Ray Cooper, and Mike Moran, who composed and orchestrated the musical score. The film's credits also list "Songs and additional material by George Harrison." This leads one to suspect that Harrison's involvement in the film probably was not limited to ***Dream Away***.

Joe Walsh

Record 384 title:
Live From Montreaux
Label / Catalog number:
Videoarts / VALJ-3369
Jacket / Inserts:
Unique / Lyric & translation insert
Recording Location / Date:
On location at Montreaux Jazz Festival, Montreaux, Switzerland / 13 Jul 92
Media:
Album 12" LVD
Producer:
Jim Beach & Louise Velazquez (film); Ringo Starr (music)

Song 384a title:
Rocky Mountain Way [live]
Release date / Country:
(probably) Nov 93 / Japan
Track details:
Side 1, track 6 / 6 min. 18 sec.
Composer:
J. Walsh - J. Vitale - K. Passarelli - S. Grace

Joe Walsh: Lead Vocals & Guitar; Ringo Starr: Drums; Todd Rundgren: Guitar; Burton Cummings: Keyboards; Nils Lofgren: Guitar; Dave Edmunds: Guitar; Timothy B. Schmit: Bass; Tim Cappello: Saxophone; Zak Starkey: Drums (Ringo Starr And His All-Starr Band)

Record 385 title:
Ringo Starr And His All-Starr Band
Label / Catalog number:
Pioneer Artists / PA-090-007
Jacket / Inserts:
Standard international design
Recording Location / Date:
On location at Greek Theatre, Los Angeles, CA, U.S.A. / 03 Sep 89
Media:
Album 12" LVD
Producer:
Tim Snow (film) Joe Walsh & Jim Nipar (music)

Song 385a title:
Life In The Fast Lane [live]
Release date / Country:
Jul 90 / U.S.A.
Track details:
Side 1, track 12 / 6 min. 13 sec.
Composer:
G. Frey - D.Henley - J. Walsh

Joe Walsh: Lead Vocals & Guitar; Billy Preston: Keyboards & B. Vocals; Jim Keltner: Drums; Ringo

Starr: Drums; Levon Helm: Drums & B. Vocals; Nils Lofgren: Guitar & B. Vocals; Rick Danko: Bass & B. Vocals; Clarence Clemons: Percussion, Saxophone & B. Vocals; Dr. John: Keyboards & B. Vocals

This song is also included on Rykodisc / RCD 10190 & RCD5-1019 / Albums 5" [2 CD set] / CD1, track 11 / released 12 Oct 90 in the U.S.A. / Unique in box set in Jewel box / 6 page CD booklet, sticker postcard & Rykodisc info. postcard & CD insert.

Song 385b title:
Rocky Mountain Way [live]
Release date / Country:
Jul 90 / U.S.A.

Track details:
Side 2, track 6 / 8 min. 11 sec.
Composer:
J. Walsh - J. Vitale - K. Passarelli - S. Grace

Joe Walsh: Lead Vocals & Guitar; Billy Preston: Keyboards; Jim Keltner: Drums; Ringo Starr: Drums; Levon Helm: Harmonica; Nils Lofgren: Guitar; Rick Danko: Bass; Clarence Clemons: Saxophone; Dr. John: Keyboards

This song is also included on Rykodisc / RCD 10190 & RCD5-1019 / Albums 5" [2 CD set] / CD2, track 3 / released 12 Oct 90 in the U.S.A. / Unique in box set in Jewel box / 6 page CD booklet, sticker postcard & Rykodisc info. postcard & CD insert.

Joe Walsh was born on November 20, 1947 in Wichita, Kansas. He first gained notoriety as the hard-rocking guitarist in the band The James Gang, which he joined in 1969, but left two years later. He turned out several fairly successful solo recordings in the early 1970s, including his trademark song ***Rocky Mountain Way***. In 1976 Walsh joined The Eagles. He remained a member until their disintegration at the end of the decade. In 1978, he scored another hit with his autobiographical song ***Life's Been Good***. Walsh has maintained a career as a solo artist, producer, songwriter, and session player.

Walsh produced, played on and wrote or co-wrote six of the ten tracks on Ringo Starr's 1983 album **Old Wave**. Walsh covered one of the songs from **Old Wave**, ***In My Car***, on his 1987 album **Got Any Gum?**, though Ringo did not contribute to Walsh's version.

Walsh was a member of Ringo Starr's All-Starr Band tour in 1989 performing ***Life In The Fast Lane*** and ***Rocky Mountain Way*** with Ringo backing him on drums. Walsh, along with Jeff Lynne*, Jim Keltner *(see Attitudes)* and Tom Petty* backed Ringo singing ***I Call Your Name*** as a contribution to **The John Lennon Scholarship Concert** held on May 5, 1990 in Liverpool, included on the 1991 laser videodisk **The World's Greatest Artists Sing LENNON A Tribute**.

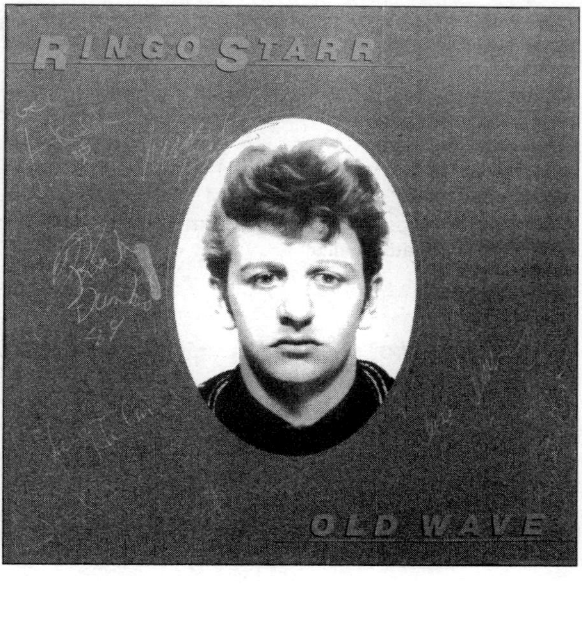

Walsh's 1991 album **Ordinary Average Guy** listed Ringo, along with a number of other familiar names, as one of "The Ordinary Average Guys," but he did not contribute to the album. Ringo's name is mentioned only because of his long association with Walsh.

Walsh was also a member of Ringo Starr's All-Starr Band tour in 1992 performing ***Rocky Mountain Way***, again with Ringo on drums. Ringo cleared the legal path for Walsh's use of a sample of The Beatles' song ***A Day In The Life***, on the song ***Decades*** from his 1992 album **Songs For A Dying Planet**. Walsh's touring with the reunited

Eagles prevented him from being a member of Ringo's 1995 All-Starr Band tour. However, Walsh did appear with the All-Starr Band for their encore at the Greek Theatre in Los Angeles on August 18, and again the following night when he performed ***Rocky Mountain Way***. Walsh also made a guest appearance during Ringo's All-Starr Band performance of ***Photograph*** and ***With A Little Help From My Friends*** at Six Flags Astro World in Houston on May 25, 1997. Walsh contributed to Ringo's 1998 album **Vertical Man**.

Cynthia Webb

Record 386 title:
None

Producer:
Klaus Voormann & Cynthia Webb

Recording Location / Date:
Stronghold & Jimmy Webb's home studio, Los Angeles, CA, U.S.A. / Nov - Dec 74 & spring 1975

Song 386a title:
Changing

Release date / Country:
[Unreleased]

Composer:
C. Webb

Cynthia Webb: Lead Vocals & Piano; Ringo Starr: Drums; Klaus Voormann: Bass; Lon Van Eaton: Guitar

Song 386b title:
Dream Baby

Release date / Country:
[Unreleased]

Composer:
C. Webb

Cynthia Webb: Lead Vocals & Piano; Ringo Starr: Drums; Klaus Voormann: Bass

Song 386c title:
I Am Sorry

Release date / Country:
[Unreleased]

Composer:
C. Webb

Cynthia Webb: Lead Vocals & Piano; Ringo Starr: Drums; Klaus Voormann: Bass; Lon Van Eaton: Guitar

Song 386d title:
Let Go Of Love

Release date / Country:
[Unreleased]

Composer:
C. Webb

Cynthia Webb: Lead Vocals; Ringo Starr: Drums; Klaus Voormann: Bass; Gary Wright: (possible) Piano; Lon Van Eaton: Guitar

Song 386e title:
Secret

Release date / Country:
[Unreleased]

Composer:
C. Webb

Cynthia Webb: Lead Vocals & Piano; Ringo Starr: Drums; Klaus Voormann: Bass; Gary Wright: (possible) Electric Piano

Song 386f title:
Take Your love

Release date / Country:
[Unreleased]

Composer:
C. Webb

Cynthia Webb: Lead Vocals & Piano; Ringo Starr: Drums; Klaus Voormann: Bass

Song 386g title:
Window Blues

Release date / Country:
[Unreleased] / U.S.A.

Composer:
C. Webb

Cynthia Webb: Lead Vocals & Piano; Ringo Starr: Drums; Klaus Voormann: Guitar & Bass

Cynthia Webb was born and raised in the Los Angeles, California area. She wrote poems as a child, and put them to melodies she created as she grew older. When she was a teenager, she took up dance, violin, and piano. Her mother was a teacher, and the schools Cynthia attended always had a strong fine arts program.

Webb began working at a number of well-known rock clubs in the Los Angeles area in the mid-1960s to break into the music business. She then moved to England where she, Karen Harvey and Nicole Tacot (Tacot later married Steve Winwood *[see Blind Faith]*) formed a folk-rock trio before making their way to the offices of Apple Records in London. George Harrison and Tony Meehan produced some demos for them for possible release on Apple, but, according to Webb, nothing ever developed beyond that.

Webb returned to the Los Angeles area in the early 1970s and met and married Klaus Voormann *(see Paul Jones)*. Being married to Klaus put her in the company of George Harrison, John Lennon and Ringo Starr. Cynthia contributed background vocals on Ringo's song ***Call Me*** from his album **Goodnight Vienna**. She played maracas on the John Lennon produced album **Pussy Cats** by Harry Nilsson*. She also wrote the song ***Fool For You***, recorded by Nilsson for his **Flash Harry** album that, in Cynthia's words, "never quite came together and was left off the album." Cynthia feels one of her best compositions is ***My Man (You Changed My Tune)***, recorded by Martha Reeves. Between the winter of 1974 and spring of 1975, Webb made some recordings with contributions from Ringo, Lon and Derrek Van Eaton*, her husband Klaus, and others, that remain unreleased.

Cynthia and Klaus were divorced in the early 1980s. She currently divides her time between working in the film industry in Los Angeles, and raising their son Otto. Now that her son is grown, she plans to resume her career as an aspiring songwriter and poet. Cynthia says, "I've always written, I turn to paper, it's my outlet!"

Jimmy Webb

Record 387 title:
Land's End

Media:
Album 12"

Label / Catalog number:
Asylum / SD 5070

Producer:
Jimmy Webb

Jacket / Inserts:
Standard international design / Lyric sheet

Recording Location / Date:
Trident Studios, London, U.K. / Jul - Aug or fall 1973

Song 387a title:
Alyce Blue Gown

Track details:
Side 2, track 3 / 4 min. 58 sec.

Release date / Country:
03 Jun 74 / U.S.A.

Composer:
J. Webb

Jimmy Webb: Lead Vocals & Piano; Tom Scott: Saxophone; Ringo Starr: Drums; Fred Tackett: Guitar; Dee Murray: Bass

Jimmy Webb, Los Angeles, CA, 1975, photo courtesy of Tom Bert

Jimmy Webb was born August 15, 1946 in Elk City, Oklahoma, and began playing keyboards at an early age. He is known primarily as a successful hit songwriter, penning classics that include Glen Campbell's ***By The Time I Get To Phoenix***, ***Wichita Lineman*** and ***Galveston***; The 5th Dimension's ***Up-Up And Away***; Richard Harris's ***MacArthur Park***; Art Garfunkel's ***All I Know***; and Brooklyn Bridge's ***The Worst That Could Happen***. He has also worked as a producer, and has written for such diverse talents as Cher, Frank Sinatra, Barbra Streisand and Johnny Rivers, among others.

By the 1970s, Webb decided to record his compositions, and began releasing a string of solo albums including **Land's End**, recorded in London with a little help from Ringo Starr. The album's credits do not list the specific musicians for each track. According to Webb, Ringo's contribution to the album was the result of their mutual friendship with Harry Nilsson. Webb recalled, "I was thrilled with the sight of Ringo and his drum kit in the studio. I had first met The Beatles at Trident Studios when they were recording **The Beatles** (the white album)." Webb said Ringo told him his drums had been packed away for some time, and that he had not played for a while. The engineer on the session felt the drums needed additional tuning, and spent hours with Ringo trying to get the right sound. The session dragged on for hours, and Webb became worried that Ringo would become discouraged and leave, so he and Ringo retreated to the lobby of the studio for some lighthearted conversation. Upon returning to the studio, Ringo laid down what Webb described as "the best-sounding drum track on the album on ***Alyce Blue Gown***. He said ***Alyce Blue Gown*** is the only song of his to which Ringo ever contributed.

Webb recalled that some months later he was hanging out with Ringo and John Lennon in Los Angeles, and that Ringo told him the drum-tuning incident had shaken his confidence and intimidated him. Webb said the events surrounding ***Alyce Blue Gown*** will always remain vivid in his mind because of the distress the session caused Ringo.

Jimmy said he occasionally bumped shoulders with George Harrison at A&M Studios, and was a guest at several of Paul McCartney's parties, including the one held on the retired ocean liner Queen Mary in 1975. The Beatles' producer, George Martin*, has also worked with Webb.

Webb is now a member of The National Song Writer's Hall Of Fame, and of The Nashville Song Writer's Hall Of Fame. He continues to write and record, and feels **Suspending Disbelief**, released in 1993, is one of his best albums.

Bobby Whitlock

Record 388 title:
Bobby Whitlock
Label / Catalog number:
Dunhill/ABC / DSX 50121
Jacket / Inserts:
Unique with Gatefold / Record label inner sleeve
Recording Location / Date:
Olympic Studios, London, U.K. / Jan 71
Media:
Album 12"
Producer:
Bobby Whitlock & Andy Johns

Song 388a title:
A Day Without Jesus
Release date / Country:
1972 (first issued Jul 71) / U.S.A.
Track details:
Side 1, track 5 / 3 min. 22 sec.
Composer:
B. Whitlock - D. Nix

Bobby Whitlock: Lead Vocals & Keyboards; George Harrison: Guitar; Carl Radle: Bass; Jim Gordon: Drums; Eric Clapton: Guitar; Delaney Bramlett: B. Vocals; Bonnie Bramlett: B. Vocals

Song 388b title:
Back In My Life Again
Release date / Country:
1972 (first issued Jul 71) / U.S.A.
Track details:
Side 2, track 1 / 3 min. 30 sec.
Composer:
B. Whitlock

Bobby Whitlock: Lead Vocals & Keyboards; George Harrison: Guitar; Eric Clapton: Guitar; Carl Radle: Bass; Jim Price: Horns; Bobby Keys: Saxophone; Jim Gordon: Drums

Song 388c title:
Where There's A Will There's A Way
Release date / Country:
1972 (first issued Jul 71) / U.S.A.
Track details:
Side 1, track 1 / 3 min. 43 sec.
Composer:
B. Whitlock - B. Bramlett

Bobby Whitlock: Lead Vocals & Keyboards; George Harrison: Guitar; Carl Radle: Bass; Jim Gordon: Drums; Eric Clapton: Guitar; Bobby Keys: Saxophone; Jim Price: Horns

Bobby Whitlock was born on March 18, 1948 in Memphis, Tennessee. Whitlock is yet another of the many musicians George Harrison worked with as a result of his association with Delaney & Bonnie & Friends*. Whitlock is best remembered as a member of Eric Clapton's band Derek And The Dominos. Derek And The Dominos contributed to George Harrison's album **All Things Must Pass**. For years there has been speculation by a number of reliable publications that Harrison might be involved in Whitlock's solo albums **Bobby Whitlock** and **Raw Velvet**, but the album credits are sparse, confusing, or cryptic. Ads for the **Bobby Whitlock** album listed Harrison as a contributor.

In Marc Roberty's book **Eric**

Clapton The Complete Recording Sessions 1963 - 1992, he lists Clapton as playing on the following Whitlock tracks recorded at Olympic Studios in January 1971: ***Where There's A Will There's A Way***, ***A Day Without Jesus***, ***Back In My Life Again***, ***The Scenery Has Slowly Changed***, ***The Dreams Of A Hobo*** and ***Hello L.A., Bye-Bye-Birmingham***. George Harrison is listed among the other musicians, but, as is the case with many of the entries in Roberty's book, it is unclear if all the musicians he lists for the sessions play on every song recorded at those sessions. There is also no way to tell from Roberty's book if Harrison plays on any other Whitlock songs that did not include Clapton. **Dreams Of A Hobo** is on the U.S. version of **Bobby Whitlock**, but on **Raw Velvet** in the U.K. ***Hello L.A., Bye-Bye-Birmingham*** is on **Raw Velvet**. The rest of the tracks are on **Bobby Whitlock**.

To the best of Whitlock's recollection, George played on only three songs: ***Where There's A Will There's A Way***, ***A Day Without Jesus*** and ***Back In My Life Again*** – all from the album **Bobby Whitlock**. ***A Day Without Jesus*** is credited as being written by Whitlock and Don Nix, but Whitlock claims he wrote the song alone in California, while Nix was in Memphis. According to Whitlock, George did not contribute to ***The Scenery Has Slowly Changed***, or any songs on **Raw Velvet**. Some of the confusion about what songs and albums of Whitlock's George contributed to is due to the difference between the U.S. and U.K. versions. Several of the songs from these two albums are actually Derek And The Dominos tracks with Whitlock on lead vocals. Whitlock lives near Memphis and continues to write and record.

John Williams

Record 389 title:
Filmtracks - The Best Of British Film Music [Various Artists]

Media:
Album 5" CD [2 CD set]

Label / Catalog number:
London / 820 252-2 (820 253-2)

Producer:
Stanley Myers & Richard Harvey & [Paul McCartney]

Jacket / Inserts:
Unique in double Jewel box / 8 page CD booklet

Recording Location / Date:
Olympic Studios, London, U.K. / 1983

Song 389a title:
Paul McCartney's Theme From The Film "The Honorary Consul"

Track details:
CD1, track 2 / 3 min. 44 sec.

Release date / Country:
Jul 85 (first issued 19 Dec 83) / Germany

Composer:
P. McCartney

Paul McCartney: Guitar; John Williams: Guitar

John Williams was born on April 24, 1941 in Melbourne, Australia. He attended courses with Segovia at the Accademia Musicale Chigiana in Siena, Italy, and studied at the Royal College of Music in London. He established himself as a classical and Spanish Flamenco guitarist. His albums **Travelling** in 1978, and **Bridges** in 1979, were in the U.K. top 20. In 1979, he formed the classical / jazz / rock fusion instrumental group Sky, whose first four albums were also in the U.K. top 20. Williams recorded a cover of ***Here Comes The Sun***, produced by George Martin*, that was released in 1998.

Williams performed Paul McCartney's instrumental title theme for the 1984 film **The Honorary Consul** (titled **Beyond The Limit** in the U.S.) The film was directed by John McKenzie, who also directed McCartney's promotional film for the ***Take It Away*** single, and was probably instrumental in McCartney's contribution to the soundtrack theme. According to Paul McCartney's fan-club magazine Club Sandwich issue # 67, Paul also produced the John Williams recording, and in McCartney's 1989 World Tour Program, McCartney states he played guitar on the recording.

Nicol Williamson

Record 390 title:
None
Recording Location / Date:
London, U.K. / 1970 or 1971

Song 390a title:
None
Release date / Country:
(probably) [Unreleased]

Nicol Williamson: Lead Vocals; one or more of the following: Roy Young: Keyboards; Ringo Starr: Drums; Eric Clapton: Guitar; Klaus Voormann: Bass; George Harrison: Guitar

Nicol Williamson was born on September 14, 1938 in Hamilton, Scotland. Williamson is an accomplished Shakespearean actor who has appeared in a number of films, and on television. He is familiar to Americans from his appearances in the films **Excalibur**, **The Goodbye Girl**, **I'm Dancing As Fast As I Can**, **Exorcist III** and an episode of the TV series **Columbo**.

According to Roy Young *(see Cliff Bennett And The Rebel Rousers, Tony Sheridan)*, he, George Harrison, Ringo and Eric Clapton played on some recordings by Williamson. Williamson has had several releases over the years, mostly easy-listening and spoken-word albums. Young did not know if the recordings were ever released, and could not recall much, other than that they were rock-oriented oldies, and were recorded in London in the early 1970s. An album titled **Nicol Williamson** was released in 1971 that contains mostly orchestrated easy listening-music that sounds nothing like the recordings Young described. Young did not recognize the recordings as being those he made with Williamson. He feels the recordings he made with Williamson were not suitable for release. This seems likely as there is no indication these recordings were released.

Johnny Winter

Record 391 title:
John Dawson Winter III
Media:
Album 12"
Label / Catalog number:
Blue Sky / PZ 33292
Producer:
Shelly Yakus
Jacket / Inserts:
Standard international design with Gatefold / Red & Black
Recording Location / Date:
Record Plant (East) Studios, New York, NY, U.S.A. / (probably) late summer or early fall 1974

Song 391a title:
Rock & Roll People
Track details:
Side 1, track 1 / 2 min. 44 sec.
Release date / Country:
25 Nov 74 / U.S.A.
Composer:
J. Lennon

Johnny Winter: Lead Vocals & Guitar; Randy Jo Hobbs: Bass & Percussion; Richard Hughes: Drums & Percussion

John Dawson Winter III was born on February 23, 1944 in Leland, Mississippi. Both he, and his equally famous younger brother Edgar, are albinos. Their parents were musicians, and sons John and Edgar soon took an interest in blues and rock music at an early age. By the late 1960s both had become stars.

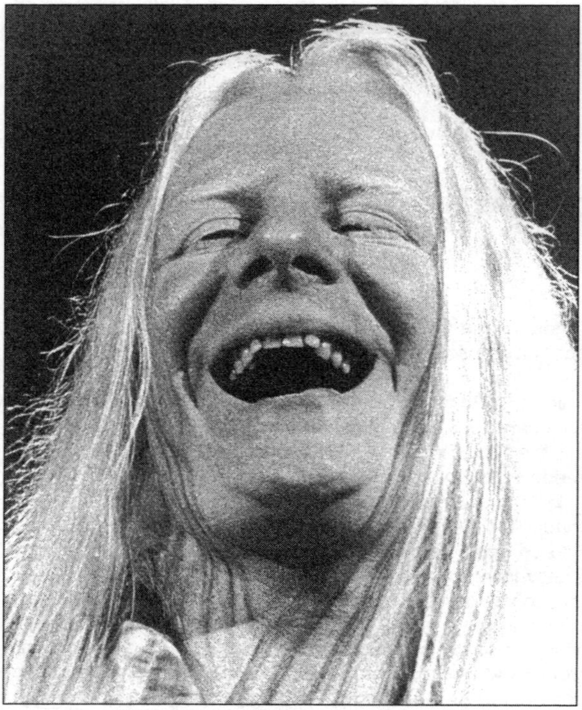

Johnny Winter, Flint, MI, mid-1970s, photo courtesy of Tom Bert

The album **John Dawson Winter III** was released in late 1974, and included the then-unreleased John Lennon composition ***Rock & Roll People***. The album was produced by Shelly Yakus, who helped engineer many of Lennon's recordings at the Record Plant in New York. Yakus felt Lennon's ***Rock & Roll People*** (which dated back to Lennon's **Mind Games** album sessions), was perfect for Winter, and Lennon agreed. (Lennon's recording of ***Rock & Roll People*** appeared on his posthumously released album **Menlove Ave**, in 1986.)

There is also a five-and-a-half-minute live version of ***Rock & Roll People*** on the U.S. CD **Johnny Winter Captured Live** (Sony / 33944) recorded in 1976. Johnny made a brief cameo appearance in Robert Stigwood's 1978 film **Sgt. Pepper's Lonely Hearts Club Band**. The two brothers continue to record and guest on other artist's records.

Ron Wood

Record 392 title:
I've Got My Own Album To Do
Label / Catalog number:
Warner Bros / 2-45692
Media:
Album 5"
Producer:
Ron Wood & Gary Kellgren
Jacket / Inserts:
Standard international design in jewel box / 4 page CD booklet
Recording Location / Date:
The Wick (Ron Wood's home studio), Richmond Hill, U.K. / Jul 74

Song 392a title:
Far East Man
Release date / Country:
13 Sep 94 (first issued 23 Sep 74) / U.S.A.
Track details:
Side 1, track 2 / 4 min. 40 sec.
Composer:
G. Harrison - R. Wood

Ron Wood: Lead Vocals & Guitar; George Harrison: Guitar & B. Vocals; Willie Weeks: Bass; Ian McLagan: Keyboards; Jean Rousseu: Keyboards; Andy Newmark: Drums

Song 392b title:
Take A Look At The Guy
Release date / Country:
13 Sep 94 (first issued 23 Sep 74) / U.S.A.
Track details:
Side 1, track 4 / 2 min. 33 sec.
Composer:
R. Wood

Ron Wood: Lead Vocals & (probable) Guitar; probably one or more of the following: Rod Stewart: B. Vocals; Willie Weeks: Bass; Ian McLagan: Keyboards; Andy Newmark: Drums

Ron Wood, Los Angeles, CA, late 1980s, photo courtesy of Tom Bert

Ronald Wood was born on June 1, 1947 in London, England. He began his music career in the early 1960s English group Birds, before joining Rod Stewart* in the Jeff Beck Group. In June 1969, he joined The Faces, a group that was formed from the Small Faces *(see Kenney Jones, Ian McLagen, Rod Stewart)*. When singer Rod Stewart's solo career took off, his band members began heading in different directions.

When preparing his album **I've Got My Own Album To Do**, "Woody," as he is known to his friends, called on George Harrison to help him finish the lyrics to the song ***Far East Man***. The two had previously worked together on the song. While driving down to Wood's home, Harrison came up with some of the lyrics, and wrote the middle eight and the remaining lyrics during the rehearsal for the song. In an article on the Small Faces in the June 21, 1996 issue of Goldmine magazine, Ian McLagan claims that he also helped write ***Far East Man***, though Wood discounts this. Harrison's involvement with Wood's recording of ***Far East Man*** was largely ignored when Harrison released his version of the song a short time later on his **Dark Horse** album (to which Wood also contributed). Though he has never been credited, Harrison shares the vocals and guitar work on Wood's version. Wood revealed that Paul McCartney "helped shape up ***Take A Look At The Guy*** on **I Got My Own Album To Do**." Wood didn't elaborate on the "shaping up" though it likely involved McCartney producing, or helping compose the song or possibly performing on it.

Wood had long been good friends with Keith Richards *(see The Rolling Stones)*, and in April 1975, he was asked to fill in for the departed Mick Taylor on The Rolling Stones Tour. By the end of the year, The Faces had finally folded up, and Ron Wood became a permanent member of The Rolling Stone.

Rumors have long persisted that Harrison or Ringo may have contributed to Wood's 1979 album **Gimme Some Neck**. However, according to Wood, none of The Beatles contributed to the album. Ringo and Wood are also long-time buddies. Ringo played drums on Wood's June 8, 1979 performance of ***Buried Alive*** from **Gimme Some Neck**, on NBC-TV's **Midnight Special**, which may be how the rumor was started that Ringo contributed to the album. Wood contributed to the songs ***Dead Giveaway*** and ***Brandy*** on Ringo's 1981 album **Stop And Smell The Roses**. Wood has issued a book of some of his drawings, and continues to maintain both his solo career and membership in The Rolling Stones.

Gary Wright

Record 393 title:
Artifacts III (Not Fade Away 1969-1971) [Various Artists]
Media:
Album 5" CD [4 CD set]
Label / Catalog number:
Big Music / 9 BIGBX 009.4 (BIG 4033) [Unauthorized Record]
Producer:
(The Dick Cavett Show)
Jacket / Inserts:
Unique in Jewel box in box set / 24 page box set booklet & (4) 2 page CD inserts
Recording Location / Date:
New York, NY, U.S.A. / 23 Nov 71

Song 393a title:
Two Faced Man [live]
Track details:
(1) Side 1, track 25 / 3 min. 48 sec.
Release date / Country:
(probably) Feb 95 / Italy
Composer:
G. Wright

Gary Wright: Lead Vocals & Acoustic Guitar; Mick Jones: Electric Guitar & B. Vocals; George Harrison: Slide Guitar; Bryson Graham: Drums; Archie Legget: Bass

Record 394 title:
First Signs Of Life
Media:
Album 5" CD
Label / Catalog number:
Worldly/Triloka / 7211-2
Producer:
Gary Wright
Jacket / Inserts:
Standard international design in jewel box / 4 page CD insert & Triloka Records insert
Recording Location / Date:
High Wave Studios, Los Angeles, CA, U.S.A. / Jul 94

Song 394a title:
Don't Try To Own Me
Track details:
Side 1, track 6 / 4 min. 18 sec.
Release date / Country:
25 Apr 95 / Canada
Composer:
G. Wright - D. Hitchings

Gary Wright: Lead Vocals & Keyboards; Terry Bozzio: Drums; Jimmy Haslip: Bass; Steve Farris: Guitar; George Harrison: B. Vocals

Record 395 title:
Footprint
Media:
Album 12"
Label / Catalog number:
A&M / SPSP-4296
Producer:
Gary Wright
Jacket / Inserts:
Standard international design / Record label inner sleeve

Song 395 title:
Stand For Our Rights
Track details:
Side 2, track 1 / 3 min. 32 sec.
Release date / Country:
01 Nov 71 (first issued 28 May 71) / U.S.A.
Composer:
G. Wright

Recording Location / Date:
Olympic Studios, London, U.K. & New York, NY† U.S.A. / (probably) Apr or May 71

Gary Wright: Lead Vocals; Jim Keltner: Drums; Jim Gordon: Drums; Hugh McCracken: Guitar; Jerry Donahue: Guitar; George Harrison: Guitar; Klaus Voormann: Bass; King Curtis: Saxophone†; Bobby Keys: Tenor Saxophone; Jim Price: Trumpet & Trombone; Doris Troy: B. Vocals; Nannette Workman: B. Vocals; Madeline Bell: B. Vocals; Barry St. John: B. Vocals; Pat Arnold: B. Vocals; Jimmy Thomas: B. Vocals; Colin Allen: Percussion; Alan White: Percussion; Nicky Hopkins: (possible) Harpsichord

Song 395b title:
Two Faced Man
Track details:
Side 1, track 2 / 3 min. 40 sec.
Release date / Country:
01 Nov 71 / U.S.A.
Composer:
G. Wright
Recording Location / Date:
Olympic Studios, London, U.K. / 1970 &/or 1971

Gary Wright: Lead Vocals & Keyboards; Alan White: Drums; Hugh McCracken: Guitar; George Harrison: Slide Guitar; Klaus Voormann: Bass; John Barham: String Arrangements

Record 396 title:
Who I Am
Media:
Album 5" CD
Label / Catalog number:
Cypress / YD0111/DIDX 003275
Producer:
Wyn Davis & Gary Wright
Jacket / Inserts:
Standard international design in jewel box / 8 page CD booklet
Recording Location / Date:
High Wave Studios, Los Angeles, CA, U.S.A. / (probably) Mar 87

Song 396a title:
(I Don't Wanna) Hold Back
Track details:
Side 1, track 8 / 4 min. 12 sec.
Release date / Country:
21 Sep 88 / U.S.A.
Composer:
R. Brookins - G. Wright

Gary Wright: Lead Vocals, Keyboards & Arrangement; Steve Farris: Rhythm Guitar; Bruce Gaitsch: Arrangement & Rhythm Guitar; George Harrison: Solo Guitar; Jimmy Johnson: Bass; Terry Bozzio: Drum Machine Programming; Mindy Lee: B. Vocals

Gary Wright's Wonderwheel

Record 397 title:
Wright's Wonderwheel
Media:
Album 12" [Test Press]
Label / Catalog number:
A&M / AMLH 64362
Producer:
Gary Wright
Recording Location / Date:
Apple Studios, London, U.K. / (probably) 1972

Song 397a title:
Goodbye Sunday
Track details:
Side 2, track 1
Release date / Country:
[Unreleased] (proposed release: Jul 72) / U.K.
Composer:
G. Wright

Gary Wright: Lead Vocals & Keyboards; Mick Jones: Guitar; George Harrison: Guitar; Bryson Graham: Drums; Tom Duffy: Bass

Gary Wright was born on April 26, 1943 in Englewood, New Jersey. Wright began his career in show business as a child actor on the **Captain Video** TV show in New York. He also appeared in a variety of TV and radio commercials before joining the cast of the Broadway play **Fanny**. Wright began playing piano and organ, and during high school he was in a number of local rock bands. He planned a career in psychology and medicine, and attended college in Berlin, Germany, but was drawn back to music.

Wright joined an English band called Art who renamed themselves Spooky Tooth in 1967. Their music combined Wright's intricate keyboards with late '60s hard rock and psychedelic blues. During the late '60s and early '70s, they were a top album-oriented, FM radio mainstay. The band included a cover of The Beatles' ***I Am The Walrus*** on their album **The Last Puff**.

Wright left Spooky Tooth between 1970 and 1973 to pursue a solo career, and formed the band Gary Wright's Wonderwheel with Mick Jones on guitar, Tom Duffy on bass, and Bryson Graham on drums. Spooky Tooth underwent numerous personnel changes (guitarist Henry McCullough was briefly a member before he joined Paul McCartney's band Wings) before disbanding in 1974. In 1975, Wright released his most commercially successful album **Dream Weaver**, which went platinum. The title track, and the song ***Love Is Alive*** from the album, reached the top five. Wright made a brief cameo appearance in Robert Stigwood's 1978 film **Sgt. Pepper's Lonely Hearts Club Band**.

Following Wright's departure from Spooky Tooth in 1970, he released his first solo album, **Extraction**. He contributed to George Harrison's album **All Things Must Pass**, and the two quickly became good friends. He released his second, and arguably his best solo album, **Footprint**, toward the end of 1971. Though **Footprint's** musical credits, which list George O'Hara (a pseudonym for Harrison), are not specific to each song, Wright stated that George played guitar on two songs on the album, ***Two Faced Man*** and ***Stand For Our Rights***. Harrison also joined Wright and Wonderwheel on **The Dick Cavett TV Show** on November 23, 1971 playing guitar on ***Two Faced Man***.

The first Gary Wright's Wonderwheel album was scheduled for release in July 1972 on A&M records, and was to be titled **Ring Of Changes** or **Wright's Wonderwheel**, but it was never released. However, acetates of the album on Apple Record's custom recording label are known to exist. Wright has no idea why A&M records canceled the release, but a few of the album's songs were issued on singles. According to Wright, George played guitar on one song ***Goodbye Sunday*** which has yet to see release. Wright accompanied Harrison on a trip to India in 1972.

Wright has contributed keyboards to Harrison's solo albums **Living In The Material World**, **Dark Horse**, **Extra Texture**, **Thirty-Three & 1/3**, **George Harrison**, and **Cloud Nine**. He helped George compose the songs ***If You Believe*** from **George Harrison**, and ***That's What It Takes*** from **Cloud Nine**. Wright also contributed keyboards to Ringo's songs ***It Don't Come Easy***, ***Back Off Boogaloo*** and ***Down And Out*** in the early 1970s.

Wright's 1988 album **Who I Am** featured Harrison contributing to the song ***(I Don't Wanna) Hold Back***. In 1995, Wright released **First Signs Of Life**, a critically acclaimed album of African and Brazilian music fused with Wright's distinctive keyboards. The album's single, ***Don't Try To Own Me***, featured Harrison on background vocals. A brief clip of Harrison and Wright recording the vocals was contained in a two-minute promotional video for the album. It is likely that George Harrison and Gary Wright, friends who share a similar spiritual view of life, will continue to work together in the future.

Darren Young with John Barry and His

Record 398 title:
My Tears Will Turn To Laughter
/ I've Just Fallen For Someone
Label / Catalog number:
Parlophone / R 4919
Jacket / Inserts:
Record label sleeve
Recording Location / Date:
EMI-Abbey Road Studios, London, U.K. / Apr 62

Media:
Single 7" (mono)
Producer:
John Burgess

Song 398a title:
I've Just Fallen For Someone
Release date / Country:
Apr 62 / U.K.

Track details:
Side 2, track 1 / 1 min. 50 sec.
Composer:
J. Askew - [J. Lennon]

Darren Young: Lead Vocals; John Barry and His Orchestra

Darren Young was born John Askew on December 8, 1936 in Liverpool, England. He was one of many singers in promoter Larry Parnes' stable in Britain in the late 1950s, then performing under the name Johnny Gentle. He was a regular on the U.K. pop music TV shows **Oh Boy** and **Drumbeat**.

Parnes hired a band then known as The Silver Beetles, including John, Paul, George, Stu Sutcliffe, and Tommy Moore on drums, to back up Gentle on a seven-date tour of Scotland in May 1960. Gentle found The Beatles' charm and energy irresistible. He said, "The first time I met The Beatles was just before they backed me on stage; the chemistry between us was great; we didn't have a bad show." He later tried, unsuccessfully, to get Parnes to sign them to a long-term contract. Gentle joined The Beatles onstage during their performance at the Grosvenor Ballroom in Liscard on July 2, 1960.

Askew, as he is again known, said, "When I was on tour with The Beatles in Scotland I was having problems with the middle eight of a song I was writing called ***I've Just Fallen For Someone***. John Lennon played something he had written that he thought would fit the song and I liked it, so I used it. It's the part 'We know that we'll get by, just wait and see, just like the song tells us, the best things in life are free.'" The song was issued as the B-side of the Parlophone single ***My Tears Will Turn To Laughter*** by Darren Young, Askew's pseudonym at the time. However, Lennon was not credited as a composer on the label, and the song was not a hit. According to Askew, Adam Faith* did a cover of ***I've Just Fallen For Someone*** on one of his albums. Askew retired from show business in the late 1960s. He still lives in England, and now earns his living as a joiner and carpenter.

Frank Zappa & The Mothers Of Invention

Record 399 title:
Playground Psychotics
Label / Catalog number:
Barking Pumpkin / D2 74244
Jacket / Inserts:
Unique in double Jewel box / 8 page CD booklet
Recording Location / Date:
On location at Fillmore East Theater, New York, NY, U.S.A. / 06 Jun 71
Media:
Albums 5" CD [2 CD set]
Producer:
Frank Zappa

Song 399a title:
A Small Eternity With Yoko Ono [aka Au] [live]
Release date / Country:
03 Nov 92 / U.S.A.
Track details:
CD1, track 26 / 6 min. 11 sec.
Composer:
J. Lennon - Y. Ono

Yoko Ono: Lead Vocals; John Lennon: Voice & Feedback Guitar; Frank Zappa: Feedback Guitar; Don Preston: Mini Moog

Song 399b title:
Aaawk [aka Jamrag] [live]
Release date / Country:
03 Nov 92 / U.S.A.
Track details:
CD1, track 24 / 2 min. 59 sec.
Composer:
J. Lennon - Y. Ono - F. Zappa

Yoko Ono: Lead Vocals; John Lennon: Voice, B. Vocals & Guitar; Frank Zappa: Guitar; Mark Volman: B. Vocals; Howard Kaylan: B. Vocals; Ian Underwood: Winds, B. Vocals & Keyboards; Aynsley Dunbar: Drums; Jim Pons: Bass; Bob Harris: Keyboards & B. Vocals; Don Preston: Mini Moog

Song 399c title:
Say Please [aka Jamrag] [live]
Release date / Country:
03 Nov 92 / U.S.A.
Track details:
CD1, track 23 / 0 min. 57 sec.
Composer:
J. Lennon - Y. Ono - F. Zappa

Yoko Ono: Lead Vocals; John Lennon: Voice, B. Vocals & Guitar; Frank Zappa: Guitar; Mark Volman: B. Vocals; Howard Kaylan: B. Vocals; Ian Underwood: Winds, B. Vocals & Keyboards; Aynsley Dunbar: Drums; Jim Pons: Bass; Bob Harris: Keyboards & B. Vocals; Don Preston: Mini Moog

Mark Volman, Bay City, MI, 1994, photo by Kristofer Engelhardt

Frank Zappa was born on December 21, 1940 in Baltimore, Maryland. His father was a Sicilian immigrant and his mother a first generation Italian-American. His family moved to southern California when Frank was ten. Like his father, Frank took an interest in music, playing in his high school orchestra, and forming his first band, The Black-Outs, in the late 1950s. Even then he was demonstrating his bizarre brand of humor and reportedly renamed his friend, Don Van Vliet, "Captain Beefheart." Unlike most of his contemporaries in the rock world, Zappa not only could read music, but studied music theory as well. Zappa's early musical influences were Edgar Varese,

Stravinsky and rhythm & blues. By the early 1960s, Zappa was playing with a variety of groups in local bars, and was scoring music for other artists and B-movies like **The World's Greatest Sinner** and **Run Home Slow**. He also wound up on the **Steve Allen TV Show** performing a ***Bicycle Concerto*** by blowing through the handlebars and plucking the spokes. He invested his earnings building a recording studio that closed after he was arrested and convicted of selling pornographic audio tapes (fake moaning noises, etc.) to an undercover vice officer.

Ringo Starr as Frank Zappa
from the film / album booklet "200 Motels"

By 1964, Zappa's professional persona was established. It consisted of a mixed bag of free form jazz, classical music, rhythm & blues, "doo-wop", and hard rock fused with political satire and bizarre, sexually oriented comedy. His band was named The Mothers of Invention. His first two albums, **Freak Out** and **Absolutely Free**, set new boundaries for the outer limits of music in the 1960s. McCartney cited **Freak Out** as having an influence on The Beatles' recordings for the **Sgt. Pepper's Lonely Hearts Club Band** album. Zappa became the talk of the underground press and music scene of the psychedelic '60s. But he avoided drugs, and openly distanced himself from the hippie drug scene that he often satirized in his music. In 1968, Zappa and the Mothers released the album **We're Only In It For The Money**. The albums' jacket was a parody of The Beatles' **Sgt. Pepper's Lonely Hearts Club Band** album jacket. By the late 1960s, Zappa, now an accomplished guitarist, was being taken seriously as a musician. Zappa was also a master of promotion, and an astute businessman, but he neither sought, nor achieved top 40 success. Zappa disbanded The Mothers toward the close of the decade.

In 1970 Zappa reformed The Mothers around the vocal and comedy talents of Mark Volman and Howard Kaylan (The Phlorescent Leech and Eddie, aka Flo & Eddie), who were the founding members of The Turtles. This more musically accessible line-up toured the world, and gained Zappa a cult following.

In 1971, Zappa released **200 Motels**, one of several ventures of his into filmmaking. **200 Motels** was a parody of a rock group on the road that featured Ringo Starr as a very convincing Frank Zappa look-alike named Larry The Dwarf and Keith Moon* as a nun who overdoses on drugs (get the picture?). Ringo's chauffeur, Martin Lickert, successfully auditioned for a role in the film as bass player and actually ended up becoming a member of The Mothers. The film premiered on November 10, 1971. The sound-

Howard Kaylan, Bay City, MI, 1994, photo by Kristofer Engelhardt

track album included a booklet that featured photos of Ringo. The film was released on VHS in 1988.

It was not very surprising when, on June 6, 1971, John and Yoko* joined Frank Zappa And The Mothers for a jam onstage at New York's Fillmore East Theater. They were, after all, the two best examples of popular performing conceptual artists of the time. The performance was a combination of John's and particularly Yoko's experimental music fused with Zappa and The Mothers' free-form jazz and comedy.

What can only be described as a confusing and delightful postscript to John and Yoko's performance with Zappa at the Fillmore East Theater, was Zappa's release of the performance in 1992 on his album **Playground Psychotics**. Zappa accurately recounts in the liner notes: "Some of you might have heard another version of this material on the John and Yoko album **Some Time In New York City**. When they sat in with us that night, we were in the process of recording the **Live At The Fillmore East, June 1971** album, and all of this insanity was captured on tape. After the show, John and I agreed we would each put out our own version of the performance, and I gave him a copy of the 16 track master tape. Here is our version...a substantially different mix from what they released." A casual listen makes it hard to believe it's the same recording. The Zappa release is a completely different edit and mix. Due to the nature of the jam (where one title begins and ends), song times vary widely from release to release, and are an approximation at best. To begin with, the song ***Well*** has a longer introduction, and is some twenty seconds longer on the fade out (the actual performance of the song was over seven minutes). The only song from the performance on the Zappa release that is substantially edited from Lennon's release is ***Jamrag***, that is at least a minute and a half shorter and is broken into two new titles, ***Say Please*** and ***Aaawk***, that seem more appropriately titled. Zappa also rightfully includes himself in the composing credits. Much of ***Jamrag*** consisted of bits and pieces of well-known Zappa compositions, including ***King Kong***. Ironically, it is the Zappa portion of ***Aaawk [Jamrag]*** that is edited on his release. Lennon's ***Scumbag*** (which, because of Lennon's lead vocals is classified as a Lennon song), restores the full backing band, including Flo & Eddie's vocals, that were eliminated from the Lennons' release. Zappa also retitled the final song ***Au***, to ***A Small Eternity With Yoko Ono***. Though it may appear from differing times (some releases include the tail end of ***Scumbag*** in the timing of ***Au***) on the Lennon release that almost two minutes of this song were edited out by Zappa, it is the same length except for a much longer audience fade-out. What Zappa has rightly presented is a Mothers performance that included a walk-on guest-spot by John and Yoko. What was essentially presented on the **Sometime In New York City** album was a bare bones Plastic Ono Band sound with Zappa and The Mothers' backing all, but eliminated from the mix.

The questions are: Why did John Lennon, Yoko Ono and Phil Spector* so radically alter the recordings they released? Why did John deface and use The Mothers' **Fillmore East** album jacket as the inner-sleeve credits for his release on **Sometime In New York City**? The Lennons' performance was not included on the **Fillmore East** album. One story has it that Allen Klein refused Zappa permission to use the John and Yoko portion of the show for his release, and that what Zappa turned over to the Lennons was minus much of The Mothers backing! Zappa stated in a Rolling Stone magazine interview in February 1988: "The deal I made with John and Yoko was that we were both to have access to the tapes and could deploy them any way we wanted. They got a duplicate copy of the master, and they mixed it their way. I had a copy of the master, and I was gonna mix it and put it out as part of the Mothers album. They put out this record that took ***King Kong*** – which obviously has a tune, and a rhythm and chord changes – and they called it ***Jamrag***, and accredited the writing and publishing to themselves." Mark Volman said, "There was a battle over the tapes. Frank was never happy about the way Lennon released our portion of the record, and he didn't like the way John changed the (Mothers') album design." Now that both are dead, we may never know the full story.

By the end of 1971, the 200 motels of touring began to take its toll on Zappa. The band lost its equipment to a fire at the Montreux Casino in Switzerland, as recounted in Deep Purple's song ***Smoke On The Water***. A week later, an audience member, jealous over his girlfriend's attention to Zappa, pushed Zappa off the stage and into the orchestra pit during the group's encore (a rendition of The Beatles ***I Want To Hold Your Hand***) at London's Rainbow Theatre. It took Zappa over a year to recover from the injuries he sustained. It would prove to be the last song Flo & Eddie performed with Zappa, who became disillusioned with touring during his nearly year-long recovery. (Zappa also performed The Beatles' song ***I Am The Walrus*** in concert.)

Flo & Eddie, backed by The Mothers, recorded their first solo album under the Flo & Eddie name during Zappa's convalescence. In the mid-1970s, Flo & Eddie hosted a radio show on Los Angeles' progressive KROQ that often featured guest rock stars including Keith Moon and Ringo Starr. (A portion of their appearance is included on the 1983 album **The History Of Flo & Eddie And the Turtles** [Rhino / RNTA 1998].) Ringo took phone calls, and did an impromptu rendition of ***Oh My My***, along with the others in the studio, while The Beatles' song ***I Wanna Be Your Man*** played in the background. Flo & Eddie continue to host syndicated radio shows from time to time, and were considered for Ringo Starr's All-Starr Band tour in 1995.

Zappa continued to record, tour, and make personnel changes throughout the 1970s, dropping The Mothers moniker. Zappa's prolific pace continued unabated throughout most of the 1980s. His daughter Moon Unit was emerging as an actress and sons Dweezil and Ahmet were following in their father's musical footsteps. Towards the end of the 1980s, Zappa became less musically, but more politically, active. Most of his new releases consisted of stockpiled live and studio out-takes.

In 1991 Frank Zappa seemed ready to re-enter the musical arena when he was diagnosed with prostate cancer that had gone undetected for nearly a decade. On December 4, 1993, he fell victim to the disease, depriving the world of one of its greatest musicians and composers. He was inducted into the Rock and Roll Hall of Fame in 1995.

Frank Zappa, Flint, MI, early 1970s, photo courtesy of Tom Bert

ARTIST INDEX

The 220 artists (individuals, bands, etc.) detailed in this book can be found on the following pages.

ARTISTS INDEX

Notes

Notes

Notes

Notes

Notes

Notes

Notes

Notes

Books to look for in 1998

The Pink Floyd Reference Encyclopedia

by Vernon Fitch
to be published by CGP 1998

The Pink Floyd Reference Encyclopedia is an in-depth reference work covering all the people, places, and history of the musical group Pink Floyd. From the earliest days of the band to the present, this book explains the band from The Abdabs to Zee. Written by **Vernon Fitch** author of the web's leading Floyd site "The Pink Floyd Archives", The book also features an appendix of unique reference works including Books, Concert Dates, Discographies, Session Work, and more. *The Pink Floyd Reference Encyclopedia* is a must for every Pink Floyd enthusiast, from the casual fan to the obsessive collector.

The Pink Floyd Archives
E-Mail: PFArchives@CompuServe.com
WWW: http://ourworld.compuserve.com/homepages/PFArchives

ABOUT THE CD

The accompanying CD contains three previously unreleased recordings, available only with this book, which were produced by John Lennon. Two of the three songs were arranged by Lennon, and the lyrics for the song Incantation were written by Lennon.

The songs were recorded in early 1975 at Record Plant Studios (New York) with a backing band originally called Bomf, who renamed themselves Dog Soldier.

The recording details are as follows:

Incantation
is performed by Dog Soldier with Patrick Jude singing lead vocals. As well as helping to produce the song, John Lennon wrote the lyrics. His lyrics were inspired by an indian he had met named Rolling Thunder. Dog Soldier took their name from Lennon's lyrics for this song. Dog Soldier backed Lennon on April 18, 1975 at the Waldorf Astoria Hotel for "A Salute to Sir Lew Grade". Roy Cicala was the owner and chief sound engineer at the Record Plant and had helped John Lennon with most of his recordings. Lori burton had previously sung backing vocals on a couple of Lennon;s recordings.

Let's Spend The Night Together
is the familiar Rolling Stones song sung as a duet by Lori Burton and Patrick Jude. This song was produced (with help from Roy Cicala) and arranged by John Lennon. Jude, who supplied hand claps to lennon's song *Whatever Gets You Through The Night*, sings lead vocals.

Answer Me, My Love
performed by Lori Burton, was was produced by John Lennon and Roy Cicala, Burton's husband at the time. The song had been a hit for Nat King Cole which Lennon had liked, and he arranged it for Lori.

For more information on these recordings, see Lori burton and Dog Soldier in this book.

Special thanks to Yoko Ono for granting permission for the use of *Incantation* and to Roy Cicala for providing the recordings.